STUDY GUIDE FOR USE WITH

Fundamentals of CORPORATE FINANCE

FIFTH CANADIAN EDITION

STEPHEN A. ROSS
Massachusetts Institute of Technology

RANDOLPH W. WESTERFIELD
University of Southern California

BRADFORD D. JORDAN
University of Kentucky

GORDON S. ROBERTS
York University

PREPARED BY
JEANNETTE A. SWITZER
Dalhousie University

McGraw-Hill Ryerson

Toronto Montréal Boston Burr Ridge, IL Dubuque, IA Madison, WI New York San Francisco
St. Louis Bangkok Bogotá Caracas Kuala Lumpur Lisbon London Madrid
Mexico City Milan New Delhi Santiago Seoul Singapore Sydney Taipei

McGraw-Hill
Ryerson

Study Guide
for use with
Fundamentals of Corporate Finance
Fifth Canadian Edition

ISBN: 0-07-092284-5

4 5 6 7 8 9 10 TRI 0 9 8 7 6 5

Printed and bound in Canada

Care has been taken to trace ownership of copyright material contained in this text; however, the publisher will welcome any information that enables them to rectify any reference or credit for subsequent editions.

Executive Sponsoring Editor: Lynn Fisher
Developmental Editor: Maria Chu
Senior Production Coordinator: Madeleine Harrington
Page Layout: JayTee Graphics, Ltd.
Printer: Tri-Graphic Printing

Table of Contents

1. Introduction to Corporate Finance 1

2. Financial Statements, Taxes, and Cash Flow 9

3. Working With Financial Statements 29

4. Long-Term Financial Planning and Corporate Growth 51

5. Introduction to Valuation: The Time Value of Money 73

6. Discounted Cash Flow Valuation 89

7. Interest Rates and Bond Valuation 115

8. Stock Valuation 141

9. Net Present Value and Other Investment Criteria 155

10. Making Capital Investment Decisions 173

11. Project Analysis and Evaluation 203

12. Some Lessons from Capital Market History 227

13. Return, Risk, and the Security Market Line 241

14. Cost of Capital 267

15. Raising Capital 285

16. Financial Leverage and Capital Structure Policy 305

17. Dividends and Dividend Policy 331

18. Short-Term Finance and Planning 349

19. Cash and Liquidity Management 373

20. Credit and Inventory Management 391

21. International Corporate Finance 417

22. Leasing 437

23. Mergers and Acquisitions 449

24. Risk Management: An Introduction to Financial Engineering 465

25. Options and Corporate Securities 473

PREFACE

Many business students find the first course in corporate finance to be one of the most challenging, as well as one of the most rewarding, courses in the undergraduate business curriculum. The underlying goal in writing this Study Guide is to supplement the preeminent text in its field, *Fundamentals of Corporate Finance*, by Stephen A. Ross, Randolph W. Westerfield, Bradford D. Jordan, and Gordon S. Roberts. I hope you will use this **Study Guide** in conjunction with *Fundamentals of Corporate Finance* in every phase of your introduction to corporate finance.

ORGANIZATION OF THE STUDY GUIDE

The Study Guide to accompany the text is designed to accomplish one major objective. It will augment and reinforce a sound grasp of modern fundamentals of finance and its underlying principles. The Study Guide contains a comprehensive treatment of each chapter from the text, providing you with **Chapter Highlights**, **Concept Tests**, and **Problems with Solutions**. To accomplish this objective, the **Study Guide** has been organized as discussed below.

APPROACH

Chapter Highlights: These cover all the essential concepts and subjects in an easily understandable narrative form. The goal of the Chapter Highlights is to reinforce the major concepts presented in the text by including summaries of the material, extensive use of numerical examples and, where appropriate, discussion of alternative perspectives designed to provide additional insight.

Concept Test: The Concept Test for each chapter is a "do-it-yourself" summary of the chapter. Completing this test will help you to create a summary of the chapter, while also testing your understanding of the material. You will be able to identify your strengths and weaknesses by comparing your answers to those provided at the end of the chapter.

Problems and Solutions: Problems, with solutions are provided for each chapter. To obtain the greatest benefit, **work the problems by yourself first**. Then, look at the solutions given in the Study Guide, located at the end of each chapter. This is the best way to prepare for an exam on the subject.

TIPS FOR THE STUDENT

The **Study Guide** is designed to enhance your understanding of corporate finance. It is essential to understand a concept before it can be properly applied to the analysis of a specific problem. Keep this goal in mind as you read and study both the text and this guide. Since much of corporate finance is mathematical in nature, you should have your calculator, as well as pencil and paper, handy as you read. This will allow you to verify your understanding of the calculations used to solve the numerous examples for each chapter.

The **Problems and Solutions** at the end of each chapter will be most helpful to you if you first try to completely solve the problem before reading the solutions we have provided. You'll get a lot more out of the problem if you try to solve it yourself and **then** compare your results to our solutions. Remember that the best way to actually learn how to solve finance problems is to do them yourself.

Most of the examples in the Study Guide and the end-of-chapter Problems and Solutions were solved using a financial calculator. If you use the financial tables in the Appendix to your text, your answer may differ slightly from ours; this is a result of rounding in the tables. In addition, you should be aware of the rounding error which can arise in problems which require a sequence of calculations. That is, if you round off an immediate result, you lose accuracy in your final answer. This problem can generally be avoided by working with the most accurate figures possible, until you have completed your solution. We have tried to take this approach throughout this guide. Therefore, for the sake of consistency with our solutions, it is important that you take the same approach. Otherwise, you may find your answers differ from ours, which may cause unnecessary confusion.

I have greatly enjoyed preparing this **Study Guide** for you. However you use it, I hope it makes the study of corporate finance more productive and enjoyable and, of course, a little easier!

Jeannette A. Switzer

1   Introduction to Corporate Finance

CHAPTER HIGHLIGHTS

The two major issues addressed in this chapter are: (1) What is corporate finance? (2) What is the goal of the financial manager? The answers require an understanding of the forms of business organization. We also explore the agency problem as it relates to both control of the firm and to Canadian financial markets.

1.1   CORPORATE FINANCE AND THE FINANCIAL MANAGER

WHAT IS CORPORATE FINANCE?

Major decisions faced by financial managers

1. **Capital budgeting decision -** What long-term investments should the firm undertake?

2. **Capital structure decision -** What is the best way to raise long-term financing for these

3. **Working capital decision -** How should the firm manage its short-term assets and liabilities?

THE FINANCIAL MANAGER

Shareholders are the owners of the firm

1. In large firms, shareholders are not involved in the day-to-day operations. Managers are employed as agents of the shareholders to make decisions on their behalf.

2. The treasurer and controller share financial functions of the firm. They typically report to a top officer of the firm (vice president of finance or chief financial officer. The controller handles financial accounting, taxes and management information systems. The treasurer handles activities related to the three major decisions listed above. Our emphasis is on the treasurer's functions.

FINANCIAL MANAGEMENT DECISIONS

Capital Budgeting: The financial manager's job is to create value for shareholders by acquiring assets with a value greater than their cost.

Steps in process:

1. Forecast cash inflows and outflows generated by an asset.

2. Use this information to determine the asset's value.

3. Manager compares the asset's value with its cost to the firm.

Any analysis of cash flows must consider

1. Size of the cash flows

2. Timing of the cash flows

3. Riskiness of the cash flows.

Capital Structure: A firm's capital structure is the specific mixture of equity and long-term debt used to finance the acquisition of fixed assets. The financial manager must decide on

1. Best combination of debt and equity

2. The least expensive sources of funds

3. How and when to raise money if funds are needed.

Working Capital Management: The concept of working capital management deals with the firm's receipt and disbursement of cash. Typically, these decisions involve management of current assets and current liabilities.

1.2   THE FORMS OF BUSINESS ORGANIZATION

Businesses can be organized in three different legal forms. Differences among these forms are related to the life of the business, the ability of the business to obtain financing, and the way in which the business is taxed.

Sole Proprietorship: One person owns the entire business and keeps all the profits from the business. This is the simplest and least regulated form of business organization.

In a sole partnership, the owner has *unlimited liability* for business debts. Personal assets can be seized to pay outstanding debts. All business profits are taxed as personal income. The life of the business life is limited to the life of the owner life; available equity financing is limited to the owner's personal wealth. Transfer of ownership may be difficult because it requires selling the entire business to a new owner.

Partnership: A partnership has two or more owners (partners).

1. *General partnership:* all partners share in any gains or losses from the business. They have unlimited liability for any debts incurred by the partnership.

2. *Limited partnership:* one or more general partners runs the business. The limited partners do not actively participate. General partners have unlimited liability for the business debts; the liability of limited partners is restricted to the amount that partner contributes to the business.

3. Partnerships are easy to form and all profits are taxed as personal income.

4. Major disadvantages include the unlimited liability of the general partners, the limited life of the business (the partnership is dissolved when any general partner wishes to leave the partnership). Therefore, it may be difficult to transfer ownership. These disadvantages may make it difficult for the business to raise the funds needed for investment opportunities.

Corporation: The corporation is the most important form of business organization in Canada. A corporation is a legal entity, separate and distinct from its owners.

1. This means a corporation can incur debts in its own name, sue or be sued, and enter into legal contracts. The liability of the owners is limited to the amount of money they have invested in the business.

2. Corporations are formed according to the *articles of incorporation* and the firm's *bylaws*. Canadian firms are incorporated under either the Federal Canada Business Corporation Act or provincial law. The articles of incorporation contain information about the corporation's name, its intended life (usually indefinite), its business purpose, and the number of shares that can be issued. The bylaws describe how the corporation regulates its own existence.

3. *The owners of a corporation are its shareholders.*

    a. Leadership interest is represented by shares of common stock. These shares can be easily transferred, or sold, from one shareholder to another. This means the life of the corporation is not limited to the life of its owners

    b. The shareholders elect the corporation's board of directors. The directors then decide on the managers for the corporation. *This separates the functions of ownership and management.*

4. The advantages of corporations are:

    a. Ownership is easily transferrable

    b. Owners' liability is limited to the amount invested in the firm

    c. The business has an unlimited life span.

    d. These advantages make it easier for a corporation to raise large amounts of financing.

5. The major disadvantage of the corporate form is double taxation. Corporate profits are subject to corporate income taxes. Then, dividends paid to the firm's owners (shareholders) are taxed as personal income for the shareholder.

1.3   THE GOAL OF FINANCIAL MANAGEMENT

Corporate finance is the study of financial decision making within a corporation. The goal of these decisions is to make money for the firm's owners, the shareholders.

1. Shareholders measure financial benefit in terms of changes in the firm's stock price. Decisions which are in the best interest of the shareholders are those which increase the value of the stock.

2. *The goal of financial management should be to maximize the current price per share of the firm's existing stock. This is equivalent to maximizing the value of shareholders' equity.*

3.   For privately held firms (no traded stock), the goal should be to maximize the value of owners' equity. For firms with publicly traded stock, maximizing shareholders' equity means maximizing the stock price.

4.   The major factors that financial managers should consider are profitability and risk. Both factors affect the value of the firm's stock. To make decisions consistent with maximizing owners' wealth, financial managers must assess the impact of these factors on the value of the firm's stock.

1.4   THE AGENCY PROBLEM AND CONTROL OF THE CORPORATION

Although the goal of financial managers should be to maximize the current stock price (the owners' wealth), managers may not always act in a manner consistent with shareholders' best interest. Conflicts between the manager's personal interests and those of the firm's owners are referred to as *agency problems*.

Agency Relationships: The relationship between shareholders and managers is an *agency relationship*. The principals (shareholders) contract with agents (managers) to perform the task of managing the firm. When the goals of managers differ from those of shareholders, an agency problem exists.

Management Goals: Goals of managers are sometimes in conflict with goals of shareholders. Managers are sometimes motivated by considerations such as organizational survival, managerial independence, and corporate self-sufficiency. These factors are related to the maximization of corporate wealth, typically related to corporate size or growth. *Decisions that increase the firm's size do not necessarily increase the value of the firm's stock.*

Do Managers Act in the Shareholders' Interests?

In general, the extent to which managers' actions are consistent with shareholders' goals depends on the nature of managerial compensation and the control of the firm.

1.   Managerial compensation plays a major role in determining the extent to which managers act in shareholders' interests. Compensation may be linked directly or indirectly to firm performance. For example, managers may have an option to purchase shares at a pre-determined price. The value of the option increases with the value of the firm's stock. Promotions and the manager's value in the labour market are often directly related to the manager's success in achieving the goals of shareholders.

2.   Control of the firm rests with the firm's owners (shareholders). Shareholders elect the firm's directors, who, in turn, hire (and fire) the firm's managers. Shareholders can also vote to remove directors / managers who do not act in their interests. Additionally, poorly-managed firms may be taken over by another firm. Then, the existing management team is usually replaced.

3.   *Stakeholders* are any parties who have an interest in the firm's decisions. Stakeholders include shareholders, creditors, employees, customers, suppliers, and the federal and provincial governments. Well-managed firms pay close attention to the needs and expectations of all stakeholders.

1.5   FINANCIAL MARKETS AND THE CORPORATION

Debt and equity securities issued by firms are bought and sold in the financial markets. The financial markets are simply a way of bringing together the buyers and the sellers of financial securities.

Money versus Capital Markets: Financial market transactions are classified according to the maturity of the financial instruments bought and sold.

1. *Money markets* are financial markets where short-term debt securities (maturity is usually one year or less) are bought and sold . It is a dealer market in which the dealers (brokers and agents) match buyers and sellers, but do not personally own the security. It has no physical location; trading facilities and market participants are linked via telephone and computers.

2. *Capital markets* are financial market where long-term debt and shares of stock are traded.

Primary versus Secondary Markets:

Primary market transactions refer to the original sale, or issue, of a security by a government or corporation. *Secondary market* transaction refers to any subsequent sale or purchase of a security.

Primary Markets: When a firm first issues a security, the sale takes place in the primary market. These transactions may be either public offerings or private placements. Most public offerings are *underwritten* by investment dealers or groups of dealers (a *syndicate*) who purchase the securities from the issuing firm and then resell them to the public (hopefully at a higher price). New public offerings must be registered with provincial authorities. The most important is the Ontario Securities Commission (OSC). Private placements do not need to be registered with the OSC and do not require an underwriter's involvement.

Secondary Markets: Securities trades *after* the initial public issue take place in the secondary markets. These are either *auction markets* or *dealer markets*. Auction markets have a physical location (an *exchange*) where trading takes place on the floor of the exchange. The largest auction market in Canada is the Toronto Stock Exchange (TSE), where the common shares of most large Canadian corporations are traded. Dealer markets have no physical location. Debt securities (bonds) usually trade in dealer markets. Shares of smaller firms often trade in the over-the-counter market (OTC), which is a dealer market.

Listing: Any stock trading on an organized exchange is said to be *listed* on the exchange. Listed firms must apply to the exchange and meet certain minimum requirements regarding asset size and number of shareholders. Listing criteria differ across the various exchanges in Canada.

FINANCIAL INSTITUTIONS

Financial institutions act as intermediaries between investors (suppliers of funds) and firms that need to raise funds (demanders of funds). These institutions provide a variety of services which promote the efficient allocation of funds. Examples of financial institutions include chartered banks, trust companies, credit unions, investment dealers, insurance companies, pension funds, and mutual funds.

1. Chartered banks operate under federal regulation. They accept deposits and make loans, earning their income on the spread between the interest paid on deposits and the higher rates charged for loans to both businesses and individuals.

2. Trust companies also accept deposits and make loans. In addition, they engage in fiduciary activities including managing assets for estates, registered retirement savings plans, etc.

3. Credit unions also accept deposits and make loans.

4.   Investment dealers are non-depository institutions. They assist firms in issuing new securities and work with investors to buy or sell securities. Their income is based on transaction fees. Insurance companies include both property and casualty, and health and life insurance. They accept funds in a form similar to deposits and also make loans.

5.   Pension funds invest contributions from employers and employees in securities offered by financial markets. Mutual funds pool individual investments to purchase a diversified portfolio of securities.

Recent deregulation affecting Canadian financial institutions now allows the above institutions to engage in most of the above activities, with one exception: chartered banks are not allowed to sell life insurance through their branch networks.

TRENDS IN FINANCIAL MARKETS AND FINANCIAL MANAGEMENT

Financial engineering is the design of new securities and processes which can reduce and control risk and minimize taxes. Examples are securitized financial instruments, derivative securities (including options and futures) . Financial engineering also tries to reduce the costs of issuing securities and compliance with government regulations. For example, the *Prompt Offering Prospectus* (POP) allows firms that frequently issue new equity to bypass most of the OSC regulation requirements.

In addition, advances in technology have created opportunities to combine different types of financial institutions to take advantage of economies of scale and scope. Current regulations allow almost unlimited scope for financial institutions to enter each others' traditional businesses.

CONCEPT TEST

1.   Corporate finance is the study of ways to answer three major questions. These three subjects are referred to as _____, _____, and _____ decisions.

2.   The _____ of large corporations are generally not involved in day-to-day operations of the firm. Consequently, _____ are employed to make decisions on behalf of the owners.

3.   The financial functions of the firm are generally shared by the _____ and the _____ .

4.   The three different legal forms of business organization are the _____, the _____, and the _____.

5.   In a sole proprietorship, the profits are kept by the _____. Unlimited liability for all business debts falls on the _____.

6.   A _____ is a business owned by two or more persons. In a _____, everyone shares in gains or losses and has unlimited liability for all debts. In a _____, one or more persons runs the business and has unlimited liability; the others have only limited liability.

7.   The primary disadvantages of the forms of business referred to in questions 5 and 6 are _____, _____ _____, and _____.

8.   The rules and procedures by which a corporation governs itself are contained in the _____ . All corporations must prepare a document called the _____ , describing the number of shares which may be issued, the business purpose, the intended life and other details.

9.   The major advantages of the corporate form of organization are _____ , _____ , and _____ . The primary disadvantage of the corporate form of organization is the _____ of corporate income.

10.   The primary goal of the corporation is maximization of _____ . Because management goals may conflict with shareholders' goals, an _____ problem is said to exist. _____ are the costs associated with aligning shareholders' goals with managers' goals.

11.   Chartered banks and investment dealers are examples of institutions which act as _____. These institutions promote the efficient _____ of funds and _____ of securities.

12.   Banks earn their income from the _____ between interest paid on deposits and the higher rate earned on _____ .

13.   _____ are non-depository financial institutions which assist firms in issuing new securities. Recent _____ allows financial institutions to engage in most of the activities of other financial institutions.

14.   When financial markets are classified according to the maturity of the financial instruments, the two types of markets are the _____ and the _____ . Short-term debt instruments are traded in the __ _____ , which is a _____ market. Long-term debt instruments and equities are traded in the _____ .

15.   Financial markets can also be classified as either primary markets or secondary markets. The original sale, or _____ , of a security takes place in the _____ of a security.

16.   The Toronto Stock Exchange is an example of a secondary market which functions as an _____ market. A stock that trades on the TSE is said to be _____ on the exchange.

17.   The creation of new securities or financial processes is referred to as _____ . This has resulted in the reduction and control of _____ and the minimization of _____ .

18.   Compensation may be either directly or indirectly linked to _____. A manager may have the _____ to purchase shares at a pre-determined price. Further, promotion and the manager's labour market value are related to the manager's success in achieving the _____.

ANSWERS TO CONCEPT TEST

1.   capital budgeting; capital structure; working capital

2.   shareholders; managers

3.   treasurer; controller

4.   sole proprietorship; partnership; corporation

5.   owner; owner

6.   partnership; general partnership; limited partnership

7.   unlimited liability; limited life; difficulty of transferring ownership

8.   bylaws; articles of incorporation

9.   ease of transferring ownership; limited liability; unlimited life; double taxation

10. current price of existing stock; agency; agency costs

11. financial intermediaries; allocation; pricing

12. spread; loans

13. investment dealers; deregulation

14. money market; capital market; money market; dealer; capital market

15. issue; primary market

16. auction; listed; dealer

17. financial engineering; risk; taxes

18. firm performance; option; goals of shareholders

2 Financial Statements, Taxes, and Cash Flow

CHAPTER HIGHLIGHTS

This chapter examines financial statements, cash flow concepts, and important tax considerations in the Canadian setting. The chapter emphasizes the *use* of accounting statements in corporate finance, rather than the actual preparation of the financial statements. Keep in mind two important distinctions as you work through the chapter: (1) the difference between accounting (book) value and market value, and (2) the difference between accounting income and actual cash flows.

2.1 THE BALANCE SHEET

The *balance sheet* is a snapshot of a firm's accounting value at a particular date. The firm's assets are listed on the left-hand side; the liabilities and shareholders' equity on the right-hand side. By definition, the value of the firm's assets is equal to the sum of its liabilities and shareholders' equity:

$$\text{Assets} \quad = \quad \text{Liabilities} \quad + \quad \text{Shareholders' Equity} \qquad [2.1]$$

Note that the book value of equity is the difference between the values of the firm's assets and its liabilities.

An Example: Abbreviated balance sheets for Tin Can, Inc. are given below.

TIN CAN, INC.
Balance Sheets as of December 31, 2002 and 2003 ($ in millions)

Assets	2002	2003	Liabilities & Owners' Equity	2002	2003
Current assets			**Current liabilities**		
Cash	$ 200	$ 503	Accounts payable	$ 500	$ 530
Accounts receivable	650	688	Notes payable	543	460
Inventory	1,045	700	Other	214	183
Total	$1,895	$1,891	Total	$1,257	$1,173
			Long-term debt	$1,097	$1,184
Fixed assets			**Owners' equity**		
Net plant			Common stock	590	720
and equipment	$1,490	$1,689	Retained earnings	441	503
			Total	1,031	1,223
Total assets	$3,385	$3,580	Total liabilities & Owners' Equity	$3,385	$3,580

The financial manager must be especially aware of the following three aspects of the balance sheet: liquidity, debt versus equity, and market versus book value. These are discussed below.

Liquidity: *Liquidity* refers to the speed and ease with which assets can be converted to cash without significant loss in value. On the balance sheets, assets are listed in order of decreasing liquidity. Current assets are relatively liquid. Fixed assets are, in comparison, relatively illiquid. Liquidity is valuable because it increases the firm's ability to meet short-term obligations. However, rates of return are usually lower for liquid assets than for fixed assets. So, there is a tradeoff between liquidity and the foregone potential of higher returns on fixed assets. Managers must consider this tradeoff in deciding on the mix of short- and long-term assets.

Debt versus Equity: Debt is a liability that obligates the firm to repay principal and interest to creditors at specified times. The firm's creditors have the first claim on any cash flows generated. Equity holders are entitled to the firm's residual value once all claims to creditors have been paid. This residual value is expressed by the equation:

$$\text{Shareholders' Equity} = \text{Assets} - \text{Liabilities}$$

From an economic standpoint, if the firm sells all of its assets and pays off all of its debts, any remaining cash belongs to the firm's shareholders. The use of debt financing is referred to as *financial leverage* because it magnifies both the firm's gains and losses that accrue to the shareholders.

Market Value versus Book Value: The firm's balance sheet shows the book value of the firm's assets, rather than the market value. These values are based on *historical cost*, as determined by Generally Accepted Accounting Principles (GAAP). Most often, an asset's *market value* (the price at which it could be sold today) is not the same as the book value. The difference between market and book values is usually higher for fixed assets than for current assets. Financial managers must consider the difference between market and book values when making capital budgeting decisions. For financial decisions, the value of an asset, the value of a firm, or the value of a firm's common stock depends on *market* value. The goal of the financial manager is to maximize the market value of the firm's existing share price.

An Example: The December 31, 2003 balance sheets of the KMS Corporation are presented below in both accounting (book value) and economic (market value) terms:

KMS CORPORATION
Balance Sheet (Market vs. Book Value)

Assets	Book	Market	Liabilities & Equity	Book	Market
Net working capital	$ 3,000	$ 4,000	Long-term debt	$ 5,000	$ 5,000
Fixed assets	8,000	12,000	Shareholders' equity	6,000	11,000
	$11,000	$16,000		$11,000	$16,000

Using market values, the firm would realize $4,000 (i.e. its NWC) if it liquidated all current assets and used the proceeds to pay off its current liabilities. The book value of net working capital, though, is only $3,000. The $1,000 difference reflects the difference between the market and book values of the firm's current assets. There is also a $4,000 difference between the market and book values of the firm's fixed assets. These differences result in the market value of the shareholders' equity exceeding the book value by $5,000 ($1,000 + $4,000).

2.2 THE INCOME STATEMENT

The firm's *income statement* measures its performance over a period of time, usually one year. The basic income statement equation is: Revenues - Expenses = Income   [2.2]

Income statements report (1) revenues and expenses related to the firm's principal operations, (2) financing expenses, and (3) income taxes. The last item on the income statement is the firm's *net income*. The firm's *earnings per share* (EPS) is the net income divided by the number of common shares outstanding.

Example: An abbreviated 2003 income statement for Tin Can, Inc. is below:

TIN CAN, INC.
2003 Income Statement

Net sales		$ 1,400
Cost of goods sold		700
Depreciation		200
EBIT		$ 500
Interest paid		150
Taxable income		$ 350
Taxes (34%)		119
Net income		$ 231
Addition to retained earnings	$ 62	
Dividends	169	

According to the income statement, $169 in dividends were paid in 2003. The remaining $62 of net income was added to the firm's retained earnings. If you go back to the balance sheet example, you will notice that the increase in accumulated retained earnings from 2002 to 2003 is the same amount, $62.

Example: Tin Can has 150 shares of stock outstanding. What are earnings and dividends per share?

EPS = Net income / Shares outstanding = $231 / 150 = $1.54

Dividends per share = Dividends / Shares outstanding = $169 / 150 = $1.13

GAAP and the Income Statement: Generally Accepted Accounting Principles (GAAP) require revenues to be recorded when they are earned (accrued), even if the cash inflow from payment has not been received. This means revenues are recognized at the time of sale. Costs are recognized based on the matching principle: they are recorded when the associated revenues are recorded. Revenues and costs recorded for a particular time period may therefore be very different from the actual cash flows during the same period.

Non-Cash Items: Non-cash items appear on the income statement as expenses deducted from income. These items affect the firm's net income, but *they do not affect the actual cash flow*. This is the major reason for the difference between accounting income and the firm's cash flows.

The major non-cash expense is *depreciation*. If a firm pays $20,000 cash for an asset, the actual cash outflow is $20,000 at the time of purchase. However, firms may depreciate assets over time, allocating a portion of the cost to each year. The portion deducted each year is recorded as an expense on the income statement. Although the expense of the asset is divided over the period during which the firms receives benefit from the asset, these annual deductions are non-cash items. The actual cash outflow occurred when the asset was purchased.

Time and Costs: For financial decision-making, we distinguish between variable and fixed costs. This distinction changes with the time period under consideration. In the long run, all costs are variable, because, given a sufficiently long period of time, even fixed assets can be bought or sold and long-term debts can be paid. In the short run though, costs such as rent or property taxes are considered to be fixed; other costs, including wages and payments to suppliers, are variable. The distinction between fixed and variable costs can be important to financial managers. Accountants, however, classify costs as either product costs or period costs, so the distinction between fixed and variable costs may be blurred. This is another reason for the difference between reported accounting net income and the firm's actual cash flows.

2.3 CASH FLOW

The cash flow a firm generates from the use of its assets is equal to the sum of the cash flows to creditors and shareholders:

$$\text{Cash flow from assets} \quad = \quad \text{Cash flow to creditors} \quad + \quad \text{Cash flow to shareholders} \qquad [2.3]$$

The three components of cash flow from assets are: operating cash flow, capital spending, and additions to net working capital.

Operating cash flow is the cash flow resulting from a firm's day-to-day operations. Operating cash flow is equal to revenues minus costs, excluding depreciation and interest. Depreciation expense is excluded because it does not represent an actual cash flow; interest expense is excluded because it represents a financing expense.

For Tin Can, Inc. EBIT for 2003 was $500, after deducting $200 depreciation. Adding back the non-cash deduction for depreciation, and subtracting the $80 in current taxes, the firm's operating cash flow is:

Earnings before interest and taxes (EBIT)	$ 500
Depreciation	200
Current taxes	(119)
Operating cash flow	$ 581

The accounting definition of operating cash flows is net income plus depreciation. For Tin Can, Inc., this is $231 + $200 = $431. The difference in the two figures is the year's interest expense ($150). This is because the accounting definition treats interest expense as an operating, rather than a financial, expense.

Capital Spending is the net amount spent on fixed assets, that is, the difference between the acquisition and sale prices of fixed assets. For 2002, Tin Can, Inc. listed fixed assets of $1,490. These assets were depreciated by $200 over the next year. Their value at the end of 2003 would have been $1,490 - $200 = $1,290. However, the 2003 balance sheet reports $1,689 in fixed assets. This means the firm acquired assets worth $1,689 - $1,290 = $399 (or ending fixed assets - beginning fixed assets + depreciation) during the year. The firm's net capital spending for 2003 was, therefore, $399. Note: net capital spending can be negative if the firm sold more assets than it purchased.

Change in Net Working Capital Firms invest in both current and fixed assets. For Tin Can, Inc., the investment in current assets decreased by $4 from 2002 to 2003 ($1,891 - $1,895 = -$4). The change in current liabilities was by $1,173 - $1,257 =   -$84. The *change in the firm's net working capital* is computed as the change in the level of current assets minus the change in the level of current liabilities: [-$4 - (-$84)] = $80.

Alternatively, the change in the firm's net working capital can be computed as the difference between the 2003 and 2002 levels of net working capital: Net working capital in 2002 is $1,895 - $1,257 = $638; for 2003 it is $1,891 - $1,173 = $718. The addition to net working capital is, therefore, $718 - $638 = $80 (or ending NWC - beginning NWC = addition to NWC).

Total Cash Flow from Assets can be calculated as [operating cash - net capital spending - additions to net working capital]. For Tin Can, cash flow from assets equals: $581 - $399 - $80 = $102.

Cash Flow to Creditors and Shareholders: The cash flow to investors in a firm consists of net payments to both creditors and shareholders. The net *cash flow to creditors* is [interest paid - net new borrowing]. For Tin Can, interest paid during 2003 was $150, and long-term debt increased by $1,184 - $1,097 = $87. The net cash flow to creditors is $150 - $87 = $63.

The *cash flow to shareholders* is [dividends paid - net new equity]. For Tin Can, Inc., 2003 dividends are $169 and net new equity financing is $720 - $590 = $130. The cash flow to shareholders is $169 - $130 = $39. The *total cash flow to investors* is $63 + $39 = $102, which is the same as the total cash flow from assets.

2.4 TAXES

Taxes are extremely important because the firm's cash flows are measured after taxes. The size of the tax bill is determined through tax laws and regulations and the annual budgets of the federal government (administered by Canada Customs and Revenue Agency) and provincial governments.

Individual Tax Rates: Individual federal tax rates and selected provincial rates for the year 2003 are below. These rates apply to income from employment (wages and salary) and from unincorporated businesses. Investment income is also taxable and includes includes interest income (taxed at individual rates) and dividend and capital gain income (taxed at special rates).

Federal Tax Rates

Taxable Income	Tax Ra te
$ 0 - 31,677	17.0%
31,678 - 63,354	22.0
63,355 - 103,00	26.0
103,001 and over	29.0

Provinces and territories follow a similar approach. Tax tables for some provinces are provided on page 36 of your text. page . Tax rates change over time. So, rather than trying to memorize the tables, it is more important to understand how the tax process works. You can apply that knowledge even if tax rates change.

Your *average tax rate* is your total tax bill divided by total income. Your *marginal tax rate* is the extra amount you would pay in tax if you earned one more dollar. Taxes on individual income in Canada are *progressive*, with higher incomes taxed at higher rates. For financial decisions, the marginal tax rate is the relevant rate because any new cash flows are taxed at the marginal rate.

Example: You live in Quebec and have a taxable income of $75,000. Find your total tax bill, your average tax rate, and your marginal tax rate. (Note: Use the tables on page 36 of your text to calculate the provincial tax.)

Federal tax = ($31,677 x 17%) + [($63,354 - 31,677) x 22.0%)] + [($75,000 - 63,354) x 26.0%]
       = $5,385.09 + $6,968.94 + $3,027.96 = $15,381.99

Provincial tax = ($26,700 x 16%) + [($53,405 - 26,700) x 20%) + [($75,000 - 53,405) x 24%]
       = $4,272.00 + $5,341.00 + $5,182.80 = $14,795.80

Total tax bill = Federal tax + Provincial tax = $15,381.99 + $14,795.80 = $30,177.79

Average tax rate = Total tax / Taxable income = $30,177.79 / $75,000 = 40.02%

Marginal tax rate = Federal rate + Provincial rate = 26% + 24% = 50%

Taxes on Investment Income: Interest income is taxed at the investor's marginal tax rate. However, there is a tax shelter for dividend income. This reduces the problem of double taxation discussed in section 1.2. The *dividend tax credit* reduces the effective tax rate on dividends for investors in each of the three federal tax brackets. Actual dividends are 'grossed up' by 25 % and federal tax is calculated on this figure. A dividend tax credit of 13 1/3 % of the *actual dividend* is subtracted from the federal tax to get the net federal tax payable. The provincial tax is then added. Below is an example of the way in which dividend income is taxed for a resident of Ontario who earned $5,000 in dividends during 2003. Regular income was $150,000. Note: in Ontario, the dividend tax credit is 5.13%.

Actual dividends	$ 5,000.00
Gross up at 25%	1,250.00
Grossed up dividends	$ 6,250.00
Federal tax at 29%	1,812.50
Less dividend tax credit (0.1333 x $6,250)	(833.13)
Federal tax payable	$ 979.37
Provincial tax at 11.16%	725.00
Less dividend tax credit (5.13% x $6,250)	(320.63)
Provincial tax payable	$ 404.37
Total tax	$ 1,383.74

Note: The effective tax rate on dividends in Ontario can also be computed with the following formula: 1.25 [(Federal tax rate − .1333) + (Provincial tax rate - .0513)]. For Ontario, this rate is 27.13%. This is lower than the effective tax rate on ordinary income. This is true for investors in all tax brackets.

$5,000 in *interest income* would be taxed as: federal tax + provincial tax = ($5,000 x 29%) + ($5,000) x 11.16) = $1,450 + $558 = $2,008.

Capital gains occur when the selling price of an asset exceeds its original cost. Taxes on capital gains are currently 50% of the applicable marginal rate. An Ontario resident with capital gains of $5,000 would pay

Capital gains	$ 5,000
Taxable capital gains (50%)	2,500
Federal tax at 29%	725
Provincial tax at 11.16%	279
Total tax	$ 1,004

In practice, income from capital gains is more attractive than either interest or dividend income because individuals pay taxes on *realized capital gains* only when the asset sale actually takes place. And, as you will see in Chapter 5, the time value of money dramatically reduces the effective tax rate on capital gains if investors hold the assets for a long time..

Corporate Taxes: Canadian corporations must pay taxes to both the federal and provincial governments. In general, small corporations and some manufacturing and processing companies receive tax breaks due to lower rates. Although corporate tax rates *appear* to be lower than individual tax rates, corporate income is subject to double taxation because individuals must pay personal income tax on any dividends received.

Since interest is a tax deductible expense for corporations, debt financing has a tax advantage over equity financing. For example, if a firm's tax rate is 40 % then it must increase EBIT by [$1 / (1 − 0.40)] = $1.67 to pay $1.00 in dividends since $0.67 goes to taxes. Because interest is tax-deductible though, firms only need only $1 more in EBIT to pay an additional $1 in interest.

For interest and dividend income *earned* by the firm, however, just the opposite is true. Interest is fully taxable, but dividends received from other Canadian corporations are tax-exempt.

Capital gains received by corporations are currently taxed at 50 % of the marginal rate. When calculating capital gains for tax purposes, a firm nets out all allowable capital losses in the same year. **Capital losses** occur when the selling price of an asset is lower than its original cost. If capital losses exceed capital gains, the net capital loss may be **carried back** to reduce capital gains in three prior years. In this case, a firm files a revised tax return and receives a refund of prior taxes. Any additional losses may be carried forward indefinitely to reduce future capital gains taxes. (For *operating losses*, the carry-back period is three years; the carry-forward period is seven years.)

Example: Acme Enterprises experienced a net capital loss of $2 million in 2003 and had net capital gains of $600,000 in 2002, $400,000 in 2001, $300,000 in 2000, and $150,000 in 1999. What is the maximum carry-back, and how much can be carried forward indefinitely?

Maximum carry-back = $600,000 + $400,000 + $300,000 = $1,300,000

Carry-forward amount = $2,000,000 - $1,300,000 = $700,000

Example: A firm sells a building for $500,000 (its original cost 5 years ago was $200,000), and a tract of land for $250,000 (its original cost 10 years ago was $300,000). If the tax rate is 40 %, what are the net capital gains and tax, if any?

Capital gain (building) = $500,000 − $200,000 = $300,000
Capital loss (land) = $250,000 − $300,000 = - $50,000
Net capital gain = $300,000 - $50,000 = $250,000
Taxes = $250,000 x (0.50 x 0.40) = $50,000

2.5   CAPITAL COST ALLOWANCE (CCA)

For tax purposes, CCA depreciation is used to determine taxable income. Depreciation calculated using CCA is not necessarily the same as accounting depreciation computed under GAAP.. For CCA calculations, every asset is assigned to a particular class ('pool') which establishes its maximum CCA rate. Most assets are depreciated using the declining balance method (intangible assets use straight-line depreciation in calculating CCA).

For a given year, the CCA is computed by multiplying the beginning balance of the asset pool, the *undepreciated capital cost* (UCC), by the appropriate rate. CCA uses the half-year rule. This means that firms only use one-half of an assets installed cost to calculate CCA depreciation during the first year of use.

As a firm buys and sells assets from a given class of assets during the year, the following scenarios are possible:
1. The firm buys assets (the half-year rule is applied).
2. The firm buys and sells assets; however, total acquisitions exceed the lower of selling price(s) and original cost(s). The half-year rule is applied to the net acquisitions.
3. The firm sells assets. Any gain or loss is applied to net income.
4. The firm buys and sells assets. However, total acquisitions are less than the lower of selling price(s) and original cost(s). The loss is deducted from income.
5. The firm does not buy or sell assets during the year.

Note: In the last three scenarios, the half-year rule does not apply.

Example: A firm will acquire class 10 assets to be depreciated at a CCA rate of 30 % with a beginning UCC balance of $50,000. Calculate the maximum CCA for each of the next 5 years.

Year	Activity
1	Buy one truck for $100,000
2	Buy two vans for $50,000 and $150,000; sell the truck bought in Year 1 for $100,000
3	Sell a truck for $15,000 that originally cost $45,000
4	Buy one van for $10,000; sell the $50,000 van both in year 2 for $40,000
5	No asset purchases or sales during the year

Year 1	UCC beginning + Acquisition (½ of $100,000)	$100,000
	CCA @ 30%	30,000
	UCC ending balance	70,000
	Year 2 beginning: add ½ of Year 1 acquisition	50,000
	Year 2 beginning	120,000

Year 2	UCC beginning balance	120,000
	Add ½ Year 2 *net* acquisitions	
	.50($50,000 + 150,000 - 100,000)	50,000
	UCC balance	170,000
	CCA @ 30%	51,000
	UCC ending balance	119,000
	For Year 3 beginning, add ½ Year 2 acquisitions ($100,000)	219,000

Year 3	UCC beginning balance	$219,000
	Asset sale (subtract, using lesser of cost or sale price)	15,000
	UCC balance	204,000
	CCA @ 30%	61,200
	UCC ending balance	142,800

Year 4	UCC beginning	142,800
	Add ½ net acquisition .50 ($10,000 - $40,000) = -$30,000*	30,000
	UCC balance	112,800
	CCA @ 30%	33,840
	UCC ending balance	78,960

Year 5	UCC beginning balance	$ 78,960
	CCA @ 30%	23,688
	UCC ending balance	55,272

*The lesser of original cost or selling price reduces acquisitions because the asset is removed from the pool. As can be seen from the above example, the half-year rule applies to the acquisition of assets and to situations where net acquisitions are positive. In all other cases, including negative net acquisitions, the rule is not applied.

The procedure illustrated above is repeated in subsequent periods for each asset class until either a "recapture" or a "terminal loss" occurs. A *recapture* occurs when the UCC balance is negative, resulting from over-depreciating the asset class. This amount is added back (recaptured) as ordinary taxable income and taxed at the corporate tax rate. A *terminal loss* occurs when both (1) the UCC class has a positive balance, and (2) there are no assets left in the class. A terminal loss reflects under-depreciation of the asset class because nothing is left in the asset pool. Firm may claim the full terminal loss as an ordinary expense for the year in which it occurs.

Example: Simple, Inc. has five asset classes. We will assume the original cost of one asset sold in each pool is $25,000. Before the sale, asset classes B and C have only one asset left. Simple also sold securities for $100,000, which originally cost $90,000. They also sold a tract of land for a $5,000 loss. All sales are in 2003; the applicable tax rate is 30%. Calculate Simple's taxes payable assuming a before-tax operating income of $30,000.

Asset Class	UCC Beginning	Sale Proceeds	Terminal Loss	Recaptured Income	Capital Gain
A	$15,000	$ 7,500			
B	15,000	7,500	$ 7,500		
C	27,500	30,000	2,500		$ 5,000
D	15,000	17,500		$ 2,500	
E	15,000	30,000		10,000	5,000

Note that, for classes D and E there is recaptured income because the UCC balance is reduced by the lower of sales proceeds and original cost ($25,000). For class D, $15,000 - $17,500 = -$2,500; for class E, $15,000 - $25,000 = -$10,000. These amounts must be added to taxable income. For asset classes C and E, sale proceeds are greater than the original cost, so capital gains must be recognized. For classes B and C, the UCC balance after the sale is positive with no assets remaining in the class; this results in terminal losses of $7,500 and $2,500.

Taxes for Simple, Inc. are calculated as follows:

Operating income	$ 30,000
+ Recapture of Depreciation ($2,500 + $10,000)	12,500
+ Net Capital Gains ($5,000 + $5,000 + $10,000* - $5,000**) (0.50)	7,500
- Terminal losses ($7,500 + $2,500)	10,000
Total taxable income	40,000
Taxes payable (30%)	$12,000

*	Capital gains from sale of securities
**	Capital loss on non-depreciable asset (land). Note that capital losses cannot exceed capital gains in any given year. Deferral provisions allow capital losses to be carried back 3 years to reduce capital gains and carried forward indefinitely.

CONCEPT TEST

1. A _____ can be thought of as a snapshot of a firm's accounting value as of a particular date. By definition, the value of a firm's assets is equal to _____ + _____ . Alternately, this definition can be thought of as _____ = assets - _____ .

2. An asset that can be converted to cash quickly and easily, without significant loss in value, is said to be a _____ asset.

3. Assets are listed on the balance sheet in the order of decreasing _____ . _____ generally earn lower rates of return than do fixed assets.

4. If a firm raises funds from investors, the first claim on cash flows is given to the _____ . The residual cash flows belong to the firm's _____ .

5. The use of debt financing is referred to as _____ because it magnifies both the _____ and the _____ accruing to the firm's shareholders.

6. The fixed asset values shown on a firm's balance sheet are not current market values. Instead, they are shown at _____ . The difference between market value and _____ is generally fairly small for the firm's _____ assets, but can be extremely large for _____ assets.

7. The income statement equation is _____ - _____ = _____ . Net income divided by the number of shares outstanding is called _____ .

8. For accounting purposes, revenue is shown on the income statement when it _____ , not necessarily when payment is received. For financial decision-making purposes, accounting income must be distinguished from _____ .

9. One of the reasons that net income is not the same as cash from operations is that some deductions are _____ deductions. The most common of these expenses is _____ .

10. Operating cash flow is calculated as _____ + _____ - _____ . Total cash flow from assets is calculated as _____ - _____ - _____ .

11. Cash flow to creditors is calculated as _____ - _____ . Cash flow to shareholders is calculated as _____ - _____ .

12. The _____ tax rate is computed by dividing total taxes paid by the total taxable income. The _____ tax rate is the tax rate applied to the last dollar earned. A _____ tax is a tax rate which is a constant percentage of income, regardless of income level.

13. The three different types of Canadian investment income, _____, _____, and _____ are taxed differently.

14. Corporate income taxes create a tax advantage for _____ over _____ financing because interest paid is tax deductible while dividends paid are not.

15.   _____ is depreciation for tax purposes in Canada. CCA rates are found by determining the _____ in which an asset belongs.

16.   The _____ rule mandates that only _____ of the net acquisition be added to the beginning _____ of the asset class.

17.   If an asset is sold from a depreciable class, the lower of _____ or _____ must be deducted from the UCC.

18.   Although the _____ reduces the firm's taxes payable dollar for dollar, CCA cannot be claimed on that amount.

19.   If a particular class of assets are over depreciated, then the firm must pay taxes on the full amount of the _____ . On the other hand, if there are no assets left in the class and the UCC balance is positive, then a _____ occurs. Terminal losses reduce _____ in the year in which they occur.

20.   Capital gains for corporations are taxed at _____ of the _____ .

21.   Generally, income from capital gains is more attractive than _____ which is fully taxed or _____ which must be grossed up by _____ . The _____ is then calculated on the grossed-up figure.

22.   A dividend tax credit of _____ of the grossed up dividend is subtracted from the federal tax to get the net federal tax payable.

PROBLEMS

Basic Questions

Problem 1

During the year 2003, the B.C. Company had sales of $1,000, cost of goods sold of $400, depreciation of $100, and interest paid of $150. Using a 34% corporate tax rate, and assuming all taxes are paid the year they are due, construct B.C.'s income statement for 2003.

Problem 2

The B.C. Company had 100 shares of common stock outstanding at the end of 2003. Total dividends paid for 2003 were $120. Compute earnings per share (EPS) and dividends per share for the year.

Problem 3

At the end of 2002, B.C. had notes payable of $1,200, accounts payable of $2,400, and long-term debt of $3,000. For 2003, those amounts are $1,600, $2,000, and $2,800, respectively. Asset values for 2002 and 2003, respectively, are $800 and $500 in cash; $400 and $300 in marketable securities; $900 and $800 in accounts receivable; $1,800 and $2,000 in inventory; $6,000 and $8,000 in net plant and equipment. Prepare balance sheets for 2002 and 2003.

Problem 4

Based on the information from Problem 1, calculate B.C.'s operating cash flow for 2003.

Problem 5

During 2003, B.C. sold $300 in net fixed assets. They also issued $2,400 worth of new stock and used the proceeds to buy new fixed assets. What was net capital spending for that year?

Problem 6

Based on the balance sheets above for B. C. Company, what was net working capital in each year? What were the additions to net working capital in 2003?

Problem 7

Having invested $50,000 in the common stock of Garden Enterprises, you receive $0.10 in cash dividends for every $1.00 invested. Compute the effective tax rate on dividend income. Then compute your total marginal tax rate on any interest income you receive. Assume your federal marginal tax rate is 29% and the provincial tax rate is16.67%

Problem 8

Emma Movers, Inc. is purchasing a $50,000 machine to replace an existing one which cost $12,000 five years ago but can be sold for $10,500 today. The new machine will have a CCA rate of 20 %. If Emma's tax rate is 35 %, what is the tax saving from claiming CCA in year 3, if the beginning UCC balance in the asset class is $70,000?

Intermediate Questions

Use the information in problems 1 - 6 to solve problems 9-11.

Problem 9

Using the information from the above problems, what was B.C.'s total cash flow from assets in 2003?
Explain your answer.

Problem 10

What was B.C.'s cash flow to long-term creditors in 2003?

Problem 11

Now assume that, iin addition to issuing $2,400 in new common shares, B.C. also repurchased $611 in common shares. What was the firm's cash flow to shareholders in 2003?

Problem 12

Based on the following information for Pascucci Corporation, calculate total cash flow from assets, cash flow to creditors, and cash flow to shareholders for 2003. Use a 34% corporate tax rate.

	2002	2003
Sales	$2,230	$2,890
Costs	1,050	1,437
Depreciation	418	418
Interest	225	276
Dividends	350	400
Current assets	1,140	1,335
Fixed assets	5,670	5,877
Current liabilities	884	1,006
Long-term debt	2,349	2,666

Problem 13

The current undepreciated capital cost of a pool of assets is $250,000. The company has decided to sell one of the 6 assets in the pool. The original capital cost of that asset was $360,000. Calculate the amount (if any) of recaptured depreciation, capital gains and terminal loss resulting from the sale of that asset at the following sale prices: $400,000; $250,000; $170,000. Calculate the new opening UCC balance for each case, using a CCA rate of 20%.

Problem 14

A firm has three asset pools. The acquisition in asset pool C is eligible for a 10% investment tax credit. Use the information below to compute amounts of recapture, capital gains, terminal losses, capital losses, and the CCA charge based on a rate of 20%, For asset pool B, no assets remain after the sale.

Asset Pool	A	B	C
UCC beginning	$ 120,000	$ 240,000	$ 100,000
Acquisitions	50,000	0	150,000
Assets sold			
Original cost	400,000	80,000	80,000
Proceeds of sale	450,000	120,000	60,000

Problem 15

Refer to the information in Problem 14. Assume the corporate tax rate is 35% and that the firm's earned net income (after-tax) *excluding* depreciation is $91,000. Compute the firm's tax liability.

Challenge Questions

Problem 16

Your federal marginal tax rate is 29%. In addition, your provincial rate is 14.7%. If you invest $50,000 for one year, which alternative would generate the highest after-tax income?

1)   Common stock with a 10% dividend yield
2)   Bonds paying a rate of 12.75%
3)   Investing in common stock that pays no dividends but is worth $55,250 at year end.

Problem 17

FYE Company has the following asset pool eligible for CCA @ 20% and is subject to a 40% tax rate. The acquisition in asset pool A is eligible for a 10% investment tax credit.

Asset Pool	A
UCC beginning	$100,000
Acquisitions	150,000
Assets sold	
Original cost	80,000
Proceeds of sale	100,000
Book value	60,000

Assume that FYE has two other assets pools. Pool B will have a positive UCC balance of $40,000 at the beginning of year 2, from which the *last* asset will be sold for $20,000 (original cost was $15,000). Pool C will have a positive UCC balance of $30,000 at the beginning of year 2, from which one asset will be sold for $65,000 (original cost was $55,000). If FYE's earnings before taxes is projected to be $80,000 in year 2, calculate the taxes payable for that year. Be sure to incorporate the impact of acquisitions and sales from all three asset pools.

Problem 18

Upon their arrival in Quebec in 2001, Marco and Polo decided to form the Marco Polo Pasta Company. At that time they purchased a small industrial pasta mixer for $6,000 and a spaghetti machine for $5,000. Due to rapidly expanding business, in 2003 they bought a larger pasta mixer for $10,000 and a new spaghetti machine for $12,500. They sold the old machines for $4,500 and $7,000, respectively. Their equipment is depreciated at a CCA rate of 20%, and they have a 40% tax rate. The firm has $200,000 of taxable income before considering CCA. Calculate their tax bill for 2003.

ANSWERS TO CONCEPT TEST

1.   balance sheet; total liabilities; shareholders' equity; shareholders' equity; total liabilities

2.   liquid

3.   liquidity; liquid (or current) assets

4.   creditors; shareholders

5.   financial leverage; gains; losses

6.   book value (or historical cost); book value; current; fixed

7.   revenues; expenses; income; earnings per share (EPS)

8.   accrues (is earned); cash flow

9.   non-cash; depreciation

10.   earnings before interest and taxes (EBIT); depreciation; taxes; operating cash flow; capital spending; additions to net working capital

11.   interest; net new borrowing; dividends; net new equity raised

12.   average; marginal; flat rate

13.   interest; dividends; capital gains

14.   debt; equity

15.   capital cost allowance (CCA); class

16.   half-year; half; undepreciated capital cost (UCC)

17.   selling price; original cost

18.   investment tax credit

19.   recaptured depreciation; terminal loss; taxable income

20.   50 %; marginal tax rate

21.   interest income, dividend income; 25 %; federal tax

22.   13 1/3 percent

PROBLEM SOLUTIONS

Problem 1:

B.C. COMPANY, INC.
2003 Income Statement

Net sales	$ 1,000
Cost of goods sold	400
Depreciation	100
Earnings before interest and taxes	$ 500
Interest paid	150
Taxable income	$ 350
Taxes (34%)	119
Net income	$ 231

Problem 2:   EPS = Net income / Number of shares outstanding   = $231 / 100 = $2.31
                          Dividends per share = Total dividends / Number of shares = $120 / 100 = $1.20

Problem 3:   B.C. COMPANY
                        Balance Sheets as of December 2002 and December 2003
                        2002   2003   2002   2003

Assets   *Liabilities & Owners' Equity*
Current assets   Current liabilities
  Cash $ 800 $ 500   Accounts payable $ 2,400 $ 2,000
  Marketable securities   400   300   Notes payable   1,200   1,600
  Accounts receivable   900   800   Total $ 3,600 $ 3,600
  Inventory   1,800   2,000
Total $ 3,900 $ 3,600
                                                      Long-term debt $ 3,000 $ 2,800
                                                      Owners' equity   3,300   5,200
Fixed assets
  Net plant & equipment $ 6,000 $ 8,000
Total assets $ 9,900 $11,600   Total liabilities & equity $ 9,900 $11,600*

*To compute owners' equity, use the balance sheet equation (assets = liabilities + owners' equity); solve for owners' equity.

Problem 4:   Earnings before interest and taxes $ 500
                 + Depreciation   100
                 - Taxes   119
                    Cash flow from operations $ 481

Problem 5: Depreciation expense of $100 (from the income statement) means the value of the fixed assets remaining from 2002 is $6,000 - $100 = $5,900. Net capital spending is $8,000 - $5,900 = $2,100. It can also be computed as: (funds raised and used on fixed assets - funds received from the sales of fixed assets) $2,400 - $300 = $2,100.

Problem 6:   For 2002: ($800 + $400 + $900 + $1,800) - ($1,200 + $2,400) = $3,900 - $3,600 = $300
                For 2000: ($500 + $300 + $800 + $2,000) - ($1,600 + $2,000) = $3,600 - $3,600 = $0

    Addition to net working capital = NWC_{2003} - NWC_{2002} = $0 - $300 = -$300

This is actually a reduction of $300 in net working capital. Alternatively, the addition to NWC can be computed as:
    Addition to NWC = Change in CA - Change in CL = ($3,600 - $3,900) - ($3,600 -$3,600) = -$300

Problem 7:   Dividends received ($50,000 x 0.10) = $5,000

    Federal tax payable $5,000 x 1.25 x (0.29 - 0.1333) = 979.38
    Provincial tax payable $5,000 x 1.25 x (0.1667- 0.0513) = 721.25
    Total tax payable $979.38 + 721.25 = $1,700.63
    Effective tax rate = Total tax / Total dividends = 1,700.63 / 5,000 = 34.01% ~ 34%
  OR
    Federal tax   = 1.25 (.29 - .1333) = 0.1959 = 19.59%
    Provincial tax = 1.25 (.1667 - .0513) = 0.1446 = 14.46%
    Effective tax rate = 19.59 + 14.46 = 34.05% ~ 34%

    Marginal tax rate on interest income = 29% + 16.67% = 45.67%

Problem 8:

Year 1		
UCC beginning Yr 1		$70,000
½ of Net acquisition		19,750
UCC balance		89,750
CCA Yr 1 @ 20 %		17,950
UCC ending		71,800

Year 2		
UCC beginning		71,800
Add ½ of net acquisition		19,750
UCC balance		91,550
CCA Yr 2 @ 20 %		18,310
UCC ending		73,240

Year 3 UCC beginning		73,240
CCA Yr 2 @ 20 %		14,648
Year 3 tax savings at 35%		$ 5,126.80

Note that the net acquisition in year 1 is the purchase price, less the lower of original cost or selling price, taking into consideration the half-year rule.

Problem 9:

Operating cash flow	$ 481	(Problem 4)
- Net capital spending	2,100	(Problem 5)
- Additions to NWC	(300)	(Problem 6)
Cash flow from assets	($1,319)	

Explanation: The firm's net income is positive, but cash flow is negative. This is because capital expenditures are not included in net income, but are included in actual cash flow. In general, net income is not equal to total cash flow.

Problem 10

Interest paid	$ 150	(2002 income statement)
- Net new borrowing	(200)	(long-term debt$_{2003}$ - long-term debt$_{2002}$)
Cash flow to creditors	$ 350	

Problem 11:

Dividends paid	$ 120	(Problem 2)
- Net new equity	1,789	(Common stock$_{2003}$ - common stock$_{2002}$)*
Cash flow to shareholders	($1,669)	

*Note: You can't compute the net new equity from the owner's equity in the balance sheets because the owner's equity section includes both common stock and retained earnings. (The items were not listed separately.) Net new equity is computed using the value of common stock, as follows:

	Change in total equity ($5,200 - 3,300) = 1,900	
Less	Change in retained earnings = (EPS - Dividends) x shares outstanding	
	= (2.31 - 1.20) x 100 = 1.11 x 100 = 111	
=	Change in common shares = $1,900 - 111 = $1,789	

Also note the total cash flow to creditors and shareholders, $350 + (-$1,669) = -$1,319, is the same as the total cash flow from assets.

Problem 12:   Cash flow from operations: $1,195
Total cash flow from assets   = $497*
Cash flow to long-term creditors   = $(41)
Cash flow to shareholders   = $497 - ($41)   = $538   i.e. $CF_{Assets} - CF_{Creditors}$

Problem 13:

	Case I	Case II	Case III
UCC beginning	$ 250,000	$ 250,000	$ 250,000
Sale	360,000	250,000	170,000
Recapture	110,000	0	0
UCC (new)		0	80,000
Capital gain	40,000	0	0
Terminal loss	0	0	0

Note: Case I: Recapture = UCC beg - original cost because cost < sale proceeds
Case II and III: Sale is recorded as because sale price < original cost
There is no terminal loss because, in each case, there were assets remaining in the pool.

Problem 14:

Asset Pool	A	B	C
Recapture	$ 200,000		
Terminal loss		$ 160,000	
Capital gain	50,000	40,000	
Capital loss			
CCA charge @ 20%			27,500

Problem 15:

Earnings before tax [$91,000 / (1 - 0.35)]	$140,000
Recapture	200,000
Capital gains ($50,000 + $40,000) x 0.50	45,000
Terminal loss	(160,000)
CCA	(27,500)
Total taxable	$197,500
Taxes payable @ 35%	69,125
Less investment tax credit	15,000
Net taxes payable	$ 54,125

Problem 16:   1)   Total tax   = $5,000 x 1.25 x [(0.2 9 - 0.1333) + (.0.1470 - 0.0513)]   = $1,577.7
Net income = $5,000 - 1,577.5   = $3,422.50

2)   Total tax   = $6,375.00 x (.29 + .1470)   = $2,785.88
Net income = $6,375 - 2.785.88   = $3,589.13

3)   Capital gain $ 5,250.00
Tax $5,250 x 0.50 x (.29 + .1470)   1,147.13
Net income $ 4102.87

The highest after-tax income comes from investing in non-dividend paying stock. Therefore, that is your best alternative. Return on investment is (1) 3,422.50 / 50,000   =   6.84% ; (2) 3,589.13 / 50,000   =   7.18% ; 4,102.87 / 50,000   =   8.21%

Problem 17: Pool A

	UCC beginning Yr 1	$ 100,000
	Net acquisition ($150,000 x 0.90 - 80,000) x 0.50	27,500
	Balance	127,500
	Year 1 CCA @ 20%	25,500
	UCC beginning Yr 2	102,000
	Year 2 CCA @ 20%	20,400

Pool B

	UCC beginning Yr 2	$ 40,000
	Sale	15,000
	Balance	25,000
	Year 2 CCA @ 20%	5000

Pool C

	UCC beginning Yr 2	$ 30,000
	Sale	55,000
	Balance	$(25,000)

Earnings before taxes	$ 80,000

Pool A

Taxable capital gain ($100,000 - $80,000) x 0.50	10,000

Pool B

Taxable capital gain ($20,000 - $15,000) x 0.50	2,500
Terminal loss	25,000

Pool C

Taxable capital gain ($65,000 - $55,000) x 0.50	5,000
Recapture	25,000
Taxable income	97,500
Taxes @ 40%	39,000

Problem 18:

UCC beginning 2001	$ 0
Acquisitions ($11,000) x 0.50	5,500
CCA @ 20%	1,100
UCC balance	4,400
Add ½ of acquisitions	5,500
UCC beginning 2002	9,900
CCA @ 20%	1,980
UCC balance	7,920
UCC beginning 2003	7,920
Net acquisitions ($10,000 + $12,500 - $4,500 - $5,000) x 0.50	6,500
Balance	14,420
CCA @ 20%	2,884
Balance	11,536
Taxable income before CCA	$ 200,000
Taxable capital gain ($2,000 on spaghetti machine) x 0.50	1,000
CCA deduction	(2,884)
Taxable amount	198,116
Tax @ 40%	$ 79,246.40

3 Working With Financial Statements

CHAPTER HIGHLIGHTS

In this chapter, we continue to examine the financial statements discussed in Chapter 2. Again, our emphasis is on the use of financial statements as a source of information for financial decisions. Remember that under ideal circumstances, financial decisions are based on market value information, rather than accounting data. However, managers rarely have full market value information about all of a firm's assets. So they (and we) must rely on accounting figures for much of our financial information. And, for privately held corporations, not-for-profit businesses and smaller firms, accounting statements may provide the only information available.

3.1   CASH FLOW AND FINANCIAL STATEMENTS: A CLOSER LOOK

In This chapter, we analyze more closely the impact of various transactions on the firm's cash flows, using the cash flow equation: Cash flow from assets = Cash flow to creditors + Cash flow to owners.

Sources and Uses of Cash: Transactions which create cash inflows for the firm are sources of cash, and transactions which create cash outflows are uses of cash. We can create a statement detailing the sources and uses of cash by analyzing successive year-end balance sheets to identify those changes in balance sheet accounts which represent sources or uses of cash.

For example, a firm whose inventory increases from $100 to $120 over a given year must have a $20 net expenditure on inventory during the year. This is a net *use* of cash. A decrease in inventory from $100 to $70 is a $30 net *source* of cash (the funds were not tied up in inventory, so they were available for other purposes). *An increase in an asset account is a use of cash. A decrease is a source of cash.*

A decrease in a liability or equity account is a net use of cash. For example, a firm with long-term debt of $200 could reduce the debt to $175 by repaying $25 of the debt. This involves paying out (using) $25 cash. If the firm's equity accounts increased from $300 to $350 during the year, the additional $50 represents cash coming into the firm, or a source of cash. *An increase in a liability or equity account is a source of cash.*

Example: Balance sheets for the K-Bec Company, for 2002 and 2003 and the 2003 income statement are below:

K-BEC CO., INC.
Balance Sheets as of December 31, 2002 and 2003

	2000	2003	Change
Assets			
Current assets			
Cash	$ 500	550	+ $ 50
Accounts receivable	1,000	975	- 25
Inventory	2,000	2,225	+ 225
Total	$ 3,500	$ 3,750	+ $ 250
Fixed assets			
Net plant and equipment	6,500	6,750	+ 250
Total assets	$10,000	$10,500	+ $ 500

Liabilities and Owners' Equity

Current liabilities				
Accounts payable	$ 1,000	$ 1,200	+ $	200
Notes payable	500	350	–	150
Total	$ 1,500	$ 1,550	+	50
Long-term debt	$ 2,500	$ 2,586	+ $	86
Owners' equity				
Common stock and paid-in surplus	3,500	3,600	+	100
Retained earnings	2,500	2,764	+	264
Total	$ 6,000	$ 6,364	+ $	364
Total liabilities and owners' equity	$10,000	$10,500	+ $	500

K-BEC CO., INC. 2003 Income Statement

Sales	$ 5,000
Cost of goods sold	3,000
Depreciation	600
Earnings before interest and taxes	$ 1,400
Interest paid	400
Taxable income	$ 1,000
Taxes (34%)	340
Net income	$ 660
Retained earnings	$ 264
Dividends	$ 396

The last column of the balance sheet statement shows the change in each account from the end of 2000 to the end of 2003. For example, the decrease in accounts receivable is a $25 source of cash; the $225 increase in inventory is a use of cash. The sources and uses of cash for K-Bec are as follows:

Sources of cash	
Decrease in accounts receivable	$ 25
Increase in accounts payable	200
Increase in long-term debt	86
Increase in owners' equity	100
Increase in retained earnings	264
Total sources	$ 675
Uses of cash	
Increase in inventory	225
Increase in net plant and equipment	250
Decrease in notes payable	150
Total uses	$ 625
Net addition to cash	$ 50

Note that the net addition to cash, $50, is the difference between total sources and total uses. It agrees with the $50 increase in the cash account from 2000 to 2003, as shown on the balance sheet.

The Statement of Cash Flows: We use income statement and balance sheet information to create the Statement of Cash Flows. This statement organizes the sources and uses of cash into three categories: operating, financing, and investment activities.

From the balance sheets, there is a $250 increase in fixed assets. However, the $600 depreciation expense on the income statement indicates that, had K-Bec not purchased additional fixed assets, the fixed asset account for 2002 would have decreased to $5,900 ($6,500 - 600). Since fixed assets increased to $6,750 in 2003, the firm actually invested $850 = $6,750 – $5,900 to acquire fixed assets. Note this amount is the same as depreciation plus change in fixed assets: $600 + $250 = $850.

Depreciation is deducted as an expense in computing net income. It is not a cash expense though, so it is added to net income as a source of cash on the statement of cash flows. Under the category of financing activities, dividends are deducted as a use of cash because payment of dividends requires the expenditure of cash.

Example: The Statement of Cash Flows for K-Bec Co., Inc. is below:

2003 Statement of Cash Flows	
Operating activities	
Net income	$ 660
Plus:	
Depreciation	600
Increase in accounts payable	200
Decrease in accounts receivable	25
Less:	
Increase in inventory	- 225
Net cash from operating activity	$ 1,260
Investment activities:	
Fixed asset acquisitions	- $ 850
Net cash from investment activities	- $ 850
Financing activities:	
Decrease in notes payable	- $ 150
Increase in long-term debt	86
Dividends paid	- 396
Increase in common stock	100
Net cash from financing activity	- $ 360
Net increase in cash	$ 50

3.2   STANDARDIZED FINANCIAL STATEMENTS

In making financial decisions, it is often helpful to standardize a firm's financial statements by comparing them with those of companies in the same industry or with its own statements from previous years. These approaches are known as common-size statements and common-base-year statements. Note that the common-size approach may be problematic if firms in the same industry differ substantially. And, common-base-year statements may not be particularly relevant if the firm has grown significantly. Both approaches are illustrated below.

Common-size statements: Financial statements are standardized by presenting balance sheet accounts as a percentage of total assets and income statement data percentage of sales.

Example: The common-size balance sheets and income statement for K-Bec are below:

K-BEC CO., INC.
Common-Size Balance Sheets
December 31, 2002 and 2003

	2002	2003	Change
Assets			
Current assets			
Cash	5.0 %	5.2 %	+ 0.2 %
Accounts receivable	10.0	9.3	- 0.7
Inventory	20.0	21.2	+ 1.2
Total	35.0	35.7	+ 0.7
Fixed assets			
Net plant and equipment	65.0	64.3	- 0.7
Total assets	100.0 %	100.0 %	0 %
Liabilities and Owners' Equity			
Current liabilities			
Accounts payable	10.0 %	11.4 %	+ 1.4 %
Notes payable	5.0	3.3	- 1.7
Total	15.0	~14.8	- ~0.2
Long-term debt	25.0	24.6	- 0.4
Owners' equity			
Common stock and paid-in surplus	35.0	34.3	- 0.7
Retained earnings	25.0	26.3	+ 1.3
Total	60.0	60.6	+ 0.6
Total liabilities and owners' equity	100.0 %	100.0 %	+ 0.0

K-BEC CO., INC.2003 Income Statement

Sales	100.0 %
Cost of goods sold	60.0
Depreciation	12.0
Earnings before interest and taxes	28.0
Interest paid	8.0
Taxable income	20.0
Taxes (34%)	6.8
Net income	13.2%
Retained earnings	5.3
Dividends	7.9

Common-Base-Year Financial Statements: Trend Analysis. Financial statements are standardized relative to statements in a previous year. A base year is selected; each financial statement item for the base year is assigned a value of 1.00. For subsequent years, each item is assigned a value reflecting the change in that item. If, for example, 2002 is selected as the base year, and the firm's inventory level $200. This $200 is assigned a value of 1.0 for the 2002 base-year statement. If inventory increases to $210 in 2003 (a 5% increase in inventory), 2003 common-base-year balance sheet displays an inventory value of ($210/$200) = 1.05.

3.3   RATIO ANALYSIS

To make comparisons over time or with similar businesses, financial statement analysis often compares ratios of various balance sheet and income statement items, rather than dollar values. This aids in comparing performance for firms of vastly different size, or for a firm which grows over time. Further, large Canadian companies usually span two or more industries, making absolute dollar comparisons difficult.

The major categories of financial ratios used for financial analysis are:

> 1.   Short-term solvency or liquidity ratios.
> 2.   Long-term solvency or financial leverage ratios.
> 3.   Asset management or turnover ratios.
> 4.   Profitability ratios.
> 5.   Market value ratios.

The financial ratios defined in this section are illustrated using the 2003 financial statements for K-Bec Co., Inc.

Short-term Solvency or Liquidity Measures: This group of ratios measures the firm's short-term liquidity - its ability to meet short-term obligations. The most commonly used measures in this category are the current ratio and the quick (acid-test) ratio. The values of these ratios for K-Bec in 2003 are below.

Current ratio   =   Current assets/Current liabilities = $3,750/$1,550 = 2.42   [3.1]
Quick ratio   =   (Current assets − Inventory)/Current liabilities = (3,750 − $2,225)/1,550 = 0.98   [3.2]

The current ratio indicates that K-Bec has $2.42 of current assets for each $1.00 of current liabilities. The quick ratio differs in that inventory is not included in the numerator. The quick ratio is a more stringent indicator of a firm's liquidity because it only incorporates those assets which are most quickly converted into cash.

Caution must be used in interpreting financial ratios such as the current ratio. For short-term creditors, a high ratio is better because it indicates liquidity. It may also indicate that the firm is using cash and other short-term assets inefficiently. Under ordinary circumstances, we should expect a current ratio of at least 1, indicating a positive net working capital. However, healthy current ratios vary from industry to industry.

Three additional measures of liquidity are computed for K-Bec:

Cash ratio   =   Cash/Current liabilities   = $550/1,550 = 0.36   [3.3]

NWC to Total assets ratio   =   NWC/Total assets   =   ($3,750 - $1,550)/10500   =   0.21   [3.4]

Interval measure   =   Current assets/Average daily operating cost   = $3,750/(3,000/365) = 456 days   [3.5]

Average daily operating cost is computed as operating costs (COGS), divided by 365 days: ($3,000/365) = $8.22. The interval measure gives an indication of how long the business could continue to operate if cash inflows were drastically reduced (in this case 456 days).

Long-Term Solvency Measures: These are used to gauge the extent to which a firm uses debt rather than equity financing. An increase in the level of debt increases the probability of default. The ratios in this section are also referred to as *financial leverage ratios* or *leverage ratios*. They are calculated below for K-Bec.

$$\text{Total debt ratio } = \text{ (Total assets } - \text{ Total equity)/Total equity } = \text{ (\$10,500 } - \text{ \$6,364)/10,500 } = \text{ 0.39} \qquad [3.6]$$

This means K-Bec obtains 39% of its financing is obtained from debt; the remaining 61% is equity financing.

$$\text{Debt / equity ratio } = \text{ Total debt/Total equity } = \text{ \$4,136/6,364 } = \text{ 0.65} \qquad [3.7]$$

The debt/equity ratio can also be computed from the total debt ratio. The total debt ratio indicates that K-Bec has $0.39 of debt and ($1.00 – $0.39) = $0.61 of equity financing for each dollar of assets, and a debt/equity ratio of ($0.39 / $0.61) = 0.64. (This result differs slightly from the direct calculation due to rounding)

$$\text{Equity multiplier } = \text{ Total assets/Total equity } = \text{ \$10,500/6,364 } = \text{ 1.65} \qquad [3.8]$$

The equity multiplier can be computed from the debt/equity ratio, using the fact that K-Bec has $0.61 of equity for each $1.00 of assets. The equity multiplier is ($1.00/$0.61) = 1.64.

The relationship between the equity multiplier and the debt/equity ratio can also be derived by substituting (Total equity + Total debt) for Total assets in the numerator of the above equation:

$$\text{Equity multiplier } = \text{ (Total equity} + \text{Total debt)/Total equity} = \text{ 1} + \text{(Total debt)/Total equity} = \text{ 1} + \text{D/E } = \text{ 1.65}$$

Other useful ratios:

$$\text{Long-term debt ratio} = \text{LT debt/(LT} + \text{Total equity)} = \text{ \$2,586/(2,586} + \text{6,364)} = \text{ 0.29} \qquad [3.9]$$

$$\text{Times interest earned ratio } = \text{ EBIT/Interest } = \text{ \$1,400/400 } = \text{ 3.50 times} \qquad [3.10]$$

The times interest earned ratio provides an indication of the firm's ability to meet its interest obligations. Deterioration in this ratio over time may be a signal that the firm is likely to encounter financial distress.

$$\text{Cash coverage ratio } = \text{ (EBIT} + \text{Depreciation)/Interest } = \text{ (\$1,400} + \text{\$600)/400 } = \text{ 5.00 times} \qquad [3.11]$$

The cash coverage ratio is often considered more meaningful than the times interest earned ratio because the firm's ability to meet its interest obligations is more closely related to its cash flow than its earnings.

Asset Management or Turnover Measures: These ratios, sometimes referred to as *asset utilization ratios*, measure how effectively the firm uses its assets to generate sales. Values of these ratios for K-Bec are below.

$$\text{Inventory turnover } = \text{ Cost of goods sold/Inventory } = \text{ \$3,000/2,225 } = \text{ 1.35 times} \qquad [3.12]$$

$$\text{Days' sales in inventory } = \text{ 365 days/Inventory turnover } = \text{ 365/1.35 } = \text{ 270 days} \qquad [3.13]$$

The *inventory turnover ratio* measures how quickly inventory is produced and sold. A high turnover ratio, relative to similar firms, may indicate that the firm is managing its inventory efficiently; high turnover ratio may mean the firm is low on inventory and possibly even foregoing sales. *Days' sales in inventory* indicates that, on average, the firm holds its inventory for 270 days before it is sold.

The *receivables turnover* and *days' sales in receivables* measure the firm's ability to manage collections of accounts from customers. Days' sales in receivables is also referred to as the *average collection period* (ACP).

Receivables turnover   =   Sales/Accounts receivable   =   \$5,000/975   =   5.13 times   [3.14]

Days' sales in receivables   =   365 days/Receivables turnover   =   365/5.13 = 71 days   [3.15]

To calculate how long, on average it takes a firm to pay its bills, we use the *payables turnover* and *average payables period*. For K-Bec, these ratios are:

Payables turnover   =   COGS/Accounts payable   =   \$3,000/1,200   =   2.5 Times

Average payables period   =   365/Payables turnover   =   365/2.5   =   146 Days

Three additional turnover ratios are:

Net Working Capital (NWC) turnover   =   Sales/NWC   =   \$5,000/(3,750 - 1,550) = 2.27 times   [3.16]

Fixed asset turnover   =   Sales/Net fixed assets   =   \$5,000/6,750   =   0.74 times   [3.17]

Total asset turnover   =   Sales/Total assets   =   \$5,000/10,500   =   0.48 times   [3.18]

The total asset turnover indicates how effectively the firm uses its total assets to generate revenues. K-Bec generates \$0.48 of sales for each \$1.00 of total assets. A low value for this ratio, in comparison with other firms in the same industry, may indicate that assets are not being used as efficiently as possible. If the total asset turnover is low, the firm should examine the inventory turnover, receivables turnover, etc., to determine the source of inefficiency.

Profitability Measures: These ratios are designed to measure a firm's profitability using accounting statement data. However, since accounting data ignore both future profitability and risk, the profitability ratios may not provide a complete indication of a firm's performance. The ratios for K-Bec are given below.

Profit margin   =   Net income/Sales   =   \$660/5,000 = 13.2%   [3.19]

K-Bec generates approximately 13 cents of profit for each dollar of sales. It might seem that a higher profit margin is preferable. However, a firm may choose to offer low prices, resulting in low profit margins, in order to increase sales and total profits.

Return on assets (ROA)   =   Net income/Total assets   =   \$660/10,500   =   6.29%   [3.20]

Return on equity (ROE)   =   Net Income/Total equity   =   \$660/6,364   =   10.37%   [3.21]

Although both ROA and ROE are often cited as important measures of a firm's profitability, it is important to recall that these ratios are based on book values rather than market values. So, it is unlikely that either of these figures accurately reflects the market return earned by the firm, or by its shareholders, on their investments.

Market Value Measures: Analysis of financial statements usually combines market value information with accounting information. The market price of a share of stock is the price paid when an investor buys or sells a share. The total market value of the firm's equity is (price per share x number of shares outstanding). Analysts frequently use ratios to make such comparisons of market value. Three commonly used ratios are the EPS ratio, the P/E ratio, and the market-to-book ratio. These values are given below for K-Bec.

Assume that K-Bec has 330 shares of common stock outstanding. The stock's market price is $25 per share. So,
Earnings per share (EPS)   =   Net income/Number of shares   = $660 = $2.00

Price earnings (P/E) ratio   =   Price per share/Earnings per share   = $25/2.00   =   12.5   [3.22]

Market-to-book ratio = Market value per share/Book value per share   = $25.00/19.28   = 1.30 times   [3.23]

3.4   THE DU PONT IDENTITY

Use of the Du Pont identity to analyse financial statements is based on the idea that return on equity (ROE) is a valid measure of the firm's performance. Although ROE is based on accounting data (not market values), the DuPont method provides some insight into the firm's performance.

First, ROA can be written as the product of profit margin and total asset turnover:

ROA   = $\frac{\text{Net income}}{\text{Total assets}}$ = $\frac{\text{Net income}}{\text{Sales}}$ x $\frac{\text{Sales}}{\text{Total assets}}$ =   Profit margin x Total asset turnover

This decomposition of ROA makes it clear that return on assets depends on operating efficiency (profit margin) and asset use efficiency.

For K-Bec Co., Inc., ROA is: (0.132 x 0.48)   =   6.34%. This differs slightly from the value of ROA computed earlier (6.29%) due to rounding. The main point is that the firm's ROA can be increased by increasing either its operating or asset use efficiency. A firm can be profitable with a low profit margin, if low prices increase turnover, or with a high profit margin, even if high prices reduce turnover.
Return on equity (ROE) can be re-written as the product of ROA and the equity multiplier:

ROE   =   ROA x Equity multiplier   = $\frac{\text{Net income}}{\text{Total assets}}$ x $\frac{\text{Total assets}}{\text{Total equity}}$

Substituting for the definition of ROA developed above,

ROE   =   Profit margin x Total asset turnover x Equity multiplier

ROE   = $\frac{\text{Net income}}{\text{Sales}}$ x $\frac{\text{Sales}}{\text{Total assets}}$ x $\frac{\text{Total assets}}{\text{Total equity}}$ [3.24]

This equation shows that the firm's ROE on its operating efficiency (profit margin), the efficiency of its asset management (total asset turnover), and its financial leverage (equity multiplier). ROE can also be rewritten as:

ROE   =   ROA x (1 + Debt/Equity)ratio

3.5 USING FINANCIAL STATEMENT INFORMATION

There are three issues associated with using financial statement information: the reasons for evaluating financial statements; the sources of benchmarks for financial statement analysis; and problems encountered in financial statements analysis.

Why evaluate financial statements? Financial statement analysis has both internal and external uses. Internal uses include performance evaluation and planning for the future. External uses include analysis performed by creditors and potential investors, evaluation of competitors, and assessment of a potential acquisition opportunity.

Choosing a Benchmark: The two major types of analysis are time-trend analysis and peer group analysis. Time-trend analysis compares a firm's current data to its historical data to determine changes in firm performance and profitability over time. Peer group analysis compares financial information for a given firm with information for other firms with similar characteristics (product lines, industry factors, type of assets, etc.).

Problems with Financial Statement Analysis: The major problem is that there is no unifying financial or economic theory which can be applied to this analysis. Consequently, there are no clear guidelines regarding the optimal values for the ratios presented here. In fact, it is often not even clear which ratios should be analysed when performing an analysis. Other problems include:

(1) identification of comparable peer groups
(2) differences in accounting procedures
(3) differences in fiscal years for financial statements
(4) unusual events which have an impact on reported financial results.

CONCEPT TEST

1. Transactions which bring in cash are referred to as _____ of cash, and transactions which involve outlays of cash are _____ of cash.

2. An increase in an asset account on the balance sheet represents a _____ of cash, and a decrease in an asset account represents a _____ of cash.

3. A decrease in a liability or equity account is a _____ of cash, while an increase in a liability or equity account is a _____ of cash.

4. The Statement of Cash Flows organizes the sources and uses of cash into three categories: _____ activities, _____ activities, and _____ activities. Since depreciation is not a cash expense, it is added to net income as a _____ of cash on the Statement of Cash Flows. Under the category of financing activities, dividends are a _____ of cash.

5. Common-size financial statements are standardized by presenting balance sheet accounts as a percentage of _____ and income statement data as a percentage of _____.

6. Common-base-year financial statements are standardized by comparing each statement item to its corresponding value during a _____ year. Each financial statement item for the base year is assigned a value of _____. Then, for subsequent years, each item is assigned a value which reflects any

increase/decrease in the item. If a firm has accounts receivable of $500, $550, and $600 for the years 2001, 2002, and 2003 respectively, and if 2001 is chosen as the base year, the common-base-year balance sheet amounts will be _____, _____, and _____ for 2001, 2002, and 2003.

7.   Ratios intended to measure the firm's short-term liquidity are referred to as _____ ratios or _____ ratios. Some important ratios in this category are: Current ratio = _____/_____; Quick ratio = _____/_____; Cash ratio = _____/_____; Net working capital to total assets = _____/_____; Interval measure = _____/_____ .

8.   Ratios which gauge the extent to which a firm uses debt financing rather than equity financing are called _____ ratios. These ratios are also referred to as _____ ratios. Some important ratios in this category are: Total debt ratio = _____/_____; Debt/equity ratio = _____/_____ Equity multiplier = _____/_____ . The equity multiplier can also be computed as follows: Equity multiplier = 1 + _____ . Long-term debt ratio = _____/_____; Times interest earned ratio = _____/_____; Cash coverage ratio = _____/_____ .

9.   Ratios designed to measure how effectively the firm uses its assets are called _____ ratios or _____ measures. These ratios are also referred to as _____ ratios. For any given category of assets, the appropriate level of investment is analysed by comparison with the firm's _____. Some important ratios in this category are: Inventory turnover = _____/_____; Days' sales in inventory = _____/_____; Receivables turnover = _____/_____; Days' sales in receivables = _____/_____; NWC turnover = _____/_____; Fixed asset turnover = _____/_____; Total asset turnover = _____/_____ .

10. Ratios designed to measure a firm's profitability using accounting statement data are _____ ratios. Some important ratios in this category are: Profit margin = _____/_____ ; Return on assets = _____/_____ ;Return on equity = _____/_____ .

11. Ratios based on market value data are called _____ ratios. Important ratios in this category are: P/E ratio = _____/_____; Market-to-book ratio = _____/_____ .

12. The use of the Du Pont identity in analyzing financial statements is based on the idea that _____ is a primary measure of the firm's performance. The importance of this ratio is diminished by the fact that it is based on _____ data, rather than _____.

13. The Du Pont identity can be derived by first expressing return on assets as: Return on assets = _____ × _____ . This decomposition of ROA makes it clear that return on assets depends on _____ efficiency and _____ efficiency. Return on equity can be written as: Return on equity = _____ × _____ . ROE can be further decomposed by substituting for ROA: ROE = _____ × _____ × _____ . This last equation highlights the fact that the firm's return on equity depends on _____ efficiency, _____ efficiency, and _____.

14. Financial statement analysis based on comparison of current data with historical data is referred to as _____ analysis. Analysis based on comparison of data for one firm with corresponding data for similar firms is called _____ analysis.

PROBLEMS

Use the following financial statements for Coogan Development Co., Inc., to solve Problems 1 through 14:

COOGAN DEVELOPMENT CO., INC.
2003 Income Statement

Sales	$ 25,000
Cost of goods sold	16,000
Depreciation	3,000
Earnings before interest and taxes	$ 6,000
Interest paid	2,000
Taxable income	$ 4,000
Taxes (34%)	1,360
Net income	$ 2,640
Retained earnings	$ 1,584
Dividends	1,056

COOGAN DEVELOPMENT CO., INC.
Balance Sheets as of December 31, 2002 and 2003

	2002	2003
Assets		
Current assets		
Cash	$ 4,000	$ 3,000
Accounts receivable	9,000	11,000
Inventory	5,000	4,500
Total	$ 18,000	$ 18,500
Fixed assets		
Net plant and equipment	30,000	31,500
Total assets	$ 48,000	$ 50,000
Liabilities and Owners' Equity		
Current liabilities		
Accounts payable	$ 3,000	$ 2,500
Notes payable	6,000	6,416
Total	$ 9,000	$ 8,916
Long-term debt	15,000	13,000
Owners' equity		
Common stock and paid-in surplus	14,000	16,500
Retained earnings	10,000	11,584
Total	$ 24,000	$ 28,084
Total liabilities and owners' equity	$ 48,000	$ 50,000

Basic Questions

Problem 1

Compute the changes in the balance sheet accounts for Coogan Development Co., and summarize the firm's sources and uses of cash as indicated by these changes.

Problem 2

Prepare a statement of changes in cash flow for Coogan Development Co., Inc.

Problem 3

Prepare common-size balance sheets for Coogan Development Co., Inc. for both 2002 and 2003.

Problem 4

Prepare a common-size income statement for Coogan Development Co.

Problem 5

Prepare common base year balance sheets for Coogan Development Co., using 2002 as the base year.

Problem 6

For Coogan Development Co., compute the five measures of short-term solvency from this chapter. (use 2003 data)

Problem 7

For Coogan Development Co., compute the six measures of long-term solvency from this chapter. (use 2003 data)

Problem 8

For Coogan Development Co., compute the seven asset management measures from this chapter. (use 2003 data.)

Problem 9

For Coogan Development Co., compute the three profitability measures from this chapter. (use 2003 data.)

Problem 10

Use the Du Pont identity to compute ROA and ROE for Coogan Development Co. for the year 2003.

Intermediate Questions

Problem 11

Suppose that Coogan Development Co. has 1,000 shares of common stock outstanding and that the market price per share is $40. Compute earnings per share, the price/earnings ratio and the market-to-book ratio for 2003.

Problem 12

Suppose that Coogan Development Co. decides to reduce its total debt ratio to 0.20 from 0.44 by selling new common stock and using the proceeds to repay principal on some of its outstanding long-term debt. Compute the resulting value for each of the following: debt/equity ratio, equity multiplier, and return on equity. How much equity financing will the firm need in order to accomplish this reduction in the total debt ratio?

Problem 13

Suppose that Coogan decides to increase its total debt ratio to 0.80 by borrowing additional long-term funds, and uses the proceeds to buy some of its own outstanding common stock. Compute the resulting value for each of the following: debt/equity ratio, equity multiplier, and return on equity. How much long-term debt financing will Coogan have to obtain in order to accomplish this increase in the total debt ratio?

Problem 14

Suppose that Coogan decides to reduce its average collection period (ACP) to 120 days from 161 days. How much of its current outstanding accounts receivable would the firm have to collect in order to accomplish this reduction? How would the firm's current and quick ratios change if (1) the collected funds were held as cash, or (2) the collected funds were used to repay notes payable?

Problem 15

The following information was taken from the financial statements of Bombitdear Corporation: Cash = $25,000; Accounts Receivable = $211,000; Inventory = $72,223.35; Sales = $2,081,486.50; Total Assets = $828,595; Shareholders Equity = $291,308.25; and the firm has no current assets other than those given. What is the firm's fixed asset turnover?

Problem 16

Your firm's financial statements indicate cash of $75,000; accounts receivable of $672,000; inventory of $96,750; total assets of $1,663,000; and shareholder's equity of $490,000. Assuming a fixed asset turnover of 3.5, what is the level of sales?

Problem 17

Concord Ltd. is a 100% equity financed firm with net fixed assets of $500,000. It has a net profit margin of 8%, a fixed asset turnover of 8 times, a total asset turnover of 5 times and earnings per share of $2.00. How many Concord common shares are outstanding?

Problem 18

Forgetit Ltd. has a gross profit margin of 25% on sales of $500,000 (90% credit). Cash and marketable securities are $10,000, accounts receivable are $40,000, inventory is $50,000, and the current ratio is 2.0.

a.   What are Forgetit's average collection period and inventory turnover? (Use a 365-day year).

b.   How much inventory should there be if management wants the inventory turnover to be 10 times a year?

c.   What would the accounts receivable be if management wants the average collection period to be 22 days?

Problem 19

Go Broke, Ltd. has a profit margin of 30% on sales of $6 million. All sales are for credit. The firm's cash and marketable securities are $130,000; accounts receivable are $240,000; inventory is valued at $700,000.

a. What is Go Broke's average collection period (days' sales in receivables)?

b. If the inventory turnover is 4 times per year, what is the firm's cost of goods sold?

Problem 20

Sam's Supply Company Limited, a small manufacturer of surgical supplies and equipment, has been plagued with low profitability in recent years. As a result, the board of directors replaced the president of the firm. The new president has asked you to conduct an analysis of the firm's financial condition. The most recent financial statements and selected industry average ratios are reproduced below:

Balance Sheet
November 30, 2003 *(thousands of dollars)*

Cash	$ 450	Accounts payable	$ 610
Marketable securities	330	Notes payable	200
Accounts receivable	660	Other current liabilities	150
Inventory	1,590	Total current liabilities	$ 960
Total current assets	$3,030		
Gross fixed assets	$2,250	Long-term debt	$1,000
Less: Depreciation	(780)	Common shares	2,100
Net fixed assets	$1,470	Retained earnings	440
Total assets	$4,500	Total liabilities & owners' equity	$4,500

INCOME STATEMENT
Year Ended November 30, 2003 *(thousands of dollars)*

Net sales	$ 7,950
Cost of goods sold	6,600
Gross profit	1,350
Operating expenses	735
Depreciation	120
Interest	45
Taxable income	$ 450
Taxes (47.1%)	212
Net income	$ 238

Selected Industry Average Ratios

Debt to total assets	40%	Fixed asset turnover	5 times
Times interest earned	7 times	Total asset turnover	3 times
Inventory turnover	9 times	Net profit on sales	3%
Avg. collection period	21 days	Return on total assets	9%
Return on equity	15%		

Use the Du Pont equation to identify whether balance sheet accounts or income statement figures seem to be primarily responsible for Sam's low return on common equity relative to the industry average of 15%.

Which specific **accounts** are most out of line in relation to other firms in the industry?

What additional information would be most useful in analyzing Sam's financial condition?

ANSWERS TO CONCEPT TEST

1. sources; uses

2. use; source

3. use; source

4. operating; investment; financing; source; use

5. total assets; sales

6. base; 1.00; 1.00; 1.10; 1.20

7. short-term solvency; liquidity; current assets; current liabilities; (current assets - inventory); current liabilities; cash; current liabilities; (current assets - current liabilities); total assets; current assets; average daily operating cost

8. long-term solvency; financial leverage; (total assets -total equity); total assets; total debt; total equity; total assets; total equity; debt/equity ratio; long-term debt; long-term debt + total equity; EBIT; interest; EBIT + depreciation; interest

9. asset management; turnover; asset utilization; sales; COGS; inventory; 365 days; inventory turnover; sales; accounts receivable; 365 days; receivables turnover; sales; net working capital; sales; net fixed assets; sales; total assets

10. profitability; net income; sales; net income; total assets; net income; total equity

11. market value; price per share; earnings per share; market value per share; book value per share

12. return on equity; accounting; market values

13. profit margin; total asset turnover; operating; asset use; return on assets; equity multiplier; profit margin; total asset turnover; equity multiplier; operating; asset use; financial leverage

14. time-trend; peer group

PROBLEM SOLUTIONS

Problem 1:   COOGAN DEVELOPMENT CO., INC.
               Balance Sheets as of December 31, 2002 and 2003 (Changes)

	Change
Assets	
Current assets	
Cash	- $ 1,000
Accounts receivable	+ 2,000
Inventory	- 500
Total	+ $ 500
Fixed assets	+ 1,500
Net plant and equipment	
Total assets	+ $ 2,000
Liabilities and Owners' Equity	
Current liabilities	
Accounts payable	- $ 500
Notes payable	+ 416
Total	- $ 84
Long-term debt	- 2,000
Owners' equity	
Common stock and paid-in surplus	+ 2,500
Retained earnings	+ 1,584
Total liabilities and owners' equity	+ $ 2,000

The sources and uses of cash are summarized as follows:

Sources of cash		Uses of cash	
Decrease in inventory	$ 500	Increase in accounts receivable	$ 2,000
Increase in notes payable	416	Decrease in accounts payable	500
Increase in common stock	2,500	Decrease in long-term debt	2,000
Increase in retained earnings	1,584	Net fixed asset acquisitions	1,500
Total sources	$ 5,000	Total uses	$ 6,000

Net decrease in cash $ 1,000

Problem 2:   COOGAN DEVELOPMENT CO., INC.
                   2003 Statement of Cash Flows

Operating activities	
Net income	$ 2,640
Plus:	
Depreciation	3,000
Decrease in inventory	500
Less:	
Increase in accounts receivable	- 2,000
Decrease in accounts payable	- 500
Net cash from operating activities	$ 3,640

Investment activities
    Fixed asset acquisitions   -\$ 4,500 Fixed Assets$_{2003}$ - (Fixed Assets$_{2002}$-Depn$_{2003}$)
Net cash from investment activities   -\$ 4,500

Financing activities
    Increase in notes payable   +\$ 416
    Decrease in long-term debt   -   2,000
    Dividends paid   -   1,056
    Increase in common stock   +   2,500
Net increase from financing activities   -\$ 140

Net decrease in cash   -\$ 1,000

Problem 3:   COOGAN DEVELOPMENT CO., INC.
Common-Size Balance Sheets December 31, 2000 and 2003

	2002	2003	Change
Assets			
Current assets			
Cash	8.3 %	6.0%	- 2.3%
Accounts receivable	18.8	22.0	+ 3.2
Inventory	10.4	9.0	- 1.4
Total	37.5	37.0	- 0.5
Fixed assets			
Net plant and equipment	62.5	63.0	+ 0.5
Total assets	100.0	100.0	0.0
Liabilities and Owners' Equity			
Current liabilities			
Accounts payable	6.3%	5.0%	- 1.3%
Notes payable	12.5	12.8	+ 0.3
Total	18.8	17.8	- 1.0
Long-term debt	31.3	26.0	- 5.3
Owners' equity			
Common stock	29.2	33.0	+ 3.8
Retained earnings	20.8	23.2	+ 2.4
Total	50.0	56.2	+ 6.2
Total liabilities and owners' equity	100.00*	100.0	+ 0.0 *

Slight difference is due to rounding.

Problem 4:   COOGAN DEVELOPMENT CO., INC
                            Common-Size Income Statement, 2003

Sales	100.0%
Cost of goods sold	64.0
Depreciation	12.0
Earnings before interest and taxes	24.0
Interest paid	8.0
Taxable income	16.0
Taxes (34%)	5.4
Net income	10.6
Retained earnings	6.3
Dividends	4.3

Problem 5: Divide each account value in 2003 by the corresponding account value in 2002

COOGAN DEVELOPMENT CO., INC.
Common Base Year Balance Sheets
as of December 31, 2002 and 2003

	2002	2003
Assets		
Current assets		
Cash	1.00	0.75
Accounts receivable	1.00	1.22
Inventory	1.00	0.90
Total	1.00	1.03
Fixed assets		
Net plant and equipment	1.00	1.05
Total assets	1.00	1.04
Liabilities and Owners' Equity		
Current liabilities		
Accounts payable	1.00	0.83
Notes payable	1.00	1.07
Total	1.00	0.99
Long-term debt	1.00	0.87
Owners' equity		
Common stock and paid-in surplus	1.00	1.18
Retained earnings	1.00	1.16
Total	1.00	1.17
Total liabilities and owners' equity	1.00	1.04

Problem 6: Current ratio = Current assets / Current liabilities = $18,500 / $8,916 = 2.07

Quick ratio = (Current assets - inventory)/Current liabilities = ($18,500 - $4,500) / $8,916 = 1.57

Cash ratio = Cash / Current liabilities = $3000 / $8,916 = 0.34

Net working capital to total assets = NWC / Total assets = ($18,500 - $8,916)/ $50,000 = 0.19

Interval measure = Current assets / Average daily operating cost = $18,500 / $43.84 = 422 days

Note: Average daily operating cost: ($16,000/365) = $43.84

Problem 7: Total debt ratio = (Total assets - Total equity) / Total assets = ($50,000 - $28,084) / $50,000 = .44

Debt/equity ratio = Total debt / Total equity = $21,916 / $28,084 = 0.78

Equity multiplier = Total assets / Total equity = $50,000 / $28,084 = 1.78

Long-term debt ratio = LT debt/(LT debt + Total equity) = $13,000 / ($13,000 + $28,084) = 0.32

Times interest earned ratio = EBIT / Interest = $6,000 / $2,000 = 3.00 times

Cash coverage ratio = (EBIT + Depreciation) / Interest = ($6,000 + $3,000) / $2,000 = 4.5 times

Problem 8: Inventory turnover = Cost of goods sold / Inventory = $16,000 / $4,500 = 3.56 times

Days' sales in inventory = 365 days / Inventory turnover = 365 / 3.56 = 103 days

Receivables turnover = Sales / Accounts receivable = $25,000 / $11,000 = 2.27 times

Days' sales in receivables = 365 days / Receivables turnover = 365 / 2.27 = 161 days

NWC turnover = Sales / NWC = $25,000 / ($18,500 - $8,916) = 2.61 times

Fixed asset turnover = Sales / Net fixed assets = $25,000 / $31,500 = 0.79 times

Total asset turnover = Sales / Total assets = $25,000 / $50,000 = 0.50 times

Problem 9: Profit margin = Net income / Sales = $2,640 / $25,000 = 10.56%

Return on assets = Net income / Total assets = $2,640 / $50,000 = 5.28%

Return on equity = Net income / Total equity = $2,640 / $28,084 = 9.40%

Problem 10: ROA = Net income / Total assets = (Net income / Sales) x (Sales / Total assets)

= Profit margin x Total asset turnover = .1056 x .50 =   .0528   =   5.28%

ROE = ROA x Equity multiplier = .0528 x 1.78 = .0940 = 9.40%

OR

ROE = Profit margin x Total asset turnover x Equity multiplier = .1056 x .50 x 1.78 = 9.40%

Problem 11: Earnings per share (EPS) = ($2,640/1,000) = $2.64

P/E ratio = $40.00 / $2.64 = 15.2

Market-to-book = $40.00 / $28.08 = 1.42 times*

*Book value per share = $28,084 / 1,000 = $28.08

Problem 12: The debt/equity ratio can be computed from the total debt ratio. The new total debt ratio indicates that Coogan would have $0.20 of debt financing and ($1.00 - $0.20) = $0.80 of equity financing for each dollar of assets.

D/E ratio = 0.20 / 0.80 = 0.25

Equity multiplier = $1.00 / $0.80 = 1.25   (because they have $0.80 equity for each $1.00 in assets)

OR   =(1 + debt/equity ratio) = 1 + 0.25 = 1.25.

ROE = Profit margin x Total asset turnover x Equity multiplier = .1056 x .50 x 1.25 = 6.60%

To determine the amount of new equity financing required, we use the new total debt ratio to determine total equity for Coogan Development after the new financing.

Total debt ratio = ($50,000 - Total equity) / $50,000 = .20 → Total equity = $40,000.

Additional equity financing = ($40,000 - $28,084) = $11,916.

Note that long-term debt is reduced to ($13,000 - $11,916) = $1,084.

Problem 13: The debt/equity ratio can be computed from the new total debt ratio. Coogan Development would have $0.80 of debt financing and ($1.00 - $0.80) = $0.20 of equity financing for each dollar of assets. Therefore, the debt/equity ratio is ($0.80/$0.20) = 4.00. The equity multiplier = (1 + 4.00) = 5.00. The new return on equity is: ROE = .1056 x .50 x 5.00 = .2640 = 26.40%. The total equity after the new financing is obtained by solving:

D/E ratio = 0.80 / 0.2 = 4.00

Equity multiplier = $1.00 / $ 0.20 = 5   (because they have $0.20 equity for each $1.00 in assets)
OR   = 1 + D/E ratio = 5

ROE = Profit margin x Total asset turnover x equity multiplier = .1056 x .50 x. 5 = 26.4%

To compute new equity financing needed:

Total debt ratio = (50,000 - equity) / 50,000 = 0.80 → Total equity = $10,000

Additional equity financing = $10,000 - $28,084 = -$18,084   (i.e. they bought back $18,084 in equity)

Long-term debt financing increases to: $13,000 + $18,084 = $31,084   (i.e. $18,084 in new debt)

Problem 14: Also called the days' sales in receivables, we can determine the required reduction in accounts receivable, by first solving the equation below for the receivables turnover required to accomplish the reduction in ACP:

ACP = 365 days / Receivables turnover = 120 days → Receivables turnover = 3.04
Solving for the required level of accounts receivable: 3.04 = $25,000 / Accounts receivable
Required level of accounts receivable = $8,223.68
Coogan must collect ($11,000 - $8,223.68) = $2,776.32 of its accounts receivable.

If the collected funds were held as cash, there is no effect on current or quick ratios total current assets and total current liabilities are not affected.

If the collected funds were used to pay outstanding notes payable, both current assets and current liabilities would be reduced by $2,776.32.

Current ratio = ($18,500 - $2,776.32) / ($8,916 - $2,776.32) = 2.56

Quick ratio = ($18,500 - $2,776.32 - $4,500) / ($8,916 - $2,776.32) = 1.83

Problem 15: Fixed asset turnover = $2,081,486.50 / ($828,595 - $25,000 - $211,000 - $72,223.35) = 4.0

Problem 16: 3.5 = Sales/($1,663,000 - $75,000 - $672,000 - 96,750) → Sales = $2,867,375

Problem 17: .08 = $500,000 / Sales → Sales = $500,000 / .08 = $4,000,000
Net income = .08 x $4,000,000 = $320,000 →Number of common shares = $320,000 / $2 =160,000

Problem 18:   a. Receivables turnover = ($500,000 x .90) / $40,000 = 11.25
Average collection period = 365 / 11.25 = 32.44 days
Inventory turnover = COGS / Inventory = ($500,000 x .75) / $50,000 = 7.5 times

b. Inventory turnover = 10 = ($500,000 x .75) / Inventory → Inventory = $37,500

c. ACP = 22 = 365 / Accounts receivable turnover → Receivables turnover = 16.59
Receivables turnover = 1.69 = ($500,000 x .90) / Receivables → Receivables = $27,125

Problem 19:   a. Receivables turnover = $6,000,000 / $240,000 = 25 → ACP = 365 / 25 = 14.6 days
b. Inventory turnover ratio = 4 = COGS / $700,000 → COGS = $2,800,000.

Problem 20:
a. ROE = (Net income / Sales) x (Sales / Total assets) x (Total assets / Common equity)
= ($238 / $7,950) x ($7,950 / $4,500) x ($4,500 / $2,100) = 3% x 1.77 x 2.14 = 11.4%

b. Balance Sheet accounts seem to be responsible for Sam's low return on common equity because there is a high investment in assets for the level of sales being generated. Also, note the lower use of debt financing (30%) versus the industry average of 40%.

c. (i)   previous years' information which would allow one to do a hard analysis.
(ii)   industry averages relating to liquidity ratios.
(iii)   number of shares outstanding, market price data, etc., in order to calculate market value ratios.

4   Long-Term Financial Planning and Corporate Growth

CHAPTER HIGHLIGHTS

This chapter discusses long-term financial planning and financial planning models. The financial planning process should identify the firm's financial goals, analyse the difference between the firm's current status and the established goals, and identify the actions required to achieve those goals. Growth rate in sales is usually a major planning component. There are explicit links among potential growth, investment decisions and financing decisions.

The basic policy elements needed to develop a financial plan are listed below. Decisions related to these four areas affect the firm's future profitability, its need for external financing, and its growth opportunities.

1.   The firm's needed investment in new assets (capital budgeting decision)
2.   The degree of financial leverage (capital structure decision)
3.   The dividend payment to shareholders (dividend decision)
4.   The firm's liquidity and working capital requirements (net working capital decision)

4.1   WHAT IS FINANCIAL PLANNING?

The financial plan identifies methods for achieving the firm's financial goals. Since the implementation of a financial decision may require substantial lead time, financial planning is required to successfully meet the firm's goals.

Growth as a Financial Management Goal: The appropriate goal for financial managers is to maximize share (equity) value. Growth, by itself, is *not* an appropriate goal. However, because growth rates are commonly used in financial planning, we use them here to summarize the elements of a firm's financial and investment policies.

Dimensions of Financial Planning: A financial plan has two dimensions: the *planning horizon* and the process of *aggregation*. A short-term is generally considered to be the next 12 months; a long-term plan usually covers two to five years. In this chapter, we are primarily concerned with a long-term planning horizon.

Creating a financial plan typically involves the combination of smaller investment proposals into larger units, so that the sum of these smaller proposals is treated as if they were one larger investment. This process is called aggregation.

Financial plans often require alternative sets of assumptions. For example, a firm might require that each of its divisions prepare alternative plans under different assumptions regarding the state of the economy and the firm's prospects. These might include a worst case, most likely (or normal) case, and best case set of assumptions.

What Can Planning Accomplish? First, the plan makes clear the link between investment proposals and the firm's financing alternatives. Second, it plan allows the firm to evaluate different investment and financing options and their long-run impact on firm value. Third, a financial plan helps identify what may happen if today's assumptions about the future are incorrect. This helps managers to develop contingency plans that may avoid unpleasant surprises. Finally, a plan helps establish whether individual objectives and goals are feasible and consistent with overall corporate objectives.

4.2 FINANCIAL PLANNING MODELS: A FIRST LOOK

The exact form and level of detail in a financial plan varies from firm to firm. In Some of the common elements of a financial plan and develop a simple financial planning model are discussed in this section.

A Financial Planning Model - The Ingredients: Most financial planning models include the following components:

1. *Sales forecast.* An externally supplied sales forecast is the foundation of most planning models. All other values in the planning model are derived from this forecast.

2. *Pro forma statements.* These are projected (forecasted) accounting statements, including balance sheet, income statement, and statement of cash flows.

3. *Asset requirements.* The financial plan describes projected capital expenditures (i.e., investments in fixed assets) and working capital needs.

4. *Financial requirements.* This part of the plan details the necessary financial arrangements. The firm's debt policy and dividend policy are also relevant here because of their impact on the required financing.

5. *The 'plug'.* The projected growth rates in sales, assets and financial requirements are generally not compatible without some adjustment; in other words, the balance sheet will not balance. Often, the 'plug' variable is the amount of external financing (i.e., new debt and/or equity) required in order to finance the projected increase in assets.

6. *Economic assumptions.* Assumptions about the future state of the economy, including such variables as interest rates, tax rates, and the general state of the economy, must be explicitly stated.

A Simple Financial Planning Model - An Example: The purpose of the financial planning model described in this section is to illustrate the relationships mentioned earlier. The approach to financial planning in the following example is highly simplified, and therefore is not necessarily practical.

The most recent income statement and balance sheet for the Tinker Corporation are presented here:

TINKER CORPORATION
Financial Statements

Income Statement

Sales	$ 2,000
Costs	1,500
Net income	$ 500

Balance Sheet

Current assets	$ 800	Current liabilities	$ 600
Fixed assets	3,600	Long-term debt	1,500
		Equity	2,300
Total	$4,400	Total	$ 4,400

Suppose Tinker forecasts a 10% increase in sales, and that all income statement and balance sheet variables will grow at the same rate as sales. These assumptions result in the following pro forma statements:

Pro Forma Income Statement

Sales	$ 2,200
Costs	1,650
Net income	$ 550

Pro Forma Balance Sheet

Current assets	$ 880 (+$ 80)	Current liabilities	$ 660	(+$ 60)
Fixed assets	3,960 (+$360)	Long-term debt	1,650	(+$150)
		Equity	2,530	(+$230)
Total	$4,840 (+$440)	Total	$ 4,840	(+$440)

The assumption that all variables grow at the same rate as sales implies that all variables maintain the same proportionate relationship after the increase in sales. In the example, costs are 75% of sales and current assets are 40% of sales. This is true for both the current and pro forma income statements. All other balance sheet items maintain the same proportionate relationships. For example, net working capital remains constant at 1.333.
Retained earnings is the link between the pro forma income statement and balance sheet. This model has not accounted for this interaction, so there is an inconsistency between the pro forma statements. Assuming no dividend payments, retained earnings should increase by the entire net income of $550, rather than the $230 shown in the pro forma balance sheet.

This inconsistency can be resolved in several ways, through the use of a "plug" figure. If dividends are used as the plug, dividend payments should be ($550 - $230) = $320. Long-term debt could also be the 'plug' figure. If no dividends are paid, equity increases to ($2,300 + $550) = $2,850. Pro forma current liabilities are $660 and total assets are $4,840. Long-term debt must be [$4,840 - ($2,850 + $660)] = $1,330. This means the firm repaid ($1,500 - $1,330) = $170 of its long-term debt. The resulting pro forma balance sheet is:

Pro Forma Balance Sheet

Current assets	$ 880 (+$ 80)	Current liabilities	$ 660	(+$ 60)
Fixed assets	3,960 (+$360)	Long-term debt	1,330	(- $170)
		Equity	2,850	(+$550)
Total	$4,840 (+$440)	Total	$ 4,840	(+$440)

Although this example is highly simplified, it demonstrates the interdependencies among the relevant variables and policies in financial planning models: growth in sales, growth in assets, dividend policy, and financing (capital structure) policy.

4.3 THE PERCENTAGE OF SALES APPROACH

The simple financial planning model above assumed that all income statement and balance sheet items increase proportionately with sales. The *percentage of sales approach* modifies the simple model be recognizing that not all accounts are likely to increase with sales.

Example: The most recent income statement and balance sheet for the Evers Corporation are presented here:

EVERS CORPORATION
Income Statement

Sales	$ 5,000
Costs	4,000
Taxable income	$ 1,000
Taxes (34%)	340
Net income	$ 660
Retained earnings	$ 495
Dividends	$ 165

EVERS CORPORATION
Balance Sheet

Current assets			Current liabilities	
Cash	$ 500	(10%)	Accounts payable	$ 1,000 (20%)
Accounts receivable	1,000	(20%)	Notes payable	500 (n/a)
Inventory	2,000	(40%)	Total	$ 1,500 (n/a)
Total	$ 3,500	(70%)		
			Long-term debt	$ 2,500 (n/a)
Fixed assets			Owners' equity	
Net plant	$ 6,500	(130%)	Common stock	$ 4,000 (n/a)
			Retained earnings	2,000 (n/a)
			Total	$ 6,000 (n/a)
Total assets	$10,000	(200%)	Total	$10,000 (n/a)

The percentages in parentheses represent the given item as a percentage of annual sales. Those items not expected to increase proportionately with sales are identified by 'n/a', so the percentage calculation is not applicable.

The Evers Corporation has projected a 20% increase in sales. The pro forma income statement is based on the assumption that costs remain a constant percentage of sales ($4,000/$5,000) = 80%. This also results in a constant profit margin of ($660/$5,000) = 13.2%.

The ratio of total assets to sales is sometimes called the *capital intensity ratio*. It indicates the level of assets needed to generate $1 in sales. The higher the ratio, the more capital intensive is the firm. (This is the reciprocal of total asset turnover.) For Evers, this ratio is $10,000 / $5,000   =   2 (i.e. 200%). Assuming this ratio is constant, it takes $2 in total assets to generate $1 in sales.

The *dividend payout ratio* is the percentage of net income paid as dividends: cash dividends / net income. For Evers the payout ratio is ($165/$660) = 25%. The *retention ratio* or *plowback ratio* is the percentage of net income which is retained: retained earnings / net income, also computed as (1 - dividend payout ratio) because everything not paid out is retained. Evers' retention ratio is ($495/$660) = 75%. If we assume the dividend payout ratio is constant, the retention ratio is also constant.

EVERS CORPORATION
Pro Forma Income Statement

Sales	$ 6,000
Costs	4,800
Taxable income	$ 1,200
Taxes (34%)	408
Net income	$ 792
Retained earnings	$ 594
Dividends	$ 198

The pro forma balance sheet is derived by applying the respective percentages of sales to the projected sales levels for those items which are expected to increase proportionately with sales. Retained earnings on the pro forma balance sheet is computed by adding the retained earnings figure from the pro forma income statement to the current balance sheet retained earnings figure. All other balance sheet accounts remain constant, and the 'plug' figure is *external financing needed* (EFN). The figures in parentheses on the following partial pro forma balance sheet represent the respective increases from the current balance sheet.

EVERS CORPORATION
Partial Pro Forma Balance Sheet

Current assets			Current liabilities		
Cash	$ 600	($ 100)	Accounts payable	$ 1,200	($ 200)
Accounts receivable	1,200	(200)	Notes payable	500	(0)
Inventory	2,400	(400)	Total	$ 1,700	($ 200)
Total	$ 4,200	(700)			
			Long-term debt	$ 2,500	($ 0)
Fixed assets			Owners' equity		
Net plant	$ 7,800	($ 1,300)	Common stock	$ 4,000	(0)
			Retained earnings	2,594	(594)
			Total	$ 6,594	(594)
Total assets	$12,000	($2,000)	Total	$10,794	($ 794)
			EFN	$ 1,206	

This statement is considered a *partial* pro forma balance sheet because the firm must still determine how to raise the $1,206 of external financing needed to generate the expected 20% increase in sales. The pro forma balance sheet is complete when the source(s) of external financing are determined and indicated on the balance sheet. The possible sources of external financing are: short-term debt, long-term debt, and new equity financing. If, for example, all of the external financing is additional long-term debt, the long-term debt would be ($2,500 +$1,206) = $3,706.

An Alternative Scenario: The assumption that assets are a fixed percentage of sales may not always be suitable. For example, suppose that Evers is using its fixed assets at only 60% of full capacity. The need for external financing will be quite different. This means that the current sales level is 60 percent of the full capacity sales level: Current sales = $5,000; Full capacity sales = $5,000/.60 = $8,333. This means that sales could increase by 67 percent [($8,333 –$5,000) / $5,000] before the firm needs to invest in new fixed assets. Operating at 67% of capacity, the amount of external financing needed is ($1,206 - $1,300) = - $94 → this amount will actually be injected into the firm (for example, it could be used to pay down debt, etc.).

4.4 EXTERNAL FINANCING AND GROWTH

Growth and external financing needed (EFN) are positively related → higher growth rates of sales (and assets) increases the need for external financing. The relationship between these two aspects of financial planning is examined by assuming a given financial policy for the firm, and then assessing the impact of that policy on the firm's financing requirements and ability to grow.

EFN and Growth: This simplified example for Chance Corporation illustrates the relationship between EFN and growth. The most recent income statement and balance sheet for the Chance

CHANCE CORPORATION
Income Statement

Sales	$ 2,000
Costs	1,400
Taxable income	$ 600
Taxes (34%)	204
Net Income	$ 396
Retained earnings	$ 99
Dividends	$ 297

CHANCE CORPORATION
Balance Sheet

Current assets	$ 2,000	Total debt	$ 1,000
Fixed assets	3,000	Owners' equity	4,000
Total assets	$ 5,000	Total liabilities	$ 5,000

Chance is forecasting a 25% increase in sales for the coming year. They predict that assets increase directly with sales, while liabilities and equity do not increase spontaneously with sales.

The following notation and data will be used in this example:

S = Previous year's sales = $2,000
A = Total assets = $5,000
D = Total debt = $1,000
E = Total equity = $4,000
g = Growth rate = 25%

The following ratios can be computed for Chance Corporation:

p = Profit margin = $396 / $2,000 = 19.80%
R = Retention ratio = $99 / $396 = 25.00%
ROA = Return on assets = $396 / $5,000 = 7.92%
ROE = Return on equity = $396 / $4,000 = 9.90%
D/E = Debt/equity ratio = $1,000 / $4,000 = 25.00%

Assuming a constant capital intensity ratio, the increase in total assets is equal to:

$A \times g$ = $5,000 × .25 = $1,250

The pro forma income statement generated by the forecasted 25% sales increase is below.

CHANCE CORPORATION
Pro Forma Income Statement

Sales	$ 2,500
Costs	1,750
Taxable income	$ 750
Taxes (34%)	255
Net Income	$ 495
Retained earnings	$ 123.75
Dividends	$ 371.25

The projected sales level is: S × (1 + g) = $2,000 × 1.25 = $2,500

Projected net income equals the profit margin times projected sales: p S × (1 + g) = .198 × $2,500 = $495

The projected addition to retained earnings is: retention ratio x projected net income = p SR × (1 + g) = $123.75

Therefore, the external financing needed is:

EFN = increase in assets - projected addition to retained earnings   [4.2]
OR
= (A × g) − [p × S × R (1 + g)] = $1,250 B $123.75 = $1,126.25

The pro forma balance sheet for Chance Corporation is:

CHANCE CORPORATION
Pro Forma Balance Sheet

Current assets	$ 2,500.00	Total debt	$ 1,000.00
Fixed assets	3,750.00	Owners' equity	4,123.75
Total assets	$ 6,250.00	Total liabilities	$ 5,123.75
		External funds needed	$1,126.25

The relationship between EFN and g can be clarified by algebraically rearranging the above equation for EFN:

EFN = (A × g) − [pSR (1 + g)]   =   Ag - pSR - pSRg = -pSR + Ag - pSRg

EFN = −(pSR) + [A − (pSR)] × g   [4.3]

Substituting the data for the Chance Corporation:

EFN = B (.198 × $2,000 x .25) + [$5,000 B (.198 × $2,000 x .25] × g   =   B$99 + ($4,901 × g)

This is the equation for a straight line with a y-intercept (dependent variable) of -$99 and a slope (independent variable) of $4,901. So, when g = 0, EFN = −$99 (i.e. if the growth rate is zero, the addition to retained earnings is the same as it was for the previous year). And, the negative EFN means that surplus financing is available.

The slope of $4,901 means that, for each 1% increase in the growth rate, ($4,901 × .01) = $49.01 of external financing is required. For our example, g is 25%, so that external financing needed is:

$$EFN = -\$99 + (\$4,901 \times .25) = \$1,126.25$$

Internal Growth Rate: The above equation can be used to determine the firm's internal growth rate; the growth rate which can be achieved without any external financing. To find this growth rate, set EFN = to zero and solve for g:

$$EFN = -\$99 + (\$4,901 \times g) = 0 \rightarrow \$99 = \$4,901 \times g \rightarrow g = \$99/\$4,901 = 2.02\%$$

The internal growth rate can also be written as: (ROA x R / [1 - (ROA x R)])   [4.5]

Financial Policy and Growth: The 2.02% growth rate computed above would allow Chance Corporation to grow indefinitely without obtaining external financing. Because all internal financing is derived from retained earnings, and the firm obtains no new external debt financing, the firm's debt/equity ratio will decrease over time. The *sustainable growth rate* (SGR) is the growth rate which the firm could maintain without issuing any new equity, while maintaining the current debt/equity ratio. That is, all external financing is debt financing, which is obtained in a sufficient amount to maintain the existing debt/equity ratio. Algebraically, the sustainable growth rate (g*) is:

$$g* = (ROE \text{ x } R)/[1 - (ROE \text{ x } R)] \qquad\qquad [4.7]$$

For Chance, the sustainable growth rate is: g* = (.099 x .25) / [1 - (.099 x .25)] = .02538

This result can be verified by preparing a pro forma statements based on the 2.538% sustainable growth rate:

CHANCE CORPORATION
Pro Forma Income Statement

Sales	$ 2,050.76
Costs	1,435.53
Taxable income	$ 615.23
Taxes (34%)	209.18
Net income	$ 406.05
Retained earnings	$ 101.51
Dividends	$ 304.54

Pro Forma Balance Sheet

Current assets	$ 2,050.76	Total debt	$ 1,000.00
Fixed assets	3,076.14	Owners' equity	4,101.51
Total assets	$ 5,126.90	Total liabilities	$ 5,101.51
		External funds needed	$ 25.39

Since the external financing is all debt, the debt/equity ratio is constant: ($1,025.39/$4,101.51) = 25.00%.

Determinants of Growth: The Du Pont identity writes the equation for return on equity (ROE) as:

$$\text{ROE} = \text{Profit margin} \times \text{Total asset turnover} \times \text{Equity multiplier} \rightarrow \text{ROE} = p \times (S/A) \times [1 + (D/E)]$$

Since ROE is a determinant of the sustainable growth rate, the three determinants of ROE are determinants of the SGR. This relationship is seen more clearly by substituting the equation for ROE into the equation for the SGR:

$$g^* = \frac{\text{ROE x R}}{1 - (\text{ROE x R})} = \frac{p \text{ x } (S/A) \text{ x } [1 + (D/E)] \text{ x R}}{1 - \{p \text{ x } (S/A) \text{ x } [1 + (D/E)] \text{ x R}\}} \qquad [4.8]$$

In this form, it is clear that the sustainable growth rate depends on four factors:

1. *Profit margin* - As profit margin (p) increases, the ability to generate internal financing increases, and the SGR increases.

2. *Dividend policy* - A decrease in the dividend payout ratio increases the retention ratio (R), retained earnings and the SGR increase.

3. *Financial policy*. An increase in the debt/equity ratio (D/E) increases financial leverage, so additional debt financing is available and SGR increases.

4. *Total asset turnover*. An increase in total asset turnover (S/A) decreases the need for financing of new assets and consequently increases the SGR.

This view of the sustainable growth rate clarifies the relationship among the four aspects of financial decision making and their respective effects on the firm's ability to grow. If management desires a growth rate higher than the sustainable growth rate, then one of the stated assumptions must be modified. In this way, firms may use the financial planning model to reconcile potentially conflicting goals and objectives.

4.5   SOME CAVEATS ON FINANCIAL PLANNING MODELS

Financial planning models do not necessarily identify optimal financial policies. Furthermore, the assumptions used in the above discussions of financial planning models to accurately represent reality. Financial planning models are useful for pointing out inconsistencies, but offer limited guidance concerning the resolution of these inconsistencies. The main reason for these deficiencies is that financial planning models are typically based on accounting relationships. They focus on matters such as the association between the debt/equity ratio and firm growth. But, they do not focus on the three basic determinants of firm value: size, risk, and timing of cash flows.

CONCEPT TEST

1.   The basic policy elements which must be established by management to develop a financial plan are:
        1. The firm's needed investment in new assets.
        2. The degree of financial leverage the firm elects to employ.
        3. The dividend payment to stockholders.
        4. The firm's liquidity and working capital requirements.

        These four areas represent, respectively, the firm's _____ decisions, _____ policy, _____ policy, and _____ decision.

2.   A financial plan which covers a period of 2 to 5 years is generally considered a _____ plan. A plan which covers only a 12-month period is considered a _____ plan.

3.   Creation of a financial plan typically involves a process of combining smaller investment proposals into larger units. This process is called _____ .

4.   A universal requirement for financial planning is the _____ forecast. Projected, or forecasted, accounting statements are referred to as _____ statements.

5.   The financial plan describes projected capital expenditures and working capital needs. These are _____ requirements. The firm's financial requirements detail the manner in which required financing will be obtained. The firm's _____ policy and _____ policy are also relevant here because of their impact on the required financing.

6.   The projected growth rates in sales, assets and financial requirements are generally not compatible without some adjustment. The amount of external financing required in order to finance the projected increase in assets is referred to as the _____ variable.

7.   Assumptions about variables such as interest rates, tax rates, and the general state of the economy, must be explicitly stated; these are called _____ assumptions.

8.   The financial planning model based on the assumption that some, but not all, accounting statement data increase proportionately with sales is called the _____ approach. Using this approach, we assume that costs, as a percentage of sales, __(do/do not)__ remain constant. A consequence of this assumption is that the profit margin __(does/does not)__ remain constant.

9.   The dividend payout ratio is the percentage of _____ paid as dividends. That is, the dividend payout ratio is equal to (_____ / _____).

10.   The retention ratio is the percentage of _____ which is _____ . That is, the retention ratio is equal to (_____ / _____).

11.   If, in preparing the pro forma income statement, we assume that the dividend payout ratio is constant, this (is/is not) equivalent to assuming that the retention ratio is constant.

12.   For the financial planning model described in the preceding question, it is generally assumed that assets __(do/do not)__ increase proportionately with sales. It is also assumed that liabilities (other than accounts payable) and owners' equity __(do/do not)__ increase proportionately with sales.

13.   Retained earnings on the pro forma balance sheet is computed by adding the retained earnings figure from the _____ statement to the current balance sheet retained earnings figure. All other balance sheet accounts remain constant, and external financing needed is the _____ figure. The pro forma balance sheet is then complete when the source, or sources, of the external financing are determined and indicated appropriately on the balance sheet. The possible sources of financing are: _____ debt, _____ debt, and _____ .

14.   Since assets are assumed to increase directly with sales, the increase in total assets is equal to: _____ . Projected sales level is equal to: _____ . Projected net income is equal to _____ times projected _____ ; that is: _____ . The projected addition to retained earnings is _____ times _____ ; that is: _____ .

15.   External financing needed is: EFN = _____ . The relationship between EFN and g can be clarified by algebraically rearranging the above equation for EFN:
EFN = – _____ + _____ × g. This is the formula for a linear equation with g as the _____ variable and EFN as the _____ variable. The y-intercept is _____ and the slope is _____ .

16.   The y-intercept in the EFN equation signifies that, when g = 0, EFN = _____ . In other words, if the growth rate is zero, the addition to retained earnings is _____ . Also, since there is no growth in sales or assets, EFN is negative, indicating that _____ .

17.   The EFN equation allows us to determine the growth rate which the firm can achieve without any external financing. This growth rate is ascertained by setting EFN equal to _____ and solving for g. This growth rate allows the firm to grow indefinitely without obtaining external financing. Since all internal financing is derived from _____ , and the firm obtains no new external debt financing, the firm's debt/equity ratio will (increase/decrease) over time.

18.   The growth rate which the firm could maintain without issuing any new equity, while maintaining the current debt/equity ratio, is called the _____ . It is computed: g* = _____ .

19.   The Du Pont identity specifies that return on equity can be written: ROE = _____ .

20.   The Du Pont identity can also be written as: ROE = _____ .

21.   By substituting the above expression for ROE into the formula for the sustainable growth rate, this latter formula is written as follows: g* = (_____)/(_____). In this form it is clear that the sustainable growth rate depends on four factors: (1) An increase in the profit margin ___ (increases/decreases) the firm's ability to generate internal financing, and, consequently, ___ (increases/decreases) the firm's SGR. (2) An increase in the retention ratio (increases/decreases) retained earnings and, thus, (increases/decreases) the SGR. (3) An increase in the debt/equity ratio ___ (increases/decreases) financial leverage, and thereby makes additional debt financing available and _ (increases/decreases) the SGR. (4) An increase in total asset turnover (increases/decreases) the need for financing of new assets and consequently (increases/decreases) the SGR.

PROBLEMS

Basic Questions

Problem 1

The most recent income statement and balance sheet for the G. T. Seaver Corporation are presented below:

G. T. SEAVER CORPORATION

Income Statement

Sales	$ 80,000
Costs	56,000
Net income	$ 24,000

Balance Sheet

Current assets	$ 15,000	Current liabilities	$ 10,000
Fixed assets	85,000	Long-term debt	25,000
		Owners' equity	65,000
Total	$100,000	Total	$100,000

Seaver expects sales to increase by 15% in the coming year. Suppose that all income statement and balance sheet variables will grow at the same rate as sales. Prepare the pro forma income statement and balance sheet. Reconcile these statements using dividends as the 'plug' figure.

Problem 2

Reconcile the pro forma statements in the solution to Problem 1, using long-term debt as the 'plug' figure, under the assumption that Seaver Corporation pays no dividends.

Problem 3

Now , reconcile the pro forma statements in the solution to Problem 1, using long-term debt as the 'plug' figure, under the assumption that Seaver Corporation has a dividend payout ratio of 80%.

Problem 4

The most recent income statement and balance sheet for DMB, Inc. are presented below:

DMB, Inc.
Income statement for the year ending December 31, 2003

Sales	$108,000
Total costs	72,000
Net income	$ 36,000
Retained earnings	$ 9,000
Dividends	$ 27,000

DMB, Inc.
Balance Sheet as of December 31, 2003

Current assets	$ 60,000	Current liabilities	$ 15,000
Fixed assets	120,000	Long-term debt	70,000
		Owners' equity	95,000
Total	$180,000	Total	$180,000

DMB expects sales to increase by 25 % in the year 2004. Prepare a pro forma income statement and balance sheet, assuming all income statement variables will grow at the same rate as sales, and that long-term debt remains constant while all other balance sheet variables increase at the same rate (25%). Assuming that DMB maintains the same retention ratio, determine the amount of external financing needed.

Problem 5

The most recent income statement and balance sheet for the T. McGraw Corporation are as follows:

T. McGRAW CORPORATION
Income Statement

Sales	$ 10,000
Costs	7,500
Taxable income	$ 2,500
Taxes (34%)	850
Net income	$ 1,650
Retained earnings	$ 660
Dividends	$ 990

Balance Sheet

Current assets	$ 5,000	Total debt	$ 6,000
Fixed assets	10,000	Owners' equity	9,000
Total	$ 15,000	Total	$ 15,000

McGraw is forecasting a 20% increase in sales for the coming year. Assets increase directly with sales, while liabilities and equity do not increase spontaneously with sales. Compute the following for McGraw: profit margin (p), retention ratio (R), return on assets (ROA), return on equity (ROE) and debt/equity ratio (D/E).

Problem 6

Use the ratios computed in the solution to Problem 6 to calculate the external financing required by T. McGraw.

Problem 7

Use pro forma statements to verify the results in the solution to Problem 7.

Problem 8

Use the solution to Problem 7 to determine the growth rate McGraw can maintain if no external financing is used.

Problem 9

Use the linear equation from the solution to Problem 9 to determine the EFN needed for a growth rate of to zero. Also, find EFN for a growth rates of 1% and 10%.

Intermediate Questions

Problem 10

The most recent balance sheet and income statement for Grote & Co., Inc., are presented here:

GROTE & CO., INC.
Income Statement

Sales	$ 20,000
Costs	17,000
Taxable income	$ 3,000
Taxes (34%)	1,020
Net income	$ 1,980
Retained earnings	$ 1,188
Dividends	$ 792

Balance Sheet

Current assets			Current liabilities		
Cash	$ 3,000	(15%)	Accounts payable	$ 6,000	(30%)
Accounts receivable	5,000	(25%)	Notes payable	3,000	(n/a)
Inventory	7,000	(35%)	Total	$ 9,000	(n/a)
Total	$15,000	(75%)			
			Long-term debt	$ 15,000	(n/a)
Fixed assets			Owners' equity		
Net plant	$30,000	(150%)	Common stock	$ 13,000	(n/a)
			Retained earnings	8,000	(n/a)
			Total	$ 21,000	(n/a)
Total assets	$45,000	(225%)	Total liabilities	$ 45,000	(n/a)

For each balance sheet item, the percentage in parentheses represents the given item as a percentage of annual sales. Those items which are not expected to increase proportionately with sales are identified by 'n / a', indicating that the percentage calculation is not applicable. Grote & Co. has projected a 25% increase in sales. The dividend payout ratio is expected to remain constant. Use the percentage of sales approach to prepare the pro forma statements and to compute the external financing needed.

Problem 11

Use the data from the solution to Problem 6 to determine the sustainable growth rate for McGraw.

Problem 12

Use the Du Pont identity to verify the calculations in the solution to Problem 11.

Problem 13

Verify the results in the solutions to Problems 11 and 12 by preparing the pro forma income statement and balance sheet for McGraw, using the 7.914% sustainable growth rate.

Use the following information to solve Problems 14 through 17:

RYAN & CO., INC.
Financial Statements

Income Statement

Sales	$ 2,000
Costs	1,800
Taxable income	$ 200
Taxes (34%)	68
Net income	$ 132
Retained earnings	$ 88
Dividends	$ 44

Balance Sheet

Current assets	$ 500		Current liabilities	$ 165
Fixed assets	1,150		Long-term debt	535
			Owners' equity	950
Total	$ 1,650		Total	$ 1,650

Problem 14

Ryan & Co. forecasts next year's sales as $2,200. Costs, assets and current liabilities increase proportionately with sales, and the retention ratio remains constant. Compute external financing needed for Ryan.

Problem 15

Assume that Ryan currently has sufficient excess capacity to support a sales level of $2,100 without any additional fixed assets. Calculate external financing needed for projected sales of $2,200.

Problem 16

Assume that Ryan is currently operating at 80% of its capacity. Calculate external financing needed for projected sales of $2,200.

Problem 17

Assume that Ryan is currently operating at 95% of its capacity. Calculate external financing needed for projected sales of $2,200.

ANSWERS TO CONCEPT TEST

1.   capital budgeting; capital structure; dividend; net working capital

2.   long-term; short-term

3.   aggregation

4.   sales; pro forma

5.   asset; debt; dividend

6.   plug

7.   economic

8.   percentage of sales; do; does

9.   net income; cash dividends; net income

10.   net income; retained; retained earnings; net income

11.   is

12.   do; do not

13.   pro forma income; plug; short-term; long-term; new equity financing

14. $(A \times g)$; $[S \times (1 + g)]$; the profit margin; sales; $[p \times S \times (1 + g)]$; the retention ratio; projected net income; $[R \times p \times S \times (1 + g)]$

15. $(A \times g) - [R \times p \times S \times (1 + g)]$; $(R \times p \times S)$; $[A - (R \times p \times S)]$; independent; dependent; $[-(R \times p \times S)]$; $[A - (R \times p \times S)]$

16. $[-(R \times p \times S)]$; $[-(R \times p \times S)]$; surplus financing is available

17.   zero; retained earnings; decrease

18.   sustainable growth rate; $(ROE \times R)/[1 - (ROE \times R)]$

19.   (Profit margin $\times$ Total asset turnover $\times$ Equity multiplier)

20. $p \times (S/A) \times [1 + (D/E)]$

21. $p \times (S/A) \times [1 + (D/E)] \times R$; $1 - \{p \times (S/A) \times [1 + (D/E)] \times R\}$; increases; increases; increases; increases; increases; increases; decreases; increases

PROBLEM SOLUTIONS

Problem 1:

G. T. SEAVER CORPORATION
Pro Forma Income Statement

Sales	$ 92,000
Costs	64,400
Net income	$ 27,600

Pro Forma Balance Sheet

Current assets	$ 17,250 (+ $ 2,250)	Current liabilities	$ 11,500 (+ $ 1,500)
Fixed assets	97,750 (+ $12,750)	Long-term debt	28,750 (+ $ 3,750)
		Owners' equity	74,750 (+ $ 9,750)
Total	$115,000 (+ $15,000)	Total	$115,000 (+ $15,000)

The figures in parentheses indicate the increase in the respective balance sheet items. The increase of $9,750 in equity is inconsistent with the net income figure of $27,600 from the pro forma income statement. If these figures are reconciled using dividends as the 'plug' figure, the dividends for the year must be ($27,600 – $9,750) = $17,850.

Problem 2: If dividends are zero, then pro forma retained earnings are $27,600 and equity is ($65,000 + $27,600) = $92,600. Equity + current liabilities = ($92,600 + $11,500) = $104,100, so that long-term debt is ($115,000 – $104,100) = $10,900. Seaver must pay off ($25,000 – $10,900) = $14,100 of long-term debt.

The pro forma balance sheet is: G. T. SEAVER CORPORATION
Pro Forma Balance Sheet

Current assets	$ 17,250 (+ $ 2,250)	Current liabilities	$ 11,500 (+ $ 1,500)
Fixed assets	97,750 (+ $12,750)	Long-term debt	10,900 (- $ 14,100)
		Owners' equity	92,600 (+ $27,600)
Total	$115,000 (+ $15,000)	Total	$115,000 (+ $15,000)

Problem 3: Dividends are ($27,600 × .80) = $22,080, and retained earnings are ($27,600 – $22,080) = $5,520. Equity on the pro forma balance sheet is equal to ($65,000 + $5,520) = $70,520. Equity plus current liabilities are equal to ($70,520 + $11,500) = $82,020. Long-term debt must be ($115,000 – $82,020) = $32,980, so that Seaver must borrow ($32,980 – $25,000) = $7,980. The pro forma balance sheet appears below:

G. T. SEAVER CORPORATION
Pro Forma Balance Sheet

Current assets	$ 17,250 (+ $ 2,250)	Current liabilities	$ 11,500 (+ $ 1,500)
Fixed assets	97,750 (+ $12,750)	Long-term debt	32,980 (+ $ 7,980)
		Owners' equity	70,520 (+ $ 5,520)
Total	$115,000 (+ $15,000)	Total	$115,000 (+ $15,000)

Problem 4:

DMB, Inc.
Pro Forma Income Statement for 2004

Sales	$135,000
COGS	90,000
Net income	$ 45,000
Retained earnings	$ 11,250
Dividends	$ 33,750

DMB, Inc.
Pro Forma Balance Sheet for 2004

Current assets	$ 75,000 (+15,000)	Current liabilities	$ 18,750 (+3,750)
Fixed assets	150,000 (+30,000)	Long-term debt	70,000
		Owners' equity	106,250 (+11,250)
Total	$225,000 (+45,000)	Total	$195,000 (+15,000)

External financing needed: EFN = $225,000 - $195,000 = $30,000
Note: Change in owners' equity is the increase in retained earnings: $95,000 x 1.25 = $11,250

Problem 5: These ratios are computed as follows:

p	=	$1,650 / $10,000	=	16.5%
R	=	$660 / $1,650	=	40%
ROA	=	$1,650 / $15,000	=	11%
ROE	=	$1,650 / $9,000	=	18.33%
D/E	=	$6,000 / $9,000	=	66.67%

Problem 6: EFN =   increase in assets -   addition to retained earnings
$\qquad$ = (A × g) - p x S x R x (1 + g) =   ($15,000 x 0.20) - 0.165 x 10,000 x 0.40 x (1.20)
$\qquad$ = $3,000 - $792 = $2,208

Problem 7:

T. Mc McGraw CORPORATION
Pro Forma Income Statement

Sales	$ 12,000
Costs	9,000
Taxable income	$ 3,000
Taxes (34%)	1,020
Net income	$ 1,980
Retained earnings	$ 792
Dividends	$ 1,188

Pro Forma Balance Sheet

Current assets	$ 6,000	Total debt	$ 6,000
Fixed assets	12,000	Owners' equity	9,792
Total	$ 18,000	Total	$ 15,792
		EFN	$ 2,208

Problem 8: EFN $= (A \times g) - [R \times p \times S \times (1+g)] = -(R \times p \times S) + [A - (R \times p \times S)] \times g$
$= -(.40 \times .165 \times \$10,000) + [\$15,000 - (.40 \times .165 \times \$10,000)] \times g$
$= -\$660 + (\$14,340 \times g) \rightarrow 660 / 14,340 = g \rightarrow g = 4.603\%$

Problem 9: growth rate $= 0$: EFN $= -\$660 + (\$14,340 \times g) = -\$660 + (\$14,340 \times 0) = -\$660$
surplus financing $= \$660$

growth rate $= 1\%$: EFN $= -\$660 + (\$14,340 \times .01) = -\$516.60$
surplus financing $= \$516.60$

growth rate $= 10\%$: EFN $= -\$660 + (\$14,340 \times .10) = \$774$
additional financing needed $= \$774$

Problem 10: The pro forma income statement assumes that costs remain a constant percentage of sales: (costs/sales) $= (\$17,000/\$20,000) = 85\%$, and the profit margin remains constant at $(\$1,980/\$20,000) = 9.9\%$. The dividend payout ratio is $(\$990/\$2,475) = 40\%$, so the retention ratio is 60%.

GROTE & CO., INC.
Pro Forma Income Statement

Sales	$ 25,000
Costs	21,250
Taxable income	$ 3,750
Taxes (34%)	1,275
Net income	$ 2,475
Retained earnings	$ 1,485
Dividends	$ 990

The partial pro forma balance sheet is below. The 'plug' figure is external financing needed (EFN). The figures in parentheses are the dollar increases over the current balance sheet accounts.

GROTE & CO., INC.
Partial Pro Forma Balance Sheet

Current assets			Current liabilities		
Cash	$ 3,750	($ 750)	Accounts payable	$ 7,500	($ 1,500)
Accounts receivable	6,250	(1,250)	Notes payable	3,000	(0)
Inventory	8,750	(1,750)	Total	$10,500	($ 1,500)
Total	$18,750	($ 3,750)			
			Long-term debt	$15,000	($ 0)
Fixed assets			Owners' equity		
Net plant	$37,500	($ 7,500)	Common stock	$13,000	($ 0)
			Retained earnings	9,485	(1,485)
			Total	$22,485	($ 1,485)
Total assets	$56,250	($ 11,250)	Total liabilities	$47,985	($ 2,985)
			EFN	$ 8,265	

Now, Grote must decide how to obtain the additional financing. If all the external financing is obtained from issuing long-term debt, the pro forma balance sheet would show long-term debt = ($15,000 + $8,265) = $23,265.

Problem 11: $g^* = [ROE \times R] / [1 - (ROE \times R)] = (.18333 \times .40) / [1 - (.18333 \times .40)] = 7.914\%$

T. McGraw can grow at 7.914% without issuing new equity and maintain the current debt/equity ratio.

Problem 12:   ROE for McGraw : $ROE = .165 \times (\$10,000/\$15,000) \times [1 + (\$6,000/\$9,000)] = .18333$

$g^* = p \times (S/A) \times [1 + (D/E)] \times R / [1 - \{p \times (S/A) \times [1 + (D/E)] \times R\}]$

$= .165 \times (.667) \times [1 + (.667)] \times .40 / [1 - \{.165 \times (.667) \times (1 + 1.667) \times .40\}]$
$= 7.914\%$

Problem 13:

T. McGRAW CORPORATION
Pro Forma Income Statement

Sales	$ 10,791.40
Costs	8,093.55
Taxable income	$ 2,697.85
Taxes (34%)	917.27
Net income	$ 1,780.58
Retained earnings	$ 712.23
Dividends	$ 1,068.35

Pro Forma Balance Sheet

Current assets	$ 5,395.70	Total debt	$ 6,000.00
Fixed assets	10,791.40	Owners' equity	9,712.23
Total	$ 16,187.10	Total	$ 15,712.23
		EFN	$ 474.87

Since the external financing is all debt, the debt/equity ratio is ($6,474.87/$9,712.23) = 66.667%; the debt/equity ratio is unchanged from the calculation in the solution to Problem 5.

Problem 14: The retention ratio is ($88/$132) = 2/3, and the growth rate for sales is ($200/$2,000) = 10%. The pro forma income statement and partial pro forma balance sheet are below.

RYAN & CO., INC.
Pro Forma Income Statement

Sales	$ 2,200.00
Costs	1,980.00
Taxable income	$ 220.00
Taxes (34%)	74.80
Net income	$ 145.20
Retained earnings	$ 96.80
Dividends	$ 48.40

Partial Pro Forma Balance Sheet

Current assets	$ 550.00	Current liabilities	$ 181.50
Fixed assets	1,265.00	Long-term debt	535.00
		Owners' equity	1,046.80
Total	$ 1,815.00	Total	$ 1,763.30

$$EFN = \$1,815.00 - \$1,763.30 = \$51.70$$

Problem 15: At the full capacity sales level of $2,100, the ratio of fixed assets to sales is:

(Fixed assets/Full capacity sales) = $1,150/$2,100 = .548

If this ratio is maintained at a sales level of $2,200, then Ryan requires (.548 × $2,200) = $1,205.60 of fixed assets. In Problem 14, the fixed asset level is $1,265. Therefore, total assets required are now ($1,265 – $1,205.60) = $59.40 less than previously calculated, so external financing needed is also $59.40 less. External financing needed is now ($51.70 – $59.40) = –$7.70. The negative figure means that Ryan now has excess financing of $7.70.

Problem 16: Full capacity sales level = $2,000 / .80 = 2,500. So, no additional fixed assets are needed to support sales of $2,200. In Problem 14, Ryan needs $115 in additional fixed assets of $115; EFN is $51.70. Since Ryan does not need additional fixed assets, EFN = ($51.70 – $115) = –$63.30, or excess financing of $63.30.

Problem 17: Full capacity sales level = $2,000 / .95 = $2,105.26.
Fixed assets / Full capacity sales = $1,150 / $2,105.26 = 0.546
Fix assets needed for sales of $2,200 = 0.546 x $2,200 = $1,201.2
Total assets required = $1,265 - $1,201.2 = $63.8 less (the $1,265 is from Problem 14)
EFN is also $63.8 less → EFN = $51.70 - $63.80 = -12.21
→ Excess financing = $12.21

5   Introduction to Valuation: The Time Value of Money

CHAPTER HIGHLIGHTS

This chapter deals with one of the most important concepts of finance: the time value of money. Time value the foundations used by corporate managers for financial decision making, and it has important applications for financial decisions made by individual consumers. Anyone who makes a bank deposit, takes out a loan, or buys a share of stock should understand the importance of the time value of money.

A thorough knowledge of the material presented in this chapter is essential to an understanding of the material which follows. Furthermore, since the topics in the chapter are developed sequentially, it is crucial that each subject in the chapter be understood before moving to the next topic.

While the mathematical concepts presented in this chapter are not especially complicated, the mechanics of the calculations often require the use of financial tables or a calculator. The tables provided in the Appendix of your text are sufficient for most problems in the chapter, but a financial calculator can be a valuable time-saving aide.

THE TIME VALUE OF MONEY

Financial managers must be able to determine the value today of cash flows that are expected in the future. This value depends on the time value of money. Put simply, the *time value of money* means that a dollar today is worth more than a dollar promised in the future. This is because today's dollar could have earned interest while you waited. So, it would grow to more than a dollar in the future. The tradeoff between money today and money later depends on several factors. One of them is the rate earned on investments.

5.1   FUTURE VALUE AND COMPOUNDING

Future value is the amount to which an initial dollar will grow over some length of time at some interest rate. We first consider investing for a single time period.

Investing for a Single Period - An Example: Consider a deposit of $500 in a savings account paying 10% interest per year. The $500 deposit is the original *principal*. The future value is the account balance at some later date. If the $500 is invested for one year, it will earn $50 interest, so you will have a balance of $550 in the account. The calculation of this future value can be thought of as principal plus interest.

$$\$500 + (.10 \times \$500) = \$500 + \$50 = \$550$$

OR

$$\$500 \times (1.10) = \$550, \text{ where } 1.10 \text{ is one plus the interest rate.}$$

These two alternative approaches are mathematically equivalent, but the second approach is more efficient, especially when performing future value calculations over more than one year. In general, the future value (FV) for an investment over a one-year period can be determined from the following equation:

$$FV = P \times (1 + r)$$

where P is the original principal and r is the annual interest rate.

Investing for More than One Period: Suppose the $500 principal above is left for two years. What is the future value (balance in the account at the end of the two-year period)? Assume the bank continues to pay 10% interest.

First, assume the $50 interest earned the first year is withdrawn and put into a non-interest bearing account. During the second year, the $500 principal amount will earn another $50 in interest. The interest paid in the first year, however, will earn nothing. At the end of the second year, the total value (from both accounts) will be:

$500   principal
  50   interest on principal, year 1
  <u>50</u>   interest on principal, year 2
$600   Total value in year 2

Note that, because the first year's interest was placed in a non-interest bearing account, the investor earns exactly $50 interest in each year. That is, the first year's interest payment is not reinvested at the 10% rate, so interest is earned only on the original principal amount invested. This is referred to as *simple interest*.

Now, assume the depositor reinvests the interest from year 1 by leaving it in the account paying 10 %. The account balance at the end of year 1 is $550, and the investor will earn 10% interest on this entire amount over the second year. Since the depositor earns interest on the previous year's interest (as well as the principal), this is referred to as *compound interest*, or the process of *compounding* interest. The value at the end of year 2 will have four components:

$500   principal
  50   interest on principal, year 1
  50   interest on principal, year 2
  <u>5</u>   interest on year 1 interest, invested for year 2
$605   Total value in year 2

It is important to compare the two calculations above: future value with simple interest, and future value with compound interest. Note that the future value using compound interest is $605, not $600 as in the simple interest case. The additional $5 future value represents the "interest earned on interest" in the second year. Although the difference may seem small in this example, over longer periods of time, the difference between compound and simple interest can become extremely large.

Remember, we wrote the future value at the end of the year 1 as:

$$FV_1 = P \times (1 + r) = \$500 \times (1.10) = \$550$$

Using the future value in year 1 as the beginning principal in year 2, the future value at the end of year 2 is:

$$FV_2 = P \times (1 + r) = \$550 \times (1.10) = \$605$$
OR
$$FV_2 = FV_1 \times (1 + r) = \$550 \times (1.10) = \$605$$

The notation FV_2 is used here to indicate the future value at the end of the second year, in order to distinguish it from the future value at the end of the first year (FV_1), which is $550. Therefore, the principal at the beginning of the second year (i.e., $FV_1 = \$550$) is the future value of the $500 deposited at the beginning of the first year.

$$FV_1 = P \times (1 + r) = \$500 \text{ x } (1.10) = \$550$$

Combining these last two equations, we have:

$$
\begin{aligned}
FV_2 &= FV_1 \times (1 + r) \\
&= [P \times (1 + r)] \times (1 + r) \\
&= [\$500 \times (1.10)] \times (1.10) = \$500 \times (1.10)^2 = \$605
\end{aligned}
$$

In general, the future value at the end of year 2 is equal to the original principal times $[(1 + r) \times (1 + r)]$, or:

$$ FV_2 = P \times (1 + r)^2 $$

To find the future value at the end of year 3 (FV_3), we compound the future value at the end of year 2 for one more year by multiplying by the factor $(1 + r)$, as follows:

$$ FV_3 = P \times (1 + r)^3 $$

For the $500 deposit, receiving 10% interest, for a three-year period:

$$ FV_3 = \$500 \times (1.10)^3 = \$500 \times (1.331) = \$665.50 $$

In general, the future value of an original principal P, invested for any given number of years t, at an interest rate r, is given by:

$$ FV_t = P \times (1 + r)^t \qquad [5.1] $$

The expression $(1 + r)^t$ is often referred to as *the future value interest factor,* or simply future value factor, and is sometimes abbreviated as FVIF(r,t).

Consider the future value of a deposit of $1,000, invested at a 5% interest rate for 7 years:

$$ FV_7 = \$1,000 \times (1.05)^7 = \$1,000 \times (1.40710) = \$1,407.10 $$

The future value interest factor is: $(1 + r)^t = (1.05)^7 = (1.40710)$. There are several alternative approaches to determining this value. Using either pencil and paper or a basic four-function calculator, we could multiply seven factors of 1.05. More efficient alternatives include the use of a calculator with a $[y^x]$ function key, or tables of future value interest factors, such as Table A.1 in the Appendix of your text.

If you are using a calculator with a $[y^x]$ function key, first realize that we must enter $(1 + r)$ as the base (that is, y on the calculator), and t as the exponent (that is, x on the calculator). For the above example, this is generally calculated using the following sequence: 1.05 $[y^x]$ 7 = 1.40710042. This value is then multiplied by the original principal to determine the future value. But, if you are using a calculator, be sure you are familiar with it, because not all calculators use exactly the same sequence just discussed.

If you are using Table A.1, the appropriate future value interest factor is in the seventh row under the 5% column. This indicates that $(1.05)^7$ is equal to 1.4071. Note that the use of the table provides a less accurate result than does the calculator. Furthermore, the use of the table is limited to problems for which the interest rate and time period are provided in the tables. Therefore, the use of a calculator with a $[y^x]$ function key is usually preferable to the use of Table A.1 because the calculator provides a more accurate answer and can also be used for any combination of interest rate and time period.

If you are using a financial calculator, the key strokes typically include:

> PV = initial amount invested
> i = interest rate
> n = number of periods
> FV = calculator computes future value

Again, not all calculators use exactly the same notation or sequence of entering the variables. So, *be sure* you read the instruction manual and understand *exactly* how to operate your calculator.

Example: You make a $2,000 deposit in a Registered Retirement Savings Plan (RRSP) at a bank which will pay 4% interest per year for the next forty years, at which time you plan to retire. The future value of your RRSP account at the end of forty years is given by:

$$FV_t = P \times (1 + r)^t$$

$$FV_{40} = \$2,000 \times (1.04)^{40} = \$2,000 \times (4.801021) = \$9,602.04$$

Table A.1 indicates that $(1.08)^{40} = 4.8010 \rightarrow FV_{40} = \$2,000 \times (4.8010) = \$9,602.00$

Clearly, the difference of $.04 in these results has little practical significance. However, keep in mind that this discrepancy arises from the fact that the future value interest factor in Table A.1 is rounded to three decimal places, and therefore is somewhat less accurate than the result obtained using a $[y^x]$ function key on a calculator.

The interest earned over the forty-year period is:

> $9,602.04 – $2,000 = $7,602.04

If the deposit earned simple interest, the interest would be (.04 × $2,000) = $80 per year, or ($80 × 40) = $3,200 for the forty-year period. Therefore, the compounding of interest, or interest paid on interest previously received, accounts for ($7,602.04 – $3,200) = $4,402.04 of the total interest received.

A Note on Compound Growth: The interest rate earned on a savings account deposit is a compound growth rate. That is, the annual interest rate is actually the rate at which the balance in the account grows each year. Since an interest rate is one specific example of a compound growth rate, the mathematics of future value calculations can be applied to any quantity which grows at a given compound rate over a period of time. For example, the population of a given geographic area may grow at a specified annual rate. Similarly, compound growth rates can be used to describe the growth of economic variables, such as Gross National Product (GNP), or financial values such as a company's sales or profits.

Example: The dividends of the TTK Corporation are expected to grow at a compound rate of 6% each year for the next five years. The most recent annual dividend was $3.50 per share. What is TTK's dividend per share expected to be five years from now?

Think of the current year's dividend as the original 'principal' ($3.50) and the compound growth rate as r (6%). Five years from now the dividend will be:

$$FV_5 = \$3.50 \times (1.06)^5 = \$4.68$$

5.2   PRESENT VALUE AND DISCOUNTING

In the previous section, the future value concept was used to answer the question: If you deposit $2,000 today in a savings account paying 4% interest per year, what is the balance in the account forty years from now? (the answer is $9,602.04) In this section, a different, but closely related question is: What deposit is required today, in an account paying 4% interest, in order to have $250,000 forty years from now? The answer is $52,072.26. The $52,072.26 is the *present value* of $250,000 to be received forty years from now, when the appropriate interest rate is 4%.

The Single Period Case: Kris can earn 5% interest in her savings account during the next year. Kris would like to be able to withdraw $1,200 from her account one year from now (i.e. she wants the future value of the account to be $1,200). How much should she deposit today to have a future value of $1,200? To find out, use the future value equation, substiting the known values for FV and r. Then solve for P:

$$FV = P \times (1 + r) \rightarrow \$1,200 = P \times (1.05)$$

$$P = \$1,200 / 1.05 = \$1,142.86$$

At an 5% rate of interest, Kris would have to deposit $1,142.86 11 today in order to receive $1,200 one year from now. So, $1,142.86 is the present value of $1,200, one year from today, when the relevant interest rate is 5%.

Note that the present value depends on three factors: the amount of the future payment (i.e., the future value), the time period, and the market rate of interest. The process of computing a present value is referred to as *discounting*. The interest rate used in a present value calculation is known as the *discount rate*.

The equation for calculating present value can be derived from the future value formula: $FV = P \times (1 + r)$. From this point, through the text, the notation P (original principal) will be replaced with the notation PV, to represent present value:

$$FV = PV \times (1 + r) \rightarrow PV = FV / (1 + r)$$

Substituting the known values of FV ($1,200) and r (.05), the result is the same:

$$PV = \$1,200 / (1.05) = \$1,1,142.86$$

The general formula for present value in the single-period case:

$$PV = FV / (1 + r)$$

Since dividing by the term $(1 + r)$ is equivalent to multiplying by the reciprocal $[1/(1 + r)]$, the above present value formula can also be rewritten as:

$$PV = FV \times [1 / (1 + r)]$$

Present Values for Multiple Periods: Suppose that Kris has two years, rather than one year, to accumulate $1,200, and that her bank will pay 5% interest per year for the next two years. What deposit would Kris have to make today in order to obtain a future value of $1,200 two years from today?

The future value formula for multiple periods is: $FV_t = PV \times (1 + r)^t$

Substituting the known values ($FV_2 = \$1,200$; $r = .05$; $t = 2$):

$$\$1,200 \ = \ PV \times (1.05)^2 \ \rightarrow \ PV \ = \ \$1,200 \,/\, (1.05)^2 = \$1,200 \,/\, 1.1025 \ = \ \$1,088.44$$

Kris would have to deposit $1,088.24 today, in an account paying 5% interest per year, in order to be able to withdraw $1,200 two years from today. Therefore, $1,088.44 is the present value of $1,200, to be received two years from today, when the appropriate interest rate (or discount rate) is 4%.

A general formula for present value in the multiple-period case is:

$$PV \ = \ FV_t \,/\, (1 + r)^t$$

Note that dividing by the term $(1 + r)^t$ is equivalent to multiplying by its reciprocal $1/(1 + r)^t$:

$$PV \ = \ FV_t \times [1 \,/\, (1 + r)^t]   \qquad\qquad [5.2]$$

The term $[1/(1 + r)^t]$ in the above formula is sometimes referred to as the *present value interest factor*, and can be abbreviated PVIF (r,t). Since the process of calculating a present value is sometimes called discounting, we also refer to the term $[1/(1 + r)^t]$ as the *discount factor*. The process of computing a present value is also referred to as *discounted cash flow* (DCF) valuation.

Note that the present value interest factor PVIF (5%,2) is equal to $[1/(1.05)^2] = (1/1.1025) = .907029$. Using Table A.2 in the Appendix, the above problem can be solved as follows:

$$PV \ = \ FV_t \times PVIF \,(r, t) \ = \ \$1,200 \times PVIF \,(5\%, 2) \ = \ \$1,200 \times .9070 \ = \ \$1,088.40$$

(The answer is slightly less accurate because the factors in Table A.2 are rounded to four decimal places.) You should be comfortable with using both the tables and a handheld calculator in order to understand and apply present value concepts and calculations.

5.3   MORE ON PRESENT AND FUTURE VALUES

This section provides more analysis of the relationship between present and future values and of some additional aspects of these concepts.

Present versus Future Value: It is important to emphasize and understand that the basic equations for prexent and future value are, in fact, two algebraically equivalent versions of the same equation. Repeating these equations:

$$FV_t = PV \times (1 + r)^t$$

$$\text{and } PV \ = \ FV_t \,/\, (1 + r)^t \ \text{ or } \ PV \ = \ FV_t \times [1 \,/\, (1 + r)^t]$$

where $[1/(1 + r)^t]$ is the present value interest factor. The present value interest factor is the reciprocal of the future value interest factor.

One of our major concerns in the study of corporate finance is the evaluation of investment opportunities. Two alternative, but equivalent, approaches to evaluating investment opportunities are based on the future value and present value concepts, as illustrated below.

Example: Suppose an investor is contemplating the purchase of an antique automobile for $60,000 today. The investor expects that it can be sold for $70,000 in one year.

The investor believes this is a very safe investment. But, the $60,000 could be invested elsewhere at 12%, also for very little risk. Which investment is better? Future-value analysis is used to calculate the value of $60,000 invested at 12% to determine the value at the end of one year.

$$FV = PV \times (1 + r) = \$60,000 \times (1.12) = \$67,200$$

In one year, the investor will have $67,200. But, the car will be worth $70,000. Since both opportunities require a $60,000 outlay today, the investor will choose the automobile because it provides a larger future return.

Present-value analysis of this problem requires that the investor determine the amount needed to invest today, at the 12% rate of interest, in order to obtain a return of $70,000 one year from today (i.e. the present value):

$$PV = FV_t / (1 + r)^t = PV = \$70,000 / (1.12) = \$62,500$$

That is, the investor can obtain a $70,000 payoff with a smaller initial investment by buying the car for $60,000.

Both the future value analysis and the present-value analysis indicate that the investment in the antique automobile is preferable to the alternative investment opportunity with a 12% interest rate. Since the two approaches are mathematically equivalent, the conclusions should be the same in both cases.

Determining the Discount Rate: A third approach to evaluating the investment opportunity is based on calculating the rate of return implicit in the automobile investment. This rate of return is then compared to the 12% interest rate available for the other investment. Since this approach is also based on the fundamental future value concept, it too is mathematically equivalent to the future-value and present-value analyses described above.

To determine the rate of return for the investment in the antique automobile, use the basic future value equation and substitute for the known values (FV = $70,000; PV = $60,000; t = 1):

$$FV_t = PV \times (1 + r)^1 \rightarrow \$70,000 = \$60,000 \times (1 + r)^1$$

Dividing both sides of the above equation by $60,000,

$$1.16667 = (1 + r) \rightarrow r = .166667 = 16.667\%.$$

This result indicates that an investment which grows in value from $60,000 to $70,000 in one year provides a 16.67% rate of return. The alternative investment opportunity available pays a 12% return, so investing in the car is the preferred investment opportunity.

The calculation to determine the rate of return is more complicated when the relevant time period is more than one year. The following example demonstrates the interest rate computation for a particular investment or loan.

Example: If you borrow $5,000 today and promise to repay $7,500 in six years, what is the annual interest rate you are paying for this loan? The answer can be determined by using the basic future value formula, Table A.1, or a financial calculator. To solve, substitute $FV_6 = \$7,500$, PV = $5,000, t = 6 in the future value formula:

$$FV_t = PV \times (1 + r)^t \rightarrow \qquad \$7,500 = \$5,000 \times (1 + r)^6 ; \qquad 1.500 = (1 + r)^6$$

An approximate value for r can be determined from Table A.1 by locating the future value interest factor for a six-year period which is closest to 1.500. The future value factor 1.5007 in the sixth row, under the 7% column, indicates that $(1.07)^6 = 1.5007$, so r is approximately 7%.

The alternative approach to solving for r is to take the sixth root of both sides of the above equation. The right hand side of the equation becomes $(1 + r)$. The sixth root of 1.500 is found by solving

$$1.5^{1/6} = 1 + r \rightarrow 1.0069913 \rightarrow r = 1.0069913 - 1 = r = 0.069913 = 6.9913\%$$

Finding the Number of Periods: The present or future value approach can be used to to determine how long it takes to have a certain amount of money. Suppose an investor has $15,000 to invest in a savings account that pays 7% interest per year. How long will it take the investor to have $25,000? Start with the same future value equation: $FV_t = PV \times (1 + r)^t$. Substitute the known values for FV ($25,000), PV($15,000), and r(7%) and solve for t.

$$\$25,000 = \$15,000 \times (1.07)^t \rightarrow 1.6667 = (1.07)^t$$

The future value factor is $25,000 / $15,000 = 1.6667. From Table A.1 under the column for 7%, the factor for 7 years at 7% is 1.6058; the factor for 8 years at 7% is 1.7182. So, it will take between 7 and 8 years to have $25,000.

CONCEPT TEST

1.   When a deposit or investment earns interest on interest previously received, it is said to be earning _____ . This process is referred to as _____ .

2.   A _____ is the amount to which an initial dollar deposit, called the _____ , will grow when interest is compounded at a specified interest rate for a specified number of years. The future value (FV_t) of an initial deposit (PV) which earns interest at the rate r for t years is given by the following formula: FV_t = _____ . The expression _____ is referred to as the future value interest factor, and is abbreviated as _____ .

3.   A present value is the amount which must be invested today, at a specified _____ , in order to grow to a specified _____ , at a specified _____ . Therefore, a present value is dependent on three things: the _____ , the amount of the _____ , and the _____ .

4.   The process of computing a present value is referred to as _____ . The interest rate used in a present value calculation is referred to as the _____ .

5.   A present value can be calculated by substituting the known values of the _____ , the _____ , and the _____ into the basic present value equation, as follows: PV = _____

6.   An alternative approach is to rearrange the basic present value equation so that the present value is determined by multiplying the future value times the _____ of the future value interest factor, as follows: PV = _____ .

7.   The term _____ is referred to as the present value interest factor, and can be abbreviated _____ . The present value interest factor can be determined from tables. The present value interest factor is also called the _____ and the process of computing a present value is also referred to as _____ valuation.

PROBLEMS

Basic Questions

Problem 1

If you deposit $10,000 today in a bank account paying 5.38%, how much will you have in one year? If you need $12,000 in one year, how much do you have to deposit today?

Problem 2

Calculate the future value for each of the following cash flows to be received one year from now:

Today's cash flow	Interest rate
$ 60,000	12.0 %
273,000	10.0
1,500	9.0
27,634	6.7
135,000	3.0

Problem 3

If you deposit $2,500 in a savings account at Tightfist Bank, how long will it take your balance to reach $5,000? The bank uses a 10% simple interest rate. What about if the interest rate is double to 20%? If instead, the bank compounds interest annually, how long will it take to have a $5,000 balance, using the 10% rate?

Problem 4

Eddie is wondering if he should invest $2,000 in a rare coin that he expects will be worth $2,500 two years from today. Alternatively, he can invest his $2,000 in a savings account and earn 10%. Using both present value and future value analysis, determine whether or not Eddie should invest in the coin.

Problem 5

After talking to a friend who is completing a business degree, you have learned about compound interest. You decide to take your money out of your account at Tightfist Bank (see Problem 3) and transfer it to JPH Direct, which offers 10% compound interest. If you leave your $2,500 in this account, how much money will you be able to withdraw in five years? What if the interest rate doubled to 20%?

Problem 6

An art collector has the opportunity to invest in paintings. The investment requires an initial outlay of $2 million today. The collector is certain that the paintings will sell for $2.06 million one year from now. Alternatively, the $2 million can be invested in bank certificates of deposit which pay 4% per year. What is the future value of the $2 million in one year if the collector elects to buy certificates of deposit? Are the paintings a good investment?

Problem 7

In Problem 6, what is the rate of return for the investment in paintings?

Problem 8

For the paintings described in Problem 6, what is the present value of the future cash flow the collector would receive if the paintings are sold one year from now? What is the value of the paintings to the collector?

Problem 9

You plan to live very well when you retire in thirty-five years and have calculated that you will require $3,000,000 at that time. If the rate of interest available is 9%, how much do you need to invest today in order to live comfortably during your retirement? What if rates are only 4.5%?

Problem 10

Calculate the present value for each of the following cash flows to be received one year from now:

Future cash flow	Interest rate
$ 10,000	10 %
153,000	12
153,200	10
2,567,450	5
120,600	9

Problem 11

What is the present value of $145 to be received in 5 years if the market interest rate is 5.3?

Problem 12

What is the future value of $235 dollars invested at 4.8% for 4 years?

Problem 13

For each of the following, compute the present value:

Future value	Years	Interest rate
$ 498	7	13 %
1,033	13	6
14,784	23	4
898,156	4	31
75,000	3	10.5
169,700	9	4.6

Problem 14

For each of the following, compute the future value:

Present value	Years	Interest rate	Future value
$ 123	13	13 %	
4,555	8	8	
74,484	5	10	
167,332	9	1	
108,350	24	3.8	
57,300	16	12.4	

Problem 15

Solve for the unknown time period in each of the following:

Present value	Future value	Interest rate	Time (years)
$ 100	$ 350	12%	
123	351	10	
4,100	8,524	5	
10,543	26,783	6	

Problem 16

Solve for the unknown interest rate in each of the following:

Present value	Future value	Interest rate	Time (years)
$ 100	$ 305		5
123	218		6
4,100	8,524		7
10,543	21,215		12

Intermediate Questions

Problem 17

You have the opportunity to acquire an asset today for $1,000 which will generate $300 income in one year, when it will then be sold for $900. What is minimum interest rate at which this investment would be attractive.

Problem 18

An entrepreneur has purchased an asset for $200,000 which will produce a cash inflow of $300,000 one year from today. He plans to issue himself 100 shares of common stock and sell 900 shares to the general public. His business, which consists entirely of this one asset, will cease to exist after one year. The market rate of interest is 20%, and the future cash inflow to the firm is guaranteed. At what price per share should the entrepreneur sell the common stock?

Problem 19

Your Aunt Nell has promised you a two week trip to Europe when you graduate from university in two years, providing your grades are good. She estimates that the trip will cost $5,000. How much money should Aunt Nell put aside today to pay for your trip? She earns 4% on her money.

Problem 20

Unfortunately, Aunt Nell just discovered that you and your friends hit several hockey pucks into her front windows. Repair costs are $2,500. Aunt Nell now has only $2,500 toward your trip. You must come up with the remaining $2,500. If you earn 3.6% interest, how much must you save this summer in order to take the trip?

Challenge Questions

Problem 21

As a recently-graduated finance major embarking on a career in investment banking, you naturally *must* own a BMW 325 IS immediately. The car costs $28,320. You also *must* spend $3,248 on blue pin-stripe suits. Your salary this year is $42,000, and next year it will be $46,000. Your routine living expenses this year will be $34,000. You plan to make up the difference between current income and current consumption by getting a loan at a rate of 14%. You intend to repay the loan, plus interest, in one year. How much will you have left to spend next year?

ANSWERS TO CONCEPT TEST

1.   compound interest; compounding

2.   future value; principal; $PV \times (1 + r)^t$; $(1 + r)^t$; FVIF(r,t)

3.   interest rate; dollar amount; future date; interest rate; future payment; time period

4.   discounting; discount rate

5.   interest rate; future payment; time period; $FV_t / (1 + r)^t$

6.   reciprocal; $FV \times [1/(1 + r)^t]$

7. $1/(1 + r)^t$; PVIF(r,t); discount factor; discounted cash flow (DCF)

PROBLEM SOLUTIONS

Problem 1: If you deposit $10,000 today, the balance in the account at the end of the year will be:

$$FV_1 = \$10,000 \times 1.0538 = \$10,538$$

If you need $12,000, the amount you will have to deposit today is: $PV = \$12,000 / 1.0538 = \$11,387.36$

Problem 2:

Today's cash flow	Interest rate	Future value
$ 60,000	12.0 %	$ 67,200.00
273,000	10.0	300,300.00
1,500	9.0	1,635.00
27,634	6.7	29,485.48
135,000	3.0	139,050.00

Problem 3: At a 10% rate, your interest each year is $2,500 x 0.1 = $250. To reach a $5,000 balance, you need a total of $2,500, so you must leave your money in the bank for $2,500 / $250 = 10 years.
At a 20% rate, you would receive $500 per year. The required investment horizon is $2,500 / $500 = 5 years.

If interest is compounded annually, use the FV equation to solve for number of years:

$$FV_t = \$2,500 \text{ x } (1.10)^t \rightarrow \$5,000 = \$2,500 \text{ x } (1.10)^t \rightarrow 2 = (1.10)^t$$

Using the Table A.3 at 10%, a future value factor of 2 relates to approximately 7 years. This means that, at an interest rate of 10%, your money will be doubled in 7 years. (The actual rate is slightly higher.)

Problem 4: Using future value analysis to calculate the value of investing $2,000 in the savings account:

$$FV_t = PV \text{ x } (1+r)^t \rightarrow FV_2 = \$2,000 \text{ x } (1.10)^2 = \$2,420.00$$

Eddy should invest in the rare coin.

Using present value analysis:

$$PV = FV / (1+r)^t \rightarrow PV = \$2,500 / (1.10)^2 = \$2,066.12$$

Present value analysis gives the same conclusion - Eddy should invest in the rare coin.
Note: The decision is the same using either future or present value analysis. This is *always* the case.

Problem 5: At 10%: $FV_5 = \$2,500 \text{ x } (1.10)^5 = \$4,026.28$

At 20%: $FV_5 = \$2,500 \text{ x } (1.20)^5 = \$6,220.80$

Note: Although the interest rate doubled, the amount of interest you received over five years *more* than doubled:
($6,220.80 - $2,500) / ($4,026.28 - $2,500) = 2.44 times. This is the magic of compound interest!

Problem 6: Invest in certificates of deposit at 4%: $FV_1 = \$2,000,000 \times 1.04 = \$2.08$ million

Consequently, the investment in the paintings is not a good investment. The collector will have a greater cash flow in one year from purchasing the bank certificates of deposit.

Problem 7: $FV_1 = PV \times (1+r)^1 \rightarrow \$2.06$ million $= \$2.00$ million $\times (1+r)^1 \rightarrow 1.03 = 1+r \rightarrow r = 3\%$

The rate of return for the paintings is less than that for the bank certificates of deposit, so the certificates of deposit are a better investment. This is the same conclusion reached in Problem 3. Since the two evaluation procedures are mathematically equivalent, the conclusions must *always* be the same.

Problem 8: PV $= \$2.06$ million $/ 1.04 = \$1.98$ million

The present value is the amount the collector would have to invest today in the alternative investment (i.e., the bank certificates) in order to duplicate the cash flow received by selling the paintings one year from today. Since the collector can duplicate the $2.06 million cash flow for only $1.98 million, the $1.98 million is value of the paintings to the collector and, thus, the maximum purchase price for the paintings.

Problem 9: At 9%   PV $= \$3,000,000 / (1.09)^{35} = \$3,000,000 / 20.413968 = \$146,958.20$

At 4.5% PV $= \$3,000,000 / (1.045)^{35} = \$3,000,000 / 4.667348 = \$642,763.33$

You need to invest $146,958.20 at 9% and $642,763.33 at 4.5% in order to have $3,000,000 when you retire.

Problem 10:

Future cash flow	Interest rate	Present value
$ 10,000	10 %	$ 9,090.91
153,000	12	136,607.14
153,000	10	139,090.91
2,567,450	5	2,445,190.48
120,600	9	110,642.20

In the second and third cases, the future cash flow is the same, but the present value is greater when the discount rate is 10% rather than 12%. This result illustrates the fact that present value and interest rates are inversely related.

Problem 11: PV $= \$145/(1.053)^{5} = \$112.00$

An investor must deposit $112.00 today, at a 5.3% interest rate, to be able to withdraw $145 in five years.

Problem 12: $FV_4 = \$235 \times (1.048)^{4} = \$283.47$

Problem 13:

Future value	Years	Interest rate	Present value
$ 498	7	13 %	$ 211.68
1,033	13	6	484.31
14,784	23	4	5,998.26
898,156	4	31	304,976.65
75,000	3	10.5	55,587.15
169,700	9	4.6	113,213.10

Problem 14:

Present value	Years	Interest rate	Future value
$ 123	13	13 %	$ 602.46
4,555	8	8	8,430.99
74,484	5	10	119,957.23
167,332	9	1	183,008.54
108,350	24	3.8	265,195.04
57,300	16	12.4	371,890.94

Problem 15:

Present value	Future value	Interest rate	Time (years)
$ 100	$ 350	12%	11.05
123	351	10	11.00
4,100	8,524	5	15.00
10,543	26,783	6	16.00

Problem 16:

Present value	Future value	Interest rate	Time (years)
$ 100	$ 305	25 %	5
123	218	10	6
4,100	8,524	11	7
10,543	21,215	6	12

Problem 17: Substitute the relevant values (PV = $1,000; FV = $1,200) into either the future value formula or the present value formula, and then solve for the interest rate r. Using the future value formula:

$$FV = PV \times (1 + r) \rightarrow \$1,200 = \$1,000 \times (1 + r) \rightarrow 1 + r = 1.20 \rightarrow r = 20\%$$

Therefore, the rate of return for the investment is 20%. If the rate of return available on alternative investments is less than 20%, then the investment opportunity described above is acceptable. On the other hand, if the rate of return available elsewhere is greater than 20%, then the investment described above is unacceptable.

Problem 18: The present value of the future cash inflow is: PV = $300,000/1.20 = $250,000

Therefore, each of the 1,000 shares is worth $250. This can be demonstrated several different ways. An individual who owns one of the shares is entitled to 1/1,000 of the future cash inflow or, (1/1,000) × $300,000 = $300. The present value of the $300 is: PV = $300/1.20 = $250

Alternatively, an individual who owns one share is the owner of 1/1,000 of the present value of the asset, or (1/1,000) × $250,000 = $250. Furthermore, an individual who buys a share for $250 today and receives $300 one year from today earns a rate of return $300 / $250 - 1 = 20%. Since this is the same as the rate of return available on alternative investments, an investor would be willing to pay $250 for a share.

Problem 19: Aunt Nell needs to save: $5,000 = PV x $(1.08)^2$. Solving for PV leaves $4,622.78.

Problem 20: You need to save: $2,500 = PV x $(1.036)^2$. Solving, you need $2,329.27

Problem 21: This year you need a total of ($28,320 + $3,248 + $34,000) = $65,568. So, you must borrow ($65,568 − $42,000) = $23,568 this year. The amount you will have to repay next year is:

$$FV_1 = \$23,568 \times 1.14 = \$26,867.52$$

Therefore, you will have ($46,000 − $26,867.52) = $19,132.48 of next year's income left to spend.

6   <u>Discounted Cash Flow Valuation</u>

CHAPTER HIGHLIGHTS

Chapter 5 iscussed the basic concept of the time value of money. These concepts form the foundation for *discounted cash flow* analysis (DCF), which is discussed in more detail in this chapter. In this chapter, DCF analysis is extended to situations which have multiple cash flows. An understanding of DCF analysis is very important because it has practical applications in everyday life.

6.1   FUTURE AND PRESENT VALUES OF MULTIPLE CASH FLOWS

To this point, our future value and present value calculations have been restricted to problems involving only a single future cash flow. We now analyze future value and present value problems with multiple cash flows.

Future Value with Multiple Cash Flows: An earlier example (Chapter 5, page) calculated the future value of a $2,000 deposit in an RRSP account paying 4% interest per year for the next forty years. The balance in the account at the end of forty years was: $FV_{40} \;=\; \$2,000 \times (1.08)^{40} \;=\; \$9,602.04$

This section discusses the computation of an account balance when several deposits are made over a period of years. For example, the depositor described above might make a $2,000 deposit each year for the next forty years, or deposits of different amounts each year. It is important to determine the future value regardless of the number, size and timing of the deposits.

For simplicity, the following example involves only three deposits: $2,000 deposited today, $1,000 deposited one year from today, and $3,000 deposited two years from today in an account paying 4 percent interest per year. If these deposits are made into an RRSP account, it is possible to compute the balance thirty or forty years from today. For the sake of simplicity, we first discuss the procedure for calculating the balance in the account three years from today.

A very useful tool to help visualize the problem is a *time line*, which illustrates the pattern of cash flows over the investment horizon. The time line for this example is:

A future value with multiple cash flows can be computed in at least two different ways. First, the account balance can be computed year-by-year, adding both the subsequent deposits and compound interest to the account each year. Alternatively, the future value of each deposit can be calculated separately; then the separate future values are added. Alternative 1: computation on year-by-year basis at 4% interest

    The future value of the first deposit, after one year, is:

$$FV_1 = \$2,000 \times (1.04) = \$2,160$$

Since the second deposit is made at the end of year 1, the account balance after one year is:

($2,080 + $1,000) = $3,080.

The depositor now earns interest on the $3,160 balance for one year, and also deposits $3,000 in the account. The balance at the end of two years is:

[$3,080 × (1.04)] + $3,000 = $3,203.20 + $3,000 = $6,203.20

This balance remains on deposit for one more year, earning 4 percent interest. No additional deposit is made, so the balance in the account at the end of three years is:

$6,412.80 × (1.04) = $6,451.33

The time line showing the calculations is:

0 (today)	end of Yr. 1	end of Yr. 2	end of Yr. 3
$2,000	$1,000	$ 3,000.00	$6,451.33
	2,080	3,203.20	
	$3,080	$ 6,203.20	

If no additional deposits are made to the account, and if the depositor continues to receive 4 percent interest per year, the future value for any given time period is computed by compounding this balance for the appropriate number of years. For example, suppose the depositor plans to retire forty years after the initial deposit is made. Then, in order to determine the account balance at retirement, the balance for year 3 is compounded for thirty-seven additional years:

$6,451.33 × (1.04)^{37} = $27,534.86

Alternative 2: calculating future value of each cash flow separately

The future value of multiple cash flows can also be determined by compounding each deposit for the appropriate number of years. That is: the $2,000 deposit is compounded for three years, the $1,000 deposit is compounded for two years, and the $3,000 deposit is compounded for one year.

$$\$2,000 \times (1.04)^3 = \$2,249.73$$
$$\$1,000 \times (1.04)^2 = \$1,081.60$$
$$\$3,000 \times (1.04)^1 = \$3,120.00$$

The time line for this method of calculation is:

0 (today)	end of Yr. 1	end of Yr. 2	end of Yr. 3
$2,000	$1,000	$ 3,000.00	$ 2,249.73
			1,081.60
			3,120.00
			$6,451.33

This is the same result derived earlier by computing the balance in the account year-by-year.

To determine the account balance the end of forty years, the three-year balance can be compounded for thirty seven more years, as shown in Alternative 1. The same result can be obtained by compounding the three deposits for forty, thirty-nine and thirty-eight years, respectively:

$$\$2,000 \times (1.04)^{40} \ = \ \$\,9,602.04$$
$$\$1,000 \times (1.04)^{39} \ = \ \$\,4,616.37$$
$$\$3,000 \times (1.04)^{38} \ = \ \$13,316.44$$

The total future value of the three deposits is $27,534.85. (The $.07 difference is due to rounding.)

Present Value with Multiple Cash Flows: The present value of multiple cash flows can be calculated in two ways.. First, future payments may be discounted year-by-year. Second, the present value of each future cash flow can be computed separately; then the separate present values are added to determine the total present value. Although the two approaches are mathematically equivalent, the second approach is simpler, so that approach is discussed here.

In a Chapter 5 example (page), Kris had two years to accumulate $1,200 in a bank account paying 5% interest per year. The present value was: $PV \ = \ FV_t / (1 + r)^t \ = \ \$1,200 / (1.05)^2 \ = \ \$1,088.44$

Example Using Multiple Cash Flows: Kris intends to make withdrawals of $1,200, $1,200, and $2,000 in one, two, and three years from now, respectively. How much should she deposit today at 5%, to make these withdrawals?

Kris can think of this as three separate problems. First, what deposit today lets her withdraw $1,200 in one year? Second, what deposit today lets her withdraw $1,200 in two years? And, third, what deposit today lets her withdraw $2,000 in three years? The answer to each question is derived from a basic present value calculation:

$$PV \ = \ \$1,200 / (1.05) \ = \ \$1,142.86$$
$$PV \ = \ \$1,200 / (1.05)^2 \ = \ \$1,088.44$$
$$PV \ = \ \$2,000 / (1.05)^3 \ = \ \$1,727.68$$

The time line for this problem is:

0 (today)	end of Yr. 1	end of Yr. 2	end of Yr. 3
$1,142.86	$1,200	$ 1,200	$2,000
1,088.44			
1,727.68			
$3,958.97			

Kris must deposit $3,958.97 today to be able to withdraw the amounts she needs in years 1, 2, and 3.

The present value of a series of cash flows *always* equals the sum of the present values of the individual cash flows.

Example: Kris' broker has suggested the following investment today: if she invests $4,000 today, she will receive $1,200 in one year, $1,200 in two years, and $2,000 in three years from today. Should she make the investment?

Using the present value calculation from the previous example, a deposit of $3,958.27 in an account paying 5 percent interest, allows Kris to withdraw the needed funds. This alternative is superior to the investment offered by the broker, because Kris can deposit ($4,000 - $3,958.27 = $41.73) fewer dollars in her account and still receive the same payment stream. How much would Kris be willing to pay for the investment offered by the broker? She would pay no more than $3,958.27, the present value of the future cash flows, discounted at the appropriate interest rate.

6.2   VALUING LEVEL CASH FLOWS: ANNUITIES AND PERPETUITIES

An *annuity* is a series of constant cash flows that occur at regular intervals for a fixed number of time periods. For example, the payments on a five-year car loan are a sixty-month annuity. Typically, the payments for a car loan begin one month after the car is purchased. When payments occur at the end of the relevant time period, the annuity is referred to as an *ordinary annuity*.

If payments are at the beginning of the time period, the annuity is referred to as an *annuity due* (or deferred annuity). Deferred annuities are common for leases, when the first payment is made immediately upon taking possession of the leased asset.

A *perpetuity* is a perpetual ordinary annuity. They are less common than   Ordinary annuities or annuities due. It might seem that the mathematics of an infinite payments would be difficult, but this is not the case. Financial calculations involving both annuities and perpetuities are discussed below.

Present Value for Annuity Cash Flows: Refer again to Kris from the previous example.

Example: Kris is evaluating another investment proposed by her broker. The investment costs $3,000 and pays a guaranteed $1,200 per year at the end of each of the next three years. This is a $1,200 3-year ordinary annuity.

Note that (1) the three $1,200 payments are guaranteed and (2) her opportunity cost for a similarly risky investment is 5%. The present value of the three payments are calculated below:

$$PV \; = \; \$1,200 \text{ x PVIF}(5\%,1) \; = \; \$1,200 \text{ x } (1 \, / \, 1.05) \quad = \; \$1,142,86$$

$$PV \; = \; \$1,200 \text{ x PVIF}(5\%,2) \; = \; \$1,200 \text{ x } (1 \, / \, 1.05^2) \; = \; \$1,088.44$$

$$PV \; = \; \$1,200 \text{ x PVIF}(5\%,3) \; = \; \; \$1,200 \times (1 \, / \, 1.05^3) \; = \; \$1,036.61$$

The present value of the investment is: $1,142.86 + 1,088.44 + $1,0036.61   = $3,267.91

Kris must deposit $3,267.91 today in order to $1,200 per year for three years. Since the investment suggested by the broker costs only $3,000 for 3 yearly payments of $1,200, she should purchase the investment from her broker.

This calculation can be simplified by (1) computing the total of the three present value interest factors, then (2) multiplying this total by $1,200 (the size of the payment):

$$0.952381 + 0.907003 + 0.863838 \; = \; 2.723222$$
$$2.723222 \times \$1,200 \quad = \quad \$3,267.90$$

The total of the present value interest factors is the *present value interest factor for an annuity*, PVIFA(r,t). This procedure is much more efficient for calculating the present value of long-term annuities. These values can also be found using financial tables. Table A.3 indicates that PVIFA(5%,3) = 3.1525. Consequently, we can compute the present value of the annuity in this example as follows:

$$PV = C \times \text{PVIFA}(r,t) \; = \; \$1,200 \times \text{PVIFA}(5\%,3) \; = \; \$1,200 \times 2.7232 = \$3,267.84 \qquad [6.1]$$

where C represents the constant annuity payment and PV is the present value of the annuity. Clearly, this approach is more efficient than calculating and then totalling the three individual present values.

A third alternative for computing the annuity present value factors uses the following formula (developed by mathematicians)to determine the value of PVIFA(r,t):

$$PVIFA(r,t) \quad = \quad [1 - 1/(1+r)^t]/r$$

Since the term in brackets in the numerator is the present value interest factor, this equation can be written as:

$$PVIFA(r,t) \quad = \quad \{1 - [PVIF(r,t)]\}/r$$

For the above example, PVIFA (5%, 3) = (1 - 0.8638)/.05 = 2.724

The present value of the annuity is $1,200 \times 2.724$ = $3,268.80

The fourth alternative is to use a financial calculator with annuity functions. If you do, **be sure to read the instruction manual for *your* calculator. And, practice solving problems with your calculator before you take an exam!!!!**

Finding the Payment - An Example: When the interest rate, the present value of the annuity, and the number of payments are known, the annuity equation is used to calculate the size of each payment.

Suppose you intend to purchase a used car for $15,000. You must put down 10% of the purchase price of the car and you can borrow 90% of the price from a bank. The bank will give you a five-year loan, to be repaid in equal monthly installments, at an interest rate of 6% per year, or 0.5% per month. What are the monthly payments?

The loan will be for (.90 × $15,000) = 13,500, so PV = $13,500. The monthly interest rate is 6% / 12 = 0.5%, and there are 5 x 12 = 60 equal monthly installments. Using the equation from above:

$$PV \quad = \quad C \times PVIFA(r,t) \quad \rightarrow \quad \$13,500 \quad = \quad C \times PVIFA(0.5\%,60)$$

$$PVIFA(0.5\%,60) \quad = \{1 - [1/(1.005)^{60}]\}/0.005 \quad = \quad (1 - .741372)/.005 \quad = \quad 51.72556$$

Substitute PVIFA(0.5%,60) into the above equation and solve for C:

$$\$13,500 \quad = \quad C \times 51.72556 \quad \rightarrow \quad C \quad = \quad \$13,500/51.72556 \quad = \quad \$260.99$$

The loan requires sixty monthly payments of $260.99 beginning one month after the loan is made. Solving the problem using financial tables or a financial calculator gives the same answer (except for rounding differences).

Finding the Interest Rate - An Example: Life insurance companies sell annuities to investors wanting constant periodic payments at retirement . For example, a 64 year old investor might purchase an annuity, to begin one year later, at age 65. Such annuities are generally paid on a monthly basis; however, in this example, we assume that the annuity payments are made annually. Suppose that, a guaranteed ten-year annuity, paying $15,000 per year, beginning one year from now, costs $120,000. What is the interest rate implicit in this annuity?

To solve, the known values are substituted into the equation for the present value of an annuity:

$$PV \quad = \quad C \times PVIFA(r,t) \quad \rightarrow \quad \$120,000 \quad = \quad \$15,000 \times PVIFA(r,10)$$

$$PVIFA(r,10) = \$120,000/\$15,000 \quad = \quad 8 \quad \text{or} \quad \{1 - [1/(1+r)^{10}]\}/r \quad = \quad 8$$

It is impossible to directly compute the solution to this equation, but an approximate answer can be determined from Table A.3, and a more precise solution can be computed using trial-and-error. A financial calculator will quickly compute the precise value of r.

Using Table A.3, an approximate solution for r uses the PVIFA value obtained from the table. Values of PVIFA(r,10) are in the tenth row of the table. The value 8 is between the factors for r = 4% (8.1109) and r=5% (7.7217). Therefore, r must be between 4% and 5%. A more precise value can be found using trial-and-error and the formula for PVIFA given earlier. The value 8 is closer to the factor for 4% than for 5%, Using the equation for PVIFA and a rate of r = 4.1%, the factor value is:

$$\text{PVIFA}(4.1\%,10) = \{1 - [1/(1.041)^{10}]\} / 0.041 = 8.070669$$

So, the value of r is greater than 4.1%. The values of PVIFA(r,10) for r = 4.2% and 4.3%, are 8.030740 and 7.991107, respectively. Consequently, r is between 4.2% and 4.3%, and closer to 4.3%. Further trial-and-error indicates that the value of r is between 4.27% and 4.28%. This procedure can be continued to any desired degree of accuracy. The precise value, easily determined with a financial calculator, is r = 4.2775%.

Finding the Number of Payments - An Example: If the interest rate, the present value, and the amount of the annuity payments are known, the number of payments can also be determined.

Assume you are buying a new living room set for $8,200.39. Annual payments, based on an interest rate of 7%, will be $2000. How many payments must you make? Using the same formula:

$$\$8,200.39 = \$2,000 \times \text{PVIFA}(7\%,t) \rightarrow \$8,200.39/ \$2,000 = 4.100195 = \text{PVIFA}(7\%,t)$$

Using the tables, you'll see that you must make five annual payments.

We can use the annuity formula to check: $\{1 - [(1/1.07)^5]\} / .07 = 4.100197$

Future Value for Annuities: The future value of an annuity can be calculated using procedures analogous to those for computing the present value. The four approaches are:

   (1)   compute and then sum the future values of the individual cash flows,

   (2)   use Table A.4 to determine the *future value interest factor for an annuity* [FVIFA(r,t)], and multiply by the constant payment amount,

   (3)   compute FVIFA(r,t) a formula (below) and multiply by the constant payment amount, and

   (4)   use a financial calculator.

The results for the approaches are the same, so only third approach is presented:

$$\text{FVIFA}(r,t) = [(1 + r)^t - 1] / r \rightarrow = \{[\text{FVIF}(r,t)] - 1 \} / r = (\text{Future value factor} - 1) / r$$

To determine the future value of an annuity, multiply FVIFA(r,t) times the constant annuity payment:

$$\text{FV} = C \times \text{FVIFA}(r,t)$$

A Note on Annuities Due - An Example: As mentioned earlier, annuity contracts sometimes specify payments or receipts at the *beginning* of each period. Suppose you want to set aside $10,000 at the beginning of each of the next three years, given an interest rate of 10% per annum. What is the future value of this annuity due? What is this annuity due worth today (i.e., the present value of the annuity due)?

The answer to the first question can be found in two ways, by using either of the following equations:

$$\text{Annuity due FV factor } = \text{FVIFA (r,t) x (1 + r)} = \text{FVIFA (10\%,3)} \times (1.10) = 3.310 \times 1.1 = 3.6410$$

The future value of this annuity due is: $10,000 \times 3.6410 = $36,410

Note that, because payments are made at the *beginning* of the year, each payment is *compounded* for one period *more*. That means the future value of an annuity due is greater than the future value of an ordinary annuity.

Alternately, the following equation can be used:

$$\text{Annuity due FV factor } = [\text{FVIFA (r\%, n + 1)}] - 1 = 4.6410 - 1 = 3.6410$$

The future value of the annuity due is the same: $36,410.

To answer the second question, again there are two alternative solutions:

$$\text{Annuity due PV factor} = \text{PVIFA(r,t)} \times (1 + r) = \text{PVIFA (10\%, 3)} \times (1.10) = 2.487 \times 1.1 = 2.735537$$
The present value of the annuity due is: $10,000 \times 2.735537 = $27,355.37

In this case, because payments are made at the *beginning* of the year, each payment is *discounted* for one period *less*. Thus, the present value of an annuity due is greater than the present value of an ordinary annuity.

Alternately,

$$\text{Annuity due PV factor} = [\text{PVIFA (r\%, n − 1)}] + 1 = 1.735537 + 1 = 2.735537$$

Again, the present value of the annuity due is $27,355.37.

Perpetuities: A *perpetuity* (or perpetual annuity) is a constant series of cash flows occurring at regular intervals forever. The series of dividend payments for a share of preferred stock is often thought of as a perpetuity. Applying the techniques described earlier, the present value of a perpetuity is:

$$PV = C/(1+r)^1 + C/(1+2)^2 + C/(1+r)^3 + \dots \quad C/(1+r)^n$$

where C is the constant payment or cash flow. This looks complicated. Mathematically, though, this is the easiest type of cash flow to value. The above formula reduces to a very simple equation:

$$PV = C \times (1/r) = C/r$$

Example: A share of preferred stock pays an annual dividend of $8 and you require a 5% return. What is the present value of the $8 perpetuity? What would an investor be willing to pay to purchase the share of preferred stock?

The investor would pay whatever price (PV) would equate the $8 payments to a 5% interest rate or, algebraically:

$$PV \times .05 = \$8 \quad \rightarrow \quad PV = \$8 / .05 = \$160$$

This equation can also be written as: $PV \times r = C$. Assuming a $160 deposit pays 5% interest forever, this equation can be used to determine the amount of the perpetual cash flow:

$$C = PV \times r = \$160 \times .05 = \$8.00$$

If the $8.00 is withdrawn every year, the account balance will always be $160.

This equation may also be re-arranged to solve for the rate of return:

$$r = C / PV = \$8 / \$160 = 0.05 = 5\%$$

Growing Perpetuities: Today, it is common to find perpetuities for which the payment *grows* over time. This is as a *growing perpetuity* - an endless, constant stream that is expected to increase indefinitely. The algebraic formula for a growing perpetuity is complicated, but it reduces to a very simple equation:

$$PV = C / (r - g)$$

C is the cash flow at the end of the first period, r is the interest rate, and g is the growth rate for future cash flows. This simplified equation requires the assumption that cash inflows and outflows occur at regular, discrete intervals.

Example: You are interested in buying a growing perpetuity issued by a major corporation. The stated cash flow is 12% of face value, or $120 per year. These cash flows are expected to grow at an annual rate of 3% forever. If the return on similar securities is 8%, what is the value of the growing perpetuity today?

$$PV = C / (r - g) = \$120 / (.08 - .03) = \$2,400 \quad \text{(and the most you would pay for it)}$$

Growing Annuity: A *growing annuity*, as opposed to a growing perpetuity, is a *finite* series of cash flows that grows over time. The equation for a growing annuity similar to that for an ordinary annuity, but there are differences:

$$PV = [C / (r - g)] \times \{1 - [(1 + g) / (1 + r)]^T\}$$

As before, C is the cash flow at the end of the first period, r is the interest rate, and g is the growth rate in cash flows. T is the number of periods for the annuity. Note that the first term, $C / (r - g)$ is the same as the equation for finding the value of a growing perpetuity. The second term adjusts for the fact the this is a finite stream of cash flows.

Example: Use the same values as in the growing perpetuity example, but assume that the payments will be made for 20 years. The value of the growing annuity is:

$$PV = [\$120 / (.08 - .03)] \times \{1 - [(1 + .03) / (1 + .08)]^{20}\}$$

$$= \$2,400 \times [1 - (1.03 / 1.08)^{20}] = \$2,400 \times (1 - 0.32874979)$$

$$= \$2,400 \times 0.612502 = \$1,470.00$$

Because the growing annuity is a *finite* stream of cash flows its value is less than that of a growing perpetuity.

6.3 COMPARING RATES: THE EFFECT OF COMPOUNDING PERIODS

The preceding discussion of future-value and present-value analysis was based on the assumption of annually compounded interest rates. However, banks and other financial institutions often compound interest on deposits more frequently. The effects of different compounding periods on financial calculations are discussed below.

Effective Annual Rates and Compounding: Consider a bank which advertises 12% interest per year, compounded quarterly. This rate is equivalent to 3% interest each quarter. The 12% interest rate in this example is sometimes referred to as the *stated interest rate*, the *quoted interest rate*, or the *nominal interest rate*. Financial institutions often refer to the 'annual rate' or simply the 'rate.' However, when interest is compounded more frequently than once a year, the actual interest rate the depositor receives is greater than the quoted interest rate. The actual interest rate is often called the *effective annual interest rate* (EAR) or the *effective annual yield*. When comparing the returns offered on two different investments, ***always*** convert to effective rates.

Calculating and Comparing Effective Annual Rates: With quarterly compounding, the depositor begins to receive interest on interest during the second quarter, rather than after the first year, as in the case of annual compounding. To calculate the future value for a deposit with the bank described above, determine the quarterly interest rate (i.e., 3% in this example) and treat the quarter, rather than the year, as the relevant time period. Therefore, the future value, after one year, of a $1,000 deposit is:

$$FV = \$1,000 \times (1.03)^4 = \$1,000 \times 1.12551 = \$1,125.51$$

With annual compounding, the future value would be $1,120. The additional ($1,125.51 − $1,120) = $5.51 is the interest on interest earned during the second, third and fourth quarters of the year. If the bank paid 12.551% interest per year, compounded annually, the future value for a $1,000 deposit over a one-year period would be the same:
$$FV = \$1,000 \times (1.12551)^1 = \$1,000 \times 1.12551 = \$1,125.51$$

Therefore, a quoted annual interest rate of 12%, compounded quarterly, is equivalent to an effective annual interest rate of 12.551%. This can be seen directly in the example by noting that: $(1.03)^4 = (1.12551)^1$, so that the effective annual interest rate is simply:

$$(1.03)^4 - 1 = (1.12551)^1 - 1.0 = .12551 = 12.551\%$$

In general, this result is presented algebraically as follows:

$$\text{effective annual rate} = \text{EAR} = [1 + (\text{quoted rate/m})]^m - 1$$

where m is the number of times per year interest is compounded.

Example: Suppose that, for the $1,000 deposit in the account described earlier, the investor would like to compare the future value at the end of thirty years for two accounts, one paying 12% interest per year, compounded annually, and the other paying 12% interest per year, compounded quarterly.

The future value for the first account is: $FV = \$1,000 \times (1.12)^{30} = \$29,959.92$

For the second account, the interest rate is (.12/4) = .03 = 3% per quarter, and the time period is (30 × 4 quarters) = 120 quarters, so the future value is: $FV = \$1,000 \times (1.03)^{120} = \$34,710.99$

The difference of ($34,710.99 − $29,959.92) = $4,751.07 future value is due to the difference in compounding period.

The calculation procedure for compounding m times per year over a period of t years can be summarized as:

$$FV = PV \times [1 + (r/m)]^{mt}$$

Quoting a Rate - An Example: As a banker, you have determined that you need a 12% percent EAR on a loan with interest compounded monthly. What rate do you quote?

Solve for q (quoted rate) as follows:

$$EAR = [1 + q/m)]^m - 1 \quad \rightarrow \quad .12 = [1 + q/12]^{12} - 1 \quad \rightarrow \quad 1.12 = [1 + q/12]^{12}$$

$$(1.12)^{1/12} = 1 + q/12 \quad \rightarrow \quad 1.0095 = 1 + q/12 \quad \rightarrow \quad .0095 = q/12 \quad \rightarrow \quad q = 11.39\%$$

Mortgages: Mortgages are an example of annuities monthly payments. Regulations for Canadian financial institutions, though, require that mortgage rates be quoted with semiannual compounding. Most mortgages are for five years or less, however payments are usually calculated to maturity (25 years).

Example: Loyal Bank is offering a $200,000, 25-year mortgage at a quoted rate of 9%. What are the monthly payments?

First, the quoted monthly rate is found by converting the quoted rate to an EAR:

$$EAR = [1 + quoted\ rate / m]^m - 1 = [1 + .09/2]^2 - 1 = 9.2025\%$$

Next, find the quoted monthly rates:

$$quoted\ rate/m = (EAR + 1)^{1/m} - 1 \quad \rightarrow \quad quoted\ rate / 12 = (1.092025)^{1/12} - 1 = .007363\%$$

Then, use the annuity present value formula to find the payments:

Annuity present value: $200,000 = $ $C \times (1 - PV\ factor) / r$

$$\$200,000 = C \times (1 - 1/1.007363^{300})/.007363 \rightarrow 200,000 = C \times 120.7777 \rightarrow C = \$1,656.04$$

Note: the number of payments is 12 × 25 = 300.

Example: Suppose that the rate of 9 % in the above example is fixed for five years and you are wondering whether to lock in this rate or take a lower rate of 8 % fixed for one year. If you choose the lower one year rate, how much lower will your payments be for the first year?

Following the steps outlined in the previous solution, your payment is $1,526.40, a reduction of $129.64 per month. By taking this alternative, you are betting that rates will not increase over the next year. This tradeoff between lower payments and the added uncertainty of interest rate fluctuations reflects the fundamental nature of most financial decisions and is discussed in more detail under risk and return in later chapters.

Annual Percentage Rate (APR): The Bank Act in Canada requires that lenders disclose an APR on virtually all consumer loans. The APR and EAR are not necessarily the same. Lenders are required by law to compute the APR as the interest rate per period multiplied by the number of periods in a year. For example, if a Trust Company charges 3% every quarter then the APR is (3% × 4) = 12%. The EAR is $[(1.03)^4 - 1] = 12.55\%$.

Example: Your credit card company quotes an interest rate of 18% APR and requires monthly payments. Your uncle is willing to lend you money at 19 percent with annual repayments. Who is offering the better rate? Your uncle, because the credit card EAR $=$ $[1 + .18/12]^{12} - 1$ $=$ 19.56%

Taking It to the Limit - A Note on Continuous Compounding: Quarterly, monthly and daily compounding are commonly used by financial institutions, and it is even possible to compound interest hourly, or each minute or second. While these latter compounding periods are not common, continuous compounding, which is equivalent to compounding over the smallest possible period of time, is frequently used in financial calculations. The following equation applies to continuous compounding: :

$$FV = PV \times e^{qt}$$

where e is a constant with an approximate value of 2.71828 and q is the quoted interest rate.

If a $1,000 deposit is compounded continuously at 12% for 3 years , the future value is:

$$FV_3 = PV \times e^{qt} = \$1,000 \times e^{(.12 \times 3)} = \$1,000 \times e^{.36}$$

The value of $e^{.36}$ is 1.43333, which can be determined using a calculator. The future value is $1,433.33.

The future value, at the end of one year, for a $1,000 deposit in an account paying 12% interest per year, compounded continuously, is:

$$FV_1 = PV \times (e^{qt}) = \$1,000 \times e^{(.12 \times 1)} = \$1,000 \times e^{.12} = \$1,000 \times 1.12750 = \$1,127.50$$

An account which paid interest compounded annually would have to pay 12.75% to provide a future value of $1,127.50. Therefore, the effective annual interest rate is 12.75%. It can be computed directly as:

$$EAR = e^{qt} - 1 \qquad \text{where q is the quoted interest rate.}$$

6.4   LOAN TYPES AND LOAN AMORTIZATION

The three basic forms of loans are: pure-discount loans, interest-only loans, and amortized loans. The present value principles studied previously can be applied to these three kinds of loans.

Pure Discount Loans: A *pure-discount loan* is a loan which is repaid in a single payment. The single payment therefore represents principal plus interest for the period of the loan. The mathematics of pure-discount loans is simply the mathematics of single cash flows.

Example: Melissa borrows $2,500 today, at an interest rate of 6% per year, and agrees to repay the loan three years from today. What is Melissa's payment in three years?

The payment is simply the future value of $2,500, compounded for three years at 6% per year:

$$FV_3 = \$2,500 \times (1.06)^3 = \$2,977.54$$

Suppose that Melissa determines that she must borrow substantially more than $2,500, but she can only afford to repay $4,500 in three years. If the interest rate is 6% per year, what is the maximum amount she can borrow today?

The maximum amount Melissa can borrow is the present value of $4,500, discounted at 6%, for three years:

$$PV \ = \ \$4,500 / (1.06)^3 \ = \ \$3,778.29$$

Now Melissa finds another lender willing to lend her $7,500. This is also a pure-discount loan; Melissa must repay $12,500 three years from today. What is the interest rate this new lender is charging?

The interest rate for the loan is determined by substituting into the basic future value equation the known values of FV, PV and t, and then solving for r:

$$FV_t \ = \ PV \times (1+r)^t \ \rightarrow \ \$12,500 \ = \ \$7,500 \times (1+r)^3 \ \rightarrow \ 1.66666 \ = \ (1+r)^3 \ \rightarrow$$

$$(1.66666)^{(1/3)} \ = \ (1+r) \ \rightarrow \ 1.1856311 \ = \ (1+r) \ \rightarrow \ r \ = \ 18.563\%.$$

An Example - Treasury Bills: Treasury Bills issued by the Government of Canada are pure discount loans with maturities typically between 3 to 12 months. If a T-Bill promises to pay $1,000 in 12 months and the market interest rate is 7 %, how much should the bill sell for in the market?

The T-Bill should sell for the present value of $1,000 to be paid in one year at 7 percent or: $1,000/1.07 = $934.58.

Interest-Only Loans: *Interest-only loans* require the payment of interest each year, and then repayment of the entire principal at a later date. The mathematics of such loans is generally fairly uncomplicated, because there is no compounding of interest for such loans.

Example: Suppose Melissa can obtain an interest-only loan at an annual rate of 11% , with the principal due in three years. What are the required payments on a $2,500 loan?

The annual payment is (.11 × $2,500) = $275. Melissa pays $275 per year at the end of each of the next three years. Then, at the end of the third year, she also repays the $2,500 principal, for a total payment of [($275 x 3) + $2,500] = $3,325. Most bonds issued by the Government of Canada and the provinces have the general form of an interest-only loan.

Amortized Loans: An *amortized loan* requires that the lender make periodic payments which include interest plus repayment of a portion of the principal. Two of the most common types of amortized loans are: (1) a loan payment schedule which requires periodic repayment of a fixed portion of the principal, plus interest, and (2) a loan payment which remains constant throughout the life of the loan, so that successive payments repay progressively increasing portions of the principal and correspondingly decreasing interest payments. The latter form of amortized loan is the typical mortgage or consumer loan.

Example: Melissa can borrow $7,500 in the form of an amortized loan which requires repayment of one-third of the principal each year, and annual interest payments equal to 15% of the remaining principal. What are the annual payments for this loan?

At the end of each year, Melissa repays (1/3 × $7,500) = $2,500 principal.

Payment: Year 1 $2,500 + (0.15 x $7,500)   = $3,625.00

                Year 2 $2,500 + 0.15 x ($7,500 - $2,500)   = $3,250

                Year 3 $2,500 + 0.15 x ($5,000 - $2,500)   = $2,875

Suppose the loan described in the preceding example is to be amortized with constant annual payments. What are the payments? How much of each payment is applied to repayment of principal? How much of each payment represents interest? This type of computation is referred to as an *amortization schedule.*

Amortization Schedules - An Example: First, the size of the payment must be determined using the equation for an annuity:

$$PV \ = \ C \times PVIFA(r,t) \ \ \rightarrow \ \ \$7,500 \ = \ C \times PVIFA(11\%,3)$$

SO

$$PVIFA(11\%,3) \ = \ \{1 - [1/(1.11)^3]\} \ / \ .11 \ = \ (1 - .731191)\ /\ .11 \ = \ 2.443715$$

$$\$7,500 \ = \ \ C \times PVIFA(11\%,3) \ \ \rightarrow \ \ \$7,500 \ = \ \ C \times 2.443715 \ \ \rightarrow \ \ C \ = \ \$3,069.10$$

The total of the payments is $(3 \times \$3,069.10) = \$9,207.30$; the total interest paid is $(\$9,207.30 - \$7,500) = \$1,707.30$.

In order to determine what portion of each payment is applied to payment of principal and what portion is interest, we prepare an *amortization schedule*, which also indicates the principal balance remaining on the loan at the end of each of the three years. Since the principal is $7,500, the interest for the first year is $(.11 \times \$7.500) = \$825$. For the first payment, the principal repayment is the difference between the size of the payment and the first year's interest, or $(\$3,069.10 - \$825) = \$2,244.10$. After the first payment is made, the principal balance is reduced to $(\$7,500 - \$2,244.10) = \$5,255.90$. This process is continued for each year. The ending balance in year 3 should be zero; the slight discrepancy is due to rounding.

Year	Beginning Balance	Total Payment	Interest Paid	Principal Paid	Ending Balance
1	$7,500.00	$3,069.10	$825.00	$2,244.10	$5,255.90
2	5,255.90	3,069.10	578.15	2,490.95	2,764.95
3	2,764.95	3,069.10	304.14	2,764.96	- .01

CONCEPT TEST

1.   A future value with multiple cash flows can be computed by separately computing the _____ of each deposit and then summing the separate _____ .

2.   A present value with multiple cash flows can be calculated by separately computing the _____ of each cash flow and then summing the separate _____ .

3.   An annuity is a series of _____ cash flows that occur at _____ intervals for a _____ number of time periods.

4.   When annuity payments occur at the end of the relevant time period, the annuity is referred to as an _____ annuity or a _____ annuity. If payments are at the beginning of the time period, we call the annuity a _____ annuity or an _____ .

5.   The present value of an annuity can be determined according to the equation: PV = _____ .
       In the equation, PV is the present value of the annuity, C represents the _____ , and PVIFA(r,t) is the _____ .

6.   PVIFA(r,t) can be determined from a table or from the formula: PVIFA(r,t) = _____ .

7.   The future value of an annuity can be determined by the equation:FV = _____ . In this equation, FV
        is the future value of the annuity, C represents the _____ , and FVIFA(r,t) is the _____

8.   FVIFA(r,t) can be determined either from a table or from the formula: FVIFA(r,t) = _____ .

9.   A perpetuity is a series of _____ cash flows, occurring at _____ intervals, which continues
        perpetually. The formula for the present value of a perpetuity is: PV = _____ .

10.   The formula can also be solved for C, and can be written as: C = _____ . This formula can also be
        presented in a third form, solving for r: r = _____ .

11.   A quoted interest rate is also referred to as a _____ interest rate or a _____ interest rate. When
        interest is compounded more frequently than once a year, the actual interest rate is _____ than the
        quoted interest rate. The actual interest rate is often called the effective annual interest rate or the
        _____ .

12.   The effective annual interest rate (EAR) is computed as follows: EAR = _____ , where m is the
        number of times per year interest is compounded .

13.   When interest is compounded m times per year, the future value is computed as follows:
        FV = _____

14.   In the case of continuous compounding the future value is determined according to the following formula:
        FV = _____ .

15.   A pure-discount loan is a loan which is repaid in a _____ which represents _____ plus
        _____ for the period of the loan. The mathematics of pure-discount loans is simply the mathematics
        of single cash flows.

16.   Interest-only loans require the payment of _____ each year, and then repayment of the _____
        at a later date. The mathematics of such loans is relatively uncomplicated, because there is no compounding
        of interest.

17.   An amortized loan requires that the borrower make periodic payments which include _____ plus
        repayment of a portion of the _____ .

18.   Two common forms of amortized loans are: a loan payment schedule which requires periodic repayment of
        a fixed portion of the _____ plus _____ ; and, a loan payment which remains constant
        throughout the life of the loan, so that successive payments repay progressively _____ portions of the
        principal and correspondingly _____ interest payments. The latter form of amortized loan is the typical
        mortgage or consumer loan.

19.   Lenders in Canada are required to disclose the Annual Percentage Rate (APR) due to the _____ . The
        APR and EAR are not necessarily the _____ . The APR is computed as the _____ multiplied
        by _____ .

PROBLEMS

Basic Questions

Problem 1

An investment requires an initial outlay of $195. The cash inflow from this investment will be $114 one year from today (year 1) and $144 two years from today (year 2). The market rate of interest is 20%. Find the present value for this investment. Is the investment acceptable?

Problem 2

Mike will deposit $3,000 into his bank account now, $4,000 in two years, and $1,000 in five years. If the account earns 7% (compounded annually), how much will his deposits be worth at the end of Year 2? Year 5? Year 10?

Problem 3

An investment requiring a cash outlay of $1,243 today will provide cash inflows of $400, $889, and $432 at the end of one year, two years, and three years, respectively. The market interest rate is 12%. Is this a good investment?

Problem 4

Below are four different investment opportunities with projected cash flows. Project 1 costs $2,000; Project 2 costs $5,000, and Project 3 costs $4,000. Using an 8 % discount rate, determine which projects are good investments.

Project	End of Yr. 1	End of Yr. 2	End of Yr. 3
1	$1,000	$ 800	$ 600
2	1,900	1,900	1,900
3	1,400	1,600	1,800

Problem 5

Your banker is trying to interest you in a small-scale investment project for the next three years. The banker says you will receive payments of $800, $1,500, and $1,600 in years 1, 2, and 3, respectively. The cost to get in on the investment is $3,000. Currently, your savings are in an account earning an annual rate of 8%. Should you take your funds out of the account to participate in this investment?

Problem 6

Refer back to the cash flows from Project 2 in Problem 4. Now, you get the cash flows at the beginning of the year, rather than at the end.. The discount is still 8%. Does this change your decision?

Problem 7

You are entering graduate school tomorrow and have saved $35,000 saved up to fund your education over the next 3 years. If your savings account pay 5% annually, how much can you withdraw at the end of each year?

Problem 8

Unfortunately, after computing the amount you can withdraw above, you realize that you need the funds at the *beginning* of each year. How much can you withdraw each year now?

Problem 9

You will receive an annuity of $1,000 per year for the next five years. The market rate of interest is 7%. Assuming you do not spend any of the income at any other time, what is the maximum you can spend at the end of year 5? What is the maximum amount you can spend today (if you borrow against the future payments)?

Problem 10

Consider a perpetuity which pays $100 per year; the market rate of interest is 10%. What is the present value of the perpetuity? What is the present value of the perpetuity three years from now? What is the present value of the perpetuity n years from now? Under what circumstances does the value of a perpetuity change?

Problem 11

A firm invests $3 million in a project which will yield a perpetuity of $1 million per year. What is the discount rate for which this project's present value is $4.5 million?

Problem 12

What is the present value of a perpetuity which pays $1,000 per year if the market rate of interest is 5%? What about a 50-year annuity with the same annual payments? What is it for a 100 year annuity?

Intermediate Questions

Problem 13

A widget machine can be purchased for $1,200 and will create cash flows of $300 per year for the first two years, $500 in Year 3, and $100 in Year 4. At the end of Year 4 the machine can be sold for $200. The market rate of interest is 8.5%. Should you buy the machine?

Problem 14

You have just joined the investment banking firm of Knot, Wirthem, *et al*. They have offered you two different salary arrangements: Option 1 is $50,000 yearly for 3 years; Option 2 is $25,000 yearly for 3 years plus a $50,000 signing bonus today. If the market interest rate is 7%, which salary arrangement do you prefer?

Problem 15

Find the present value of the following series of cash flows, using a discount rate of 10%.

Year	Cash Flow
1	$100
2	200
3	300
4	300
5	300

Problem 16

WeGrow.com is going public with a perpetuity that offers 150% of the $100 face. They will use an interest rate of 9% in the analysis. Managers anticipate that the recent slow-down in dot.com securities will be short-lived, so they think it might be less expensive to issue the security as a *growing perpetuity* with a constant annual growth of 4%. Are they right that issuing a growing perpetuity will be less expensive? What will happen if they issue the security as a 25-year *growing annuity*?

Problem 17

A local bank is offering 9% interest, compounded monthly, on savings accounts. If you deposit $700 today, how much will you have in 2 years? How much will you have in 2.5 years?

Problem 18

For each of the following, calculate the effective annual rate:

Stated Rate	Number of Times Compounded
5%	semiannually
11%	quarterly
16%	daily
20%	continuously

Problem 19

A bank pays interest compounded monthly; the effective annual interest rate is 8%. What is the quoted rate?

Problem 20

Mike, from Problem 2, just learned that his bank is offering to change his account so that interest is compounded semi-annually, rather than annually. Redo Problem 2 to find the value of Mike's account after 2, 5, and 10 years.

Problem 21

Calculate the sum you would need to deposit today at 12% interest, in order to pay out the following amounts in the periods indicated. Note: The solution below uses PFIV factors from the tables in the Appendix.

Period	Amount Paid (at the end of the period)
6	$1,000,000
7	2,000,000
8	2,500,000

Problem 22

A lease financing company has determined that it must charge 14% on amortized loans in order to be profitable. What semiannual payment would be required from a borrower who would repay a four-year loan of $25,000 assuming beginning-of-period payments?

Problem 23

You intend to open a business 3 years from today, after you have finished your bachelor's in business administration. You currently have $30,000 in your savings account and estimate that capital expenditures of $27,500 per year-end for six years after the business opens, will be necessary. The only other source available to you (other than your own funds) will be a loan from your generous Aunt Looney. How much will Aunt Looney need to lend you the day the business opens? Assume the appropriate interest rate is 12% throughout the period.

Problem 24

Your corporation wishes to borrow cash to fund a project. A lender offers you two choices. Choice 1: borrow at an Annual Percentage Rate (APR) of 10%. Choice 2: borrow at an Effective Annual Rate (EAR) of 10.5%. If both choices require monthly interest payments, which do you prefer?

Problem 25

You wish to invest for a one year period. Two investment opportunities exist. Opportunity 1: Receive an Annual Percentage Rate (APR) of 4.65%, compounded semi-annually. Opportunity 2: Receive an Effective Annual Rate (EAR) of 4.75%. Which should you choose?

Challenge Questions

Problem 26

A local loan shark offers 'four for five on payday.' This means you borrow $4 today and you must repay $5, 6 days from now, when you get your next paycheck. What is the effective annual interest rate for this loan?

Problem 27

A local bank is offering an account that has an effective annual interest rate of 12.75%. If the bank is using continuous compounding, what is the quoted rate?

Problem 28

Your new investment pays 13.98% continuously compounded. How long will it take your money to double?

Problem 29

An investment will increase in value by 270% over the next 17 years. What is the annual interest rate which, when compounded quarterly, provides this return?

Problem 30

Attempt the following two parts independently from each other:

a)   The Bank of Notreal offers a 2-year Investment Certificate (IC) that pays 10% compounded annually. The Bank of Goners offers a 2-year Investment Certificate compounded semiannually. The IC's have identical risk. What is the stated, or nominal, rate that the Bank of Goners would have to offer to make you indifferent between the two investments?

b)   For a 10-year deposit, what annual rate payable semiannually will produce the same effective rate as 4% compounded continuously?

Problem 31

Your firm is planning to invest in a project expected to generate the following income stream: a negative flow of $250,000 per year for 5 years, a positive flow of $450,000 in the sixth year, and a positive flow of $650,000 per year in years 7 through 9. What is the present value of this income stream if the appropriate discount rate is 10% for the first 5 years and 12% thereafter?

Problem 32

Expansion of your business has resulted in moving to a new building. This entails obtaining a new 25 year mortgage of $100,000 at an annual rate of 12 % fixed for a five year term. What is the effective monthly interest rate? the monthly payments?

Problem 33

Given the information in problem 30, attempt the following two parts independently from each other.

a)   What portion of the first payment will be for interest and what portion represents the payment of principal?

b)   Suppose the mortgage was variable-rate where interest is compounded monthly. Assuming that interest rates do not fluctuate during the first year, what are the monthly payments? Are you better or worse off with the variable rate mortgage?

Problem 34

Suppose your firm needs $100,000 in working capital and your bank manager has responded with the following three alternatives:

1)   A lump sum repayment at the end of three years equal to $133,100.

2)   An interest only loan where your firm must pay $10,500 for each of the next two years plus $110,500 at the end of the third year.

3)   Annual end-of-period payments of $40,921.31 for each of the next three years.

Which alternative should your firm choose?

ANSWERS TO CONCEPT TEST

1.   future value; future values

2.   present value; present values

3.   constant; regular; fixed

4.   ordinary; regular; deferred; annuity due

5.   C × PVIFA (r,t); constant annuity payment; present value interest factor for an annuity

6. $\{1 - [1/(1 + r)^t]/r\}$

7.   C × FVIFA(r,t); constant annuity payment; future value interest factor for an annuity

8. $[(1 + r)^t - 1]/r$

9.   constant; regular; C/r

10.   PV × r; C/PV

11.   stated; nominal; greater; effective annual yield

12. $[1 + (\text{quoted rate}/m)]^m - 1$

13. $PV × [1 + (r/m)]^{mt}$

14. $PV × (e^{qt})$

15.   single payment; interest; principal

16.   interest; principal

17.   interest; principal

18.   principal; interest; larger; smaller

19.   Bank Act; same; interest rate per period; number of periods per year

PROBLEM SOLUTIONS

Problem 1: This solution calculates the present value by finding the present value of each cash flow separately, then finding the total. You should confirm this result by also calculating the present value year-by-year.

Year	Cash Flow	PV (at 20%)
1	$114	$ 95
2	144	100
		$ 195

The present value ($195) is the same as its cost, so the investor is indifferent between the investment opportunity described here and an investment at the market rate of interest.

Problem 2: The time line for this problem is:

0 (today)	end of Yr. 2	end of Yr. 5	end of Yr. 10
$3,000	$4,000 + FV (from Yr. 0)	$1,000 + FV (from Yr. 2)	FV (from Yr. 5)

The future value of the first deposit, after 2 years is:

$$FV_2 \ = \ \$3,000 \times (1.07)^2 \ = \ \$3,000 \times 1.1449 \ = \ \$3,434.70$$

The account balance includes the $4,000 deposited in Year 2: FV = $3,434.70 = $4,000 = $7,434.70. This balance will earn interest for 3 years until we make the $1,000 deposit in Year 5. At the end of Year 5, the total account balance will be:

$$FV_5 \ = \ \$7,434.70 \times (1.07)^3 \ + \ \$1,000 \ = \ \$7,434.70 \times 1.2250 \ + \ \$1,000 \ = \ \$10,107.83.$$

This amount will earn interest for another 5 years. The balance in Year 10 will be:

$$FV_{10} \ = \ \$10,107.83 \times 1.4123 \ = \ \$14,176.75.$$

Alternatively, the future value of each cash flow can be calculated and all future values can be added together:

$$FV \ (\$3,000 \ deposit) \ = \ \$3,000 \times (1.07)^{10} \ = \ \$5,901.45$$
$$FV \ (\$4,000 \ deposit) \ = \ \$4,000 \times (1.07)^8 \ = \ \$6,872.74$$
$$FV \ (\$1,000 \ deposit) \ = \ \$1,000 \times (1.07)^5 \ = \ \$1,402.55$$

$$Total: FV \ = \ \$14,176.75$$

Problem 3: $PV \ = \ (\$400/1.12) \ + \ (\$889/1.12^2) \ + \ (\$432/1.12^3) \ = \ \$1,373.34$

The investment described above requires an outlay of $1,243, but provides cash flows of $400, $889 and $432 at the end of years 1, 2, and 3, respectively. Therefore, this investment is preferable to the alternative opportunity at the market interest rate of 12%.

Problem 4: Find the present value of each investment opportunity. If the present value is greater than the cost, the project is a good investment.

Project 1: $PV \ = \ \$1,000/1.08 \ + \ \$800/(1.08)^2 \ + \ \$600/(1.08)^3 \ = \ \$2,088.10$

The project costs $2,000, so it is a good investment.

Project 2: $PV \ = \ \$1,900/(1.08) \ + \ \$1,900/(1.08)^2 \ + \ \$1,900/(1.08)^3 \ = \ \$4,896.48$

The project costs $5,000, though, so it is not a good investment.

Project 3: $PV \ = \ \$1,400/(1.08) \ + \ \$1,600/(1.08)^2 \ + \ \$1,800/(1.08)^3 \ = \ \$4,096.94$

Since the project only costs $4,000, it is a good investment.

Problem 5: Find the present values of the cash flows from the investment:

$$PV = \$800 / (1.08) + \$1,500 / (1.08)^2 + \$1,600 / (1.08)^3 = \$3,296.88$$

Your banker is giving you good advice. You would earn less by leaving the funds in your savings account.

Problem 6: Effectively, you are receiving each cash flow one year earlier, so the discount period is one year less for each cash flow. The present value is:

$$PV = \$1,900 / (1.08)^0 + \$1,900 / (1.08) + \$1,900 / (1.08)^2 = \$5,288.20$$

The project is now a good investment. Note: $(1.08)^0 = 1$

Problem 7: PVIFA(5%,3) $= \{1 - [1/(1.05)^3]\} / .05 = \{1 - .772183\} / .09 = 2.723248$

Use the formula for the present value of an annuity to solve for C, the amount to withdraw:

$$PV = \$ 35,000 = C \times 2.723248 \rightarrow C = \$35,000 / 2.723248 = 12,852.30$$

So, you can withdraw $12,852.30 each year while you are in school.

Problem 8: This is an annuity due with bdginning-of-year withdrawals. The problem can be solved two ways.

Alternative 1: compute the annuity due PV factor as:

$$PVIFA (r\%, n - 1) + 1 = \{1 - [1/(1.05)^2]\} / .05 + 1 = 1.859410 + 1 = 2.859410$$

The withdrawals are: $\$35,000 = C \times 2.859410 \rightarrow \$35,000 / 2.859410 = \$12,240.29$
Alternative 2: compute the annuity due PV factor as:

$$PVIFA(5\%,3)(1 + r) = 2.723248(1.05) = 2.859410 \rightarrow C = \$12,240.29$$

Problem 9: For the first question, find the future value of the annuity:

$$FV = \$1,000 \times (1.07^4 + 1.07^3 + 1.07^2 + 1.07^1 + 1.07^0) = \$1,000 \times (5.75074) = \$5,750.40$$

For the second question, find the present value of the annuity:

$$PV = \$1,000 \text{ x } [1/(1.07)^1 + 1/(1.07)^2 + 1/(1.07)^3 + 1/(1.07)^4 + 1/(1.07)^5]$$
$$= \$1,000 \text{ x } (4.1002) = \$4,100.20$$

The maximum to spend in 5 years is $5,750.40; the maximum to spend today is $4,100.20

Problem 10: The present value is: $PV = C / r = \$100 / .10 = \$1,000$

Three years from now (or n years from now) the value of the perpetuity is still $1,000; the above calculation applies in either case, as long as the market rate of interest is 10%. The value of the perpetuity changes only if the market rate of interest changes.

Problem 11: Using the perpetuity present value equation: $\$1,000,000 / r = \$4,500,000 \rightarrow r = .2222 = 22.22\%$. For values of r less than 22.22%, the present value of the project is greater than \$4,500,000.

Problem 12: The present value of the perpetuity is: $PV = C / r = \$1,000 / .05 = \$20,000$

The 50-year annuity: $PV = \$1,000 \times PVIFA (5\%, 50) = \$1,000 \times 18.25593 = \$18,255.93$

The 100-year annuity: $PV = \$1,000 \times PVIFA (5\%, 100) = 1,000 \times 19.84791 = \$19,847.91$

Note: The longer the life of an annuity, the more its value approaches that of a perpetuity. This is because the present value interest factor, PVIF, gets smaller as t increases. For example:

$$PVIF (5\%, 250) = 1 / (1.05)^{250} = 0.00000504$$

That makes the present value factor 5 millionths. So, the present value of the 250th payment $=$ $\$1,000 \times 0.00000504 = 5.04$ thousandths of a cent!

Problem 13: Note: the net cash flow in Year 4 is the \$100 from use of the machine plus the \$200 from selling it.

$$PV = \$300 / (1.085) + \$300 / (1.085)^2 + \$500 / (1.085)^3 + \$300 / (1.085)^4$$

$$= \$276.50 + \$254.84 + \$391.45 + \$216.47 = \$1,139.26$$

The present value of the cash inflows is less than the \$1,200 purchase price, so this is not a good investment.

Alternatively, solved the problem can also be solved another way by recognizing that all 4 years have a cash flow of \$300 (an annuity), with an extra \$200 cash flow in year 3. The present value equation becomes:

$$PV = \$300 \times PVIFA (8.5\%, 4) + \$200 / (1.085)^3 = \$982.68 + \$156.58 = \$1,139.26$$

The present value of the cash flows, and the investment decision, are the same with either approach.

Problem 14: To compare, compute the present value of each salary option.

Option 1: $PVIFA(7\%,3) = 2.624316 \rightarrow PV = \$50,000 \times 2.624316 = \$131,215.80$

Option 2: $PVIFA(7\%,3) = 2.624316 \rightarrow PV = \$25,000 \times 2.624316 + \$5,000 = \$115,607.90$.

You should select the \$50,000 per year option.

Problem 15: The most efficient way to find the present value is to recognize that the cash flows in years 3, 4, 5 constitute a 3-year annuity. Find the value of the annuity at the beginning of year 3 (end of year 2). Then, that value is discounted for two more years in order to find the value today. Find the present values of the cash flows for the first two years, then compute the total of the separate present values.

Year	Calculation	Present Value
1	$\$100 \times PVIF(10\%,1) = 100 \times .909091$	\$ 90.91
2	$200 \times PVIF(10\%,2) = 200 \times .826446$	165.29
3-5	$300 \times PVIFA(10\%,3) \times PVIF(10\%,2)$	
	$= 300 \times 2.486852 \times .826446$	616.57
	Total present value	\$ 872.77

Problem 16: Cost of an ordinary perpetuity: $PV = C / r = \$150 / .09 = \$1,666.67$

Cost of a growing perpetuity: $PV = C / (r - g) = \$150 / (.09 - .04) = \$3,000$

Cost of a growing annuity: $PV = [C / (r - g)] \times \{1 - [(1 + g) / (1 + r)]^t \}$
$= [\$150 / (.09 - .04)] \times [1 - (1.04 / 1.09)^{25}]$
$= (\$150 / .05) \times (1 - 0.30915) = \$3,000 \times .69085 = \$2,072.55$

WeGrow.com has it backwards. Their best alternative is to issue an ordinary perpetuity. The worst alternative is to issue a growing perpetuity. This makes sense, because as the value to investors increases, the cost to the company must increase. Looks like WeGrow.com managers need a refresher course in finance!

Problem 17: The interest rate is actually $(.09/12) = .0075 = .75\%$ per month. Since there are 24 months in two years, the future value factor is: $(1.0075)^{24} = 1.1964$. Multiplying the future value factor times the $700 deposit; leaves \$837.49 after 2 years.

This problem can also be solved by first calculating the effective annual rate: $[1 + (.09/12)]^{12} - 1 = 9.38069\%$

After 2 years, you will have: $\$700 \times (1.0938069)^2 = \$837.49$

After 2.5 years (or 30 months), you will have: $\$700 \times (1.0938069)^{2.5} = \$875.89$

Problem 18:

Stated Rate	Number of Times Compounded	Effective Rate
5%	semiannually	5.063%
11%	quarterly	11.462%
16%	daily	17.347%
20%	continuously	22.140%

Problem 19: Solving for the quoted rate:

$[1 + (\text{quoted rate}/12)]^{12} - 1 = .08 \rightarrow [1 + (\text{quoted rate}/12)]^{12} = 1.08$

$1 + (\text{quoted rate}/12) = (1.08)^{1/12} \rightarrow 1 + (\text{quoted rate}/12) = 1.006434$

$\text{quoted rate}/12 = 1.006434 - 1 = .006434 \rightarrow \text{quoted rate} = 12 \times .006434 = 7.7208\%$

Problem 20: The periodic interest rate is now $.07 / 2 = 0.035 = 3.5\%$

After 2 years (4 periods), the balance will be: $FV_4 = \$3,000 \times (1.035)^4 + \$4,000 = \$7,442.57.$

After 5 years (6 additional periods), the balance will be: $FV_5 = \$7,442.75 \times (1.035)^6 + \$1,000 = \$10,148.82.$

After 10 years (10 additional periods), $FV_{10} = \$10,148.82 \times (1.035)^{10} = \$14,315.91$

Note: The subscripts on the term FV refer to the value in the *actual* year. However, when computing that value, the *compounding interval* (the exponent) is multiplied by 2 to reflect semi-annual compounding.

Problem 21: $1,000,000 (.5066) + $2,000,000 (.4523) + $2,500,000 (.4039) = $2,420,950

Problem 22: Semiannual payment = $25,000 / [(PVIFA 7%,8-1) + 1] = $25,000 / 6.3893 = $3,912.79

Problem 23: Funds required at end of year 3: $27,500 (PVIFA 12%, 6) = $27,500 (4.1114) = $113,063.50

Savings by end of year 3: = $30,000 (FVIF 12%, 3) = $30,000 (1.4049) = $42,147

Borrow (113,063.50 – 42,147) = $70,916.5

Problem 24: The APR associated with the first choice is 10%, compounded monthly. The EAR is equal to $[1 + .1/12]^{12} – 1 = 10.47\%$. This EAR of 10.47% is less than the EAR of 10.5% associated with choice 2. Since a borrower should choose the lower rate, choice 1 is preferable.

Problem 25: The APR associated with the first opportunity is 4.65%, compounded semi-annually. The EAR is equal to $[1 + .0465/2]^{2} – 1 = 4.7\%$. This EAR of 4.7% is less than the EAR of 4.75% associated with opportunity 2. Since an investor should choose the higher rate, opportunity 2 is preferable.

Problem 26: The interest rate is $[(5/4) – 1] = 25\%$ for 6 days. There are about $(365/6) = 60.8333$ such periods in a year. The effective rate is thus 1.25 raised to the power 60.8333, minus 1. This works out to be a nice round 78.59 million percent. Yes, it's a might high, but it beats having your legs broken (or worse yet, "feedin' the fishies").

Problem 27: Solve for q in the following equation: $e^q – 1 = .1275 \rightarrow e^q = 1.1275$

where e is the constant 2.7183. The solution requires finding the natural logarithm of both sides of the above equation. The natural logarithm of e^r is r. The natural logarithm of 1.1275 is determined by using the following sequence on a financial calculator: 1.1275 [1n]. Thus, $r = .12 = 12\%$.

If logarithms make you nervous, then it may help to know that compounding 5,000 times per year is nearly the same as continuous compounding. With this in mind, you can solve this problem the same way that Problem 15 was solved. The five thousandth root of 1.1275 is 1.000024, and $(5,000 \times .000024)$ is approximately .12.

Problem 28: There are two ways to solve this problem.

Alternative 1: Calculate the EAR and use that rate to determine when your money will be doubled.

$$EAR = e^{.1398} - 1 = 2.71828^{.1398} - 1 = 15\%$$

$$PVIF(15\%, t) = 2 \rightarrow t = 4.96 \ (\sim5) \text{ years to double your money.}$$

Alternative 2: Solve the following equation for t: $\$1 \times (e^{.1398\,t}) = \$2$

Take the natural log of 2 and divide by .1398 (i.e. 0.693147 / .1398). The solution is 4.96 years.

Problem 29: Set $1 as the beginning amount and $270 as the amount in 17 years. There are 68 quarterly compounding periods in 17 years. Then solve for the value of r:

$$\$1 \times (1 + r/4)^{68} = \$270 \rightarrow (1 + r/4)^{68} = \$270 \rightarrow (1 + r/4) = (270)^{1/68} \rightarrow r/4 = .085814$$

$$r = .343255 = 34.3255\%. \text{ This is very easily done on a financial calculator.}$$

Problem 30:

a)   To be indifferent between the two alternatives, the returns must be equal. So, set the effective annual rate
      for Goners equal to the known 10% rate for Notreal. Then solve for q:

$$(1 + q/2)^2 - 1 = .10 \rightarrow q = 9.76\%.$$

b) $e^{.04 \times 10} = (1 + q/2)^{20} \rightarrow 1.491825 = (1 + q/2)^{20} \rightarrow 1.020201 = 1 + q/2 \rightarrow q = 4.04\%$

Problem 31: Using DCF analysis, investment opportunities can be evaluated when discount rates change over time.
      PV = –$250,000 (PVIFA 10%, 5) + $450,000 (PVIF 12%, 1)(PVIF 10%,5) +
            $650,000 (PVIFA 12%,3)(PVIF 12%,1)(PVIF 10%, 5)

      = -$250,000 (3.7908) + $450,000 (.8929)(.6209) + $650,000 (2.4018)(.8929)(.6209)

      = –$947,700 + $249,480.72 + $865,515.16 = $167,295.88

      Note: PV interest factors are from the tables in the Appendix.

Problem 32:   First, convert the quoted semiannual rate to an EAR: EAR = $[1 + .12/2]^2 - 1$ = 12.36%

      Then the effective monthly rate: $(1.1236)^{1/12} - 1$ = .009759

      Use the annuity present value formula to calculate payments:

      $100,000 = C \times (1 - 1/1.009759^{300})/.009759 \rightarrow $100,000 = C \times 96.906953 \rightarrow C = $1,031.92$

Problem 33:

   a) Interest = $100,000 \times .009759 = 975.90; payment on principal = $1,031.92 – $975.90 =
       $56.02.

   b) Using monthly compounding the payments would be:

       $100,000 = C \times \{1 - [1/(1.01)^{300}]\}/0.01 \rightarrow C = $1,053.22$

   You are worse off by ($1,053.22 - $1,031.92) = $21.30 if the variable rate mortgage is chosen.

   Note: The effective monthly rate is $[1 + (0.12/12)]^{12} - 1 = 0.01$.

Problem 34:   Alternative 1 is a pure discount loan. The interest rate is $[$133,100/(1 + r)^3] = 10\%$.

      Alternative 2 is an interest only loan. The interest rate is ($10,500/$100,000) = 10.5%.
      Alternative 3 is an amortized loan; the interest rate is $40,921.31 = $100,000/PVIFA r%, 3 \rightarrow 11\%.
      Note: PVIFA (r%, 3) = 2.4437 is about halfway between the factors for 10% and 12%.

      Your firm should select alternative 1.

7   Interest Rates and Bond Valuation

CHAPTER HIGHLIGHTS

This chapter extends the present value concepts introduced in Chapters 5 and 6 to the valuation of bonds. It then discusses the basic features of bonds and how they are traded in financial markets. Finally, it explains the way in which bond values depend on interest rates. The function of interest rates in our economy, and the factors that cause them to change, are discussed also.

It is important while studying this chapter to remember that *the value of a bond, or any other security, is simply the present value of the future cash payments to the holder of the security.*

7.1   BONDS AND BOND VALUATION

Bonds are long-term debt securities issued by corporations as well as governmental units, including the Bank of Canada, and provincial and municipal governments. The *issuer* of the bond is the *borrower*; the *investor* who buys the bond is the *lender*. Although bonds can take many different forms, the basic form discussed in this section is the level-coupon bond. The valuation of these securities is based on the present value concepts developed in the preceding chapter.

Bond Features and Prices: Bond owners are typically paid only the interest on the loan every period; the principal is not repaid until the end of the loan. A *level-coupon bond* promises regular interest payments (either annually or semi-annually), as well as a specified principal payment, or *face value*, at the *maturity date*. The face value is also referred to as the *par value* or *maturity value* of the bond. The annual interest payment is called the bond's *coupon interest payment*, or simply *coupon* for short. The coupon payment remains constant during the life of the bond.

Example: Consider a corporate bond issued by MAM industries. The bond promises a 6% coupon rate and has a face value of $1,000, payable on January 1, 2024. The annual interest payment to the bondholder is the coupon rate times the face value: $.06 \times \$1,000 = \$60$ per year. The *maturity date* is January 1, 2024. This is the date of the last interest payment and the date of the principal repayment to the bondholder. If today is January 1, 2004, there are still 20 years of coupon payments left. Therefore, the *maturity* of the bond is 20 years. So, bondholders will receive $60 interest per year for 20 years, and they will also receive the $1,000 face value at the end of 20 years. The *discount rate*, used to value bonds, is the rate investors would earn on other bonds of similar risk and maturity. For MAM, the appropriate discount rate is 10%.

For most bonds, the coupon payment is made in the form of two semiannual payments. In this case the semi-annual coupon payment would be $60/2 = $30. Most of the examples and problems in this study guide will be based on semiannual payments.

Note: When working problems based on semiannual coupon payments, remember to make three adjustments:

     1.   coupon payment = ½ the annual payment (for MAM: $60 / 2 = $30)
     2.   number of periods = 2 × years to maturity (for MAM: 20 × 2 = 40)
     3.   discount rate = ½ annual rate (for MAM: 0.10/2 = .05)   5%

Bond Values and Yields: The value of the MAM Industries bond is the present value of the future coupon payments and principal payment discounted at the appropriate opportunity cost for bonds of similar characteristics. The *opportunity cost* is the rate of return, or yield, available on other corporate bonds with approximately twenty years to maturity and risk level comparable to that of the MAM bond. If the market interest rate for such bonds is 10%, then the value of the MAM bond is given by:

$$PV = \$30/(1.05)^1 + \$30/(1.05)^2 + ... + \$30/(1.05)^{40} + \$1,000/(1.05)^{40} = \$656.82$$

In general, the above calculation can be represented as follows:

$$P = C/(1+r)^1 + C/(1+r)^2 + ... + C/(1+r)^t + \$1,000/(1+r)^t$$

Where C is the semi-annual coupon payment, t is the number of semi-annual time periods to the maturity date, r is the appropriate semi-annual opportunity cost, and $1,000 is the principal payment at maturity. Since the coupon payments are in the form of an annuity, the above equation can be rewritten as:

$$PV = C \times PVIFA(r,t) + \$1,000/(1+r)^t$$

where: $PVIFA(r,t) = \{1 - [1/(1+r)^t]\}/r$

Recall that PVIFA(r,t) can be determined by using either the above formula or Table A.3. Using the formula, the value of PVIFA(r,t) for the MAM Industries bond is:

$$PVIFA(3\%,40) = \{1 - [1/(1.05)^{40}]\}/.05 = \{1 - .142046\}/.05 = 17.159086$$

Therefore, the present value of the bond is calculated as follows:

$$\begin{aligned} PV &= [\$30 \times PVIFA(5\%,40)] + \$1,000/(1.05)^{40} \\ &= (\$30 \times 17.159086) + (\$1,000 \times .142046) = \$656.82 \end{aligned}$$

Notice that the bond value is simply the present value of the stream of coupon payments plus the present value of the face value paid when the bond matures.

The interest rate required in the market (10 percent in the example above) is also known as the bond's *yield to maturity,* or YTM. Bond yields are quoted like APRs; the quoted rate is equal to the actual rate per period multiplied by the number of periods per year. In our case, the yield is 5 percent every six months, or $.05 \times 2 = .10 = 10\%$ per year. To calculate the effective yield on this bond, note that 5 percent every six months is equivalent to: Effective annual rate $= (1 + .05)^2 - 1 = 10.25\%$. The effective yield, therefore, is 10.25 percent.

Further discussion of the level-coupon bond described above can provide insight into two other aspects of bond valuation: the relationship between interest rates and bond prices, and the concept of a bond's yield to maturity, which is the rate of return for a bond.

A change in the market interest rate changes the value of the bond. Suppose an investor purchased the bond for $656.82 and, immediately after, market interest rates increased from 10% to 12%. If the investor wants to sell the bond, he will no longer be able to sell it for the same price. The bond, if bought at $656.82 is providing a 10% return. Other investors will find this unacceptable since other similar bonds return 12%. Therefore, they will no longer pay $656.82 for the bond. The new price of the bond will be:

$$PV = [\$30 \times PVIFA(6\%,40)] + \$1,000 / (1.06)^{40} = (\$30 \times 15.046297) + (\$1,000 \times .097222)$$
$$= \$548.61$$

Mathematically, it is clear that the value of the bond decreases when the market rate of interest increases, because the interest rate is in the denominator of the basic present value formula. An increase in the denominator reduces the present value.

A decrease in the market rate of interest increases the value of the bond. For example, if YTM = 8%, then the value of the bond is:

$$PV = [\$30 \times PVIFA(4\%,40)] + \$1,000 / (1.04)^{40}$$

$$= (\$30 \times 19.792774) + (\$1,000 \times .208289) = \$802.07$$

The fact that the bond's value increases with the decrease in interest rates is consistent with both a mathematical and an intuitive understanding of the relationship between interest rates and bond values. From a mathematical perspective, the decrease in the appropriate discount rate from 10% to 8% results in an increase in the value of the bond because the discount rate is in the denominator of the basic present value calculation; a decrease in the size of the denominator increases the present value.

Suppose an investor bought the bond at a price of $656.82, when the market rate of interest was 10%. If the market rate of interest then declines to 8%, the holder of the bond is not willing to sell the bond for $656.82. At that price, a subsequent buyer would be earning a 10% rate of interest at a time when the rate available on comparable bonds is only 8%. Therefore, the holder of the bond would be able to sell the bond at a higher price (i.e., $802.07). The price is determined such that a subsequent buyer would earn the new 8% market rate of interest. A subsequent buyer would not be willing to pay a price higher than $802.07, because the buyer would then earn less than the 8% market interest rate. On the other hand, the current owner of the bond has no incentive to sell it for less than $802.07, since a subsequent buyer would be satisfied with a price at which he earns the current 8% market rate.

When the bond value is greater than its $1,000 face value, the bond is said to be selling at a *premium* and is referred to as a *premium bond*. A bond which sells for less than face value is selling at a *discount* and is called a *discount bond*. When the market rate of interest is equal to the bond's coupon rate, the bond value is $1,000 (i.e. 6% in this case). An investor who pays $1,000 for a bond and receives annual coupon payments of $60 earns a 6% rate of return on the investment.

Interest Rate Risk: An investor buying a bond is faced with the possibility that the value of the bond will change if market interest rates change. The risk that arises for bond owners from fluctuating interest rates is called *interest rate risk*. The amount of interest rate risk depends on how sensitive the bond's price is to changes in interest rates. This sensitivity depends on two things:

1)   time left until maturity: interest rate risk increases as time to maturity increases
2)   coupon rate: interest rate risk increases as coupon rates are lowered

The reason that longer-term bonds have greater interest rate sensitivity is that a large portion of the bond's value comes from the $1,000 face amount. The present value of the amount isn't greatly affected by a change in interest rate if it is to be received in one year, as opposed to 20 years. Similarly, if two bonds with different coupon rates have the same maturity, the value of the lower-coupon bond is proportionately more dependent on the face amount to be received at maturity. As a result, its value will fluctuate more as interest rates change. In other words, the higher-coupon bond has a larger cash flow early in its life, so its value is less sensitive to changes in the discount rate.

Finding the Yield to Maturity: An understanding of the relationship between interest rates and bond values is essential in determining the rate of return, or yield to maturity, for a given bond. For example, suppose that the MAM bond described earlier is known to be selling for $720. What yield to maturity will an investor who purchases the bond for this price earn? To simplify, assume that coupon payments are made *annually*. Therefore, the values calculated in the above example will change slightly. Specifically, when r = 8%, PV = $803.63; when r = 12%, PV = $548.61. The answer to this question is the value of r which solves the equation:

$$PV = [C \times PVIFA(r,t)] + \$1,000 / (1 + r)^t \rightarrow \$720 = [\$60 \times PVIFA(r,20)] + \$1,000 / (1 + r)^{20}$$
OR
$$\$720 = \$60 \times \{1 - [1/(1 + r)^{20}]\} / r + \$1,000 / (1 + r)^{20}$$

Even though there is only one unknown in this equation, it is not mathematically possible to solve for r directly. The solution can, however, be obtained in three ways: using a trial-and-error approach; using a financial calculator; or, using a shortcut formula.

Given the inverse relationship between interest rates and bond prices, it is clear that the yield to maturity for the bond selling at a price of $720 is between 8% and 10%. Starting with a midway point, if r = 9%, the bond's value is: PV = $726.14. Since an increase in r decreases PV, the next 'guess' should be slightly higher than 9% - maybe 9.2%, resulting in PV = $712.00. The rate is between 9% and 9.2%f; the actual yield is just under 9.1%.

The precise yield to maturity can be found using a financial calculator. But again, if you're using a calculator **be sure you know to how solve the problems using your calculator before taking a test!**

There is also a shortcut to guessing the yield on a bond; it uses the following approximate yield formula:

$$\text{Yield} = \frac{[\text{Coupon} + (\text{Face Value} - \text{Price})/\text{Maturity}]}{(\text{Price} + \text{Face Value})/2}$$

In the example above, the approximate yield is:

$$\text{Yield} = \frac{[\$60 + (\$1,000 - \$720)/20]}{(\$720 + \$1,000)/2} = 8.61\%$$

Although the shortcut approximation is a good starting point, it ignores the time value of money and can be significantly different from the true yield when the bond is selling at a large premium or discount. (In the MAM case, there is nearly .5% difference.)

7.2   MORE ON BOND FEATURES

A debt is a promise to repay principal (i.e., the original amount of the loan) plus interest at a specified time to the *lender,* or *creditor.* The corporation is the *debtor* or *borrower,* and the amount owed to the creditor is a liability of the corporation.

Debt is different from equity in three main ways:

1.   Debt does not represent an ownership interest; creditors have no voting power.
2.   Interest paid on debt is tax-deductible; dividends paid to shareholders are not.
3.   Failure to pay creditors can result in bankruptcy; the cost of financial failure is a cost of issuing debt

Is it Debt or Equity?   With the many types of securities available to corporations and investors today, it is not always clear whether a particular security is debt or equity. In general though, equity represents an ownership interest in the firm. Shareholders have a residual claim, meaning that they are paid after debt holders. This affects both the risks and benefits of holding one security or the other.

Long-term Debt - The Basics: Debt securities are often classified according to the maturity of the debt, which is the length of time that an unpaid balance remains outstanding. Debt that matures within one year is considered short-term debt; debt with a maturity greater than one year is considered long-term debt.

Typically, corporate debt securities are either notes, debentures, or bonds. Strictly speaking, a *bond* is secured debt; however, the word 'bond' is often used generically. A note is a debt security with a maturity less than ten years.

A long-term debt security can also be classified by whether it is a public issue or a private placement. Publicly issued debt is sold to the general public. The terms of privately placed debt are negotiated directly between the borrower and the lender, and the security is issued directly to the lender, rather than to the general public.

Other features of long-term debt are discussed below.

The Indenture: The *indenture* is the written agreement between the corporation and its bondholders. The indenture includes

1. the terms of the loan (interest rate, maturity date, etc.),
2. the amount of debt issued,
3. any property used as collateral,
4. repayment arrangements
5. call provisions
6. information on all protective covenants

Terms of a Bond: Long-term corporate debt is usually issued as a bond with a principal (face) value of $1,000. Annual interest is generally specified as a coupon rate equal to a percentage of face value. Interest payments are made semi-annually. A bond with interest payments equal to 8.4% of face value might pay $42 on March 1 and September 1 of each year. Principal, plus the last interest payment, is repaid to the bondholder on the maturity date. Bonds are issued in two forms:

Registered bonds: The company mails the interest payment and principal directly to the owner of record. The firm's registrar records ownership and any changes in ownership. These bonds frequently have attached coupons which must be sent to the firm's registrar to receive interest payments. (Hence the term "coupon clipping".)

Bearer bonds: The certificate is considered proof of evidence; whoever has the certificate or coupons is considered to be the owner of the bond. These bonds have dated coupons attached. The bondholder must detach a coupon and mail it to the company; the company mails the interest payment to the coupon holder. Ownership of a bearer bond is not registered with the company. Therefore, recovery is more difficult if the bonds are lost or stolen. However, since bearer bonds are not easily traceable, they may have advantages to some investors (i.e. crooks, tax dodgers, drug traders, and the "mob").

Security: Debt securities differ with regard to the collateral pledged as security for the repayment of debt.

Mortgage securities are secured by a mortgage on real property (usually real estate). The mortgage is described in a legal document called the mortgage-trust indenture or trust deed. Public utilities and railroads issue primarily mortgage bonds.

> *Chattel mortgages* are mortgages against a specific piece of property (a building, for example). The firm's other assets cannot be seized for repayment of debt.

> *Blanket mortgages* pledges all of the company's real property. In the case of financial failure, creditors can seize any or all of the firm's assets (except cash and inventories). This is the most common type of mortgage security.

Debentures are not secured by specific property. Holders of debentures are paid only when all claims to secured debt have been satisfied. Most of the corporate bonds issued today are debentures, although as stated earlier, public utilities issue mostly mortgage bonds.

Seniority: *Seniority* determines the order in which creditors are paid if the firm becomes bankrupt. Some debt is *subordinated* - other creditors must be repaid first before these debtholders can collect anything in the event that the firm is liquidated.

Repayment: The face value of most corporate bonds is repaid prior to maturity. For public issues, repayment takes place through the use of a sinking fund or a call provision (described in the next section). A *sinking fund* requires the corporation to make annual payments to the bond trustee, who then repurchases bonds. Bonds may be either repurchased in the open market or selected by lottery and redeemed at a specified price.

Sinking fund arrangements vary. Most start between five and ten years after the original issue date. Some call for equal annual payments throughout the life of the bond. The amount paid into the sinking fund may be insufficient to redeem the entire issue so that the corporation must make a large 'balloon' payment at maturity. Sinking funds provide additional security to bondholders by providing for the orderly retirement of debt and by serving as an early warning system regarding potential problems.

The Call Provision: A *call provision* allows the company to repurchase, or call, the entire debt issue prior to maturity at a specified price. Most debentures are callable. The call price is usually the face value of the bond plus a *call premium*. The call premium might be one year's interest initially and decrease every year as maturity approaches. Often, bonds cannot be called for some number of years following issue (a *deferred call*) and are said to be *call protected* during this period.

Protective Covenants: A *protective covenant* restricts certain actions of the company. A *negative covenant* (ex: a dividend restriction) prevents managers from taking certain actions that might put bondholders at increased risk. A *positive covenant* (ex: minimum level of working capital) requires that certain actions be taken by the corporation to protect the value of bondholders' investment.

7.3   BOND RATINGS

Firms typically pay to have a credit rating assigned to their bonds by either one or both of the two leading bond rating firms in Canada:. Standard & Poor's (S+P) and Dominion Bond Rating Service (DBRS). The largest U.S. rating agencies are Moody's Investor Services and Standard & Poor's Corporation (S&P). Bonds are rated according to the likelihood of default and the protection afforded the bondholders in the event of default. The two highest ratings for DBRS are AAA and AA. (S&P uses a similar ranking system). These ratings indicate a very low probability of default. Bonds rated at least BBB (DBRS) are considered investment grade, while lower-rate bonds are referred to as low-grade or high-yield bonds, commonly called 'junk' bonds. A bond in default is given a C rating. Because of their higher risk, bonds with lower ratings pay higher interest rates.

7.4 SOME DIFFERENT TYPES OF BONDS

Bonds issued in recent years frequently have some unusual, more innovative features than traditional debentures. Some of these are discussed below.

Financial Engineering: The design of new securities is referred to as *financial engineering*. The goal of financial engineering is to minimize taxes and to reduce and control risk. In addition, financial engineering may help reduce costs associated with issuing and servicing debt and complying with various regulations. Some debt instruments created through the process of financial engineering are described below.

Stripped Bonds: Bonds that pay no coupons are called stripped bonds or zero-coupon bonds. These bonds sell at a price much lower than the par value. Consider a 10-year stripped bond issued when the market rate of interest is 10%. The bond price is $1,000, discounted at 10% for 10 years:

$$PV = [\$1,000/(1.10)^{10}] = \$385.54$$

Over the life of the bond, the issuer effectively pays ($1,000 - $385.54) = $614.46 in interest. The issuer deducts interest every year for tax purposes, even though no interest is actually paid out. And, the owner pays taxes on accrued interest every year, even though no interest is actually received until maturity. Stripped bonds are popular with tax-exempt investors.

Floating-Rate Bonds: The coupon interest payments on a *floating-rate* bond are adjusted as interest rates change. This adjustment is based on an interest rate index such as the Treasury-bill interest rate. The value of a floating-rate bond depends on the nature of the adjustment mechanism and the frequency of the adjustments. Most 'floaters' have a 'put' provision giving the holder the option to redeem the bond at face value. Usually, a put provision takes effect following a specified time period after the bond is issued. Another feature of most floaters is a floor-and-ceiling provision, specifying the minimum and maximum coupon rates payable throughout the life of the bond.

Other Types of Bonds: The coupon payment for an *income bond* depends on corporate income. The firm is obligated to make interest payments only if income is sufficient. Income bonds offer the advantage of the tax deduction for interest expense without the risk of financial distress; an income bond is not in default when a coupon payment is omitted due to insufficient income. Despite these advantages, corporations rarely issue income bonds.

Other kinds of bonds include *convertible bonds* and *retractable bonds* (put bonds), which are discussed in more detail in Chapter 25.

7.5 BOND MARKETS

There is a huge trading volume in bonds every day, much larger than the trading volume in stocks. In fact, the largest securities market in the world, in terms of volume, is the U.S. Treasury market, which oversees the trading of U.S. government securities.

How Bonds Are Bought and Sold: Most bonds are traded *over the counter* (OTC). Dealers all around the world are connected electronically. While most firms have only one stock issue outstanding, they typically have many bond issues outstanding, and that the number of bond issues is far greater than the number of stock issues. We say that the bond market has very little *transparency*, mostly because it is an OTC market. So, it is difficult for investors to observe trading prices and volume. Transactions are often privately negotiated, and there is little centralized reporting of transactions. Although the trading volume of bonds exceeds that of stocks, only a small portion of total bond issues trade on a given day. This makes it more difficult to get current and accurate bond prices.

7.6   INFLATION AND INTEREST RATES

This section discusses the importance of inflation on interest rates, bond yields, and returns.

Real versus Nominal Rates: *Nominal rates* are interest rates that *have not* been adjusted for the effect of inflation. *Real rates*, on the other hand, *have* been adjusted for inflation. If prices are increasing by 3% a year, the inflation rate is 3%. The real rate is concerned with whether or not $1 will purchase the same amount of goods after adjusting for inflation. When inflation is increasing, the nominal rate is adjusted downward to reflect that prices are higher in real dollar terms. For example, if you invest $50 in an account paying a nominal rate of 10%, you will have $55.00 at the end of the year. The return on your investment is clearly 10%, but the impact of inflation has not been considered. Suppose that inexpensive winter scarves sell for $10 each at the beginning of the year. With $50, you could buy five scarves. By the end of the year, the price of the scarves has increased by 3% to $10.30 each. Your $55 will now buy you $55 / $10.30 = 5.34 scarves. The rate of return on the scarves is (5.34/5) - 1 = 6.8%. So, even though the nominal return on the investment was 10%, buying power went up only 6.8%. So, your real rate of return is 6.8%. (The remaining 3.2% is due to inflation).

The Fisher Effect: The Fisher effect describes mathematically the relationship between the real and nominal rates of interest and the rate of inflation. This relationship is expressed by the equation:

$$1 + R = (1 + r) \times (1 + h)$$

where R is the nominal rate of interest, r is the real rate, and h is the inflation rate. Rearranging,:

$$R = r + h + (r \times h)$$

This equation tells us that the three components of the nominal rate are: the real rate, the inflation rate (which compensates for the decrease in the purchasing value of money), and (r x h), which compensates for the loss in value on your investment earnings due to inflation. The third term is very small and is usually dropped from the equation. So, the Fisher effect is usually stated simply as:

$$R \approx r + h$$

Example: Investors require a 12 % rate of return, and the inflation rate is 4%. What is the exact nominal rate? The approximate nominal rate?

Exact rate: $1 + R = (1.12 \times 1.04) = 1.1648$ Or   16.48%

Approximate rate $R = .12 + .04 = .16 = 16\%$

7.7   DETERMINANTS OF BOND YIELDS

Bond yields depend on many factors. These are discussed below.

The Term Structure of Interest Rates: The *term structure of interest rates* establishes the relationship between short-term and long-term interest rates. Specifically, it tells us the nominal interest rates on default-free, pure discount bonds with different maturities. It represents the 'pure' time value of money for different lengths of time.

The Yield Curve: The graphical representation of the term structure is referred to as the *yield curve*. Usually, the yield curve is upward-sloping because long-term rates are higher than short-term rates. It can also be downward-sloping if short-term rates are higher. A 'humped' term structure occurs when rates rise at first, then fall with increasing maturity.

Determinants of the Level and Shape of the Term Structure: Three basic factors influence the shape of the term structure:

> 1.   The real rate of interest
> 2.   The rate of inflation
> 3.   The interest rate risk premium

The real rate of interest compensates investors for the pure time value of money. It influences the *level* of interest rates, rather than the actual shape of the term structure. Term structure *shape* is strongly influenced by investors' expectations about future inflation rates. If they expect inflation to increase, they will demand a higher nominal rate as compensation for the loss of future purchasing power. This addition to the real rate is referred to as the *inflation premium*. Finally, longer-term bonds are more subject to price changes due to changes in interest rates. The compensation required by investors for bearing this additional risk is referred to as the *interest rate risk premium*.

Bond Yields and the Yield Curve: So far, the discussion has involved essentially default-free bonds. The typical yield curve uses the default-free Government of Canada bonds. In determining an appropriate yield for a corporate or municipal bond, investors consider the probability of default. The additional compensation for bearing this default risk is referred to as the *default risk premium*. An additional consideration is that Canadian bonds are taxable; corporate bonds are not. Taxability, therefore, is another concern for investors.

Finally, investors prefer liquid, rather than illiquid, securities. Therefore, they also demand additional compensation if they buy a relatively less liquid bond. This compensation is referred to as the *liquidity risk premium*.

7A.   ON DURATION

Duration is a measure of a bond's *effective maturity*. As discussed above, bond values fluctuate when interest rates change, depending on the bond's coupon and its maturity. Duration incorporates both these factors to measure how sensitive a bond's price is to changes in interest rates.

First, note that for pure discount bonds, only the time to maturity affects interest rate sensitivity (because there are no coupon payments). So, time to maturity is an appropriate measure of volatility. For bonds that pay coupons, duration is essentially an *effective maturity* which measures interest rate sensitivity for these bonds. Duration is used to determine the *average maturity* of the various payments received by the bondholders.

Duration is computed as follows:

1.   Compute the present value of each payment
2.   Calculate the relative value of each payment as the ratio of the
      payment's present value to the value of the bond
3.   Weight the maturity of each payment by its relative value

The bond's duration is the sum of these weighted payments. In general, bonds with a higher duration have more sensitivity to interest rate changes than those with lower durations.

Example: Calculate the duration of a three-year bond paying a $90 coupon. The interest rate is 9%.

Calculate the present value of each payment:

$$\text{PV (Pymt 1)} \quad = \quad \$90 \,/\, 1.09 \quad = \quad \$82.57$$

$$\text{PV(Pymt 2)} \quad = \quad \$90 \,/\, (1.09)^2 \;=\; \$75.75$$

$$\text{PV(Pymt 3)} \quad = \quad \$1{,}090 \,/\, (1.09)^3 \;=\; \$841.68$$

$$\text{Total} \quad = \quad \$1{,}000$$

Find the relative weight of each payment:

$$\text{Pymt 1} \;=\; \$82.57 \,/\, \$1{,}000 \;=\; .082570$$

$$\text{Pymt 2} \qquad = \; \$75.75 \,/\, \$1{,}000 \;=\; .075750$$

$$\text{Pymt 3} \;=\; \$841.68 \,/\, \$1{,}000 \;=\; .841680$$

$$\text{Total} \;=\; \qquad 1.000$$

3.   Multiply the maturity of each payment by its relative weight to calculate duration

$$\text{Duration} \;=\; 1 \times .082570 \;+\; 2 \times .075750 \;+\; 3 \times .841680 \;=\; 2.759 \text{ years}$$

The percentage price fluctuations for this bond should be the same as those of a zero coupon bond with the same duration.

7B.   CALLABLE BONDS AND BOND REFUNDING (APPENDIX 7C)

The Call Provision: *Bond refunding* is the process of replacing all or part of a bond issue. Call provisions have value to the issuing firm. If interest rates decline after the bond is issued, the firm has the option to replace the bond issue with bonds paying a lower interest rate. On the other hand, a call provision is disadvantageous for bondholders. Bonds are called when interest rates decline, so that bondholders are forced to sell their bonds back to the issuing company and are then unable to earn a return on their investment equal to that earned on the called bond. Consequently, bondholders require compensation for the possibility that their bonds may be called away. As a result, a firm must pay a higher interest rate on a callable bond than on a comparable non-callable bond.

Cost of the Call Provision: Suppose a firm plans to issue a perpetual bond paying 9% interest. There is an equal chance that the market interest rate will be either 11.25% or 7.5% one year from now. What is the price of the bond today if it is not callable? The price is the present value of next year's coupon interest payment plus the present value of next year's expected price. Since the bond is a perpetuity, its value at the end of the year will be:

$$\$90/.1125 \ = \ \$800 \qquad\qquad OR \qquad\qquad \$90/.075 \ = \ \$1,200.$$

The expected value of the future price is: $[.5(\$800) + .5(\$1,200)] = \$1,000$.

Therefore, the price of the bond today is: $P_{NC} \ = \ (\$90 + \$1,000) / 1.09 \ = \ \$1,000$
(P_{NC} is the bond price if it is not callable.)

Suppose the above bond is callable next year at $1,090, and that it will be called if the interest rate drops to 7.5%. What must the coupon interest payment (C) be in order for the firm to be able to issue the bond at the par value of $1,000? At the end of the year, the bondholder will have an interest payment of C dollars plus either $1,090 (the call price) or a bond worth $(C/.1125)$. The expected value of the future price is therefore:

$$.50(\$1,090) + .50(C/.1125)$$

In order for the bond to sell for $1,000 today, the present value of the coupon interest payment (C) plus the present value of the expected future price must equal $1,000 ($P_C$ is the price of the callable bond):

$$P_C \ = \ \$1,000 \ = \ \{C + [(.50)(\$1,090) + (.50)(C/.1125)]\} \ / \ 1.09$$

$$\$1,000 \, (1.09) \ = \ C + 545 + 4.4444C \ \rightarrow \ 545 \ = \ 5.4444C \ \rightarrow \ C \ = \ \$100.10$$

The coupon payment must be $100.10 (or 10.01%) in order to sell the callable bond for $1,000.

The cost of the call provision to the issuing firm can be determined by computing the price of a similar but *noncallable* bond with C = $100.10.

Expected value of next year's price: $.50 \times (\$100.10 / 0.75) + 0.50 \times (\$100.10 / .1155) = \$1,112.225$

$$P_{NC} \ = \ (\$100.10 + \$1,112.225) / 1.09 \ = \ \$1,112.23$$

$$P_{NC} - P_C \ = \ \$1,112.23 - \$1,000 \ = \ \$112.23 \ \rightarrow \ \text{the firm is paying \$112.23 for the option.}$$

Value of the Call Provision: The value of the call provision is :

$$\text{Call value} \ = \ \text{PV (firm's interest savings)} \ - \ \text{PV (call premium)}$$

If the bond above is called one year from now,

New coupon payment $= \ \$1,000 \times 0.75 \ = \ \$75$

Interest savings $= \ \$100.10 - \$75 \ = \ \$25.10$

PV (interest savings) $= \ \$25.10 / .075 \ = \ \$334.67$ (this is a pertuity)

Net savings $=$ PV (interest savings) - call premium $= \ \$334.67 - \$990 \ = \ \$244.67$

Since there is only a 50% probability that the interest rate will decline, there is only a 50% probability that the savings will be realized.

Expected value of interest savings = .50 x $224.67 = $112.34 ~ cost of call provision

This result demonstrates that the net present value of the call provision, to either the issuer or the bondholders, is zero, because the bondholders require compensation for the call provision which exactly offsets their expected loss.

THE REFUNDING ISSUE

When Should Firms Refund Callable Bonds? A firm should refund callable bonds when the net present value of the refunding is positive. In other words, the firm will refund the callable bonds next year if the net present value of the transaction, at that time, is positive. If the market rate of interest declines to 7.5% one year from now, the net present value of calling (refunding) the bond is $224.67, as computed earlier. The bond should be refunded next year if the market interest rate declines to 7.5%, because the net present value of refunding, at that time, is positive.

Assume that: 1.   Bonds are perpetuities
               2.   No taxes
               3.   No refunding costs except the call premium, and refunding is instantaneous (no overlap period)
               4.   The refunding takes place today

The following notation is used: C_O = Coupon rate on outstanding bonds
               C_N = Coupon rate on new issue (current market rate)
               CP = Call premium per bond
               $[(C_O - C_N) (\$1,000)] / C_N$ = PV (interest savings)
               NPV = $[(C_O - C_N) \times (\$1,000)] / C_N$ -   CP

Example: Assume that Minerva, Inc., has outstanding bonds originally issued with a 16.3 % coupon. The market interest rate is 7 % and the call premium is 18 %. What is the NPV of refunding?

NPV = $[(.163 - .07) (\$1,000)] / .07 - [(\$1,000) (.18)]$ = $1,328.57 - $180 = $1,148.57 per bond

Relaxing the Assumptions: Realistically, the refunding procedure must incorporate finite maturities, taxes, flotation costs and an overlap period that incorporates the timing problem of issuing new bonds while the outstanding issue comes in. These can be best understood by following the procedure outlined in the solution to the example below.

Example: In 1987, WeCall Inc. issued $25 million in 15% coupon bonds. The bonds mature in 2006 but are callable today at a 6% premium. Investment bankers have assured WeCall that a new $30 million, 9 year issue, also maturing in 2006, can be sold with a 10% coupon. The new bonds will be sold two months before the old bonds are called, in order to eliminate timing problems with the two issues. Although WeCall has to pay the coupons on both issues during these two months, the new issue can be invested at the 8% short-term interest rate. The flotation costs for the $25 million issue would be $1,406,250 and the firm's tax rate is 30 %. Should the bonds be refunded?

Note: The call premium is *not* tax-deductible. Flotation costs are amortized (depreciated) over 5 years or the life of the bond, whichever is shorter. This depreciation *is* tax-deductible. The after-tax incremental interest paid is the difference between the interest earned from investing the new issue at the short-term rate and the interest paid on the old issue during the overlap period. *The discount rate for the analysis is always the after tax cost of the new debt issue.* For this example the discount rate is 10% x (1 - .30) = 7%

The analysis can be broken down into three steps: the cost of refunding, interest savings, and the NPV.

Cost of Refunding: The cost included the call premium, flotation costs (and associated tax savings), and any interest that must be paid or can be earned.

Call premium (6% of old issue)	0.06 x $25,000,000	$1,500,000.00
Flotation costs	$1,406,250	
Yearly depreciation for 5 years	$1,406,250 / 5 = $281,250	
Tax shield on depreciation	$281,250 x .30 = $84,375	
PV tax shield	$84,375 x (PVIFA 7%, 5)	
	= $345,954.12	
Net flotation costs	$1,406,250 - $345,954.12	$1,060,295.88
Incremental interest		
Extra interest paid on old issue	$25,000,000(.15) (2/12)	
After tax cost	$625,000 (.70) = $437,500	
Extra interest earned on new issue	$25,000,000(.08) (2/12)	
After tax earnings	$333,333.33 (.70) = $233,333.33	
Total additional interest	$437,500 - $233,333.33	$ 204,166.67
Total cost of refunding:		$2,764,462.55

Benefit of Refunding: The benefit from refunding a bond issue is that the firm will have lower coupon rates. These savings occur over the remaining years to maturity for the old bond issue. The present value of these savings is an annuity. As before, all calculations are done on an after-tax basis.

Interest Savings		
After tax interest on old issue	$25,000,000 (.15)(1- .30)	
	= $ 2,625,000.	
After-tax interest on new issue	$25,000,000 (.10) (1-.30)	
	= $ 1,750,000	
Annual interest savings	$(2,625,000 - $1,750,000)	
PV (interest savings)	$875,000 (PVIFA 7%, 9)	$5,700,828.22

NPV of Refunding: The NPV consists of interest savings less the cost of refunding:

Interest savings	$ 5,700,828.00
Cost of refunding	$ 2,764,462.55
NPV	$ 2,936,365.45

WeCall can save almost $3 million by calling the old bond issue and refunding it with the new issue. So, they should call the bonds. This example illustrates the importance of a call provision when interest rates are relatively high.

CONCEPT TEST

1.   A long-term debt instrument issued by a corporation is called a _____.

2.   A long-term debt instrument promising regular interest payments and a specified principal payment at a specified date is called a _____. The regular interest payment is called the _____ payment and the principal payment is called either the _____ value, the _____ value or the _____ value.

3.   The principal payment for most corporate bonds is $_____. The regular interest payment is indicated by the _____, which is multiplied by the principal to determine the dollar amount of the payment. The date of the principal payment (and of the last regular interest payment) is called the _____ date.

4.   The value of a bond (or of any asset) is equal to the _____ of the future _____ to the holder of the bond. The valuation of a bond requires that we determine the relevant future _____ and the appropriate market rate of interest, or _____ for the bond. Then the _____ of the future _____ is calculated, using the appropriate opportunity cost, or _____ rate.

5.   The _____ is the amount an individual would have to invest at the relevant _____ today in order to duplicate the future cash payments promised to the holder of the security.

6.   Bond prices and interest rates are said to have an inverse relationship. That is, when the relevant market interest rate for a particular bond increases, the price of the bond _____, and when the market interest rate decreases, the bond price _____.

7.   This relationship can be understood mathematically by noting that the interest rate is in the _____ of the basic present value equation, so that when the interest rate increases (or decreases) the size of the denominator _____ (or _____), resulting in a(n) _____ (or _____) in the present value of the bond. Tthis result means that investors will pay less (more) for bonds with fixed annual payment when the level of interest rates available on comparable investments _____ (or _____).

8.   When the market rate of interest is equal to the _____ for a particular bond, the present value of the bond is equal to its _____. When the market rate of interest is greater than the coupon interest rate, the present value of the bond is _____ than its face value, and the bond is called a _____ bond. When the market rate of interest is less than the coupon interest rate, the present value of the bond is _____ than its face value, and the bond is called a _____ bond.

9.   A bond with a market value equal to its face value is equivalent to an _____ loan. The mathematics of such a bond are summarized by the equation: C = _____. Alternatively, this equation can be expressed as PV = _____ or r = _____.

10.   The yield to maturity for a bond is the bond's _____. Unless the market value of the bond is equal to its _____, the yield to maturity is determined by using a _____ approach. The process requires taking successive 'guesses' at the _____ which equates the _____ of the bond's future _____ with its current market value.

11.   A corporate debt is a promise by a corporation to repay the original amount of a loan, called the _____, plus interest, at a specified time. The lender is also called the _____, and the corporation is the borrower or _____.

12. Three features distinguish debt from equity. First, debt (does/does not) represent an ownership interest. Second, interest paid on a debt (is/is not) tax-deductible while dividends paid on common stock (are/are not) tax-deductible. Third, failure to pay creditors can result in _____.

13. Debt securities are often classified according to the length of time that an unpaid balance remains outstanding; this time period is called the _____ of the security. A debt security is considered _____ if its _____ is less than one year; a debt security is considered _____ if its _____ is greater than one year.

14. A _____ is secured by a mortgage on specific property, whereas a _____ is unsecured.

15. The written agreement between the corporation and its bondholders is called the _____.

16. Bonds can be either registered bonds or bearer bonds. If a bond is _____, the company's appointed registrar mails the interest payment directly to the owner of record. _____ bonds have dated coupons attached; every six months, the bondholder detaches a coupon and mails it to the company, which then makes the interest payment to the bondholder. The ownership of a _____ bond is not recorded with the company.

17. _____ governs priority of payment to creditors in the event of bankruptcy. Some debt is _____ which means that other creditors must be repaid first in the event of bankruptcy.

18. Most corporate bonds (are/are not) repaid prior to maturity. Repayment takes place through the use of a _____, which is an arrangement requiring the corporation to make annual payments to the bond trustee, who then repurchases bonds.

19. A _____ provision allows the company to repurchase the entire debt issue prior to maturity. The call price is equal to the _____ of the bond plus a _____. Often, bonds cannot be called for some number of years following issue; this is a _____ call, and the bonds are _____ during this period.

20. A _____ restricts certain actions of the company. A _____ disallows certain actions. A _____ requires that certain actions be taken by the corporation.

21. Firms typically pay to have a credit rating assigned to their bonds. Bonds are rated according to the likelihood of _____ and the protection afforded the bondholders in the event of _____. The highest ratings indicate a _____ probability of default.

22. A stripped bond does not pay annual _____; _____ and _____ are paid at maturity. The price of a stripped bond is the present value of its _____, discounted at the appropriate market rate of interest. The difference between the price at which the bond is issued and the _____ of the bond is the interest paid by the issuing corporation. For tax purposes, the implicit interest expense for any given year is the difference between the _____ and the _____. This amount (is/is not) taxable income for the holder of the bond.

23. The coupon interest payments on a _____ bond are adjusted as interest rates change. This adjustment is based on an _____ index. The coupon payment for an _____ bond is dependent on corporate income; that is, the company is obligated to make interest payments only if _____.

24.   A call provision has value to the issuing firm because it gives the firm the option to replace a bond issue with bonds paying a _____ interest rate if interest rates _____ subsequent to the original issue of the bond. A call provision is disadvantageous for bondholders because bonds are called when interest rates _____ .

25.   The cost of a call provision, to the issuing firm, is equal to the price at which the firm could sell a comparable _____ bond minus the price at which the firm could sell the _____ bond. The value of the call provision, to the issuing firm, is equal to the present value of the firm's _____ minus the present value of the _____ . The _____ of the call provision is equal to the _____ of the call provision, so that the net present value of the call provision, to either the issuer or the bondholders, is _____ . Consequently, a firm should generally be indifferent as to whether it issues callable bonds.

26.   A firm should refund callable bonds if the NPV of refunding is _____ . The NPV of the refunding is equal to the present value, as of the date of the refunding, of _____ , minus the _____ .

27.   The effective maturity of a bond is measured by its _____ . This provides information about how sensitive bond value is to changes in the _____ .

28.   In general, bonds with _____ are more sensitive to changes in interest rates than bonds with _____ .

29.   The graphical representation of the term structure is know as a _____ .

PROBLEMS

Basic Questions

Problem 1

Verbrugge Company has a level-coupon bond outstanding that pays coupon interest of $120 per year and has 10 years to maturity. The face value of the bond is $1,000. If the yield for similar bonds is currently 14%, what is the bond's value? (Assume that interest is paid annually).

Problem 2

Find the value of the Verbrugge bond from Problem 1 if the yield for similar bonds decreases to 12%.

Problem 3

Find the value of the Verbrugge bond from Problem 1 if the yield for similar bonds decreases to 9%.

Problem 4

Suppose Verbrugge pays semiannual coupon interest payments. What would its value be if the yield is 14%?

Problem 5

Now find the value of the Verbrugge bond if rates drop to 9%, assuming semiannual coupon interest payments.

Problem 6

For your birthday, your great uncle has given you a choice between a bond with a face value of $1,000 and 8% coupon paid annually, and a vintage chardonnay which will sell for $2,500 in 10 years. You can sell the wine the same year the bond matures. The market rate of interest is 12%. Which gift should you pick?

Problem 7

A corporation issues a bond today with a $1,000 face value, maturity in 25 years, and an 8% coupon interest rate; interest is paid annually. An investor purchases the bond for $1,000. What is the yield to maturity?

Problem 8

Suppose that the investor bought the bond described in the previous problem for $900. What is the yield to maturity?

Problem 9

Suppose that the bond described in the previous two problems has a price of $1,100 five years after it is issued. What is the yield to maturity at that time?

Problem 10

A level coupon bond paying 8% interest semi-annually has a face value of $1,000 and 10 years left to maturity. If the present market rate of interest is 6%, what is the present value of this bond?

Problem 11

Calculate the value of the bond in the previous problem assuming the market interest increases to 10%.

Intermediate Questions

Problem 12

Sasha Company has a level-coupon bond outstanding with a 9% coupon rate, payable annually. The bond has 20 years to maturity and a face value of $1,000; similar bonds currently yield 7%. By prior agreement the company will skip the coupon interest payments in years 8, 9, and 10. These payments will be repaid, without interest, at maturity. What is the bond's value?

Problem 13

Calculate the *approximate* yield to maturity, on an annual basis, of an 8% coupon, 10-year bond that pays interest semi-annually if its price now is $770.60. Use your results to calculate the effective yield on the bond.

Problem 14

A bond pays annual interest of 8% and has a face value of $1,000. The life of the bond is 20 years. If you purchase the bond for $700, what is its YTM? Find the YTM using the approximate formula also.

Problem 15

In December 1995, Campough Inc. issued $400,000,000 in long-term debt with a 10-year maturity (i.e. it matures in December 2005). The annual interest rate was 14% with semiannual interest paid on June 1 and December 1. In December 1999, interest rates on similar debt of equivalent risk had fallen to 10%. What was the total value of the Campough Inc. 14% debt on December 1999?

Problem 16

A corporate bond with a face value of $1,000, is currently quoted at 90. The coupon interest rate is 8%. What is the price of the bond? What coupon interest payment does the holder of the bond receive?

Problem 17

A corporation issued a five-year stripped bond, with a $1,000 face value, at a time when the market rate of interest was 12%. At what price did the bond originally sell?

Problem 18

Gilliam Industries has decided to float a perpetual bond issue. The coupon interest payment will be 12%, which is the current market interest rate. There is an equal chance that, in one year, the market rate of interest for the Gilliam Industries bond will be either 8% or 24%. What will the market value of the bonds be one year from now if they are noncallable? At what price can the bonds be sold today if they are noncallable?

Problem 19

Suppose that the Gilliam Industries bonds described in Problem 19 are callable at par value plus $120. At what price can the bonds be sold today?

Problem 20

If the Gilliam Industries bond in Problem 10 is callable and sells at par, what is the coupon interest payment (C)?

Problem 21

What is the cost of the call provision to Gilliam?

Problem 22

What is the value of the call provision to Gilliam Industries?

Problem 23

Suppose that Gilliam Industries issues the callable bonds described in Problem 21, and that, one year later, the market rate of interest declines to 8%. Should Gilliam refund the bonds at that time?

Challenge Questions

Problem 24

Find the duration of a four-year, 10% coupon bond .

Problem 25

Fundit Inc. is considering whether to refund a $40 million, 14% coupon, 30-year bond issue that was sold 5 years ago. Fundit's investment dealers have indicated that current yields on 25-year bonds of similar risk are 11.67%. A call premium of 7.5% would be required to retire the old bonds, and flotation costs on the new issue would amount to $3.5 million. Fundit's marginal tax rate is 40%. The new bonds would be issued 1.5 months before the old bonds were called, with the proceeds being invested in short-term government securities returning 9% annually. What is the bond refunding's NPV? Should Fundit call the bonds?

Problem 26

Your firm is considering refunding $16,000,000 face-value, 12% preferred shares outstanding with a similar issue but a lower dividend rate. Current dividend yields on 20-year term-preferred shares of similar risk are 9%, but you estimate that potential preferred shareholders investing in a perpetuity would require a premium of 1% above the term preferred shares. The outstanding preferred shares were issued 44 months ago costing the firm a total of $235,000 in before-tax issue costs and have a call premium equal to a rate that is 4% higher than the prevailing yield on perpetual preferred shares. The new preferred shares would be issued 3 months before the old ones are called, with before tax issue costs amounting to $300,000 where the proceeds of the issue would be invested in a bank deposit that yields 6%. Issue costs could be amortized over five years. The applicable discount rate is 8%. The firm's tax rate is 40%. Should they refund? (Note: Dividends are *not* tax-deductible; preferred shares are perpetuities.)

ANSWERS TO CONCEPT TEST

1.   bond

2.   level-coupon bond; coupon interest; face; par; maturity

3. $1,000; coupon interest rate; maturity

4.   present value; cash payments; cash payments; opportunity cost; present value; cash payments; discount

5.   present value; market rate of interest

6.   decreases; increases

7.   denominator; increases; decreases; decrease; increase; increases; decreases

8.   coupon interest rate; face value; less; discount; greater; premium

9.   interest-only; $PV \times r$; C/r; C/PV

10.   rate of return; face value; trial-and-error; discount rate; present value; cash payments

11.   principal; creditor; debtor

12.   does not; is; are not; bankruptcy

13.   maturity; short-term; maturity; long-term; maturity

14.   mortgage security; debenture

15.   indenture

16.   registered; bearer; bearer

17.   seniority; subordinated

18.   are; sinking fund

19.   call; face value; call premium; deferred; call-protected

20.   protective covenant; negative covenant; positive covenant

21.   default; default; low

22.   interest; interest; principal; face value; face value; value of the bond at the end of the year; value of the bond at the beginning of the year; is

23.   floating-rate; interest-rate; income; income is sufficient

24.   lower; decline; decline

25.   non-callable; callable; expected future interest savings; call premium; cost; value; zero

26.   positive; future interest savings; call premium

27.   duration; interest rates

28.   higher duration; lower duration

29.   yield curve

PROBLEM SOLUTIONS

Problem 1: PV $= \dfrac{\$120}{(1.14)^1} + \dfrac{\$120}{(1.14)^2} + ... + \dfrac{\$120}{(1.14)^{10}} + \dfrac{\$1,000}{(1.14)^{10}}$

$= \$120$ x PVIFA(14%,10) $+ \$1,000 / (1.14)^{10} = \$120$ x 5.216116 $+ \$1,000$ x .2697438
$= \$895.68$

The bond sells for less face value because the yield is greater than the coupon rate. This bond is a discount bond.

Problem 2: PV $= \$120$ x PVIFA(12%,10) $+ \$1,000 / (1.12)^{10}$

$= \$120$ x 5.650233 $+ \$1,000$ x .3219732 $= \$1,000.00$

This bond sells at par (coupon and market interest rates are equal). Therefore, no calculations are necessary.

Problem 3: PV $= \$120$ x PVIFA(9%,10) $+ \$1,000 / (1.09)^{10}$

$= \$120$ x 6.417658 $+ \$1,000$ x .4224108 $= \$1,192.53$

This is a premium bond, because its yield is less than its coupon rate. As the yield decreases, bond value increases.

Problem 4: PV $= \dfrac{\$60}{(1.07)} + \dfrac{\$60}{(1.07)^2} + ...+ \dfrac{\$60}{(1.07)^{20}} + \dfrac{\$1,000}{(1.07)^{20}}$

PV $= \$60$ x PVIFA(7%,20) $+ \$1,000 / (1.07)^{20}$

$= \$60$ x 10.594014 $+ \$1,000$ x .2584190 $= \$894.06$

This value differs somewhat the value in Problem 1due to the use of semiannual, not annual coupon payments.

Problem 5: PV $= \$60 \times$ PVIFA(4.5%,20) $+ \$1,000/(1.045)^{20}$
$= \$60 \times 13.007936 + \$1,000$ x .414643 $= \$1,195.12$

Problem 6: PV (wine) $= \$2,500$ x $[1 / (1.12)^{10]} = \$804.93$

PV (bond) $= \$80$ x PVIFA (12%, 10) $+ \$1,000 / (1.12)^{10} = \$773.99$

The wine is the better gift (unless you plan to drink it rather than sell it).

Problem 7: The yield to maturity is the value of r which solves the equation:

$\$1,000 = [\$80$ x PVIFA(r,25)] $+ \$1,000/(1 + r)^t$ OR $\$1,000 = \$80$ x $\dfrac{1 - [1 / (1 + r)^{25}]}{r} + \dfrac{\$1,000}{(1 + r)^{25}}$

Using trial-and-error, the solution is r = .08 = 8%. However, this is a par bond; it sells for face value. For par bonds, the coupon and market interest rates must be equal. Therefore no calculations are necessary.

Problem 8: The yield to maturity is the value of r in the following equation:

$$\$900 \; = \; [\$80 \times PVIFA(r,25)] \; + \; \$1,000 / (1+r)^t$$

The $900 price is less than face value, so the yield must be higher than 8%. This is a trial-and-error process.

At 10%:   PV = $80 x PVIFA(10%,25) + $1,000 / (1.10)^{25} = $818.46

Since $818.46 is less than the $900 purchase price, the yield to maturity is less than 10%.

At 9%   PV = $80 x PVIFA(9%, 25) + $1,000 / (1.09)^{25} = $901.77

The yield to maturity is slightly greater than 9%. The precise value (using a financial calculator) is 9.01969%.

Problem 9: The yield to maturity is the value of r in the following equation:

$$\$1,100 \; = \; [\$80 \times PVIFA(r,20)] \; + \; \$1,000 / (1+r)^t$$

The yield to maturity is less than the coupon rate because this is a premium bond. Using trial and error:

At 6% : PV = $1,229.40   →   6% is too low because $1,229.40 is greater than the market price.

At 7%:   PV = $1,105.94   →   7% is too high because $1,105.94 is less than the market price.

Therefore, the yield to maturity is slightly greater than 7%. The exact value is 7.05224%.

Problem 10: The semi-annual interest payment is $1,000 x (.08 / 2) = $40. The discount rate is 0.06 / 2 = 0.03, and the number of periods is 10 x 2 = 20.

PV = $40 x PVIFA (3%, 20) + $1,000 / 1.03^{20} = $40 x 14.877475 + $1,000 x 0.553675

= $1,148.78

Note: This is a *premium bond* because the coupon rate is higher than the current discount rate.

Problem 11: This should be a discount bond because the discount rate is higher than the coupon rate.

PV = $40 x PVIFA (5%, 20) + $1,000 / 1.05^{20} = $40 x 12.462210 + $1,000 x 0.376890

= $875.38

Problem 12: This problem can be solved by calculating the present value of each coupon interest payment, plus the present value of the face value. An easier approach is to

1. Calculate the present value of the bond under the assumption that all the coupon interest is paid
2. Deduct the present value of the skipped payments
3. Add the present value of the payments made at maturity.

PV (bond) from step 1: PV $=$ $90 (PVIFA 7%, 20) $+$ $1,000 (PVIF 7%, 20) $=$ $1,211.88

PV (skipped coupons): PV $=$ $90/(1.07)^8 +$90/(1.07)^9 +$90/(1.07)^{10} =$ $147.09
PV(extra payment at maturity): PV $=$ PV (3 x $90) $=$ $270 x (PVIF 7%, 20) $=$ $69.77

$\Rightarrow$ Bond Value $=$ $1,211.88 $-$ $147.09 $+$ $69.77) $=$ $1,134.56.

Problem 13: The semi-annual yield is: $\dfrac{40 + [(1,000 - 770.6) / 20]}{(1,000 + 770.6)/2} = 5.8138\%$

The annual yield is 5.8138% $\times$ 2 = 11.63% ; the effective yield is $(1 + .1163/2)^2 - 1 = 11.97\%$

Problem 14:

$700 $=$ $80 x PFIVA (r%, 20) + $1,000 / (1 + r)^{20}$

This is a discount bond, so the YTM is greater than 8%. Use trial and error.

At 10%:   PV $=$ $80 x (PVIFA 5%, 20) + $1,000 x (PVIF 5%, 20) $=$ $829.73

At 12% PV $=$ $80 x (PVIFA 12%, 20) $+$ $1,000 x (PVIF 12%, 20) $=$ $710.22

The YTM is slightly higher than 12%. By financial calculator, the actual YTM is 12.02187%

Using the approximate formula:

YTM $=$ $\dfrac{$80 + ($1,000 - $700) / 20}{($700 + $1,000) / 2} = 0.111765 = 11.18\%$

Problem 15: Calculate the market value of 1 bond:

Price $=$ $70 $\times$ PVIFA(5%,12) $+$ $1,000 x PVIF(5%, 12) $=$ $70 x (8.86325) + $1,000 x .55684
   $=$ $ 620.428 + $556.837 $=$ $1,177.265

Number of bonds outstanding: $400,000,000 / $1,000 $=$ 400,000 bonds outstanding

Total value of issue: 400,000 x $1,177.265 $=$ $470,906,000
Note: Rounding differences may result in slightly different answers.

Problem 16: The 90 quote means the bond is selling at 90% of face value. So, bond price $=$ .90 x $1000 $=$ $900. Annual coupon = .08 4 $1,000 $=$ $80. Payments are usually semiannual, paying $40 twice yearly.

Problem 17: The market value of a stripped bond is the present value of the face value, discounted at the market rate of interest. Therefore, the price of the five-year zero-coupon bond is: $1,000 / (1.12)^5 = $567.43.

Problem 18: The bond is a perpetuity. Year-end value is;

$$\$120 \,/\, .08 \;=\; \$1,500 \qquad \text{OR} \quad \$120 \,/\, 0.12 \;=\; \$500$$

Expected value of future price $=\quad [.5(\$1,500) + .5(\$500)] = \$1,000.$

$$P_{NC} \;=\; (\$120 + \$1,000) \,/\, 1.12 \;=\; \$1,000$$

Problem 19: If rates fall to 8%, the bond will be called at $1,120; if rates rise to 24%, the market value will be $500.

Expected value of future price $=\; .5\,(\,\$1,120) \;+\; .5\,(\$500) \;=\; \$810.$

$$P_C \;=\; (\$120 \;+\; \$810) \,/\, 1.12 \;=\; \$830.36.$$

Problem 20: At the end of the year, the bondholder will have an interest payment of C dollars plus either $1,120 (the call price) or a bond worth (C/.24). The expected value of the future price is:

$$.50(\$1,120) \;+\; .50(C/.24)$$

In order for the bond to sell for $1,000 today, the present value of the coupon interest payment (C) plus the present value of the expected future price must equal $1,000. Algebraically:

$$P_C \;=\; \$1,000 \;=\; \frac{C + [(.50)\,(\$1,120) + (.50)\,(C/.24)]}{1.12}$$

$$\$1,120 \;=\; C + (\$560) + (.50)(C/.24) \quad\rightarrow\quad \$560 \;=\; C + (.50)(C/.24)$$

$$\$134.40 \;=\; .24C + .50C = .74C \quad\rightarrow\quad C \;=\; \$134.40/.74 \;=\; \$181.62$$

If the coupon interest payment is $181.62, then the bond will sell for $1,000.

Problem 21: Step 1: compute price for non-callable bond with $181.62 coupon:

Expected value next year: $.5\,(\$181.62 \,/\, .08) \;+\; .5\,(\$181.62 \,/\, .24) \;=\; \$1,513.50$

$$P_{NC} \;=\; (\$181.62 \;+\; \$1,513.50) \,/\, 1.12 \;=\; \$1,513.50$$

Cost of call $=\; \$1,513.00 \,-\, \$1,000 \;=\; \$513.50$

Problem 22: Call value $=\; $ PV (interest savings) $-$ PV (call premium)

Interest payment on new issue: $\$1,000\,(\,.08) \;=\; \$80$

PV (Interest savings) $=\; (\$181.62 \,-\, \$80)/08 \;=\; \$2,270.25 \,/\, .08 \;=\; \$1,270.25$

Net savings $=\;$ PV (savings) $-$ Call Premium $=\; \$1,270.25 \,-\, \$120 \;=\; \$1,150.25$

Expected value of savings $=\; (.50 \times \$1,150.25) = \$575.125$

PV = $575.125 / 1.12 = $513.50

⇒ NPV = 0   (For either the issuer or the bondholders), because call cost = call value

Because the NPV of a call provision is zero, this questions can be answered with no calculations.

Problem 23: Gilliam will refund the callable bonds if the NPV is positive. Using a market interest rate of 8%:

PV (interest savings) = $101.62 / .08 = $1,270.25

Call premium = $120
NPV = ($1,270.25 - $120) = $1,150.25

⇒   They should refund the issue

Problem 24: Step 1: Calculate the present value of each payment:

PV (Pymt 1) = $100 / 1.10   = $ 90.9091
PV (Pymt 2) = $100 / (1.10)^2   =   82.6446
PV (Pymt 3) = $100 / (1.10)^3   =   75.1315
PV (Pymt 4) = $1,100 / (1.10)^4   =   751.3148

Step 2: Determine the relative weights

Pymt 1 = $90.9091 / $1,000   =   .090909
Pymt 2 = $82.6446 / $1,000   =   .082645
Pymt 3 = $75.1315 / $1,000   =   .075132
Pymt 4 = $751.3148 / $1,000 =   .751315

Step 3: Calculate the duration

Duration = 1 x .090909 + 2 x .082645 + 3 x .075132 + 4 x .751315 = 3.4869 years

Problem 25: Cost of Refunding:

Call premium:	$40,000,000 (.075)	$3,000,000

Flotation costs:
   Annual tax shield after tax: ($3,500,000/5)(.40) = $280,000

PV (tax shield): $280,000 (PVIFA 7%, 5) = $1,148,055.28
         Net flotation costs: $3,500,000 - $1,148,055.28 $2,351,944.72

Additional interest:
   Extra interest on old issue: $40,000,000 (.14)(1.5/12)(1 - .40) = $420,000
   Extra interest on new issue: $40,000,000 (.09)(1.5/12)(1 - .40) = $270,000
         Total additional interest $ 150,000
Total cost of refunding $5,501,944.72

Benefit of Refunding

    Extra interest on old issue: ($40,000,000)(.14) = $5,600,000

    Interest earned on new issue: ($40,000,000)(.1167) = $4,668,000

    Annual savings: $5,600,000 - $4,668,000 = $932,000

    After-tax savings: $932,000 (1 - .4) = $559,200

        PV (Interest savings) = $559,200 x PVIFA (7%, 25) $6,516,683.71

        NPV = $6,516,683.71   - $5,501,944.72 $1,014,738.99

NPV is positive, so Fundit Inc. should proceed with the refunding.

Problem 26: Cost of Refunding:

        Call premium: (.09% + .01% + .04%) $16,000,000 $2,240,000

    Flotation costs:

     Annual tax shield after tax: ($300,000/5)(.40) = $24,000

     PV(tax shield): $24,000 x PVIFA (8%, 5) = $95,825.04

        Total flotation costs: $300,000 - $95,825.04 $204,174.96

    Incremental interest

     Extra dividend on old issue: $16,000,000 (.12)(3/12) = $480,000

     Extra interest on new issue: $16,000,000(.06)(3/12)(1-.4) = $144,000.

        Total

                                $336,000.00

        Total cost of refunding $2,780,174.96

Benefit of refunding:

    Dividend savings: $16,000,000 (.12 - .10) = $320,000

        PV (savings): $320,000 / .08 $4,000,000

        NPV   = $4,000,000 - $2,780,174.96 $1,219,825.04

    Refund the old issue

8   Stock Valuation

CHAPTER HIGHLIGHTS

It is more difficult to value shares of common stock than to value bonds because (1) unlike bonds, the promised cash flows are not known in advance, (2) bonds have a fixed maturity date, but the life of a share of stock is essentially forever, and (3) there is no easy way to observe the return required by investors. This chapter discusses the estimation future cash flows and uses them to determine the value of shares of stock.

Common Share Cash Flows: Investors who purchase common shares expect returns either as dividends and/or future price appreciation.. It is not immediately apparent which cash flows are relevant for valuation. For example, an investor who plans to hold a share of stock for one year might compute the value of a share as follows:

$$P_0 \; = \; D_1 \, / \, (1+r) \; + \; P_1 \, / \, (1+r) \; = \; (D_1 + P_1) \, / \, (1+r) \qquad\qquad [8.1]$$

P_0 and P_1 are share prices today and one year from today, respectively. D_1 is next year's dividend. To determine the price of the share *next* year (P_1), the investor must calculate the present value, as of next year, of dividends and the future selling price to be realized in following years. However, any future selling price is the present value of all subsequent dividend payments. So, regardless of an investor's time horizon, *the value of a share of common stock is the present value of all future dividends*. Algebraically, this conclusion is represented as:

$$P_0 \; = \; D_1 / (1+r)^1 \; + \; D_2 / (1+r)^2 \; + \; D_3 / (1+r)^3 \; + \; D_4 / (1+r)^4 \; + \; \dots$$

It is virtually impossible to accurately forecast dividend payments far into the future. Consequently, in applying the present value approach to stock valuation, a simplifying assumption is generally made regarding the pattern of dividend payments. Alternative approaches to stock valuation are discussed in the next section.

8.1   COMMON STOCK VALUATION

Some Special Cases: There are three alternative, simplifying assumptions regarding the pattern of future dividend payments. They are:

(1)   zero growth in dividends, or constant dividends,
(2)   constant growth in dividends, and
(3)   nonconstant growth in dividends.

Zero growth: A stock with constant dividends (i.e. zero growth) is a perpetuity. The equation for valuing a zero growth stock is similar to the equation for valuing a perpetuity: $PV \; = \; C \, / \, r$. For valuing shares, the dividend payment is equivalent to the variable C in the perpetuity equation. So, the value of a share of stock is:

$$P_0 = \quad PV = D \, / \, r \;\; (D \text{ is the constant annual dividend; r is the required rate of return}) \qquad\qquad [8.2]$$

Example: Consider a preferred stock that pays an annual of $12. If the relevant opportunity cost is 12%, what is the value of a share of preferred stock? Using the equation for the present value of a perpetuity:

$$P_0 \; = \; D \, / \, r \; = \; \$12 \, / \, .12 \; = \; \$100 \qquad \text{This is the price of a share of the preferred stock}$$

Constant Growth: In some cases, the series of dividend payments a share of stock take the form of a *growing perpetuity*, as long as the size of the dividend payment increases at a constant rate. For example, an investor intends to purchase a share of Furillo Farms common stock, which has recently paid an annual dividend of $2 per share. The investor expects dividends to increase at the rate of 5% per year indefinitely. Next year's dividend is expected to be:

$$D_1 = D_0 \times (1 + g) = \$2 \times (1.05) = \$2.10$$

where D_0 and D_1 are the dividends this year and next year, respectively, and g is the annual growth rate in dividends. Similarly, the dividend expected two years from now (D_2) is:

$$D_2 = D_0 \times (1 + g)^2 = \$2 \times (1.05)^2 = \$2.21$$

and the dividend at any future date (D_t) is:

$$D_t = D_0 \times (1 + g)^t$$

If the appropriate opportunity cost is 12%, the present value calculation for Furillo Farms stock is:

$$P_0 = \$2 (1.05)^1 / (1.12)^1 + \$2 (1.05)^2 / (1.12)^2 + \$2 (1.05)^3 / (1.12)^3 + ... + \$2 (1.05)^t / (1.12)^t$$

In general, this formula is:

$$P_0 = D_0(1 + g)^1 / (1 + r)^1 + D_0(1 + g)^2 / (1 + r)^2 + D_0(1 + g)^3 / (1 + r)^3 + ... + D_0(1 + g)^t / (1 + r)^t$$

As long as r is greater than g, the above formula is equivalent to:

$$P_0 = D_0 (1 + g) / (r - g) = D_1 / (r - g) \qquad [8.3]$$

Applying this result to the Furillo Farms example above, the present value is:

$$P_0 = \$2 (1.05) / (.12 - .05) = \$30.00$$

Note: this result is the exact present value of the growing perpetuity; not an approximation of the present value.

Nonconstant Growth: The assumption of nonconstant (supernormal) growth is best illustrated with an example.

Suppose that Husky Corporation's dividend this year is $1.20 per share and that dividends will grow at 10% per year for the next three years, followed by 6% annual growth. The appropriate discount rate for Husky common stock is 12%. What is the value of a share of Husky Corporation common stock?

(1) Compute the present value of the first three dividend payments:

Year	Growth rate (g)	Expected dividend	Present value
1	10%	$1.3200	$1.1786
2	10%	$1.4520	$1.1575
3	10%	$1.5972	$1.1369
		PV:	$3.4730

(2) Compute dividend for *Year 4*, use it to calculate stock value in *Year 3*

$$D_4 = \$1.20 \times (1.10)^3 \times (1.06) = \$1.6930$$

$$P_3 = D_4 / (r - g) = \$1.6930 / (.12 - .06) = \$28.2167$$

In general, the stock price at any time t can be found using this equation:

$$P_t = D_{t+1} / (r - g) \qquad\qquad [8.4]$$

(3) Find the present value of Year 3 stock price

$$PV = \$28.2167 / (1.12)^3 = \$20.0841$$

(4) Compute the share value as the sum of *all* the present values

$$P_0 = (\$3.4730 + \$20.0841) = \$23.5571 \quad \text{or} \quad \$23.56.$$

i.e. The stock price today is the present value of the dividends for the next three years plus the present value of the expected stock price in year 3.

Components of the Required Return: This section demonstrates that the rate of return for an investment in a stock whose dividends grow at a constant rate can be thought of as having two components: a dividend component and a capital gains component. This result uses the constant growth model as a starting point: $P_0 = D_1 / (r - g)$

Solving for r: $r - g = D_1 / P_0 \rightarrow r = D_1 / P_0 + g$ \qquad\qquad [8.4]

The first component, D_1 / P_0, is referred to as the *dividend yield*. The second component, g, is the *capital gains yield*. From the Furillo Farms example, it was assumed that the company recently paid an annual dividend of $2 per share, that dividends would increase at the rate of 5% per year, and that the relevant opportunity cost is 12%. Given a 5% growth rate in dividends, what is the growth rate in the value of the common stock? For example, what is the price of the common stock four years from now, and what is the growth rate for the price of the stock?

To determine the value of P_4, compute the dividend to be paid in year 5 (D_5):

$$D_5 = D_0 \times (1 + g)^5 = \$2 \times (1.05)^5 = \$2.5526$$

Using the constant growth formula, P_4 is:

$$P_4 = D_5 / (r - g) = \$2.5526 / (.12 - .05) = \$36.47$$

What is the growth rate for Furillo Farms common stock? From the earlier example, $P_0 = \$30.00$. An increase in value from $30.00 to $36.47 over a four-year period is an annual growth rate of 5%, as shown below:

$$\$30.00 \times (1.05)^4 = \$36.47$$

Note that the stock price grows at the same rate as the dividend. In fact, for any time period, the capital gains yield, or the rate of growth in the price of the stock, is equal to the rate of growth of the dividends.

The required return for Furillo Farms was 12%, and the stock price was $30. From equation [8.5]:

$$r \;=\; D_1/P_0 \;+\; g \;=\; \$2.10\,/\,\$30 \;+\; 0.05 \;=\; .07 + .05 \;=\; .12 \;=\; 12\%$$

8.2   COMMON STOCK FEATURES

In general, *common stock* refers to a share that has no priority in either dividend payments or bankruptcy.

Shareholders' Rights: As the owners of the firm, shareholders essentially control the corporation through their right to elect the directors. This usually occurs at the annual shareholders meeting. Directors are elected by shareholder vote. Election requires winning the vote of the holders of a majority of shares present and entitled to vote. The mechanics of electing directors may vary from firm to firm.

Other Rights: In addition to the right to elect the directors, shareholders have three other primary rights:

1. The right to a proportionate share of dividends paid
2. The right to a proportionate share of assets remaining in a liquidation
3. The right to vote on important matters, usually at the annual meeting or a special meeting.

Sometimes shareholders have a *preemptive right*, the right to share proportionately in any new shares sold. If a firm wishes to issue new stock, they must first offer shares to the existing shareholders. This allows shareholders to protect their proportionate ownership position in the firm.

Dividends: Dividends provide shareholders with a return on the capital they have contributed to the corporation. Dividends are paid at the discretion of the board of directors. Important characteristics of dividends include:

1. Dividends are not a corporate liability until declared by the board of directors.
2. Dividends are *not* tax-deductible because they are not considered a business expense.
3. Individuals receive a dividend tax credit which partially shelters income received. This avoids the problem of double taxation discussed in Chapter 2.

Classes of Stock: Many firms have more than one class of common shares, typically with different voting rights. Some firms also issue *restricted stock*, which is non-voting. The main reason for dual classes of stock has to do with retaining control of the firm. Issuing shares with limited voting rights allows managers to raise equity capital without losing control of the firm.

8.3   PREFERRED STOCK FEATURES

Preferred stock differs from common stock in that preferred shareholders must be paid a stated dividend before dividends can be paid to common shareholders. If the firm liquidates, the claim of preferred shareholders has priority over that of common shareholders. Preferred shares usually do not have voting rights.

Stated Value: A preferred share normally has a stated liquidating value. The cash dividend is quoted either as dollars per share or as a percentage of the stated share value. For example, a share of preferred stock might be identified as an '$8 preferred,' indicating a dividend yield equal to 8% of the stated value.

Cumulative and Noncumulative Dividends: A corporation is not legally obligated to pay dividends on preferred stock. If dividends are *cumulative,* then any dividends not paid are accumulated, and the entire amount must be paid before any dividends on common stock can be paid. Usually, preferred shareholders are granted voting rights if some specified number of dividends have not been paid.

Is Preferred Stock Really Debt? In many ways, preferred stock resembles a perpetual bond. The dividend is fixed, and preferred shareholders receive a stated value in the event of liquidation. Preferred shares are often rated, as are bonds. In addition, preferred stock is frequently callable or convertible into common stock. In recent years, many preferred issues have also had sinking funds. This provision effectively creates a maturity date for the preferred stock since some portion of the original issue is retired each year. Preferred stock sometimes has "floating-rate" dividends. Corporations like to invest in preferred stock, however, because they pay "dividends" which are 100% tax-deductible. Firms pay a premium for this opportunity, so returns on preferred stock are typically low.

Preferred Stock and Taxes: However, preferred dividends are not tax-deductible for the issuing corporation, as is interest on a debt security. Corporations with low (or no) taxes, though, have no need of tax deductions. So, they can issue preferred shares and take advantage of the low yields, which translates into lower issuing costs. Since individual investors do not receive this exclusion, most preferred stock is held by corporations.

Beyond Taxes: The fact that the dividend is not deductible creates a tax disadvantage, relative to debt, for the issuing firms that have higher taxes. For many firms, this is a serious disadvantage. However, there are other reasons for a corporation to issue preferred shares. The most commonly cited reasons are:

1. Preferred stock, unlike debt, does not increase the firm's risk of bankruptcy.
2. Preferred shareholders do not have voting rights; firms can issue preferred shares without affecting control of the corporation.

8.4 STOCK MARKET REPORTING

If you look in a financial newspaper, you would see information on many stocks in different markets. Suppose you encounter the following in the *Globe and Mail:*

52 Week							
High	**Low**	**Stock**	**Div**	**High**	**Low**	**Close Change**	**Vol**
32 1/8	19 3/8	Cdn Pacific	.93	$23 5/8	23 ½	23 7/8 –3/8	258,641

The first two columns indicate the highest and lowest share prices during the last 52 weeks. The third column indicates the company (Canadian Pacific in our example). The Dividend Column indicates the annual cash dividend. The next three columns indicate the high, low, and closing (last) price for the day. Change indicates the difference between the quoted closing price and the closing price on the preceding day. In our case, closing price was down three-eighths (or $0.375) from the closing price of the previous trading day. Notice that shares are quoted in dollars and fractions down to 1/8 whereas bonds are quoted in dollars, percents and basis points. The volume column indicates the number of shares traded on the trading day reported.

Growth Opportunities: Suppose a company has a level stream of earnings in perpetuity and pays all earnings out as dividends. Therefore, EPS = Div (dividend per share). From the perpetuity formula, the value of a share is:

$$PV \ = \ EPS \,/\, r \ = \ Div \,/\, r$$

Now consider that many firms have growth opportunities, that is, opportunities to invest in profitable projects.

Since these investment projects can represent a significant fraction of the firm's value, it would be unwise to forego them in order to pay out all earnings as dividends.

Assume that the set of growth opportunities means investment in a single project and that the firm will retain the entire dividend at date 1 in order to invest in a particular project. If the net present value *per share* of the project as of date 0 is *NPVGO* (net present value,per share, of the growth opportunity), what is the price of a share at date 0 if the firm decides to take on the project at date 1? Because the per share value of the project is added to the original share price, the new share price (after the firm commits to the new project) must be:

$$P_0 = (EPS/r) + NPVGO$$

Therefore, the price of a share is equal to the value of the firm if it distributed all earnings to the shareholders (EPS/r) plus the *additional* value if the firm retains earnings in order to finance new projects.

Application - The Price Earnings Ratio: A common application of this equation is to the price earnings ratio. Dividing the above equation by EPS yields:

$$\frac{\text{Price per Share}}{\text{EPS}} = \frac{1}{r} + \frac{\text{NPVGO}}{\text{EPS}}$$

The left hand side is the P/E ratio which is obviously related to NPVGO. For example, assume two firms have EPS of $2 but only one of them has valuable growth opportunities. Consequently, the one with growth opportunities will sell at a higher price because an investor is buying both $2 income and growth opportunities. If this price is $24 and assuming a price of $16 for the firm with no growth opportunities, and since $2 appears in the denominator of the P/E ratio for both, the P/E is 12 for the firm with growth. ($24/$2) but only 8 for the firm without any opportunities ($16/$2).

Thus, investors who expect a higher growth in one firm over another explains why the higher growth firm will have a higher P/E ratio. Other factors causing a high P/E are low risk, a low discount rate, r, and conservative accounting.

Note however, that P/E ratios by themselves are not a shortcut for stock analysis, but should be followed up with cash flow analysis using the dividend valuation model.

CONCEPT TEST

1.   Theoretically, the value of a share of common stock is equal to the _____ of the future _____ to the holder of the stock. The relevant cash flows for a share of common stock are future _____ and future _____ value of a share.

2.   Application of the present value concept to common stock valuation is more difficult than for bond valuation because each of the following is unknown for a share of common stock: (1) future _____ payments (2) future _____ value; and (3) appropriate _____.

3.   Three alternative simplifying assumptions sometimes made for the purpose of common stock valuation are:(1) zero growth in dividends, or _____ dividends; (2) constant _____ in dividends; and, (3) _____ in dividends.

4.   The mathematics of a zero-growth stock are summarized by the equation: $P_0 = PV = $ _____.
      Alternatively, this equation can be expressed as D = _____ or r = _____.

5.   The mathematics of a constant-growth stock are summarized by the equation: $P_0 = PV = $ _____.

6.   The case of nonconstant growth requires the calculation of the _____ of several initial dividend
      payments and then the application of the equation for _____ to subsequent dividend payments.

7.   The rate of return for a _____ stock can be thought of as having two components: the dividend yield
      and the capital gains yield. The former is equal to _____ and the latter is equal to the _____.

8.   The capital gains yield is equal to the _____ because the rate at which the _____ of a constant
      growth stock increases is equal to the rate of growth in dividends.

9.   If a firm pays out all of its level, perpetual earnings as dividends, then the value of the stock is equal to
      _____ or _____. The firm with growth opportunities will have a stock price comprised of two
      components; _____ + _____. The firm with higher growth opportunities will also tend to have
      a higher _____ ratio.

10.   Because they are the owners of the firm, the shareholders have the right to _____ the _____ of
      the firm.

11.   Three other rights important to shareholders are: the right to share _____ in _____ paid;
      the right to share _____ in remaining assets after a _____ ; and the right to _____
      on matters of _____ at either the annual or a special meeting.

12.   The right stating that firms must first offer any new equity issue to existing shareholders it called the
      _____ . This allows shareholders to protect their _____ in the firm.

13.   Dividends do not become a _____ of the corporation until they have been _____ by the
      board of directors.

14.   Unlike interest payments, dividends paid are not _____ . This is because they are not considered
      to be a _____ .

15.   Dividend payments to individuals are partially sheltered by a _____ . This is to avoid the problem
      of _____ associated with dividend payments.

16.   The primary reason firms issue dual classes of stock is so that they can _____ without
      _____ of the firm.

17.   Preferred shareholders must be paid a _____ dividend before _____ can be paid to
      _____ shareholders , and preferred shareholders have preference over _____
      shareholders to the _____ value of assets following _____ of the company.

18.   A corporation (is/is not) legally obligated to pay dividends on preferred stock. If dividends are
      _____ , then any dividends not paid are accumulated. The entire amount must be paid before any
      dividends on common stock can be paid.

19.   In many ways, preferred stock resembles a _____ bond. For example, the dividend is _____ and preferred shareholders receive a _____ value in the event of _____ .

20.   On the other hand, the preferred dividend (is/is not) tax-deductible for the issuing corporation.

PROBLEMS

Basic Questions

Problem 1

Security analysts have forecasted the dividends of Hodges Enterprises for the next 3 years as: $D_1 = \$1.50$; $D_2 = \$1.75$; $D_3 = \$2.20$. The forecasted selling price in 3 years is $48.50. The rate of return for common stock with a risk level comparable to that of Hodges Enterprises is 14%. What is the value of Hodges common stock?

Problem 2

A share of TTK Corporation preferred stock pays a $10 annual dividend. What is the price of a share of TTK preferred stock if preferred stock with comparable risk has a yield of 8%? What is the price if comparable preferred stock has a yield of 11%?

Problem 3

If a share pays a constant annual dividend of $10 and is selling for $50, what is the rate of the return for the share? What if the share price changes to $65?

Problem 4

A share of preferred stock with a $12 annual dividend is selling for $75. What is the rate of return?

Problem 5

Hilliard, Inc. has just paid a $2 annual dividend on its common stock. The dividend is expected to increase at a constant rate of 8% per year indefinitely. If the required return on Hilliard's stock is 16%, what is its current value?

Problem 6

Jeff is considering buying shares in PMG Corporation. PMG has just paid dividends of $2.25 per share. Dividends are expected to grow at a constant annual rate of 5%. What would Jeff be willing to pay for a share of PMG? The market rate of interest is 10%.

Intermediate Questions

Problem 7

The dividend just paid on a share of common stock is $10. If grow at a 5% rate for the foreseeable future, and that the required rate of return is 10%, what is the value of the share today? Last year $(t-1)$? Next year $(t+1)$?

Problem 8

The current price of a share (P_0) is $20 and last year's price (P_{-1}) was $18.87. This year's dividend (D_0) is $2. Assume a constant growth rate (g) in dividends and share price. What is the rate of return for the coming year?

Problem 9

The current year's dividend (D_0) for a share of common stock is $2 and the current share price (P_0) is $30. Dividends are expected to grow at a 5% rate for the foreseeable future. What is the current rate of return for this stock? What is the capital gain (or loss) on the stock over the past year if the required rate of return was 10% last year?

Problem 10

Pettway Corporation's next annual dividend (D_1) is expected to be $4. The growth rate in dividends over the following three years is forecasted at 15%. After that, Pettway's growth rate is anticipated to be equal to the industry average of 5%. If the required rate of return is 18%, what is the current value of the stock?

Challenge Questions

Problem 11

A company pays a current dividend (D_0) of $1.20 per share on its common stock. The annual dividend will increase by 3%, 4%, and 5%, respectively, over the next three years, and then by 6% per year thereafter. The appropriate discount rate is 12%. What is the current price of the stock? What is the capital gain (or loss) on the stock over the past year?

Problem 12

JPH Corporation has just signed a large deal with one of its customers. Dividends are expected to grow at rates of 10%, 15%, and 20% over the next three years. The fourth year and all following years, growth is expected to be 10%. If Pat is interested in purchasing 20 shares of JPH, how much would he be willing to pay if the market rate of interest is 12% and JPH has just paid dividends of $2.00 per share?

Problem 13

A company's dividend this year is $2.25 per share, and dividends are expected to grow at 12% for the next four years and at 5% indefinitely after that. If the firm's discount rate is 8%, what is the value of one share today?

Problem 14

The NoCanDo Company has been hit hard due to increased competition. The company's analysts predict that earnings (and dividends) will decline at a rate of 5% annually for an indefinite period of time. Assume that the required return consists of a 3 % dividend yield and 8 % capital gain components, and that the most recent dividend per share was $2.00. What will be the price of the company's stock in three years?

ANSWERS TO CONCEPT TEST

1.   present value; cash payments; dividends; market

2.   dividend; market; opportunity cost

3.   constant; growth; nonconstant growth

4.   D/r; PV×r (or P_0/r) ; D/PV (or D/P_0)

5. D_1 / (r–g)

6.   present value; constant growth

7.   constant growth; (D_1/P_0); dividend growth rate

8.   dividend growth rate; price

9.   EPS/r; Div/r; EPS/r; NPVGO; P/E

10.   elect; directors

11.   proportionately; dividends ; proportionately; liquidation; vote; importance

12.   preemptive right; proportionate ownership

13.   liability; declared

14.   tax-deductible; business expense

15.   dividend tax credit; double taxation

16.   raise equity capital; losing control

17.   stated; dividends; common; common; residual; liquidation

18.   is not; cumulative

19.   perpetual; fixed; stated; liquidation

20.   is not

SOLUTIONS TO PROBLEMS

Problem 1: $P_0 = \dfrac{D_1}{(1+r)^1} + \dfrac{D_2}{(1+r)^2} + \dfrac{D_3}{(1+r)^3} + \dfrac{P_3}{(1+r)^3}$

$= \dfrac{\$1.50}{(1.14)^1} + \dfrac{\$1.75}{(1.14)^2} + \dfrac{\$2.20}{(1.14)^3} + \dfrac{\$48.50}{(1.14)^3} = \$36.88 =$ stock price

Problem 2:   At an 8% yield: $P_0 \quad = \quad D/r \quad = \quad \$10/.08 \quad = \quad \$125$

At an 11% yield: $P_0 \quad = \quad D/r \quad = \quad \$10/.11 \quad = \quad \$90.91$

Problem 3: $P_0 = D/r$ can be rearranged as: $r = D/P_0 \quad \rightarrow \quad r \quad = \quad \$10/\$50 \quad = \quad 0.20 \quad = \quad 20\%$

Problem 4: $P_0 \quad = \quad D/r, \quad \rightarrow \quad \$75 \quad = \quad \$12/r \quad \rightarrow \quad r \quad = \quad .16 \quad = \quad 16\%.$

Problem 5: $D_1 \quad = \quad \$2.00 \times 1.08 \quad = \quad \$2.16$

$P_0 \quad = \quad D_1/(r-g) \quad = \quad \$2.16/(.16-.08) \quad = \quad \$2.16/.08 \quad = \quad \$27.00$

Problem 6: $P_0 \quad = \quad D_0(1+g)/(r-g) \quad = \quad (\$2.25 \times 1.05)/(0.10-0.05) \quad = \quad \$2.36/0.05 \quad = \quad \$47.20$

Problem 7:   Today: $P_0 \quad = \quad D_1/(.10-.05) \quad = \quad \$10 \times (1.05)/.05 \quad = \quad \$210$

Last year: $P_{-1} \quad = \quad D_0/(.10-.05) \quad = \quad \$10/.05 \quad = \quad \$200$

Next year: $P_1 \quad = \quad D_2/(.10-.05) \quad = \quad \$10(1.05)^2/.05 \quad = \quad \$220.50$

Notice that the price increases at the same growth rate that the dividends increase.

Problem 8:   This problem can be solved by finding the solution for r in the following equation:

$$P_0 \quad = \quad \frac{D_1}{r-g}, \quad \text{so} \quad r \quad = \quad \frac{D_1}{P_0} \quad + \quad g$$

We know that $P_0 = \$20$. We can determine the values of both g and D_1 from the information given. The growth rate for dividends is the same as the growth rate for share price. Solve for g in the following equation:

$$P_0 \quad = \quad P_{-1} \times (1+g) \rightarrow \$20 = \$18.87 \times (1+g) \rightarrow \quad g = \$20/\$18.87 - 1 = 05988 = 6\%$$

$$\rightarrow \quad D_1 \quad = \quad \$2 \times 1.06 \quad = \quad \$2.12 \quad \rightarrow \quad r \quad = \quad D_1/P_0 + g \quad = \quad \$2.12/\$20 + .06 \quad \rightarrow \quad r = 16.6\%$$

Problem 9: $r \quad = \quad D_1/P_0 \quad + \quad g \quad = \quad \$2.00(1.05)/\$30 \quad + \quad .05 \quad = \quad .07 + .05 \quad = \quad 12\%$

To compute the capital gain, find the stock price the previous year (P_{-1}):

$$P_{-1} \quad = \quad D_0/(r-g) \quad = \quad \$2.00/(.10-.05) \quad = \quad \$40$$

$$\text{Capital gain} \quad = \quad P_0 - P_{-1} \quad = \quad \$30 - \$40 \quad = \quad -\$10 \quad \text{**** so this is actually a capital loss}$$

Problem 10: The current value of the stock is equal to the present value of the dividends from the high growth phase plus the present value of the share price when the high growth phase ends. Notice that the next dividend (D_1) is forecasted at $4. Calculate the present value of the first four dividend payments as follows:

Year	Growth rate (g)	Expected dividend	Present value
1	15%	$4.000	$3.3898
2	15%	$4.600	$3.3036
3	15%	$5.290	$3.2197
4	15%	$6.084	$3.1381

Total of present values for dividends in Years 1 - 4 $13.0512

Now, calculate the dividend for year 5; use that amount to calculate the value of the share in year 4.

$$D_5 = \$4 \times (1.15)^3 \times (1.05) = \$6.39$$

$$\rightarrow \quad P_4 = D_5 / (r - g) = \$6.39 / (.18 - .05) = \$49.15$$

$$PV(P_4) = \$49.15 / (1.18^4) = \$25.35.$$

Add PV(dividends) + PV (Year 4 stock price)   = $25.34 + $13.05   = $38.39   =   current stock price

Problem 11: Today's stock price is determined as follows:

$$D_1 = \$1.20 \times (1.03) = \$1.24$$
$$D_2 = \$1.20 \times (1.03) \times (1.04) = \$1.29$$
$$D_3 = \$1.20 \times (1.03) \times (1.04) \times (1.05) = \$1.35$$

$$P_3 = D_4 / (r - g) = \$1.35 (1.06) / (.12 - .06) = \$23.85$$

$$(P_0) = PV (3 \text{ dividends}) + PV (P_3) \text{ discounted at } 12\% \quad \rightarrow \quad P_0 = \$20.06$$

To find the capital gain:

Discount P_0 for 1 year at 12% : $PV(P_0) = \$20.06 / 1.12 = \$17.91$

Discount D_0 for 1 year at 12%: $PV(D_0) = \$1.20 / 1.12 = \$1.07$

$$P_{-1} = \$17.91 + \$1.07 = \$18.98 \quad \rightarrow \quad \text{Capital gain} = \$20.06 - \$18.98 = \$1.08.$$

Problem 12: Dividends for the next 4 years are:

$$D_1 = \$2.00 \times 1.10 = \$2.20$$
$$D_2 = \$2.00 \times 1.10 \times 1.15 = \$2.53$$
$$D_3 = \$2.00 \times 1.10 \times 1.15 \times 1.20 = \$3.04$$
$$D_4 = \$2.00 \times 1.10 \times 1.15 \times 1.20 \times 1.10 = \$3.34$$

$$P_3 = \$3.32 / (.12 - .10) = \$167$$

$$\rightarrow \quad P_0 = PV (\text{dividends} + \text{year 3 price}) = \$125.02$$

Pat will pay 20 x $125.02   = $2,500.40 for 20 shares.

Problem 13: PV (dividend payments):

Year 1: expected dividend = $2.5200; PV = $2.3333
Year 2: expected dividend = $2.8224; PV = $2.4198
Year 3: expected dividend = $3.1611; PV = $2.5094
Year 4: expected dividend = $3.5404; PV = $2.6023

PV at 8% = $9.86

P_4 = $D_5 / (r - g)$ = $3.7174 / (.08 - .05) = $123.91

PV at 8% = $123.91 / (1.08)^4$ = $91.08

$\rightarrow P_0$ = $9.8648 + $91.08 = $100.94.

Problem 14: D_4 = $2.00 (1 - .95)^4$ = $1.63

P_3 = $1.63/ [.11 - (-.05)] = $10.19

9   <u>Net Present Value and Other Investment Criteria</u>

CHAPTER HIGHLIGHTS

Many of the criteria used for capital budgeting decision-making are discussed in this chapter. The criteria analyzed include: net present value, the payback period, the discounted payback period, the average accounting return, the internal rate of return, and the profitability index. Our major conclusion is that net present value (NPV) is unequivocally the appropriate criterion for capital budgeting decisions. Consequently, we begin with a discussion of net present value and then compare each of the alternative approaches to the present value. Each of the alternative criteria is deficient in some important ways. However, we must consider these alternatives and understand their deficiencies because they are used in practice.

9.1   <u>NET PRESENT VALUE</u>

The chapter demonstrates that the use of the net present value criterion in making capital budgeting decisions is consistent with the goal of financial managers examined in Chapter 1. That is, the manager who uses the net present value criterion in making capital budgeting decisions is maximizing the current price of the firm's common shares.

The Basic Idea: Consider an investment in an asset (e.g., a piece of real estate) for a price of $2,000. Assume that the asset can be sold for $2,500 one year from today. Alternatively, the investor has the opportunity to earn an 8% rate of return on an investment of similar risk. To decide whether to acquire the real estate, we compare the acquisition of the asset vs. the investment at 8%. The comparison may be based on: (1) future value; (2) present value; or (3) rate of return. Comparisons based on future value and present value are below. The use of rate of return for decision-making is discussed later in the chapter.

Again, the investor's options are to: (1) invest $2,000 at 8% for one year, or (2) invest $2,000 to acquire the real estate today, receiving $2,500 in one year. If he selects the first alternative, then one year from today he will receive:

$$FV_1 \ = \ PV \times (1 + r) \ = \ \$2,000 \times (1 + .08) \ = \ \$2,160$$

Clearly, alternative (2) is preferable since the investor will have $2,500, rather than $2,160, one year from today. Therefore, the investor should acquire the real estate today for $2,000.

The investment opportunities can also be compared using present value analysis. The investor must answer this question: At an 8% opportunity cost, what deposit must be made today in order to receive $2,500 in one year? Using the present value equation developed in Chapter 5:

$$PV \ = \ FV / (1 + r) \ = \ \$2,500 / (1.08) \ = \ \$2,314.81$$

At the 8% opportunity cost, $2,314.81 invested today in a one-year certificate of deposit will return $2,500 in one year. Consequently, the investor would select the real estate investment opportunity that only costs $2,000 but still returns $2,500 in one year.

The present value approach to investment decision-making can also be described in terms of the difference between the present value of the investment (i.e., $2,314.81 in the above example) and the cost of the investment ($2,000).

This difference ($314.81 in this example) is called the *net present value*. The NPV for this example is:

$$NPV \quad = \quad PV - Cost \quad = \quad \$2,314.81 - \$2,000 \quad = \quad \$314.81$$

NPV not only provides a criterion for determining whether an investment is acceptable, but it is also an unambiguous measure of the value of the investment. Note that the investor could sell the real estate for $2,314.81 immediately after purchasing it. The $2,314.81 represents the market value of the asset. Thus, the NPV is the difference between an investment's market value and its cost. An investment with a positive NPV provides a net benefit equal to the NPV; an investment with a negative net present value is unacceptable.

The above interpretation of NPV applies to corporate investment decision-making as well. This is demonstrated by the following simplified example.

Example: Suppose you want to form a corporation with a one-year life. The corporation is being formed in order to acquire an asset costing $200,000; it can be sold in one year $250,000. You would like to convince each of 100 investors (including yourself) to purchase a share in this corporation for $2,000. Since each investor is a 1% owner, each investor would then receive 1% of $250,000, or $2,500, one year from now. Assume that the market rate of interest is 8%. Is this investment opportunity attractive to potential investors?

$$PV \quad = \quad \$250,000 / (1.08) \quad = \quad \$231,481.48$$

The entire corporation consists of this one asset; the $231,481.48 is thus the value of the corporation once the asset is purchased. An investor who purchases one share for $2,000 and then immediately sells the share in the financial market will be able to sell his share for $2,314.81. This is 1% of the value of the firm ($.01 \times \$231,481.48$), and also the present value of 1% of the $250,000 future value of the asset:

$$PV \quad = \quad \$250,000 \, (.01) / (1.08) = \$2,314.81$$

The NPV of one share is the difference between the present value and the cost of a share:

$$NPV \quad = \quad \$2,314.81 - \$2,000 \quad = \quad \$314.81$$

This example demonstrates that corporate investments with positive NPVs provide a net benefit to the shareholder equal to his proportionate share of the NPV of the corporate investment. Investments with positive NPVs, provide value to the shareholders. Consequently, the NPV criterion indicates that corporate financial managers should seek to maximize the current share value by choosing investments with positive net present value.

Estimating Net Present Value - An Example: The example below further develops some aspects of the net present value concept introduced in the previous section.

Campanella Construction, Inc. is considering buying new construction equipment. Management estimates that the equipment will cost $10,000 and will increase the firm's cash revenues by $9,000 per year for each of the next two years. Cash expenses, however, will increase by $4,000 per year, including labour costs and additional income taxes. (Depreciation is not a cash expense and is not included here; it is discussed in Chapter 10). The equipment is expected to have a useful life of two years; the expected salvage at the end of two years is $3,000. Assuming an opportunity cost of 12%, should Campanella invest in the new equipment?

When calculating NPV, it is critical that only *incremental* cash flows are used in the analysis. That is, the difference between any cash flow increases and any cash flow decreases (or revenue increases – cost increases). The net cash inflow to Campanella is expected to be ($9,000 – $4,000) = $5,000 per year for each of the next two years. In addition, Campanella expects to be able to sell the equipment for $3,000 at the end of the two-year life of the asset. Therefore, the relevant cash inflows are $5,000 at the end of the first year and $8,000 at the end of the second year. Next, compute the present value of the cash inflows, using the 12% discount rate specified above:

$$PV = \$5,000 / 1.12 + (\$5,000 + \$3,000) / (1.12)^2 = \$4,464.29 + \$6,377.55 = \$10,841.84$$

So, Campanella needs to invest $10,841.84 at the 12% market interest rate in order to receive payments of $5,000 and $8,000 in year 1 and 2, respectively. Since Campanella has the opportunity to invest only $10,000 in the new equipment to receive the same cash inflows, the latter alternative is clearly preferable to the market alternative.

The difference between the present value calculated above ($10,841.84) and the $10,000 cost of the asset is the net present value of the asset ($841.84). In the earlier example, it was assumed that the acquired asset represented the total assets of the firm. However, NPV analysis applies even in cases where a given investment represents only a portion of a firm's assets. The acquisition of *any* asset with a positive NPV increases the amount that prospective investors would be willing to pay to acquire ownership in the firm. The net benefit of this increased value accrues to the existing shareholders of the firm. For each shareholder, the net benefit is equal to his/her proportionate share of the NPV of the corporate investment.

Algebraically, the net present value calculation for this example can be summarized as follows:

$$NPV = -C_0 + C_1 / (1 + r)^1 + C_2 / (1 + r)^2$$

where C_0 is the initial $10,000 outlay, C_1 is the $5,000 payment one year from now, C_2 is the $8,000 payment two years from now and r is the 12% market interest rate. The more general formula for net present value is:

$$NPV = -C_0 + C_1 / (1 + r)^1 + C_2 / (1 + r)^2 + ... + C_t / (1 + r)^t$$

where t represents the last period during which a payment is received.

To summarize the NPV rule, *an investment should be accepted if the NPV is positive and rejected if it is negative.*

9.2   THE PAYBACK RULE

The *payback period* is the length of time required to recover the initial investment for a capital budgeting project. The payback period is easy to calculate. The payback period rule is simple to apply, but it has several major deficiencies which generally make it an inappropriate criterion for capital budgeting decisions.

Defining the Rule: The *payback period rule* specifies that an investment is acceptable if the sum of its undiscounted cash flows equals the initial investment before some specified cutoff time period.

Example: An investment expects the following cash flows: an initial investment of $10,000, and cash inflows of $2,000, $5,000, $3,000, and $6,000 at the end of years 1, 2, 3 and 4, respectively. What is the payback period? According to the payback period rule, should the investment be accepted?

The initial investment is $10,000. After three years, the sum of the cash inflows equals $10,000, so the payback period for this investment is three years. Consequently, this investment would be rejected if the cutoff time period were, for example, two years. Managers would accept the project if their cutoff date was greater than three years.

If the initial investment was $13,000 instead of $10,000, what is the payback?   Clearly, another $3,000 must be recovered in the fourth year during which the cash inflow is $6,000. To figure out the fractional year, divide $3,000 by $6,000 (=.50). So, the payback is 3.50 years. Note: the payback rule assumes that the cash inflows and outflows occur at a *constant rate throughout the year.*

Analyzing the Payback Period Rule: The deficiencies of the payback rule are:

1.   The timing of cash flows within the payback period is ignored, thereby treating all cash flows as equally valuable; NPV properly discounts these cash flows.
2.   All cash flows after the cutoff time period are ignored; NPV considers all cash flows.
3.   There is no objective criterion for choosing the cutoff time period (i.e. it is subjective); the NPV criterion is based on market interest rates and the creation of wealth.

The primary advantage of the payback rule is its simplicity; it is both easy to compute and easy to understand. It is often used in practice for making low-level, relatively small investment decisions.

The Discounted Payback Rule: The *discounted payback period rule* specifies that a project is acceptable if the sum of the *discounted* cash flows equals the initial investment before a specified cutoff time period. This rule is identical to the payback period rule except that the time value of money is considered because the cash flows are discounted.

Example: Using the cash flow data from the preceding problem and a 10% discount rate, would the investment be acceptable for a company that requires a discounted payback period of three years?

The sum of the discounted cash flows is the present value of the future cash inflows. For years 1 - 3, the sum is $8,204.35; for year 4, it is $12,302.44. Therefore, the discounted payback period is between three and four years, and it would be rejected because the cutoff is 3 years. The exact discounted payback is (3 + $1795.65 / $4098.08) = 3.44 years. The fractional year is computed by dividing the amount needed to be recovered in the fourth year, [($10,000 - $8,204.35 = $1,795.64] by the present value of year 4's cash flow: [$6,000/(1.1)^4] = $4098.08. Notice that the NPV is positive: ($12,302.44 – $10,000) = $2,302.44. The investment should have been accepted.

The discounted payback period rule may appear preferable to the payback period rule because cash flows are discounted. However, two of the three deficiencies of the payback period criterion also apply to the discounted payback period. Cash flows after the cutoff period are ignored, and the choice of cutoff period is subjective. Consequently, discounted payback lacks the simplicity of the simple payback method and is still inferior to NPV.

9.3   THE AVERAGE ACCOUNTING RETURN

The *average accounting return* (AAR) is defined as average net income attributed to an investment divided by the average book value of the asset. The *average accounting return rule* specifies that an investment is acceptable if its average accounting return exceeds a specified target level.

Example: Suppose the cash inflow data of the preceding problems represent accounting net income rather than cash flows. What is the average accounting return? According to the average accounting return criterion, is the capital budgeting project acceptable?

The average net income is:

$$(\$2,000 + \$5,000 + \$3,000 + \$6,000) / 4 \quad = \quad \$4,000$$

If the \$10,000 investment is depreciated to a value of zero, on a straight-line basis, over four years, the book value decreases by (\$10,000/4) = \$2,500 per year. The average book value is:

$$(\$10,000 + \$7,500 + \$5,000 + \$2,500 + \$0) / 5 \quad = \quad \$5,000$$

Note that even though the asset is depreciated over a four-year period, the average book value is the average of five observations, beginning with the year 0 book value, and ending with the year 4 book value. So, if an asset will be fully depreciated over the project's life, the average book value is always the investment divided by 2.

$$AAR \quad = \quad \text{Avg. Net Income / Avg. Book Value} \quad = \quad \$4,000 / \$5,000 \quad = \quad 80\%$$

The project is acceptable if the firm's target AAR is less than 80%.

The AAR rule has several serious deficiencies:

1. It uses accounting income and book value data, which generally are not closely related to cash flows
2. It ignores the time value of money. Income received in three years, for example, is treated as equivalent to income received in one year.
3. The target AAR is arbitrary specified because it is not a rate of return in the financial market sense.

The redeeming features of the AAR rule are that it is easy to calculate and that the needed information is almost always available. Nevertheless, these features do not compensate for the disadvantages of this method.

9.4   THE INTERNAL RATE OF RETURN

The *internal rate of return* (IRR) criterion is the most significant alternative to the net present value criterion. For any investment, the IRR is the rate of return (or discount rate) which equates the present value of the cash inflows with the cash outlay, or cost, of the investment. In other words, the IRR is the unique discount rate that makes the NPV of an investment zero. Alternatively, the IRR is defined as the rate of return for an investment. Algebraically, the IRR is the solution for the discount rate in the following equation:

$$NPV \quad = \quad 0 \quad = \quad -C_0 \ + \ C_1 / (IRR)^1 \ + \ C_2 / (1 + IRR)^2 \ + \ ... + \ C_t / (1 + IRR)t$$

Example: Consider the investment described earlier in this chapter; the cash outlay (C_0) is \$10,000, and the cash inflows are $C_1 = \$2,000$, $C_2 = \$5,000$, $C_3 = \$3,000$, $C_4 = \$6,000$. What is the IRR for this investment?

To calculate the IRR, substitute the known C_i values into the above equation:

$$NPV = 0 = -\$10,000 \ + \ \$2,000/(1 + IRR)^1 \ + \ \$5,000/(1 + IRR)^2 \ + \ \$3,000/(1 + IRR)^3 \ + \ \$6,000/(1 + IRR)^4$$

or

$$\$10,000 = \$2,000/(1 + IRR)^1 \ + \ \$5,000/(1 + IRR)^2 \ + \ \$3,000/(1 + IRR)^3 \ + \ \$6,000/(1 + IRR)^4$$

Solving this equation for r is equivalent to solving for the yield to maturity of a level coupon bond, as discussed in Chapter 7. The value of r can be determined by using either trial-and-error or a financial calculator.

Using trial-and-error, a first 'guess' might be IRR is 5%. To determine whether the guess is correct, find the present value of the cash inflows, discounted at 5%:

$$\$2,000/(1.05)^1 + \$5,000/(1.05)^2 + \$3,000/(1.05)^3 + \$6,000/(1.05)^4 = \$13,967.64$$

The present value is greater than C_0, (\$10,0000), so the IRR must be greater than 5% (i.e. we have not discounted the cash flows enough).

$$\text{At } 10\%: \$2,000/(1.10)^1 + \$5,000/(1.10)^2 + \$3,000/(1.10)^3 + \$6,000/(1.10)^4 = \$12,302.44$$

Again, the discount rate is too low. Actually is appears that the IRR must be substantially greater than 10%.

$$\text{At } 20\%: \$2,000/(1.20)^1 + \$5,000/(1.20)^2 + \$3,000/(1.20)^3 + \$6,000/(1.20)^4 = \$9,768.52$$

The IRR is between 10% and 20% and closer to 20%. Using discount rates of 18% and 19%, the present values are \$10,206.46 and \$9,983.76, respectively, so the IRR is between 18% and 19%. At   18.5%, the present value is \$10,094.16. Therefore, the IRR is between 18.5% and 19%. This procedure can be continued until the desired degree of accuracy is reached, but the trial-and-error process is both tedious and time consuming. An accurate solution can be reached quickly with a financial calculator; the IRRto is 18.9259%. If you use a financial calculator, read the instruction manual for examples of how to work these problems on your particular calculator. **Be sure you know how to use the calculator before an exam.**

In part, the appeal of IRR is that it is fairly simple to apply and understand the criterion. An investment project is acceptable if the IRR is greater than the rate of return the firm could earn on investments of equal risk. An investment project is unacceptable if the IRR is less than the rate of return required by the firm.

A useful tool in understanding the relationship between NPV and IRR is the *net present value profile* for a given investment opportunity. The NPV profile summarizes the relationship between the discount rate (r) and the NPV of the investment.

Clearly, as the discount rate increases, the NPV decreases. The IRR is the value of r for which the NPV is zero.

The NPV profile illustrates the reason why, under certain circumstances, the IRR and the NPV criteria lead to identical decisions regarding the acceptability of an investment. If the IRR for a particular investment is greater than the required rate of return, the following conclusions apply:

1.   According to the IRR criterion, the investment is acceptable
2.   The NPV discounted at the required rate of return is positive (i.e. on the NPV profile, NPV is positive for any discount rate less than the IRR)
3.   The investment is also acceptable according to the NPV criterion
4.   The same conclusion applies when the IRR is less than the required rate of return. That is, both criteria indicate that the investment is unacceptable.

Problems with the IRR: The above discussion seems to imply that the IRR criterion is equivalent to the NPV criterion in its ability to identify acceptable investments. However, under certain circumstances, the IRR criterion does not correctly indicate whether an investment is acceptable. Problems with applying the IRR criterion are associated with the following situations: nonconventional cash flows and mutually exclusive investments. These situations are analyzed below.

Nonconventional Cash Flows: Projects with *conventional* cash flows have either (1) a negative cash flow(s) followed by positive cash flows, or (2) a positive cash flow(s) followed by negative cash flows. *There is only one sign change in the cash flow stream* (i.e from negative to positive or vice versa). A *nonconventional* series of cash flows changes sign (from negative to positive, vice versa) more than once.

Consider the following cash flows for an investment: (–$80, $500, –$500). NPV is calculated as:

$$\text{NPV} = -\$80 + \$500/(1+\text{IRR})^1 - \$500/(1+\text{IRR})^2$$

To find the IRR, the equation must be solved for the value of r at which the NPV equals zero. The NPV for this series of cash flows is zero when the discount rate is 25%, - *but is also zero at a discount rate of over 400%.* There are two internal rates of return. This is an example of the *multiple rates of return* problem. Since there is no basis for choosing either one of these rates as the relevant IRR for such an investment, it is impossible to apply the IRR criterion when cash flows change sign more than once. In such cases, NPV must be used as the decision rule.

Mutually Exclusive Investments: An *independent investment project* is an investment whose acceptance or rejection does not affect, and is not affected by, the acceptance or rejection of any other projects. A set of *mutually exclusive investment projects* is a set of projects for which the acceptance of any one project in the set implies the rejection of all other projects in the set. For example, a company which is considering the purchase of a delivery truck may have under consideration numerous models produced by several manufacturers. Since only one truck will be purchased, the alternatives under consideration comprise a set of mutually exclusive investments.

The difficulties encountered in applying the IRR criterion to mutually exclusive projects arise when the projects being compared differ with respect to either (1) project scale or (2) timing of cash flows. In the former case, there are differences in the size of the initial outlay for the projects under consideration. In the latter case, the differences are generally between one project whose cash flows are concentrated in the early years of the project's life and another project whose cash flows are concentrated in the later years. The scale problem is discussed in detail here.

Consider two mutually exclusive investments, X and Y, with the following respective cash flows:

X: (–$200, $100, $300, $400)
Y: (–$5,000, $4,000, $1,000, $2,000)

Project X requires an outlay of $200 today and for returns $100, $300 and $400 in Years 1, 2 and 3, respectively. The two investments differ in scale because the cash flows for Y are substantially larger than those for X. Further, suppose that the relevant opportunity cost is 10%. Since these investments are mutually exclusive, we must determine

1.   Whether either investment is acceptable
2.   If both are acceptable, which is preferable

At the 10% discount rate, the NPVs are $439.37 and $965.44 for X and Y, respectively, so both investments are acceptable. The internal rates of return are 87.20% and 22.81%. X has the higher IRR while Y has the higher NPV, so that it is not immediately apparent which is the preferable alternative.

Remember that NPV analysis provides managers with the change in firm value because of its investment decision; it also provides shareholders with clear information about how the decision will affect the value of their shares. Given those conclusions, it is clear that Y is the preferable alternative, because firm value (and , hence, shareholder value) increases more with this investment.

To understand why the IRR criterion can sometimes be misleading, the choice between X and Y is often analysed in terms of the *cross-over rate*. This analysis is based on the *incremental* cash flows that investors would receive from investing in Y, rather than X (i.e. the difference in cash flows from Y - X). (Y–X) requires an additional ($5,000 – $200) = $4,800 be invested and will generate incremental cash flows of $3,900 $700, and $1,600.

$$NPV(Y\text{-}X) \quad = \quad \text{-}\$4,800 \quad + \quad \$3,900 / (1.10)^1 \quad + \quad \$700 / (1.10)^2 / \quad + \quad \$1,600 / (1.10)^3 \quad = \quad \$526.07$$

From above, X was an acceptable project if treated independently, based on both NPV and IRR. In addition, the project (Y - X) is also acceptable; the NPV = $526.07 and the IRR = 17/70%. These results show that both X and (Y–X) are acceptable. Viewed in this way, accepting project Y amounts to accepting project X plus another acceptable investment (Y–X). Therefore, Y is the preferable alternative.

The internal rate of return for (Y–X) is referred to as the *cross-over rate*. In this example and as shown in the figure below, it indicates that we are indifferent between investments X and Y if the opportunity cost is equal to the 17.70% cross-over rate. If the opportunity cost is less than the cross-over rate, then investment Y is preferable; if the opportunity cost is greater than the cross-over rate, then investment X is preferable.

The timing problem mentioned at the beginning of this section occurs when two investments requiring the same initial outlay differ substantially in terms of the timing of the cash inflows. That is, the larger cash inflows for one investment occur early in the life of the asset, while the larger inflows for the other occur later; or in the case when two projects have different lives. As is the case for the scale problem, it is possible that the IRR criterion will mislead the decision-maker into selecting the less desirable alternative. As described above for the scale problem, this can be avoided by: (1) applying the NPV criterion; or, (2) comparing the incremental IRR with the required rate of return.

Redeeming Qualities of the IRR: Although NPV is the superior tool for analysing investment opportunities, IRR is actually more widely used. This is largely because investors and financial analysts prefer to discuss rates of return; this is a concept most people are familiar with. In addition, IRR is an easily understood way to communicate information about the profitability of a project.

IRR actually has one advantage over NPV. Using NPV requires being able to estimate an appropriate discount rate. We can compute the IRR without this information.

9.5   THE PROFITABILITY INDEX

The *profitability index* (PI), also known as the *benefit/cost ratio,* is defined as the present value of the future cash flows divided by the initial investment. In one sense, the profitability index is comparable to the NPV criterion, because it provides an indication of whether the present value of the future cash flows exceeds the initial investment. If this ratio is greater than one, the investment is desirable, because the present value of the future cash flows is greater than the initial outlay. Any independent investment shown to be acceptable according to the PI criterion is also acceptable according to the NPV criterion. However, as in the case of the IRR, problems may arise in applying the PI to mutually exclusive investment projects. For example, a smaller project may have a higher PI, but a lower NPV than a larger project. Incorrect decisions are avoided by: (1) applying the NPV criterion; or, (2) applying the PI criterion to the incremental cash flows.

For example, if the present value of future cash flows is $12,302.44 for an initial investment of $10,000, the PI is simply ($12,302.44/$10,000) = $2,302.44. This tells us that for every $1 invested, $.23 in NPV is created ($.23 is the value created per dollar invested). Note that the NPV is ($12,302.44 - $10,000) = $2,302.44.

9.6   THE PRACTICE OF CAPITAL BUDGETING

In surveys of large corporations, discounted cash flow approaches (i.e., NPV, IRR, PI) are the most commonly used capital budgeting techniques. It appears that 80% or more use discounted cash flow (NPV and/or IRR), but not necessarily to the exclusion of other procedures.

CONCEPT TEST

1.   Present value analysis of an investment opportunity specifies that the investment is _____ if the present value of the future cash inflows is _____ the cash outlay. The investment is_____ if the present value of the future cash inflows is _____ the cash outlay.

2.   The net present value of an asset is equal to the difference between the present value of the future_____ produced by the asset and the _____ of the asset.

3.   An investment is acceptable if its net present value is _____. This is consistent with present value analysis because an asset with a _____ net present value has a present value greater than its cost, which makes the investment _____.

4.   An investment is unacceptable if its net present value is _____. This is consistent with present value analysis because an investment with a_____ net present value has a present value less than its cost, which makes the investment _____.

5.   The net present value of an asset measures the _____ which accrues to the _____ of the firm if the asset is acquired. Therefore, the use of the net present value criterion is consistent with the financial manager's goal of maximizing the _____ of the firm's common shares.

6.   The payback period is the amount of time required to recover the _____ for a capital budgeting project from the future _____ produced by the project. The payback period rule specifies that an investment is _____ if the payback period is less than a specified _____.

7.   The deficiencies of the payback rule are: the _____ of cash flows within the payback period is ignored, thereby treating these cash flows as _____; all cash flows after the _____ are ignored; there is no objective criterion for choosing the _____.

8.   The primary advantage of the payback rule is its _____.

9.   The discounted payback period for an asset is the time period required for the sum of the discounted future _____ to equal the _____ for the asset. The discounted payback period rule specifies that a project is _____ if the discounted payback period is less than a specified _____.

10.   The deficiencies of the discounted payback period rule are: cash flows after the_____ are ignored; and there is no objective criterion for choosing the _____.

11.   The average accounting return (AAR) for an investment project is defined as _____ attributed to the asset divided by _____ of the asset. The average accounting return rule specifies that an investment is _____ if its average accounting return exceeds a _____.

12.   The deficiencies of the AAR are: the AAR method uses _____ income and _____ value data, rather than _____; the AAR ignores the _____; and, the_____ must be arbitrarily specified.

13.   The internal rate of return is the rate of return (or discount rate) which equates the _____ of the future _____ for an investment with the _____ of the investment. The IRR can also be defined as the rate of return which equates the net present value of an investment to _____.

14.   An investment project is _____ if the IRR is greater than the rate of return which could be earned in the financial markets on investments of equal risk. An investment project is _____ if the IRR is less than the relevant rate of return in the financial markets.

15.   The IRR criterion may not correctly indicate whether an investment is acceptable. The problems which arise in applying the internal rate of return criterion are associated with the following situations: _____ cash flows and _____ investments.

16.   A conventional cash flow for a capital budgeting project has a _____ cash flow (i.e., an outlay) followed by _____ cash flows (i.e., inflows). A _____ series of cash flows changes sign more than once, and may have more than one IRR. It is impossible to apply the IRR criterion in the case of a _____ series of cash flows.

17.   An _____ investment project is an investment whose acceptance or rejection does not affect, and is not affected by, the acceptance or rejection of any other projects. A set of mutually exclusive investment projects is a set of projects for which the acceptance of any one project in the set implies the _____ of all other projects in the set.

18.   The difficulties encountered in applying the IRR criterion to mutually exclusive projects arise when the projects being compared differ with respect to either _____ or _____. Incorrect decisions are avoided by: (1) applying the_____ criterion; or, (2) applying the IRR criterion to the _____ cash flows.

19.   The profitability index is defined as the _____ of the future _____ divided by the _____. If the PI is greater than _____, then the investment is_____, because the present value of the future cash inflows is greater than the _____. Any _____ investment shown to be acceptable according to the PI criterion is also acceptable according to the NPV criterion.

20.   Problems may arise in applying the PI to_____ investment projects. Incorrect decisions are avoided by: (1) applying the_____ criterion; or, (2) applying the PI criterion to the _____ cash flows.

PROBLEMS

Basic Questions

For Problems 1–7, use the following cash flows for projects A and B:

        A: (−$2,000, $500, $600, $700, $800)
        B: (−$2,000, $950, $850, $400, $300)

Problem 1

Calculate the payback period for projects A and B. If the target payback period is 3 years for each project, will the projects be accepted?

Problem 2

If the discount rate is 12%, what is the discounted payback period for project A? For project B?

Problem 3

Calculate (by trial-and-error) the internal rate of return for projects A and B.

Problem 4

If A and B are mutually exclusive and the required rate of return is 5%, which project should be accepted?

Problem 5

If the discount rate is 12%, and A and B are mutually exclusive, which project should be accepted?

Problem 6

Pete is considering two investment opportunities. Investment P requires an initial cash outflow of $900 and is expected to return $225 for each of the following six years. Investment J requires an initial investment of $1,200 and will provide cash inflows of $300 for the next five years. Use the profitability index criterion to determine which investment Pete should choose, given that his required rate of return is 8%.

Problem 7

Use the following abbreviated financial statements to calculate the average accounting return for a proposed investment:

	Year				
	0	1	2	3	4
Gross book value	$160	$160	$160	$160	$160
Less: Accumulated Depreciation		40	80	120	160
Net book value	$160	$120	$ 80	$ 40	$ 0
Sales		$ 95	$ 90	$ 97	$ 80
Costs		33	30	25	10
Depreciation		40	40	40	40
Taxes (50%)		11	10	16	15
Net income		$ 11	$ 10	$ 16	$ 15

Problem 8

What is the internal rate of return for the investment described in Problem 7?

Problem 9

What is the IRR of a project with a cash outflow of $600 in year 0, followed by yearly cash inflows of $200, $200, and $400?

Problem 10

You have the opportunity to borrow $8,000, to be repaid in yearly installments of $2,200 at the end of each of the next five years. Use the IRR criterion to determine whether this loan is preferable to borrowing at the market rate of 11.5%.

Intermediate Questions

Problem 11

Christine is considering purchasing a new piece of equipment for her factory. The equipment costs $10,000 and will increase revenues by $4,000 per year for the next three years, and $2,000 per year for two years after that. It will cost Christine $1,000 per year to run the equipment, and at the end of the five years the equipment is expected to have a salvage value of $2,500. Use the net present value criterion to determine whether Christine should invest in this equipment, assuming an opportunity cost of 10%.

Problem 12

Compute the internal rate of return for investments with the following cash flows in years 0, 1 and 2, respectively:

   A: (–$60, $155, –$100)
   B: ($60, –$155, $100)

How do you interpret these results?   Draw an NPV profile of the two investments on the same graph. Label the IRRs and the crossover point. Be sure to include the points at which the NPV profiles cross the x- and y- axes.

Problem 13

Refer back to the information for problems 1 - 5. At what discount rate will you be indifferent between A and B?

Problem 14

A firm is considering the following mutually exclusive investment projects: Project A requires an initial outlay of $500 and will return $120 per year for the next seven years; Project B requires an initial outlay of $5,000 and will return $1,350 per year for the next five years. The required rate of return is 10%. Use the net present value criterion to determine which investment is preferable.

Problem 15

Calculate the internal rate of return for each of the investment projects described in Problem 14.

Problem 16

Calculate the profitability index for each of the investment projects described in Problem 14.

Problem 17

Again, refer to the two investments identified in Problem 15. Calculate the internal rate of return, the profitability index and the net present value for the incremental investment (B–A).

Challenge Questions

Problem 18

You have been asked to analyse an investment with the following cash flows in years 0, 1 and 2, respectively: (–$51, $100, –$50). Compute the internal rate of return for this investment. Is the investment acceptable? The required return is unknown.

ANSWERS TO CONCEPT TEST

1.   acceptable; greater than; unacceptable; less than

2.   cash flows; cost

3.   positive; positive; acceptable

4.   negative; negative; unacceptable

5.   value; shareholders; current price

6.   initial investment; cash inflows; acceptable; cutoff time period

7.   timing; equally valuable; cutoff time period; cutoff time period

8.   simplicity

9.   cash inflows; initial investment; acceptable; cutoff time period

10.   cutoff time period; cutoff time period

11.   average net income; average book value; acceptable; specified target level

12.   accounting; book; cash flows; time value of money; target AAR

13.   present value; cash inflows; cost; zero

14.   acceptable; unacceptable

15.   nonconventional; mutually exclusive

16.   negative; positive; nonconventional; nonconventional

17.   independent; rejection

18.   scale; timing; net present value; incremental

19.   present value; cash inflows; initial investment; one; acceptable; initial investment; independent

20.   mutually exclusive; net present value; incremental

SOLUTIONS TO PROBLEMS

Problem 1: The sum of Projects A's cash flows for years 1 - 3 is $1,800, and the sum for years 1- 4, so the payback period for A is between three and four years. After three years, A is within $200 of paying back the initial cost. The fractional year is thus ($200/$800) = .25, so the payback period is 3.25 years. This is greater than the target cutoff, so the project will be rejected. The payback period for project B is 2.5 years, so it will be accepted.

Problem 2: The sum of the four discounted cash flows for project A is $1,931.41, so A does not pay back its initial cost (the payback period is greater than 4 years). For B, the sum of the four discounted cash flows is $2,001.20, so the payback period is almost exactly four years.

Problem 3: The solution to Problem 1 provides useful information for solving this problem. For project B, the discounted payback period is almost exactly equal to the life of the project, so the IRR must be slightly greater than the 12% discount rate. The exact value of the IRR is 12.0351%. For project A, the NPV is –$68.59 at a 12% discount rate, so the IRR is somewhat less than 12%. At discount rates of 10% and 11%, the NPV is $22.74 and –$23.76, respectively. Therefore, the IRR must be between 10% and 11%. The exact value is 10.4845%.

Problem 4: Using a discount rate of 5%, the NPV for A is $283.26 and the NPV for B is $268.08. Therefore, A is preferred even though it has the lower IRR (10.485% vs. 12.0351% for project B).

Problem 5: In Problem 2, A has a negative NPV at a 12% discount rate (–$68.59), making it unacceptable. B has an NPV of $1.20, so it is acceptable and preferred.

Problem 6: First, calculate the present value of the future cash flows for each option at an 8% discount rate. Then divide that present value by the initial investment to determine the profitability index.

For project P: PV   = $225 x PVIFA (8%, 6)   = $225 x 4.6229   = $1,040.15

                PI   = $1,040.15 / $900   =   1.1557   →   Accept project P (Note: NPV   = $140.15)

For project J: PV   = $300 x PVIFA (8%, 5)   = $300 x 3.9927   = $1,197.81

                PI   = $1,197.81 / $1,200   =   0.9982   →   Reject project J (Note: NPV   =   - $2.19)

Problem 7: Avg. Net income   =   ($11 + $10 + $16 + $15) / 4 = $13

           Avg. Book Value   ($160 + $120 + $80 + $40 + $0) / 5 = $80

        AAR   =   ($13 / $80)   =   .1625   =   16.25%

Problem 8: First, compute cash flows by adding depreciation to net income:

$51, $50, $56, $55 for years 1 - 4, respectively; initial investment = $160.

By the IRR is approximately 12%. For a 12% discount rate, the present value of the cash flows is $160.21 and the net present value is ($160.21 – $160) = $.21. The exact value of the IRR is 12.0608%.

Problem 9:

$$NPV = 0 \quad -\$600 + \$200 / (1 + IRR) + \$200 / (1 + IRR)^2 + \$400 / (1 + IRR)^3$$

Using a trial and error approach, the following IRRs can be found:

Discount rate	NPV
12%	$22.72
13%	10.84
14%	- 0.68

So, the IRR is between 13% and 14% and very close to 14%. By financial calculator, the exact answer is 13.9402%.

Problem 10: The IRR is the solution for r in the following equation:

$$PV = C \times PVIFA(r,t) \rightarrow \$8,000 = \$2,200 \times PVIFA(r,5) \rightarrow PVIFA(r,5) = 3.63636$$

Using Table A.3, the IRR is between PVIFA(10%,5) = 3.7908 and PVIFA(12%,5) = 3.6048. To find PVIFA (11%, 5) it is necessary to interpolate. The PVIFA for 11% is exactly halfway between the two, it is 3.6978. By trial and error, the IRR is between 11.6% and 11.7%. By financial calculator, IRR = 11.6488%. Therefore, borrowing at the market rate of 11.5% is the preferred alternative

Problem 11: Remember that net present value is concerned with *incremental* cash flows. During the first three years, the equipment will generate cash flows of (4,000 - $1,000) = $3,000 per year, and during the fourth and fifth years it will generate cash flows of ($2,000 - $1,000) = $1,000 per year. The salvage of $2,500 must be added to the year 5 cash flows. The NPV can then be calculated as:

$$NPV = -\$10,000 + [\$3,000 \text{ x } PVIFA (10\%, 3)] + \$1,000 / (1.10)^4 + \$3,500 / (1.10)^5$$

$$= -\$10,000 + \$7,460.56 + \$683.01 + \$2,173.22 = \$316.79$$

Christine should accept the investment and purchase the equipment, because the NPV was positive.

Problem 12: Since the cash flows for each of these investments change sign more than once, each investment has more than one internal rate of return. These can be determined by trial and error, but since these cash flows extend over only three time periods, it is possible to solve algebraically for the two IRR values. Consider, for example, the first of the two investments. The IRR is the rate r which is the solution to the following equation:

$$\$60 = \$155 / (1 + IRR) - \$100 / (1 + IRR)^2$$

Algebraically, this is a quadratic equation. In general, a quadratic equation has two solutions, which can be determined directly by using the quadratic formula. The two solutions for Project A are $IRR_1 = .25 = 25\%$ and $IRR_2 = .3333 = 33.33\%$. These same values are also the two solutions for Project B.

To interpret these results, compute the net present value at a rate between the two IRRs. At a discount rate of 30%, for example, the NPV is +$.06 for the first investment and – $.06 for the second. The first investment is acceptable only if the required rate of return is between 25% and 33.33%. The second investment is acceptable only if the required return is outside the range 25% to 33.33%. This conclusion derives from the fact that a quadratic equation, when graphed, has the shape of a parabola, so that the net present value must be either exclusively negative or exclusively positive between the two solutions identified here, and has the opposite sign outside the range of the two solutions.

Problem 13: The crossover rate is found by using the incremental cash flows from (B-A) and solving for the rate at which the projects have the NPV. That is: $NPV_A = NPV_B$. This is equivalent to finding the rate at which $NPV_A - NPV_B = 0$

The incremental cash flows for (A-B) are: $0, -$450, -$250, $300, $500. The IRR of this stream of cash flows is the crossover rate.. This rate is found by trial and error or with the use of a financial calculator. A financial calculator that the rate is 6.0654%. At this discount rate, both A and B have an NPV of $223.51. Note: Using the incremental cash flows from (B-A) will give the same results.

Problem 14: Project A: NPV $= ($120 \times 4.8684) - $500 = 84.21

Project B: NPV $= ($1,350 \times 3.7908) - $5,000 = 117.58

Project B is the preferred alternative. (Note: there may be an additional problem be cause the two assets have different life spans. If the assets perform a comparable task, the shorter life of project A may imply that a new investment in a replacement is required sooner for A than for B. This possibility is addressed in the next chapter.)

Problem 15: The IRR can be found using either trial and error (as in Problem 14) or by financial calculator. By financial calculator, the IRRs for Projects A and B are 14.9500% and 10.9162%, respectively, so Project A is preferred. However, according to the NPV analysis in Problem 15, project B is preferred because it has the higher NPV. This is an example of the scale problem discussed earlier. Remember that, if there is a question, the decision should always be based on NPV.

Problem 16: Project A: PI $= $584.21/$500 = 1.1684$.

Project B: PI $= $5,117.58/$5,000 = 1.0235$.

If these were independent projects, both would be acceptable according to the profitability index criterion. because each of the above values is greater than 1. This conclusion is consistent with that implied by the NPV and IRR criteria for independent projects. However, since these are mutually exclusive projects, the profitability index criterion should not be used. Instead NPV analysis should be used and Problem B is preferred.

Problem 17: The cash flows for the incremental investment (B–A) are:

(–$4,500, $1,230, $1,230, $1,230, $1,230, $1,230, –$120, –$120)

The IRR for (B–A) is 10.3009%, the present value is $4,533.35, the profitability index is 1.0074 and the net present value is $33.35. (Note that the internal rate of return computed here is also referred to as the cross-over rate.) All three criteria indicate that the incremental investment (B–A) is acceptable. It is always true that the three criteria applied to the incremental investment result in the same decision. Consequently, since project A is acceptable and the incremental investment (B–A) is acceptable, then project B is preferred.

Problem 18: This is a problem designed to keep students out of trouble by keeping them   busy. There is no IRR!!! (i.e. There is no positive number for which NPV = zero. Even at r = 0, the NPV is:

$$NPV = -\$51 + \$100 / (1.1) - \$50 / (1.10)^2 = -\$1$$

At any positive discount rate, the NPV becomes more negative. Because the NPV is always negative, the required return is irrelevant.

10 Making Capital Investment Decisions

CHAPTER HIGHLIGHTS

The major emphasis of this chapter is the identification of the relevant cash flows for NPV analysis of a capital budgeting problem. Although financial managers use accounting income data in their decision-making, financial decisions must be based on cash flows rather than income. Consequently, it is important to correctly interpret accounting data in order to identify relevant cash flows.

10.1 PROJECT CASH FLOWS: A FIRST LOOK

When it undertakes a capital budgeting project, a firm changes its current and future cash flows. Capital investment decision-making requires that financial managers determine whether these changes add value to the firm.

Relevant Cash Flows: The relevant cash flows for analysis of a capital budgeting project are the *incremental cash flows* associated with the project. The incremental cash flows consist of any and all changes in the firm's cash flows *that are a direct consequence of accepting the project.* Even though accounting income data is used, it must interpreted in such a way as to identify the incremental cash flows.

The Stand-Alone Principle: The incremental cash flows for a project are defined as the difference between the firm's current and future cash flows, depending on whether or not the project is undertaken. For practical purposes, this is an unwieldy definition because it requires the examination of the firm's total cash flows. Fortunately, a particular project can generally be viewed as having its own cash flows. That is, the stand-alone principle specifies that the financial manager can view the incremental cash flows from the perspective of the project, rather than from the perspective of the entire firm.

10.2 INCREMENTAL CASH FLOWS

The financial manager encounters numerous difficulties in the process of identifying incremental cash flows for a capital budgeting project. Some of the most frequently encountered complications relate to the interpretation of the following concepts: sunk costs, opportunity costs, side effects, net working capital, and financing costs.

Sunk Costs: A *sunk cost* is money the firm has already spent, or is committed to spend, regardless of whether it accepts the project under consideration. For instance, the cost of a feasibility study undertaken before the accept/reject decision is made is a sunk cost, because it must be paid regardless of the decision made. This sunk cost is *not* an incremental cost. Therefore it is not relevant to the capital budgeting decision. Sunk costs are *always* excluded from the analysis.

Opportunity Costs: Suppose a firm is considering a project that involves building a new factory on land owned by the firm. The price paid for the land, at some time in the past, is a sunk cost and is therefore not relevant to the current decision. However, by building a factory on the land, the firm would lose the opportunity to use the land for some alternative project. One alternative to building the factory would be to sell the property. By using the property to build the factory, the firm forgoes the proceeds from a sale of the property. Hence, the market value of the property (net of any capital gains taxes) is an opportunity cost which is an incremental cost to the project.

Side Effects: Capital budgeting projects often have side effects. One example of a side effect is *erosion*. When a consumer products manufacturer introduces a new product, some portion of the new product's sales might come at the expense of sales of the company's existing products. The resulting reduction in cash flow to other product lines is a direct consequence of introducing the new consideration and must be considered in the analysis.

Net Working Capital: As defined in Chapter 2, net working capital is the difference between current assets and current liabilities. A capital budgeting project often requires an increase in net working capital during the life of the project. For example, the development of a new product necessitates increases in cash balances, inventory and accounts receivable. Some of the financing needed for this expansion of current assets is provided by increases in accounts payable. However, the increase in accounts payable is typically not sufficient to finance the increase in current assets; hence, additional outlays are normally required to finance the increase in net working capital. This investment in net working capital is an incremental cash outflow. At the termination of a project, this outflow is typically recovered, and is therefore an inflow at that time.

Financing Costs: Financing costs are *not included* in the computation of incremental cash flows. These costs are important for an NPV analysis in that they determine the appropriate discount rate for the NPV calculations. This issue is discussed in detail in later chapters. In this chapter, it is assumed that all financing costs are already incorporated in the discount rate.

Inflation: Because capital budgeting projects span many years, inflation may have an impact on a project's cash flows. It was discussed earlier that nominal rates are adjusted for expected inflation. Similarly cash flow estimates must also be adjusted. Ignoring the impact of inflation could bias against accepting a positive NPV project.

Government Intervention: In Canada, various levels of government offer incentives to promote certain types of capital investment including grants, investment tax credits and favourable rates for capital cost allowance (CCA) and subsidized loans. Since these change a project's cash flows, they must be factored into capital budgeting analysis.

Other Issues: Two additional issues associated with the identification of the relevant incremental cash flows are:

1.   Cash flows are measured when they *occur*, not when they accrue in the accounting sense
2.   Since taxes are clearly cash outflows, *we are concerned with after-tax incremental cash flows.*

10.3 PRO FORMA FINANCIAL STATEMENTS AND PROJECT CASH FLOWS

For a typical capital budgeting project, current cash outflows are followed by future cash inflows. Therefore, it is necessary to forecast, or project, these incremental cash inflows. Projected cash flows for a capital budgeting project are derived from *pro forma financial statements*. These are projected financial statements for future time periods.

Example: This section discusses how to determine the NPV for a proposed capital budgeting project for KMS Corporation. The first step is to determine the incremental cash flows. Assume KMS is considering the purchase of new manufacturing equipment, expected to produce a better quality product at a lower cost. Sales revenue is expected to increase by $40,000 the first year, and 10 % a year for each of the next four years. Operating costs will decrease by $20,000 per year. The equipment costs $150,000 and is expected to have a useful economic life of five years. The market value at the end of five years will be $60,000. Assume straight line depreciation and a 40% tax rate for both ordinary income and capital gains. KMS projects an investment of $15,000 in working capital. This investment will be completely recovered at the end of year five.

Recall that cash flow from the firm's assets has three components: operating cash flow, capital spending, and additions to net working capital. The capital spending for the new equipment is the $150,000 outlay to purchase the equipment. The addition to net working capital is the $15,000 investment in working capital. Therefore, the total outlay at year 0 is ($150,000 capital expenditure + $15,000) = $165.000. Operating cash flow is defined as:

Earnings before interest and taxes + Depreciation – Taxes   (From Chapter 2)

The sum (EBIT + depreciation) is equivalent to earnings before depreciation, interest and taxes. Taxes are deducted because they are a cash outflow. (Note: KMS has no interest expense.) For KMS, operating cash flows are:

	Year 1	Year 2	Year 3	Year 4	Year 5
Sales revenue	$40,000	$44,000	$48,400	$53,240	$58,564
-Operating costs	- 20,000	- 20,000	- 20,000	- 20,000	- 20,000
-Depreciation	18,000	18,000	18,000	18,000	18,000
EBIT	$42,000*	$46,000	$50,400	$55,240	$60,564
Plus Depreciation	18,000	18,000	18,000	18,000	18,000
-Tax on EBIT(at 40%)	16,800	18,400	20,160	22,096	24,225.60
Operating cash flow	$43,200	$45,600	$48,240	$51,144	$54,338.40

*Note that we are subtracting a *decrease* in costs. This actually *increases* the EBIT.

For year 5, in addition to operating cash flows, we have cash flows related to the sale of the asset and the recovery of working capital. KMS will receive $60,000 for selling the equipment. In addition, KMS $15,000 of the working capital investment will be recovered.

The total cash flow for year 5 is: $54,338.40 + $60,000 + $15,000 = $129,338.40

The NPV of the cash flows must be computed to determine the acceptability of the investment. For simplicity, assume that all cash flows occur at year end. Assuming a 16% opportunity cost, the present value of the cash inflows for years 1 through 5 is $191,861.01. The net present value of the investment is $26,861.01. Clearly the NPV criterion indicates that the investment in new equipment is acceptable to KMS.

10.4 MORE ON PROJECT CASH FLOW

Two important aspects of the previous example are: (1) the relationship between our treatment of net working capital and the issue of the timing of cash flows; and (2) various aspects of the tax treatment of depreciation.

A Closer Look at Net Working Capital: Recall (from Chapter 2) that Generally Accepted Accounting Principles (GAAP) require that revenue is recorded on the income statement when it is accrued. Furthermore, for income statement purposes, costs are determined according to the 'matching' principle, which requires that expenses are recognized at the time of the sale. It is important to adjust this accounting information to reflect the actual timing of cash flows. The manner in which additions to net working capital were treated in the KMS incorporate the necessary adjustment.

Depreciation and Capital Cost Allowance (CCA): Chapter 2 introduces the CCA system. The CCA system is Canada Customs and Revenue Agency's (CCRA) method of determining accounting depreciation. Accounting depreciation does not represent an actual change in cashflow, except for the changes in taxes caused by the depreciation. The depreciation calculation performed in this chapter use the CCA system.

Example: Suppose that, when KMS makes sales of $40,000 during year 1, 20% of the sales are on credit; the credit terms require payment in the month following the sale. Also assume that sales are equally distributed throughout the year, i.e. $40,000 / 12 = $3,333.33 per month. Therefore, at the end of the first year, (.20 × $3,333.33) = $666.67 of sales revenue has not yet been collected, but the full $3,333.33 has been recorded on the accounting income statement for December sales. Actual cash inflows in December, though, are only $2,666.67. Consequently, even though year 1 revenue is $40,000, the cash inflow should be $39,333.33. How does the treatment of net working capital correctly account for this fact?

The $666.67 of revenue which appears on the income statement but has not been received by the end of year 1 is recorded as accounts receivable on the balance sheet. This is an increase in net working capital and, assuming there are no additional changes in current assets or current liabilities during year 1, the $666.67 increase in net working capital is an outflow for year 1. So, the net result is $40,000 in revenue, as an inflow, and a $666.67 addition to net working capital, as an outflow, for a net $39,333.33 inflow. This is the correct cash flow, as indicated above, so the treatment of additions to net working capital correctly adjusts for the difference between accrued revenue and actual cash inflow. A comparable conclusion results from an evaluation of other changes in net working capital, which arise from changes in other current assets, such as inventory, or current liabilities, such as accounts payable.

Example: Assume that W.C. Inc. is investing in a new project that will affect certain of the firm's working capital accounts in the next three periods (see table below). Presently total current assets are $20,000 and total current liabilities are $12,000. If we assume that the firm's net working capital will revert to its original levels after three years and given a 10 % discount rate, what is the impact on cash flow and on NPV?

Period	Account	$ Increase	$ Decrease
0	Accounts Receivable	9,000	
1	Inventory		7,000
2	Accruals		3,000
3	Accounts Payable	8,000	
3	Accounts Receivable	5,000	

The table below summarizes the effect on cash flow given changes in working capital.

Working Capital Effects on Cash Flow

Funds Required (−)	Funds Released (+)
Increase in current assets	Increase in current liabilities
Decrease in current liabilities	Decrease in current assets

Applied to our example, the cash flow would change in present value by [− $9,000 + $7,000 (.9091) − $3,000 (.8264)] + [$8,000 − $5,000 × (.7513)] = −$2,861.60 where the brackets represent present value factors. Therefore, W.C. Inc. will require a net increase in working capital of $2,861.76 over the life of the project. To understand the recovery of working capital, consider the cumulative changes in the working capital accounts:

	Current Assets	-	Current Liabilities	=	Net Working Capital	Cumulative Change
Current level	$20,000		$ 12,000		$ 8,000	
Time 0	9,000				17,000	$ 9,000
1	–7,000				10,000	2,000
2			- 3,000		13,000	5,000
3	5,000		8,000		10,000	2,000

The cumulative change in net working capital is $2,000 at the end of year 3. This $2,000 increase represents the net increase in working capital levels (undiscounted) at the end of the project. Since the problem stated that working capital levels would revert back to the original levels at the end of the project, the net increase in working capital (–$2,000) becomes an inflow (+$2,000) and in present value is: $2,000 × .7513 = $1,502.60, which should be added to cash flow.

In summary the effect on cash flow, in present value, of changes in working capital is – $2,861.60 + $1,502.63 = – $1,359.00 so that NPV would be reduced by this amount.

10.5 ALTERNATIVE DEFINITIONS OF OPERATING CASH FLOW

In the KMS example above, each year's operating cash flow was calculated according to the following definition:

$$\text{Operating Cash Flow} = \text{Earnings before interest and taxes} + \text{Depreciation} - \text{Taxes}$$

For example,   Year 1 OCF = $42,000 + $18,000 – $16,800 = $43,200

This section develops several alternative, but equivalent, approaches to computing operating cash flow. These alternatives provide insight into various aspects of the cash flow calculation. The following notation is used:

OCF	=	project operating cash flow	D	=	depreciation
S	=	sales (in dollars)	T_c	=	corporate tax rate
C	=	operating costs			

$$\text{EBIT} = (S - C - D); \quad \text{taxes are: EBIT} \times T_c = (S - C - D) \times T_c$$

Substituting these definitions into the above equation for operating cash flow:

$$\text{OCF} = \text{EBIT} + D - \text{Taxes} = (S - C - D) + D - [(S - C - D) \times T_c] \tag{10.1}$$

This is simply a restatement of the definition of operating cash flow in terms of the algebraic notation. This definition can be rearranged to derive alternative approaches to the computation of operating cash flow.

The Bottom-Up Approach: The *bottom-up approach* to defining operating cash flow accentuates the relationship between net income and operating cash flow. Using the notation introduced earlier, net income is defined as follows:

$$\text{Net income} = \text{EBIT} - \text{Taxes} = (S - C - D) - [(S - C - D) \times T_c] = (S - C - D) \times (1 - T_c)$$

This definition of net income ignores financing costs; the original definition of OCF can be rearranged to emphasize this bottom-up interpretation, as follows:

$$\text{OCF} = \text{EBIT} + \text{D} - \text{Taxes} = \text{Net income} + \text{Depreciation} = [(\text{S} - \text{C} - \text{D}) \times (1 - T_c)] + \text{D} \quad [10.2]$$

Using this bottom-up definition for the KMS example for Year 1:

$$\text{OCF} = \text{Net income} + \text{Depreciation} = \$25,200 + \$18,000 = \$43,200$$

This is the same value for OCF, but it on *how* net income and depreciation determine operating cash flow.

The Top-Down Approach: The *top-down approach* is derived from the basic definition of operating cash flow:

$$
\begin{aligned}
\text{OCF} &= \text{EBIT} + \text{D} - \text{Taxes} = (\text{S} - \text{C} - \text{D}) + \text{D} - [(\text{S} - \text{C} - \text{D}) \times T_c] \\
&= (\text{S} - \text{C}) - \text{D} + \text{D} - [(\text{S} - \text{C} - \text{D}) \times T_c] \\
&= (\text{S} - \text{C}) - [(\text{S} - \text{C} - \text{D}) \times T_c] = \text{Sales} - \text{Costs} - \text{Taxes}
\end{aligned}
\quad [10.3]
$$

OCF is sales less expenses, including taxes, but excluding depreciation (non-cash expense). For KMS, Year 1:

$$\text{OCF} = \$40,000 - (-\$20,000) - \$16,800 = \$43,200$$

The Tax Shield Approach: The *tax shield* approach to defining operating cash flow emphasizes the manner in which depreciation affects cash flow. Since depreciation is a non-cash expense, its only impact on cash flow is through its effect on taxes; the tax shield approach accentuates this fact. The tax shield approach is derived from the basic definition of operating cash flow as follows:

$$
\begin{aligned}
\text{OCF} &= \text{EBIT} + \text{D} - \text{Taxes} = (\text{S} - \text{C} - \text{D}) + \text{D} - [(\text{S} - \text{C} - \text{D}) \times T_c] \\
&= (\text{S} - \text{C}) - [(\text{S} - \text{C}) \times T_c] + (\text{D} \times T_c) = [(\text{S} - \text{C}) \times (1 - T_c)] + (\text{D} \times T_c)
\end{aligned}
\quad [10.3]
$$

This definition of operating cash flow has two terms. The first term can be thought of as the project's cash flow in the absence of depreciation. That is, $[(\text{S} - \text{C}) \times (1 - T_c)]$ would be the project's after-tax income if depreciation were zero. In the absence of depreciation, operating cash flow would equal net income after taxes. Note that this refers to net operating income. That is, interest costs have been excluded from consideration. The second term is referred to as the *depreciation tax shield*. Since depreciation is a non-cash expense, its only impact on operating cash flow calculations is its impact on taxes. The tax savings associated with the tax-deductibility of depreciation expense is equal to the depreciation expense (D) multiplied by the tax rate (T_c); this tax savings is the depreciation tax shield.

For the KMS example, the calculation of operating cash flow using the tax shield approach is:

$$
\begin{aligned}
\text{OCF} &= [(\text{S} - \text{C}) \times (1 - T_c)] + (\text{D} \times T_c) = [\$40,000 - (-\$20,000) \times (1 - .40)] + (\$18,000 \times .40) \\
&= [\$60,000 \times .60] + (\$18,000 \times .40) = \$36,000 + \$7,200 = \$43,200
\end{aligned}
$$

Notice that this value of OCF is identical to that derived earlier. The tax shield approach emphasizes the fact that the $18,000 depreciation expense produces a $7,200 tax savings for the firm.

10.6 APPLYING THE TAX SHIELD APPROACH: CCA

Canada Customs and Revenue Agency (CCRA) requires firms to compute capital cost allowance (CCA) instead of book depreciation. CCA actually allows for faster depreciation of the asset. Each asset is assigned to a particular asset when it is purchased. The asset is depreciated according to CCA (not GAAP) rules, and the half-year convention is applied. Depreciation percentages are given for each asset class. In the KMS example, the firm invested $150,000. If the applicable CCA rate is 30% , what are the annual CCA charges that KMS can claim?

Year	Beginning UCC	CCA	Ending UCC
1	$ 75,000	$22,500	$52,500
2	127,500*	38,250	89,250
3	89,250	26,775	62,475
4	62,475	18,742.50	43,732.50
5	43,732.50	13,119.75	30,612.75

*$127,500 $=$ $52,500 + $75,000 ($75,000 is due to half-year convention)

The problem with calculating annual CCA is that, although the investment project has a finite life, the CCA charges can continue indefinitely since these are calculated by applying a rate on the declining balance. Moreover, in addition to calculating the tax savings that result from claiming CCA, the future tax savings must be converted into their present value equivalent. Fortunately, the following formula calculates the present value of infinite CCA tax savings incorporating the half-year rule:

$$\frac{CdT_c}{k+d} \quad \times \quad \frac{1+.5k}{1+k}$$

where   C = change in the UCC pool (net of any tax credits)
d = CCA rate
T_c = tax rate
k = discount factor
$\dfrac{1+.5k}{1+k}$ = adjustment for the half-year rule

Example: Considering the $150,000 investment by KMS Corporation, what is the present value of tax savings they will earn from CCA charges. Assume a 30 % CCA rate, 16 % discount rate and a 40 % tax rate?

$$PV \text{ (tax savings)} \quad = \quad \frac{\$150,000 \times .30 \times .40}{.16 + .30} \quad \times \quad \frac{1.08}{1.16} \quad = \quad \$36,431.78$$

KMS will save $36,431.78 in taxes (today's dollars) by claiming CCA on the investment indefinitely.

Salvage: Since salvage value represents a recoverable amount from the depreciable asset and will reduce the UCC pool, the perpetual CCA tax savings will also be reduced. These lost tax savings, which reduce net cash flow, are quantifiable in the same way as the declining balance formula, but must then be multiplied by the present value formula to convert the lost CCA tax savings in today's dollars. The present value of lost CCA tax savings due to expected salvage can be computed by using the following formula:

$$PV \text{ (lost tax savings)} \quad = \quad \frac{- SdT_c}{k+d} \quad \times \quad \frac{1}{(1+k)^n}$$

where S = incremental salvage value. Apart from reducing CCA tax savings, the salvage value will also increase future cash inflows as noted earlier in the KMS example.

Example: For KMS, what is the impact of the $60,000 salvage value on the firm's cash flow?

$$\text{PV (lost tax savings)} \quad = \quad \frac{-\$60,000 \times .30 \times .40}{.16 + .30} \times \frac{1}{(1.16)^5} \quad = \quad -\$15,652.17 \times .476113 \quad = \quad -\$7,452.20$$

$$\text{PV (salvage)} \quad = \quad \$60,000 \times (.477113) \quad = \quad \$28,566.78$$

Therefore, the impact of salvage value on cash flow is $-\$7,452.20 + \$28,566.78 = \$21,114.58$.

Also, there are tax implications associated with the sale of an asset whenever the asset is sold for a price which differs from its UCC (undepreciated capital cost) value at the time of the sale. When the asset is sold for more than its UCC value, a tax obligation is created; when the asset is sold for less than its UCC value and there are no assets left in the class, the difference between the two figures is a tax deduction for the firm. These situations correspond to the definitions of recaptured income and terminal loss in Chapter 2.

To complicate matters, the implication of these tax effects is not only that the tax liability will be increased (in the case of a recapture) or reduced (in the case of a terminal loss), but the lost CCA tax savings formula must be slightly modified by substituting the value of S by the remaining UCC balance. In other words, since a recapture or terminal loss results in a zero UCC balance, the infinite CCA tax savings must be reduced by the UCC balance at the time the asset sold.

Example: Carefully reconsider the previous example when KMS sold the equipment for $60,000. Are there any tax implications?

If there were no other assets in the class in which the equipment was placed, the answer is yes. Notice that by investing $150,000 in a class 10 asset where the CCA rate is 30%, KMS was left with $43,732.5 beginning UCC balance in the fifth year. The sale of equipment for $60,000 reduces the UCC pool to a negative amount of ($43,732.50 – $60,000) = -$16,267.50 which must be *recaptured* as income. KMS must pay taxes of ($16,267.50 × .40) = $6,507 on the recapture, which will reduce the cash flow of the project. The NPV would be reduced by ($16,267.5 × PVIF(16%,5) = $7,745.17. The second impact of a recapture is that the UCC balance reverts to zero for period 6 and onwards, which means that instead of reducing the infinite CCA tax savings by the salvage value, the UCC beginning balance in the year in which the recapture occurred is used. That is, calculate the lost CCA tax savings using the same formula introduced earlier, except substituting UCC for S.

$$\text{PV (lost CCA tax savings)} \quad = \quad \frac{-(\$43,732,50) \, (.30) \, (.40)}{.16 + .30} \times \frac{1}{(1.16)^5} \quad = \quad -\$5,431.73$$

To summarize, the tax implications of a recapture are that KMS must pay taxes on the recaptured amount ($7,745.17 in present value) and the present value of lost CCA tax savings are reduced to $5,431.73 (instead of $7,452.20 when salvage was used in the formula).

In general, the entire formula can be written as:

$$\text{PV tax shield on CCA} \quad = \quad \frac{CdT_c}{d + k} \times \frac{1 + .5k}{1 + k} \quad - \quad \frac{SdT_c}{d + k} \times \frac{1}{(1 + k)^n}$$

10.7 SOME SPECIAL CASES OF DISCOUNTED CASH FLOW ANALYSIS

Three special capital budgeting problems are analyzed in this section. These examples are illustrative of the wide variety of specific circumstances which can arise in the application of DCF to capital budgeting.

Replacing an Asset: Instead of cutting costs by automation, companies often attempt to enhance productivity by replacing existing equipment with newer models of advanced technology. Consider the replacement decision below:

Example: Firm Publishing Company is considering replacing two of its many printing presses which were purchased five years ago for $40,000 each with an estimated remaining useful life of five years and a salvage value of $1,500 per press. One new press is needed to replace the two old ones which could be sold today for $3,500 each. The new press normally retails for $62,500 but you have found a manufacturer who is willing to sell the same model for a 20 % discount. The new press is expected to increase sales by $9,000 per year and economize on annual operating expenses, which were $4,500 per press ($9,000 total), but would be $7,000 per year for the new press. Furthermore, each of the existing presses requires one operator who is currently paid $15,000 per year but would not be needed if the new press is purchased. The new press could be sold for $8,000 at the end of the fifth year. The company also foresees a decrease in working capital requirements of $6,000 at the end of the first year of operations, but this decrease will revert to its original level once the project is completed in five years. The applicable discount rate is 16 %, the CCA rate is 30 % and the tax rate is 40 %. Assuming that the sale of the new printing press will not result in any recaptured depreciation or terminal loss, should your company replace the two existing printing presses?

The first step is to identify the initial investment; then the relevant cash flows are discounted to calculate the NPV: The initial investment consists of the discount price of the new press less the market value of the old presses: ($62,500 × .80) – ($3,500 × 2) = $43,000. The after tax operating income in present value is: {$9,000 – [$7,000 – ($4,500 × 2) – $15,000]} (1 – .4) [PVIFA(16%,5)], = $51,078.99. The incremental salvage value in today's dollars is: [$8,000 – ($1,500 × 2)](PVIF(16%,5) = $2,380.57.

The present value tax shield for CCA is:

$$\frac{\$43,000\,(.30)\,(.40)}{.16 + .30} \quad \times \quad \frac{1.08}{1.16} \quad - \quad \frac{\$5,000\,(.30)\,(.40)}{.16 + .30} \quad \times \quad \frac{1}{(1.16)^5}$$

$$= \quad \$10,443.78 \quad - \quad \$621.02 \quad = \quad \$9,822.77$$

Finally, the present value of working capital requirements are:

$$\$6,000\,(PVIF_{16\%,1}) - \$6,000\,(PVIF_{16\%,5}) \ = \$6,000\,(.862069) - \$6,000\,(.476113) = \$2,315.74$$

Notice that a decrease in working capital requirements means that cash flow increases and, when working capital requirements revert to their original levels, cash flow decreases.

The NPV is: –$43,000 + $51,078.98 + $2,380.57 + $9,822.76 + $2,315.74 = $22,598.05

The new press should be purchased since the NPV is positive.

Evaluating Equipment with Different Lives: The NPV analysis of a replacement decision becomes more complicated if the two machines (or any asset under consideration) have different operating lives. The problem is resolved by using the *equivalent annual cost* (EAC) method.

Example: Consider the purchase of either Machine X or Machine Y. The two machines provide the same benefit to the company and the machine selected will be replaced at the end of its useful life. The lives and annual costs for each are:

Year	Machine X	Machine Y
0	- $100	- $70
1	- 10	- 15
2	- 10	- 15
3	- 10	

The firm's opportunity cost is 10%. Assuming no taxes, which machine should be selected?

At a 10% discount rate, the present values of the costs for X and Y are $124.87 and $96.03, respectively. Ignoring the fact that Machine Y would have to be replaced earlier than Machine X, Y would be selected because the present value of the costs are less.

The two present values, however, cannot be compared because they cover a different period of years. The question is: what constant dollar amount, paid each year, has exactly the same present value as the machine's purchase price plus operating costs? This amount is the *equivalent annual* cost, EAC. For Machine X, this value is determined by solving for C in the following annuity formula:

$$PV = C \times PVIFA(r,t) \rightarrow \$124.87 = C \times PVIFA(10\%,3) \rightarrow \$124.87 = C \times 2.486852$$
$$C = \$124.87 / 2.486852 = \$50.21$$

The equivalent annual cost for Machine X is $50.21.

The equivalent annual cost (EAC) for machine Y is:

$$\$96.03 = C \times PVIFA(10\%,2) = C \times 1.73554 \rightarrow C = \$55.33$$

The EAC for X is less than the EAC for Y, so that X has the lower cost. Therefore, X is the preferable alternative.

Setting the Bid Price: Under certain circumstances, a supplier of a product or service submits a bid price to a prospective customer who then purchases the product or service from the supplier who has submitted the lowest bid. This procedure might be used by a governmental unit or agency which is required by law to purchase from the lowest bidder. The problem for the supplier is to set the bid price at the lowest price which still provides the required rate of return. To derive this price, the supplier must solve the capital budgeting problem 'backwards.' That is, rather than using price and cost data to determine cash flows and net present value, the supplier identifies the operating cash flow and then the price which provides the required rate of return.

Example: Reese Sporting Goods (RSG) is submitting a bid to supply baseballs to a high school athletic league. The league will buy 5,000 baseballs per year for the next five years. To supply the baseballs, RSG must purchase $20,000 for manufacturing equipment. The equipment has a five-year life and no salvage value at the end of five years. For simplicity, assume that the equipment will be depreciated on a straight-line basis. Additional fixed costs will total $3,000 per year and variable costs will be $2 per baseball. An additional investment of $5,000 in net working capital will be required; this investment will be recovered at the end of five years. The firm's tax rate is 40% and the required rate of return is 15%. What is the lowest price Reese can charge for the baseballs?

To solve this problem, work *backwards,* as follows:

    1.   Find the minimum annual operating cash flow (OCF) needed to yield a 15% return.
          Note: this means NPV will be zero at that level of OCF
    2.   Compute the net income for that level of OCF
    3.   Find the required price per unit

1. To find the minimum required OCF, use the basic formula for NPV. Substitute for r = 15%. The initial outlay, C_0 = –$20,000 – $5,000 = –$25,000 (cost of machine plus investment in net working capital). Cash flows for years 1 through 5 are $C_1 = C_2 = C_3 = C_4 = C_5$ = OCF. Finally, the $5,000 investment in net working capital will be recovered in year 5.

At the required return of 15%, NPV equals zero. So,

$$0 = -\$25{,}000 + \frac{OCF}{(1.15)^1} + \frac{OCF}{(1.15)^2} + \frac{OCF}{(1.15)^3} + \frac{OCF}{(1.15)^4} + \frac{OCF}{(1.15)^5} + \frac{\$5{,}000}{(1.15)^5}$$

The present value of the $5,000 recovery of net working capital is $\$5{,}000/(1.15)^5 = \$2{,}485.88$. Also note that the OCF is actually a five-year annuity. The NPV can be rewritten as:

$$0 = -\$25{,}000 + OCF \times PVIFA(15\%,5) + \$2{,}485.88 = -\$22{,}514.12 + OCF \times 3.352155$$

Now solve for OCF: $22,514.12 / 3.352155 = OCF = $6,716.31. So, with an operating cash flow of $6,716.31, NPV equals zero and Reese will earn exactly the required 15% return.

2. Now, use the bottom-up definition of operating cash flow to determine net income:

$$OCF = \text{Net income} + \text{Depreciation} \rightarrow \$6{,}716.31 = \text{Net income} + \$20{,}000/5 \rightarrow \text{Net income} = \$2{,}716.31$$

3. Now, use the definition of net income to solve for S, the required sales level. Note that C is the sum of fixed and variable costs: C = $3,000 + $2 × 5,000 = $13,000.

    Net income = $(S - C - D) \times (1 - T_c) \rightarrow$ $2,716.31 = (S - \$13{,}000 - \$4{,}000) \times (1 - .40)$
    $2,716.31 = (S - \$17{,}000) \times (.60) \rightarrow$ $2,716.31 / .60 = S - \$17{,}000$
    $4,527.18 + 17,000 = S = \$21{,}527.18$

That is, sales of $21,527.18 will generate the required cash flow of $2,716.31. The bid is for 5,000 baseballs, so the price per unit must be:

    Sales Revenue / units = price per unit $\rightarrow$ $21,527.18 / 5,000 = price = $4.31

CONCEPT TEST

1.   In evaluating a capital budgeting project, the relevant cash flows are the incremental cash flows, which consist of all _____ in the firm's cash flows that are a direct consequence of _____ the project.

2. The incremental cash flows for a project can be defined as the firm's cash flows if the project is undertaken minus _____. Alternatively, the _____ principle specifies that incremental cash flows can be analysed from the perspective of the_____, rather than from the perspective of the _____.

3. A sunk cost for a capital budgeting project is money the firm has already _____, or is_____, regardless of whether it accepts the project under consideration. A sunk cost _(is/is not)_ incremental to a capital budgeting project, and therefore _(is/is not)_ relevant to the capital budgeting decision.

4. An opportunity cost for a capital budgeting project is a benefit which the firm would_____ if it _____ the project. An opportunity cost _(is/is not)_ an incremental cost for a capital budgeting project.

5. A _____ is the impact which a given capital budgeting project might have on cash flows in another area of the firm. These changes in cash flows _(are/are not)_ incremental cash flows for the project under consideration.

6. Net working capital is equal to _____ minus _____. A capital budgeting project typically requires an _____ in net working capital during the life of the project.

7. The investment in net working capital is an incremental cash _____. At the termination of a project, this investment is typically recovered, and is therefore an incremental cash _____ at that time. This treatment of changes in net working capital adjusts accounting data to a cash flow basis. Generally Accepted Accounting Principles require that revenue is recorded on the income statement when it _____, and that costs are determined according to the _____ principle. Consequently, it is essential to adjust accounting information, which is reported on an_____ basis, in such a way that it reflects the actual timing of _____.

8. Depreciation is a _____ expense; it is relevant to the computation of incremental cash flows only because it affects _____.

9. Depreciation affects cash flow calculations in two ways: first, depreciation expenses affect operating cash flows, since the deduction of depreciation expense reduces _____; and, second, depreciation affects the _____ value of an asset, and the difference between _____ value and _____ value has tax implications when an asset is sold.

10. There are tax implications associated with the sale of an asset whenever the asset is sold for a price which differs from its _____ value at the time of the sale. When the asset is sold for more than its _____ value, a tax obligation is created; when the asset is sold for less than its _____ value, the difference between the two figures is a _____ for the firm.

11. Projected cash flows for a capital budgeting project are derived from _____ financial statements, which are projected financial statements for future time periods. Operating cash flow is defined as: _____ + _____ – _____.

12. We do not deduct either interest or depreciation in computing operating cash flow. Interest is not deducted because it is not an_____ expense. Financing costs have an impact on our net present value analysis in that these costs determine the appropriate _____ in our net present value calculations. We do not deduct depreciation in computing operating cash flow because depreciation is a _____ expense.

13. Algebraically, we define EBIT as _____; taxes as _____; and operating cash flow (OCF) as: _____ + _____ − _____.

14. The bottom-up approach to defining operating cash flow accentuates the relationship between_____ and operating cash flow. The bottom-up interpretation of operating cash flow can be derived as follows: OCF = _____ + _____ − _____ = (EBIT − Taxes) + D = _____ + Depreciation = _____ + D

15. The top-down approach is derived from the basic definition of operating cash flow as follows: OCF = _____ + _____ − _____ = _____ + D − _____ = $(S − C) − [(S − C − D) × T_c]$ = Sales − Costs − Taxes. The top-down approach emphasizes the fact that operating cash flow is equal to _____ minus _____.

16. The tax shield approach to defining operating cash flow emphasizes the manner in which_____ affects cash flow. The tax shield approach is derived from the basic definition of operating cash flow as follows: OCF = _____ + _____ − _____ = (S − C − D) + D − $[(S − C − D) × T_c]$ = _____ + _____ . The first term in this definition is the project's _____ in the absence of _____. The second term in this definition of operating cash flow is referred to as the _____.

17. A supplier of a product or service sometimes submits a bid price to a prospective customer who then purchases the product or service from the supplier who has submitted the lowest bid. The problem for the supplier is to set the bid price at the _____ price which still provides the_____. To derive this price, the supplier must solve the capital budgeting problem 'backwards.' The supplier first determines the annual operating cash flow which makes the net present value of the project equal to _____. This value of OCF would provide the supplier with the_____. The supplier then determines the level of _____, and the price per unit, which would provide the required OCF. This price per unit is the supplier's _____.

18. A special capital budgeting problem arises when a firm compares two different machines that provide the same essential service, but differ with respect to purchase price and operating costs. This is an example of a choice between _____ alternatives. Such choices can be made on the basis of the _____ criterion. Since the machines provide the same essential service to the firm, the cash inflows can be ignored because they are not _____ cash flows for either machine.

19. If the machines have the same operating life, this choice between mutually exclusive alternatives is resolved by choosing the machine with the _____ present value of _____. If the two machines have different operating lives and if the firm will be replacing the selected machine at the end of its useful life, then the problem is resolved by the use of the _____ method.

PROBLEMS

Basic Questions

Use the following information to solve Problems 1 - 2:

Frizzle, Inc. manufactures imitation Persian rugs (as opposed to hand-knotted ones). Its owner, Matt Frizzle, has spent $30,000 travelling to Persia to study rugs. On his return he purchased a new weaving machine for $400,000. The machine will be depreciated using a 20% CCA rate. The machine will increase sales by $300,000 in each of the next 3 years. Annual fixed costs will be $40,000 and variable costs will be 55% of sales. The tax rate is 34%.

Problem 1

What are the CCA charges and ending UCC for the project?

Problem 2

Prepare the pro forma income statements for years 1 to 3.

Use the following information to solve Problems 3-15:

Aunt Sally's Sauces, Inc., is considering expansion into a new line of all-natural, cholesterol-free, sodium-free, fat-free, low-calorie tomato sauces. Sally paid $50,000 for a marketing study which indicates that sales for the new product line will be $650,000 per year for the next six years. Manufacturing plant and equipment would cost $500,000. The appropriate CCA rate is 20% . Salvage value will be zero. Annual fixed costs are projected at $80,000, and variable costs are projected at 60% of sales. Net working capital requirements are $75,000 for the six-year life of the project; the outlay for working capital will be recovered at the end of six years. Aunt Sally's tax rate is 34%, and the firm requires a 16% return on capital budgeting projects.

Problem 3

Compute the annual CCA charges and the ending UCC value for the fixed assets.

Problem 4

Prepare pro forma income statements for years 1 through 6.

Problem 5

Compute operating cash flow for the project for years 1 through 6.

Problem 6

Compute total projected cash flows for year 0 through 6 for the project.

Problem 7

Compute the net present value and the internal rate of return for the new product line.

Problem 8

Use the tax-shield approach to compute the operating cash flow for years 1 through 6.

Problem 9

Use the 'bottom-up' approach to compute the operating cash flow for years 1 through 6.

Intermediate Questions

Problem 10

Use the 'top-down' approach to compute the operating cash flow for years 1 through 6.

Problem 11

Assume that fixed assets have a salvage value of $100,000 after six years. Calculate total cash flow for Year 6.

Problem 12

Using the information in problem3 10 and 11, compute the net present value, the benefit-cost ratio and the IRR for the new product line. Use the 16% discount rate. Note: This incorporates a $100,000 salvage value.

Problem 13

Once again, solve Aunt Sally's capital budgeting problem assuming the fixed assets have a salvage value of $100,000. This time, use the declining balance formula to calculate the present value of CCA tax savings.

Problem 14

Now go back to problem 13 and assume that there will be other assets in class 8 so that a terminal loss will not occur in year six. Using a salvage value of $100,000, how should the NPV of the project be adjusted?

Problem 15

To replace an existing non-depreciable asset whose market value is $30,000 requires the purchase of a new asset which costs $60,000 and is expected to generate before-tax cash savings of $11,111.11 per year for each of the next five years. If the discount rate is 10 % and the tax rate 46 %, what is the NPV of this project? What is the IRR?

Problem 16

Turtle Speed is considering the acquisition of production equipment which will reduce both labour and materials costs. The cost of the equipment is $100,000. For simplicity, assume this asset can be depreciated straight line over four years for tax purposes. However, the useful life of the equipment is five years, and it will have a $20,000 salvage value at the end of five years. Operating costs will be reduced by $30,000 in the first year and the savings will increase by $5,000 per year for years 2, 3 and 4. Due to increased maintenance costs, savings in year 5 will be $10,000 less than the year 4 savings. The equipment will also reduce net working capital by $5,000 throughout the life of the project. The firm's tax rate is 34% and the firm requires a 16% return on capital budgeting projects. Prepare the pro forma income statement for years 1 through 5. Then, Compute operating cash flow for the project.

Problem 17

Compute total projected cash flows for years 0 through 5 for the project.

Problem 18

Compute the net present value and the internal rate of return for the production equipment.

Problem 19

Sky High Mfg. is considering the acquisition of a new machine which must have an IRR of at least 15%. This new machine will have an expected useful life of 10 years and zero salvage value. The firm takes maximum CCA tax savings each year and annual total cash flow (after CCA deductions and taxes), resulting from the addition of the new machine, will begin at the end of the year in which the initial investment has been made (i.e. year 0) and are estimated to be $9,962.60. What is the maximum amount your firm should be willing to pay for the new machine?

Problem 20

Rinki Dink Inc., is considering the purchase of a new ice-making machine that costs $55,500. The firm expects the machine to generate before-tax revenues of $21,500 per year for four years and increase operating costs by $4,500 per year for each of the next four years. At the end of the year 4, the machine will be sold for its remaining UCC . A CCA rate of 30% on the declining balance is applicable. In order to support the machine, an additional $7,000 is needed in working capital immediately and another $3,500 is required at the end of the second year of operations. Working capital additions are *not* subsequently recovered. Assume that there will be other assets in the UCC pool so that there will be no recapture or terminal loss. The tax rate is 40%.

a.   Compute the total after-tax cash flow for each of the next four years, incorporating the half year rule.

b.   Compute the payback period.

Problem 21

Referring to problem 20, determine the NPV of the investment if Rinky Dink's opportunity cost is 10%. Should the machine be purchased?

Problem 22

TJR Corporation is going to invest $100,000 in equipment with an applicable CCA rate of 30%. There are no other assets in this pool. The equipment has a useful life of five years. Calculate the annual CCA charges the corporation can claim. Next, assume the equipment has a salvage value of $40,000 and that TJR uses a 14% discount rate. Using a 40% tax rate, apply the tax shield approach to determine the present value of future CCA savings.

Problem 23

WeCan Corporation is considering the replacement of existing equipment that is listed on its books for $10,000 but would probably sell for half as much today, with another machine belonging in the same asset class that would cost $65,000. The firm expects this replacement to generate incremental after-tax revenues of $28,000 per year for three years and increase before-tax operating costs by $3,000 per year for each of the next three years. At the end of the third year, the new machine is expected to be scrapped (sold) for $8,750 which is 75% more than the expected salvage value of the old machine, had the old machine been used for another three years. Assume that there will always be another asset in the UCC pool. CCA rate of 20% on the declining balance is applicable. In order to support the machine, an additional $6,000 is needed in working capital immediately. Working capital additions are recovered at the end of the investment project. Compute the total after-tax cash flow for each year of the investment project, using a 40% tax-rate and incorporating the half-year rule.

Problem 24

Referring to problem 22, if the firm's cost of capital is 8%, determine the NPV of the investment. Should the machine be purchased?

Problem 25

A firm is deciding between purchasing Machines A or B. The two machines provide the same benefit to the company and the machine selected will be replaced at the end of its useful life. The lives and annual costs for each are:

Year	Machine A	Machine B
0	$5,000	$4,000
1	800	1,200
2	800	1,200
3	800	1,200
4	800	1,200
5	800	

The firm's opportunity cost is 12%. If we assume no taxes, which machine should be selected? Solve this problem by computing the equivalent annual cost for each machine.

Problem 26

Suppose that, in the previous problem, all costs are before-tax costs and the tax rate is 34%; the company will depreciate either machine using straight-line depreciation over the life of the asset, and the salvage value of either asset is zero at the end of the life of the asset. Compute the EAC for each asset. Which asset is preferable?

Problem 27

A firm is considering the purchase of either Machine X or Machine Y. The two machines provide the same benefit, and the machine selected will be replaced at the end of its useful life. The lives and annual costs for each are:

Year	Machine X	Machine Y
0	$800	$600
1	150	200
2	150	200
3	150	200
4	150	

The firm's opportunity cost is 15%. If we assume no taxes, which machine should be selected? Solve this problem by computing the equivalent annual cost for each machine.

Problem 28

Ace Hand Tools, Inc. (AHT) is submitting a bid to supply hammers for Canada's Department of Defense (DOD). The DOD will buy 1,000 hammers per year for the next three years. To supply the hammers, AHT must buy $150,000 of manufacturing equipment. The equipment has a five-year life and will be depreciated for tax purposes on a straight-line basis. The DOD contract is for three years, and ACT plans to sell the equipment at the end of three years for an estimated $50,000. Additional fixed costs will total $38,000 per year and variable costs are expected to be $2 per hammer. An additional investment of $25,000 in net working capital will be required. This investment will be recovered at the end of three years. The firm's tax rate is 34% and the required rate of return is 18%. What is the lowest price the manufacturer can charge for the hammers?

Problem 29

FlyAway Airlines, Inc. (FAAI) currently generates sales revenues of $254,450,000 per year. However, recent regulation has resulted in the entry of several low-fare air carriers into the industry, and FAAI's management is concerned that competition from these new entries into the industry will threaten FAAI. They are particularly concerned about the difference between FAAI's fares and the fares charged by the new airlines. To address the threat, management proposes the creation of its own discount airline, RockBottom Air, Inc. (RBAI), which would offer fares comparable to the low-fare competitors. Management provides the following estimates: the cash flows from RBAI; the erosion that RBAI will cause to FAAI's cashflows; and the erosion of FAAI's cash flows due to the entry of the low-fare air carriers that will occur if RBAI is not created, as follows:

	Year 1	Year 2	Year 3	Year 4	Year 5
Cashflows from RBAI	$17,500,000	$28,750.00	$40,000,000	$40,000,000	$45,000,000
Erosion of FAAI due to RBAI	$20,000,000	$25,000,000	$30,000,000	$40,000,000	$40,000,000
Erosion due to competition if RBAI is not created	$5,000,000	$20,000,000	$20,000,000	$30,000,000	$30,000,000

What are the incremental cashflows associated with RBAI?

Problem 30

Fun & Free, Inc. (FFI) currently generates sales revenues of $3,543,234 per year selling low-fat pastries. However, a new competitor, Blissful Health, Inc. (BHI), has introduces a new low-fat, low-sugar and low-carbohydrate pastry to the industry, which could significantly hurt FFI's sales. To address the potential competition from BHI, FFI's management proposes the introduction of a new line of low-fat, low-sugar and low-carbohydrate pastries to the market, under the brand name Endless Flavor (EF). Management provides the following estimates: the cash flows from EF; the erosion that EF will cause to FFI's existing cashflows; and the erosion of FFI's cash flows due to the new BHI product that will occur if EF is not created, as follows:

	Year 1	Year 2	Year 3
Cashflows from EF	$35,453	$60,765	$76,765
Erosion due to EF	$28,870	$54,000	$54,000
Erosion due to competition if EF is not created	$10,000	$15,000	$15,000

What are the incremental cashflows associated with EF?

ANSWERS TO CONCEPT TEST

1. changes; accepting

2. the firm's cash flows if the project is not undertaken; stand-alone; project; entire firm

3. spent; committed to spend; is not; is not

4.   forego; accepts; is

5.   side effect; are

6.   current assets; current liabilities; increase

7.   outflow; inflow; accrues; matching; accrual; cash flows

8.   non-cash; taxes

9.   taxes; book; book; market

10.   book; book; book; tax deduction

11.   pro forma; earnings before interest and taxes (EBIT); depreciation; taxes

12.   operating; discount rate; non-cash

13. $(S-C-D)$; $[(S-C-D) \times T_C]$; $(S-C-D)$; D; $[(S-C-D) \times T_C]$

14.   net income; EBIT; D; Taxes; Net income; $[(S-C-D) \times (1-T_c)]$

15.   EBIT; D; Taxes; $(S-C-D)$; $[(S-C-D) \times T_c]$; sales; expenses

16.   depreciation; EBIT; D; Taxes; $[(S-C) \times (1-T_c)]$; $(D \times T_c)$; cash flow; depreciation; depreciation tax shield

17.   lowest; required rate of return; zero; required rate of return; sales; bid price

18.   mutually exclusive; net present value; incremental

19.   lower; operating costs; equivalent annual cost

PROBLEM SOLUTIONS

Problem 1:

Year	Beginning UCC	CAA	Ending UCC
1	$200,000	$40,000	$160,000
2	360,000	72,000	288,000
3	288,000	57,600	230,400

Problem 2:

	Year 1	Year 2	Year 3
Sales	$300,000	$300,000	$300,000
- Variable costs	$165,000	$165,000	165,000
- Fixed costs	40,000	40,000	40,000
- Depreciation	40,000	72,000	57,600
EBIT	$ 55,000	$ 23,000	$ 37,400
- Tax @ 34%	18,700	7,820	12,716
Net income	$ 36,300	$ 15,180	$ 24,684

Problem 3:

Year	Beginning UCC	CCA	Ending UCC
1	$250,000	$50,000	$200,000
2	450,000	90,000	360,000
3	360,000	72,000	288,000
4	288,000	57,600	230,400
5	230,400	46,080	184,320
6	184,320	36,864	147,456

Problem 4: The pro forma income statements are presented in the following table:

	Year 1	Year 2	Year 3	Year 4	Year 5	Year 6
Sales revenue	$ 650,000	$ 650,000	$ 650,000	$650,000	$ 650,000	$ 650,000
−Variable Costs	390,000	390,000	390,000	390,000	390,000	390,000
−Fixed Costs	80,000	80,000	80,000	80,000	80,000	80,000
−Depreciation	50,000	90,000	72,000	57,600	46,080	36,864
EBIT	$ 130,000	$ 90,000	$108,000	$122,400	$ 133,920	$ 143,136
	44,200	30,600	36,720	41,616	45,532.80	48,666.24
Net Income	$ 85,800	$ 59,400	$ 71,280	$ 80,784	$ 88,387.20	$ 94,469.76

Problem 5: The operating cash flows are computed in the following table, using data from the pro forma income statements in problem 2:

	Year 1	Year 2	Year 3	Year 4	Year 5	Year 6
(EBIT)	$130,000	$ 90,000	$108,000	$122,400	$133,920	$143,136
+Depreciation	50,000	90,000	72,000	57,600	46,080	36,864
−Tax (at 34%)	44,200	30,600	36,720	41,616	45,532.80	48,666.24
OCF	$135,800	$149,400	$143,280	$138,384	$134,467.20	$131,333.76

Problem 6: Net working capital remains constant from years 1 through 5 and capital expenditures take place only in year zero. Consequently, for years 1 through 5, total cash flow is the same as operating cash flow. For year zero, additions to net working capital are $75,000 and capital expenditures are $500,000. Therefore, year zero cash outflow is $575,000. For year 6, recovery of net working capital results in a cash inflow of $75,000. The ending UCC value is $147,456 and if there are no assets left in this pool, then the company can realize a terminal loss equal to this amount. The resulting tax savings are equal to $50,135.04 ($147,456 × .34). Note we are assuming that the company will scrap the investment for zero salvage at the end of the sixth year, and claim CCA that year. Total cash inflow for year 6 is equal to the sum of the operating cash flow, the recovery of net working capital, and tax savings from the terminal loss: ($131,333.76 + $75,000 + $50,135.04 = $256,468.80)

Note: The cost of the marketing study ($50,00) is a sunk cost and has no bearing on our calculations

Problem 7: The present value of the future cash flows is:

$$\frac{\$135,800}{(1.16)} + \frac{\$149,400}{(1.16)^2} + \frac{\$143,280}{(1.16)^3} + \frac{\$138,384}{(1.16)^4} + \frac{\$134.467.20}{(1.16)^5} + \frac{\$256,468.80}{(1.16)^6}$$

$$k = \$565,606.40$$

The net present value is ($565,606.40 – $575,000) = –$9,393.60. Since the net present value is negative, the new product line is not an acceptable investment.

The IRR can be computed using the trial-and-error procedures described in the previous chapter. It is necessary to determine the discount rate for which the present value of the future cash flows is equal to the current cash outlay. Alternatively, the IRR is the discount rate which makes the net present value of the project zero. For a discount rate of 16%, the present value is $565,606.40 and the net present value is –$9,393.60. For a discount rate of 15%, the present value and net present value are +$582,117.75 and +$7,117.75, respectively. Therefore, the IRR is between 15% and 16% indicating an unacceptable investment because it is less than the appropriate discount rate. The precise value of the IRR is 15.4255%.

Problem 8: the tax-shield approach defines the operating cash flow as follows:

$$OCF = [(S - C) \times (1 - T_c)] + (D \times T_c)$$

This equation is used in the following table to compute operating cash flow for each year of the project's life:

	Year 1	Year 2	Year 3	Year 4	Year 5	Year 6
Sales revenue	$650,000	$650,000	$650,000	$650,000	$650,000	$650,000
–Total Costs	470,000	470,000	470,000	470,000	470,000	470,000
(S - C)	180,000	180,000	180,000	180,000	180,000	180,000
(S – C) × (1 – Tc)	118,800	118,800	118,800	118,800	118,800	118,800
Depreciation	50,000	90,000	72,000	57,600	46,080	36,864
(D x Tc)	17,000	30,600	24,480	19,584	15,667.20	12,533.76
OCF = [(S – C) × (1–Tc)+ (D × Tc)	$135,800	$149,400	$143,280	$138,384	$134,467.20	$131,333.76

These figures for operating cash flow are identical to those computed in Problem 3.

Problem 9: The 'bottom-up' approach defines the operating cash flow as follows:

$$OCF = [(S - C - D) \times (1 - T_c)] + D = \text{Net Income} + \text{Depreciation}$$

This equation, and data from Problem 2, are used to compute OCF for each year of the project's life.

	Year 1	Year 2	Year 3	Year 4	Year 5	Year 6
Net income	85,800	59,400	71,280	80,784	88,387.20	94,469.76
+Depreciation	50,000	90,000	72,000	57,600	46,080.00	36,864.00
OCF	135,000	149,400	143,280	138,384	134,467.20	131,333.76

These figures for operating cash flow are identical to those computed in Problems 5 and 8.

Problem 10: The 'top-down' approach defines the operating cash flow as follows:

$$OCF = (S - C) - [(S - C - D) \times T_c] = \text{Sales} - \text{Costs} - \text{Taxes}$$

This equation and data from Problem 4 are used to compute OCF for each year of the project's life:

	Year 1	Year 2	Year 3	Year 4	Year 5	Year 6
Sales	$650,000	$650,000	$650,000	$650,000	$650,000	$650,000
–Total Costs	470,000	470,000	470,000	470,000	470,000	470,000
–Taxes	44,200	30,600	36,720	41,616	45,532.80	48,666.24
OCF	$135,800	$149,400	$143,280	$138,384	$134,467.20	$131,333.76

Problem 11: From Problem 3, we know the beginning UCC value in year 6 is $184,320. If the fixed assets are sold for $100,000, the terminal loss is reduced to $84,320. The resulting tax savings are: $84,320 × .34 = $28,668.80. For year 6, the total cash flow components consist of salvage value (-$100,000), terminal loss tax savings ($28,668.80), recovery of working capital ($75,000) and operating cash flow ($131,333.76) which add up to $335,002.56.

Problem 12: The present value of the future cash flows us:

$$\frac{\$135,800}{(1.16)} + \frac{\$149,400}{(1.16)^2} + \frac{\$143,280}{(1.16)^3} + \frac{\$138,384}{(1.16)^4} + \frac{\$134,467.2}{(1.16)^5} + \frac{\$335,002.56}{(1.16)^6}$$

The net present value is: $597,839.98 – $575,000 = $22,839.98 and the investment project is acceptable (mainly because of the large salvage value that is recovered at the end of six years).

The benefit-cost ratio is $597,839.98 / $575,000 = 1.03972, or approximately 4 cents of value created for every 1 dollar invested.

The IRR must be greater than 16 %, since the NPV is positive. The exact IRR is 17.32 %.

Problem 13: Calculate the present value of CCA tax savings. The problem can be solved sequentially by calculating the present value of six different cash flow components:

First, identify the initial investment: –$500,000.

Second, calculate the present value of after tax operating income excluding CCA:

$$(\$650,000 – \$470,000)(1 – .34)(PVIFA_{16\%,6}) = (\$180,000)(.66)(3.684736) = \$437,746.64$$

Third, calculate the present value of working capital requirements:

$$-\$75,000 + (\$75,000 × PVIF_{16\%,6}) = -\$75,000 + (\$75,000 × .410442) = -\$44,216.85$$

Fourth, calculate the present value of CCA tax savings:

$$\frac{\$500,000(.20)(.34)}{.16 + .2} × \frac{1.08}{1.16} - \frac{\$147,456(.20)(.34)}{.16 + .2} × .410442$$

$$= \$87,931.03 – \$11,431.96 = \$76,499.07$$

Note, $147,456 has been used for S (not, $100,000). This is to reduce the infinite CCA tax savings ($87,931.03) by the ending UCC value ($147,456) since there is a terminal loss at the end of the project. If a terminal loss was not anticipated, the infinite CCA tax savings would have been reduced by the salvage amount ($100,000) in the formula.

Fifth, compute the present value of salvage: $100,000 (.410442) = $41,044.2. Finally, calculate the present value of the terminal loss tax savings: $84,320 (.34) (.410442) = $11,766.88.

Note, the terminal loss is equal to the beginning UCC value in year 6 less the salvage value ($184,320 – $100,000).

The NPV is therefore: $–500,000 + $437,746.64 – $44,216.85 + $76,499.07 + $41,044.20 + $11,766.88 = $22,839.94 which is the same result as the solution to Problem 12.

Problem 14: The fourth component of cash flow in problem 13, the present value of CCA tax savings, needs to be recomputed:

$$\frac{\$500,000\,(.20)\,(.34)}{.16 + .2} \times \frac{1.08}{1.16} - \frac{\$100,000\,(.20)\,(.34)}{.16 + .2} \times .410442 = \$80,178.24$$

This amount is greater than the CCA tax savings when a terminal loss was expected ($76,499.07) because the reduction in CCA tax savings was based on the ending UCC balance ($147,456) which is greater than the salvage value ($100,000). NPV will increase by: $80,178.24 – $76,499.07 = $3679.17,   At the same time, NPV will be reduced by $11,766.88, which represents the terminal loss tax savings that will *not* occur. The overall reduction in NPV is: $3,679.17 – $11,766.88 = $8,087.71. The NPV is $22,839.95 – $8,087.71 = $14,752.23.

Problem 15: The initial investment is: $60,000 - $30,000 = $30,000. The total cash flows after taxes are: $11,111.11 (1 – .46) = $6,000 per year. The NPV is is: $–30,000 + ($6,000 × PVIFA$_{10\%,5}$) = –$7,255.28

The IRR of the project is found by trial and error, a financial calculator, or using the following equation:

$$- \$30,000 + \$6,000 \times [1 - 1/(1 + IRR)^5]/IRR = 0$$

The IRR works out to 0.0%. This implies that the present value factor for each of the next five years is 1.0. Therefore, at a zero percent discount rate (IRR) the NPV is zero: –30,000 + $6,000 × 5 = 0.

Problem 16: The pro forma income statements are presented in the following table:

	Year 1	Year 2	Year 3	Year 4	Year 5
Sales revenue	$ 0	$ 0	$ 0	$ 0	$ 0
–Operating costs	– 30,000	–35,000	–40,000	–45,000	–35,000
–Depreciation	25,000	25,000	25,000	25,000	0
(EBIT)	$ 5,000	$10,000	$15,000	$20,000	$35,000
–Tax (at 34%)	1,700	3,400	5,100	6,800	11,900
Net Income	$ 3,300	$ 6,600	$ 9,900	$13,200	$23,100

Note: sales revenue does not change, and only incremental cash flows are used in the analysis. So, the relevant sales revenue is zero. The negative sign for operating costs reflects that these numbers represent a *decrease* in costs. So, for example, EBIT for year 1 is:EBIT = $0 - (- $30,000) - $25,000 = The decrease in operating costs results in an increase in EBIT and net income. Operating cash flows based on the pro forma income statements are below:

	Year 1	Year 2	Year 3	Year 4	Year 5
(EBIT)	$ 5,000	$10,000	$15,000	$20,000	$35,000
+Depreciation	25,000	25,000	25,000	25,000	0
–Tax (at 34%)	1,700	3,400	5,100	6,800	11,900
(OCF)	$28,300	$31,600	$34,900	$38,200	$23,100

Problem 17: For years 1 - 4, total cash flow is the same as operating cash flow. For year zero, NWC is reduced by $5,000 and capital expenditures are $100,000. The reduction in NWC is a cash *inflow*, so that the year zero cash outflow is $100,000 – $5,000 = $95,000. In year 5, the reduction in NWC is terminated and returns to the pre-project level. The resulting increase in NWC at the end of year 5 is a cash *outflow*. Also at the end of year 5, fixed assets have a salvage value of $20,000 and a book value of zero. The after-tax cash inflow resulting from the sale of fixed assets is: ($20,000 – $0) × (1 – .34) = $13,200.

Total cash inflow for year 5 is: $23,100 – $5,000 + $13,200 = $31,300

Problem 18: The present value of the future cash flows is:

$$\frac{\$28,300}{(1.16)} + \frac{\$31,600}{(1.16)^2} + \frac{\$34,900}{(1.16)^3} + \frac{\$38,200}{(1.16)^4} + \frac{\$31,300}{(1.16)^5} = \$106,239.31$$

The NPV is: $106,239.31 – $95,000 = $11,239.31. Since the NPV is positive, the acquisition of the new production equipment is an acceptable investment.

By trial-and-error, an IRR of 20% yields a present value of $96,725.37 and an NPV of $1,725.37. For a discount rate of 21%, the present value and NPV are: $94,559.88 and –$440.12, respectively. Therefore, the IRR is between 20% and 21%, indicating an acceptable investment. The precise value of the IRR is 20.794%. (This can also be solved with a financial calculator.)

Problem 19: The maximum investment (Co) occurs when NPV is equal to zero.

$9,962.60 × PVIFA$_{15\%,10}$ (1.15) – Co = 0 → Co = $9,962.60 × 5.018769 (1.15) = $57,499.98

Note: the cash flows st at the *end* of Year 0, or the *beginning* of Year 1. This is an *annuity due*.

Problem 20: *All numbers are rounded off to the nearest dollar*

a.   First calculate a schedule for CCA charges:

t	UCC Beginning	CCA	UCC ending
1	$27,500	$ 8,250	$19,250
2	46,750	14,025	32,725
3	32,725	9,818	22,907.5
4	22,907.5	6,872.25	16,035.25

Next, identify the components for total cash flow:

	Year 0	Year 1	Year 2	Year 3	Year 4
Investment	$–55,000				
Revenue		$21,500	$21,500	$21,500	$21,500
Costs		4,500	4,500	4,500	4,500
CCA		8,250	14,025	9,818	6,872
EBIT		8,750	2,975	7,182	10,128
–Tax (at 40%)		3,500	1,190	2,873	4,051
+CCA		8,250	14,025	9,818	6,872
Operating cash flow		13,500	15,810	14,127	12,949
Working capital	– 7,000		– 3,500		
Salvage value					16,035
Total cash flow	$–62,000	$13,500	$12,310	$14,127	$28,984

b.   To calculate the payback period (undiscounted) add the total cash flows:

	Year 0	Year 1	Year 2	Year 3	Year 4
Total cash flows	$–62,000	$13,500	$12,310	$14,127	$28,984
Cumulative	$–62,000	– 48,500	–36,190	–22,063	+ 6,921

Rinki Dink, needs to recover only $22,063 from year four cash flows. The fraction of year four in which the payback occurs is ($22,063/$28,984) = .7612. Therefore, the payback period is 3.75 years.

Problem 21: Initial investment: – $62,000

$$PV \text{ (working capital requirements): } –\$7,000 –\$3,500 \ (PVIF_{10\%,\ 2}) \ = \ –\$9,892.56$$

The present value of after-tax operating income (using the basic approach):

$$\text{Operating income (after tax)} = EBIT \ - Tax \ - Depn \ = \ EBIT \ (1 - T_c) + Depn$$

	Year 0	Year 1	Year 2	Year 3	Year 4
EBIT (1 - T^c)		5,250	1,785	4,309	6,077
+CCA		8,250	14,025	9,818	6,872
After-tax OCF		13,500	15,810	14,127	12,949

PV(CFAT) at 10% : $44,947

The present value of CCA tax savings are: $\dfrac{\$55,000\ (.30)\ (.40)}{.10 + .30} \ \text{x} \ \dfrac{1.05}{1.10} \ = \ \$15,750$

The present value of CCA tax savings lost due to salvage:

$$- \ \ \frac{\$16,035\ (.30)\ (.40)}{.10 + .30} \ \ \text{x PVIF (10\%,4)} \ = \ -\$3,285.64$$

The present value of salvage proceeds received:

$$= \$16,035 \ (PVIF \ 10\%, 4) = \$16,035 \ (.6830) = \$10,952.12$$

NPV: $-\$55,000 - \$9,892.76 + \$44,947 + \$15,750 - \$3,285.64 + \$10,952.12 = \$3,470.72$

Decision: Purchase the machine.

Problem 22:

Year	Beginning UCC	CCA	Ending UCC
1	$50,000	$15,000	$35,000
2	85,000*	25,500	59,500
3	59,500	17,850	41,650
4	41,650	12,495	29,155
5	29,155	8,746.50	20,408.50

$* \ \$85,000 = \$35,00 + \$50,000$

Next, calculate the present value of the tax shield:

$$PV = \frac{\$100,000 \ (.30) \ (.40)}{.14 + .30} \times \frac{1 + (0.5) \ (0.14)}{1 + .14} - \frac{\$29,155 \ (.30) \ (.40)}{.14 + .30} \times \frac{1}{(1.14)^5}$$

$$= \$25,598.09 - \$4,129.69 = \$21,468.40$$

Note that the salvage value used to solve this equation is the UCC balance in the beginning of year 5 because there are no other assets in the pool. TJR Corporation will have a tax savings of $21,447.40 from the depreciation and subsequent sale of the equipment.

Problem 23: First, calculate a schedule for CCA changes:

t	UCC beginning	CCA	UCC ending
1	* $30,000	$ 6,000	$24,000
2	54,000	10,800	43,200
3	43,200	8,640	34,560

Note, the UCC beginning balance for the first year is $30,000. This is because the net acquisition is: $65,000 − ($10,000 × ½) = $60,000 of which only half is added when it is put in use.

Next, identify the components of total cash flow:

	Year 0	Year 1	Year 2	Year 3
Net Investment	–$60,000			
Revenue		$28,000	$28,000	$28,000
Costs		3,000	3,000	3,000
CCA		6,000	10,800	8,640
EBIT		19,000	14,200	16,360
+CCA		6,000	10,800	8,640
–Tax		7,600	5,680	6,544
Operating cash flow		17,400	19,320	18,456
Working capital	– 6,000			6,000
Salvage value				3,750
Total cash flow	–$66,000	$17,400	$19,320	$28,206

To calculate the change in revenues, convert the after-tax amount of $16,800 to its before-tax equivalent of $16,800/(1 – .4) = $28,000. The salvage value is the difference between the salvage values of the new equipment ($8,750) and the old equipment, if it had been kept ($5,000); i.e. S_{old} = $8,750 / 1.75 - $5,000 = $3,725.

Problem 24:   Initial investment: $60,000

PV (working capital):   – $6,000 + $6,000 (PVIF$_{8\%,3}$)   =   –$1,237

PV (after-tax Op Inc): ($28,000 – $3,000) (1 – .4) (PVIFA 8%,3)   = $38,656.46

PV (CCA tax savings): $\dfrac{\$60,000\,(.20)\,(.40)}{.08\ +\ .20} \times \dfrac{1.04}{1.08}\ -\ \dfrac{\$3,750\,(.20)\,(.40)}{.08\ +\ .20} \times .793832$

$=$ $16,507.94 - $850.53 = $15,657.41

PV (salvage): $3,750 (.793832)   = $2,976.87

NPV: –$60,000 + $38,656.46 – $1,237 + $15,657.41 + $2,976.87   =   –$3,946.26.

Since the NPV is negative, the equipment should not be purchased.

Problem 25: At a 12% discount rate, the present values of the costs for A and B are -$7,883.82 and -$7,644.82, respectively (Remember, these are costs!). Ignoring the fact that Machine B would have to be replaced earlier than Machine A, Machine B would be selected because the PV(costs) is less. Proper evaluation involves computing the equivalent annual cost (EAC) for each:

For A: PV (costs) = - $7,883.82 = EAC × PVIFA$_{12\%,5}$ → EAC = - $2,187.05

For B: PV (costs) = -$7644.82 x PVIFA$_{(12\%,4)}$ → EAC = - $2,516.94.

EAC(A) < EAC(B), so A has the lower cost, on an annual basis, and is therefore the preferable alternative.

Problem 26: In order to compute the EAC, we first determine the operating cash flows for each asset. In this problem, operating cash flow is most easily computed using the tax-shield approach.

$$\text{Machine A: OCF} = [(\$0 - \$800) \times (1 - .34)] + (\$5,000 / 5) \times .34 = -\$188$$

$$\text{PC (OCF)} = -\$188 \times \text{PVIFA}_{12\%,5} = -\$188 \times 3.604776 = -\$677.70$$

$$\text{PV (Total cash outflows)} = -\$5,000 - \$677.70 = -\$5,677.70$$

$$\rightarrow \quad -5,677.70 = \text{EAC} \times 3.604776 \rightarrow \text{EAC} = -\$1,575.05$$

Machine B: OCF = –\$452; PV(OCF) = -\$1,372.88;
PV (Total cash outflows) = -\$6,372.88; $\rightarrow$ EAC = -\$2,098.17.

Therefore, Machine A is the preferable alternative because it involves lower cash outflows.

Problem 27: PV (costs) for X and Y are \$1,228.25 and \$1,056.65, respectively.

$$\text{Machine X: } \$1,288.25 = \text{EAC} \times \text{PVIFA}_{15\%,4} \rightarrow \text{EAC} = -\$430.21$$

$$\text{Machine Y: } \$1,056.65 = \text{EAC} \times \text{PVIFA}_{15\%,3} \rightarrow \text{EAC} = -\$462.79$$

X has the lower cost, on an annual basis, and is therefore the preferred alternative.

Now, determine the net income and price per unit that will provide the necessary OCF. Using the bottom-up approach:

$$\text{OCF} = [(S - C - D) \times (1 - T_c)] + D \rightarrow \$58,540.64 = (S - C - D) \times (1 - T_c) + \$30,000$$

$$\$28,540.64 = (S - C) \times (1 - T_c)$$

$$\rightarrow \quad \text{Net income} = [(S - C - D) \times (1 - T_c)] \rightarrow \$28,540.64 = (S - \$40,000 - \$30,000) \times (1 - .34)$$

$$\$28,540.64 = (S - \$70,000) \times (.66) \rightarrow (\$28,540.64 / .66) = (S - \$70,000)$$

$$\rightarrow \quad S = \$113,243.39$$

Note: The value of C is the sum of variable (\$2 x 1,000) and fixed (\$38,000) costs = \$40,000. S is the total sales required to generate the required OCF. Since the bid is for 1,000 hammers, the price per unit is (\$113,243.39/1,000) = \$113.24. This price will provide AHT with an annual OCF of \$58,540.64 and NPV for the project equal to zero, so that AHT would earn the required 18% rate of return.

Problem 28: The minimum annual operating cash flow (OCF) needed to yield an 18% return is determined using the NPV formula. At the required return of 18%, NPV will equal zero. The initial outlay is the cost of the manufacturing equipment plus the working capital = \$150,000 + \$25,000 = \$175,000. The \$25,000 of working capital plus \$50,000 from the sale of the equipment = \$75,000 will be recovered in year 3. It follows:

$$0 = -\$175,000 + \frac{\text{OCF}}{(1.18)^1} + \frac{\text{OCF}}{(1.18)^2} + \frac{\text{OCF}}{(1.18)^3} + \frac{\$75,000}{(1.18)^3}$$

The present value of the $75,000 recovered in year 3 is $75,000/(1.18)^3 = $45,647.32$. Noting that the OCF is actually a three-year annuity, the NPV can be rewritten as:

$$0 = -\$175,000 + OCF \times PVIFA(18\%,3) + \$45,647.32 = -\$129,352.68 + OCF \times 2.174273$$

We solve for OCF: $\$129,352.68 / 2.174273 = OCF = \$59,492.39$. Next, since OCF = Net Income + Depreciation, it follows that $\$59,492.39$ = Net Income + $\$150,000/5$. Solving, it follows that Net Income = $\$29,492.39$. And since

$$\text{Net Income} = (\text{Sales} - \text{Fixed Costs} - \text{Variable Costs} - \text{Depreciation}) \times (1 - T_c),$$

it follows:

$$\$29,492.39 = (\text{Sales} - \$38,000 - \$2 \times 1,000 - \$150,000/5) \times (1 - 0.34)$$

Solving, we find Sales = $\$114,685.44$. Since the bid is for 1,000 hammers, the lowest price the manufacturer can charge is $\$114,685.44/1,000 = \$114.69$.

Problem 29: The incremental cashflows are equal to the cashflows from the project, adjusted downward for the erosion caused by the project, and adjusted upwards due to erosion caused by competition if the project is not implemented. It follows:

Incremental cashflows = Cashflows from RBAI - Erosion of FAAI due to RBAI + Erosion due to competition if RBAI is not created

It follows:

	Year 1	Year 2	Year 3	Year 4	Year 5
Incremental cashflows	$2,500,000	-$4,971,250	$30,000,000	$30,000,000	$35,000,000

Problem 30: The incremental cashflows are equal to the cashflows from the project, adjusted downward for the erosion caused by the project, and adjusted upwards due to erosion caused by competition if the project is not implemented. It follows:

Incremental cashflows = Cashflows from RBAI - Erosion of FAAI due to RBAI + Erosion due to competition if RBAI is not created

It follows:

	Year 1	Year 2	Year 3
Incremental cashflows	$16,583	$21,765	$37,765

11   Project Analysis and Evaluation

CHAPTER HIGHLIGHTS

The focus of Chapter 10 was on identifying and computing cash flows for capital budgeting projects. Remember though, the individual cash flows themselves, as well as the resulting net present value calculations, are estimates. These must be evaluated more closely. This chapter discusses how to assess these forecasts and estimates and their impact on the firm.

11.1 EVALUATING NPV ESTIMATES

Remember that, although a capital budgeting project is acceptable if its market value exceeds its cost, most of the time, market value cannot be directly observed. Therefore, it is estimated, usually using discounted cash flow (DCF) analysis. If the present value of the project exceeds its cost, then the project's NPV is positive. Although this is a good sign, remember that the numbers used to compute the NPV are only estimates. Therefore, the NPV calculations are subject to error. A potential source of error is in the forecast of future cash flows. There is always a possibility that actual cash flows will deviate from the forecasts. All NPV calculations, therefore, must be evaluated to determine their reliability.

The first step in evaluating the reliability of an NPV estimate is to understand the nature of the cash flow forecasts. In general, these forecasts can be thought of in terms of the expected value concept. For example, consider a forecasted cash flow of $5,000 one year from now. This does not mean that the actual cash flow will be $5,000 or even very close to $5,000. Rather, the expected value refers to a weighted average of all the cash flows which *might* possibly occur. Therefore, the actual cash flow could be a great deal more or less than $5,000. In interpreting the DCF analysis, keep in mind that the actual cash flow can, and most likely will, differ from the expected value.

Forecasting risk is the risk that the financial manager will make an incorrect decision because of errors in forecasting future cash flows. If forecasted cash inflows are overly optimistic, a project may appear to have a positive NPV when, in fact, it is negative. Many of the techniques described in this chapter are designed to identify sources of potential errors in cash flow forecasts.

11.2 SCENARIO AND OTHER WHAT-IF ANALYSES

Capital budgeting deals with the uncertain future. If assumptions about future cash flows are incorrect, the estimates of NPV will be incorrect as well. *Scenario analysis*, *sensitivity analysis*, and *simulation analysis* are commonly used to evaluate the critical assumptions of net present value calculations.

Getting Started: Assume a firm is considering the production of a new product. The project requires an investment of $1,000,000 in plant and equipment which has a ten-year life and no salvage value. For simplicity, assume that, for tax purposes, fixed assets will be depreciated on a straight-line basis. The required rate of return is 16% and the tax rate is 34%. The firm has made the following forecasts:

	Base case	Lower bound	Upper bound
Unit sales	10,000	9,000	11,000
Price per unit	$200	$190	$210
Variable costs per unit	$130	$125	$135
Fixed costs per year	$425,000	$410,000	$440,000

The 'base case' forecast represents the expected values for each forecasted item. The 'lower bound' and 'upper bound' forecasts are values such that the firm believes it is unlikely that actual values will be outside these bounds. What is the net present value of the project using the base case forecast?

First, compute the net income and operating cash flow:

Sales	$2,000,000
– Variable costs	1,300,000
– Fixed costs	425,000
– Depreciation	100,000
EBIT	$ 175,000
– Taxes (34%)	59,500
Net income	$ 115,500

EBIT	$ 175,000
+ Depreciation	100,000
– Taxes	59,500
Operating Cash Flow	$ 215,500

Next, compute the present value of an annuity of $215,500 per year for ten years, discounted at 16%:

$$PV = \$215,500 \times PVIFA(16\%,10) = \$215,500 \times 4.833227 = \$1,041,560$$

The net present value of the project is:

$$\$1,041,560 - \$1,000,000 = \$41,560$$

This net present value can be thought of as the *expected* net present value, the NPV managers deem most likely.

Scenario Analysis: Since the NPV computed in the preceding example is positive, the projectg may appear to be acceptable. However, a more careful analysis, reflecting the lower and upper bound forecasts may yield different results. *Scenario analysis* examines the effect on all variables, and consequently on NPV, of a hypothetical sequence of events.

An Example: For our scenario analysis, we examine both the worst case scenario and the best case scenario, as indicated in the following table:

	Worst case	Best case
Unit sales	9,000	11,000
Price per unit	$190	$210
Variable costs per unit	$135	$125
Fixed costs per year	$440,000	$410,000

The worst case scenario indicates the least favourable outcome for each of the four forecasted variables while the best case scenario indicates the most favourable outcome for each of the variables. For example, the worst case scenario will use the lower bound for unit sales and price per unit but the upper bound for variable and fixed costs. The best case scenario will use the upper bound for sales and price, and the lower bound for variable and fixed costs. For each scenario, we now compute net income, cash flow, net present value and internal rate of return for the proposed project. The results are presented in the following table:

Scenario	Net income	Cash flow	NPV	IRR
Base case	$115,500	$215,500	$ 41,650	17.11%
Worst case	– 29,700	70,300	–660,224	–5.94
Best case	280,500	380,500	839,043	36.33

What conclusions can we draw from these results? The major conclusion seems to be that further analysis is required. While the net present value is positive for the base case scenario, there is some possibility that the net present value will be significantly negative (the NPV for the worst case scenario is –$660,224). In the next section, we use a variant of scenario analysis to evaluate these results further.

Sensitivity Analysis: *Sensitivity analysis* is designed to determine the sensitivity of one variable to changes in another variable. For our purposes, we are interested in the sensitivity of NPV to variation in the level of each of the four forecasted variables. For example, we might attempt to determine the change in NPV which results if actual sales are at the lower bound of our forecasted range, while all other variables are held at their base case levels. Sensitivity analysis is a variant of scenario analysis in which each scenario represents a change in only one variable, rather than a number of variables.

An Example: Assume that all variables, except unit sales, take on their base case levels. What is the effect on net present value and internal rate of return if unit sales are at their lower bound?

The answer to this question is provided in the following table:

Scenario	Unit sales	Cash flow	NPV	IRR
Base case	10,000	$215,500	$ 41,650	17.11%
Worst case	9,000	169,300	–181,735	10.93
Best case	11,000	261,700	264,856	22.82

Although the problem posed here concerns the effect on NPV and IRR if unit sales are at their lower bound, we have also included results for the case in which sales are at their upper bound. For both the worst case and best case scenarios here, we assume that price, variable costs and fixed costs take on their base case values. Before we analyze these results, we perform sensitivity analysis for additional variables.

An Example: What is the effect on NPV and IRR if variable costs are at their lower bound and all other variables are at their base value?

Sensitivity analysis of variable costs is performed in the following table:

Scenario	Variable costs	Cash flow	NPV	IRR
Base case	$130	$215,500	$ 41,650	17.11%
Worst case	135	182,500	–117,936	12.76
Best case	125	248,500	201,057	21.22

These results are derived by varying only variable costs. In the worst case scenario, variable costs are $135 per unit and in the best case scenario, variable costs are $125 per unit. For both scenarios, unit sales, price and fixed costs take on their base case values.

An Example: What is the effect on NPV and IRR if fixed costs are at their lower bound?

Sensitivity analysis of fixed costs is performed in the following table:

Scenario	Fixed costs	Cash flow	NPV	IRR
Base case	$425,000	$215,500	$ 41,650	17.11%
Worst case	440,000	205,600	– 6,288	15.83
Best case	410,000	225,400	89,409	18.36

We have now performed sensitivity analysis for three of our forecasted variables. What conclusions can we derive from this analysis? The first important conclusion is that net present value is more sensitive to changes in the unit sales forecast than to either the variable cost or the fixed cost forecasts. When sales are at the lower bound, net present value is –$181,735; when variable costs and fixed costs are at the lower bound, net present values are –$117,936 and –$6,288, respectively. These are typical results; they reflect the fact that sales are typically more difficult to forecast than costs. In this example, the range of sales levels deviates from the base case sales level by 10 % in either direction. The cost forecasts vary by less than 4 % in either direction, thereby contributing to the lower sensitivity of NPV to cost forecasts.

The second important conclusion is that, for each of the three variables subjected to sensitivity analysis, the net present value is negative for the worst case scenario. That is, net present value is negative if any one of the variables takes on its lower bound forecast. This is not a particularly encouraging result. A reasonable conclusion suggested by this outcome might be that further evaluation of the forecasts is appropriate. Especially worthy of attention are the unit sales and variable cost forecasts. The goal of this additional analysis is to obtain more accurate forecasts which might clarify the likelihood that the net present value will be negative.

Simulation Analysis: This is another variant of scenario analysis in which we consider a large number of different combinations of the forecasted variables. Unlike scenario analysis, however, the combinations of the variables are selected randomly, rather than with an hypothesized scenario in mind. For each combination of values, net income, cash flow, and net present values are computed. The financial analyst then uses the resulting data to derive estimates of the likelihood that net present value will take on some particular values. For example, the analyst might be interested in estimating the probability that the NPV is negative. Simulation analysis is typically performed with the aid of a computer because it involves a large number of calculations. Furthermore, the manner in which the computer selects combinations of variables must be carefully specified according to reasonable rules of probability if the results are to be meaningful.

11.3 BREAK-EVEN ANALYSIS

In the example analyzed in the previous section, we concluded that unit sales forecast is the crucial variable in ascertaining whether the project is likely to have a positive net present value; this is often the case for a capital budgeting project, especially if the project involves development of a new product. Consequently, the relationship between sales volume and profitability warrants additional attention. In this section, we develop several forms of break-even analysis. In general, the goal of break-even analysis is to identify the level of sales below which a project is unacceptable.

Fixed and Variable Costs: Break-even analysis requires that we first distinguish between fixed and variable costs. Variable costs are costs that vary with production. They are frequently assumed to be proportional to the level of production. Direct labour cost is an example of a variable cost. Total variable costs (VC) are equal to variable cost per unit of output (v) multiplied by the number of units of output (Q). This relationship is summarized by:

$$VC \;=\; v \times Q$$

Fixed costs do not change over a specified time interval and must be paid regardless of production levels. Rent is an example of a fixed cost. Fixed costs are considered fixed during a given period of time, such as a quarter or a year. However, in the long run, all costs are ultimately variable. Rent, for example, may be fixed over a given time period specified in the lease (for example 5 years). However, it is variable over a longer period because the contractual obligation may be terminated.

Total costs (TC) for a given level of output in a given period of time are defined as the sum of total variable costs (VC) and fixed costs (FC):

$$TC \;=\; VC + FC$$

Since $VC = v \times Q$, the above equation can be rewritten as:

$$TC \;=\; (v \times Q) + FC$$

Accounting Break-Even: The *accounting break-even point* is the sales level at which net income is zero.

An Example: Heggestad, Inc. has forecasted sales of a new product at 4,400 units per year, with a selling price of $5.95 per unit. Fixed assets will be acquired for $40,000. The fixed assets have a ten-year life and will be depreciated on a straight-line basis; depreciation will be $4,000 annually. Variable costs are $3.45 per unit. Fixed costs will be $2,000 per year. The firm's required rate of return is 18% and the corporate tax rate is 34%. What is the accounting break-even point for Heggestad?

If EBIT is zero, then taxes and net income are also zero. Therefore, we can solve this problem by finding the sales level for which EBIT is zero. First, suppose that sales are zero. Then, EBIT is ($0 – $2,000 – $4,000) = –$6,000. Now suppose that Heggestad increases sales from zero units to one unit, so that EBIT increases by the difference between the selling price and the variable cost per unit: ($5.95 – $3.45) = $2.50. Each additional unit sold will increase EBIT by $2.50, so that, in order to increase EBIT to zero, Heggestad must sell ($6,000/$2.50) = 2,400 units. This example illustrates the fact that, in general, the accounting break-even occurs when the number of units (Q) is equal to:

$$Q \;=\; \frac{\text{Total fixed costs} + \text{Depreciation}}{\text{Unit price} - \text{Unit variable cost}}$$

This formula for the accounting break-even point can be derived from the algebraic definition of net income:

$$\text{Net income} \;=\; (S - VC - FC - D) \times (1 - t)$$

where S = sales, VC = total variable costs, FC = fixed costs, D = depreciation and t = the tax rate. If we let P = selling price per unit, v = variable cost per unit, and Q = total units sold, then:

$$S \;=\; P \times Q \quad \text{and} \quad VC \;=\; v \times Q$$

Net income can be rewritten as:

$$\text{Net income} = [(P \times Q) - (v \times Q) - FC - D] \times (1 - t)$$
$$= \{[(P - v) \times Q] - FC - D\} \times (1 - t)$$

Since accounting break-even is the sales level for which net income is zero, then accounting break-even is the value of Q for which:

$$\{[(P - v) \times Q] - FC - D\} \times (1 - t) = 0$$

Dividing both sides of this equation by $(1 - t)$, we have:

$$[(P - v) \times Q] - FC - D = 0$$

The left side of this equation is EBIT, so this statement indicates that the value of Q for which net income is zero is the same value of Q for which EBIT is zero, as we observed earlier. This equation is solved as follows:

$$[(P - v) \times Q] - FC - D = 0$$
$$(P - v) \times Q = FC + D$$

$$Q = \frac{FC + D}{P - v}$$

This statement is the algebraic equivalent of our earlier definition of the accounting break-even point.

Although the accounting break-even point is widely used for analysis of capital budgeting projects, there is some question as to its usefulness. The primary reason for this skepticism is the fact that a project whose sales level exceeds the accounting break-even point does not necessarily have a positive net present value. On the other hand, the accounting break-even point is relatively simple to calculate and understand, and may be useful as a rough guide to the acceptability of a project. As an example of this latter point, a project which is not expected to break even in the accounting sense is also unacceptable from net present value perspective.

11.4 OPERATING CASH FLOW, SALES, VOLUME, AND BREAK-EVEN

In this section, we consider the accounting break-even point from an alternative perspective, and we develop two additional break-even concepts: cash break-even point and financial break-even point. In order to simplify our analysis somewhat, we assume that the firm pays no income tax.

Accounting Break-Even and Cash Flow: In the example of the previous section, Heggestad, Inc. had an accounting break-even point of 2,400 units. Therefore, if Heggestad sells 2,400 units per year, both EBIT and net income are zero. At this level of sales, what is the firm's operating cash flow? Recall that the 'bottom-up' approach defines operating cash flow as net income plus depreciation. For this example:

$$OCF = EBIT + D - T = 0 + \$4,000 - 0 = \$4,000$$

If sales remain at the breakeven level, the IRR is zero. The project will return a cash flow of $4,000 per year for ten years, on an initial outlay of $40,000. At any positive discount rate, the NPV is less than zero. Thus it is easily seen that, even if sales exceed the breakeven point, NPV is not necessarily positive.

Sales Volume and Operating Cash Flow: Operating cash flow has been defined as:

$$\text{OCF} \quad = \quad \text{EBIT} + D - \text{Taxes}$$

$$= \quad (S - C - D) + D - [(S - C - D) \times T_c]$$

In this section, we have chosen to ignore taxes. Therefore, the above definition becomes:

$$\text{OCF} \quad = \quad \text{EBIT} + D \quad = \quad (S - C - D) + D$$

In addition, earlier in this chapter, we defined EBIT as follows:

$$\text{EBIT} \quad = \quad [(P - v) \times Q] - FC - D$$

Therefore, the above definition of OCF can be rewritten as:

$$
\begin{aligned}
\text{OCF} \quad &= \quad \text{EBIT} + D \\
&= \quad (S - C - D) + D \\
&= \quad \{[(P - v) \times Q] - FC - D\} + D \\
&= \quad [(P - v) \times Q] - FC
\end{aligned}
$$

Cash Flow, Accounting, and Financial Break-Even Points: The above definition of OCF can be rearranged by solving for Q:

$$\text{OCF} \quad = \quad [(P - v) \times Q] - FC$$

$$FC + \text{OCF} \quad = \quad (P - v) \times Q$$

$$Q \quad = \quad \frac{FC + \text{OCF}}{P - v}$$

This relationship specifies the level of Q required in order to achieve any given level of OCF.

For the accounting break-even point, OCF = D. Therefore, the accounting break-even can be defined in terms of the relationship between Q and OCF by simply replacing OCF by D. This verifies that the accounting break-even is:

$$Q \quad = \quad \frac{FC + D}{P - v}$$

The *cash break-even point* is the level of sales for which the operating cash flow is zero. This is easily derived by substituting OCF = 0 in the above relationship between Q and OCF:

$$Q \quad = \quad \frac{FC + 0}{P - v} \quad = \quad \frac{FC}{P - v}$$

An Example: Compute the cash break-even point for the Heggestad example.

The cash break-even point is:

$$Q \; = \; \frac{FC}{P - v} \; = \; \frac{\$2,000}{\$5.95 \; - \$3.45} \; = \; 800$$

Heggestad must sell 800 units to have operating cash flow equal to zero. A project with sales equal to the cash break-even level throughout its life has an internal rate of return of –100%. That is, the $40,000 investment produces no cash inflow, so the investment represents a total loss of the original investment.

The most significant break-even point for the financial manager is the *financial break-even point*, which is the level of sales such that the net present value of the project is zero.

An Example: Compute the financial break-even for Heggestad.

We solve the problem by first identifying the level of operating cash flow (OCF) for which net present value is zero. Then, substituting this value of OCF in the earlier equation, we solve for Q. Heggestad's operating cash flow is in the form of a ten-year annuity. The present value of this annuity must equal the initial outlay of $40,000. Solve the following equation for OCF:

$$
\begin{aligned}
\$40,000 &= \; OCF \times PVIFA(18\%,10) \\
\$40,000 &= \; OCF \times 4.494086 \\
OCF &= \; \$40,000 \, / \, 4.494086 \; = \; \$8,900.59
\end{aligned}
$$

Substitute this value of OCF into the earlier equation to determine the financial break-even point:

$$Q \; = \; \frac{\$2,000 \; + \; \$8,900.59}{\$5.95 \; - \; \$3.45} \; = \; 4,360.24$$

Therefore, sales must be 4,361 units in order for the project to have a net present value greater than zero.

11.5 OPERATING LEVERAGE

The level of fixed costs for a capital budgeting project, or for a company as a whole, has an important impact on the break-even concepts developed in the previous section. The precise nature of the relationship between fixed costs and break-even points is described in this section.

The Basic Idea: *Operating leverage* is the extent to which a capital budgeting project, or a firm as a whole, relies on fixed production costs. A firm or project with a relatively high level of fixed costs has high operating leverage. Generally, a high level of fixed costs is also associated with a relatively large investment in plant and equipment; such a situation is said to be capital-intensive.

Measuring Operating Leverage: The *degree of operating leverage* (DOL) is defined as:

$$DOL \; = \; \frac{\text{Percentage change in OCF}}{\text{Percentage change in Q}}$$

This is equivalent to:

$$DOL = 1 + FC / OCF$$

An Example: Suppose sales for the project under consideration by Heggestad increase from 2,400 units to 3,000 units. What is the effect on operating cash flow? What is the degree of operating leverage?

Remember, OCF is equal to $4,000 at the accounting break-even point of 2,400 units. To find the DOL, the percentage change in OCF and Q are measured using the break-even point as the base quantity. Operating cash flow for an output of 3,000 units can be computed as follows:

$$OCF = [(P - v) \times Q] - FC$$
$$= [(\$5.95 - \$3.45) \times 3,000] - \$2,000 = \$5,500$$

The percentage change in operating cash flow is:

$$\frac{\$5,500 - \$4,000}{\$4,000} = .375 = 37.5\%$$

The percentage change in output is:

$$\frac{3,000 - 2,400}{2,400} = .25 = 25\%$$

Therefore, the degree of operating leverage is (37.5%/25%) = 1.5. The alternative calculation of DOL provides the same result:

$$DOL = 1 + FC / OCF = 1 + \$2,000 / \$4,000 = 1.5$$

The following examples illustrate additional aspects of the DOL calculation.

An Example: Suppose that sales for the project under consideration by Heggestad increase from 2,400 units to 3,600 units. What is the effect on operating cash flow?   What is the degree of operating leverage?

Using OFC = $4,000 when Q = 2,400 units, for Q = 3,600 units:

$$OCF = [(P - v) \times Q] - FC = [(\$5.95 - \$3.45) \times 3,600] - \$2,000 = \$7,000$$

The percentage change in operating cash flow is:

$$\frac{\$7,000 - \$4,000}{\$4,000} = .75 = 75\%$$

The percentage change in output is:

$$\frac{3,600 - 2,400}{2,400} = .50 = 50\%$$

Therefore, the degree of operating leverage is $(75\%/50\%) = 1.5$. This example illustrates the fact that, for a given level of output (in this case, $Q = 2,400$ units), the degree of operating leverage remains constant regardless of the size of the increase in Q. This conclusion can be verified by observing the alternative formula for the calculation of DOL. For a given level of Q, both FC and OCF remain constant regardless of the size of the increase in Q.

An Example: If sales increase from 3,000 units to 3,600 units, what is the degree of operating leverage?

When $Q = 3,000$ units, OCF = \$5,500; when $Q = 3,600$ units, OCF = \$7,000. The percentage change in operating cash flow is:

$$\frac{\$7,000 - \$5,500}{\$5,500} \quad = \quad .272727 \quad = \quad 27.2727\%$$

The percentage change in output is:

$$\frac{3,600 - 3,000}{3,000} \quad = \quad .20 \quad = \quad 20\%$$

The degree of operating leverage is $(27.2727\%/20\%) = 1.3636$. The alternative calculation of DOL is:

$$DOL \;=\; 1 + FC / OCF \;=\; 1 \;+\; \$2,000 / \$5,500 \;=\; 1.3636$$

This example illustrates the fact that the DOL changes when the level of Q changes. When we consider changes in Q from a base of 2,400 units, DOL = 1.5. For changes in Q from a base of 3,000 units, DOL decreases to 1.3636. This is representative of the general result that DOL decreases when the base level of Q increases.

An Example: Heggestad has determined that an alternative manufacturing process can be used to produce the new product. The alternative process is less capital-intensive, so that fixed costs are reduced but variable costs per unit are increased; annual fixed costs are \$800 and variable costs are \$4.45 per unit. The required investment in fixed assets is \$25,000. Heggestad is using straight-line depreciation to depreciate the asset over its ten-year life. Compute the accounting break-even, the cash break-even and the financial break-even for the alternative process. Also, compute the degree of operating leverage and the net present value for each production process at a forecasted sales level of 4,400 units per year.

Depreciation for the alternative process is $D = (\$25,000/10) = \$2,500$ and $(P - v) = (\$5.95 - \$4.45) = \$1.50$. The accounting break-even point is:

$$Q \;=\; \frac{FC + D}{P - v} \;=\; \frac{\$800 \;+\; \$2,500}{\$1.50} \;=\; 2,200$$

The cash break-even point is:

$$Q \;=\; \frac{FC \;+\; OCF}{P - v} \;=\; \frac{\$800 + 0}{\$1.50} \;=\; 533.33 \;=\; 534 \text{ units}$$

To compute the financial break-even, first solve for OCF in the following equation:

$$\$25,000 \;=\; OCF \times PVIFA(18\%,10)$$
$$\$25,000 \;=\; OCF \times 4.494086$$

$$OCF = \$25,000 / 4.494086 = \$5,562.87$$

Substitute this value of OCF into the earlier equation to determine the financial break-even point:

$$Q = \frac{FC + OCF}{P - v} = \frac{\$800 + \$5,562.87}{\$5.95 - \$4.45} = 4,241.91 = 4,242 \text{ units}$$

Notice that each break-even point has decreased relative to the corresponding calculation for the original, capital-intensive process.

At Q = 4,400 units, OCF for the original production process is:

$$OCF = [(P - v) \times Q] - FC = [(\$5.95 - \$3.45) \times 4,400] - \$2,000 = \$9,000$$

The degree of operating leverage is:

$$DOL = 1 + FC / OCF = 1 + \$2,000 / \$9,000 = 1.222$$

The net present value for the original capital-intensive process is:

$$NPV = -\$40,000 + [\$9,000 \times PVIFA(18\%,10)] = -\$40,000 + (\$9,000 \times 4.494086) = +\$446.77$$

For the alternative process:

$$OCF = [(P - v) \times Q] - FC = [(\$5.95 - \$4.45) \times 4,400] - \$800 = \$5,800$$

$$DOL = 1 + \$800 / \$5,800 = 1.138$$

$$NPV = -\$25,000 + (\$5,800 \times 4.494086) = +\$1,065.70$$

The alternative production process has a higher net present value and a lower DOL at the forecasted sales level. Also, as noted earlier, the financial break-even point is lower. Does this mean that the alternative process should be implemented by the firm? There is no simple answer to this question. Clearly, if we were certain that sales would be precisely 4,400 units, this is the preferable alternative. However, as discussed earlier, the forecasting risk can be substantial when a new product is introduced.

Suppose that there is a possibility that sales could be higher than 4,400 units. Does this possibility change our conclusion? The higher degree of operating leverage for the capital-intensive production process indicates that operating cash flow and net present value increase more rapidly with an increase in sales. For example, at a sales level of 5,000 units, the NPV for the original process is +\$7,187.90 while NPV for the alternative is +\$5,110.38. The original process now has the higher NPV and is therefore preferable. On the other hand, if sales are below the forecasted level, the higher DOL for the capital-intensive process implies a more rapid decline in net present value. There is no clear preference between the two alternatives in this problem.

11.6 ADDITIONAL CONSIDERATIONS IN CAPITAL BUDGETING

The additional considerations discussed in this section are managerial options and capital rationing.

Managerial Options: So far, we have assumed that all basic features of a capital budgeting project will not change throughout the life of the project. This ignores *managerial options* that might change the course of the project. Management can, for example, change product price, expand production, modify the production process, or even abandon an unsuccessful project. Ignoring these managerial options may incorrectly estimate the net present value of a project. A dynamic analysis incorporates the value of managerial options.

Two particularly important managerial options are the option to expand a successful project and the option to reduce the scale of a project, or even abandon a project, if it is unsuccessful. Since these options have value to the firm, they must be considered in capital budgeting analysis.

In a static analysis, NPV calculations are based on forecasted sales levels throughout the life of the project. In dynamic capital budgeting, we incorporate the fact that our estimates of projected sales will be revised over the life of the project. For example, if sales forecasts are revised upward, a firm might expand production and sales. This implies that cash flows and NPV are greater than initially anticipated. Since static analysis ignores this possibility, it underestimates the net present value of the project.

Similar conclusions apply to the option to abandon an unsuccessful project. If demand for a new product is significantly below original expectations, it might be less expensive to abandon the project than to proceed with it. Static analysis assumes that an unsuccessful project will continue for a specified number of years. If abandonment of the project is less expensive than continuing at low sales levels, then the net present value increases if the project is abandoned. In other words, static analysis again underestimates a project's NPV because it ignores the managerial option to abandon an unsuccessful project. The analysis of managerial options is difficult because we must predict the probability that a project will be expanded or abandoned.

Suppose a project will be expanded if first-year sales exceed 10,000 units, and it will be abandoned if first-year sales are less than 5,000 units. Dynamic analysis forecasts the probability that these events will occur. Then the NPV is determined for each possibility, as well as the possibility that the project is maintained at its expected level. The net present value of the project is the weighted average (i.e., expected value) of the possible NPVs for each event. The major difficulty with this analysis is making reasonable forecasts of the probabilities for each possible outcome. Both forecasting and computation can be quite complicated.

Capital Rationing: Capital rationing exists if a firm, or a unit of a corporation, has identified positive NPV capital budgeting projects but is unable to obtain the financing required for the projects. One approach to resolving such a problem is to accept the set of projects which maximizes the NPV with the funds available. This is generally equivalent to accepting those projects with the highest profitability index. However, the existence of capital rationing raises questions as to whether the firm is employing appropriate discounted cash flow analysis. For example, if a corporation limits the financing available to a division of the firm, without regard for whether additional positive NPV projects exist, it is questionable whether the corporation is attempting to maximize shareholder value.

CONCEPT TEST

1.   The risk that a financial manager makes an incorrect decision because of errors in forecasting future cash flows is called _____ .

2.	An analysis of the effect on all forecasted variables, and on NPV, of a hypothetical sequence of events is referred to as _____ .

3.	An assessment of the sensitivity of one variable to changes in another variable is called _____ .

4.	Capital budgeting is concerned about the sensitivity of _____ to variation in the level of a forecasted variable. For example, the financial managers evaluate the change in _____ which results if actual sales are at the lower bound of a forecasted range, while all other variables are held constant. The process of analyzing the impact of different forecasted variables on the acceptability of a capital budgeting project is called _____ . In this process, the combinations of the variables are not selected with any particular scenario in mind, but rather are selected _____ .

5.	Variable costs are costs that vary with the level of _____ and are generally assumed to be proportional to the level of _____ . Total variable costs (VC) are equal to _____ multiplied by _____ . This relationship is summarized algebraically as : VC = _____ .

6.	Costs which do not change over a specified time interval and must be paid regardless of production levels are called _____ .

7.	Total costs (TC) for a given level of output in a given period of time are defined as the sum of _____ and _____ . This relationship can be expressed algebraically as: TC = _____ .

8.	The accounting break-even point is the sales level at which a project's _____ is equal to _____ . The accounting break-even point is computed as Q = _____ . If sales are equal to the accounting break-even point, then both _____ and _____ are equal to zero.

9.	The 'bottom-up' approach defines operating cash flow as _____ plus _____ . At the break-even sales level, operating cash flow is equal to _____ . If sales remain at the break-even level throughout the life of a project, then the internal rate of return is equal to _____ . Therefore, at any positive discount rate, the net present value of such a project is _____ .

10.	In the absence of corporate income taxes, the level of output (Q) required to achieve a given level of operating cash flow (OCF) can be written as: Q = _____ .

11.	The cash break-even point is the level of sales for which the _____ is equal to _____ . The formula for the cash break-even point is derived from the previous equation by substituting _____ = _____ , resulting in the following: Q = _____ .

12.	 A project with sales equal to the cash break-even level throughout the life of the project has an internal rate of return equal to _____ because the initial outlay produces no cash inflow.

13.	The most significant break-even point for the financial manager is the financial break-even point, which is the level of sales such that the _____ of the project is equal to _____ . The financial break-even point is computed by first identifying the level of operating cash flow (OCF) for which _____ is equal to _____ and then substituting this value of OCF in the equation which describes the relationship between Q and OCF.

14.   The extent to which a capital budgeting project, or a firm as a whole, relies on fixed production costs is called _____ . A firm or project with a relatively high level of fixed costs is said to have high _____ . A high level of fixed costs is typically associated with a relatively large investment in plant and equipment; such a situation is said to be _____ .

15.   The degree of operating leverage (DOL) is defined as: DOL = _____ .   It can be demonstrated algebraically that this definition is equivalent to: DOL = _____ .

16.   For a given level of output, the degree of operating leverage (increases/decreases/remains constant) as the size of the increase in Q increases. When the base level of Q increases, the degree of operating leverage (increases/decreases/remains constant) . A capital-intensive production process has a (higher/ lower) DOL than a less capital-intensive process, so that operating cash flow and net present value increase (more/less) rapidly with an increase in sales; if sales are below the forecasted level, then net present value decreases (more/less) rapidly for the capital-intensive process.

17.   If capital budgeting analysis ignores managerial options, then the net present value of a project is _____ . Such analysis is said to be _____ , because it assumes that changes during the life of a project are not possible. Capital budgeting analysis which acknowledge the value of managerial options is said to be _____ .

18.   If a firm, or a unit of a corporation, has identified positive NPV capital budgeting projects but is unable to obtain the financing required for the projects, then _____ is said to exist. One approach to resolving such a problem is to accept the set of projects which maximizes the _____ with the funds available. This is generally equivalent to accepting those projects with the highest _____ . However, the existence of capital rationing raises questions as to whether the firm is employing appropriate discounted cash flow analysis.

PROBLEMS

Use the following information on SDC Corporation to solve Problems 1-4:

	Base case	Lower bound	Upper bound
Unit sales	1,000	800	1,200
Price per unit	$95	$90	$100
Variable costs per unit	$50	$40	$ 60
Fixed costs per year	$10,000	$9,000	$11,000

SDC's required rate of return is 12%, and a $15,000 investment in a new machine is required. The corporate tax rate is 34%. The machine is expected to last 5 years with no salvage value and will be depreciated on a straight-line basis.

Problem 1

Compute the annual operating cash flow for the project associated with each of the three cases.

Problem 2

Calculate the NPV of the project using each of the scenarios.

Problem 3

What are the operating cash flows and the NPV for the project if all variables are from the base case except fixed costs which take on the lower bound values?

Problem 4

What are the operating cash flows and the NPV for the project if all variables are from the base case except variable costs which take on the upper bound values?

Use the following information to solve Problems 5–17:

D. Newcombe & Associates, Inc. is considering the introduction of a new product. Production of the new product requires an investment of $140,000 in equipment with a five-year life. The equipment has no salvage value at the end of five years and will be depreciated on a straight-line basis. Newcombe's required rate of return is 15% and the tax rate is 34%. The firm has made the following forecasts:

	Base case	Lower bound	Upper bound
Unit sales	2,000	1,800	2,200
Price per unit	$55	$50	$60
Variable costs per unit	$22	$21	$23
Fixed costs per year	$10,000	$9,500	$10,500

Problem 5

Compute the annual operating cash flow for the project, using the base case forecast for each variable.

Problem 6

Compute the net present value for the project, using the base case forecast for each variable.

Problem 7

Compute the net present value and the internal rate of return for the Newcombe project under the best case scenario and then under the worst case scenario.

Problem 8

Assume that all variables, except unit sales, take on their base case levels. What is the effect on net present value and internal rate of return if unit sales are at their lower bound? Also, compute net present value and internal rate of return under the assumption that unit sales are at their upper bound.

Problem 9

Assume that all variables, except price per unit, take on their base case levels. What is the effect on net present value and internal rate of return if price per unit is at its lower bound? Also, compute net present value and internal rate of return under the assumption that price per unit is at the upper bound.

Problem 10

Assume that all variables, except variable costs per unit, take on their base case levels. What is the effect on net present value and internal rate of return if variable costs per unit are at their upper bound? Also, compute net present value and internal rate of return under the assumption that variable costs per unit are at their lower bound.

Problem 11

Assume that all variables, except fixed costs, take on their base case levels. What is the effect on net present value and internal rate of return if fixed costs are at their upper bound? Also, compute net present value and internal rate of return under the assumption that fixed costs are at their lower bound.

Problem 12

Assume the base-case forecasts for the Newcombe project. Compute the accounting break-even point for the project.

Problem 13

Assume the base-case forecasts and no income taxes for the Newcombe project. Compute the cash break-even point for the project.

Problem 14

Assume the base-case forecasts and no income taxes for the Newcombe project. Compute the financial break-even point for the project.

Problem 15

Suppose that sales for the project under consideration by Newcombe increase from 2,000 units to 2,200 units per year. Compute the degree of operating leverage for the project at sales of 2,000 units. Use both the definition of the degree of operating leverage and its algebraic equivalent for this calculation. Assume Newcombe does not pay income taxes on this project.

Problem 16

Suppose that sales for the project under consideration by Newcombe decrease from 2,000 units to 1,600 units per year. Compute the degree of operating leverage for the project, using the definition of the degree of operating leverage. Assume Newcombe does not pay income taxes on this project.

Problem 17

Assume that sales increase from 1,600 units to 2,000 units for the project. Compute DOL for the project at sales of 1,600 units. Use both the definition of the degree of operating leverage and its algebraic equivalent for this calculation. Assume Newcombe does not pay income taxes on this project.

Problem 18

The following data have been computed for a firm: when output is 20,000 units, operating cash flow is $50,000 and operating leverage is 2.5. Suppose output increases to 23,000 units. What is the new level of operating cash flow?

Problem 19

For the data in Problem 18, compute the firm's fixed costs.

Problem 20

Suppose an investor is considering a piece of property to use as a parking lot. The cost of the property is $10,000. The investor expects that the value of the property will remain constant for the foreseeable future; no depreciation expense will be taken on the property. The investor expects that, for the foreseeable future, 6,000 cars per year will use the parking lot at a rate of $3 per car.

Variable costs are zero, but an attendant must be paid $16,000 per year. Assume that the required rate of return is 25% and that there are no taxes. Compute the net present value for the investment. Is the project acceptable?

Problem 21

Suppose that in the previous problem, the investor intends to re-evaluate her forecast at the end of the first year. She believes that usage of the parking lot during the first year will be either 5,500 or 6,500 cars per year, and that the volume of business during the first year will indicate which of these figures will continue beyond the first year. In addition, she believes that each of these figures is equally likely. Compute the net present value of the project. Is the project acceptable?

ANSWERS TO CONCEPT TEST

1.   forecasting risk

2.   scenario analysis

3.   sensitivity analysis

4.   net present value; net present value; simulation analysis; randomly

5.   production; production; variable costs per unit of output; number of units of output; $(v \times Q)$

6.   fixed costs

7.   total variable costs; fixed costs; $(v \times Q) + F]$

8.   net income; zero; $(FC + D)/(P - v)$; EBIT; net income

9.   net income; annual depreciation expense; annual depreciation expense; zero; negative

10. $(FC + OCF)/(P - v)$

11.   operating cash flow; zero; OCF; zero; $FC/(P - v)$

12. -100%

13.   net present value; zero; net present value; zero

14.   operating leverage; operating leverage; capital intensive

15.   (% change in OCF)/(% change in Q); $1 + (FC/OCF)$

16.   remains constant; decreases; higher; more; more

17.   underestimated; static; dynamic

18.   capital rationing; net present value; profitability index

PROBLEM SOLUTIONS

Problem 1: First, compute the net income and operating cash flow for the different scenarios.

	Base case	Lower bound	Upper bound
Sales	$95,000	$72,000	$120,000
– Variable costs	50,000	32,000	72,000
– Fixed costs	10,000	9,000	11,000
– Depreciation	3,000	3,000	3,000
EBIT	$32,000	28,000	34,000
– Taxes (34%)	10,880	9,520	11,560
Net income	$21,120	$18,480	$ 22,440
EBIT	$32,000	28,000	34,000
+ Depreciation	3,000	3,000	3,000
– Taxes	10,880	9,520	11,560
Operating Cash Flow	$24,120	$21,480	$ 25,440

Problem 2: The NPV for each scenario is calculated by treating each operating cash flow as the present value of a five-year annuity with a 12 % required rate of return.

Base case: PV   = $24,120 x PVIFA (12%, 5) = $24,120 x 3.604776 = $86,947.20

               NPV   = $86,947.20 - $15,000 = $71,947.20

Lower bound: PV   = $21,480 x PVIFA (12%, 5) = $21,480 x 3.604776 = $77,430.59

               NPV   = $77,430.59 - $15,000 = $62,430.59

Upper bound: PV   = $25,440 x PVIFA (12%, 5) = $25,440 x 3.604776 = $91,705.51

               NPV   = $91,705.51 - $15,000 = $76,705.51

Problem 3:

Sales	$95,000
– Variable costs	50,000
– Fixed costs	9,000
– Depreciation	3,000
EBIT	$33,000
– Taxes (34%)	11,220
Net income	$21,780
EBIT	$33,000
+ Depreciation	3,000
– Taxes	11,220
Operating Cash Flow	$24,780

NPV   = $24,780 x PVIFA (12%, 5) - $15,000   = $89,326.35 - $15,000   = $74,326.35

Note: Because the project is not very capital intensive, the majority of costs are variable. Changes in fixed costs don't cause a large change in the NPV.

Problem 4:

Sales	$95,000
– Variable costs	60,000 ($60 x 1,000 base case units)
– Fixed costs	10,000
– Depreciation	3,000
EBIT	$22,000
– Taxes (34%)	7,480
Net income	$14,520
EBIT	$22,000
+ Depreciation	3,000
– Taxes	7,480
Operating Cash Flow	$17,520

NPV   = $17,520 x PVIFA (12%, 5) - $15,000   = $63,155.68 - $15,000   = $48,155.68

Problem 5: We first compute the net income and then the operating cash flow, as follows:

Sales		$110,000
– Variable costs	44,000	
– Fixed costs		10,000
– Depreciation		28,000
EBIT		$ 28,000
– Taxes (34%)		9,520
Net income		$ 18,480
EBIT		$ 28,000
+ Depreciation		28,000
– Taxes		9,520
Operating Cash Flow		$ 46,480

Problem 6: The present value of the project is the present value of an annuity of $46,480 per year for five years, discounted at the 15% required rate of return:

$$PV = \$46,480 \times PVIFA(15\%,5) = \$46,480 \times 3.352155 = \$155,808$$

The net present value of the project is: $155,808 – $140,000 = $15,808

Problem 7: The worst case scenario is comprised of the least favourable outcome for each of the four forecasted variables, while the best case scenario is comprised of the most favourable outcome for each of the variables. These scenarios are described in the following table:

	Worst case	Best case
Unit sales	1,800	2,200
Price per unit	$50	$60
Variable costs per unit	$23	$21
Fixed costs per year	$10,500	$9,500

For each scenario, we compute net income, cash flow, net present value and internal rate of return for the proposed project. The results are presented in the following table:

Scenario	Net income	Cash flow	NPV	IRR
Base case	$18,480	$46,480	$15,808	19.68%
Worst case	6,666	34,666	–23,794	7.57
Best case	31,878	59,878	60,720	32.16

The net present value for the base case scenario is positive, so the project appears to be acceptable. However, the negative net present value for the worst case scenario indicates that further analysis is necessary. Sensitivity analysis might be useful at this point so that Newcombe can identify those forecasted variables which most clearly contribute to the possibility that the net present value will be negative.

Problem 8: The solution is provided in the following table:

Scenario	Unit Sales	Cash flow	NPV	IRR
Base case	2,000	$46,480	$15,808	19.68%
Worst case	1,800	42,124	1,206	15.36
Best case	2,200	50,836	30,410	23.85

For both the worst case and best case scenarios here, we assume that price, variable costs and fixed costs take on their base case values. These results indicate that net present value is relatively sensitive to the unit sales forecasts. However, even assuming the lower bound sales level, net present value is still positive. This is an encouraging result, but Newcombe's optimism regarding this result must be tempered by the fact that we assume base case levels for all variables other than sales. If, in fact, any additional variable takes on its 'worst case' value, then it seems likely that net present value would become negative.

Problem 9: Sensitivity analysis of unit price is performed in the following table:

Scenario	Price per unit	Cash flow	NPV	IRR
Base case	$55	$46,480	$15,808	19.68%
Worst case	50	39,880	– 6,316	13.08
Best case	60	53,080	37,932	25.95

Comparison of these results to those in Problem 8 reveals the fact that net present value of the project is more sensitive to changes in unit price than it is to changes in sales level; when unit price is at its lower bound, the net present value of the project is negative. It is essential for Newcombe to further assess the sensitivity of net present value to both sales level and unit price. For example, the likelihood that sales and price both take on their lower bound values may be an important consideration because such a scenario would have a significant impact on the net present value of the project.

Problem 10: Sensitivity analysis of variable costs is performed in the following table:

Scenario	Variable costs	Cash flow	NPV	IRR
Base case	$22	$46,480	$15,808	19.68%
Worst case	23	45,160	11,383	18.39
Best case	21	47,800	20,233	20.95

Net present value is relatively insensitive to changes in variable costs. Therefore, in assessing the acceptability of the project, it may not be particularly important for Newcombe to further evaluate this forecast.

Problem 11: Sensitivity analysis of fixed costs is presented in the following table:

Scenario	Fixed costs	Cash flow	NPV	IRR
Base case	$10,000	$46,480	$15,808	19.68%
Worst case	10,500	46,150	14,702	19.35
Best case	9,500	46,810	16,914	20.00

Net present value is not particularly sensitive to changes in fixed costs. This result follows from the fact that, first, the percentage change in fixed costs from the base case to the upper bound is relatively small, and, second, fixed costs are a relatively small portion of the total costs for the project. It is probably not worthwhile for Newcombe to analyze the fixed costs forecast more closely.

Problem 12: The accounting break-even point is computed as follows:

$$Q = \frac{FC + D}{P - v} = \frac{\$10,000 + \$28,000}{\$55 - \$22} = 1,151.52$$

Net income (and EBIT) will be zero if Newcombe produces and sells 1,151.52 units. In order for the project to produce net income (and EBIT) approximately equal to zero, sales must be 1,152 units.

Problem 13: The cash break-even point is the sales level for which operating cash flow is equal to zero. The relationship between Q and OCF is:

$$Q = \frac{FC + OCF}{P - v} = \frac{FC + 0}{P - v} = \frac{FC}{P - v} = \frac{\$10,000}{\$55 - \$22} = 303.03$$

At sales of 303.03 units, operating cash flow is zero; therefore, Newcombe must sell at least 304 units for cash flow to be positive.

Problem 14: The OCF for the project is a five-year annuity. At the financial break-even point, the net present value of the project is zero, which is equivalent to stating that the present value of the annuity is equal to the $140,000 cash outflow. Therefore, we solve the following equation for OCF:

$$\$140,000 \ = \ OCF \times PVIFA(15\%,5) \ = \ OCF \times 3.352155$$

$$OCF \ = \ \$140,000 \,/\, 3.352155 \ = \ \$41,764.18$$

Substitute this value of OCF into the following equation to determine the financial break-even point:

$$Q \ = \ \frac{FC \ + \ OCF}{P \ - \ v} \ = \ \frac{\$10,000 \ + \ \$41,764.18}{\$55 \ - \ \$22} \ = \ 1,568.61$$

Therefore, sales must be 1,569 units in order for the project to have a net present value greater than zero.

Problem 15: The degree of operating leverage (DOL) is defined as follows:

$$DOL \ = \ \frac{Percentage \ change \ in \ OCF}{Percentage \ change \ in \ Q}$$

Operating cash flow for output of 2,000 units can be computed as follows:

$$OCF \ = \ [(P-v) \times Q] - FC \ = \ [(\$55 - \$22) \times 2,000] - \$10,000 \ = \ \$56,000$$

OCF for output of 2,200 units is $62,600. The percentage change in operating cash flow is:

$$\frac{\$62,600 \ - \ \$56,000}{\$56,000} \ = \ .11786 \ = \ 11.786\%$$

The percentage change in output is:

$$\frac{2,200 \ - \ 2,000}{2,000} \ = \ .10 \ = \ 10\%$$

Therefore, the degree of operating leverage is (11.786% / 10%) = 1.1786. The alternative calculation of DOL provides the same result.

Problem 16: Operating cash flow for output of 2,000 units is $56,000, as computed in the solution to Problem 11. Operating cash flow for output of 1,600 units is:

$$OCF \ = \ [(P-v) \times Q] - FC \ = \ [(\$55 - \$22) \times 1,600] - \$10,000 \ = \ \$42,800$$

The percentage change in operating cash flow is:

$$\frac{\$42,800 \ - \ \$56,000}{\$56,000} \ = \ -.23571 \ = \ -23.57\%$$

The percentage change in output is:

$$\frac{1,600 \ - \ 2,000}{2,000} \ = \ -.20 \ = \ -20\%$$

Therefore, the degree of operating leverage is:

$$\text{DOL} \quad = \quad \frac{\text{Percentage change in OCF}}{\text{Percentage change in Q}} \quad = \quad \frac{-23.57\%}{-20\%} \quad = \quad 1.1786$$

This is the same result obtained in the solution to Problem 11. DOL depends on the current level of Q and OCF, and is constant for any change from that level.

Problem 17: The solutions to Problems 15 and 16 indicate the following: when Q = 1,600, OCF = $42,800; when Q = 2,000, OCF = $56,000. The percentage change in operating cash flow is:

$$\frac{\$56,000 - \$42,800}{\$42,800} \quad = \quad .30841 \quad = \quad 30.84\%$$

The percentage change in output is:

$$\frac{2,000 - 1,600}{1,600} \quad = \quad .25 \quad = \quad 25\%$$

Therefore, the degree of operating leverage is:

$$\text{DOL} \quad = \quad \frac{30.84\%}{25\%} \quad = \quad 1.2336$$

The alternative calculation of DOL provides the same result:

$$\text{DOL} \quad = \quad 1 \; + \; \text{FC} / \text{OCF} \quad = \quad 1 \; + \; \$10,000 / \$42,800 \quad = \quad 1.2336$$

The degree of operating leverage is higher for the increase in Q from 1,600 units to 2,000 units than it is for the decrease in Q from 2,000 units to 1,600 units. Operating leverage decreases as the level of Q increases.

Problem 18: The definition of the degree of operating leverage is:

$$\text{DOL} \quad = \quad \frac{\text{Percentage change in OCF}}{\text{Percentage change in Q}}$$

The percentage change in output is:

$$\frac{23,000 - 20,000}{20,000} \quad = \quad .15 \; = \; 15\%$$

Substituting this percentage change in output, and DOL = 2.5, into the definition of the degree of operating leverage, we can solve for the percentage change in operating cash flow:

$$2.5 \quad = \quad \frac{\text{Percentage change in OCF}}{.15}$$

Therefore, the percentage change in OCF = (2.5 × .15) = .375 = 37.5%. OCF increases by 37.5%, so that the new level of operating cash flow is (1.375 × $50,000) = $68,750.

Problem 19: The alternative formula for computing DOL is:

$$DOL = 1 + FC / OCF$$

Substituting DOL = 2.5 and OCF = $50,000, solve for FC as follows:

$$2.5 = 1 + FC / \$50,000$$

$$1.5 = FC / \$50,000$$

Fixed costs therefore equal (1.5 × $50,000) = $75,000.

Problem 20: Sales are ($3 × 6,000) = $18,000 and net income is ($18,000 – $16,000) = $2,000. Since depreciation and taxes are zero, operating cash flow is also $2,000. Treating this cash flow as a perpetuity, the present value is ($2,000/.25) = $8,000. The net present value is ($8,000 – $10,000) = –$2,000, so the project is unacceptable.

Problem 21: If the volume of business is 5,500 cars per year, then sales will be ($3 × 5,500) = $16,500; net income and operating cash flow will be ($16,500 – $16,000) = $500. At 6,500 cars per year, net income and operating cash flow are $3,500. Since the two figures are considered equally likely, the expected value of the first year's operating cash flow is [(.5 × $500) + (.5 × $3,500)] = $2,000.

If the volume of business during the first year is 5,500 cars, then the operating cash flow will be $500 for all subsequent years. The value of this perpetuity, as of the end of the first year, is ($500/.25) = $2,000. Since the property can be sold for $10,000, the investor would sell the property at the end of the first year. On the other hand, at 6,500 cars per year, operating cash flow will be $3,500 and the value of the business would be ($3,500/.25) = $14,000. Under these circumstances, the investor will continue to operate the business. Therefore, at the end of the first year, the investor will have an expected cash flow of $2,000, plus either $10,000 in cash or a business worth $14,000. The expected value at the end of the first year is therefore:

$$\$2,000 + [(.5 × \$10,000) + (.5 × \$14,000)] = \$14,000$$

The present value of this $14,000 is ($14,000/1.25) = $11,200, and the net present value of the investment is ($11,200 – $10,000) = $1,120. The investment is acceptable. The option to abandon the investment at the end of the first year has added value to the project, compared to the solution to Problem 16.

12   Some Lessons from Capital Market History

CHAPTER HIGHLIGHTS

The capital budgeting concepts discussed so far have mostly ignored the issue of risk. However, risk is a critical element in determining the required rate of return used to discount a project's cash flows. Put simply, the greater the risk, the greater the required return. This chapter begins the task of understanding the relationship between risk and return. We begin with a perspective on risk and return as provided by capital market history. In general, we learn two major lessons: (1) investors earn a reward for taking risk, and (2) the higher the potential reward, the higher the risk.

12.1 RETURNS

In order to understand the relationship between risk and return, we must be able to measure both risk and return for an investment. In this section, we introduce the measurement of returns, both as dollar returns and as percentage returns.

Dollar Returns: The return on an investment has two components: the income component, and the capital gain (or capital loss) component. It is possible for an investment to have only a capital gain component. For example, a collectible antique produces no periodic income, but increases in value, providing its owner with a capital gain. Assets purchased for business purposes (machinery, for example) typically produce periodic income but no capital gains. If you buy common stock, however, your return on the investment usually comes in two forms: dividends (periodic income) and capital gains.

Suppose you buy 100 shares of Ahlers Corporation's common stock for $25 per share. Over the course of a year, Ahlers pays a cash dividend of $2 per share and the value of the share rises to $30. At the end of the year, you have received ($2 × 100) = $200 in dividends. In addition, you own 100 shares of stock worth $30 per share. The capital gain is [($30 − $25) × 100] = $500. The total dollar return is therefore:

Total dollar return = Dividend income + Capital gain (or loss) = $200 + $500 = $700

The total value of your position is $3,200, the total investment is $2,500, and the total return is $700.

Percentage Returns: For financial decision-making, percentage returns are easier to work with because the results apply regardless of the amount invested in a particular asset. In the case of the investment in Ahlers common stock, you received $700 on a $2,500 investment, so your total percentage return is:

[$200 + ($3,000 - $2,500)] / $2,500 = .28 = 28%

This calculation can also be expressed on a per share basis. An investor who purchases one share for $25 receives a $2 dividend during the year and has a share worth $30 at the end of the year. Therefore, the investor's total percentage return can be computed as:

[$2 + ($30 - $25)] / $25 = .28 = 28%

This 28% total return is comprised of the dividend yield plus the percentage capital gain (or capital gains yield).

The dividend yield is:

$$D_t / P_t \ = \ \$2 / \$25 \ = \ .08 \ = \ 8\%$$

where P_t is the price of the stock at the beginning of the year, and D_t is the dividend paid during the year.

The capital gains yield is:

$$(P_{t+1} \ - \ P_t) / P_t \ = \ (\$30 - \$25) / \$25 \ = \ .20 \ = \ 20\%$$

where P_t is the price of the stock at the beginning of the year and P_{t+1} is the price at the end of the year. The total percentage return is the sum of the dividend yield and the capital gains yield:

$$\text{Total percentage return} \ = \ 8\% + 20\% \ = \ 28\%$$

12.2 THE HISTORICAL RECORD

Historical returns of a variety of portfolios can be reviewed to provide insight into capital market history. Consider the following portfolios, assembled by William M. Mercer Ltd.:

1. *Canadian common stocks* composed of Canadian stocks with the largest market value;
2. *U.S. common stocks* composed of the 500 largest U.S. stocks.
3. *Small stocks* composed of small capitalization Canadian stocks.
4. *Long bonds* composed of long-term and high-quality government (provincial and federal) and corporate bonds.
5. *Canada Treasury bills* composed of 3-month Canadian T-bills.

In addition, Statistic Canada's Consumer Price Index (CPI) is used as a measure of inflation through which to calculate real returns.

A First Look: Over the period 1957-2002, $1 invested in Canadian common stocks grew into $54.01. During the same period, $1 invested in Canada Treasury bills and long bonds grew into $20.87 and $43.41, respectively. These values are not adjusted for inflation: over the same period, the value of $1 in 1957 grew to $6.94 in 2002 after adjusting for inflation. These results strongly suggest that investment in common stock is superior to investment in either Treasury bills or long bonds. However, these values do not account for the variability associated with each investment. The historical record indicates that returns associated with common stocks are much more volatile than those associated with Treasury bills and long bonds.

A Closer Look: To demonstrate the variability of historical returns, note that some years are characterized by extremely high returns. For example, long bonds earned 45.82% in 1982, the S&P 500 earned 52.62% in 1954, and T-bills earned 19.11% in 1981.

12.3 AVERAGE RETURNS: THE FIRST LESSON

To use historical stock market returns for financial decisions, we must summarize percentage return data for individual stocks or for the stock market as a whole. To do this, we calculate the average return. The average (mean) return is simply the sum of all returns divided by the number of observations.

Consider an investment which has a guaranteed 100% return the first year and a guaranteed 60% loss the second. The average return is [100% + (–60%)]/2 = 20%. Financial managers are often interested in the answer to the question: "What rate can I expect to earn next year?" In this case, one possible forecast of this expected return may be the average return for some historical period.

A common benchmark used in comparing returns is the return on securities issued by the Canadian government. One form of government security is the Treasury bill or T-bill, which is a security sold by the Bank of Canada maturing in less than one year. We refer to the T-bill rate as the risk-free rate of return.

From 1948 to 1990, the average return on T-bills was 6.1% per year. During the same time period, a portfolio consisting of Canadian common stocks (the TSE 300 Composite Index) had an average return of 12.92%. The difference between the 12.92% return for the common stock portfolio and the 6.1% earned on T-bills is called the excess return for the risky asset. Since the excess return is due to the greater riskiness of stock investments, the excess return is also called the risk premium. The historical risk premium for the Canadian common stock portfolio is (.1292 – .061) = .0682 = 6.82%. The historical existence of risk premiums is the basis for our first lesson: *Risky assets, on average, earn a risk premium.* In other words, there is a reward for bearing risk.

12.4 THE VARIABILITY OF RETURNS

Since riskiness affects returns, we must be able to measure the degree of risk associated with an investment in order to understand the relationship between risk and return. The most common measures are the *variance* and the *standard deviation*.

The Historical Variance and Standard Deviation: Suppose that a particular investment returned 8%, 14%, –4%, and 6% over the last 4 years. The average return is:

$$\text{Avg. Return} = (.08 + .14 - .04 + .06) / 4 = .06 = 6\%$$

Financial economists equate risk with the statistical concept of variability. The most commonly used statistical measures of variability are the variance and the standard deviation. In the financial context, we use the variance to measure the variability of returns from the average return; the greater the deviation from the average, the more variable the rate of return and the higher the level of risk.

To calculate the variance, we first find the squared deviations from the mean (average) return. The sum of these amounts is then divided by the number of returns less 1.

The calculation of the variance is summarized in this table:

Rate of return	Average return	Deviation from average return	Squared value of deviation
.08	.06	.02	.0004
.14	.06	.08	.0064
- .04	.06	- .10	.0100
.06	.06	.00	.0000

The variance is the average squared deviation, or [.0168/(4 – 1)] = .0056. The standard deviation is the square root of .0056, which equals .07483. This calculation of the variance is summarized by the following formula:

$$\text{Var}(R) = \sigma^2 = [1 / (T\text{-}1)] [(R_1 - E(R))^2 + (R_2 - E(R))^2 + ... + (R_T - E(R))^2]$$

where Var(R) and σ^2 represent alternative notations for variance, R_1, R_2, and R_T are the returns for each year, and T is the number of observations. The standard deviation is the square root of the variance, and is denoted as either SD(R) or σ.

Normal Distribution: For many random events, the normal distribution (or bell curve) is useful for deriving the probability that the value of a variable falls within a certain range. For example, if stock returns have a normal distribution, the probability that the return in a given year is within one standard deviation of the mean is about 68%, or approximately 2/3. The probability that the return is within two standard deviations of the mean is about 95%. Figure 12.6 on page 393 of your text illustrates a normal return distribution for a portfolio of large common shares.

For the Canadian common stock portfolio, the standard deviation of returns from 1948 to 1999, is approximately 16.62%. The mean return during this period was 13.20%. The probability that the return in a given year is in the range –.0342 to .2982, (.1392 plus or minus one standard deviation, .1662) is approximately 2/3. Put another way, there is one chance in three that the rate of return would fall outside this range. This result illustrates that the stock market can be quite volatile. However, there is only a 5% chance (approximately) that the mean rate of return would be outside the range –.2004 to .4644 [.1320 plus or minus (2 x .1662)]. Assuming that the return on the Canadian common stock portfolio is normally distributed, these points are illustrated on the graph in your text.

That graph tells us that if you buy stocks in large Canadian corporations, you will be outside the range of –3.42 % to 29.82 % one time in three (or one year out of every three years). This is an important observation about the stock market's volatility. However, there is only a 5 % chance (approximately) that you would end up outside the range of –20.04 % to 46.44 % . Thus, this year to year volatility is the basis for our second lesson: *the greater the potential for reward, the greater is the risk.*

Suppose we are interested in evaluating an investment that is about as risky as the Canadian common stock portfolio. What discount rate should we use for out present value analysis? Recall that the difference between the return on a risky asset and the risk-free return is the risk premium, so that the appropriate discount rate for evaluating a risky investment is the sum of the risk-free rate plus a risk premium. The historic risk premium for the Canadian common stock portfolio is 6.82%. If T-bills are currently yielding 7%, then the appropriate rate to use in evaluating this investment would be (6.82% + 7%) = 13.82%.

Clearly, not all risky investments have the same risk level as the Canadian common stock portfolio. Therefore, we can not use the above procedure for evaluating all risky investments. So, it is necessary to analyze the relationship between risk and return in the financial markets. We will complete this discussion in the next chapter.

12.5 CAPITAL MARKET EFFICIENCY

The financial markets in Canada have very low trading costs and many buyers and sellers, all of whom have ready access to relevant information. In such a market, all transactions have exactly zero NPV. That is, assets are worth exactly what they cost. This premise is the basis for the notion that financial markets are efficient. We briefly discuss the concept of market efficiency in this section.

The Efficient Markets Hypothesis: An *efficient capital market* is a market in which all transactions have net present value equal to zero. Alternatively, it can be said that the price of any asset is always equal to its present value, so that the return for an investment is equal to the equilibrium return for a given level of risk. All that is required for a market to be efficient is that current market prices reflect available information. If a market is efficient with respect to some piece of information, then that piece of information can not be used to identify a positive NPV investment.

The *efficient markets hypothesis* (EMH) asserts that prices for assets in Canadian capital markets are efficient with respect to available information. The hypothesis implies that no investment strategy based on current or historical information produces extraordinarily large profits. With thousands of investment advisory services, mountains of information, and millions of investors (all of whom have the same goals), the adjustment of prices to new information is almost instantaneous.

There are two important implications of market efficiency for investors and firms. First, investors buying stocks and bonds should expect to earn an equilibrium return commensurate with the level of risk they assume. Second, firms issuing securities should expect to receive from investors a price equal to the present value of the securities.

Some Common Misconceptions About the EMH: Two objections to the efficient markets hypothesis are frequently raised. The first is based on the observation that security prices fluctuate every day. However, this observation is not inconsistent with market efficiency. On the contrary, since new information arrives every day, the efficient markets hypothesis predicts that prices adjust rapidly to the new information. The second criticism is that the market cannot be efficient because only a fraction of the outstanding shares are traded every day. Once again, however, this result is actually consistent with the hypothesis. Investors trade only when they expect to benefit from doing so. In a market with transaction costs, such as brokerage fees, there is little incentive for trades to take place if securities are correctly valued.

The efficient markets hypothesis does not suggest that the determinants of price changes are unknown. Prices depend on expected future cash flows. It is the expectations of these future cash flows that change when new information arrives. The hypothesis also does not imply that we should select stocks randomly. The result could be an undiversified portfolio of securities with an undesirable level of risk. Finally, the EMH does not imply that investors are uninformed. To the contrary, the hypothesis is based on the assumption that investors are quite rational, and are not easily fooled or manipulated.

Market Efficiency - Forms and Evidence: Financial economists generally identify three forms of market efficiency, based on the kinds of information which might be expected to influence stock prices. A market is said to be *weak-form efficient* if current security prices completely incorporate the information contained in past prices. This means that it is pointless to analyze past prices in an attempt to predict future prices. Such an evaluation procedure is called technical analysis or 'charting'. Weak-form efficiency implies that technical analysis can not be used successfully to forecast future prices and therefore that technical analysts do not earn extraordinary profits. There is a great deal of evidence indicating that financial markets are weak-form efficient.

A market is said to be *semistrong-form efficient* if current prices incorporate all publicly available information. Semistrong-form efficiency implies that the analysis of published financial statements, for example, does not result in earning excess profits. Notice that a semistrong efficient market is also weak-form efficient, since past prices are a form of publicly available information.

At the extreme, a market is *strong-form efficient* if current prices reflect *all* information, including inside information; inside information is information about a firm which is available only to 'insiders', including corporate executives and major shareholders. There seems to be little reason to believe that markets are strong-form efficient; that is, available evidence seems to indicate that valuable inside information does exist. At the other extreme, there are compelling reasons for believing that markets are weak-form efficient. There is a great deal of debate, however, over semistrong-form efficiency. A reasonable compromise view might be summarized as follows: some prices, some of the time, might not reflect all publicly available information, but most assets, most of the time, do reflect this information.

CONCEPT TEST

1. The return on an investment comes in either or both of two general forms; these are the _____ component, and the _____ gain or loss.

2. The return on an investment in common stock usually comes in two forms; _____ and _____ gains. _____ , which are cash payments by a corporation to its shareholders, represent the income component of the return. _____ gains (or losses) for an investment in common stock result from _____ or _____ in the value of the stock.

3. The total percentage return for an investment is the sum of the _____ yield and the percentage _____ gain (or _____ gains yield). The _____ yield is defined algebraically as _____ . The _____ gains yield is defined algebraically as _____ .

4. The _____ return or _____ return is simply the ordinary average: the total of the returns divided by the number of observations. The calculation of the average return is summarized algebraically as follows: $E(R) =$ _____ , where T is the number of time periods, and R and E(R) are alternative notations for the average return.

5. Treasury bills are considered virtually _____ , so that the T-bill rate is often referred to as the _____ . The difference between the rate of return for a particular risky investment and the rate of return earned on T-bills is called the _____ or the _____ for the risky asset.

6. Financial economists equate risk with the statistical concept of _____ , which is commonly measured by the variance and the standard deviation. The variance is used to measure the variability of return from the average return. The variance is the average of the _____ deviations from the _____ return. This calculation of the variance is summarized by the formula: $Var(R) = \sigma^2 =$ _____ , where Var(R) and σ^2 are alternative notation for variance, R_1, R_2, and R_T are the returns for each year, and T is the number of observations.

7. The _____ is the square root of the variance, and is denoted as either _____ or _____ .

8. For many random events, the _____ distribution or the bell curve, is useful for deriving the probability that the value of a variable falls within a certain range. If stock returns have this distribution, then the probability that the rate of return in a given year is within one standard deviation of the mean is _____ . The probability that the return is within two standard deviations of the mean is _____ .

9. An efficient capital market is a market in which all transactions have net present value equal to _____ . Alternatively, it can be said that in an efficient market, the price of an asset is always equal to its _____ , so that the rate of return for an investment is equal to the equilibrium rate of return for a given level of risk. All that is required for a market to be efficient is that current market prices reflect _____ . If a market is efficient with respect to some piece of information, then that piece of information can not be used to identify an investment with a _____ .

10. The _____ hypothesis asserts that prices for assets in Canadian capital markets are efficient with respect to available information. The hypothesis implies that no investment strategy based on current or historical information produces extraordinarily large profits. The adjustment of prices to new information is _____ .

11. Financial economists identify three forms of market efficiency. A market is said to be _____-form efficient if current security prices completely incorporate the information contained in past prices. A market is said to be _____-form efficient if current prices incorporate all publicly available information. A market is _____-form efficient if current prices reflect all information, including inside information.

12. Available evidence seems to indicate that valuable inside information does exist, so that financial markets (are/are not) strong-form efficient. At the other extreme, there are compelling reasons for believing that markets (are/are not) weak-form efficient. There is a great deal of debate, however, over _____-form efficiency.

13. Value at Risk VaR measures the _____ loss associated with a portfolio, though it is _____ for the actual loss to exceed the VaR. Financial institutions use VaR to manage _____ and to determine adequate _____ levels.

PROBLEMS

Problem 1

Adam bought 100 shares of TJR Corporation's common stock for $18 per share. In the following year, he received a cash dividend of $2.50 per share, and the value of the stock increased to $22 per share. What is Adam's total dollar return? Also calculate his dividend and capital gains yield, and his total percentage return.

Problem 2

Suppose that, one year ago, you bought 100 shares of Bradley Corporation common stock for $32 per share. During the year, you received dividends of $2.50 per share. Bradley common stock is currently selling for $33.50 per share. What was your total dividend income during the year? How much did you earn in capital gains? What was your total dollar return? Use these dollar returns to calculate the dividend yield, capital gains yield and total percentage return for this investment.

Problem 3

For the Bradley common stock investment described in Problem 2, compute the dividend yield, the capital gains yield, and the total percentage return on a per share basis.

Problem 4

Suppose that, one year from today, you expect the Bradley Corporation common stock described in Problem 2 to be selling for $33 per share, and that during the coming year, you expect to receive dividends of $2 per share. What is the total dividend income expected during the year? What is the total capital gain expected during the year? What is the total dollar return expected during the year? Use these dollar returns to calculate the dividend yield, capital gains yield and total percentage return expected during the year.

Problem 5

For the investment described in Problem 4, compute the dividend yield, the capital gains yield, and the total percentage return on a per share basis.

Problem 6

Last year Jacky bought 50 shares of JAG Corporation common stock for $19.73 per share. During the year, she received dividends of $2.70 per share. JAG Corp is now selling for $24.27 per share. What was Jacky's total dividend income during the year? How much did she earn in capital gains? What was her total dollar return? What were the dividend yield and capital gains yield? What was the total percentage return on Jacky's investment?

Problem 7

For JAG Corporation's information in Problem 6, calculate the dividend yield, the capital gains yield, and the total percentage return on a per-share basis.

Problem 8

The following table contains information on the rates of return for common shares of the Healy Tire Corporation (HT) and the Smooth Ride Wheel Company (SR) over a five-year period.

	Returns	
Year	HT	SR
1	7%	10%
2	9	12
3	-8	8
4	4	-6
5	8	6

What is the mean return for HT common stock and for SR common stock? Also, calculate the variance and standard deviation for each common stock.

Use the information the following table to solve Problems 9–12:

Suppose that the following information represents the rate of return for General Motors Canada (GM) common stock and Bell Canada (BC) common stock over a five-year period:

Year	Returns	
	GM	BC
1	.10	.12
2	.04	.06
3	-.09	-.10
4	.20	.22
5	.05	.05

Problem 9

What is the mean return for GM common stock? For BC common stock?

Problem 10

What is the variance of the return for GM common stock? For BC stock?

Problem 11

What is the standard deviation of the return for GM common stock? For BC common stock?

Problem 12

Suppose the returns for GM and BC each have a normal distribution with the means and standard deviations calculated in Problem 6 and 7, respectively. For each stock, determine the range of returns within one standard deviation of the mean and the range of returns within two standard deviations of the mean. Interpret these results.

Use the following information to solve Problems 13–15:

The returns for the TTK Corporation common stock and the MAX Corporation common stock during the past 5 years are listed below:

Year	Returns	
	TTK	MAX
1	12%	6%
2	15	14
3	4	7
4	- 5	0
5	9	13

Problem 13

Calculate the average return for TTK and for MAX common stock.

Problem 14

Calculate the variance for TTK and for MAX common stock.

Problem 15

Calculate the standard deviation for TTK and for MAX common stock.

Problem 16

Money and More, Inc. (MMI) is a large financial institution that has $1,000,000,000 invested in stocks. The average return associated with the portfolio is 12.5% while the portfolio standard deviation is 23.5%. What is the Value at Risk (VaR) associated with this portfolio, assuming you require that 97.5% of the time the actual loss does not exceed the VaR?

Problem 17

Bank of Azoka, Inc. (BAI) is a small bank with $2,700,000 invested in a portfolio of stocks. The average return associated with the portfolio is 8.5% while the portfolio standard deviation is 10.5%. What is the Value at Risk (VaR) associated with this portfolio, assuming you require that 97.5% of the time the actual loss does not exceed the VaR?

ANSWERS TO CONCEPT TESTS

1.   income; capital

2.   dividends; capital; dividends; capital; increases; decreases

3.   dividend; capital; capital; dividend; (D_t/P_t); capital; $[(P_{t+1} - P_t)/P_t]$

4.   average; mean; $[(R_1 + R_2 + ... + R_T)/T]$

5.   risk-free; risk-free rate of return; excess return; risk premium

6.   variability; squared; average; $[1/(T - 1)] [(R_1 - R)^2 + (R_2 - R)^2 + ... + (R_T - R)^2]$

7.   standard deviation; SD(R); σ

8.   normal; about 68%, or about 2/3; about 95%

9.   zero; present value; available information; positive NPV

10.   efficient markets; almost instantaneous

11.   weak; semistrong; strong

12.   are not; are; semistrong

13.   maximum, possible, risk exposure, capital

PROBLEM SOLUTIONS

Problem 1: Total dollar return   =   Dividend income + Capital gain (loss)

$$= (100 \times \$2.50) + [100 \times (\$22 - \$18) = \$250 + \$400 = \$650$$

Dividend yield = D_t / P_t = $\$2.50 / \$18$ = 0.138889 = 13.89%

where P_t is the share price at the beginning of the year and D_t is the dividend paid during the year.

Capital gains yield = $(P_{t-1} - P_t) / P_t$ = $(\$22 - \$18) / \$18$ = 0.22222 = 22.22 %

Total percentage return = Dividend yield + Capital gains yield   =   13.89% + 22.22%   =   36.11%

OR

Total percentage return = (Dividend + Capital gain) / Original Investment

$$= (\$2.50 + \$4) / \$18 = 0.3611 = 36.11\%$$

Problem 2: The total dividend income is ($2.50 × 100) = $250. Capital gains are equal to [($33.50 – $32) × 100] = $150 and total dollar return is ($250 + $150) = $400. The dividend yield is [$250/($32 × 100)] = .0781 = 7.81%. The capital gains yield is [$150/($32 × 100)] = .0469 = 4.69%. The total percentage return is [($150 + $250)/($32 × 100)] = .1250 = 12.50% = (4.69% + 7.81%).

Problem 3: The dividend yield is:

$$D_t / P_t \;=\; \$2.50 / \$32 \;=\; .0781 \;=\; 7.81\%$$

where P_t is the price of the stock at the beginning of the year, and D_t is the dividend paid during the year. The capital gains yield is:

$$\frac{P_{t+1} - P_t}{P_t} \;=\; \frac{\$33.50 - \$32}{\$32} \;=\; .0469 \;=\; 4.69\%$$

where P_t is the price of the stock at the beginning of the year and P_{t+1} is the price at the end of the year. The total percentage return is the sum of the dividend yield and the capital gains yield:

$$\text{Total percentage return} \;=\; 7.81\% + 4.69\% \;=\; 12.50\%$$

Problem 4: The total dividend income expected is ($2 × 100) = $200. The expected capital gains are equal to [($33 – $33.50) × 100] = –$50; this is a capital loss of $50. The total dollar return expected is ($200 – $50) = $150. The expected dividend yield is [($200/($33.50 × 100)] = .0597 = 5.97%. The expected capital gains yield is [–$50/($33.50 × 100)] = –.0149 = –1.49%. The total percentage return is [($200 – $50) / ($33.50 × 100)] = .0448 = 4.48% = (5.97% – 1.49%).

Problem 5: The dividend yield is: $2.00 / $33.50 = .0597 = 5.97%. The capital gains yield is: ($33 – $33.50) / $33.50 = -.0149 = -1.49%. The total percentage return is the sum of the dividend yield and the capital gains yield: 5.97% – 1.49% = 4.48%

Problem 6: Total dividend income is ($2.70 x 50) = $135.00, and capital gains were [($24.27 - $19.73) x 50] = $227.00. Total dollar return is $135 + $227 = $362. Dividend yield was $135 / ($19.73 x 50) = 0.1368 = 13.68%. Capital gains yield was $227 / ($19.73 x 50) = 0.2301 = 23.01%. Total percentage return was 13.68% + 23.01% = 36.69%.

Problem 7: The dividend yield, capital gains yield, and total percentage return are the same for one share as they are for a group of shares. There are no calculations required to answer this problem. That means the percentage values are the same as those in Problem 6.

Problem 8: The mean returns are:

For HT: (.07 + .09 - .08 + .04 + .08) / 5   =   0.04   =   4.0%

For SR: (.10 + .12 + .08 - .06 + .06) / 5   =   0.06   =   6.0%

The variance calculations are summarized in the following table:

Year	Rate of Return		Deviation from Average Return		Squared value of Deviation	
	HT	SR	HT	SR	HT	SR
1	.07	.10	.03	.04	.0009	.0016
2	.09	.12	.05	.06	.0025	.0036
3	-.08	.08	-.12	.02	.0144	.0004
4	.04	-.06	.00	-.12	.0000	.0144
5	.08	.06	.04	.00	.0016	.0000
Total	.20	.30	.00	.00	.0194	.0200

For HT: $\sigma^2 = 0.0194 / 4 = .00485$; For SR, $\sigma^2 = .0200 / 4 = .0050$

The standard deviation of the return for each stock is the square root of the variance.

For HT: $\sigma = .00485^{1/2} = 0.06964 = 6.964\%$; For SR, $\sigma = 0.0050^{1/2} = 0.07071 = 7.071\%$

Problem 9: For GM: $R = (.10 + .04 - .09 + .20 + .05) / 5 = .06 = 6\%$
For BC: $R = (.12 + .06 - .10 + .22 + .05) / 5 = .07 = 7\%$

Problem 10: The calculations are summarized in the following table:

Year	Rate of return		Deviation from average return		Squared value of deviation	
	GM	BC	GM	BC	GM	BC
1	.10	.12	.04	.05	.0016	.0025
2	.04	.06	-.02	-.01	.0004	.0001
3	-.09	-.10	-.15	-.17	.0225	.0289
4	.20	.22	.14	.15	.0196	.0225
5	.05	.05	-.01	-.02	.0001	.0004
Total	.30	.35	.00	.00	.0442	.0544

For GM: $\sigma^2 = .0442 / 4 = 0.01105$. For BC: $\sigma^2 = .0544 / 4 = .0136$

Problem 11: The standard deviation is the square root of the variance. The standard deviation for GM is:
$\sigma = (.01105)^{.5} = .10512 = 10.512\%$. For BC: $\sigma = (.0136)^{.5} = .11662 = 11.662\%$.

Problem 12: For GM, the range of returns within one standard deviation of the mean is from $[.06 - (1 \times .10512)]$ to $[.06 + (1 \times .10512)]$, or -4.512% to 16.512%. The range of returns within two standard deviations of the mean is from $[.06 - (2 \times .10512)]$ to $(.06 + (2 \times .10512)]$, or -15.024% to 27.024%. These results indicate that there is approximately a 68% probability that, in any given year, the return for GM common stock will be between -4.512% and 16.512% and approximately a 95% probability that the return will be between -15.024% and 27.024%.

For BC common stock, the probability is approximately 68% that the return will be between -4.662% and 18.662%, and approximately 95% that the return will be between -16.324% and 30.324%.

Problem 13: The average returns are $R = (.35/5) = .07 = 7\%$ for TTK common stock and $R = (.40/5) = .08 = 8\%$ for MAX common stock.

Problem 14: The variances are: $\sigma_{TTK}^2 = (.0246/4) = .00615$ and $\sigma_{MAX}^2 = (.0130/4) = .00325$.

Problem 15: The standard deviations are: $\sigma_{TTK} = (.00615)^{.5} = .078422$ and $\sigma_M = (.00325)^{.5} = .05701$.

Problem 16: There is a 97.5% probability that the actual portfolio return will be greater than the return associated with two standard deviations below the average portfolio return = 12.5% - 2 x 23.5% = -34.5%. On a portfolio of $1,000,000,000, this means the VaR is $1,000,000,000 x (-34.5%) = - $345,000,000.

Problem 17: There is a 97.5% probability that the actual portfolio return will be greater than the return associated with two standard deviations below the average portfolio return = 8.5% - 2 x 10.5% = -12.5%. On a portfolio of $2,700,000, this means the VaR is $2,700,000 x (-12.5%) = - $337,500.

13 Return, Risk, and the Security Market Line

CHAPTER HIGHLIGHTS

We have established that investments with greater risk provide, on average, a higher rate of return. In this chapter, we establish a more precise description of the relationship between risk and return in the securities markets. The relationship between risk and return is called the *security market line* (SML). First, we discuss the appropriate procedures for measuring rates of return and risk.

13.1 EXPECTED RETURNS AND VARIANCES

In the previous chapter, we discussed the calculation of average returns and variances based on historical data. In this chapter, the focus is on rates of return that might occur in the future.

Expected Return: The rate of return that might occur in the future is referred to as the *expected return*. Actually, an expected value is an average, or mean, of possible future outcomes. Here, the term *expected return* refers to the expected value of all possible future rates of return. The *actual* return an investor earns, however, will most likely differ from the expected return.

An Example: The table below summarizes data for GM and Exxon stocks.

State of economy	Probability of state of economy (Pr)	Rate of return if state occurs (R) GM	Rate of return if state occurs (R) Exxon
1	.20	.10	.03
2	.20	.04	- .08
3	.20	- .09	.07
4	.20	.20	.12
5	.20	.05	.21
Total	1.00	.30	.35

The table represents forecasts of possible returns for each stock during the coming year. The forecasts are based on five equally likely possible states of the economy; a state of the economy might be a severe recession, or a depression, or moderate growth of the economy, for example. For each state of the economy, we have predicted the rate of return which is likely to occur for each common stock. This example is oversimplified. First, we have assumed only five states of the economy. Second, we have assumed that each state is equally likely to occur. Nevertheless, the concepts presented hold even when the 'real-world' situation becomes more complicated.

Since there are five equally-likely possible states of the economy, the probability for any one state is 0.20 or 20%; the total of the probabilities is 1.00, or 100%, indicating that one of the five states must occur during the coming year.

The expected return $E(R_U)$ is computed as the sum of each possible return multiplied by its probability of occurrence. For GM and Exxon, the expected returns are:

$$E(R_{GM}) = .20 \times .10 + .20 \times .04 + .20 \times -.09 + .20 \times .20 + .20 \times .05 = .06$$

$$E(R_{Exxon}) \quad = .20 \times .03 \;+\; .20 \times -.08 \;+\; .20 \times .07 \;+\; .20 \times .12 \;+\; .20 \times .21 \;=\; .07$$

When the probability of each return is equally likely (as above), the expected return can simply be computed as an average of the possible returns.

$$E(R_{GM}) \quad = \quad (.10 + .04 - .09 + .20 + .05)/5 \;=\; .06$$

$$E(R_{Exxon}) \quad = \quad (.03 - .08 + .07 + .12 + .21)/5 \;=\; .07$$

In general, though, each state of the economy is not equally likely to occur. Under these circumstances, expected return is calculated as a weighted average of the possible returns. Each possible return is multiplied (weighted) by its probability of occurrence. The expected return is the sum of these weighted returns:

$$E(R) \quad = \quad (Pr_1 \times R_1) \;+\; (Pr_2 \times R_2) \;+\; (Pr_3 \times R_3) + \ldots + (Pr_T \times R_T)$$

where T is the number of possible states of the economy, Pr_1, Pr_2, Pr_3, and Pr_T are the probabilities of the respective states of the economy, and R_1, R_2, R_3, and R_T are the possible rates of return.

We can revise the above table to consider the fact that all states of the economy are not equally likely:

State of economy	Probability of state of economy (Pr)	Rate of return if state occurs (R)	
		GM	Exxon
1	.10	.10	.03
2	.30	.04	- .08
3	.30	-.09	.07
4	.20	.20	.12
5	.10	.05	.21
Total	1.00	.30	.35

Computing the new expected returns for GM and Exxon, we have:

$$E(R_{GM}) \quad = .10 \times .10 \;+\; .30 \times .04 \;+\; .30 \times -.09 \;+\; .20 \times .20 \;+\; .10 \times .05 \;=\; .040$$

$$E(R_{Exxon}) \quad = .10 \times .03 \;+\; .30 \times -.08 \;+\; .30 \times .07 \;+\; .20 \times .12 \;+\; .10 \times .21 \;=\; .045$$

Variance: Our focus in this section is on the calculation of the variance for data representing future possible rates of return. To calculate the variance, we determine the squared deviations from the expected return. Each possible squared deviation is multiplied by its probability of occurrence. These are added; the sum is the variance. The standard deviation is simply the square root of the variance.

The generalized equations for the variance and standard deviation are:

$$\sigma^2 \quad = \quad \Sigma_J \, [R_j - E(R)]^2 \times P_j$$

$$\sigma \quad = \quad (\sigma^2)^{1/2}$$

The calculation of the variances for the GM and Exxon example is summarized in the following table. NOTE: for this example, we are using the scenario where each state of the economy is equally likely to occur. That is, $Pr_1 = Pr_2 = \ldots = Pr_5 = .20$.

State of economy	Rate of return if state occurs (R)		Deviation of return from expected return [R - E(R)]		Squared deviation of return from expected return [R - E(R)]^2	
	GM	Exxon	GM	Exxon	GM	Exxon
1	.10	.03	.04	-.04	.0016	.0016
2	.04	-.08	-.02	-.15	.0004	.0225
3	-.09	.07	-.15	.00	.0225	.0000
4	.20	.12	.14	.05	.0196	.0025
5	.05	.21	-.01	.14	.0001	.0196
Total	.30	.35	.00	.00	.0442	.0462

The variance (σ_{GM}^2) and standard deviation (σ_{GM}) for GM are (.0442 / 45) = 0.01105 and $[(0.01105)^{.5}] = 0.10512 = 10.512\%$, respectively . The variance (σ_{EX}^2) and standard deviation (σ_{EX}) for Exxon are (.0462 / 4) = 0.01155 and $[(0.01155)^{.5}] = 0.10747 = 10.747\%$, respectively.

Note that, if the probabilities of each state occurring were not equal, we would have to multiply each squared deviation by its probability. The sum would then be the variance.

13.2 PORTFOLIOS

Most investors own a portfolio of assets, rather than one individual asset. An investor's portfolio is the combination of assets the investor owns. Therefore, investors are more concerned about the characteristics of the portfolio than the characteristics of the individual assets which comprise the portfolio. In this section we discuss the expected return and variance of a portfolio.

Portfolio Weights: The respective percentages of a portfolio's total value invested in each of the assets in the portfolio are referred to as the portfolio weights.

An Example: An investor has a three-asset portfolio with a total value of $1,000. The values of assets A, B and C are $450, $250, and $300, respectively. What are the portfolio weights for this portfolio?

Weight invested in Asset A = $450 / $1,000 = 45%
Weight invested in Asset B = $250 / $1,000 = 25%
Weight invested in Asset C = $300 / $1,000 = 30%

Portfolio Expected Returns: Consider an individual who invests 60% of his money in GM stock and 40% in Exxon stock (the portfolio weights are 60% and 40%, respectively). For each of the five possible states of the economy indicated in the earlier example, the investor's return on his investment will be equal to a weighted average of the returns in that state for the respective stocks. For example, if state 1 occurs, the portfolio return (R_p) would be:

$$R_p = (.60 \times .10) + (.40 \times .03) = .072 = 7.2\%$$

The table below indicates the return for the portfolio in each of the five states of the economy, and the calculations required to compute the expected return for the portfolio, $(E(R_p)$ when each state has an equal probability of occurring:

State of economy economy	Probability of state of economy (Pr)	Rate of return if state occurs (R_{GM})	(R_{exxon})	(R_p)	(Pr x R_p)
1	.20	.10	.03	.072	.0144
2	.20	.04	-.08	-.008	-.0016
3	.20	-.09	.07	-.026	-.0052
4	.20	.20	.12	.168	.0336
5	.20 .05	.21	.114	.0228	
Total	1.00	.30	.35	.320	.0640

The expected return for the portfolio is $0.0640 = 6.4\%$. Notice that we have used the weighted-average procedure here to compute $E(R_p)$. Since the five possible values of R_p are equally likely, we could have computed $E(R_p)$ as a simple average of the values of R_p. That is, $E(R_p) = (.320/5) = 0.0640 = 6.4\%$.

A more direct approach computes the expected return for a portfolio as a weighted average of the expected returns of the securities in the portfolio. The weights are the portfolio weights. The formula for this calculation is:

$$E(R_p) = [x_1 \times E(R_1)] + [x_2 \times E(R_2)] + [x_3 \times E(R_3)] + \ldots + [x_n \times E(R_n)]$$

where n is the number of assets in the portfolio, x_1, x_2, x_3, and x_n are the portfolio weights for the assets, and $E(R_1)$, $E(R_2)$, $E(R_3)$, and $E(R_n)$ are the expected returns for the assets. For the GM-Exxon example:

$$E(R_p) = [x_{GM} \times E(R_{GM})] + [x_{EXXON} \times E(R_{EXXON})] = (.60 \times .06) + (.40 \times .07) = .064 = 6.4\%$$

Portfolio Variance: The expected return for a portfolio is a weighted average of the expected returns of the individual securities in the portfolio. However, the variance and standard deviation of a portfolio are *not* weighted averages of the variances and standard deviations of the individual securities. In fact, the way in which assets are combined into a portfolio can significantly change the risks faced by an investor. This is a very important concept.

Portfolio Standard Deviation and Diversification: Combining assets into portfolios in oerder to reduce portfolio risk is know as *diversification*. In general, the process of diversification reduces portfolio risk. This is because of the *correlation* between the returns of the securities in the portfolio. The correlation coefficient tells us the extent to which the returns of two securities move together over time. The correlation coefficient (CORR) can range from +1 (perfectly positive) to –1 (perfectly negative). A coefficient of 0 indicates that there is no relationship.

The graphs in Figure 13.1, on page 417 of your text show three cases for combining two assets, A and B (assume these are returns of securities). The left-hand graphs plot the separate returns for the two securities through time. The right-hand graphs represent the returns for *both* A and B over a particular time interval. The correlation of returns for A and B, CORR(R_A, R_B) ranges from –1.0 to 1.0.

The significance of different degrees of correlation on the standard deviation of a portfolio is intuitively obvious in the extreme case of perfectly negative correlation between the returns of two securities. Whenever security returns are not moving in exactly the same direction over time, then by investing equal amounts in A and B, the portfolio returns are smoothed out and the portfolio standard deviation is reduced. Mathematically, it can be shown that the portfolio variance for a two stock portfolio (Stock A and B) is:

$$\sigma^2_p \;=\; x^2_A\,\sigma^2_A \;+\; x^2_B\,\sigma^2_B \;+\; 2x_A\,x_B\,CORR_{AB}\,\sigma_A\,\sigma_B$$

where x =   proportion of wealth invested in A or B
        $CORR_{AB}$ =   Correlation between the returns for A and B
        $CORR_{AB}\,\sigma_A\,\sigma_B$ =   Covariance between the returns of A and B

An Example: The standard deviation of the rate of return for CP is 12 % and 26 % for CAE. If the correlation between their rates of return is .65, what is the standard deviation of a portfolio consisting of 20 % of CAE and the remainder in CP stock? What is the covariance between the returns of CP and CAE?

The variance of the two stock portfolio is:

$$\sigma^2_p = (.80)^2(.12)^2 + (.20)^2(.26)^2 + 2\,(.80)(.20)(.65)(.12)(.26) = .01841$$

The standard deviation is the square root of the variance: $\sigma_p \;=\; (.01841)^{1/2} \;=\; .135682$ or 13.57 %.

Note, if the correlation coefficient is 1.0, the standard deviation of this portfolio would be 14.8%, which is simply a weighted average of the individual standard deviations : $(.80)(.12) + (.20)(.26) = 14.8\%$. Any time the correlation coefficient is *less* than +1, the portfolio standard deviation is less than a weighted average of the individual standard deviations. This means that, any time the correlation coefficient is less than +1, diversification will reduce portfolio risk.

An Example: In the preceding example, what is the standard deviation of the two stock portfolios if the correlation coefficient is zero? What is it if CORR is –1.0?

$$\text{If } CORR_{A,B} = 0: \sigma_p{}^2 \;=\; (.80)^2(.12)^2 + (.20)^2(.26)^2 + 2(.80)(.20)(0)(.12)(.26)$$
$$= .00922 + .00270 + 0 = .011920$$
$$\sigma_p = (.011920)^{1/2} = .10918 = 10.92\%$$

$$\text{If } CORR_{A,B} = -1: \sigma_p{}^2 \;=\; (.80)^2(.12)^2 + (.20)^2(.26)^2 + 2(.80)(.20)(-1.0)(.12)(.26) = .001936$$
$$\sigma_p = 4.4\,\%$$

From the above examples it should be clear that as long as *CORR is less than 1.0, the standard deviation of a portfolio of two securities is <u>less</u> than the weighted average of the standard deviation of the individual securities.* Notice that the most risk reduction occurred when CORR = –1.0.

Combining securities (or assets) whose CORR is less than +1.0 offers the investor the opportunity to reduce portfolio risk as measured by the portfolio standard deviation. This process is commonly known as *diversification.*

As investors diversify their portfolios by adding securities that have correlation coefficients less than +1.0, and continue to adjust the respective weights in these portfolios, the many possible combinations can be represented in a *feasible set or the efficient set* of portfolio combinations.

13.3 ANNOUNCEMENTS, SURPRISES, AND EXPECTED RETURNS

Our measurement of risk, using variance and standard deviation, is based on the size of the differences between actual returns, R, and expected returns, E(R). In this section, we discuss the reasons why differences between R and E(R) exist.

Expected and Unexpected Returns: The actual return (R) on a security consists of two parts: the expected return, which is predicted by participants in the financial markets; and, a 'surprise,' or unexpected, part. The expected return is based on the market's understanding of a large number of factors that may influence a given company's share price.

The second part of the return, the risky part, comes from unexpected information that is revealed during the year. For a given stock, we can write:

$$R = E(R) + U$$

where R is the actual total return, E(R) is the expected part of the return and U is the unexpected part of the return. The difference between the actual return, R, and the expected return, E(R), is attributed to surprises reflected in the unexpected return, U.

Announcements and News: Consider the example of Texxon, a large oil company. The expected return on Texxon common stock is partially determined by the expected price of oil. Suppose the price of oil is currently $12 per barrel and the price is completely controlled by the OPEC cartel. It is generally expected that the cartel will raise the price to $20 per barrel. Unexpectedly, however, the cartel announces that the price will be $22. The price changes by $10 per barrel, but $8 of this change was expected and was reflected in Texxon's expected return. It is the $2 deviation from the expected price that is the 'surprise' portion of the announcement.

In general, an announcement has two components: the expected part and the surprise, or innovation:

Announcement = Expected part + Surprise

In the Texxon example, if a price hike to $20 had actually been announced, there would have been no surprise. In the language of Wall Street, the market has already 'discounted' the news of a price increase to $20, which means that the value of the Texxon shares already reflects this information because it is anticipated by market participants. Therefore, there should be no change in Texxon's stock price if the cartel announces the $20 price. If, however, a $22 price is announced, Texxon's stock price will change.

13.4 RISK: SYSTEMATIC AND UNSYSTEMATIC

The risk of owning an asset, such as common stock, results from unexpected events. If events always occurred exactly as predicted, there would be no risk. In this section, we identify two types of unexpected events which give rise to two categories of risk; systematic risk and unsystematic risk.

Systematic and Unsystematic Risk: A *systematic* risk tends to affect a large number of assets to a greater or lesser degree; systematic risks are also called *market risks*. An *unsystematic* risk affects only a single asset or a small group of assets. Systematic risks arise from uncertainty about economy-wide factors, such as inflation and interest rates, whereas the possibility of a labour strike or lawsuit involving a single company is an unsystematic risk. These risks are also referred to as unique or asset-specific risk.

Systematic and Unsystematic Components of Return: Remember, the actual return on a security consists of its expected and surprise components: $R = E(R) + U$, where U is the surprise component. The surprise component is influenced by two kinds of risk. Therefore, we can rewrite U as follows:

$$U = \text{Systematic portion} + \text{Unsystematic portion} = m + \varepsilon$$

where m represents the systematic, or market, portion of U, and ε represents the unsystematic portion of U. Substituting $(m + \varepsilon)$ for U, we can now rewrite R as follows:

$$R = E(R) + U = E(R) + m + \varepsilon$$

The unsystematic risk is particular to an individual asset. As an example, the unsystematic risk for General Motors is unrelated to the unsystematic risk for IBM. This fact has important implications for the risk of a portfolio.

13.5 DIVERSIFICATION AND PORTFOLIO RISK

As we noted earlier, diversification is the process of investing in a portfolio of several assets in order to reduce risk. We will discuss the extent to which risk is reduced by diversification, and the reason why diversification reduces risk.

The Effect of Diversification - Another Lesson from Market History: Studies of common stock listed on the Toronto Stock Exchange (TSE) demonstrate that the standard deviation of a portfolio decreases as the number of securities in the portfolio increases. Significant decreases in standard deviation occur as the number of stocks in the portfolio increases from one to approximately ten. On average, the standard deviation of a ten-stock portfolio is approximately half the standard deviation of a single TSE stock. Further decreases in standard deviation are observed as the number of stocks in the portfolio increases, but decreases in risk become smaller as additional securities are added to the portfolio. The graph in Figure 13.6 on page 427 of your text shows the way in which adding stocks to a portfolio reduces the standard deviation of the portfolio.

The Principle of Diversification: The principle of diversification indicates that spreading an investment across many assets eliminates some of the risk. The risk which is eliminated by diversification is called *diversifiable* risk. However, there is a minimum level of risk in a portfolio which cannot be eliminated by diversification. This minimum risk level is called *nondiversifiable* risk.

Diversification and Unsystematic Risk: Why isn't all risk diversifiable? The answer is found in the distinction between *unsystematic* and *systematic* risk.

In a large portfolio of common stocks, the unsystematic risk associated with one stock typically has no impact on the unsystematic risk associated with any other stock. Therefore, in a large portfolio, we would not expect to observe any particular relationship between the unsystematic risks for the individual stocks in the portfolio. In a portfolio of thirty or more stocks, the effects of unsystematic risk of various stocks usually offset each other, thereby eliminating the risk arising from each individual source. The risk which can be eliminated is diversifiable risk; it is the same as unsystematic risk.

Diversification and Systematic Risk: Systematic risk has an impact on all the stocks in a portfolio. For example, a recession will have a negative impact on virtually all the securities in the portfolio, and consequently on the investor's return from the portfolio. Systematic risk cannot be diversified away; hence, the terms systematic risk and nondiversifiable risk are synonymous.

13.6 SYSTEMATIC RISK AND BETA

The Systematic Risk Principle: We know that investors will not accept risk without compensation in the form of a higher expected return. We have established that investors can eliminate unsystematic risk by diversifying. Therefore, it is not necessary for any investor to bear the unsystematic risk of an investment. The market will not reward investors for taking unnecessary risks. So, investors are not paid for bearing unsystematic risks. In other words, the reward for bearing risk depends only on the systematic risk of an investment. This means that *the expected return for an asset depends only on that asset's systematic risk.*

Measuring Systematic Risk: The systematic risk of an asset is measured by its beta coefficient, represented by the Greek letter β. Beta measures the systematic risk for a particular asset, relative to the systematic risk for the average asset. For example, the average TSE common stock has a beta value equal to 1.0, so a stock with $\beta = 0.50$ has half the systematic risk of the average TSE stock. Or, a stock with $\beta = 1.25$ has 25% more systematic risk than the average stock. It is important to remember that, since systematic risk is the relevant risk for an investor, the expected return for an asset is dependent on β. A stock with a high value of β has a high expected return; a stock with a lower value of β has a lower expected return. This conclusion is true regardless of the standard deviation for a stock.

Portfolio Betas: The value of beta for a portfolio (β_p) is a weighted-average of the betas of the securities which comprise the portfolio, as indicated in the following formula:

$$\beta_p \;=\; (x_1 + \beta_1) \;+\; (x_2 + \beta_2) \;+\; (x_3 + \beta_3) \;+\; \ldots + \; (x_n \times \beta_n)$$

where n is the number of assets in the portfolio, x_1, x_2, x_3, and x_n are the portfolio weights, and β_1, β_2, β_3, and β_n are the beta values for the assets in the portfolio.

An Example: For the GM-Exxon example presented earlier in the chapter, suppose that $\beta_{GM} = 1.10$ and $\beta_{TEXXON} = 0.70$. What is the value of β_p for a portfolio with portfolio weights of $x_{GM} = 0.40$ and $x_{TEXXON} = 0.60$?

$$\beta_p \;=\; (x_{GM} \times \beta_{GM}) \;+\; (x_{TEXXON} \times \beta_{TEXXON}) \;=\; (.40 \times 1.10) \;+\; (.60 \times .70) \;=\; .86$$

13.7 THE SECURITY MARKET LINE

We now develop the precise relationship between systematic risk, measured by beta and the expected return. The graphic representation is called the security market line (SML) and the algebraic representation is the *capital asset pricing model* (CAPM).

Beta and the Risk Premium: Let's look at an example. Let asset A be an individual security with $\beta_A = 1.2$ and $E(R_A) = 16\%$. Assume the risk-free rate (R_f) is 5%. Note that beta for the risk-free asset is zero; since the risk-free asset does not have any risk, it clearly does not have any systematic risk. If x is the percentage of the portfolio invested in asset A, then $(1 - x)$ is the percentage invested in the risk-free asset, because the total of the portfolio weights must be 1.0 (100%). The expected return for a portfolio consisting of asset A and the risk-free asset is:

$$E(R_p) \;=\; [x \times E(R_A)] \;+\; [(1 - x) \times R_f] \;=\; (x \times 16\%) + [(1 - x) \times 5\%]$$

Beta for this portfolio is:

$$\beta_p \;=\; (x \times \beta_A) \;+\; [(1 - x) \times 0] \;=\; (x \times 1.2) \;+\; (0) \;=\; 1.2x$$

By selecting various values of x, and then computing the corresponding values of $E(R_p)$ and β_p, we can plot expected returns and beta can be plotted on a graph. Some values of x, $E(R_p)$ and β_p are indicated in the following table:

Percentage of portfolio invested in Asset A (x)	Portfolio expected return $E(R_p)$	Portfolio Beta β_p
0 %	5.0%	0.00
20	7.2	0.24
50	10.5	0.60
90	14.9	1.08
100	16.0	1.20
150	21.5	1.80
200	27.0	2.40

If you plot these points, the important thing to remember is that the relationship between $E(R_p)$ and β_p is a *straight line* through the point R_f and the point represented by $\beta_A = 1.2$ and $E(R_A) = 16\%$.

If x is greater than 100%, the portfoliowas formed by borrowing at the rate R_f and then investing the borrowed money in Asset A. For example, if an individual has $1,000 to invest, she might borrow $500 at the rate $R_f = 5\%$, and then invest $1,500 in Asset A. The total amount invested in Asset A is equal to 150% of her own funds (i.e., x = 1.50) and the value of $(1 - x)$ is $-.50$, indicating that an amount equal to half of the investor's funds is borrowed.

The Reward-to-Risk Ratio: The slope of the line in the graph is called the *reward-to-risk ratio*. The slope of this straight line can be computed between any two points on the line. We will use the following points to compute the slope: the intercept (i.e., R_f), and the point representing Asset A [i.e., the point where $\beta = \beta_A = 1.2$, and $E(R) = E(R_A) = 16\%$]. The slope is the change in the 'y' value (expected return) divided by the change in the 'x' value (β):

$$\text{Slope} = \frac{E(R_A) - R_f}{\beta_A} = \frac{.16 - .05}{1.2} = .09167 = 9.17\%$$

This reward-to-risk ratio can be interpreted by first assuming that an investor is considering placing her entire investment portfolio in the risk-free asset. Prior to making this decision, the investor might want to know what her compensation would be for taking on risk. The answer is indicated by the reward-to-risk ratio; for each one unit increase in systematic risk (i.e., by increasing the systematic risk in her investment from $\beta = 0$ to $\beta = 1$), she will increase her expected rate of return by 9.167%. Of course, increases in the value of β by more or less than one result in proportionate increases in expected rate of return.

The Basic Argument: Assume we have identified Asset B, with $\beta_B = .6$ and $E(R_B) = 10\%$. Should an investor consider purchasing this asset? In order to answer this question, we compare a portfolio of Asset B and the risk-free asset to the portfolio formed earlier with Asset A and the risk-free asset. We can prepare a table similar to the one above:

Percentage of portfolio invested in Asset A (x)	Portfolio expected return $E(R_p)$	Portfolio Beta β_p
0 %	5.0%	0.00
20	6.0	0.12
50	7.5	0.30
90	9.5	0.54
100	10.0	0.60
150	12.5	0.90
200	15.0	1.20

If you graph the portfolios using Asset A and Asset B in combination with the risk-free asset, you will see that, at each point, investors receive a higher return given the risk, if they choose the portfolio with Asset A. This means that the portfolio comprised of Asset A and the riskless asset is superior to the one with Asset B.

We can also demonstrate this result mathematically by computing the reward-to-risk ratio for Asset B:

$$\text{Slope} = \frac{E(R_B) - R_f}{\beta_B} = \frac{.10 - .05}{0.6} = .08333 = 8.33\%$$

Asset B provides a lower reward-to-risk ratio than does Asset A. Consequently, an investor would not consider purchasing Asset B. The reward-to-risk ratio is the slope of the graph of all possible portfolios formed by combining Asset B with the risk-free asset. Since the slope for Asset B is less steep than the slope for Asset A, while the intercepts are the same (i.e., R_f is the intercept for each line), all portfolios combining Asset A with R_f are preferable to corresponding portfolios combining Asset B with R_f.

Calculating Beta: A security's beta measures the responsiveness of the security's return to changes in the return on the market as a whole. We can calculate a firm's beta by graphing the relationship between a stock's expected return to different returns on the market. The resulting line, the *characteristic line*, has the same slope as the stock's beta.

The Security Market Line: The line that describes the relationship between systematic risk and expected return is the *security market line* (SML). This is one of the major concepts in finance. The SML is shown in graphic form on the following page.

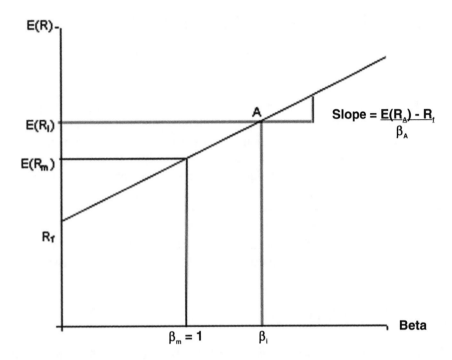

Market Portfolios: The most common way of deriving the equation of the SML involves the concept of a *market portfolio*. This is a portfolio made up of all assets in the market. The market portfolio itself is an asset, so its expected return [$E(R_M)$] and beta (β_M) must be on the security market line. What then is the value of β_M? We have defined beta as the level of systematic risk for a particular asset relative to the systematic risk of the average asset in the market. The market portfolio is comprised of all assets in the market; furthermore, a portfolio beta is a weighted-average of the betas of the securities in the portfolio. Therefore, the beta for the market portfolio must be equal to beta for the average security; that is, $\beta_m = 1.0$. The beta and expected return for the market portfolio are plotted on the SML graph above. Using the market portfolio, we can write the slope of the SML as:

$$\text{SML Slope} \quad = \quad \frac{E(R_M) - R_f}{\beta_M} \quad = \quad \frac{E(R_M) - R_f}{1} \quad = \quad E(R_M) - R_f$$

Since this slope is the excess return on the market over the risk-free rate, it is often called the *market risk premium*.

The Capital Asset Pricing Model: If $E(R_i)$ and β_i represent the expected return and beta for any asset on the market, this point must plot on the SML. The reward-to-risk ratio must be the same as that for the market in general. That means,

$$\frac{E(R_i) - R_f}{\beta_i} \quad = \quad E(R_M) - R_f$$

We can rearrange this to write the equation for the SML:

$$E(R_i) \quad = \quad R_f + [E(R_M) - R_f] \times \beta_i$$

where $E(R_i)$ and β_i are the expected return and beta for any asset. This equation is referred to as the Capital Asset Pricing Model (CAPM), and it indicates the expected return for any asset for a given level of systematic risk.

This model shows that the expected return for a given asset depends on (1) the pure time value of money, (2) the reward for bearing systematic risk, and (3) the amount of systematic risk.

13.8 THE SML AND THE COST OF CAPITAL: A PREVIEW

So far, we have discussed risk in terms of investments in securities. However, the same concepts also apply to the capital budgeting process.

The Basic Idea: The security market line describes investors' opportunities in financial markets in terms of systematic risk (i.e., β) and expected return. A capital budgeting project under consideration by management must provide an expected return to shareholders which exceeds that for other investments with comparable risk. For example, suppose the capital budgeting project has a beta of 0.9, and the expected return in the financial markets for investments with $\beta = 0.9$ is 15%; the capital budgeting project is acceptable only if its expected return exceeds the 15% which investors could earn on their own in the financial markets.

The Cost of Capital: The cost of capital associated with a capital budgeting project is the minimum required return for the investment. Since that return is the expected return available in the financial markets for investments with a specified risk level, it is the shareholders' opportunity cost. Cost of capital is discussed in Part VI.

13.9 ARBITRAGE PRICING THEORY

An alternative model of risk and return is the *arbitrage pricing theory* (APT). The major advantage of the APT model is that it can handle multiple factors that are not included in CAPM. Like CAPM, the APT model assumes that stock returns depend on both expected and unexpected returns. Unlike CAPM, the unexpected return in the APT model is related to several market factors. Assuming those factors are unanticipated changes in inflation, GNP, and interest rates, the expected return would be written as:

$$E(R) \; = \; R_r \; + \; E[(R_1) - R_f] \times \beta_1 \; + \; E[(R_2) - R_f] \times \beta_2 \; + \; E[(R_3) - R_f] \times \beta_3 \; + \; E[(R_4) - R_f] \times \beta_4$$

Using this concept, the APT model can be expanded to include as many factors as we want.

CONCEPT TEST

1. The expected return is the _____ of possible future returns for an investment.

2. When possible future returns are equally likely to occur, the expected return can be computed in two equivalent ways. The first is the same as the procedure for computing the average of historical data and is given by the formula $E(R) = $ _____ , where T is the number of possible future returns, R_1, R_2, and R_T are the _____ and $E(R)$ is the _____ . The alternative calculation is a _____ average of the possible future returns: $E(R) = $ _____ , where T is the number of possible future returns, Pr_1, Pr_2, and Pr_T are the probabilities of the respective possible returns and R_1, R_2, and R_T are the _____ . If the returns are not equally likely to occur, then the _____ procedure must be used to compute the expected return.

3. To calculate the variance of returns, we first compute the _____ of the possible returns from the expected return. Each of these is then multiplied by the _____ . Finally, the variance is the _____ of all these terms.

4.   An investor's portfolio is the _____ which the investor owns. The respective percentages of a portfolio's total value invested in each of the assets in the portfolio are referred to as the _____ .

5.   The expected return for a portfolio is a weighted average of the _____ of the securities which comprise the portfolio, as indicated by the formula $E(R_p) =$ _____ , where n is the number of assets in the portfolio x_1, x_2, and x_n are the _____ for the assets, and $E(R_1)$, $E(R_2)$, and $E(R_n)$ are the _____ for the assets.

6.   The _____ represents the statistical relationship between two series of numbers and can range from _____ to _____ .

7.   If the correlation between two securities is +1.0 then the _____ of this portfolio would be equal to a _____ of the individual standard deviations.

8.   The covariance term for securities A and B includes the product of _____ × _____ × _____ .

9.   As long as the correlation coefficient is less than _____ the standard deviation of a two stock portfolio is _____ than the weighted average of the _____ of the individual securities.

10. Combining securities whose correlation is _____ than _____ in order to reduce portfolio risk is known as the process of _____ .

11. The actual return (R) on a security consists of two parts: the _____ return, which is the part of the return predicted or expected by participants in the financial markets, and, a 'surprise' or _____ , part.

12. The risk for a particular asset comes from the _____ part of the return. For a given stock, we can write that $R = E(R) + U$, where R is the actual total return, $E(R)$ is the _____ part of the return and U is the _____ part of the return.

13. The difference between the actual return and the expected return is attributed to surprises which are reflected in the _____ part of the return. The surprise component is influenced by two kinds of risk, so that we can write U as: U = _____ portion + _____ portion = _____ , where m represents the _____ , or market, portion of U, and ε represents the _____ portion of U.

14. Substituting (m + ε) for U, the actual return on a security is: $R = E(R) + U = E(R) +$ _____ .

15   A _____ risk tends to affect a large number of assets to a greater or lesser degree; this kind of risk is also called a _____ risk, and it arises from uncertainty about economy-wide factors. An _____ risk affects only a single asset or a small group of assets.

16. As the number of assets in a portfolio increases, the standard deviation of the portfolio _____ . A significant reduction in portfolio risk occurs by combining as many as ___ assets. As more assets are added to the portfolio further reductions in risk are _____ .

17. Increasing the number of assets in a portfolio eliminates a significant portion of the risk to which the investor would be subjected if he held only one stock. The risk which is eliminated by diversification is called _____ risk. However, there is a minimum level of risk in a portfolio of common stocks which can not be eliminated by diversification; this minimum level is referred to as _____ risk.

18. In a large portfolio of common stocks, the _____ risk associated with one stock typically has no impact on the _____ risk associated with any other stock. In a portfolio of thirty or more stocks, it would be reasonable to expect that the effects of _____ risk on various stocks would offset each other, thereby eliminating the risk to the investor arising from this source. This source of risk is synonymous with _____ risk.

19. _____ risk has an impact on all the stocks in a portfolio, and cannot be diversified away; hence, the terms _____ risk and _____ risk are synonymous.

20. Financial markets do not reward investors for taking on risks which can be eliminated by _____ . Investors are not rewarded for taking on _____ risk, because this risk is _____ .

21. The systematic risk principle states that the reward for bearing risk depends only on the _____ risk of an investment. Consequently, the expected return for an asset depends on that asset's _____ risk.

22. The systematic risk of an asset is measured by its _____ . This measures the amount of systematic risk for a particular asset, relative to the amount of _____ risk for the average asset. The average common stock has a beta value equal to _____ .

23. The value of a portfolio beta (β_p) is a weighted-average of the _____ of the securities which comprise the portfolio, as indicated by $\beta_p =$ _____ , where n is the number of assets in the portfolio, x_1, x_2, and x_n are the _____ , and β_1, β_2, and β_n are the beta values for the assets in the portfolio.

PROBLEMS

Use the following information to solve Problems 1 through 3:

The information below represents possible future returns for Canadian Pacific (CP) common shares next year:

State of economy	Probability of state of economy (PR)	Rate of return if state occurs (R)
1	.20	12%
2	.20	6
3	.20	- 10
4	.20	22
5	.20	5
Total	1.00	

Problem 1

What is the expected rate of return for CP common stock?

Problem 2

What is the variance of the return for CP common stock?

Problem 3

What is the standard deviation of the return for CP common stock?

Use the information to solve Problems 4 - 5

The information below provides the possible future returns for common stock for Verine Corporation (VC) and for Xavier Technologies Corporation (XT) during the next year.

State of economy	Probability of state of economy (PR)	Rate of return if state occurs	
		VC	**XT**
1	.20	10%	5%
2	.30	- 8	9
3	.15	14	14
4	.35	11	-2

Problem 4

What is the expected rate of return for VC and XT common shares, respectively?

Problem 5

What is the variance and standard deviation for VC's shares? For XT's?

Problem 6

You have the following information about returns for two securities, Asset X and Asset Y. Each return has an equal probability of occurring.

Asset X	Asset Y
11 %	- 3 %
9 %	15 %
25 %	2 %
7 %	20 %

Calculate the expected return and standard deviation of return for each asset.

Problem 7

The probability that the economy will experience a recession next year is .3, while the probabilities of moderate growth or rapid expansion are .5 and .2, respectively. The common stock of Firm A is expected to return 5%, 15% or 20%, depending on whether the economy experiences a recession, moderate growth or rapid expansion, respectively. The returns for Firm B are expected to be 0%, 16%, or 30%, respectively. Calculate the expected rate of return for each firm's common stock.

Problem 8

What is the variance of the return for Firm A common stock?   For Firm B common stock?

Problem 9

What is the standard deviation of the rate of return for Firm A common stock? For Firm B common stock?

Use the following information for Stocks K and M to solve Problems 10 - 14

State of economy	Probability of state of economy (Pr)	Rate of return if state occurs (R)	
		K	M
1	.10	.25	.18
2	.20	.10	.20
3	.50	.15	.04
4	.20	-.12	.00

Problem 10

What is the expected return for Stock K? For Stock M?

Problem 11

What is the variance for Stock K? For Stock M?

Problem 12

What is the standard deviation for Stock K? For Stock M?

Problem 13

An individual plans to invest $5,000; she will invest $3,000 in Stock K and $2,000 in Stock M. What are the portfolio weights for this portfolio?

Problem 14

Using the portfolio weights computed in Problem 13, what is the expected return for the portfolio?

Use the following information on WAK Corporation and ALH Corporation to answer Problems 15 - 16

State of economy	Probability of state of economy	Rate of return if state occurs	
		WAK	ALH
1	.20	.25	.18
2	.10	.10	.20
3	.50	.15	.04
4	.30	-.12	.00

Problem 15

What are the expected returns for WAK and ALH?

Problem 16

What is the variance and standard deviation for WAK? For ALH?

For WAK: σ^2 $=$ $.2 (.10 - .144)^2$ $+$ $.1 [(.14 - .144)^2 + .5 (.19 - .144)^2 + .5 (.05 - .144)^2]$
                    $=$ $.004098$
                σ $=$ $(.004098)^{\frac{1}{2}}$ $=$ 6.40%

For WLH: σ^2 $=$ $.2 (-.05 - .152)^2$ $+ [.1 (.08 - .152)^2 + .5 (.20 - .152)^2 + .5 (.18 - .152)^2]$
                    $=$ $.010007$
                σ $=$ $(.010007)^{\frac{1}{2}}$ $=$ 10.04%

Problem 17

Refer to the information for Assets X and Y in Problem 6. Assume that $CORR_{X,Y}$ is 0.8. Find the expected return, the variance, and the standard deviation for a portfolio invested 30% in Asset X, and the rest in Asset Y. (Note: The actual correlation coefficient must be found by finding the actual covariance of Assets X and Y. We are assuming CORR = 0.8 to keep the computation simple.)

Problem 18

Two assets have expected returns of 10% and 4.5%, respectively. Their standard deviations are 8% and 6.8%. If you invest 50% in each asset, what is the expected return for the portfolio? What is the standard deviation of the portfolio's return if the correlation coefficient between the assets is 1.0? 0.50? 0.10? 0.0? -0.6? -1.0?

Problem 19

An individual plans to invest in Stock A and Stock B. The expected returns are 9% and 10% for Stocks A and B, respectively. The beta values are 0.95 and 1.25 for Stocks A and B, respectively. Find the expected return and beta for the portfolio if she invests 75% of her funds in Stock A.

Problem 20

Suppose the investor in Problem 19 wants to construct a portfolio with expected return equal to 9.5%. What are the portfolio weights for this portfolio? What is the beta for this portfolio?

Problem 21

Suppose the investor described in Problem 19 decides to form a portfolio consisting of three assets, as follows: 10% invested in Stock A, 30% invested in Stock B and 60% invested in a risk-free asset with a return of 6%. What is the expected return for this portfolio? What is the standard deviation of return?

Problem 22

Market research has shown that the expected returns for Alpha, Inc. and Beta, Inc. are perfectly correlated. The standard deviation of the expected return is 10 % for Alpha and 5 % for Beta. A portfolio consisting of the stocks of both firms is expected to have a standard deviation of 8 %. What percent of the portfolio is invested in each asset?

Problem 23

Use the following information to compute the reward-to-risk ratio for Stocks A, B, and C:

	Expected return	Beta
Stock A	10.5%	0.90
Stock B	13.0	1.15
Stock C	14.5	1.20
Risk-free Asset	6.0	0.00

For Problems 24-28, assume the risk-free rate is 6% and the expected return for the market portfolio is 14%.

Problem 24

Write the basic equation for the capital asset pricing model. Using the information above, what is the intercept of the CAPM? What is the slope of the CAPM? What is the market risk premium?

Problem 25

Speiss Corporation has a beta of 2. What is its expected return?

Problem 26

Suppose an individual invests $4,000 in a portfolio as follows: $2,800 invested in Speiss common stock and $1,200 invested in the risk-free asset. What are the portfolio weights for this portfolio? What is the expected return for the portfolio? What is the beta for the portfolio?

Problem 27

What are the portfolio weights for a portfolio comprised of Speiss common stock and the risk-free asset which has a portfolio beta equal to 1.5? What is the expected return for this portfolio?

Problem 28

Dorigan Corporation has a beta of 1.45 and an expected return of 15%. Given the CAPM equation of Problem 20, is Dorigan common stock correctly priced?

Problem 29

Assume the four stocks below plot on the SML. What is the equation for the SML? Fill in the missing numbers.

Security	$E(R_j)$	$Var(R_j)$	β_j
1	.07	.0225	
2	.14	.0400	0.8
3	.10	.1225	
4	.07	.0000	

Use the following information to solve Problems 30–32:

The possible rates of return for assets X and M for five possible states of the economy are listed in the table below, along with the probability of occurrence:

State of economy	Probability of state of economy (Pr)	Rate of return if state occurs (R)	
		X	M
1	.20	.03	.09
2	.20	.17	.16
3	.30	.28	.10
4	.20	.05	.02
5	.10	.04	.16

Work these problems on your own. The answers are given below.

Problem 30

Calculate the expected return for asset X and asset M.

Problem 31

What is the standard deviation for asset X? For asset M?

Problem 32

Assume that Asset M is the market portfolio, and that Asset X is a capital budgeting project under consideration by a corporation. If Asset X is to be financed with equity, and β_x is equal to 1.25, then what is the required rate of return for Asset X, according to the CAPM? (The risk-free rate is 6%.)

ANSWERS TO CONCEPT TEST

1.   average

2. $(R_1 + R_2 + \ldots + R_T)/ T$; possible future returns; expected return; weighted; $(Pr_1 \times R_1) + (Pr_2 \times R_2) + \ldots + (Pr_T \times R_T)$; possible future returns; weighted-average

3.   squared standard deviations; probability of occurrence; sum

4.   combination of assets; portfolio weights

5.   expected returns; $[x_1 \times E(R_1)] + [x_2 \times E(R_2)] + \ldots + [x_n \times E(R_n)]$; portfolio weights; expected returns

6.   correlation coefficient; $+ 1.0; - 1.0$

7.   standard deviation; weighted average

8. $CORR_{A,B}$; standard deviation of A; standard deviation of B

9.   +1.0; less; standard deviation

10.   less; +1.0; diversification

11.   expected; unexpected

12.   unexpected; expected; unexpected;

13.   unexpected; systematic; unsystematic; $m + \varepsilon$; systematic; unsystematic

14. $(m + \varepsilon)$;

15.   systematic; market; unsystematic;

16.   decreases; ten; smaller

17.   diversifiable; nondiversifiable

18.   unsystematic; unsystematic; unsystematic; diversifiable

19.   systematic; nondiversifiable; systematic

20.   diversification; unsystematic; diversifiable

21.   systematic; systematic

22.   beta; systematic; 1.0

23.   betas; $(x_1 \times \beta_1) + (x_2 \times \beta_2) + \ldots + (x_n \times \beta_n)$; portfolio weights

PROBLEM SOLUTIONS

Problem 1:

$$E(R) = (.12 + .06 - .10 + .22 + .05) / 5 = 0.07 = 7\%$$

$$OR \quad E(R) = (.20 \times .12) + (.20 \times .06) + (.20 \times -.10) + (.20 \times .22) + (.20 \times .05) = .07 = 7\%$$

Problem 2:

$$\sigma^2 = .2 \times (.12 - .07)^2 + .2 \times (.06 - .07)^2 + .2 \times (-.10 - .07)^2 + .2 \times (.22 - .07)^2 + .2 \times (.05 - .07)^2$$
$$= .2 \times .0025 + .2 \times .0001 + .2 \times .0289 + .2 \times .0225 + .2 \times .0004$$
$$= .01088$$

Problem 3: $\sigma = (.01088)^{1/2} = 0.104307 = 10.4307\%$

Problem 4:

For VC: $E(R) = (.20 \times .10) + (.30 \times -.08) + (.15 \times .14) + (.35 \times .11) = .0555 = 5.55\%$

For XT: $E(R) = (.20 \times .05) + (.30 \times .09) + (.15 \times .14) + (.35 \times -.02) = .0510 = 5.10\%$

Problem 5:

For VC: $\sigma^2 = .20 (.10 - .0555)^2 + .30 (-.08 - .0555)^2 + .15 (.14 - .0555)^2 + .35 (.11 - .0555)^2$

$= .0080$

$\sigma = (.0080)^{1/2} = 8.953\%$

For XT: $\sigma^2 = .20 (.05 - .0510)^2 + .30 (.09 - .0510)^2 + .15 (.14 - .0510)^2 + .35 (-.02 - .0510)^2$

$= .003409$

$\sigma = (.003409)^{1/2} = 5.839\%$

Problem 6:   For Asset X: $E(R) = (0.11 + 0.09 + 0.25 + 0.07) / 4 = 0.13 = 13\%$

$\sigma^2 = [(0.11 - 0.13)^2 + (0.09 - 0.13)^2 + (0.25 - 0.13)^2 + (0.07 - 0.13)^2] / 4 = 0.005$

$\sigma = 0.0707 = 7.07\%$

For Asset Y: $E(R) = (-0.03 + 0.15 + 0.02 + 0.20) / 4 = 0.085 = 8.5\%$

$\sigma^2 = 0.008725$

$\sigma = 0.0934 = 9.34\%$

Note that in this solution, we used the average way to compute the expected return and standard deviation because the probabilities of each state occurring were the same.

Problem 7: The expected rates of return must be computed using a weighted average, because the possible returns are not equally likely.

$E(R_A) = (.3 \times .05) + (.5 \times .15) + (.2 \times .20) = .13 = 13\%$

$E(R_B) = (.3 \times .00) + (.5 \times .16) + (.2 \times .30) = .14 = 14\%$

Problem 8: For A: $\sigma^2 = .3 \times (.05 - .13)^2 + .5 \times (.15 - .13)^2 + .2 \times (.20 - .13)^2 = 0.00310$
For B: $\sigma^2 = .3 \times (.00 - .14)^2 + .5 \times (.16 - .14)^2 + .2 \times (.30 - .14)^2 = 0.01120$

Problem 9: Firm A: $\sigma = (.00310)^{1/2} = .05568 = 5.568\%$
Firm B: $\sigma = (.01120)^{1/2} = .10583 = 10.583\%$.

Problem 10: For K: $E(R) = (.10 \times .25) + (.20 \times .10) + (.50 \times .15) + (.20 \times -.12) = .096 = 9.6\%$

For M: $E(R) = (.10 \times .18) + (.20 \times .20) + (.50 \times .04) + (.20 \times .00) = .078 = 7.8\%$

Problem 11: For K: $\sigma^2 = .1 \times (.25 - .096)^2 + .2 \times (.10 - .096)^2 + .5 \times (.15 - .096)^2 + .2 \times (-.12 - .096)^2$
$= 0.013164$

For B: $\sigma^2 = .1 \times (.18 - .078)^2 + .2 \times (.20 - .078)^2 + .5 \times (.04 - .078)^2 + .2 \times (.00 - .078)^2$
$= 0.005956$

Problem 12: For K: $\sigma = (0.013164)^{1/2} = 0.11473 = 11.473\%$
For M: $\sigma = (0.005956)^{1/2} = 0.077175 = 7.718\%$

Problem 13: The portfolio weights are: $x_K = (\$3,000/\$5,000) = .60 = 60\%$ invested in Stock K
$x_M = (\$2,000/\$5,000) = .40 = 40\%$ invested in Stock M.

Problem 14: The easiest approach is to calculate the weighted average of the expected returns for the individual securities in the portfolio:

$$E(R_p) = [x_1 \times E(R_K)] + [x_2 \times E(R_M)] = (.60 \times .096) + (.40 \times .078) = .0888 = 8.88\%$$

Problem 15:

For WAK: $E(R) = (.2 \times .1) + (.1 \times .14) + (.5 \times .19) + (.3 \times .51) = .144 = 14.4\%$

For ALH: $E(R) = (.2 \times -.05) + (.1 \times .08) + (.5 \times .20) + (.3 \times .18) = .152 = 15.2\%$

Problem 16:

For WAK: $\sigma^2 = .2 (.10 - .144)^2 + .1 [(.14 - .144)^2 + .5 (.19 - .144)^2 + .5 (.05 - .144)^2]$
$= .004098$
$\sigma = (.004098)^{1/2} = 6.40\%$

For WLH: $\sigma^2 = .2 (-.05 - .152)^2 + [.1 (.08 - .152)^2 + .5 (.20 - .152)^2 + .5 (.18 - .152)^2]$
$= .010007$
$\sigma = (.010007)^{1/2} = 10.04\%$

Problem 17: $E(R_p) = (.30 \times .13) + (.70 \times .085) = .0985 = 9.85\%$

$\sigma^2 = x_1^2\sigma_1^2 + x_2^2\sigma_2^2 + 2x_1x_2CORR_{1,2}\sigma_1\sigma_2$
$= (.30)^2(0.005) + (.70)^2(0.008725) + 2 (.30)(.70)(0.8)(0.0707)(0.0934)$
$= 0.006944$
$\sigma = (0.006944)^{1/2} = 0.8333 = 8.333\%$

Problem 18: The expected return is always a weighted average of the expected returns of the assets in the portfolio:

$$E(R_p) \quad = \quad 0.50 \times 10\% \quad + \quad 0.50 \times 4.5\% \quad = \quad 7.25\%$$

For a correlation of 1.0, standard deviation is a weighted of standard deviations of assets in the portfolio::

$$\sigma \quad = \quad 0.50\,(8\%) \quad + \quad 0.50\,(6.8\%) \quad = \quad 7.4\%$$

For a correlation of 0.50, the standard deviation of the portfolio's expected return is:

$$\sigma = [(0.50)^2\,(0.08)^2 + (0.50)^2\,(0.068)^2 + 2\,(0.50)(0.50)(0.50)(0.08)(0.068)]^{.5}$$
$$= \quad 0.064 \quad = \quad 6.4\%$$

For correlations of 0.1, 0.0, -0.6, and -1.0, the standard deviations are 0.055 (5.5%), 0.0525 (5.25%), 0.0335 (3.35%), and 0.006 (0.6%), respectively.

Problem 19: $E(R_p) = [x_A \times E(R_A)] + [x_B \times E(R_B)] \qquad = (.75 \times .09) + (.25 \times .10) = .0925 = 9.25\%$

$$\beta_p \quad = \quad (x_A \times \beta_A) + (x_B \times \beta_B) = (.75 \times .95) + (.25 \times 1.25) \quad = \quad 1.025$$

Problem 20: In order to form a portfolio with expected return equal to 9.5%, the investor must solve the following equation for x_A (the weight to invest in Asset A):

$$E(R_p) \quad = \quad [x_A \times E(R_A)] \quad + \quad [x_B + E(R_B)]$$
$$.095 \quad = [x_A \times .09] \quad + \quad [(1 - x_A) \times .10]$$

where x_A is the proportion of the portfolio invested in Stock A and $(1 - x_A)$ is the proportion invested in Stock B. The solution for x_A is .50, so that the portfolio weights are $x_A = .50 = 50\%$ and $x_B = (1 - x_A) = .50 = 50\%$. The beta for this portfolio is: $\beta_p \quad = \quad (x_A \times \beta_A) + (x_B \times \beta_B) \quad = \quad (.50 \times .95) + (.50 \times 1.25) \quad = \quad 1.10$

Problem 21: The expected return for the portfolio is:

$$E(R_p) = [x_A \times E(R_A)] + [x_B \times E(R_B)] + [x_C \times E(R_C)] \quad = (.10 \times .09) + (.30 \times .10) + (.60 \times .06) = .075 = 7.5\%$$

Beta for the risk-free asset is zero, so the portfolio beta is:

$$\beta_p = (x_A \times \beta_A) + (x_B \times \beta_B) + (x_C \times \beta_C) \quad = (.10 \times .95) + (.30 \times 1.25) + (.60 \times 0) = .470$$

Problem 22: We know the expected return for the portfolio. If we let x_1 be the return for Alpha and x_2 be the return for Beta, we can say that: $x_1 + x_2 \quad = \quad 1, \quad$ so $\quad x_2 = 1 - x_1$

We also know the formula for the variance of a portfolio of two assets:

$$\sigma^2 \quad = \quad x_1^2\sigma_1^2 \quad + \quad x_2^2\sigma_2^2 \quad + \quad 2x_1 x_2\ CORR_{1,2}\ \sigma_1\sigma_2$$

Substituting, we have:

$$(0.08)^2 = x_1^2(0.1)^2 + (1 - x_1)^2(0.05)^2 + 2x_1(1 - x_1)(1)(0.10)(0.05)$$

$$(0.08)^2 = [\, 0.1\, x_1 + 0.05\, (1 - x_1)\,]^2$$

$$0.08 = 0.1\, x_1 + 0.05\, (1 - x_1)$$

$$0.08 = 0.05 x_1 + 0.05$$

$$0.03 = 0.05 x_1$$

$$x_1 = .60; \quad 1 - x_1 = 0.40$$

So, 60% is invested in Alpha, and 40% is invested in Beta.

Problem 23: For Stock A: $\dfrac{E(R_a) - R_f}{\beta_A} = \dfrac{.105 - .06}{0.90} = .050 = 5.0\%$

For Stocks B and C, the reward-to-risk ratios are 6.087% and 7.083%, respectively.

Problem 24: The equation for the CAPM is: $E(R_i) = R_f + [E(R_M) - R_f] \times \beta_i$, where $E(R_i)$ and β_i are the expected return and beta, respectively, for any asset. The intercept of the CAPM is $R_f = 6\%$, and the slope is:

$$[E(R_M) - R_f] = 14\% - 6\% = 8\%$$

Therefore, in this example, the equation for the CAPM is: $E(R_i) = 6\% + 8\% \times \beta_i$

The market risk premium is the same as the slope of the CAPM: $[E(R_M) - R_f] = 14\% - 6\% = 8\%$

Problem 25: $E(R_i) = 6\% + (8\% \times \beta_i) = .06 + (.08 \times 2) = .22 = 22\%$

Problem 26: $x_{risk\text{-}free} = (\$1,200 / \$4,000) = .30 = 30\%$ $\qquad x_{Speiss} = (\$2,800 / \$4,000) = .70 = 70\%$

The expected return for the portfolio is: $E(R_p) = (.30 \times .06) + (.70 \times .22) = .172 = 17.2\%$

Beta for the risk-free asset is zero, so the portfolio beta is: $\beta_p = (.30 \times 0) + (.70 \times 2) = 1.4$

Note: If we substitute this portfolio beta of 1.4 into the CAPM equation, we get the same expected return of 17.2%.

Problem 27: To form a portfolio with beta equal to 1.5, the investor must solve the following equation for x_1:

$$\beta_p = (x_1 + \beta_1) + [(1 - x_1) \times \beta_2)] = 1.5 = [x_1 \times 0] + [(1 - x_1) \times 2]$$

where x_1 is the proportion of the portfolio invested in the risk-free asset and $(1 - x_1)$ is the proportion invested in Speiss common stock. The solution for x_1 is .25, so the portfolio weights are $x_1 = .25 = 25\%$ and $x_2 = (1 - x_1) = .75 = 75\%$. That is, the individual invests 25% of his money in the risk-free asset and 75% in Speiss common stock.

The expected return for the portfolio is:

$$E(R_p) = 6\% + (8\% \times \beta_p) = .06 + (.08 \times 1.5) = .18 = 18\%$$

Alternatively,

$$E(R_p) = 0.25 \times .06 + .75 \times .22 = .18 = 18\%$$

Problem 28: The expected return for a stock with beta equal to 1.45 is:

$$E(R_i) = 6\% + (8\% \times \beta_i) = .06 + (.08 \times 1.45) = .176 = 17.6\%$$

According to the CAPM, a security with $\beta = 1.45$ should have $E(R_i)$ equal to 17.6%. Dorigan Corporation common stock has an expected return of only 15%. Consequently, Dorigan's common stock is over-priced; we would expect that demand for Dorigan will be low, resulting in a lower price and higher expected return.

Problem 29: Security 4 has a 7% expected return and zero variance. Thus Security 4 is a risk-free asset, and the risk-free rate is 7%. Beta for Security 4 must be zero. Security 1 also has an expected return of 7%. Therefore, Security 1 must also be a risk-free asset and must have beta equal to zero. Security 2 has beta equal to 0.8.

Note: In a strictly theoretical sense, Security 1, being a risk-free asset should have a variance of zero. However, in practical terms, the risk-free asset may have a slight variance (in practice, even T-bills are not completely without risk of any kind). However, the beta of the risk-free asset is always zero.

We can solve for the expected return on the market using the information for Security 2. We know the risk-free rate, the expected return, and the beta. We solve the equation:

$$.14 = .07 + [E(R_M) - .07] \times .8; \quad \text{Solving, } E(R_M) = 15.75\%$$

Security 3 has an expected return $[E(R_3)]$ of 10%. We can solve for the beta value of Security 3 (β_3) by substituting into the CAPM, as follows:

$$.10 = 7\% + (.1575 - .07) \times \beta$$
$$.03 = (.0875 \times \beta_3)$$
$$\beta_3 = (.03/.0875) = .343$$

Problem 30: Asset X: $E(R) = 13\%$;   Asset M: $E(R) = 10\%$

Problem 31: Asset X: 11.507%;   Asset M: 4.879%

Problem 32: The intercept of the CAPM is $R_f = 6\%$ and the slope is: $[E(R_M) - R_f] = 10\% - 6\% = 4\%$

In this example, the CAPM equation is: $E(R_i) = 6\% + (4\% \times \beta_i)$

For Asset X: $E(R_X) = 6\% + (4\% \times \beta_X) = .06 + (.04 \times 1.25) = .11 = 11\%$

Therefore, the required return, or cost of capital, is 11%. Since Asset X has an expected return of 13%, it is an acceptable investment.

14   <u>Cost of Capital</u>

CHAPTER HIGHLIGHTS

The appropriate discount rate for evaluating a capital budgeting project depends on the riskiness of the project. In this chapter, we establish the relationship between the risk level of a capital budgeting project and the relevant discount rate for the project. This required rate of return is the weighted average cost of capital.

14.1 THE COST OF CAPITAL: SOME PRELIMINARIES

Remember that firms should undertake investments which have positive NPVs. Another way to state this is that the return provided by the project is greater than the return required by investors for providing the firm with the capital to undertake the project. When the project is risky, the return required by investors increases to compensate for the additional risk. We refer to the return demanded by investors as the *required return*, the *appropriate discount rate*, and the *cost of capital*. The main concept is that the cost of capital for a given investment depends on the risk of that particular investment. In other words, *the cost of capital depends on the use, not the source, of funds.*

In determining the firm's cost of capital, we will assume that the firm's capital structure is fixed. That is, the firm will maintain a fixed debt/equity ratio that reflects the firm's target capital structure. The firm's overall cost of capital reflects the required return on the firm's total assets. So, we must consider the costs of both debt and equity in determining the overall cost of capital.

14.2 THE COST OF EQUITY

There are two approaches for computing the cost of equity capital: the dividend growth model approach and the security market line approach.

The Dividend Growth Model Approach: The constant dividend growth model for a firm's stock price is:

$$P_0 = \frac{D_0 \times (1 + g)}{R_E - g} = \frac{D_1}{R_E - g}$$

where P_0 is the current price of the firm's stock, D_0 is the most recent dividend paid, D_1 is next year's projected dividend, and R_E is the required return on the firm's stock. Solving this equation for R_E:

$$R_E = (D_1 / P_0) + g$$

Therefore, if D_0, P_0 and g are known, the cost of equity capital, R_E, can be determined. Note that if D_0 and g are known, then D_1 can be computed. The variable g is not directly observable and therefore must be estimated. If historical data are representative of future growth rates, g can be estimated from historical dividend data. Alternatively, an estimate of g can be based on forecasts of future dividend payments or growth rates.

An Example: A firm has recently declared and paid a dividend of $2.50 per share of common stock. The current price of the common stock is $20 per share, and it is estimated that the dividend will increase at a rate of 4% per year for the foreseeable future. Compute the cost of equity capital.

First, compute D_1: D_1 = $D_0 \times (1 + g)$ = $\$2.50 \times 1.04$ = $\$2.60$

Next, using the dividend growth model:

$$R_E = (D_1 / P_0) + g = (\$2.60 / \$20) + .04 = .17 = 17\%$$

Estimating g: There are three ways of estimating the growth rate g.

1)   Using historical growth rates.

An Example: Suppose you observe the following dividends:

Year	Dividend per share
1993	$1.87
1994	2.24
1995	2.24
1996	2.48
1997	2.74
1998	3.01

What is the compound growth rate in dividends?

The historical compound growth rate (five periods of growth) is approximately 10% (exactly 9.9879%). Then, $1.87 × FVIF(g%, 5) = $3.01. Solving for g%, we get 10% as an estimate of the growth rate.

2)   Estimate based on retention rate. This can be used when the firm's investment rate is less than its retention rate. The retention ratio is the percentage of earnings *not* paid out as dividends. It is defined as retained earnings divided by net revenue (or 1 – payout ratio, payout ratio being dividends divided by net income) and the ROE is net income after interest and taxes divided by common shareholders' equity. The following equation can be used to solve for the estimated growth rate:

$$1 + g = 1 + \text{Retention ratio x Return on retained earnings}$$

3)   Analysts' forecasts of future growth rates (available from the research departments of investment dealers) may also be used to estimate the growth rate.

The deficiencies of the dividend growth model approach are: (1) it is based on an assumption of constant growth in dividends, (2) the value of g must be estimated, and forecasting errors have a direct impact on the estimate of R_E and, (3) the dividend growth model does not explicitly consider risk.

The SML Approach: The SML approach is based on the CAPM equation for the expected (required) return on an asset: $E(R_i) = R_f + \beta_i \times [E(R_M) - R_f]$. In using the CAPM to compute the cost of equity capital, we assume the required return (R_E) is the same as the expected return, $E(R_i)$, so the above equation is now written:

$$R_E = R_f + \beta_E \times (R_M - Rf)$$

An Example: Suppose the market risk premium is 8.5%, the risk-free rate is 5.5%, and the Pettway Company has β equal to 0.7. Use the SML to compute the firm's cost of equity capital.

The expected return is:

$$R_E = R_f + \beta_E \times (R_M - R_f) \quad = \quad .055 + (.7 \times .085) = .1145 = 11.45\%$$

Investors expect a return of 11.45% for investing in Pettway common stock.

The advantages of the SML approach are: (1) it explicitly adjusts for risk; and, (2) it is applicable to any firm for which the value of β can be determined. However, this approach requires that both β and the market risk premium $(R_M - R_f)$ be determined. Again, this requires estimation because these values are not known with certainty. And, as with the dividend growth model approach, we are relying on the past to predict future betas and returns.

14.3 THE COSTS OF DEBT AND PREFERRED STOCK

In addition to equity financing, corporations also use debt and preferred stock financing. The costs of these types of financing are discussed below.

The Cost of Debt: The cost of debt financing (R_D) is the market interest rate the firm would pay on new debt. This cost can be observed directly in the financial markets in the following ways:

1)   The rate on new debt will equal the current yield on the firm's existing debt.
2)   The rate on new debt will equal the current yield on debt securities issued by other firms of similar risk.

In each case, the yield to maturity can be determined using the trial-and-error approach described in Chapter 7.

An Example: Suppose BC Ltd. will issue bonds with 15-year maturity and a coupon rate of 9.75 % for $950.50 each. What is BC's cost of debt?

We can use the approximation formula from Chapter 7 to calculate the yield to maturity on this bond:

$$YTM = \frac{Coupon + (Face\ value\ -\ Price)\ /\ Maturity}{(Price + Face\ value)\ /\ 2} = \frac{\$97.50 + (\$1,000 - \$950.50)\ /\ 15}{(\$950.50 + \$1,000)\ /\ 2} = 10.34\%$$

The exact yield using a financial calculator is 10.42% . This is the cost of new debt issued by the firm.

The Cost of Preferred Stock: The cost of preferred stock financing (R_p) can also be observed in the financial markets. A firm which expects to issue preferred stock would compute the yield for either its own currently outstanding preferred stock issue or for preferred stock issued by other firms with ratings similar to that which the firm expects to issue. Since the dividend paid on preferred stock is a perpetuity, the expected return can be computed using the valuation equation from Chapter 8: $R_p \quad = \quad D\ /\ P_0$, where D is the constant annual dividend payment and P_0 is the current price per share of the preferred stock.

An Example: As of September 21, 1995, the Island Lighting Company (ILCo), a gas and electric utility, had several issues of preferred stock outstanding. One of these issues paid an annual dividend of $4.35 per share and was trading at a price of $42 per share. Two other issues paid dividends of $8.12 and $8.30 and had market prices of $78.50 and $80.50, respectively. What is ILCo's cost of preferred stock financing on September 21?

The return for the first issue is: $4.35 / $42   =   10.357%. The returns for the other two issues are 10.344% and 10.311%, respectively. So, the cost of preferred stock financing for ILCo is between 10.3% and 10.4%.

14.4 THE WEIGHTED AVERAGE COST OF CAPITAL

The firm's overall cost of capital is its weighted average cost of capital (WACC). Although the WACC can incorporate many financing sources, our discussion will concentrate on long-term debt and equity as the two major components of the WACC. The discussion will also assume that the firm's optimal mix of debt and equity has already been established.

The Capital Structure Weights: For a firm that uses both debt and equity financing, the average cost of capital is the total amount the firm expects to pay, to both shareholders and bondholders, per dollar of financing obtained. The total cost of debt, measured in dollars, is $(D \times R_D)$, where D is the market value of the firm's debt. The total cost of equity is $(E \times R_E)$, where E is the market value of the firm's equity. The average cost of capital is the total cost of equity $(E \times R_E)$ plus the total cost of debt $(D \times R_D)$, divided by V, the total value of the firm's capital, where V = (E + D). The firm's *average cost of capital* is:

$$\text{WACC (unadjusted)} = (E/V) \times R_E + (D/V) \times R_D$$

This expression indicates that the average cost of capital is a weighted average of the firm's cost of equity (R_E) and the firm's cost of debt (R_D). The weights are the proportion of the total firm value represented by equity (E/V) and the proportion represented by debt (D/V). This weighted average is the *unadjusted* weighted average cost of capital (WACC). It is 'unadjusted' in the sense that it ignores the effect of taxes on the firm's cost of debt.

Taxes and the Weighted Average Cost of Capital: Interest is a tax-deductible expense, while dividends paid to shareholders are not tax-deductible. Consequently, the above calculation of the WACC must be adjusted to reflect this difference in tax treatment. Consider a firm with $R_D = 10\%$ and a corporate tax rate (T_c) equal to 34%. If the firm pays 10% interest on $1,000 of debt, the before-tax cost of the debt is: $D \times R_D = \$1,000 \times 10\% = \$100$. Since the $100 interest expense is tax-deductible, it reduces the firm's taxable income by $100 and consequently reduces the firm's taxes by: $D \times R_D \times T_C = \$1,000 \times .10 \times .34 = \$34$. The after-tax cost of debt, measured in dollars, is therefore: $D \times R_D \times (1 - T_c) = \$1,000 \times .10 \times (1 - .34) = \$66$

The after-tax cost of debt, as an interest rate, is $[R_D \times (1 - T_c)]$, and the unadjusted WACC developed in the preceding section must be adjusted as follows:

$$\text{WACC} = (E/V) \times R_E + (D/V) \times R_D \times (1 - T_C)$$

The WACC is the rate of return which the firm must earn on its investments in order to be able to exactly compensate the debt holders and equity holders who provide the financing to the firm. The WACC is thus the required return for the firm's investments, and it is the appropriate discount rate to use in analysis of capital budgeting projects.

One important qualification to this interpretation of the WACC must be kept in mind, however. The calculation of both the cost of debt and the cost of equity is based on the implicit assumption that *the risk level of a proposed capital-budgeting project is the same as the existing risk level of the firm.* Therefore, using the WACC as computed above is only appropriate when the project under consideration has the same risk as the overall risk of the firm. If the proposed project has a different risk level, adjustments in the discount rate must be made.

An Example: Assume Pettway's cost of equity is 11.45%. The yield to maturity on Pettway's debt is 8%. The total market value of Pettway's equity is $240 million, and the value of the debt is $160 million. Pettway's corporate tax rate is 34%. Compute the WACC for Pettway.

The WACC is: WACC $=$ ($240 / $400) x .1145 $+$ ($160 / $400) x .08 x (1 - .34) $=$ 0.08982 $=$ 8.982%

The WACC can be used as the discount rate for determining the NPV of a proposed capital budgeting project. Consider the following example:

An Example: Pettway is considering moving its operations from Quebec to Ontario to obtain a more geographically central location. The cash flows derived from this investment are expected to be $25,000 per year for the next 25 years. The cost of the move is estimated at $175,000. Should Pettway move its operations?

The cash inflows for this investment are in the form of an annuity. The WACC computed in the preceding example is the appropriate discount rate here because this investment can be considered to be in the same risk class as the firm. The present value of the investment is: PV = C × PVIFA(WACC, t) $=$ $25,000 x 9.836922 = $245,923.05. The NPV is: $245,923.05 - $175,000 $=$ $70,923.05. Since the net present value is positive, Pettway should relocate.

14.5 DIVISIONAL AND PROJECT COSTS OF CAPITAL

The SML and WACC: When a proposed investment is in a risk class different from the firm's risk class, we determine the expected return on financial market investments in the same risk class as the proposed investment, and use that rate to discount the cash flows from the new project. We do *not* use the firm's WACC when the risk of the investment differs from that of the firm. Using the same WACC for projects with varying risk can lead to two types of errors: either accepting projects that should be rejected, or rejecting projects that should be accepted. To illustrate, consider a graph of the Security Market Line (SML), which slopes upwards due to the positive relation between Beta and expected return. Using WACC for all levels of Beta can result in two errors: situations where the SML is higher than WACC, resulting in incorrect acceptance, and situations when SML is lower than WACC, resulting in incorrect rejection.

Using the WACC to evaluate projects in a different risk class may lead to poor decisions. The firm will accept risky projects because they have been evaluated at too low a discount rate, and the firm will reject less risky projects because the cost of capital used to evaluate them was too high.

Divisional Cost of Capital: Similarly, projects undertaken by a division cannot be properly evaluated using the firm's WACC. Since the riskier division is likely to have higher returns, it will tend to win competitions for resources if the riskiness of the divisions is ignored. This leads to incorrect acceptance of projects for the riskier division, and an incorrect rejection of projects for the less risky division.

The Pure Play Approach: We have critiqued WACC, yet determining the correct discount rate remains a challenge as beta is unobservable for projects within a firm. One method through which we can determine the correct discount rate is to identify the discount rate associated with similarly risky projects in the marketplace. This method is called the pure play approach.

The Subjective Approach: An alternative method through which the correct discount rate can be determined is to implement subjective adjustments to the firm's WACC. This method is called the subjective approach. While identifying the discount rate for the project separately may be better in principle, in practice subjective adjustments are often used due to the lack of the necessary information or resources required to separately identify the discount rate.

14.6 FLOTATION COSTS AND THE WEIGHTED AVERAGE COST OF CAPITAL

If the firm must issue new securities to obtain the required financing for a new project, then any flotation costs associated with the new issue are incremental costs. They must be incorporated into the NPV analysis.

An Example: The Brite Lites Production Company, an all-equity firm, is evaluating an investment in a new production studio with a ten-year useful life. The cost of the studio is $460,000, which would be financed by an issue of new common stock. Flotation costs are 8% of the amount of stock issued. The incremental after-tax cash inflow is expected to be $95,000 per year throughout the life of the studio. The corporate tax rate is 34% and the firm's cost of equity capital is 15%.

Brite Lites is an all-equity firm, so the WACC is equal to the cost of equity capital. Because the cash inflows are in the form of an annuity, the present value is computed as follows:

$$PV = C \times PVIFA(WACC, t) \; = \; \$95,000 \times PVIFA\,(15\%, 10) \; = \; \$95,000 \times 5.018769 \; = \; \$476,783.05$$

If we ignore flotation costs for the new stock issue, then the net present value would be:

$$NPV = \$476,783.05 - \$460,000 = +\$16,783.05$$

However, the flotation costs represent an additional expense associated with the capital budgeting project, and must be incorporated into the analysis. First, we compute the flotation costs for the new stock issue. Since Brite Lites requires $460,000 of financing, the firm will have to issue more than $460,000 of equity in order to net from the issue the required amount of financing. The dollar value of the stock issue is the value of X in the following equation: $\$460,000 \; = \; (1 - .08) \times X$

That is, in order to obtain $460,000 in financing, after paying the 8% flotation costs, the firm must issue $500,000 of common stock to net $460,000 after paying flotation costs. The flotation costs are ($500,000 − $460,000) = $40,000, and the true cost of the studio is $500,000. The actual net present value is:

$$NPV = \$476,783.05 - \$500,000 = -\$23,216.95$$

Therefore, when flotation costs are taken into consideration, the investment in the studio is unacceptable.

In the preceding example, the firm is an all-equity firm. For a firm which uses both debt and equity financing, it is necessary to compute a weighted-average flotation cost.

An Example: Suppose the Brite Lites Production Company has a capital structure of 75% equity and 25% debt. Assume all other relevant data are as presented in the preceding example. The cost of debt capital is 10%, with flotation costs equal to 4% of the amount of debt issued. Compute the net present value of the investment in the production studio.

First, the WACC is: $WACC \; = \; 0.75 \times .15 \; + \; 0.25 \times 0.10 \times (1 - .34) \; = \; 12.90\%$

The weighted average flotation costs are:

$$f_a \; = \; (E/V) \times f_E \; + \; (D/V) \times f_D \; = \; .75 \times .08 \; + \; .25 \times .04 \; = \; 7\%$$

The firm must raise $460,000 / (1 - .07) = $494,623.66 in order to net the $460,000 necessary to finance the investment. So, the project's NPV is:

$$NPV = \$95,000 \text{ x PVIFA}(12.90\%, 10 \text{ yrs}) - \$494,623.66 = \$517,559.96 - \$494,623.66$$
$$= \$22,936.30$$

The NPV is positive even after taking into consideration the flotation costs, so the firm should proceed with the investment.

14.7 CALCULATING WACC FOR BOMBARDIER

As an example, we calculate the WACC for Bombardier. Bombardier's revenue for the year ending January 2003 are $23.7 billion. Its net loss is $615.2 million. There are 12 million preferred shares and 1,378 million common shares. Average series market price of the preferred stock is $19.91 and average series market price of common stock is $3.89. The market value of Bombardier's preferred stock series 3 is $18.25, and pays a dividend of $1.36. For one of the common stock series, the dividend is $0.09 and the market price is $3.81, with a growth rate for dividends of 9.9%. The yield to maturity (YTM) associated with its bonds is 7.07%. Its average tax rate is 28%. Assume that Bombardier's Beta is equal to 1.79, the market risk premium is 3.4%, and the risk free rate is 3.2%. Bombardier's balance sheet is as follows:

Assets:

Current	$17,578.0
Long-term	11,431.4
Total	29,009.4

Liabilities and Equity:

Current	2,563.6
Deferred taxes and other	13,391.0
Long-term debt	10,313.8
Equity	
Preferred shares	535
Common equity	2,206
Total	29,009.4

Estimating Financing Proportions: It is common to ignore short-term financing, and we ignore short-term debt that is not a permanent source of financing. Changes in current liabilities are therefore netted against changes in current assets. We treat leases as long-term debt.

Market Value Weights for Bombardier: We next find the market value weights of interest bearing debt and preferred and common stocks. Market value = number of shares x share price for the stocks. It follows:

Market value (in $ millions):
Interest-bearing debt = Book value = $10,314
Preferred stock = $19.91 x 12 = $426
Common stock = $3.89 x 1,378 = $5,359
Total = $10,314 + $426 + $5,359 = $16,099

<u>Market value weights</u>
Debt = $10,314/$16,099 = 64.06%
Preferred stock = $426/$16,099 = 2.65%
Common stock = $5,359/$16,099 = 33.29%

Cost of Debt: The cost of debt is calculated as follows:

R_D = YTM x *(1- T_C)* = 7.07% x (1-0.28) = 5.09%

Cost of Preferred Stock: The cost of the preferred stock is calculated as follows:

$R_P = D_P/P_P$ = $1.36 / $18.25 = 7.45%

Cost of Common Stock: We calculated the cost of common stock as the average of the valuation based on the dividend valuation model and CAPM.

Dividend Valuation Model: We calculate the cost of the common stock using the dividend valuation model as follows:

$R_E = D_1/P_0 + g$ = $0.09 x 1.099 / $3.81 +0.099 = 12.52%

CAPM: We calculate the cost of the common stock using CAPM as follows:

$R_E = R_f + \beta$ *(*Market Risk Premium) =3.2% + 1.79 x 3.4% = 9.29%

It follows that the cost of common stock is (12.52% + 9.29%) / 2 = 10.91%

Bombardier's WACC: We can now calculate Bombardier's WACC, as follows:

WACC = *(E/V) x R_E + (P/V) x R_P+ (D/V) x R_D*
$\qquad$ = 0.3329 x 10.91% + 0.0265 x 7.45% + 0.6406 x 5.09%
$\qquad$ = 7.09%

CONCEPT TEST

1. For a specified level of β, the CAPM specifies the _____ available in the financial markets. Since the cost of capital specifies the minimum acceptable return for a capital budgeting project, it is also referred to as the _____ .

2. Since some financing is obtained through debt and some through equity, the firm's overall cost of capital must reflect both sources. This overall cost of capital is referred to as the _____ .

3. Under the assumption that dividends grow at a constant rate (g), the dividend growth model specifies that the price of a share of stock (P_0) is given by the equation: P_0 = _____ . Solving this equation for R_E, the cost of equity capital is: R_E = _____ . Of the required data, only _____ is not directly observable and therefore must be estimated.

4.   The deficiencies of the dividend growth model approach to computing the cost of equity capital are: (1) it is based on an assumption of _____ ; (2) the value of _____ must be estimated, and forecasting errors have a direct impact on the estimate of R_E; and, (3) the dividend growth model does not explicitly consider _____ .

5.   The expected or required return for a share of stock can be determined by using CAPM as: $E(R_i)$ = _____ .

6.   The advantages of the SML approach to computing the cost of equity capital are: (1) it explicitly adjusts for _____ ; and, (2) it is applicable to any firm for which the value of _____ can be determined. However, this approach requires that both _____ and the _____ be determined. Since neither of these quantities can be known with certainty, the value of R_E may be inaccurate.

7.   The cost of debt financing (R_D) is the interest rate that the firm will have to pay on new debt. The interest rate investors expect on a new bond issue can be determined by computing the _____ for the company's _____ . Alternatively, it is possible to determine the cost of new debt financing by computing the _____ for bonds with a _____ similar to that of the bonds the firm would issue.

8.   The cost of preferred stock financing (R_p) can be observed in the financial markets. A firm which expects to issue preferred stock would compute the yield for either _____ or for _____ . Since the dividend paid on preferred stock is in the form of a _____ , the dividend yield can be computed directly as: R_p = _____ .

9.   The overall measure of the cost of capital for the firm is the _____ . For a firm that uses both debt and equity financing, the average cost of capital is the total amount the firm expects to pay, to both shareholders and bondholders, per dollar of financing obtained. For a firm with debt level D and cost of debt R_D, the before-tax cost of debt, measured in dollars, is _____ . For a firm with equity level E and cost of debt R_E, the total cost of equity is _____ . The average cost of capital is the total cost of equity plus the total cost of debt, divided by _____ . The unadjusted weighted average cost of capital (WACC) for the firm is computed as follows: WACC(unadjusted) = _____ .

10. Interest (is/is not) a tax-deductible expense, and dividends paid to shareholders (are/are not) tax-deductible. For a firm with debt level D and cost of debt R_D, the before-tax cost of the debt is _____ . The payment of this amount of interest reduces the firm's taxes by _____ . The after-tax cost of debt, measured in dollars, is therefore equal to _____ . The after-tax cost of debt, as an interest rate, is _____ .

11. The (adjusted) weighted average cost of capital (WACC) is: WACC = _____

12. The calculation of both the cost of debt and the cost of equity is based on the implicit assumption that the risk level of a proposed capital-budgeting project is the same as the _____ . Consequently, application of the WACC to a proposed capital-budgeting project is appropriate if the risk level of the proposed project does not differ significantly from the _____ . The net present value criterion requires that we determine the NPV for an investment, using the appropriate discount rate. The appropriate discount rate to use in computing the NPV depends on the _____ .

13. When a proposed investment is in a risk class different from the firm's risk class, we determine the expected return on financial market investments in the same _____ as the proposed investment, and use that

rate to discount the cash flows from the new project. What we require of a new investment is that its return must be at least as great as the return for other investments of _____ .

14.   Comparable conclusions apply to corporations which have divisions engaged in different businesses with significantly different risk levels; in this case, the relevant cost of capital for each division of the firm depends on the _____ .

15.   If a firm uses its WACC to evaluate projects that do not belong in the same risk class as the firm's other projects, the firm will make incorrect accept/reject decisions. The firm will tend to _____ riskier projects because the discount rate used was too _____ . The firm will tend to _____ less risky projects because the discount rate used was too _____ .

16.   If a capital budgeting project requires the issue of new securities in order to obtain the required financing, then the flotation costs _(are/are not)_ incremental costs associated with the project and _(are/are not)_ considered in the net present value analysis. For a firm which uses both debt and equity financing, it is necessary to compute a weighted-average flotation cost: f_A = _____ .

17.   Economic value added (EVA) is a _____ measure that is based on the _____ . Unlike ROA, which is a percentage value, EVA is a _____ value. EVA can be perceived as _____ after _____ costs. _____

PROBLEMS

Problem 1

PMR Corporation's current common stock price is $25 per share, and it recently paid a cash dividend of $3.00 per share. If the estimated dividend growth rate is 5% per year, compute the cost of equity capital.

Problem 2

On January 1, 1985 MAM Industries issued a thirty-year bond with a 9% coupon and a $1,000 face value, payable on January 1, 2015. The bond is currently selling for $915. Use the outstanding MAM bond to determine the firm's after-tax cost of debt capital if today's date is January 1, 1995. (Assume annual interest payments and a 34% corporate tax rate.)

Problem 3

Suppose MAM Industries (see Problem 2) also issued a thirty-year bond five years ago (in 1990). The bond has a $1,000 face value and a 10% coupon interest rate. If the bond currently sells for $1,000, what is the after-tax cost of debt capital, as indicated by the market value of this outstanding bond?

Problem 4

Suppose that, five years from now, the MAM bond described in Problem 2 has a market price of $1,100. What is the after-tax cost of debt capital at that time?

Problem 5

MAM Industries has recently declared a dividend of $3.50 per share of common stock. The current price of the firm's common stock is $25 per share, and it is estimated that the dividend will increase at a rate of 4% per year for the foreseeable future. Use the dividend growth model approach to compute the cost of equity capital for MAM Industries.

Problem 6

Suppose that the market risk premium is 8.5%, the risk-free rate is 7.0%, and MAM Industries has β equal to 1.35. Use the SML to compute the firm's cost of equity capital.

Problem 7

MAM industries has paid the following dividends over the last five years: $2.83, $3.05, $3.27, $3.44, and $3.50. Use the dividend growth model to compute the cost of equity capital.

Problem 8

Suppose that MAM Industries has a debt/equity ratio of 0.50. Use the data in Problems 2, 3, 6, and 7 to compute the unadjusted weighted average cost of capital for MAM Industries.

Problem 9

Use the data above to compute the adjusted weighted average cost of capital for MAM Industries.

Problem 10

Filimon Corporation needs to purchase $400,000 worth of new machinery. The machinery will be financed by issuing $150,000 of new equity, the rest in bonds. The firm's required return on equity is 15%, and the return on its bonds is 10%. The corporate tax rate is 34%. What are the unadjusted and adjusted weighted average costs of capital?

Problem 11

Coprez Corporation has issued dividends of $3.15, $3.59, $3.90, and $4.37 over the past four years. Use the dividend growth model to calculate the firm's cost of equity capital if the price per share is currently $27.

Problem 12

If Coprez Corporation's cost of debt is 8.33% and the firm has a debt / equity ratio of 0.75, what is the firm's WACC if the corporate tax rate is 34%?

Problem 13

Omega Electronics needs to buy $350,000 worth of new equipment. The equipment will be financed by issuing new debt and equity. Omega plans to issue $150,000 in bonds; the remainder will be equity financing. The firm's required return on equity is 17%, and the return on its bonds is 9%. The corporate tax rate is 40%. What are the unadjusted and adjusted weighted average costs of capital?

Problem 14

Suppose that MAM Industries is considering an expansion of its facilities. This expansion requires that MAM obtain $690,000 of financing. Flotation costs for debt and equity are 6 % and 9 %, respectively. If flotation costs are considered, what is the true cost of the expansion?

Problem 15

Rainy Days real estate development company plans to borrow $900,000 to acquire new properties. The company's cost of debt is 12%, and its corporate tax rate is 30%. If flotation costs are expected to be 2%, how much does Rainy Days need to borrow? What is the after-tax cost of debt financing?

Problem 16

MAM Industries has an issue of preferred stock outstanding. It pays an annual dividend of $3.25 per share and currently has a market price of $25 per share. Compute the cost of preferred stock capital for MAM.

Problem 17

Suppose that MAM's capital structure is 30% debt, 10% preferred stock and 60% equity. Use the information from problems 8 and 16 to compute weighted average cost of capital.

Problem 18

Refer to the information on MAM in Problems 8 and 14. If the proposed investment generates after-tax cash flows of $100,000 for the next 10 years, should MAM undertake the project? Be sure to consider flotation costs.

Problem 19

As of November 19, 1995, Illinois Power had several outstanding issues of preferred stock listed on the New York Stock Exchange. On November 19, 1995, one issue of Illinois Power preferred stock had a market price of $39 5/8 and paid an annual dividend of $4 per share. As of the same date, two other issues of Illinois Power preferred stock had prices of $21 1/4 and $39 7/8, respectively, and paid annual dividends of $2.13 and $4.12, respectively. What is Illinois Power's cost of preferred stock financing on November 19, 1995?

Use the following information to solve Problems 20 through 23:

Margo Corporation is a major producer of lawn care products. Margo stock currently sells for $80 per share; there are 10.5 million shares outstanding. Margo also has debt outstanding with an aggregate book value of $400 million. The bonds issued by Margo are currently yielding 10%, and are trading at 90% of face value. The risk-free rate is 8%, the market risk premium is 9%, and Margo has a β equal to 2. The corporate tax rate is 34%.

Problem 20

Margo is considering expansion of its facilities. Use the SML approach to determine the cost of equity capital for Margo.

Problem 21

Compute the weighted average cost of capital for Margo.

Problem 22

The project under consideration by Margo requires an outlay of $1,000,000. The expansion will produce incremental after-tax cash inflows of $350,000 per year for the next five years. Compute the net present value of the investment, assuming the project has the same risk as Margo's other projects.

Problem 23

Flotation costs are 5% of the amount of common stock issued and 2% of the amount of debt issued. Using the data from the previous problems, compute the weighted average flotation cost for Margo. Also, compute the net present value of the investment when flotation costs are taken into account. Should they undertake the project?

Problem 24

Now assume that the project under consideration is riskier than Margo's existing projects. The beta for the new project is 2.4. How should this affect their decision? (Ignore flotation costs.)

Problem 25

Now assume that the proposed project only has a beta of 1.8. How does the firm's decision change?

Problem 26

Distinct Meats, Inc. (DMI) produces deli products for restaurants. Currently, the ROA associated with DMI is 25% and the WACC is 18%. Further, DMI's total capital is equal to $25,000,000. DMI is considering introducing a new vegetarian hotdog to its line of products. If this project would lead to an ROA of 20% and total capital of $30,000,000, do you recommend tat DMI implement the project from an economic value added perspective?

Problem 27

Loose Clothing, Inc. (LCI) produces uniforms for police and fire departments. Currently, LCI's earnings after tax are equal to $456,600 and its total capital is equal to $2,000,000. LCI is considering introducing a line of uniforms for nurses, which would raise LCI's earnings after tax to $1,000,000 and its total capital to $2,500,000. If LCI's WACC is 20%, should LCI introduce the new line of uniforms from an economic value added perspective?

ANSWERS TO CONCEPT TEST

1.   expected return; required return

2.   weighted average cost of capital (WACC)

3. $D_1/(R_E - g)$; $(D_1/P_0) + g$; g, the dividend growth rate

4.   constant growth in dividends; g; risk

5. $R_f + \beta_E \times [R_M - R_f]$

6.   risk; β; β; market risk premium

7.   yield to maturity; outstanding bonds; yield to maturity; risk level

8.   its own currently outstanding preferred stock issue; preferred stock issued by other firms of similar risk; perpetuity; (D/P_0)

9.   weighted average cost of capital; $(D \times R_D)$; $(E \times R_E)$; the total value of the firm's capital; $[(E/V) \times R_E] + [(D/V) \times R_D]$

10.   is; are not; $(D \times R_D)$; $(D \times R_D \times T_c)$; $D \times R_D \times (1 - T_c)$; $R_D \times (1 - T_c)$

11. $[(E/V) \times R_E] + [(D/V) \times R_D \times (1 - T_c)]$

12.   existing risk level of the firm; risk level of the firm; risk level of the investment

13.   risk class; similar risk

14.   risk level of the division

15.   accept; low; reject; high

16.   are; are; $[(E/V) \times f_E] + [(D/V) \times f_D]$

17.   performance, WACC, dollar, earnings, capital

PROBLEM SOLUTIONS

Problem 1:

$$D_1 = D_0 \times (1 + g) = \$3.00 \times 1.05 = \$3.15$$

Use the dividend growth model to determine the cost of equity capital (R_E)

$$R_E = (D_1 / P_0) + g = (\$3.15 / \$25) + .05 = .176 = 17.6\%$$

Problem 2: The firm's pre-tax cost of debt capital is the yield to maturity for the outstanding bond issue. Although the bond had thirty years to maturity when it was issued, the relevant time period is now the remaining twenty years to maturity. The yield to maturity is the value of r which solves the equation.

$$\$915 = [\$90 \times \text{PVIFA}(r, 20 \text{ years})] + \$1,000 / (1 + r)^{20}$$

Trial and error (or financial calculator) gives a before-tax cost of debt equal to 9.998%. The after-tax cost of debt is: $.09998 \times (1 - .34) = .06599 = 6.599\%$

Problem 3: Since the thirty-year bond was issued five years ago, the current maturity of the bond is 25 years. The pre-tax cost of debt is the yield to maturity for the bond, or the value of r which solves the equation:

$$\$1,000 = [\$100 \times PVIFA(r, 25 \text{ years})] + \$1,000 / (1 + r)^{25}$$

The required before-tax return is 10%. Note: because the bond is selling at par, the yield must be the same as the coupon rate. So, no actual calculations were necessary. The after-tax cost of debt is $.10 \times (1 - .34) = 6.6\%$

Problem 4: Five years from now, the bond will be a twenty-year bond. The yield to maturity at that time would be the value of r in the following equation:

$$\$1,100 = [\$100 \times PVIFA (r, 20 \text{ years})] + \$1,000 / (1 + r)^{20} \; ; \; r = 8.911\%.$$

The after-tax cost of debt is $8.911 \times (1 - .34) = 5.881\%$

Problem 5: In order to compute the cost of equity capital (R_E), first compute D_1 as follows:

$$D_1 = D_0 \times (1 + g) = \$3.50 \times 1.04 = \$3.64$$

Using the dividend growth model to compute R_E, we find:

$$R_E = D_1 / P_0 + g = \$3.64 / \$25 + .04 = .1856 = 18.56\%$$

Problem 6: The cost of equity capital (R_E) is:

$$R_E = R_f + \beta_E \times [R_M - R_f] = .070 + (1.35 \times .085) = .18475 = 18.475\%$$

Problem 7: First, we need to calculate the historical growth rate based on the firm's dividend payouts. The growth rate is found by solving for g in the following equation: $\$3.50 = \$2.83 (1 + g)^5$

The growth rate is $.0434 = 4.34\%$. Then, using the dividend growth model, the required return on equity is:

$$R_E = \$3.50 / \$25 + .0434 = .1834 = 18.34\%$$

Problem 8: Problem 2 indicates the pre-tax cost of debt capital, based on the yield to maturity for a twenty-year MAM Industries bond, is 9.998%. In Problem 3, we also determined that the pre-tax cost of debt capital, based on the yield for a twenty-five year bond, is 10.0%. Therefore, the cost of debt capital (R_D) for MAM is essentially equal to 10%. Problems 6 and 7 indicate that the cost of equity capital is 18.56% (using the dividend growth model approach) or 18.475% (using the SML approach). Consequently, it is appropriate to estimate that the cost of equity capital (R_E) is 18.5%.

A debt/equity ratio of 0.50 indicates that the firm has $0.50 of debt financing for each $1.00 of equity financing. Therefore, $(E/V) = [\$1.00/(\$.50 + \$1.00)] = 2/3$, and $(D/V) = [\$.50/(\$.50 + \$1.00)] = 1/3$. The unadjusted weighted average cost of capital (WACC) is:

$$WACC \text{ (unadjusted)} = 2/3 \times .185 + 1/3 \times .10 = .15667 = 15.667\%$$

Problem 9: The values of (E/V) and (D/V) are the same as in the solution to Problem 6. The value of R_E is 18.5%, and the value of R_D is 10%. The WACC, after adjusting for the effect of taxes, is computed as:

$$\text{WACC}_{\text{(adjusted)}} = 2/3 \times .185 + 1/3 \times .10 \times (1 - .34) = .14533 = 14.533\%$$

Problem 10:

$$\begin{aligned}
\text{WACC}_{\text{unadjusted}} &= (E/V) \times R_E + D\,(D/V) \times R_D \\
&= (\$150{,}000 / \$400{,}000) \times .15 + (\$250{,}000 / \$400{,}000) \times .10 = .11875 = 11.88\%
\end{aligned}$$

$$\begin{aligned}
\text{WACC}_{\text{adjusted}} &= (E/V) \times R_E + D\,(D/V) \times R_D \times (1 - T_C) \\
&= (\$150{,}000 / \$400{,}000) \times .15 + (\$250{,}000 / \$400{,}000) \times .10 \times (1 - .34) = .0975 \\
&= 9.75\%
\end{aligned}$$

Problem 11: The growth rate of Coprez can be found using $\$4.37 = \$3.15 \times (1+g)^4$. Solving for g, the growth rate is 8.5%. The cost of equity capital is therefore:

$$R_E = \$4.37 / \$27 + 0.085 = .2469 = 24.69\%$$

Problem 12: A debt / equity ratio of 0.75 means that the firm has \$0.75 of debt finance for each \$1.00 of equity of equity financing. E/V is therefore $[\$1.00 / (\$1.00 + \$0.75)] = 4/7$, and $D/V = [\$0.75 / (\$1.00 + \$0.75)] = 3/7$. It follows that:

$$\text{WACC} = 4/7 \times 0.2469 + 3/7 \times 0.0833 \times (1 - .34) = .1646 = 16.46\%$$

Problem 13:

$$\text{WACC}_{\text{(unadjusted)}} = (\$200{,}000 / \$350{,}000) \times .17 + (\$150{,}000 / \$350{,}000) \times .09 = .1357 = 13.57\%$$

$$\text{WACC}_{\text{(adjusted)}} = (\$200{,}000 / \$350{,}000) \times .17 + (\$150{,}000 / \$350{,}000) \times .09 \times (1 - .4) = 12.03\%$$

Problem 14: The weighted average flotation cost for MAM is:

$$f_A = (2/3 \times .09) + (1/3 \times .06) = .08 = 8\%$$

The total financing required is the value of X in the following equation: $\$690{,}000 = (1 - .08) \times X$. Solving, we find that the firm must obtain total financing of $(\$690{,}000/.92) = \$750{,}000$. This is the true cost of the expansion.

Problem 15: They must borrow $\$900{,}000 / .98 = \$918{,}367.35$. The after-tax cost of debt financing is $.12 \times (1 - .30) = 8.4\%$.

Problem 16: The yield for the outstanding issue is: $R_P = D / P_0 = \$3.25 / \$25 = .13 = 13\%$

Problem 17: The weighted average cost of capital is computed using the weights for all three sources of capital:

$$\text{WACC} = .60 \times .185 + .10 \times .13 + .30 \times .10 \times (1 - .34) = .1438 = 14.38\%$$

Problem 18: The weighted average cost of capital, established earlier is 15.667%. The actual investment, considering flotation costs, is $750,000. So, the NPV of the proposed project is:

$$\text{NPV} = \$100,000 \times \text{PVIFA}(15.667\%, 10 \text{ yrs}) - \$750,000 = \$489,375.81 - \$750,000$$
$$= -\$260,624.19$$

The NPV is negative, so they should not take the project.

Problem 19: The return for the first issue is computed as follows:

$$R_p = \$4.00 / \$39.625 = .100946 = 10.096\%$$

Returns for the other issues are 10.02% and 10.33%, respectively. So, a good estimate for the required rate of return on preferred stock is between 10.0% and 10.35%.

Problem 20: $R_E = .080 + (2.00 \times .090) = .2600 = 26.00\%$

Problem 21: The market value of Margo's equity is (10.5 million × $80) = $840 million. The market value of Margo's debt is (.90 × $400 million) = $360 million. The total market value of the firm is ($840 million + $360 million) = $1.2 billion.

The weighted average cost of capital is:

$$\text{WACC} = (\$840 / \$1,200) \times .26 + (\$360 / \$1,200) \times .10 \times (1 - .34) = .2018 = 20.18\%$$

Problem 22: The weighted average cost of capital is the appropriate discount rate for this investment since the expansion is in the same risk class as the firm itself. The net present value of the investment is:

$$\text{NPV} = \$350,000 \times \text{PVIFA}(20.18\%, 5 \text{ yrs}) - \$1,000,000 = \$1,042,582 - \$1,000,000 = \$42,582$$

They should accept the project.

Problem 23: The weighted average flotation cost is: $f_A = (\$840 / \$1,200) \times .05 + (\$360 / 1,200) \times .02 = .041 = 4.1\%$. So, the actual cost of the investment is $1,000,000 / (1 - .041) = $1,042,752.87. And, the NPV is $1,042,582 - $1,042,752.87 = -$170.87. They should not accept the project.

Problem 24: The appropriate cost of equity is $R_E = .08 + .09 \times 2.4 = 29.6\%$. The appropriate discount rate is: ($840 / $1,200) × .296 + ($360 / $1,200) × .10 × (1 - .34) = 22.7%.

The NPV is: $350,000 × PVIFA(22.7%, 5 yrs) - $1,000,000 = $987,455.13 - $1,000,000 = -$12,544.87.

They should not take the project. Evaluating the project at the firm's weighted average cost of capital (20.18%) would cause them to accept an unprofitable project.

Problem 25: The appropriate cost of equity is $R_E = .08 + .09 \times 1.8 = 24.2\%$. The appropriate discount rate is: ($840 / $1,200) × .242 + ($360 / $1,200) × .10 × (1 - .34) = 18.92.

The NPV is: $350,000 x PVIFA(18.92%, 5 yrs) - $1,000,000 = $1,072,086.29 - $1,000,000 = $72,086.29. They should take the project. Evaluating the project at the firm's weighted average cost of capital (20.18%) would cause them to reject a profitable project.

Problem 26: EVA = [ROA –WACC] x Total capital. It follows that the current EVA and the EVA should the project be implemented can be calculated as follows:

$$\text{Current EVA} = [0.25\text{-}0.18] \times \$25,000,000 = \$1,750,000$$

$$\text{EVA with project implementation} = [0.20\text{-}0.18] \times \$30,000,000 = \$600,000$$

Since the EVA is lower with project implementation, the project should not be implemented.

Problem 27: EVA = Earnings after tax - WACC x Total capital. It follows that the current EVA and the EVA should the new line be introduced can be calculated as follows:

$$\text{Current EVA} = \$456,600 – 0.2 \times 2,000,000 = \$56,600$$

$$\text{EVA with new line} = \$1,000,000 – 0.2 \times \$2,500,000 = \$500,000$$

Since the EVA is higher with the new line, the new line should be introduced.

15 Raising Capital

CHAPTER HIGHLIGHTS

The sale of securities to the investing public is an essential source of long-term financing for a corporation. To a great extent, the procedures described in this chapter apply to new issues of both debt and equity, but the emphasis is on equity.

Corporations typically use an investment dealer to assist them in a new security issue. The assistance from the investment dealer may include a variety of services including advice on which securities to issue, how to structure and price a deal, complying with disclosure requirements and guaranteeing the amount of funds the issuer will receive from the new issue.

Securities may be public issues, offered to investors on the primary market. Alternatively, they may be private placements, sold directly to a small number of buyers. Public issues account for the majority of new financing, comprising almost 79% of new Canadian issues in 1998.

15.1 THE FINANCING LIFE CYCLE OF A FIRM: EARLY-STAGE FINANCING AND VENTURE CAPITAL

Start-up companies typically have no assets except for their idea about what their new firm will deliver. That is, they have no track record. Entrepreneurs very often find funding in the *venture capital* market.

Venture capital: In general, *venture capital* refers to financing for new, typically high-risk ventures. Venture capital firms pool funds from different sources and invest them in start-up companies. Most often, the source of funds is 'private equity.'

The risk associated with funding a start-up project is quite high. Most will fail. However, when a start-up company succeeds, the profits are huge. To limit their risk, venture capitalists usually supply their funding in stages. That allows the venture capitalist (VC) to get out of the deal if, at any given stage, the venture does not look promising.

Some Venture Capital Realities: There is quite a large market for venture capital. However, access to this market is very limited. Much of the access to these markets requires 'networking'; personal contacts are extremely important in gaining access to funds for starting up a business.

Choosing a Venture Capitalist: The following should be considered:

1. Financial strength - Can the venture capitalist support the project through successive phases needed to bring the product to market?
2. Style - Will the VC be involved in day-to-day operations or be involved on a monthly or yearly basis?
3. References for the VC - What is their success record?
4. Contacts - Who does the VC firm know? Specialization may be important here.
5. Exit strategy - Given that VCs are typically short-term investors, how do you negotiate the terms under which they can 'cash out' of the project?

15.2 THE PUBLIC ISSUE

In 1983, the Ontario Securities Commission (OSC) introduced the *Prompt Offering Prospectus* (POP), a streamlined reporting and registration system for large companies that frequently issue securities. Since POP was introduced, *bought deals* have become the most common way to raise new equity. In these offerings, the underwriter takes all the pricing risk.

The Canadian securities market is regulated by provincial commissions and provincial securities acts. Only five provinces have such commissions. In contrast, the U.S. securities market is regulated by a federal body, the Securities and Exchange Commission (SEC). The goal of regulation is an efficient flow of information about securities and the smooth function of securities markets.

The Toronto Stock Exchange (TSE) is Canada's largest securities market, and the major regulatory body in Canada is the Ontario Securities Commission (OSC). The OSC's goal is to ensure that investors receive any relevant information about new issues, through the registration statement and the prospectus.

The OSC also regulates the trading of securities to ensure adequate disclosure of information, establishes disclosure rules for asset transitions between related parties, publishes *insider reports* filed by major shareholders, officers and directors of TSE listed firms, and oversees training and supervision of investment dealers and monitors their capital positions.

15.3 THE BASIC PROCEDURE FOR A NEW ISSUE

The first step in issuing new securities is to obtain approval from the board of directors to increase the number of authorized shares. The firm then distributes a *preliminary prospectus* to the OSC and potential investors. This contains much of the financial information that will be included in the final prospectus, but it does not give the offer price. The preliminary prospectus is sometimes called a *red herring*, in part because bold red letters are printed on the cover warning that the OSC has neither approved nor disapproved of the offering. Once the revised, final prospectus meets with the OSC's approval, an offer price is determined and the selling effort gets under way.

Tombstone advertisements are used by underwriters during and after the waiting period. They contain information about the issue and list the investment dealers involved in selling the issue. The investment dealers are divided into groups called *brackets* on the tombstone; the higher the bracket, the greater the underwriter's prestige.

An *initial public offering* (IPO), as opposed to a *seasoned new issue* for companies already trading on the TSE, represents a company's first equity issue made available to the public (also known as an unseasoned new issue). Researchers have found that IPOs with prestigious underwriters perform better.

The *Prompt Offering Prospectus* (POP) system has reduced repetitive filing requirements for large companies by allowing them to file interim and annual financial statements regardless of whether they plan an issue during a given year. To use the POP system, issuers must have complied with the continuous disclosure requirements for a period of 36 months. This gives the firms prompt access to capital markets without the need to file detailed financial statements before the issue. A *Multi-Jurisdictional Disclosure System* (MJDS) allows issuers easier and frequent access to both the U.S. and Canadian markets.

15.4 THE CASH OFFER

For a cash offer, *underwriters* help to formulate the method used to issue the securities, price the securities, and sell the securities to the public. The underwriter normally buys the securities from the firm and offers them to the public at a higher price. The difference between the underwriter's buying price and the price at which the underwriter offers the security to the public is called the *spread* or the discount. For large issues, the risk associated with selling the securities to the public is shared by forming a group of investment dealers, called a *syndicate* or *banking group*, headed by a lead underwriter.

Types of Underwriting: If the underwriter purchases the entire issue, the issuing firm receives a fixed price for the securities, and all the risk associated with the sale of the securities is transferred to the underwriter. This procedure is called *firm-commitment underwriting*. The underwriter accepts the risk of not being able to sell the securities, in exchange for compensation received in the form of the spread. A related procedure, *regular underwriting*, differs from firm-commitment underwriting in that the banking group has the option to drop the issue if the price drops significantly.

In a *best-efforts offering*, the underwriter does not purchase the securities, but rather acts as an agent and receives a commission for each share sold. The issuing firm bears the risk that the securities cannot be sold at the offer price. This type of underwriting is mostly used for IPOs.

In a *bought deal*, the issuer sells the entire issue to one investment dealer or to a group who then attempts to resell it. Although bought deals are the most popular form of underwriting in Canada today, some investment dealers criticize bought deals for excluding retail investors from access to many new issues and from due diligence investigation. With a bought deal, all the risk of selling the issue is transferred to the underwriter.

The Selling Period: The time period immediately after the sale is called the *aftermarket*. The principal underwriter is allowed to buy shares in the aftermarket in order to 'support' or stabilize the price.

The Overallotment Option: Underwriting contracts frequently contain an overallotment option (*Green Shoe Provision*), allowing the investment dealer to buy additional shares at the offer price to cover any excess demand. This option is beneficial to the underwriter if the stock price quickly rises above the initial offer price.

Investment Dealers: The services of underwriters include providing advice to the issuing firm, underwriting the issue, and marketing the securities. The leading underwriters in Canada are RBC Dominion Securities and BMO Nesbitt Burns. The setting of an appropriate issue price is essential to the investment banker's business. Mispricing affects the issuing firm and the investor, as well as the investment banker's ability to attract underwriting business in the future.

The Offering Price and Underpricing: One of the most difficult tasks for an investment banker is the pricing of an IPO. If the price is too low, the firm's existing shareholders incur an opportunity loss; if it is too high, the issue fails to sell. New issues are typically underpriced, which is beneficial to new shareholders, but detrimental to existing shareholders. Existing shareholders are, in effect, selling a portion of the firm they own at a price below its market value. The degree of underpricing varies considerably, but underpricing is usually greater for smaller issues.

15.5 THE DECISION TO GO PUBLIC

The major advantages of going public are: greater access to new capital, more information available to new investors because of disclosure requirements, and the possibility for owners to diversify their personal portfolios by selling some shares yet retaining control of the firm. The disadvantages are: stricter (and costly) disclosure and regulatory requirements, and the time spent by management in complying with these requirements and providing information to investment analysts.

Pricing IPOs: In general, firms providing lots of high-quality information get higher prices for their IPOs. This implies that larger firms have an advantage in going public. The reputation of the underwriter has an impact on the IPO price. Higher offering prices are associated with prestigious underwriters. Investors also assume that, if owners retain a substantial portion of the firm's stock after the offering, they must expect the firm to do well in the future. So, the IPO price is higher when managers keep a larger portion of the firm's shares.

Why does underpricing exist?   Consider the following analogy. Suppose 1,000 used Chevrolets are for sale at $600 each. On average, used Chevys are worth $600. So if you buy all of them, your profit will be zero. However, some are worth more than $600, and some are worth less. Suppose you are unable to make this distinction, but car dealers can. They bid on the good ones. If you try to buy all of the cars, the good ones will be rationed because demand will exceed supply, and you will be able to purchase only a percentage of them. On the other hand, you will get all the bad ones, and, on average, you will lose money. As a result of this 'winner's curse,' you will not bid at all unless the price is less than $600. This reasoning is thought to be at least part of the explanation for the fact that new issues are, on average, underpriced. If they were not underpriced, ordinary investors would not buy them.

15.6 NEW EQUITY SALES AND THE VALUE OF THE FIRM

The announcement of a new equity issue is often regarded as a negative signal to the securities market. Managers with special inside information about the future of their firm may issue new equity when they know the firm's stock is overvalued. Additionally, firms that choose an equity issue may be those that have excess debt. In both cases, an equity issue signals this negative information to investors. There are also substantial costs associated with issuing new shares. Therefore, the response to the announcement of an equity issue is a drop in the firm's stock price.

15.7 THE COSTS OF ISSUING SECURITIES

Flotation costs are the costs incurred in bringing a new issue to market. These costs include the underwriter's spread, other direct expenses (such as legal fees), indirect costs (managers' time), abnormal returns (the drop in stock price), and costs to existing shareholders resulting from underwriting and the overallotment option. Direct costs typically average 13% of the issue value. Indirect costs, although difficult to precisely quantify, are also substantial. Total costs of going public, including underpricing, have been estimated at 14% from 1984 through 1997.

Based on issuer experience, three observations have been made: (1) raising equity is less expensive for larger firms; (2) costs associated with underpricing can be substantial; and (3) issue costs are higher for IPOs than for seasoned offerings.

15.8 RIGHTS

A firm's articles of incorporation may contain a preemptive right, specifying that any new issue of common stock must first be offered to existing shareholders. The preemptive right gives shareholders the opportunity to maintain their percentage ownership of the firm when new securities are sold.

In a rights offering, a shareholder receives one right for each share owned. For a specified number of rights, the shareholder has the option to purchase a new share of stock at a fixed price (the subscription price) for a given period of time. Shareholders can exercise their rights by purchasing the stock, or they can sell the rights to someone else.

The Mechanics of a Rights Offering: The financial manager must determine the following for a rights offering: (1) the subscription price; (2) the number of shares to be sold; (3) the number of rights required to purchase a new share; and, (4) the impact of the rights offering on the value of the existing common stock.

An Example: The MRR Corporation intends to raise $20 million in new equity financing through a rights offering. The firm's outstanding common stock currently sells for $40 per share; 10 million shares are outstanding. What is the subscription price for the rights offering? How many new shares must be sold? How many rights are required to purchase a new share? What is the value of a right? How does the rights offering affect the value of the existing shares?

Number of Rights Needed to Purchase a Share: The subscription price must be set below the market price in order for the rights offering to succeed. If the subscription price for the new issues is set at $20 per share, 1 million new shares will be sold in order to raise the $20 million. The number of new shares to be issued is computed by dividing the total funds to be raised by the subscription price. For the MRR Corporation:

$$\text{Number of new shares} = \frac{\text{Funds to be raised}}{\text{Subscription price}} = \frac{\$20,000,000}{\$20} = 1,000,000 \text{ shares}$$

Each shareholder receives one right for each share owned. Since there are 10 million shares outstanding, the firm will issue 10 million rights. These rights will be used to purchase the 1 million new shares issued. For MRR, the number of rights needed to buy one share is:

$$\text{Number of rights} = \frac{\text{Old shares}}{\text{New shares}} = \frac{10,000,000}{1,000,000} = 10 \text{ rights}$$

That is, it will take 10 rights to buy one new share at the subscription price of $20.

The Value of a Right: The holder of ten shares of MRR Corporation stock has the right to purchase, for $20 a share, stock which is currently selling for $40 per share. Clearly, this offer has value to the existing shareholders. Consider an investor who buys ten shares of MRR common stock for $400, receives ten rights, and then exercises the rights to obtain another share for $20. In this way, the investor will have obtained eleven shares for a total cost of $420. Since any investor can acquire eleven shares for $420, the price per share must fall to ($420/11) = $38.18 following the exercise of the rights.

The original ten shares each carried a right, whereas the new share does not. Also, after the ten rights are exercised, none of the eleven shares include a right. Therefore, the difference between the value of one of the original shares and the value of the shares after the rights are exercised is ($40 – $38.18) = $1.82. Since the only difference between the shares is that each of the original ten shares entitles its holder to one right, then the difference between the prices is the value of a right. This means the value of each right is $1.82.

Theoretical Value of a Right: Mathematically, the equation for the theoretical value of a right during the rights-on period is:

$$R_o = (M_o - S) / (N + 1)$$

where

M_o =   Common share price during the right-on period

S   =   Subscriptions price

N   =   Number of rights required to buy one new share

For MRR the value of one right is:

R_o =   ($40 – $20) / (10 + 1)   = $1.82, which is the same answer we got earlier.

Ex-Rights: For rights offerings, the firm establishes the holder-of-record date. An investor who is a 'holder-of-record' on that date receives one right for each share owned. According to stock exchange rules, the *ex-rights date* is four trading days prior to the holder-of-record date. An investor must purchase the stock prior to the ex-rights date in order to be considered the owner of the stock on the holder-of-record date. If a share is sold before the ex-rights date, it is said to be trading 'rights-on' or 'cum rights,' and the purchaser receives the right. At the close of trading on the fifth day prior to the holder-of-record date, the stock goes ex-rights, so that any subsequent purchaser does not receive the right (the right goes to the original owner). At the start of trading on the next day, which is the ex-rights date, the price of the stock decreases by the value of the right. In the MRR example above, the price of the stock will decline from $40 to $38.18 on the ex-rights date.

Value of Rights after Ex-Rights Date: When the stock goes ex-rights, we saw that its price drops by the value of one right. However, even when the stock sells 'ex-rights,' investors can exercise their rights, and buy new shares, until the rights offering expires. The value of a right during the ex-rights period is:

R_e = $(M_e – S) / N$

where M_e =   common share price during the ex-rights period. In the case of MRR, M_e = $40 – $1.82 = $38.18.

R_e =   ($38.18 – $20) / 10 = $1.82

The Underwriting Arrangements: A rights offering often involves *standby underwriting*. The underwriter is paid a *standby fee* and agrees to purchase any unsubscribed shares. Only a small portion of a rights offering would normally not be subscribed. Furthermore, shareholders are usually given an *oversubscription privilege*, which gives them the option to buy additional shares at the subscription price, should any be available. Thus it is generally unlikely that the standby underwriter will need to 'take up' any unsold shares.

Effects on Shareholders: As long as shareholders either exercise or sell their rights, they are not harmed by the rights offering and the subsequent decline in stock price. Suppose that, in the MRR Corporation example, an owner of ten shares exercises the ten rights and purchases a share for $20. Prior to the announcement of the rights offering, the ten shares were worth a total of $400. After exercising the rights and paying an additional $20, the investor owns eleven shares worth $420. Therefore, at a cost of $20 the total value of the holdings has increased by $20. So, there is no gain or loss as a result of the transaction.

On the other hand, the investor may choose to sell the rights for (10 × $1.82)   = $18.20. The ten shares will be worth (10 × $38.18) = $381.80, which, when added to the $18.20 value of the rights, leaves total wealth unchanged at $400. Consequently, exercising or selling the rights does not affect the investor's total wealth. If, however, the investor allows the rights to expire, there is a loss equal to the decline in the value of the stock, or ($40 – $38.18) = $1.82 per share. As computed earlier, this is the same as the value of a right. In this case, the investor loses 10 x $1.82   = $18.20, and total wealth drops from $400 to $381.80.

15.9 DILUTION

Dilution is a decrease in the value of the common shareholders' position resulting from the issue of new common stock. There are three aspects of dilution: (1) dilution of proportionate ownership; (2) dilution of book value and earnings per share; and (3) dilution of market value. Each of these concepts are illustrated in the following example.

An Example: The Polo Company currently has 100 shares outstanding. Of these, R. Branca owns 40 shares and B. Thompson owns 30 shares. The market value of the firm's stock is $40 per share. The book value of the firm is $5,000, so that book value per share is $50. The firm's return on equity, ROE, is 20%. The firm intends to issue 50 new shares. How does this new issue affect the current shareholders?

First, we can solve for net income in the following equation for ROE:

$$ROE = \text{Net income / Common equity}; \quad .20 = \text{Net income / \$5,000, and Net income} = \$1,000.$$

This means that EPS is $1,000 / 100 = $10.

Dilution of Proportionate Ownership: The impact of the issue of 50 new shares on the voting rights of the current shareholders depends on the nature of the new issue. If the new issue is a rights offering, then each existing shareholder will be able to purchase one new share for each two shares currently owned. For example, Thompson will be able to purchase 15 new shares and, after the rights offering, will own 45 of 150 shares outstanding, or 30% of the outstanding shares, the same percentage currently owned. In this case, there is no dilution of ownership. If the new issue is a general cash offer, however, Thompson does not purchase any of the new shares. The ownership stake decreases to (30/150) = 20%, reducing Thompson's influence on corporate decisions.

Dilution of Value - Book versus Market Values: The impact of the new stock issue on book value and earnings per share depends on the price at which the new shares are sold and the firm's ROE before and after the new issue. If ROE remains constant at 20% , and the new shares are sold for a price equal to the current book value per share ($50 in the Polo example), then there is no dilution of book value and earnings per share. Book value for the firm will increase by (50 × $50) = $2,500 to ($5,000 + $2,500) = $7,500 and net income will be (.20 × $7,500) = $1,500. Book value per share will be ($7,500/150) = $50 and EPS will be ($1,500/150) = $10. The fact that book value per share remains constant results from the fact that the book value per share for both the old shares and the newly issued shares is $50. That is, since the new shares are sold at a price equal to the book value of the old shares, and the price of the new shares becomes their book value once they are sold, the book value per share does not change. Furthermore, the ROE for both the old shares and the new shares is 20%, so that EPS can be thought of as (.20 × $50) = $10 for both the old and new shares.

On the other hand, if the new shares are sold for a price below the book value of the old shares, then the book value per share and EPS are diluted. This reduction in both book value per share and EPS is referred to as accounting dilution. Suppose the new shares are sold for $40 per share and ROE remains at 20%. Clearly, book value per share is reduced, since 50 shares with a book value of $40 per share are now added to the existing equity of 100 shares with a book value of $50 per share. Book value of the firm is increased by (50 × $40) = $2,000, to a total of ($5,000 + $2,000) = $7,000, and the book value per share is ($7,000/150) = $46.67. EPS is also reduced because the new shares contribute only (.20 × $40) = $8 per share to the firm's total earnings, which is less than the $10 EPS of the firm's existing shares. After the new issue, total earnings are (.20 × $7,000) = $1,400 and EPS equals ($1,400/150) = $9.33. Thus, accounting dilution occurs if the firm issues new shares at a price below the current book value per share while ROE remains constant.

Market value dilution is a decrease in the market value per share of the firm's stock following the issue of new shares of common stock. Whether market value dilution occurs depends on the purpose of the additional financing obtained by Polo.

Suppose the $2,000 obtained from this issue will be used to finance a capital budgeting project whose net present value is zero. How will this affect the market value of the firm's stock? The market value of the existing stock is $40 per share, so that the market value of the firm is ($40 × 100) = $4,000. The assets for the new capital budgeting project will increase the firm's market value to ($4,000 + $2,000) = $6,000 and the market price per share will be ($6,000/150) = $40. If, however, the net present value of the capital budgeting project is +$2,450, then the market value of the firm will increase to ($4,000 + $2,450) = $6,450 and the price per share will be ($6,450/150) = $43. Market value increases because the project being financed has a positive net present value. If, however, the project had a negative NPV, we would see dilution of market value.

For our purposes, we are concerned with market value dilution, not with accounting dilution.

15.10   ISSUING LONG-TERM DEBT

A public issue of bonds requires the issuing firm to register the issue with the OSC and other relevant provincial securities commissions. The registration process is similar to that required for a common stock issue. However, for bonds, the registration statement must indicate an indenture.

More than 50% of all debt is directly placed, either as *term loans* or *private placements*. A term loan is a direct business loan that is normally amortized over a period of one to five years. The major lenders are commercial banks and insurance companies. A private placement is similar to a term loan except for the fact that the maturity is generally longer and comes under OSC regulation. A private placement does not require a full prospectus. Instead, the firm and its investment dealer draw up an *offering memorandum* briefly describing the issuer and the issue. Most privately placed debt is sold to *exempt purchasers* who are large insurance companies, pension funds and other institutions who do not require protection provided by studying a full prospectus.

Private placements tend to have higher interest rates than public issues and are also more likely to have restrictive covenants. The benefits of private placements are that they are easier to renegotiate, and incur lower distribution costs. The interest rates on term loans and private placements are usually higher than those on equivalent public issues. This reflects the trade-off between a higher interest rate and more flexible arrangements in the event of financial distress, as well as lower costs associated with private placements.

Syndicated loans are loans provided by a group of financial institutions to an individual borrower. Why do lenders form syndicates? One explanation is that an imbalance exists in the loan market: large financial institutions face greater demand for loans than they can supply, while small financial institutions face difficulty finding suitable borrowers. The formation of loan syndicates can overcome this imbalance. For example, a large financial institution may arrange a loan which is then funded by a syndicate of small financial institutions.

The characteristics of syndicated loans can vary widely. For example, syndicated loans may or may not be publicly traded. Another example is that a syndicated loan may be a line of credit that is rarely used or a term loan that is immediately used to finance a project. Syndicated loans can differ in riskiness as well. While syndicated loans are typically investment grade, a class of syndicated loans called *leveraged syndicated loan*s are speculative grade.

CONCEPT TEST

1. When a firm sells a new issue of securities in Ontario, the firm must file a _____ statement with the _____. This statement is a detailed financial disclosure. The OSC studies the registration statement during the _____. The buyer of the securities must receive a _____, which contains much of the information in the registration statement.

2. A public offering of a new issue may be either a _____ offer or a _____ offer. Some equity securities, and almost all debt securities, are sold through a _____ offer, which is an offer to sell securities to the general public.

3. A _____ offering is an offer to sell common stock to the firm's existing shareholders.

4. A company's first public offering of equity securities is called an _____ offering or an _____. A _____ new issue is a new issue by a company that has previously issued securities.

5. For a cash offer, the underwriter, or _____, normally buys the securities from the firm and offers them to the public at a higher price. The difference between the underwriter's buying price and the price at which the underwriter offers the security to the public is called the _____ or the _____.

6. If the underwriter purchases the entire issue, then the issuing firm receives a fixed price for the securities, and all the risk associated with the sale of the securities is transferred to the _____. This procedure is called _____ underwriting.

7. For a _____ offering, the underwriter does not purchase the securities, but rather acts as an agent and receives a commission for each share. The _____ bears the risk that the securities cannot be sold at the specified price.

8. One of the most difficult tasks for an investment banker is the pricing of an initial public offering. If the price is set too low, the firm's existing shareholders incur an _____ loss; if it is set too high, the issue _____. New issues are typically _____, which is beneficial to new shareholders, but detrimental to existing shareholders.

9. The announcement of a new issue is often regarded as a _____ signal to the securities markets. If the firm has a superior opportunity, it (is/is not) beneficial to existing shareholders to share this information by selling new shares of stock.

10. A firm's _____ may contain a preemptive right, which specifies that any new issue of common stock must be first offered to existing shareholders. A common stock issue offered to existing shareholders is called a _____ offering. A specified number of rights gives the shareholder the option to buy a new share at a fixed price, called the _____ price, during a specified time period, after which the rights _____.

11. In order for a rights offering to succeed, the subscription price must be set below the _____. The number of new shares to be issued is: Number of new shares = _____. The price per share after the rights are exercised can be computed as $[(N \times \underline{\hspace{1.5cm}}) + (\underline{\hspace{1.5cm}})] / (\underline{\hspace{1.5cm}})$ where N is the number of rights required to purchase one new share. The value of a right is equal to the _____ minus the _____.

12.   For a rights offering, an investor who is a 'holder-of-record' on the holder-of-record date receives _____ right(s) for each share owned. The _____ date is four business days prior to the holder-of-record date. An investor must purchase the stock prior to the _____ date to be considered the owner of the stock on the holder-of-record date. At the close of trading on the fifth day prior to the holder-of-record date, the stock goes _____, so that any subsequent purchaser does not receive the right.

13.   As long as shareholders either _____ or _____ their rights, they are not harmed by the rights offering and the subsequent decline in stock price. That is, if the investor either _____ or _____ the rights, total wealth is unchanged. If the investor allows a right to expire, the loss is equal to _____.

14.   Dilution is a decrease in the value of the common shareholders' position which results from the issue of new common stock. Dilution of voting rights (does/does not) occur if the new issue is a rights offering. If the new issue is a public offering, and if an existing shareholder does not purchase any of the new shares, dilution of voting rights (does/does not) occur.

15.   Accounting dilution is a reduction in both _____ per share and _____. Whether a new stock issue results in accounting dilution depends on the _____ and the firm's _____. If ROE remains constant after the new issue is sold, and the new shares are sold for a price equal to the current book value per share then accounting dilution (does/does not) occur. If the new shares are sold for a price below the book value of the old shares, then dilution of book value per share and EPS (does/does not) occur.

16.   Market value dilution is a decrease in the _____ of the firm's stock following the issue of new shares of common stock. Market value dilution (does/does not) occur if the funds obtained are used to finance a capital budgeting project whose net present value is zero or positive. It does occur when the net present value of a capital budgeting project is _____.

17.   A public issue of bonds requires that the issuing firm file a _____ statement with the SEC. More than 50% of all debt is directly placed, either as _____ loans or _____ placements.

18.   A _____ loan is a direct business loan that is normally amortized over a period of one to five years. A _____ placement is similar to a term loan except for the fact that the _____.

19.   A corporation may register with the OSC an offering it expects to sell in the near future. This _____ procedure permits large corporations to reduce repetitive filing requirements.

20.   To use the POP system, issuers must have been reporting for _____ months and have complied with continuous _____.

21.   In 1991, securities regulators in Canada and in the U.S. introduced a _____ where large issuers are allowed to issue securities in both countries under disclosure documents satisfactory to regulators in the _____ country.

22.   Underwriting contracts often contain an _____ which allows the _____ to purchase additional shares in order to cover excess demand.

23.   In a _____ the issuer sells the entire issue to one investment dealer who takes all the risk of _____.

24.   For debt, a _____ does not require a full prospectus. Instead an _____ briefly describes the issuer and the issue.

25.   Syndicated loans are loans made by a _____ of financial institutions to a single _____. Syndicated loans are typically rated _____ grade, though _____ syndicated loans are rated speculative grade.

PROBLEMS

Problem 1

Yul Company has just floated an IPO. Under a firm-commitment underwriting agreement, Yul received $10 for each of the 1 million shares sold. The initial offering price was $11 per share, and the stock price rose to $14 per share in the first few minutes of trading. Yul paid $60,000 in direct legal and other costs; indirect costs were $40,000. What was the flotation cost as a percentage of funds raised?

Problem 2

The Canuck Corporation plans to raise $10 million in new equity financing through a rights offering. The firm's stock is valued at $30 per share, and 20 million shares ore outstanding. If the firm sets the subscription price at $20 per share, how many new shares must be sold? How many rights are required to purchase a new share? What is the value of a right? How does the rights offering affect the value of Canuck Corporation's existing shares?

Problem 3

Suppose a shareholder with 120 shares of Canuck Corporation decides to sell the rights to the new offering. Does doing this harm the shareholder? What if the shareholder decides to exercise the rights?

Problem 4

A company requires $15 million in equity financing. Direct costs of a cash offering (including the spread, but excluding underpricing) are equal to 12% of the financing obtained. How large does the issue have to be in order to provide the company with the $15 million of required financing? What is the dollar amount of the flotation costs for this offering?

Problem 5

Dumas Corporation needs $19 million in equity financing. Direct costs of the cash offering (including the spread, excluding underpricing) are equal to 11% of the financing obtained. How large does the issue need to be in order to raise the required $19 million? What is the dollar amount of flotation costs?

Problem 6

Firms A and B have announced IPOs. Each firm's stock will be sold for $10 per share. One of these issues is undervalued by $1, while the other is overvalued by $.50. You are not able to determine which is undervalued and which is overvalued. You plan to buy 100 shares of each firm's stock. If an issue is rationed, you will be able to purchase only half of your order. If you are able to buy 100 shares of each firm's stock, what is your profit? What profit do you actually expect?

Problem 7

Emery Enterprises has announced a rights offering to obtain $10 million of equity financing for a new publishing project. The stock currently sells for $80 per share, and there are 2 million shares outstanding. If Emery sets the subscription price at $20 per share, how many shares must be sold? How many rights are required in order to buy one share?

Problem 8

For the rights offering described in Problem 7, what is the ex-rights price? What is the value of a right?

Problem 9

Suppose that an investor who owns 100 shares of Emery common stock intends to sell the rights, rather than purchase additional shares of stock. Demonstrate the fact that the shareholder is not harmed by the rights offering described in Problem 7.

Problem 10

Suppose that the investor described in Problem 9 decides to exercise, rather than sell, the rights. How does this course of action affect the investor's total wealth?

Problem 11

Suppose that the rights described in Problems 7 and 8 are trading for less than the $12 value computed in the solution to Problem 8. For example, assume that the market value of a right is $10. How will this affect the investor who owns 100 shares of Emery common stock? What action would you recommend to an investor who does not own Emery common stock?

Problem 12

Suppose that the rights described in Problems 7 and 8 are trading for more than the $12 value computed in the solution to Problem 8. For example, assume that the market value of a right is $13. How will this affect the investor who owns 100 shares of Emery common stock? What action would you recommend to an investor who does not own Emery common stock?

Problem 13

Try this one on your own, referring to the information in Problem 7. Suppose that Emery Enterprises had set the subscription price at $50. How many shares of stock must Emery sell? How many rights are required in order to buy one new share?

Problem 14

Based on your answer to Problem 13, what is the ex-rights price? What is the value of one right?

Problem 15

An investor owns 100 shares of Emery common stock. Demonstrate the fact that the investor's wealth is unchanged by the rights offering described in Problem 13, regardless of whether the investor sells or exercises the rights.

Problem 16

Assume that an investor owns 100 shares of Emery common stock, and will sell the rights regardless of the subscription price. Demonstrate that the investor's wealth is unaffected by a rights offering, regardless of the subscription price.

Problem 17

What is the maximum possible subscription price for the Emery Enterprises rights offering? What is the minimum price?

Problem 18

Delefes Enterprises has announced a rights offering to raise $15 million in equity financing for a new theatre in the downtown core. Shares currently cost $34 and there are 1.2 million shares outstanding. How many shares must be sold if the subscription price is $25? How many rights are required to buy one share? What is the ex-rights price and the value of a right?

Problem 19

Aardvark Industries needs to raise $270 million in capital. They plan a rights offering with a subscription price of $75 per share. The firm's stock is currently trading at $90 per share and there are 9 million shares outstanding. Find the value of a right and the ex-rights share price.

Problem 20

Demonstrate that an investor with 180 shares of Aardvark is equally well off by exercising or selling the rights.

Problem 21

Now suppose the investor in Problem 20 decides to sell half the rights and exercise the rest. How does this affect the investor's financial position?

Problem 22

Finally, assume that the investor lets the Aardvark rights expire. How does this affect the financial position?

Use the following information to solve Problems 23-26:

Ebbets Manufacturing Company has been experiencing financial difficulties ever since its major customer moved to Chavez Ravine. However, Ebbets is considering expansion into a new line of business. The expansion requires $4,500,000 of financing, which will be obtained through a cash offering of common stock. Ebbets currently has 5,000,000 shares of common stock outstanding and no debt. The firm's book value is $60,000,000 and net income is currently $7,500,000. Ebbets common stock currently sells for $9 per share.

Problem 23

Calculate each of the following for Ebbets, without the expansion: book value per share, earnings per share (EPS), price earnings (P/E) ratio, return on equity (ROE), and market-to-book value ratio.

Problem 24

Assume that the firm's P/E ratio and ROE remain constant. Calculate each of the following for Ebbets, after the expansion: book value per share, EPS, market price per share, market-to-book ratio.

Problem 25

What is the net present value of the expansion under consideration by Ebbets?

Problem 26

Suppose that the net present value of the expansion is $1,000,000. What is the market value of the firm's common stock after the expansion?

ANSWERS TO CONCEPT TEST

1.   registration; Ontario Securities Commission; waiting period; prospectus

2.   cash; rights; cash

3.   rights

4.   initial public; unseasoned new issue; seasoned

5.   investment dealer; spread; discount

6.   underwriter; firm-commitment

7.   best-efforts; issuing firm

8.   opportunity; fails to sell; underpriced

9.   negative; is not

10.   articles of incorporation; rights; subscription; expire

11.   market price; (Funds to be raised/Subscription price); price per share before the rights offering; subscription price; N + 1; price per share before the rights offering; price per share after the rights are exercised

12.   one; ex-rights; ex-rights; ex-rights

13.   exercise; sell; exercises; sells; the value of a right

14.   does not; does

15.   book value; earnings per share; price at which the new shares are sold; return on equity; does not; does

16.   market value; does not; negative

17.   registration; term; private

18.   term; private; maturity is longer

19.   prompt offering prospectus (POP)

20.   36; disclosure requirements

21.   Multi-Jurisdictional Disclosure System (MJDS); home

22.   overallotment option (or green shoe provision); investment dealers

23.   bought deal; selling the issue

24.   private placement; offering memorandum

25.   group, borrower, investment, leveraged

PROBLEM SOLUTIONS

Problem 1: Yul obtained financing of ($10 × 1,000,000) = $10 million. Flotation costs included:

Underwriter's spread ($11 − $10) × 1,000,000	$ 1,000,000
Direct costs	60,000
Indirect costs	40,000
Underpricing ($14 - 11) x 1,000,000	3,000,000
Total	$ 4,100,000

Flotation costs were $4,100,000 / $10,000,000 = 41% of the financing obtained.

Problem 2: The number of new shares to be issued in order to raise the required funds is:

Number of new shares = Funds to be raised / Subscription price
      = $10,000,000 / $20 = 500,000 shares

The number of rights required to purchase a new share is:

Number of rights = Olds shares / New shares = 20,000,000 / 500,000 = 40

It will take 40 rights to buy one new share at a subscription price of $20 per share.

To determine the value of a right, use the following equation:

$$R_0 = (M_0 - S) / (N + 1) = (\$30 - \$20) / (40 + 1) = \$0.24$$

Therefore, the price per share will fall to ($30 - $.24) = $29.76 on the ex-rights day.

Problem 3: Prior to the rights offering, the shareholder owns stock with a value of (120 x $30) = $3,600. Selling the rights will yield (120 x $.24) = $28.80, plus the value of the shares (120 x $29.76) = $3,571.20. The total value of the investment is $28.80 + $3,571.20 = $3,600. Therefore, the shareholder is not harmed, as the total wealth is unchanged. If the shareholder exercises the rights, he/she can purchase new shares of (120 / 40) = 3 for (3 x $20) = $60. The holdings would be worth (123 x $29.76) = $3,660.48. Subtracting $60 paid for the new shares, the position is worth $3,600.48. (The difference is due to rounding errors).

Problem 4: We need to solve for issue size in the equation: $(1 - .12) \times$ issue size = $15 million. That is, $(1 - .12)$ = .88 = 88% of the size of the issue is financing available to the firm. The firm must issue ($15 million / .88) = $17,045,455 in equity. The flotation costs are $17,045,455 – $15,000,000 = $2,045,455.

Problem 5: The size of the issue is equal to (1 - .11) x issue size = $19 million. Issue size is equal to $21,348,314.61. The flotation costs are therefore ($21,348,314.61 - $19,000,000) = $2,348,314.61.

Problem 6: If you are able to purchase all the shares for which you bid, you would earn a profit of $100 on the undervalued stock, while you would lose $50 on the overvalued stock, for a total profit of ($100 – $50) = $50. However, the undervalued issue will be rationed while the overvalued issue will not be rationed. You should therefore expect to get 50 shares of the undervalued issue, for a profit of $50, and 100 shares of the overvalued issue, for a loss of $50. Therefore, you expect to earn no profit. Notice that, on average, these new issues are underpriced by ($.25 / $10) = 2.5%. The fact that you expect to earn a zero profit, even though the two issues are, on average, underpriced, illustrates the winner's curse.

Problem 7: At a subscription price of $20 per share, ($10,000,000/$20) = 500,000 shares must be sold. There are 2 million shares outstanding, so that (2,000,000/500,000) = 4 rights are required in order to buy one new share.

Problem 8: An investor could buy four shares of Emery common stock for ($80 × 4) = $320, and then exercise the rights to acquire a fifth share for $20. Thus, five shares can be purchased for $340, or ($340/5) = $68 per share. Therefore, the ex-rights price is $68 per share, and the value of one right is ($80 – $68) = $12.

Using the equation for the value of a right: M_o = ($80 - $20) / (4 + 1) = $12. The ex-rights price is $80 -$12 = $68.

Problem 9: Before the rights offering, the 100 shares were worth ($80 × 100) = $8,000. The solution to Problem 8 indicates that the ex-rights price of the Emery stock is $68. Therefore, after the offering, the shares are worth ($68 × 100) = $6,800. The solution to Problem 8 indicates that the value of a right is $12, so that the 100 rights can be sold for ($12 × 100) = $1,200. Therefore, after the rights offering, the investor has stock whose value is $6,800, plus $1,200 in cash, for a total of $8,000. The total wealth is unchanged.

Problem 10: The solution to Problem 7 indicates that the investor will be able to purchase one additional share for every four shares currently owned. Thus, the holder of 100 shares will be able to purchase 25 new shares for ($20 × 25) = $500. From Problem 8, the ex-rights price of the stock is $68. Therefore, after exercising the rights, the value of the investor's stock is ($68 × 125) = $8,500. The investor originally owned $8,000 of Emery stock. After purchasing $500 of additional stock, the total value of the stock is now $8,500. The investor's wealth is $8,500 less the $500 spent on new shares, or $8,000. The rights offering has not affected the shareholder's wealth.

Problem 11: An investor who owns 100 shares of Emery common stock would lose ($2 × 100) = $200 by selling the rights. That is, as described in the solution to Problem 9, the stock would be worth ($68 × 100) = $6,800, but the value of the rights would be only ($10 × 100) = $1,000, for a total value of only ($6,800 + $1,000) = $7,800. Therefore, it would be preferable for this investor to exercise the rights, as described in the solution to Problem 10.

An investor who does not own Emery common stock could purchase four rights for ($10 × 4) = $40, and then exercise the rights to acquire a share for $20. The total cost to the investor would be ($40 + $20) = $60 per share. Since the ex-rights price of the stock is $68, the investor could then sell the share for an $8 gain. This transaction could be repeated many times, by any investor, whether or not they currently own Emery common stock. The demand for the rights at a price of $10 would result in an increase in the price of the rights. Furthermore, as described in the first part of this problem, those who own stock would not be willing to sell their rights at the $10 price. The conclusion here is that the rights could not have a price of less than $12, because there would be an extremely large demand for, and essentially no supply of, rights at the $10 price. The equilibrium price for the rights would be the $12 established in the above problems.

Problem 12: An investor who owns 100 shares of Emery common stock should sell the rights for $13. This would result in a $100 gain, compared to the result described in the solution to Problem 9. That is, the investor would have 100 shares worth ($68 × 100) = $6,800, plus ($13 × 100) = $1,300, for a total of ($6,800 + $1,300) = $8,100. An investor who does not own Emery stock would not be willing to purchase a right for $13. Four rights would cost ($13 × 4) = $52. In order to exercise the rights, the investor would pay the subscription price of $20, for a total cost of ($52 + $20) = $72 per share. Since the ex-rights price is $68, this would not be a reasonable investment. Consequently, Emery shareholders would be willing to sell a right for $13, but a rational investor would not be willing to buy a right for this price. Thus, the price of the rights cannot be greater than the $12 value computed in the solution to Problem 8.

Problem 13: Number of shares to sell = 200,000. Number of rights to buy 1 share = 10.

Problem 14: R_o = $2.73; Ex-rights price = $77.27.

Problem 15: Prior to the rights offering, the investor owns stock whose value is ($80 × 100) = $8,000. The investor can sell the rights and receive ($2.73 × 100) = $273.00 cash. In addition, the shares are worth ($77.27 × 100) = $7,727.00. Therefore, total wealth is unchanged: ($7,727.00 + $273.00) = $8,000.

The investor can exercise the rights and purchase ten new shares for ($50 × 10) = $500. Then, the investor owns 110 shares worth ($77.27 × 110) = $8,499.70. This value differs slightly from $8,500 due to rounding error in computing the ex-rights price in Problem 14. Total wealth is ($8,499.70 - $500) = $7,999.70. That is, it is unchanged.

Problem 16: Assume that an investor owns one share of Emery common stock. The value of the share is M_o, the rights-on price. On the ex-rights date, the value of the share decreases to the ex-rights price, M_e, so that the loss to the investor is $(M_o - M_e)$. However, the value of the right is the difference between the rights-on price and the ex-rights price, that is, $(M_o - M_e)$. Therefore, the value of the right exactly compensates the investor for the loss in the value of the stock, so that the investor's wealth is left unchanged by selling the right. Since this conclusion applies to the holder of one share, it applies to the holder of any number of shares, and it is unaffected by the subscription price of the rights offering.

Problem 17: The solution to Problem 16 demonstrates that the subscription price does not affect the existing shareholders of Emery. That is, regardless of whether the existing shareholders exercise or sell their rights, their wealth is unchanged by the rights offering, regardless of the subscription price. Theoretically, then, the minimum subscription price could be arbitrarily small, as long as it is not zero. This illustrates the fact that a rights offering cannot be underpriced, although, as a practical matter, extremely low values are unreasonable. The maximum subscription price is $80, because the issue would not sell at a price higher than the current market value. In practice, a subscription price close to $80 would be too high because the market price could decline during the offer, so that the issue would not sell.

Problem 18: The number of shares to be sold is ($15,000,000 / $25) = 600,000 and (1,200,000 / 600,000) = 2 rights are required to buy one share.

Value of one right = ($34 - $25) / (2+1) = $3

Ex-rights price = $34 - $3 = $31

Problem 19: Aardvark must sell ($270,000,000 / $90) = 3 million shares. Investors need 9 million / 3 million = 3 rights to buy one share. The value of one right is R_o = ($90 - $75) / (3 + 1) = $3.75. The ex-rights stock price is $90 - $3.75 = $86.25.

Problem 20: Before the rights offering, the value of the investor's position is 180 x $90 = $16,200. If the investor exercises the rights, the investor's total wealth will be:

Value of old shares (180 x $86.25)	$15,525
Value of new shares (180 / 3) x $86.25	5,175
Less cash to buy shares (60 x $75)	(4,500)
Total wealth	$16,200

If the investor sells the rights, the total wealth will be:

Old shares (180 x $86.25)	$15,525
Cash from selling rights (180 x $3.75)	675
Total wealth	$16,200

In either case, the investor's wealth remains unchanged at $16,200.

Problem 21: The investor's wealth will be:

Old shares (180 x $86.25)	$15,525.00
New shares (90 / 3) x $86.25	2,587.50
Cash from selling rights (90 x $3.75)	337.50
Less cash for new shares (30 x $75)	(2,250.00)
Total wealth	$16,200.00

Problem 22: The investor's wealth will be: 180 x $86.25 = $15,525. This is a loss of $16,200 - $15,525 = $675, which is equal to the value of the rights, (180 x $3.75) = $675.

Problem 23: Book value per share = ($60,000,000/$5,000,000) = $12. EPS = ($7,500,000/5,000,000) = $1.50. The P/E ratio equals market value per share divided by EPS: ($9/$1.50) = 6. ROE equals EPS divided by book value per share: ($1.50/$12.00) = .125 = 12.5%. The market-to-book ratio is market value per share divided by book value per share: ($9/$12) = .75.

Problem 24: Total book value is ($60,000,000 + $4,500,000) = $64,500,000. The number of shares issued equals ($4,500,000/$9) = 500,000. Total shares outstanding equal (5,000,000 + 500,000) = 5,500,000. Book value per share is ($64,500,000/5,500,000) = $11.73. If ROE remains constant at 12.5% (as computed in Problem 23), then net income is (.125 × $64,500,000) = $8,062,500. EPS equals ($8,062,500/5,500,000) = $1.47. If the P/E ratio remains constant at 6 (as computed in Problem 23), then the market price per share is ($1.47 × 6) = $8.82. The market-to-book ratio equals ($8.82/$11.73) = .75. Notice that both accounting dilution and market value dilution have taken place here. Accounting dilution is the reduction in book value per share and earnings per share which results from the sale of a new issue of common stock at a price below the book value per share of the firm's outstanding common stock. Book value per share decreases because the book value of the new shares is $9, which is less than the book value of the existing shares. Given a constant ROE, then EPS for the new shares can be thought of as $(.125 \times \$9)$ = $1.125; since this is less than the EPS computed in Problem 23, EPS must decrease. Accounting dilution is not relevant to the shareholder, but market value dilution is relevant. The dilution of market value is not caused by the accounting dilution; the cause of the market value dilution is the fact that the expansion under consideration by Ebbets has a negative net present value. This result is developed in the next problem.

Problem 25: The market value of the firm prior to the expansion is $(\$9 \times 5,000,000)$ = $45,000,00. After the expansion, the market value is $(\$8.80 \times 5,500,000)$ = $48,400,000. This represents an increase in market value of $3,400,000. Ebbets proposes spending $4,500,000 on a capital budgeting project which increases the firm's market value by only $3,400,000. This project has a net present value of $(\$3,400,000 - \$4,500,000) = -\$1,100,000$. It is this negative net present value which causes the dilution in the market value of the firm's common stock. The loss per share of stock is -$1,100,000 / 5,500,000 = -$.20. This is reflected in the drop in share price from $9 to $8.80 per share.

Problem 26: The market value of the firm will be $(\$45,000,000 + \$1,000,000 + \$4,500,000)$ = $50,500,000. Market value per share will be ($50,500,000/5,500,000)= $9.18. Note that the accounting dilution and the market value dilution are independent of each other. The accounting dilution occurs because the new shares are sold for a price which is below the book value of the firm's existing shares. Market value dilution occurs only if the project being financed has a negative net present value. In this problem, we hypothesize that the project has a positive net present value; the negative net present value computed in Problem 25 results from the assumptions that the firm's P/E ratio and ROE remain constant after the expansion. There is no reason to believe that these ratios will necessarily remain constant simply because the firm sells shares for a price below their book value. Therefore, there is no reason to believe that market value dilution occurs whenever accounting dilution occurs.

Note that the gain per share is NPV / number of shares = $1,000,000 / 5,500,000 = $.18. This is reflected in the increase in share price from $9 to $9.18.

16 Financial Leverage and Capital Structure Policy

CHAPTER HIGHLIGHTS

Firms have considerable flexibility in choosing their capital structure–that is, the way they finance their assets. To simplify the choice of capital structure, our discussion is limited to the choice between debt and equity. The objective of the capital structure decision, like any corporate objective, should be to maximize the wealth of the firm's owners, the shareholders. In this chapter, we will assume the firm's investment decision is already made. That is, the firm is choosing the appropriate capital structure to finance a given set of assets.

16.1 THE CAPITAL STRUCTURE QUESTION

There are two major issues related to the capital structure decision. First, should shareholders be concerned about maximizing the value of the entire firm, rather than maximizing the value of the firm's equity? And, second, what is the ratio of debt to equity that maximizes shareholders' interests?

Firm Value and Stock Value: First, we can demonstrate that maximizing the value of the firm's equity is equivalent to maximizing the value of the firm.

Consider an all-equity firm with a market value of $100,000. That is, both the firm's existing assets and its common stock are valued at $100,000. Managers are considering the possibility $40,000 and using the proceeds of the loan to pay dividends to the shareholders.

If this financial restructuring does not affect the value of the firm's assets, then the wealth of the shareholders is unaffected. Before the restructuring, they owned 100% of a firm worth $100,000. After the restructuring, they own 60% of a firm worth $100,000 = $60,000 + $40,000 in dividends = $100,000. Their total wealth is the same.

If restructuring increases the value of the firm, then shareholders benefit. If, for example, restructuring increases the value of the firm to $110,000, the shareholders now own equity in the firm worth ($110,000 – $40,000) = $70,000 plus dividends of $40,000, for a total of $110,000. In other words, the increase in firm value accrues to the shareholders. Likewise, any loss in value also accrues to the firm's shareholders. Consequently, maximizing the value of the firm is equivalent to maximizing the value of the shareholders' position.

Therefore, from the shareholders' point of view, if there is a capital structure which maximizes the value of the firm, the same capital structure also maximizes the value of the shareholders' position.

Capital Structure and the Cost of Capital: Remember that the value of a firm is the present value of the firm's cash flows, discounted at the WACC. If capital structure decisions have an impact on the WACC, then these decisions affect the value of the firm. The capital structure which minimizes the WACC is also the capital structure which maximizes the value of the firm.

16.2 THE EFFECT OF FINANCIAL LEVERAGE

Financial leverage is the extent to which a firm uses debt, rather than equity, financing. In this section, we investigate the relationship between financial leverage and the returns to the firm's shareholders.

The Basics of Financial Leverage: We discuss the impact of leverage on shareholders in terms of the effect on earnings per share (EPS) and return on equity (ROE). For now, we will ignore the impact of taxes.

An Example: W. Reed & Company is an all-equity firm with 20,000 shares of common stock outstanding. The market value per share is $25, so the firm's market value ($25 × 20,000) = $500,000. The CFO has proposed to issue $300,000 of debt in order to repurchase ($300,000/$25) = 12,000 shares of the firm's outstanding stock. The interest rate on the debt is 10%. The restructuring would leave (20,000 – 12,000) = 8,000 shares outstanding. The current and proposed capital structures are summarized in the following table:

	Current	Proposed
Assets	$500,000	$500,000
Debt	0	300,000
Equity	500,000	200,000
Debt/equity ratio	0.0	1.5
Share price	$25	$25
Shares outstanding	20,000	8,000
Interest rate		10%

The following table illustrates the impact of the restructuring on ROE and EPS under each of three alternative scenarios (i.e., recession, expected, and expansion):

Current capital structure: No debt			
	Recession	Expected	Expansion
EBIT	$40,000	$60,000	$100,000
Interest	0	0	0
Net income	$40,000	$60,000	$100,000
ROE	8.00%	12.00%	20.00%
EPS	$2.00	$3.00	$5.00

Proposed capital structure: Debt = $300,000			
	Recession	Expected	Expansion
EBIT	$40,000	$60,000	$100,000
Interest	30,000	30,000	30,000
Net income	$10,000	$30,000	$70,000
ROE	5.00%	15.00%	35.00%
EPS	$1.25	$3.75	$8.75

Since the current capital structure of Reed & Company is 100% equity, the net income is the same as earnings before interest and taxes (EBIT) for each of the three possible scenarios. ROE is equal to net income divided by total equity. For example, ROE in a recession would be ($40,000/$500,000) = .08 = 8%. EPS is equal to net income divided by the number of shares outstanding. In a recession, EPS would be ($40,000/20,000) = $2.00.

For the proposed capital structure, interest is (.10 × $300,000) = $30,000, so net income is $30,000 less for each scenario than it would be with the current capital structure. In a recession: ROE = $10,000/$200,000 = .05 = 5%. EPS = $10,000/8,000 = $1.25

Notice that, for each capital structure, both ROE and EPS change as EBIT changes. For the expected EBIT, both ROE and EPS are higher under the proposed plan. However, in the event of a recession, ROE and EPS are lower under the proposed structure. The reverse is true for an economic expansion.

In general, leverage has a beneficial impact on shareholders when EBIT is high and a detrimental impact when EBIT is low. This is due to the fixed interest cost associated with debt financing. When EBIT is low, the fixed obligation to creditors consumes a substantial portion of the firm's earnings, so the return to shareholders is relatively low. However, at higher levels of EBIT, the return to creditors remains constant, while the shareholders derive a proportionately larger benefit from the increased earnings. Financial leverage magnifies both the benefits and the losses to shareholders. In other words, the variability in returns to shareholders increases with increases in financial leverage.

Degree of Financial Leverage: Financial leverage measures how much earnings per share respond to changes in EBIT. Financial leverage is an extension of our discussion of operating leverage in Chapter 2. The *degree of financial leverage* (DFL) can be computed with the following formula:

$$\text{DFL} = \frac{\text{Percentage change in EPS}}{\text{Percentage change in EBIT}}$$

If there is debt in the capital structure, the DFL varies for different ranges of EPS and EBIT. For example, given the current capital structure, the DFL for Reed & Company for each possible EBIT will be:

EBIT = $40,000: $\quad \text{DFL} = \dfrac{(\$3.00 - \$2.00) / \$2.00}{(\$60,000 - \$40,000) / \$40,000} = \dfrac{0.50}{0.50} = 1.0$

EBIT = $60,000: $\quad \text{DFL} = \dfrac{(\$5.00 - \$3.00) / \$3.00}{(\$100,000 - \$60,000) / \$60,000} = \dfrac{0.67}{0.67} = 1.0$

Because there is no debt in the capital structure, the DFL is the same regardless of the level of EBIT. However, for the *proposed* capital structure, the DFL changes as EBIT increases from $40,000 to $60,000:

EBIT = $40,000: $\quad \text{DFL} = \dfrac{(\$3.75 - \$1.25) / \$1.25}{(\$60,000 - \$40,000) / \$40,000} = \dfrac{2.0}{0.5} = 4.0$

EBIT = $60,000: $\quad \text{DFL} = \dfrac{(\$8.75 - \$3.75) / \$3.75}{(\$100,000 - \$60,000) / \$60,000} = \dfrac{1.33}{0.67} = 2.0$

The following formula may also be used to calculate DFL:

$$\text{DFL} = \frac{\text{EBIT}}{\text{EBIT} - \text{Interest}}$$

Recalculating the DFL for the proposed capital structure and EBIT of $40,000 and $60,000, you see that the results are the same using either equation.

$$\text{DFL}_{\$40,000} = \frac{\$40,000}{\$40,000 - \$30,000} = 4.0 \qquad \text{DFL}_{\$60,000} = \frac{\$60,000}{\$60,000 - \$30,000} = 2.0$$

The importance of calculating DFL is apparent when this result is used in the context of changes in EBIT and net income. For example, under the proposed capital structure, the EBIT increased by 67 % (from $60,000 to $100,000). Since the DFL at EBIT of $60,000 is 2.0 we can conclude that Net Income will increase by 134 % (67% × 2). This means that ROE and EPS will also increase by 134 %. In other words, given a DFL, the analyst can predict the impact on net income (magnification or demagnification), given his forecast of changes in EBIT. If EBIT were to decrease by a given percentage, net income would decrease by that given percentage times the DFL factor.

Indifference EBIT: The results for Reed & Company imply that, at some level of EBIT between $40,000 and $60,000, EPS will be the same for either capital structure. We can determine the Indifference EBIT (the level of EBIT at which EPS is the same). For the current capital structure, EPS is equal to (EBIT - $0) / 20,000. For the proposed capital structure, EPS is equal to (EBIT – $30,000) / 8,000. The indifference EBIT is found by equating these two expressions and solving for EBIT:

$$\frac{(EBIT - \$0)}{20,000} = \frac{(EBIT - \$30,000)}{8,000}$$

$$8,000 \times EBIT = 20,000 \times EBIT - \$600,000,000$$

$$-12,000 \times EBIT = -\$600,000,000$$

$$EBIT = \$50,000$$

When EBIT is $50,000,   EPS is equal to $2.50 for either capital structure. The implication of the result can be seen from the graph below.

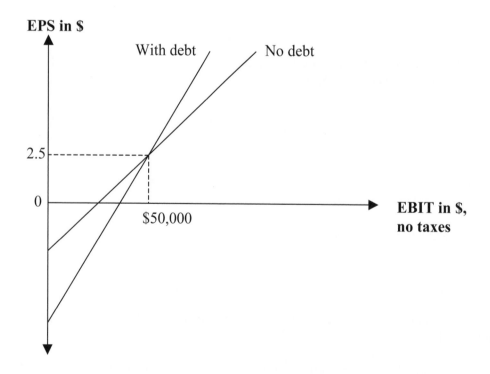

Clearly, if the analyst is forecasting higher levels of EBIT (above $50,000), this favours debt financing since EPS will be increased.

Corporate Borrowing and Homemade Leverage: The discussion above seems to suggest that the firm's capital structure is important to the shareholders. However, in a world of perfect capital markets, this conclusion is incorrect. Shareholders can adjust the amount of leverage in their position by borrowing or lending on their own, thereby creating *homemade leverage*. In these situations, investors are indifferent to the firm's choice of capital structure because their total wealth is unchanged.

An Example: Using Reed & Company again, assume that an investor owns 100 shares of stock. The table below shows the investor's financial position if the firm adopts the proposed capital structure. The next table shows that the investor can create homemade leverage by borrowing and purchasing additional shares, thus achieving the same level of wealth even if the firm does not adopt the proposed plan.

	Proposed	capital	structure
	Recession	Expected	Expansion
EPS	$ 1.25	$ 3.75	$ 8.75
Total earnings (100 shares)	125.00	375.00	875.00

Net cost   =   (100 x $25)   = $2,500.00

	Original capital structure and homemade leverage		
	Recession	Expected	Expansion
EPS	$ 2.00	$ 3.00	$ 5.00
Earnings for 250 shares	500.00	750.00	1,250.00
Less interest ($3,750 @ 10%)	375.00	375.00	375.00
Net earnings	$ 125.00	$375.00	$ 875.00

Net cost   =   (250 x $25) - Amount borrowed   = $6,250 - $3,750 = $2,500

The homemade leverage in the second section exactly duplicates the leverage of the Reed & Company roposed capital structure. The proposed capital structure has a debt/equity ratio of ($3,750 / $2,500) = 1.50. The shareholder can create the same financial leverage by *borrowing* an amount equal to 1.50 times the equity in the 100 share position, and investing this amount in additional shares. That is, borrow (1.50 × $2,500) = $3,750 and then purchase ($3,750/$25) = 150 additional shares of stock. The total number of shares owned is then (100 + 150) = 250 shares. In the event of a recession, for example, the shareholder's total earnings on this position would be ($2.00 × 250) = $500, and the total interest paid would be (.10 × $3,750) = $375. The net earnings would then be ($500 – $375) = $125, the same as the total earnings under the proposed capital structure.

If the firm adopts the proposed capital structure, a shareholder who prefers less leverage can *unlever* the position by *lending* an amount sufficient to duplicate the earnings the shareholder would receive under the original capital structure. The table below demonstrates that these earnings could be duplicated if the shareholder were to sell 60 shares, for a total of ($25 × 60) = $1,500, and then lend this $1,500 at a 10% interest rate.

	Original capital structure		
	Recession	Expected	Expansion
EPS	$ 2.00	$ 3.00	$ 5.00
Total earnings(100 shares)	$ 200.00	$300.00	$500.00

Net cost   =   (100 x $25)   = $2,500.00

	Proposed	capital	structure	and	homemade
	leverage	Recession	Expected		Expansion
EPS	$ 1.25		$ 3.75		$ 8.75
Earnings for 40 shares	50.00		150.00		350.00
Plus interest ($1,500 @ 10%)	150.00		150.00		150.00
Net earnings	$ 200.00		$300.00		$ 500.00

Net cost   =   (40 x $25) + Amount loaned   = $1,000   + $1,500   = $2,500

Thus, an investor is indifferent to the capital structure decisions of the firm since the shareholder can duplicate the preferred capital structure, regardless of the firm's actual capital structure, by borrowing or lending.

16.3 CAPITAL STRUCTURE AND THE COST OF EQUITY CAPITAL

The discussion above indicates that, under certain circumstances, the price of a firm's common stock is not dependent on the firm's capital structure. This conclusion was initially derived by Modigliani and Miller (M&M) in 1958. We refer to this result as **M&M Proposition I.** Their derivation of this result is based on the following two assumptions: first, there are no taxes; and second, investors can borrow on their own account at the same rate that the firm pays on its debt.

M&M Proposition I - The Pie Model: Recall that the market value of a firm (V) is equal to the sum of the equity value (E) and the debt value (D). The value of the firm can be viewed as a pie, and the firm's capital structure is represented by the way in which the pie is sliced; this is referred to as the pie model. The slices of the pie are the equity and debt portions. M&M Proposition I states that the size of the pie is not affected by the manner in which the pie is sliced. That is, the total value of the firm's assets is not affected by the manner in which the financing is obtained. It is the assets of a firm that generate cash flow and determine the firm's value. The firm's capital structure is simply a way of packaging those cash flows and selling them in financial markets.

Proposition I is expressed in the following formula:

$$V_u   =   EBIT / R_e^u   =   V_L   =   E_L + D_L$$

where: V_u =   Value of the unlevered firm
$\quad\quad\quad V_L$ =   Value of the levered firm
$\quad\quad\quad EBIT$ =   Perpetual operating income
$\quad\quad\quad R_e^u$ =   Equity required return for the unlevered firm
$\quad\quad\quad E_L$ =   Market value of equity for a levered firm
$\quad\quad\quad D_L$ =   Market value of debt for a levered firm

An Example: AA International is an all-equity firm that generates EBIT of $3 million per year. The required rate of return, R_E^u, is 15 %. If Proposition I holds, how would the market value of AA International change if it issued $4 million in debt, using the proceeds to retire equity?

Currently the market value of the firm is equal to the market value of equity, since there is no debt: $V_u = \$3,000,000 /$ .15 = $20,000,000. According to Proposition I, the value of AA would remain the same since $V_u = V_L$. In other words, V_L would be the sum of E_L and D_L ($16,000,000 + $4,000,000 = $20,000,000). Note that, because the market value of the firm doesn't change, the equity value drops by $4,000,000 to $16,000,000.

The Cost of Equity and Financial Leverage - M&M Proposition II: M&M Proposition II addresses the relationship between the firm's debt/equity ratio (i.e., the capital structure) and the firm's cost of equity capital. Specifically, M&M Proposition II establishes a positive relationship between leverage and the expected return on equity. That is, the risk (and the cost) of a firm's equity increases as the degree of leverage increases.

The equation for the weighted average cost of capital (WACC) is below. Also, because the WACC represents the firm's required return on its overall assets, we can replace the WACC in the equation with R_A, the return on assets.

$$WACC = R_A = (E/V) \times R_E + (D/V) \times R_D$$

Solving for the return on equity (R_E), we have:

$$R_E = R_A + (R_A - R_D) \times (D/E)$$

This relationship indicates that the required return on equity is a linear function of the firm's debt/equity ratio. We know from Proposition I that the value of the firm is not affected by changes in the debt/equity ratio, so that it must also be true that the firm's overall cost of capital R_A does not change with changes in the firm's financial structure. Also, if R_A is greater than R_D, the R_E increases with the debt/equity ratio. Intuitively, this last conclusion results from the fact that additional debt increases the risk of the firm's equity, and consequently increases the required return on equity.

M&M Proposition II states that the cost of equity is given by a straight line with a slope of ($R_A - R_D$) and a y-intercept of R_A. The y-intercept indicates that $R_E = R_A$ for a firm with no debt (i.e., for a firm with D/E = 0). As the debt/equity ratio (D/E) increases, the cost of equity (R_E) rises in a linear fashion, but the increased cost of equity is exactly offset by the increased use of cheaper debt. The overall cost of capital (R_A) is the same regardless of the value of the debt/equity ratio. Since R_A never changes, and the firm's cash flows are constant, the value of the firm is unaffected by changes in the capital structure.

An Example: Reconsider AA International by assuming that the new issue of debt could cost the firm 8 %. What is the required equity return for the levered firm and its overall weighted average cost of capital?

The debt to equity ratio is 25 % ($4,000,000 / $16,000,000). Using Proposition II, the equity required return for the levered firm is $R_E = 15\% + [(15\% - 8\%) \times (.25)] = 16.75\%$. The weighted average cost of capital will remain unchanged at 15%:

$$WACC = R_A = .1675 \times (.80) + .08 \times (.20) = 0.15 = 15\%$$

WACC does not change because the use of cheaper debt is exactly offset by the increase in the cost of equity.

Business and Financial Risk: Combining the results of Proposition II and the SML (used earlier to estimate the cost of equity), we can rewrite the required return on the firm's assets as: $R_A = R_f + (R_M - R_f) \times \beta_A$.

The beta coefficient here, β_A is called the *asset* beta as it measures the systematic risk of the firm's assets. If we combine the above equation with the cost of equity from the SML, $R_E = R_f + (R_M - R_f) \beta_E$, we can write the relationship between the equity beta, β_E, and the asset beta, β_A: $\beta_E = \beta_A \times (1 + D/E)$.

The term $(1 + D/E)$ is the same as the equity multiplier in chapter 3. Here, though, it is measured in market, instead of book values. The result is that the risk premium for the firm's equity is equal to the risk premium on the firm's assets times the equity multiplier. The real insight of this equation appears when it is rewritten in the following manner: $\beta_E = \beta_A + \beta_A \times (D/E)$.

The first component, β_A, is a measure of the riskiness of the firm's assets. In other words, it measures the *business risk* of the firm. The second component, $\beta_A \times (D/E)$ depends upon the firm's financial policy or the *financial risk* of the equity.

Therefore, the total systematic risk of the firm's equity has two parts; business risk and financial risk. As we saw earlier, the cost of equity rises when the firm increases its use of financial leverage (debt) because the financial risk of the stock increases.

16.4 M&M PROPOSITIONS I & II WITH CORPORATE TAXES

The conclusions of the previous section are derived under a set of fairly unrealistic assumptions. In addition, the conclusion that the debt-equity ratio does not affect value cannot explain the fact that debt-equity ratios seem to vary with industry characteristics. These observations make it necessary to assess the validity of the M&M conclusions under a more realistic set of assumptions. Specifically, we consider how the introduction of corporate taxes affects the M&M propositions.

Remember that interest payments on debt are tax deductible. Therefore, if corporate income is taxed, the *tax subsidy* for debt increases the attractiveness of debt in the firm's capital structure.

An Example: Two firms, Firm U and Firm L, both have earnings before interest and taxes (EBIT) of $1,000 in perpetuity. Firm L has issued perpetual bonds in the amount of $500 on which it pays 12% interest, and the corporate tax rate is 30%. Firm U has 100% equity. We can summarize this information as follows:

	Firm U	Firm L
EBIT	$1,000	$1,000
Interest	0	60
Taxable income	$1,000	$ 940
Taxes (30%)	300	282
Net income	$ 700	$ 658

The Interest Tax Shield: Since depreciation, capital spending and changes in net working capital are all zero, the cash flow from each firm's assets is equal to (EBIT – Taxes), as indicated in the following table:

Cash flow from assets	Firm U	Firm L
EBIT	$1,000	$1,000
- Taxes	300	282
Total	$ 700	$ 718

We can now compute the total cash flow to both shareholders and bondholders:

Cash flow	Firm U	Firm L
To shareholders	$ 700	$ 658
To bondholders	0	60
Total	$ 700	$ 718

The total cash flow for Firm L is $18 greater than the cash flow for Firm U. This occurs because Firm L's tax bill, which is a cash outflow, is $18 less. The interest expense has generated a tax saving equal to the interest payment ($60) multiplied by the corporate tax rate (30%). This tax saving is called the *interest tax shield*.

Taxes and M&M Proposition I: Since the debt is perpetual, this same interest tax shield will be generated every year forever. The after-tax cash flow to Firm L will be the same $700 that accrues to Firm U, plus the $18 tax shield. Because the tax shield is generated by paying interest, it has the same risk as the firm's debt, so that 12% is the appropriate discount rate for valuing the tax shield. The value of the tax shield is thus:

$$PV(\text{tax shield}) = \$18 / .12 = (.30 \times .12 \times \$500) / .12 = \$150$$

In general, the value of the interest tax shield is computed as: Tax shield $= T_C \times D$.

The after-tax cash flow to the shareholders of the unlevered firm is $[EBIT \times (1 - T_C)]$. If we assume that all cash flows are perpetual and constant, then the value of the unlevered firm is:

$$V_U = \frac{EBIT(1 - T_C)}{\rho}$$

where ρ is the unlevered cost of capital. This means that ρ is the cost of capital the firm would have if it had no debt.

Suppose that the cost of capital for Firm U is 20% (i.e., $\rho = 20\%$). The value of Firm U is:

$$V_U = \frac{\$1,000 (1 - .30)}{.20} = \$3,500$$

M&M Proposition I (with corporate taxes) states that the value of a levered firm, V_L, is equal to the value of the unlevered firm plus the value of the interest tax shield:

$$V_L = V_U + (T_C \times D)$$

For Firm L: $V_L = \$3,500 + \$150 = \$3,650$

These results demonstrate that, in a world with corporate taxes, the firm has an incentive to increase its debt/equity ratio. A higher debt/equity ratio lowers taxes and increases the total value of the firm. In fact, the above results indicate that a firm should move as close as possible to an all-debt capital structure. Clearly, this conclusion is inconsistent with reality, since firms do not choose capital structures which are virtually all debt. It is important to keep in mind here that this conclusion is derived under the assumption that there are no bankruptcy costs. These are discussed later in the chapter.

Taxes, the WACC, and Proposition II: M&M demonstrates that, in a world with corporate taxes, the following equation describes the relationship between the debt/equity ratio and the cost of equity capital:

$$R_E = \rho + (\rho - R_D) \times (D / E) \times (1 - T_C)$$

This result is known as M&M Proposition II (with corporate taxes). It indicates a positive relationship between expected return on equity and the debt-equity ratio. It also implies that the firm's overall cost of capital decreases as the amount of debt increases, which leads to the conclusion that a capital structure of 100% debt is optimal. This is the same conclusion implied by M&M Proposition I (with corporate taxes). Note that, again, the cost of equity is a linear function of the firm's debt/equity ratio.

An Example: We can use this equation to compute the WACC for Firm L in the above example.

Since $V_L = \$3,650$, and the firm's debt has a value of $D = \$500$, the equity for Firm L has a value of $E = (\$3,650 - \$500) = \$3,150$. The cost of equity for Firm L is:

$$R_E = .20 + (.20 - .12) \times (\$500 / \$3,150) \times (1 - .30) = .20889 = 20.889\%$$

The weighted average cost of capital is:

$$WACC = (\$3,150 / \$3,650) \times .20889 + (\$500 / \$3,650) \times .12 \times (1 - .30) = .1918 = 19.18\%$$

The weighted average cost of capital for an unlevered firm is 20% (i.e., $WACC = \rho = 20\%$), while the WACC for Firm L is 19.18%. Since the cash flows are the same for the two firms, the firm with the lower WACC (Firm L) has the greater value.

16.5 BANKRUPTCY COSTS

The M&M Propositions (with taxes) state that a firm can increase its value by increasing leverage. This implies that firms should be financed largely by debt. Most firms, though, are not highly leveraged. In part, the explanation for this discrepancy lies in the fact that we have ignored the cost of bankruptcy, which increases with the firm's level of debt. The impact of bankruptcy costs is discussed below.

The obligation to pay principal and interest on debt puts pressure on the firm since failure to meet the obligation results in *financial distress*. The ultimate financial distress is bankruptcy, in which case ownership of the firm's assets is transferred to the bondholders. Costs of financial distress offset the advantages of debt under certain circumstances.

Direct Bankruptcy Costs: Economically, bankruptcy occurs when the value of a firm's assets is equal to or less than the value of its debt. Legally, though, bankruptcy occurs when the firm's assets are turned over to the firm's bondholders. This process involves significant expenses, referred to as *direct bankruptcy costs*, which include attorneys' fees, administrative and accounting fees, and, in the event of a trial, fees to expert witnesses. These costs represent a disadvantage to debt financing, which, to some extent, offsets the advantage of tax-deductibility of interest.

Indirect Bankruptcy Costs: Bankruptcy often results in an impaired ability to conduct business. Customers may question the ability of the firm to provide service subsequent to a purchase, and are consequently less likely to buy from a firm in bankruptcy. Although these costs are difficult to estimate, they are generally thought to be much greater than the direct costs cited above.

Agency Costs of Equity: Bankruptcy costs are agency costs of debt that increase as financial leverage increases. Agency costs of equity can result from shirking by owner-managers and can work in the opposite manner. The implication here is that, when the firm issues equity, the owner-entrepreneur's stake is diluted, with the effect that the entrepreneur works shorter hours and consumes more perquisites (a big office, company car, larger expense account, etc.) than if the firm issues debt.

16.6 OPTIMAL CAPITAL STRUCTURE

Financial distress costs are insignificant for a firm with little or no debt. If the firm adds a small amount of debt to its capital structure, it derives the benefit of the tax shield on debt without incurring significant costs of financial distress. As a firm uses more and more debt, however, the tax savings are eventually offset by the increased likelihood that financial distress costs will be incurred. Conceivably, there exists a point where these two factors exactly offset each other, and the value of the firm is maximized.

The *static theory of capital structure* states that a firm uses additional debt financing in its capital structure up to the point where the tax benefit derived from an additional dollar of debt exactly offsets the cost associated with an increased likelihood of financial distress. An optimum (or target) capital structure exists when the benefit of another dollar in debt is exactly balanced by the increased likelihood of financial distress.

The graph below demonstrates this discussion in terms of the value of the firm. If we begin with no debt, the value of the firm increases as debt is added. The incremental gains from additional debt begin diminishing, however, because of the increased likelihood of financial distress. An optimal capital structure occurs when the present value of the tax saving from an additional dollar of debt (the marginal benefit of leverage) equals the increase in the present value of expected bankruptcy costs (the marginal cost of leverage). At this point, the value of the firm is maximized.

Two qualitative conclusions are derived from this analysis: firms with higher tax rates should borrow more, and firms with higher risks of financial distress (perhaps those with higher operating risks) should borrow less.

16.7 THE PIE AGAIN

We initially viewed the value of the firm as being equal to the value of the stock plus the value of the debt. A way of reconciling much of the discussion in this chapter is to recognize that the pie representing the firm is actually comprised of much more than just the debt and equity portions. For example, the government takes a substantial slice in the form of taxes. In the event of bankruptcy, many other parties will take a slice. Therefore, many different types of claims on the firm's cash flow may exist at any time.

All the claims to the firm's cash flow can nonetheless be divided into two groups. The debt and equity are the *marketed claims* and the rest are *nonmarketed claims*. When we speak of the capital structure issue, we are really investigating whether the total value of the marketed claims can be increased by decreasing the size of the nonmarketed claims. For example, the interest tax shield increases the size of the marketed claims by decreasing the size of the nonmarketed government claim. It is important to keep in mind that the size of the pie is constant when we include all the claims. The issue under consideration is how the cash flow from operations is paid out. The optimum capital structure minimizes the 'nibbling' by those who hold nonmarketed claims.

16.8 OBSERVED CAPITAL STRUCTURES

The results of this chapter do not provide an exact formula for evaluating the relationship between leverage and firm value. So, it is important to also consider evidence from the real world in establishing capital structure policy.

There are certain observed regularities in corporate capital structures which indicate that the firm's choice of capital structure does matter. First, most firms do not use a great deal of debt, and many of these firms pay substantial taxes. There appears to be a limit on the ability of firms to exploit the interest tax shield. Second, firms in similar industries tend to have similar capital structures, but capital structures appear to vary widely across industries. This fact suggests that capital structure is influenced by the nature of a firm's assets.

16.9 LONG-TERM FINANCING UNDER FINANCIAL DISTRESS AND BANKRUPTCY

One of the disadvantages of the use of debt is the possibility of financial distress. Financial distress includes:

1. *Business failure* is the termination of a business, resulting in a loss to the firm's creditors.
2. *Legal bankruptcy* is a legal proceeding resulting in the liquidation or reorganization of the firm.
3. *Technical insolvency* results from a firm's default on a legal obligation to pay a debt.
4. *Accounting insolvency* occurs when the firm's liabilities exceed the firm's assets, so the firm's net worth is negative.

Liquidation and Reorganization: Liquidation and reorganization are the two possible outcomes of a legal bankruptcy. *Liquidation* is the termination of a firm, following a bankruptcy proceeding. The firm's assets are sold and the proceeds of the sale are distributed to those who have claims against the firm, including employees, consumers, governments, creditors and shareholders. *Reorganization* is a plan that allows the firm to continue to operate, but generally requires a restructuring of the firm's debts. The restructuring includes some payments to creditors and shareholders, and often includes the issuing of new securities to replace existing securities.

APPENDIX 16A: CAPITAL STRUCTURE AND PERSONAL TAXES

Earlier we saw that the value of a levered firm equals the value of an identical unlevered firm, V_u, plus the present value of the interest tax shield, $T_C \times D$. The following equation represents the value of a levered firm taking into account personal as well as corporate taxes.

$$V_L \;=\; V_U \;+\; 1 \;-\; \frac{(1 - T_C)\,(1 - T_S)}{(1 - T_b)} \; \times \; D$$

where T_b = personal tax rate on ordinary income, such as interest

T_S = personal tax rate on equity distributions – dividends and capital gains

Note that, if T_b and T_s are equal, the above equation simplifies to the case when there are no personal taxes:

$$V_L = V_u + T_C \times D$$

This means that personal taxes do not affect our valuation formula as long as equity distributions are taxed identically to interest at the personal level. However, the gain from leverage is reduced when equity distributions are taxed more lightly than interest (i.e., when T_s is less than T_b). In other words, more taxes are paid at the personal level for a levered firm than for an unlevered firm. The reason why there is no gain from leverage is that the lower corporate taxes for a levered firm are *exactly* offset by higher personal taxes.

An Example: Black, Inc. expects a perpetual pre-tax earning stream of $500,000 and faces a 46 % corporate tax rate. Investors discount the earnings stream after corporate taxes at 14 %. The personal tax rate on equity distributions is 25 % and the personal tax rate on interest is 48 %. Black has an all equity capital structure but is considering borrowing $250,000 at 8 %. What is the advantage of leveraging if personal taxes are considered and if personal taxes are ignored?

The value of the all equity firm is:

$$V_U = \frac{\$500{,}000 \times (1 - .46)}{.14} = \$1{,}928{,}571.43$$

The value of the levered firm, after considering personal taxes, is:

$$V_L = \$1{,}928{,}571.43 + 1 - \frac{(1 - .46)(1 - .25)}{(1 - .48)} \times \$250{,}000 = \$1{,}983{,}859.89$$

If there are no personal taxes, the value of the levered firm is:

$$V_L = \$1{,}928{,}571.43 + .46 \times \$250{,}000 = \$2{,}043{,}571.43$$

Therefore, the advantage of leverage with personal taxes ($55,288.46) is less than with no personal taxes ($115,000).

CONCEPT TEST

1. In making capital structure decisions, the firm considers whether or not the way it _____ its assets makes any economic difference. That is, we are focusing only on the issue of how a firm _____ a given collection of _____.

2. Shareholders benefit from a financial restructuring only if _____. This occurs because any increase in the value of the firm as a result of restructuring accrues to the _____. Consequently, maximizing the value of the shareholders' position is equivalent to maximizing the _____.

3. The value of a firm is the _____ of the firm's cash flows discounted at the _____. The capital structure which maximizes the value of the firm is the capital structure which minimizes the _____.

4. Financial leverage is the extent to which a firm uses _____ financing. Leverage has a beneficial impact on stockholders when EBIT is (high/low) and a detrimental impact when EBIT is (high/low). It is said that financial leverage _____ both the benefits and the losses to shareholders. The variability in the return to shareholders is (greater/less) for a firm that uses debt financing than for an all-equity firm. The variability in returns to shareholders (increases/decreases) with increases in financial leverage.

5. In a world of perfect capital markets, the firm's capital structure (is/is not) important to the shareholders. Shareholders can adjust the amount of leverage in their position by _____ or _____ on their own, thereby creating _____. A shareholder who prefers a capital structure with more leverage than that which the firm has adopted can duplicate the preferred capital structure by _____ an amount sufficient to create a personal debt/equity ratio equal to that of the preferred capital structure. A shareholder who prefers a capital structure with less leverage than that which the firm has adopted can duplicate the preferred capital structure by _____ an amount sufficient to create a personal debt/equity ratio equal to that of the preferred capital structure.

6. Under the above circumstances, the price of a firm's common stock (is/is not) dependent on the firm's capital structure. This conclusion is referred to as _____. This result is based on the following two assumptions: first, _____; and, second, investors can borrow on their own account at the _____.

7. According to the pie model, the value of the firm can be viewed as a pie, and the firm's capital structure is represented by _____. M&M Proposition I states that the size of the pie is not affected by the manner in which the pie is sliced; that is, the total value of the firm's assets is not affected by the manner in which _____. The firm's cash flow is generated by its _____; the firm's capital structure is a way of packaging those cash flows and selling them in financial markets.

8. Proposition I is expressed in the following formula, where V_u = _____ and V_L = _____.

9. M&M Proposition II addresses the relationship between the firm's debt/equity ratio and the firm's _____. M&M Proposition II establishes a positive relationship between leverage and the _____.

10. M&M Proposition II (no taxes) is stated algebraically as: R_E = _____ . This relationship indicates that the required return on equity is a linear function of the _____. M&M Proposition II states that the cost of equity is given by a straight line with a slope of _____ and a y-intercept of _____. The y-intercept indicates that, for a firm with no debt, R_E = _____ .

11. As the debt/equity ratio increases, the cost of equity rises in a _____ fashion, but the increased cost of equity is exactly offset by the _____. As a result, the overall cost of capital (does/does not) change as the debt/equity ratio changes. Therefore, the value of the firm (is/is not) affected by changes in the capital structure.

12. A primary difference between debt and equity is that interest (is/is not) tax-deductible, whereas dividends (are/are not) tax deductible. The tax subsidy on interest (increases/decreases) the attractiveness of debt. The capital structure (does/does not) have an impact on the firm's cash flows. The interest expense on debt generates a tax saving equal to the _____ multiplied by the _____. This tax saving is called the _____, and its value is computed in either of the following alternative ways: _____ = _____ .

13. The after-tax cash flow to the shareholders of an unlevered firm is equal to _____ × _____. If we assume that all cash flows are perpetual and constant, then the value of an unlevered firm is: V_U = _____ .

14. M&M Proposition I (with corporate taxes) states that the value of a levered firm, V_L, is equal to the value of the _____ plus the value of the _____: V_L = _____ . These results demonstrate that, in a world with corporate taxes, the firm has an incentive to (increase/decrease) its debt/equity ratio. A higher debt/equity ratio (increases/decreases) taxes and (increases/decreases) the total value of the firm. In fact, the above results indicate that a firm should move as close as possible to _____. This conclusion is derived under the assumption that there are no _____.

15. M&M Proposition II (with corporate taxes) describes the relationship between the debt/equity ratio and the cost of equity capital as: R_E = _____ . It indicates a positive relationship between expected return on equity and the _____. It also implies that the firm's overall cost of capital (increases/decreases) as the amount of debt increases.

16. The M&M Propositions (with taxes) state that a firm can increase its value by (increasing / decreasing) leverage. However, these propositions ignore the cost of _____, which (increases / decreases) with increases in the firm's level of debt.

17. When we combine the SML and Proposition II, the relationship between the equity beta, β_E, and the asset beta, β_A is: _____ . This can be rewritten as: _____ .

18. β_A is a measure of the riskiness of the firm's assets, as it measures the _____ of the firm. $\beta_A \times (D/E)$ measures the _____ of the firm's equity.

19. The ultimate financial distress is _____, in which case ownership of the firm's assets is transferred to the _____. The legal interpretation of bankruptcy is the process whereby the firm's assets are turned over to the firm's _____. This process involves significant expenses, referred to as _____, which include attorneys' fees, administrative and accounting fees, and, in the event of a trial, fees to expert witnesses. Bankruptcy often results in an impaired ability to conduct business; costs associated with this impaired ability are referred to as _____.

20. The _____ theory of capital structure states that a firm uses additional debt financing up to the point where the _____ benefit derived from an additional dollar of debt exactly offsets the cost associated with an increased likelihood of _____. The _____ capital structure occurs when the present value of the tax savings from an additional dollar of debt equals the increase in the present value of expected bankruptcy costs; at this point, the value of the firm is _____.

21. A large number of different types of claims to the firm's cash flow may exist at any time. All the claims to the firm's cash flow can nonetheless be divided into two groups; the debt and equity are the _____ claims and the rest are _____ claims. The capital structure issue is really the question of whether the total value of the _____ claims can be increased by decreasing the size of the _____ claims.

22. The value of the levered firm taking into account personal taxes is: _____ . However, if T_b and T_s are equal, then the value of the levered firm is: _____ .

23. The reason why there may be no gain from leverage is that the lower corporate taxes for a levered firm are exactly offset by higher _____ .

24. It is important to consider evidence from the real world in establishing capital structure policy. Most firms (do/do not) use a great deal of debt; there would appear to be limits on the ability of firms to exploit the _____. Firms in similar industries (do/do not) tend to have similar capital structures, while capital structures (do/do not) vary widely across industries. This fact suggests that capital structure is influenced by the nature of a firm's _____.

25. _____ is the termination of a business which results in a loss to the firm's creditors. ____is a legal proceeding which results in the liquidation or reorganization of the firm.

26. _____ results from a firm's default on a legal obligation to pay a debt. _____ is a condition in which the firm's liabilities exceed the firm's assets, so that the firm's net worth is negative.

27. _____ is the termination of a firm, following a bankruptcy proceeding. The firm's assets are sold and the proceeds of the sale are distributed to those with claims against the firm. _____ is a plan that allows the firm to continue to operate, but generally requires a restructuring of the firm's debts.

28. Financial distress costs are the _____ and _____ costs associated with going bankrupt and/or avoiding a _____. Types of financial distress include _____ failure, legal bankruptcy, and technical or accounting _____.

PROBLEMS

Problem 1

Vancom Corporation is an all-equity firm with 10,000 shares of stock outstanding. The market value per share is $20, making the market value of the company 10,000 x $20 = $200,000. The CFO is recommending issuing $80,000 of debt in order to repurchase ($80,000 / $20) = 4,000 shares of the firm's outstanding stock. The interest rate on debt is 15%. Given the different EBIT scenarios for Vancom Company below, calculate net income, ROE, and EPS with its current capital structure and under the CFO's proposal.

	Scenario		
	Recession	Expected	Unexpected
EBIT	$25,00	$50,000	$75,000

Problem 2

Given the above findings, use the DFL to determine the Indifference EBIT for Vancom Company.

Use the information below to solve Problems 3 through 11:

Maxlever and Nolever are identical firms in all ways except that Maxlever employs debt in its capital structure and Nolever does not. Earnings before interest and taxes (EBIT) for each firm are expected to be $10,000. The total value of equity is $40,000 for Maxlever and $80,000 for Nolever. Maxlever has 1,000 shares outstanding; Nolever has 2,000 shares outstanding. Maxlever's bonds have a market value and a face value of $40,000. The interest rate is 10% and there are no taxes.

Problem 3

Compute earnings per share (EPS), return on equity (ROE) and price per share for Nolever and for Maxlever.

Problem 4

In the event of a recession, both Maxlever and Nolever will have EBIT equal to $5,000. EBIT will be $20,000 in the event of an economic expansion. Compute EPS and ROE for each firm under each of these scenarios.

Problem 5

Compute the level of EBIT such that Maxlever and Nolever have the same earnings per share.

Problem 6

Suppose that an investor purchased 200 shares of Maxlever. Compute the cost of this investment and the earnings for this position under each of the three scenarios described in Problems 1 and 2.

Problem 7

Explain how the investor described in Problem 6 can duplicate the earnings from the investment in Maxlever by borrowing and investing in the shares of Nolever.

Problem 8

Suppose that increased leverage increased the value of the firm, so that the market value of Maxlever is $90,000, while the market value of Nolever remains at $80,000. How would the investor above react to this information?

Problem 9

Suppose that an investor purchased 200 shares of Nolever. Compute the cost of this investment and the earnings for this position under each of the three scenarios described in Problems 1 and 2.

Problem 10

Explain how the investor described in Problem 9 can duplicate the earnings from the investment in Nolever by lending and investing in the shares of Maxlever.

Problem 11

Suppose that increased leverage decreased the value of the firm, so that the market value of Maxlever is $70,000, while the market value of Nolever remains at $80,000. How would the investor described in Problems 7 and 8 react to this information?

Problem 12

Ice King Industries makes artificial snow for use on movie sets. It is an all-equity firm with cash flow of $275,000 per year forever. Its discount rate is 10 %. In a perfect market setting, what is the value of the firm?   What would be the value of an identical, but levered firm?

Problem 13

Now assume Ice King borrows $500,000 to repurchase equity. The cost of debt is 7 %. The firm's asset beta equals one, and the market portfolio returns 10 %. What is the new value of the equity when adjusted for the increased financial risk?

Problem 14

Island Cruises expects pre-tax cash flows of $2 million in perpetuity. The company has no debt. The asset beta of cruise lines is 1.5. Assuming perfect markets with a riskless interest rate of 5 % and a 12 % return on the market index, what is the required return on assets and on equity? If the company has 1 million shares outstanding, what is the value of a single share?

Problem 15

If Ice King (from problems 12 and 13 above) shares traded for $10 each before the capital restructuring, what is the price per share after the firm issues $500,000 in debt?

Problem 16

Assume that you own 2,250 shares or 1 % of Ice King stock after the capital restructuring. Demonstrate that, even if Ice King decides not to restructure, you could use personal leverage to receive the same net cash flows as you now receive.

Problem 17

Show that, for Ice King, both the unlevered company and the new leveraged company have the same weighted average cost of capital.

Use the information below to solve Problems 18 through 21.

The North Company, a major manufacturer of document shredders, has a perpetual expected EBIT of $200. The interest rate for North's debt is 12%.

Problem 18

Assuming that there are no taxes or bankruptcy costs, what is the value of North Company if its debt/equity ratio is .25 and its weighted average cost of capital is 16%? What is the value of North's equity? What is the value of North's debt?

Problem 19

What is the cost of equity capital for North Company?

Problem 20

Suppose the corporate tax rate is 30%, there are no personal taxes or bankruptcy costs, and North has $400 in debt outstanding. If the unlevered cost of equity is 20%, what is the value of North Company? What is the value of the firm's equity?

Problem 21

What is the weighted average cost of capital for North Company?

Problem 22

Coprez Corporation has an EBIT of $400 per year. The interest rate on debt is 10% and Coprez does not pay taxes. If there are no bankruptcy costs and the debt/equity ratio is 0.5, what is the value of Coprez's debt and equity if the WACC is 12%?

Problem 23

What is the cost of equity capital for Coprez Corporation?

Use the following information to solve Problems 24 through 28:

Merrick Motors is an all-equity firm with earnings expected to be $450,000 in perpetuity. The firm has 100,000 shares outstanding. The cost of capital is 15%. MM is considering a major expansion of its facilities which will require an initial outlay of $400,000 and is expected to produce additional annual earnings of $150,000 per year in perpetuity. Management considers the expansion to have the same risk as the firm's existing assets. Assume throughout that there are no taxes and no costs of bankruptcy.

Problem 24

What is the value of the firm's assets prior to undertaking the proposed expansion? What is the value of the firm's equity? What is the price per share of the firm's stock?

Problem 25

Suppose MM plans to finance the expansion by issuing common stock. How many shares of stock must be issued? What is the value of the firm's equity after the new stock issue? What is the price per share of the firm's stock?

Problem 26

Suppose MM plans to finance the expansion by issuing bonds with an interest rate of 10%. What is the value of the firm after the new bond issue? What is the value of the firm's equity? What is the price per share of the firm's stock?

Problem 27

Calculate the expected yearly income after interest for the equityholders. Use the expected yearly income to calculate the expected return for the equityholders.

Problem 28

Use M&M Proposition II (no taxes) to determine the expected return for the equityholders.

Problem 29

Maestro Frozen Foods expects to earn $365,000 in perpetuity before interest and taxes from its line of gourmet TV dinners. The company has a debt to assets ratio of 40 %. The cost of debt is 10 %. If the company had no debt, its cost of capital would have been 15 %. The firm's tax rate is 30 %. What is the value of the firm? The value of its equity? The required rate of return on equity? The weighted average cost of capital?

Problem 30

Now suppose that Maestro decides to issue equity and retire its debt. What will happen to the value of the firm? Assume that, under the current capital structure, there are 100,000 shares outstanding.

Problem 31

Now, using the information for Maestro above, assume that the personal tax rate on equity income is 20 % and the tax rate on interest income is 35 %. How will this affect the value of the company?

Problem 32

David, a financial consultant, is advising Dilettante, Inc. (DI), a 2-year old company in the volatile nanotechnology research industry, regarding optimal capital structure. The CEO of DI chose David as his financial consultant following a recommendation by the CEO of ValleyFlour, Inc. (VFI), a 100-year old company in the non-volatile flour-producing industry. After receiving David's report on optimal capital structure, the CEO of DI immediately e-mailed David. He noted that his company is highly similar to VFI, with similar tax rates, accumulated losses, and tax shields. Why then, he asked in the e-mail, was the level of debt that David suggested DI include in its capital structure so much lower than the level of debt that David had advised VFI to use?

How should David respond?

ANSWERS TO CONCEPT TEST

1. finances; finances; assets

2. the value of the firm increases; shareholders; value of the firm

3. present value; weighted average cost of capital; weighted average cost of capital

4. debt; high; low; magnifies; greater; increases

5. is not; borrowing, lending; homemade leverage; borrowing; lending

6. is not; M&M Proposition I (no taxes); there are no taxes; same rate that the firm pays on its debt

7. the way in which the pie is sliced; financing is obtained; assets

8. $EBIT / R_E^U$; $E_L + D_L$

9. cost of equity capital; expected return on equity

10. $R_A + (R_A - R_D) \times (D/E)$; debt/equity ratio; $(R_A - R_D)$; R_A; R_A

11. linear; increased use of cheaper debt; does not; is not

12. is; are not; increases; does; interest payment; corporate tax rate; interest tax shield; $[(T_C \times R_D \times D)/R_D]$; $(T_C \times D)$

13. EBIT; $(1 - T_C)$; $[EBIT \times (1 - T_C)]/\rho$

14. unlevered firm; interest tax shield; $V_U + (T_C \times D)$; increase; decreases; increases; an all-debt capital structure; bankruptcy costs

15. $\rho + [(\rho - R_D) \times (D/E) \times (1 - T_C)]$; debt/equity ratio; decreases

16. increasing; bankruptcy; increases

17. $\beta_E = \beta_A \times (1 + D/E)$; $\beta_E = \beta_A + \beta_A (D/E)$

18. business risk; financial risk

19. bankruptcy; bondholders; bondholders; direct bankruptcy costs; indirect bankruptcy costs

20.   static; tax; financial distress; optimal; maximized

21.   marketed; nonmarketed; marketed; nonmarketed

22. $V_L = V_U + 1 - \dfrac{(1 - T_C)(1 - T_S)}{(1 - T_b)} \times D$; $V_L = V_u + (T_c \times D)$

23.   personal taxes

24.   do not; interest tax shield; do; do; assets

25.   business failure; legal bankruptcy

26.   technical insolvency; accounting insolvency

27.   liquidation; reorganization

28.   direct, indirect, bankruptcy filing, business, insolvency

PROBLEM SOLUTIONS

Problem 1:

	Current structure: no debt		
	Recession	Expected	Unexpected
EBIT	$25,000	$50,000	$75,000
Interest	0	0	0
Net income	$25,000	$50,000	$75,000
ROE	12.5%	25.0%	37.5%
EPS	$ 2.50	$ 5.00	$ 7.50

	Proposed structure: Debt = $80,000		
	Recession	Expected	Unexpected
EBIT	$25,000	$50,000	$75,000
Interest	12,000	12,000	12,000
Net income	$13,000	$38,000	$63,000
ROE	10.8%	31.7%	52.5%
EPS	$ 2.17	$6.33	$10.50

Problem 2: The Indifference EBIT is determined by equating the two expressions for EPS with all equity, and with debt, and then solving for EBIT:

$$\frac{\text{EBIT} - \$0}{10,000} = \frac{\text{EBIT} - \$12,000}{6,000}$$

$$6,000 \times EBIT = 10,000 \times EBIT - \$120,000,000$$

$$-4,000 \times EBIT = -\$120,000,000$$

$$EBIT = \$30,000$$

At an EBIT of $30,000, EPS is $3.00 for either capital structure For an EBIT below $30,000, Vancom will prefer an all-equity structure, while for any EBIT above $30,000, debt financing will be preferred, because EPS is higher.

Problem 3: For a firm with no debt, net income equals EBIT. Nolever's EPS is ($10,000/2,000) = $5.00. ROE is ($10,000/$80,000) = .125 = 12.5%. The price per share is ($80,000/2,000) = $40.

For Maxlever, net income is EBIT less interest. The firm's interest payment is (.10 × $40,000) = $4,000, and net income is ($10,000 – $4,000) = $6,000. EPS is ($6,000 / 1,000) = $6.00. ROE is ($6,000 / $40,000) = 15%. Price per share is ($40,000 / 1,000) = $40.

Problem 4: The calculations for this problem and the results from Problem 3 are summarized in below:

	Nolever: No debt		
	Recession	Expected	Expansion
EBIT	$ 5,000	$ 10,000	$ 20,000
Interest	0	0	0
Net income	$ 5,000	$ 10,000	$ 20,000
ROE	6.25%	12.50%	25.00%
EPS	$2.50	$5.00	$10.00

	Maxlever: Debt = $40,000		
	Recession	Expected	Expansion
EBIT	$ 5,000	$10,000	$ 20,000
Interest	4,000	4,000	4,000
Net income	$ 1,000	$ 6,000	$ 16,000
ROE	2.50%	15.00%	40.00%
EPS	$1.00	$6.00	$16.00

Problem 5: The level of EBIT such that the two firms have the same earnings per share is the indifference EBIT discussed in the chapter. For Nolever, EPS is (EBIT - $0)/2,000)); for Maxlever, EPS is (EBIT – $4,000)/1,000. Equating these two expressions and solving for EBIT, we find the indifference level of EBIT as follows:

$$\frac{EBIT - \$0}{2,000} = \frac{EBIT - \$4,000}{1,000}$$

$$1,000 \times EBIT = 2,000 \times EBIT - \$8,000,000$$

$$EBIT = \$8,000$$

When EBIT is $8,000, EPS is equal to $4.00 for both Maxlever and Nolever.

Problem 6: The net cost of this investment is ($40 × 200) = $8,000. In the event of a recession, the total earnings for this investment will be ($1.00 × 200) = $200. Earnings for the expected scenario and the recession scenario are $1,200 and $3,200, respectively.

Problem 7: The debt/equity ratio of Maxlever is 1.00. Therefore, the investor must purchase $8,000 of the equity of Nolever, and borrow an amount equal to the equity investment. That is, the investor borrows $8,000 and purchases an additional $8,000 of Nolever common stock. The returns for this position, and for the investment described in Problem 6 are summarized in the following table:

	Maxlever		
	Recession	Expected	Expansion
EPS	$ 1.00	$ 6.00	$ 16.00
Total earnings (200 shares)	200.00	1,200.00	3,200.00

Net cost = (200 x $40) = $8,000.00

	Nolever		
	Recession	Expected	Expansion
EPS	$ 2.50	$ 5.00	$ 10.00
Earnings for 400 shares	1,000.00	2,000.00	4,000.00
Less interest ($8,000 @ 10%)	800.00	800.00	800.00
Net earnings	$ 200.00	$1,200.00	$3,200.00

Net cost = (400 x $40) - Amount borrowed = $16,000 - $8,000 = $8,000

Problem 8: The investor's return is the same for the two strategies in Problems 4 and 5. However, if the market value of Maxlever is $90,000, rather than $80,000, the cost of buying 200 shares of Maxlever is now higher. The market value of equity is now ($90,000 – $40,000) = $50,000; the value of a share is ($50,000/1,000) = $50. The cost of 200 shares of Maxlever is ($50 × 200) = $10,000. The strategy of Problem 5 duplicates the cash flows from 200 shares of Maxlever, but the cost is only $8,000. As a result, a rational investor would pursue the strategy of Problem 5. This would increase the value of Nolever and decrease the value of Maxlever. Prices will adjust until the market values of the two firms are equal. The interpretation of this result is that corporate leverage does not have value to the shareholder, since the same effect can be created with homemade leverage.

Problem 9: The net cost of this investment is ($40 × 200) = $8,000. In the event of a recession, the total earnings for this investment will be ($2.50 × 200) = $500. Earnings for the expected scenario and the recession scenario are $1,000 and $2,000, respectively.

Problem 10: The investor would purchase 100 shares of Maxlever, and lend $4,000 at 10% interest. The returns for this position, and for the investment described in Problem 9, are summarized in the following table:

	Nolever		
	Recession	Expected	Expansion
EPS	$ 2.50	$ 5.00	$ 10.00
Total earnings (200 shares)	$ 500.00	$1,000.00	$ 2,000.00

Net cost = (200 x $40) = $8,000.00

	Nolever		
	Recession	Expected	Expansion
EPS	$ 1.00	$ 6.00	$ 16.00
Earnings for 100 shares	100.00	600.00	1,600.00
Plus interest ($4,000 @ 10%)	400.00	400.00	400.00
Net earnings	$ 520.00	$ 1,000.00	$ 2,000.00

Net cost = (100 x $40) + Amount loaned = $4,000 +$4,000 = $8,000

Problem 11: The solutions to Problems 7 and 8 indicate that the investor can earn the same returns from either strategy. The net cost of purchasing 200 shares of Nolever is $8,000. If the market value of Maxlever is $70,000, then the market value of the firm's equity is ($70,000 – $40,000) = $30,000, and the market value of a share is ($30,000/1,000) = $30. Consequently, the cost of the strategy of Problem 8 is $7,000. Since the same returns can be earned for a lower cost, any rational investor would purchase the stock of Maxlever, rather than the stock of Nolever. This would result in an adjustment of the values of the two firms, until the values are equal. As in Problem 6, this example demonstrates the fact that leverage does not affect the value of the firm.

Problem 12: V_U = $275,000 / .10 = $2,750,000. The value of the levered firm is the same $2,750,000 because, in a perfect market setting, capital structure has no effect on the value of the firm.

Problem 13: New cash flow = $275,000 - ($500,000 x 0.07) = $240,000. The new equity value is the value of the levered firm less the value of the debt: Equity value = $2,750,000 - $500,000 = $2,250,000. The firm's new equity beta is: Equity Beta = 1 x [1 + ($500,000 / 2,250,000)] = 1.2222. The new required return on equity = .070 + (0.10 - 0 .07) x 1.2222 = .10667. The new value of the equity = $240, 000 / 0.10667 = $2, 250, 00.

Problem 14: R_A = 0.05 + (0.12 - 0.05) x 1.5 = 0.155 = 15.5%
$\quad\quad\quad\quad$ R_E = R_D = 15.5% because the firm has no debt
$\quad\quad\quad\quad$ V_u = $2,000,000 / 0.155 = $12,903,225.81
$\quad\quad\quad\quad$ Value of each share = $12.90

Problem 15: When Ice King was an all-equity firm, there were $2,750,000 / 10 = 275,000 shares outstanding. The firm repurchased $500,000 / $10 = 50,000 shares, so there are now 225,000 shares outstanding. The new share price is $2,250,000 / 225,000 = $10. As expected, the price per share was not affected by the change in capital structure.

Problem 16: After the restructuring, your share of Ice King's cash flow is $240,000 x .01 = $2,400. Before the restructuring, the value of your equity position was $10 x 2,250 shares = $22,500. In order to have the same D/E ratio as the leveraged firm, you should borrow 0.01 x $500,000 = $5,000, which you will use to buy new shares. You now own [2,250 + ($5,000 / $10)] = 2,750 shares.

Your ownership percentage is 2,750 / 275,000 = 0.01 of the firm. Therefore, your net cash flow (after subtracting interest on your debt) will be ($275,000 x .01) - ($5,000 x .07) = $2,400. This is the same cash flow whether the firm decides to issues debt or to remain as an all-equity firm.

Problem 17: The WACC for the unlevered firm is (0 / $2,750,000) x 0.07 + ($2,750,000 / $2,750,000) x 0.10 = 0.10 = 10 %. The WACC for the levered firm is ($500,000 / $2,750,000) x 0.07 + ($2,250,000 / $2,750,000) x 0.10667 = 0.10 = 10 %.

Problem 18: If there are no taxes, then M&M Proposition I (no taxes) applies and North's capital structure is irrelevant. The value of the firm is: EBIT / R_A = $200 / .16 = $1,250. A debt/equity ratio of .25 indicates that the firm has $0.25 of debt for each dollar of equity. Therefore, North's capital structure is 80% equity, and the value of the equity is (.80 × $1,250) = $1,000. The value of the debt is ($1,250 – $1,000) = $250.

Problem 19: The cost of equity capital can be computed using M&M Proposition II as: R_E = .16 + [(.16 – .12) × .25] = .17 = 17%. Alternatively, we can compute the cash flow to shareholders as: $200 – (.12 × $250) = $170. Since the value of the equity is $1,000, the cost of capital is ($170 / $1,000) = .17 = 17%.

Problem 20: The value of North as an unlevered firm is: V_U = [EBIT x (1 - T_C)] / ρ = [$200 x .70] / .20 = $700. Proposition I (with corporate taxes) states that the value of a levered firm, V_L, is equal to the value of the unlevered firm plus the value of the interest tax shield: V_L = V_U + (T_C x D) = $700 + (.30 x $400) = $820. The value of the firm's equity is ($820 – $400) = $420.

Problem 21: Following M&M Proposition II (with corporate taxes), the cost of equity for North is: R_E = ρ + (ρ - R_D) x (D / E) x (1 - T_C) = .20 + (.20 - .12) x ($400 / $420) x (1 - .30) = .25333 = 25.33%. Alternatively, the cost of equity capital can be computed by first calculating the cash flow to shareholders as: [$200 – (.12 × $400)] × (1 – .30) = $106.40. Using this method, the return on equity is ($106.40/$420) = 25.333%, as previously calculated.

The weighted average cost of capital is: WACC = ($420 / $820) x .25333 + ($400 / $820) x .12 x .70 = .17073 = 17.07%. Therefore, the weighted average cost of capital for an unlevered firm is 20% (i.e., WACC = ρ = 20%), while the WACC for North Company is 17.073%.

Problem 22: The value of the firm is EBIT / R_A = $400 / 0.12 = $3,333. With a 0.5 debt/equity ratio, Coprez's capital structure is 1/3 debt and 2/3 equity. The value of the debt is therefore $3,333 x 1/3 = $1,111. The value of the equity is $3,333 - $1,111 = $2,222.

Problem 23: R_E = 0.12 + [(0.12 - 0.10) x 0.5] = 0.13 = 13%

The cost of equity can also be computed as $400 - (0.10 x $1,111) / $2,222 = $289 / $2,222 = 0.13 = 13%

Problem 24: The value of the firm is ($450,000/.15) = $3,000,000. Since MM is an all-equity firm, the value of the firm's equity is also $3,000,000. Price per share is ($3,000,000/100,000) = $30.

Problem 25: The NPV of the expansion is:–$400,000 + ($150,000/.15) = $600,000. Therefore, when the firm announces the expansion, the value of the firm increases to ($3,000,000 + $600,000) = $3,600,000. That is, the value of the firm's assets and the value of the equity each increase to $3,600,000. Price per share increases to ($3,600,000/100,000) = $36. Note that this increase in value occurs immediately following the announcement of the expansion, but before financing is obtained. To obtain $400,000 in equity financing, the firm sells ($400,000/$36) = 11,111 shares of stock. The proceeds of the stock issue are used to acquire the new assets, so that the value of the firm becomes ($3,000,000 + $600,000 + $400,000) = $4,000,000, which is the value of the firm's equity. The price per share is still $36 after the financing; that is, ($4,000,000/111,111) = $36. Note that the $6 gain in share price is the project's NPV divided by the original number of shares outstanding: $600,000 / 100,000 = $6.

Problem 26: As in Problem 25, the value of the firm increases to $3,600,000 after the announcement of the expansion. When the firm issues $400,000 of new debt, the value of the firm's assets increases to $4,000,000, but the value of the firm's equity remains at $3,600,000. The value of the firm is the same as under the equity financing arrangement, as indicated by M&M Proposition I (no taxes). The price per share of the firm's stock is $36 after the announcement and before the financing is obtained, and remains at $36 after the financing is obtained. Again, the gain in share price is equal to the project's NPV divided by the original number of shares outstanding, $6.

Problem 27: Expected yearly income is $450,000 + $150,000 - (.10 × $400,000) = $560,000. The expected return for the equityholders is ($560,000/$3,600,000) = 15.556%.

Problem 28: M&M Proposition II (no taxes) indicates that the return to equityholders is: $560,000 / $3,600,000 = .15556 = 15.556%.

Problem 29: V_u = $365,000 x (1 - 0.30) / 0.15 = $1,703,333. To find the value of the levered firm, you should recognize that debt is 40 % of total asset value. So, for the present value of the interest tax shield (T_c x D), we can substitute (V_L x 0.40) for D. V_L = $V_u + T_c$ x D = $1,703,333 + 0.30 x V_L (0.4). Solving, $0.88V_L$ = $1,703,333 and V_L = $1,935,606.

We know that the value of the debt is 40% of total firm value, so D = $1,935,606 x (0.4) = $774,242.40. This means the equity value is: E = $1,935,606 - $774,242.40 = $1,161,364.

The return on equity and WACC are:

$$R_E = 0.15 + (0.15 - 0.10) \times [(0.40 / 0.60) \times (1 - 0.30)] = 0.173 = 17.3\%$$
$$WACC = 0.15 \times [1 - (0.30 \times 0.40)] = 0.132 = 13.2\%$$

Problem 30: With debt, the share price is $1,161,363 / 100,000 = $11.61 per share. The firm's current debt level is $774,242.40, so they need to issue $774,242.49 / $11.61 = 66,687.55 shares. The entire after-tax cash flow goes to the shareholders: $365,000 x (1 - 0.30) = $255,500. Each share receives $255,500 / 166,687.55 = $1.5328. The present value is $1.5328 / 0.15 = $10.2187. The value of the equity (and the unlevered firm) is $10.2187 x 166,687.55 = $1,703,333. This is the same answer we would have obtained using the equation for the value of the levered firm. (Note: You may have slightly different answers, due to rounding.)

Problem 31: V_L = $1,703,333 + $774,242.40 x [1 - (1 - .30) x (1 - .20) / (1 - .35)] = $1,810,536

Problem 32: While DI and VFI share similar tax rates, accumulated losses, and tax shields, they differ in the level of financial distress they face as a result of borrowing. First, DI is more volatile than VFI, hence DI is more likely than VFI to face financial distress. Second, as a young research company, a large proportion of DI's assets are intangibles, such as its investment in nanotechnology research. VFI, on the other hand, is primarily focused on flour production, hence a large proportion of its assets are tangibles such as land, buildings, and equipment. Intangible assets typically have less resale value than tangible assets, hence DI is less prepared to deal with financial distress relative to VFI. To sum, DI is both more likely than VFI to face financial distress, and is less prepared to deal with financial distress. Given these considerations, David's recommendation that DI borrow less than VFI is reasonable.

17 Dividends and Dividend Policy

CHAPTER HIGHLIGHTS

Simple intuition suggests that dividend policy should not matter a great deal. Investors wishing a cash payout from their stock portfolios can simply sell some stock and pay themselves a cash 'dividend.' Investors who do not want a cash dividend can simply reinvest dividends received. However, the argument is slightly more complicated. Certain factors favour high dividend payouts; others favour low payouts. Then, some argue that dividend policy is irrelevant. These points of view are addressed below.

17.1 CASH DIVIDENDS AND DIVIDEND PAYMENT

A *dividend* is a cash payment, made to shareholders, from the firm's earnings. If the payment is from sources other than current earnings, it is called a *distribution from capital* or a *liquidating dividend*. The basic types of cash dividends are:

1. Regular cash dividends
2. Extra dividends
3. Liquidating dividends

Cash Dividends: Typically, a corporation pays a *regular cash dividend* four times a year. An *extra cash dividend* may also be paid periodically, but not on a regular basis. A *liquidating dividend* results from the liquidation of all or part of the corporation.

Standard Method of Cash Dividend Payment: A cash dividend can be expressed as either dollars per share (*dividends per share*), a percentage of market price (*dividend yield*), or as a percentage of earnings per share (*dividend payout*). A dividend becomes a liability of the firm once it is declared by the board of directors.

Dividend Payment - A Chronology: The chronology of a dividend payment involves the following four dates: the *declaration date*, the *ex-dividend date*, the *date of record*, and the *date of payment*. On the declaration date, the board of directors announces the amount of the dividend and the date of record. The dividend is paid to shareholders who are holders of record as of the date of record. The dividend checks are mailed to these owners on the date of payment.

If you buy a share the day before the date of record, this fact would not be reflected in the corporation's records on the date of record because of processing delays; the previous owner would be the shareholder of record. To avoid inconsistencies created by such delays, brokerage firms set the ex-dividend date four business days prior to the record date. Anyone purchasing a share on or after the ex-dividend date does not receive the dividend. Prior to the ex-dividend date, the stock is said to be trading *cum dividend* (with dividend). Subsequently, it trades *ex-dividend*.

More on the Ex-Dividend Date: Suppose a stock pays a $1 dividend and goes ex-dividend on Wednesday. If you buy the stock on Tuesday, just before the market closes, you will receive the dividend. If you buy on Wednesday, just as the market opens, you will not. The price of the stock declines overnight by approximately the amount of the dividend. Since dividends are taxed as ordinary income, the price decline is actually closer to the after-tax value of the dividend, rather than the full amount of the dividend.

17.2 DOES DIVIDEND POLICY MATTER?

A firm's dividend policy determines the pattern of dividend payment over time. A firm can choose to pay a large percentage of earnings to shareholders in the form of dividends, or to pay a small percentage of earnings as dividends and to reinvest a large portion of earnings with the expectation that larger dividend payments will be made in the future. The issue of dividend policy concerns the question of whether one or the other of these approaches is more advantageous to the shareholders.

An Illustration of the Irrelevance of Dividend Policy: The basic argument for dividend irrelevance can be illustrated with a simple numerical example. Consider a corporation with 100 shares outstanding and which will have a certain cash flow of $110 at date 1, and will liquidate for a certain $242 at date 2. If 10% is the required rate of return, then the total value of the firm is:

$$\frac{\$110}{1.10} + \frac{\$242}{(1.10)^2} = \$300$$

Each share is worth ($300/100) = $3.00.

One possible dividend policy is to pay $110 at date 1 and $242 at date 2. Suppose that, instead, the shareholders prefer a $200 dividend at date 1. To pay this amount, the firm could sell $90 worth of new stock at year's end and pay out a total of $200. What dividend would be paid to the old shareholders at date 2? There is $242 available at date 2. The new shareholders require a 10% return, so they would have to be paid ($90 × 1.10) = $99, leaving ($242 − $99) = $143 for the old shareholders. The present value of the dividends the old shareholders receive is:

$$\frac{\$200}{1.10} + \frac{\$143}{(1.10)^2} = \$300$$

The present value of this dividend policy is therefore identical to the present value of the previous policy. In fact, no matter how the available cash is paid out as dividends, the present value is always $300.

Homemade Dividends: Suppose you own 10 shares of stock in the company described above, and the firm has decided to pay out $110 and $242 at date 1 and date 2, respectively. You will receive $11 and $24.20, respectively. Also, suppose that you would rather receive $20 and $14.30, at dates 1 and 2. Given the firm's dividend policy, you can create the cash flows you prefer by selling enough shares at the end of the first year to receive the extra $9. In doing so, you forfeit ($9 × 1.10) = $9.90 at date 2. Thus, you will receive ($24.20 − $9.90) = $14.30, effectively creating a new dividend policy or *homemade dividend*.

Some corporations assist their shareholders by offering *automatic dividend reinvestment plans* (ADPs or DRIPs), which give the shareholder the option to automatically reinvest some or all of their cash dividend in shares acquired at a small discount. Investment dealers have also created homemade dividends (or homemade capital gains) called *Stripped Common Shares* which entitle holders to receive either all the dividends of one or a group of well-known companies which packages any capital gain in the form of a call option. The investor has the right to buy the underlying shares at a fixed price. The option value increases as share price increases.

It is important to keep in mind that we are not saying that dividends themselves are irrelevant; rather, the decision to pay dividends now or later is irrelevant. It is also important to note that it is assumed here that the firm's dividend policy does not affect its investment policy. That is, we assume that the firm accepts all positive NPV investment opportunities prior to making the dividend decision.

17.3 REAL-WORLD FACTORS FAVOURING A LOW PAYOUT

The irrelevance of dividend policy established in the previous section is based on the assumption that there are no taxes or flotation costs. Clearly, these assumptions are inconsistent with reality. The current section is devoted to a discussion of how existing tax laws affect the earlier conclusions.

Taxes: Under current tax laws in Canada, both dividend income and capital gains are taxed at effective rates *less than* the marginal tax rates on ordinary income. Investors receiving dividend income face a lower tax rate due to the dividend tax credit. Capital gains are taxed at 75 % of the marginal rate. Since taxation takes place only when capital gains are realized, capital gains are very lightly taxed in Canada and generally taxed lower than dividends.
A policy of low dividend payout means that earnings are reinvested in the firm. The value of the firm increases, resulting in capital gains for the shareholders. Consequently, the taxation of capital gains has implications for the firm's dividend policy. The lower effective tax rate for capital gains is a factor encouraging a low dividend payout.

Suppose a firm has adopted all available capital-budgeting projects with a positive net present value, and still has $1,000 in cash. This excess cash is sometimes referred to as *free cash flow*. Should such a firm pay the $1,000 in dividends to its shareholders, in spite of the tax implications and transactions costs noted above? Consider some alternatives to a dividend payment: (1) select additional capital-budgeting projects; (2) repurchase shares; (3) acquire other companies; (4) purchase financial assets.

Since the firm has already taken all positive NPV projects, any additional capital budgeting projects have negative NPVs. Therefore, alternative (1) is unacceptable. Alternative (2), repurchasing shares, may be viewed as dividends for tax purposes, so this alternative may not be very attractive. Alternative (3), acquisition of another company is generally not profitable for the acquiring firm. If the only motive for the acquisition is to avoid dividends, the acquisition will probably not succeed.

Alternative (4), the purchase of financial assets, may be advantageous to shareholders under certain circumstances. When the corporate tax rate exceeds the individual tax rate, investors would prefer to receive dividend income. Consider the following example:

Assume a firm has $10 extra cash, the corporate tax rate is 30%, and the individual tax rate is 20%. If the firm pays a $10 dividend, shareholders receive [$10 × (1 − .20)] = $8 after tax. If this is invested for five years at a 10% rate, investors will earn 8% on an after-tax basis. The investment will be worth [$8 × (1.08)^5] = $11.75 in five years. If the firm invested the $10 at a 10% rate instead of paying a dividend, the after-tax return would be 7%. After five years, the investment would be worth [$10 × (1.07)^5] = $14.03. If this amount is paid to shareholders, they will be able to keep the after-tax amount of [$14.03 × (1 − .20)] = $11.22. Clearly, the investors in this case would prefer the firm to pay the dividend today, so that they could invest for themselves.

On the other hand, if individual taxes are higher, the firm has an incentive to reduce dividend payouts.

Flotation Costs: In an earlier example, we noted that a firm could issue common stock in order to pay dividends. However, we ignored the fact that this would require the firm to pay flotation costs. These flotation costs can be substantial. So, this is an additional incentive in favour of a low dividend payout policy.

Dividend Restrictions: Bond indentures often limit a corporation's dividend payout. This protects bondholders in the event shareholders want pay themselves a large dividend, possibly limiting their ability to meet interest payment to bondholders. Dividend restriction help resolve the agency conflict between bondholders and shareholders.

17.4 REAL-WORLD FACTORS FAVOURING A HIGH PAYOUT

Some have argued that shareholders prefer a high dividend payout policy because of the desire for current income and the resolution of uncertainty.

Desire for Current Income: Some investors, including many on fixed incomes, undoubtedly desire current income. These investors might conceivably pay a premium for stocks with high dividends. Selling a portion of the stock each period in order to produce current income may be undesirable because of brokerage fees, among other reasons. However, a mutual fund could very easily provide this service by regularly selling its holdings of low-dividend stocks to pay dividends to its shareholders. Therefore, high dividend payout is not necessarily preferable, even for shareholders who desire current income.

Uncertainty Resolution: A dollar received in the form of a dividend has a known value, while a dollar reinvested by the corporation has an uncertain future value. The 'bird-in-hand' story argues that the cash dividend reduces the risk of owning the stock. However, this conclusion is erroneous because a shareholder can accomplish the same result by selling shares of a low-dividend stock in order to create homemade dividends.

Tax and Legal Benefits from High Dividends: Tax considerations which reduce the effective tax rate for capital gains generally lead individual investors to prefer common stocks with low dividend payouts. However, other investors are not subjected to higher tax rates on dividends. For corporations which own the securities of other corporations, 100% of dividend income received is excluded from the firm's taxable income. Consequently, these investors often prefer to own common stocks, or preferred stocks, with high dividend payouts, rather than either common stocks with low dividend payouts or corporate bonds. In addition, pension funds, endowment funds, and trust funds favour stocks with high dividend payouts because these institutions are tax-exempt.

17.5 A RESOLUTION OF REAL-WORLD FACTORS?

The general consensus is that several factors are important in establishing dividend policy. Tax effects and flotation costs lead some investors to favour a low payout, whereas the desire for current income influences others to favour a high payout. Although the issue has been studied extensively, it is not possible to determine which of these factors dominates, so the policy question is unresolved. As explained below, the evidence is not easy to interpret.

Information Content of Dividends: The *information content effect* is the market's reaction to a change in corporate dividend payout. It is generally established that stock prices increase following an announcement of a dividend increase. This fact seems to support the contention that investors prefer a high dividend payout. However, financial actions by the firm are sometimes regarded as a way of signalling future prospects to the financial markets. Firms resist cutting dividends, so an announcement of an increase in dividends indicates that the firm expects future cash flow to be sufficient to support a higher level of dividends. This is a positive signal, and consequently the stock price increases. It is difficult to separate the information content of the announcement from the dividend itself.

The Clientele Effect: Some investors prefer high dividend payouts while others prefer low payouts. Different firms may cater to one group (or clientele) or the other. As long as both groups are satisfied, the corporation does not benefit from a change in its dividend policy; doing so simply attracts a different clientele. This scenario is called the *clientele effect*. A natural type of clientele is based on tax brackets. Evidence suggests that investors in low tax brackets tend to hold high payout stocks, and investors in high brackets hold low payout stocks.

17.6 ESTABLISHING A DIVIDEND POLICY

In this section, we discuss alternative approaches to establishing a dividend policy.

Residual Dividend Approach: Firms with low dividend payout ratios require less external financing than firms with high payout ratios. Since external financing requires that the firm pay flotation costs, it is less expensive to obtain financing by retaining earnings; that is, by adopting a low dividend payout ratio. In this section, we assume that the firm seeks to minimize the need to issue new common stock. We also assume that the firm will maintain its existing capital structure.

A firm which adopts the *residual dividend approach* relies primarily on internally generated funds to finance positive NPV projects while maintaining a desired debt-to-equity ratio. After allocating internally generated equity funds to all positive NPV projects, the firm pays dividends from any residual funds which remain after financing these projects.

An Example: A firm with a residual dividend approach has $5,000 in earnings and a debt/equity ratio of 0.25. What is the maximum amount of capital spending possible if the firm does not obtain any new equity financing and maintains the current debt/equity ratio? If the firm has positive NPV projects available which require the investment of $4,000, how much will the firm pay in dividends?

A debt/equity ratio of 0.25 indicates the firm has $0.25 of debt for each dollar of equity. The $5,000 in earnings represents available equity financing so that the firm must raise (.25 × $5,000) = $1,250 of debt financing. Therefore, the total financing available, if the firm does not obtain any new equity financing, is ($5,000 + $1,250) = $6,250.

The debt/equity ratio of 0.25 means that the firm's capital structure is comprised of $0.25 of debt and $1.00 of equity for each $1.25 of total financing. The capital structure is therefore ($0.25/$1.25) = 20% debt and ($1.00/$1.25) = 80% equity. In order to finance capital expenditures of $4,000, while maintaining the existing capital structure, the firm will use debt financing of (.20 × $4,000) = $800, and equity financing of (.80 × $4,000) = $3,200. Since the firm has $5,000 of internal equity financing available, dividends are ($5,000 – $3,200) = $1,800.

Since the total financing available is $6,250, the firm will obtain additional equity financing only if positive NPV projects require financing greater than this total. Twenty percent of any additional financing in excess of the available $6,250 is debt financing, and 80% is equity financing.

Now assume the firm requires $10,000 of financing for positive NPV projects and $5,000 of equity financing is derived from retained earnings. This $5,000 of equity financing implies debt financing of $1,250 in order to maintain the firm's debt/equity ratio, as described earlier. Additional financing equal to ($10,000 – $6,250) = $3,750 is then obtained as follows: (.20 × $3,750) = $750 of additional debt financing and (.80 × $3,750) = $3,000 of additional equity financing. Therefore, total equity financing consists of $5,000 of internally generated funds and $3,000 of new equity. Total debt financing is equal to ($1,250 + $750) = $2,000.

Dividend Stability: Under the residual dividend approach, the dividend paid depends on both the firm's earnings for the quarter and the firm's investment opportunities. Because these quantities can vary significantly over time, the actual dividend paid can be very unstable. Since investors seem to value stability in dividends, alternative dividend policies might be preferable. Dividend stability complements investor objectives of information content, income, and reduction in uncertainty. Institutional investors often follow 'prudence' tests which restrict investment in firms that do not pay regular dividends. One such policy is a cyclical dividend policy which sets each quarter's dividend equal to a fixed fraction of the quarter's earnings; this policy is cyclical because earnings, and consequently dividends, may vary throughout the year, but total annual dividends might remain relatively stable.

A second alternative policy sets quarterly dividends equal to a specified fraction of annual earnings, rather than quarterly earnings. This is a stable dividend policy if earnings are relatively stable from one year to the next.

A Compromise Dividend Policy: Many firms follow a compromise dividend policy based on the following goals:

1.   Avoid the rejection of positive NPV projects in order to pay a dividend.
2.   Avoid reducing dividends.
3.   Avoid issuing new equity.
4.   Maintain a target debt/equity ratio.
5.   Maintain a target dividend payout ratio.

For this kind of compromise dividend policy, both the target debt/equity ratio and the target dividend payout ratio are regarded as long-term goals, rather than strict requirements. The long-run *target payout ratio* is the fraction of earnings the firm normally expects to pay as dividends. If earnings are unusually low in a given quarter, the firm might choose to temporarily increase the payout ratio in order to avoid reducing dividends.

17.7 STOCK REPURCHASE: AN ALTERNATIVE TO CASH DIVIDENDS

As an alternative to paying cash dividends, a firm can pay cash to its shareholders by a *repurchase* of its own stock from the shareholders. This alternative to cash dividends is discussed below.

Cash Dividend versus Repurchase: In the absence of taxes and transactions costs, a share repurchase has the same effect on shareholders as a dividend payment of the same dollar amount. Consider an all-equity firm with the following market value balance sheet:

Market value balance sheet			
Excess cash	$ 60,000	Debt	$ 0
Other assets	240,000	Equity	300,000
Total	$ 300,000	Total	$ 300,000

The firm has 6,000 shares outstanding, so the market value per share is ($300,000/6,000) = $50.

The firm is considering the following alternative uses of the excess cash: (1) pay a dividend of ($60,000/6,000) = $10 per share; or, (2) repurchase ($60,000/$50) = 1,200 shares of its common stock. The firm's balance sheet and the impact on an individual shareholder are the same for these two alternatives.

For the first alternative, the firm's balance sheet appears as follows after paying the dividend:

Market value balance sheet : Pay cash dividend			
Excess cash	$ 0	Debt	$ 0
Other assets	240,000	Equity	240,000
Total	$ 240,000	Total	$ 240,000

For a shareholder who owns 200 shares of stock, the market value prior to the dividend payment is ($50 × 200) = $10,000. After the dividend is paid, each share of stock has a value of ($240,000/6,000) = $40. Consequently, the shareholder who owns 200 shares now owns stock whose value is ($40 × 200) = $8,000. In addition, the investor receives dividends of ($10 × 200) = $2,000. The total value is unaffected by the dividend payment.

If instead, the firm repurchases 1,200 shares, its market value balance sheet is identical to its appearance after the dividend payment. There would be $(6,000 - 1,200) = 4,800$ shares outstanding, each with a market value of $(\$240,000/4,800) = \$50$. Assuming shareholders keep their shares, the market value of their position is unchanged after the share repurchase. The investor has 200 shares with a total value of $(\$50 \times 200) = \$10,000$. Selling all 200 shares would also leave the investor with $10,000 cash. Alternatively, the investor could sell a portion of the shares, creating homemade dividends. If, for example, 40 shares were sold, the homemade dividends would be $(\$50 \times 40) = \$2,000$. The remaining stock would be worth $(\$50 \times 160) = \$8,000$. In other words, the value of the position is still $10,000.

Real-World Considerations in a Repurchase: As demonstrated above, in the absence of taxes and transactions costs, shareholders are indifferent between a dividend payment and a stock repurchase. However, existing tax laws may lead shareholders to favour a stock repurchase.

Consider the previous case. If the firm elected to pay dividends, the investor would receive $2,000 in dividends. Assuming a tax rate of 28%, the taxes on dividends would be $560. However, if the firm repurchases stock, the investor might pay no taxes. For example, if the investor chooses not to sell any shares, then there is no taxable income. If the investor creates homemade dividends by selling 40 shares, the tax liability will still be less than if the investor received $2,000 in dividends because the tax is paid only on capital gains resulting from the sale. If the shares were bought for $30, the capital gain would be $(\$50 - \$30) = \$20$ per share. Taxable income would be $(\$20 \times 40) = \$800$. Taxes would be only $(\$800 \times .28) = \$224$.

17.8 STOCK DIVIDENDS AND STOCK SPLITS

A *stock dividend* is paid in the form of additional shares of stock. A 10% stock dividend, for example, increases by 10% the number of shares held by each shareholder. Suppose an individual owns 200 shares of the common stock of a firm which has 1,000 shares outstanding. If a 10% stock dividend is declared, this shareholder receives an additional $(.10 \times 200) = 20$ shares. Since all shareholders receive the same 10% stock dividend, the number of shares outstanding increases to $(1.10 \times 1,000) = 1,100$. Shareholders who owned 200 shares prior to the 10% stock dividend owned $(200/1,000) = 20\%$ of the outstanding shares. After the stock dividend, they still own $(220/1,100) = 20\%$ of the outstanding shares. The total value of the firm does not change when a stock dividend is declared. Since there are no cash flows associated with a stock dividend, the total value of the firm is not affected. Consequently, the investor who owned 20% of the firm prior to the stock dividend still owns 20% of the firm after the stock dividend. Since the value of the firm is unchanged, the value of the individual's holdings is also unchanged by the stock dividend. Because the number of shares outstanding is increased by 10%, without any change in the total value of the firm, each share is worth correspondingly less.

A *stock split* is essentially equivalent to a stock dividend, except that a split is expressed as a ratio rather than as a percentage. Under the TSE rules, the maximum stock dividend is 25 %; anything larger is considered a stock split. For example, a five-for-four stock split gives a shareholder five shares for every four owned prior to the split. Since a five-for-four stock split results in the distribution of one additional share for every four the shareholder owns, it is equivalent to a $(1/4) = 25\%$ stock dividend. Stock splits and stock dividends are, for the most part, just paper transactions which do not change either the total value of the firm or the value of the shareholder's position.

Some Details on Stock Splits and Stock Dividends: For accounting purposes, stock splits and stock dividends are classified as: (1) small stock dividends; (2) large stock dividends; and, (3) stock splits. Stock dividends of less than approximately 20% to 25% are classified as small stock dividends. For each of these categories, accountants adjust the firm's balance sheet somewhat differently. However, in all three cases, the total owners' equity is unaffected by the distribution. Furthermore, the total market value of the firm or individual's holdings does not change.

Value of Stock Splits and Stock Dividends: Consider the earlier example of a 10% stock dividend declared by a firm with 1,000 shares outstanding. If the market value of a share prior to the stock dividend is $22, then the total market value of the firm's equity is ($22 × 1,000) = $22,000. After the 10% stock dividend, the 1,100 outstanding shares must have the same market value because the value of the firm cannot change by simply sending pieces of paper (i.e., additional stock certificates) to the shareholders. Therefore, each of the 1,100 shares must now have a market value of $20, so the total value of the firm is still ($20 × 1,100) = $22,000. Also consider the shareholder with 200 shares prior to the stock dividend; the value is ($22 × 200) = $4,400. After the stock dividend, the investor has 220 shares with a total market value of ($20 × 220) = $4,400. Clearly, the value of the holdings has not changed.

The individual shareholder's position can also be viewed from the perspective of proportionate ownership of the firm before and after the stock dividend. Prior to the stock dividend, the investor owns (200/1,000) = 20% of the equity in the company. Since the total market value of the firm's equity is $22,000, the value is (.20 × $22,000) = $4,400. After the stock dividend, the investor still owns (220/1,100) = 20% of the equity, so that the value is still $4,400.

Popular Trading Range: Those who contend that stock splits and stock dividends have value to shareholders often argue that the value of a stock is enhanced if its price is within a certain trading range. Investors may be more likely to buy round lots (i.e., multiples of 100 shares) of a stock whose price is within the appropriate trading range. The reasoning is that broker's commissions are lower for stocks traded in round lots, and investors are more likely to be able to afford 100 shares of a stock priced in a moderate range (say, less than $100 per share) than for shares priced above this trading range. There is, however, little empirical evidence to support this contention.

Reverse Splits: A less frequently encountered manoeuvre is the reverse split, in which a firm's number of shares outstanding is *reduced*. In a one-for-three reverse split, each investor exchanges three old shares for one new share.

CONCEPT TEST

1.   A dividend is a cash payment, made to shareholders, from earnings. If the payment is from sources other than current earnings, it is called a(n) _____ or a(n) _____ dividend.

2.   A dividend which is typically paid four times a year is a(n) _____ cash dividend. A dividend which is paid periodically, but which may not continue in the future, is a(n) _____ dividend. A dividend paid subsequent to the liquidation of part or all of the corporation is a(n) _____ dividend.

3.   When the size of a cash dividend is expressed as dollars per share, it is identified in terms of _____ . When the size of the dividend is stated as a percentage of market price, it is called the _____ . When the size of the dividend is expressed as a percentage of earnings per share, it is referred to as the _____ .

4.   The date on which the board of directors announces the amount of the dividend is called the _____ . The dividend is paid to shareholders who are holders of record as of the _____ . The dividend checks are mailed to these owners on the _____ .

5.   The _____ date is four business days before the record date. Anyone purchasing a share before the ex-dividend date <u>does/does not</u> receive the dividend. Prior to the ex-dividend date, the stock is said to be trading _____ . Subsequently, it trades _____ . Prior to the ex-dividend date, the price of the stock declines overnight by approximately _____ .

6.   A stock dividend is paid in the form of _____ . Therefore, a stock dividend (is/is not) a true dividend. The total value of the firm (does/does not) change when a stock dividend is declared, and the total value of an individual's holdings (does/does not) change.

7.   A stock split (is/is not) essentially equivalent to a stock dividend. A split is expressed as a _____ , while a stock dividend is expressed as a _____ .

8.   When a 20% stock dividend is declared, an investor who owns 100 shares of stock receives _____ new shares, so the total number of shares he owns after the stock dividend is _____ .

9.   When a three-for-two stock split is declared, an investor who owns 100 shares of stock receives _____ new shares, so the total number of shares he owns after the stock split is _____ . A three-for-two stock split is equivalent to a _____ % stock dividend. A 20% stock dividend is equivalent to a _____ -for-_____ stock split.

10.   Those who contend that stock splits and stock dividends have value to shareholders often argue that the value of a stock is enhanced if its price is within a certain _____ .

11.   The argument for the irrelevance of dividend policy is based on the conclusion that an investor can create a new dividend policy, or _____ dividends, if the firm's pattern of dividend payments does/does not match the investor's preferences.

12.   The irrelevance of dividend policy is based on the assumptions that there are no _____ or _____ . Under current tax laws in Canada, dividend income and capital gains (are/are not) both taxed as ordinary income and (are/are not) subject to the same tax rates. They are taxed at _____ than the ordinary income tax rate. Capital gains taxes are deferred until the stock is sold, so that effective tax rates are (lower/higher) for capital gains.

13.   A policy of (low/high) dividend payout means that earnings are reinvested in the firm, so that the value of the firm (increases/ decreases) , resulting in capital gains for shareholders. Consequently, the taxation of capital gains has implications for the firm's dividend policy. The lower effective tax rate for capital gains is a factor encouraging a (low/high) dividend payout.

14.   The existence of flotation costs provides an incentive for firms to adopt a policy of (low/high) dividend payout.

15.   Some have argued that a (low/high) dividend payout policy is preferable because of the desire for current income and the resolution of uncertainty. It has been argued that the payment of a cash dividend (increases/decreases) the risk of owning a stock. However, a shareholder can accomplish the same result by _____ in order to create _____ dividends.

16.   Some investors are not subjected to higher tax rates on dividends than on capital gains. One such group of investors consists of corporations which own the securities of other corporations. For such investors, _____ % of dividend income received is excluded from the firm's taxable income. Consequently, these investors often prefer to own common stocks with (low/high) dividend payouts. In addition, pension funds, endowment funds, and trust funds favour stocks with (low/high) dividend payouts because these institutions are _____ .

17. Some investors prefer high dividend payouts while others prefer low payouts. Different firms may end up catering to one group or the other; this is called the _____ . Evidence suggests that investors in low tax brackets tend to hold (low/high) payout stocks, and investors in high brackets hold (low/high) payout stocks.

18. Firms with low dividend payout ratios require (less/more) external financing than firms with high dividend payout ratios. Since external financing requires that the firm pay flotation costs, it is less expensive to obtain financing by retaining earnings and consequently adopting a (low/high) dividend payout ratio.

19. A firm which adopts the _____ approach relies primarily on internally generated funds to finance positive NPV projects. After allocating internally generated equity funds to all positive NPV projects, the firm pays dividends only from any _____ funds which remain after financing these projects.

20. Under the residual dividend approach, the dividend paid to shareholders each quarter depends on both the firm's _____ and the firm's _____ . Therefore, the actual dividend paid can be very unstable. Since investors seem to value stability in dividends, alternative dividend policies which lead to more stability in dividends might be preferable. One such policy, which sets each quarter's dividend equal to a fixed fraction of the quarter's earnings, is referred to as a _____ dividend policy. A second alternative policy sets quarterly dividends equal to a specified fraction of annual earnings; this is a _____ dividend policy if earnings are relatively stable from one year to the next.

21. Many firms seem to follow a compromise dividend policy based on the following goals:

    1.   Avoid the rejection of _____ projects in order to pay a dividend.
    2.   Avoid reducing _____ .
    3.   Avoid issuing _____ .
    4.   Maintain a target _____ .
    5.   Maintain a target _____ .

    For this kind of compromise policy, both the target _____ and the target _____ are regarded as long-term goals, rather than strict requirements.

22. As an alternative to paying cash dividends, a firm can pay cash to its shareholders by a repurchase of its own stock from the shareholders. In the absence of _____ and _____ , shareholders are indifferent between a dividend payment and a stock repurchase. However, existing tax laws lead shareholders to favour a _____ .

PROBLEMS

Problem 1

The market value balance sheet for Agee Jones Associates, Inc., is shown below:

Market value balance sheet			
Cash	$ 20,000	Debt	$ 10,000
Fixed assets	30,000	Equity	40,000
Total	$ 50,000	Total	$ 50,000

The firm has 1,000 shares outstanding and has declared a 25% stock dividend. T. Agee owns 400 shares of the firm's common stock. What is the effect of the stock dividend on the firm's market value? How does the stock dividend affect the value of a share of stock? How does the stock dividend affect the value of T. Agee's holdings?

Problem 2

An all-equity firm has the following market-value balance sheet:

Market value balance sheet			
Excess cash	$ 80,000	Debt	$ 0
Other assets	360,000	Equity	440,000
Total	$ 440,000	Total	$440,000

The firm currently has 13,750 common shares outstanding. Market value per share os $440,000 / 13,750 = $32. The firm is considering using the excess cash to either repurchase ($80,000 / $32) = 2,500 shares or pay a dividend of ($80,000 / 13,750) = $5.82 per share.

Maureen owns 300 shares of stock in the firm. Assuming no transaction costs, show that either action by the firm has no impact on Maureen's wealth.

$w_M = 300 \times 32^9 = 9600$

① Repurchase : 11,250 outstanding

② $\frac{80,000}{13750} = D\text{V} = 5.81/\text{share}$

$(440-80) = 832/\text{share}$
$\overline{11,250}$

Problem 3

① L_0 $300 \times 32 = 9600$

$\Rightarrow 300 \times (32-5.82) = 7854.84$ $+D\text{IV}. \frac{26.18}{9600}$ $\frac{11,250}{}$

In the scenario from Problem 2, suppose that Maureen sold 80 of her shares, creating homemade dividends. Does her total wealth change?

$(300-80) \times 32 = 220 \times 32 = 7040$

$80 \times 32 = 2560$

$\overline{9600}$

Problem 4

Suppose that, for the data of Problem 1, Agee Jones declares a two-for-one stock split. What is the effect of the stock split on the firm's market value? How does the stock split affect the value of a share of stock? How does the stock split affect the value of T. Agee's holdings?

2000 shares : $\frac{40,000}{2000} = $20 /\text{share}$ $\Rightarrow$ same wealth

L_0 $800 \times 20 = 1600$

Problem 5

Glennie's VCR Company has 2,500 shares outstanding and is debt-free. Glennie expects to pay dividends of $3,000 one year from now and will pay liquidating dividends of $123,000 three years from now. If Glennie's required rate of return is 16.5%, what is the value of the firm and the value of one share of Glennie?

Problem 6

The Krane Pools Company is an all-equity firm with 1,000 shares outstanding. The firm expects to pay total dividends of $6,000 one year from now and total liquidating dividends of $72,000 two years from now. The required rate of return for Krane Pools is 20%. What is the total value of the firm? What is the value of a share of common stock?

Problem 7

Suppose that the shareholders of Krane Pools prefer total dividend payments of $30,000 at the end of one year, rather than dividend payments described in Problem 6. What dividend payment will the firm make at the end of the second year? What is the value of the firm if it adopts the new dividend payment schedule? What is the value of a share of stock?

Problem 8

E. Charles owns 100 shares of Krane Pools common stock. The firm plans to pay dividends as described in Problem 6, but E. Charles would like to receive the dividend payments he would receive if the firm paid dividends as described in Problem 7. How can E. Charles use homemade dividends to duplicate his desired dividend payments?

Problem 9

Lankester Corporation has a debt/equity ratio of 1/5 and earnings of $55,000. What is the maximum amount of capital spending for Lankester if the current debt/equity ratio must be maintained and the firm doesn't want to obtain additional equity financing?

Problem 10

A firm which has adopted a residual dividend approach has $30,000 in earnings and a debt/equity ratio of 1/3. What is the maximum amount of capital spending possible if the firm does not obtain any new equity financing and maintains the current debt/equity ratio?

Problem 11

Suppose that the firm described in Problem 10 has positive NPV projects available which require the investment of $24,000. How will these projects be financed? How much will the firm pay in dividends?

Problem 12

Suppose that the firm described in Problem 10 has $60,000 of positive NPV projects available. How will these projects be financed? How much will the firm pay in dividends?

Problem 13

An all-equity firm has the following market value balance sheet:

Market value balance sheet			
Excess cash	$ 10,000	Debt	$ 0
Other assets	90,000	Equity	100,000
Total	$ 100,000	Total	$ 100,000

The firm has 2,000 shares outstanding and is considering paying dividends with the excess cash. What is the impact on the firm's market value balance sheet? How does the dividend payment affect a stockholder who owns 500 shares of stock?

Problem 14

Suppose that the firm described in Problem 13 is considering a stock repurchase rather than the dividend payment. What is the impact on the firm's market value balance sheet? How does the stock repurchase affect a shareholder who owns 500 shares of stock?

Use the following information to solve Problems 15 through 19:

The balance sheet for Reebop Corporation is shown. Reebop has 1,000 shares outstanding.

Market value balance sheet			
Cash	$ 10,000	Debt	$ 0
Fixed assets	50,000	Equity	60,000
Total	$ 60,000	Total	$ 60,000

Problem 15

Reebop has declared a dividend of $3.00 per share. The stock goes ex-dividend tomorrow. What is the price of the stock today? What will its price be tomorrow? Assume no taxes.

[handwritten: $\frac{60,000}{1000} = \$60$. Today. $\$7$ Tom]

Problem 16

Reebop has declared a 20% stock dividend, rather than the cash dividend described in Problem 15. The stock goes ex-dividend tomorrow. What is the ex-dividend price?

[handwritten: 1200 stocks = 50 old,   New: $50 ×1.2 = 60]

Problem 17

Instead of paying a cash dividend, Reebop has announced that it is going to repurchase $3,000 of stock. What is the effect of this repurchase? Ignoring taxes, show how this repurchase is effectively the same as a $3.00 dividend per share.

[handwritten: $\frac{57,000}{950} = \$60/share$ → $57 after div.]

Problem 18

Suppose that capital gains are not taxed, but dividends are taxed at a 40% rate, and that taxes are withheld at the time the dividend is paid. If Reebop is going to pay a $4.00 dividend per share, what is the ex-dividend price?

[handwritten: $\$60 - 4(1-.4) = \$57.6$]

Problem 19

Suppose that, in Problem 18, capital gains are taxed at a 20% rate. What is the ex-dividend price?

Problem 20

Dadadas Company is in the same risk class as Old Balance Company. Dadadas has an expected dividend yield over the next year of 10%, while Old Balance pays no dividends. The required return on Old Balance is 20%. Capital gains are not taxed, but dividends are effectively taxed at 40%. What is the required pre-tax return on Dadadas?

Problem 21

You own 20 shares of stock in King Aircraft. You are certain you will receive a $.50 per share dividend at date 1. At date 2, King will pay a liquidating dividend of $13.80 per share. The required return is 20%. Assuming no taxes, what is the price per share of the common stock? Suppose that you would rather have equal dividends in each of the next two years. How can you accomplish this by using homemade dividends?

Problem 22

Try this one on your own. Suppose that, in Problem 21, you wanted only $5 at date 1. What is your homemade dividend at date 2?

ANSWERS TO CONCEPT TEST

1.   distribution from capital; liquidating

2.   regular; extra; liquidating

3.   dividends per share; dividend yield; dividend payout

4.   declaration date; date of record; date of payment

5.   ex-dividend; does; cum dividend; ex-dividend; the after-tax value of the dividend

6.   additional shares of stock; is not; does not; does not

7.   is; ratio; percentage

8.   20; 120

9.   50; 150; 50; six; five

10.   trading range

11.   homemade

12.   taxes; flotation costs; are not; are not; less; lower

13.   low; increases; low

14.   low

15.   high; decreases; selling shares of stock; homemade

16.   100; high; high; tax-exempt

17.   clientele effect; high; low

18.   less; low

19.   residual dividend; residual

20.   earnings for the quarter; investment opportunities; cyclical; stable

21.   positive NPV; dividends; new equity; debt/equity ratio; dividend payout ratio; debt/equity ratio; dividend payout ratio

22.   taxes; transaction costs; stock repurchase

PROBLEM SOLUTIONS

Problem 1: Prior to the stock dividend, the market value of the firm's equity is $40,000 and the market value per share is ($40,000/1,000) = $40. The stock dividend does not affect the total market value of the firm's equity, so that the market value balance sheet does not change. However, since there are now an additional (.25 x 1,000) = 250 shares outstanding, the value per share declines. After the stock dividend, the market value per share is:

        Price per share x 1,250 = $40,000

The market value per share is ($40,000/1,250) = $32 after the stock dividend.

Prior to the stock dividend, the market value of T. Agee's holdings is ($40 x 400) = $16,000. Alternatively, since T. Agee owns (400/1,000) = 40% of the firm, the market value of his position is (.40 x $40,000) = $16,000. After the stock dividend, T. Agee owns (1.25 x 400) = 500 shares, which still represents (500/1,250) = 40% of the firm. The market value of his position is: $32 x 500 = .40 x $40,000 = $16,000.

Problem 2: The market value of Maureen's shares before the dividend payment is (300 x $32) = $9,600. After the dividend is paid Mareen has shares worth ($32 - $5.82) x 300 + $5.82 x 300 in cash. The total is $7,854 + $1,746 = $9,600, the same as before.

If the firm repurchases 2,500 shares, there would be 13,750 - 2,500 = 11,250 shares outstanding with a market value of $360,000 / 11,250 = $32 per share. If Maureen keeps her shares, they are worth 300 x $32 = $9,600. Regardless of which alternative the firm chooses, the value of Maureen's position stays the same.

Problem 3: By selling 80 shares, Maureen receives homemade dividends (cash) of ($32 x 80) = $2,560. Her remaining shares are worth (220 x $32) = $7,040. Her total wealth is still $9,600 = ($2,560 + $7,040).

Problem 4: As in the case of the stock dividend, the stock split does not affect the total market value of the firm's equity. The stock split results in the distribution of one new share for each existing share. Therefore, it is equivalent to a 100% stock dividend and results in the distribution of 1,000 new shares. The total number of shares is then (1,000 + 1,000) = 2,000. The market value per share, after the stock split, is:

        Market value per share x 2,000 = $40,000

The market value per share is ($40,000/2,000) = $20 after the stock dividend.

After the stock split, T. Agee owns (2.00 x 400) = 800 shares. The market value of his position is:

        $20 x 800 = .40 x $40,000 = $16,000

Problem 5: The value of Glennie is:

$$\$3,000 / 1.165 \ + \ \$123,000 / 1.165^3 \ = \ \$80,365.75$$
The value of one share is $\$80,365.85 / 2,500 \ = \ \$32.15$

Problem 6: The total value of Krane Pools is:

$$\frac{\$6,000}{1.20} \ + \ \frac{\$72,000}{(1.20)^2} \ = \ \$55,000$$

The market value of a share is ($\$55,000/1,000$) = $55. Alternatively, the market value of one share can be computed as the present value of the dividends per share to be paid at the end of each of the next two years:

$$\frac{\$6.00}{1.20} \ + \ \frac{\$72.00}{(1.20)^2} \ = \ \$55$$

Problem 7: In order to pay $30,000 in dividends at the end of one year, Krane Pools could sell ($30,000 - $6,000) = $24,000 of common stock at the end of the year. The holders of this new common stock require a 20% rate of return, so that they will require ($24,000 x 1.20) = $28,800 in dividends. The dividend payment to the existing shareholders at the end of the second year will therefore be ($72,000 - $28,800) = $43,200. The value of the firm today is the present value of the future dividends to be paid to the existing shareholders:

$$\frac{\$30,000}{1.20} \ + \ \frac{\$43,200}{(1.20)^2} \ = \ \$55,000$$

The value of the firm does not change with the change in dividend payments. Furthermore, the value per share remains $55 under the new dividend policy.

Problem 8: The dividend payments in Problem 7 imply dividends per share of ($30,000/1,000) = $30 and ($43,200/1,000) = $43.20 at the end of one and two years, respectively. Therefore, Charles prefers to receive the following dividend payments at the end of one and two years: ($30 x 100) = $3,000 and ($43.20 x 100) = $4,320. According to the dividend payments in Problem 6, dividends paid to Charles at the end of one year will be ($6 x 100) = $600. Therefore, Charles will sell ($3,000 - $600) = $2,400 of common stock at the end of the first year. By doing so, he forfeits ($2,400 x 1.20) = $2,880 at the end of the second year. Therefore, his total payment at the end of the second year is ($7,200 - $2,880) = $4,320. This is the same payment he would have received at the end of year two if Krane Pools followed the dividend policy described in Problem 7.

Problem 9: To maintain the current capital structure, Lankester must borrow $1 for every $5 of equity financing (from earnings) used. So, they must borrow 1/5 x $55,000 = $11,000. Total capital spending possible is $66,000.

Problem 10: The debt/equity ratio of 1/3 signifies that the firm has $1.00 of debt for every $3.00 of equity. If the firm retains all of the available $30,000 as the equity financing portion, to maintain the existing debt/equity ratio, the firm must raise (1/3 x $30,000) = $10,000 of debt financing. Therefore, the total financing available, if the firm does not obtain any new equity financing, is ($30,000 + $10,000) = $40,000.

Problem 11: The debt/equity ratio of 1/3 signifies that the firm's capital structure consists of $1.00 of debt and $3.00 of equity for each $4.00 of total financing. The capital structure is ($1.00 / $4.00) = 25% debt and ($3.00 / $4.00) = 75% equity. In order to finance expenditures of $24,000, while maintaining the existing capital structure, the firm will use debt financing of (.25 x $24,000) = $6,000, and equity financing of (.75 x $24,000) = $18,000. The firm has $30,000 of internal equity financing available, so that dividends are ($30,000 - $18,000) = $12,000.

Problem 12: From Problem 10, if no external equity financing is obtained, the total financing available is $40,000. To maintain the debt/equity ratio of 1/3, any additional financing is obtained as follows: 25% is debt financing and 75% is equity financing. The firm requires additional financing of ($60,000 - $40,000) = $20,000, which is obtained as follows: (.25 x $20,000) = $5,000 of additional debt financing and (.75 x $20,000) = $15,000 of additional equity financing. Total equity financing consists of $30,000 of internally generated funds and $15,000 of new equity. Total debt financing is equal to ($10,000 + $5,000) = $15,000. In this situation, the firm pays no dividends.

Problem 13: Prior to the payment of the dividend, the market value per share is ($100,000/2,000) = $50. The owner of 500 shares owns stock with a total market value of ($50 x 500) = $25,000. After the payment of the dividends, the market value balance sheet appears as follows:

Market value balance sheet			
Excess cash	$ 0	Debt	$ 0
Other assets	90,000	Equity	90,000
Total	$ 90,000	Total	$ 90,000

Dividends are ($10,000 / 2,000) = $5 per share. The market value per share is now ($90,000 / 2,000) = $45. The owner of 500 shares owns stock with a market value of ($45 x 500) = $22,500, and he has received dividends of ($5 x 500) = $2,500. Therefore, the market value of his position is ($22,500 + $2,500) = $25,000, which is the same as it was prior to the dividend payment.

Problem 14: The firm's market value balance sheet is identical to the balance sheet in the solution to Problem 13. At a market value of $50 per share, the firm can repurchase ($10,000 / $50) = 200 shares. Since there are now (2,000 - 200) = 1,800 shares outstanding, the value of a share of stock is ($90,000/1,800) = $50. The shareholder who owns 500 shares has a position with a total market value of ($50 x 500) = $25,000. Since this market value is the same as that computed in Problem 13, the shareholder is unaffected by either the dividend payment or the stock repurchase. However, the advantage of the stock repurchase is that the shareholder's tax payments are less than they would be with a dividend payment. In Problem 13, the shareholder pays income taxes on the total dividend payment of $2,500.

With the stock repurchase, the shareholder does not pay any income taxes, unless he chooses to create homemade dividends by selling a portion of his holdings. If, for example, he chooses to sell stock in an amount sufficient to duplicate the $2,500 dividend payment he would have received with the dividend payment described in Problem 13, he would sell ($2,500/$50) = 50 shares.

However, even in this case, his tax payment is less than it would be in the event of the dividend payment. Here, he would pay taxes only on the capital gain resulting from the sale of stock, rather than on the full $2,500.

Problem 15: Since the balance sheet shows market values, the stock is worth ($60,000/1,000) = $60 per share today (cum dividend). The ex-dividend price will be ($60 - $3) = $57. Notice that once the dividend is paid, Reebop has $3,000 less cash, so the total equity is worth $57,000, or ($57,000/1,000) = $57 per share.

Problem 16: After the stock dividend is distributed, (1,000 x 1.20) = 1,200 shares will be outstanding. The total value of the shares is still $60,000. That is, the total market value of the equity is unchanged. Therefore, the per share value is ($60,000/1,200) = $50. Notice that this is not 20% less than the old price. Rather the old price is 120% of the new price: ($50 x 1.20) = $60.

Problem 17: Reebop will purchase ($3,000/$60) = 50 shares, leaving 950 outstanding. The total equity value will be $57,000, so that the market price is still ($57,000/950) = $60 per share.

Consider an investor who owns 100 shares. With the cash dividend, this investor receives ($3.00 x 100) = $300 in cash and has 100 shares with a total value of ($57 x 100) = $5,700. Using the $300, the investor could purchase ($300/$57) = 5.263 more shares and have 105.263 shares worth $57 each, for a total value of $6,000. With the repurchase, the investor has 100 shares worth $60 each, if she does not sell any shares. Alternatively, she could sell ($300/$60) = 5 shares. As a result, she would have 95 shares, with a total value of ($60 x 95) = $5,700, and $300 in cash, for a total of $6,000 again.

Problem 18: The price will decrease by the after-tax amount of the dividend, or [$4.00 x (1 - .40)] = $2.40. The ex-dividend price will be ($60.00 - $2.40) = $57.60.

Problem 19: This problem is somewhat more difficult. Consider the following scenario: suppose you buy a share just before the stock goes ex-dividend, and then sell immediately thereafter. You will have an after-tax dividend of $2.40 and a capital loss of D, the decline in the stock price. Since this loss is tax deductible, your after-tax loss is [D x (1 - .20)]. You will be indifferent with regard to buying the share with the dividend only if:

$$\$2.40 \ = \ D \times \ (1 - .20)$$

In this scenario, the price decrease will be D = ($2.40/.80) = $3.00. In reality, capital gains are only taxed when the gain (loss) is realized. In the case of a realized capital loss, the loss is only applied against realized capital gains, so the size of the price decline is more difficult to determine. However, it would probably be less than the amount of the dividend but more than the after-tax value of the dividend.

Problem 20: The 10% dividend yield is equivalent to a 6% after-tax return. Since the total expected after-tax return is 20%, the expected capital gain is (20% - 6%) = 14%. The after-tax return is thus 'grossed up' to a pre-tax return of (10% + 14%) = 24%.

Problem 21: The value of your position is the present value of the dividends, ($.50 / 1.20) + (13.80 / 1.20^2) = $10 per share. Therefore, the total value of your position is $200. An annuity of $130.91 per year for two years has the same present value. At date 1, your stock will be worth the present value of the liquidating dividend, or $11.50 per share. You will receive $10 in total dividends at date 1. You will have to sell $120.91 worth of stock, or ($120.91/11.5) = 10.514 shares, leaving you with 9.486 shares. At the end of the second year, you will receive (9.486 x $13.80) in dividends, for a total of $130.91, thereby accomplishing your goal.

Problem 22: Your liquidating dividend will be $282, which is $6 greater than it would have been.

18 Short-Term Finance and Planning

CHAPTER HIGHLIGHTS

This chapter introduces the fundamentals of short-term financial management: the analysis of decisions involving cash flows which occur within a year or less. Because they affect the firm's current assets and current liabilities, these decisions are referred to as working capital management. Some examples of short-term financial decisions are questions such as: How much inventory should be kept on hand? How much cash should be kept on hand? Should goods be sold on credit? How should the firm borrow short-term?

18.1 TRACING CASH AND NET WORKING CAPITAL

Current assets include cash and other assets expected to be converted to cash within one year. The four major categories of current assets are: cash, marketable securities, accounts receivable, and inventory. Current assets appear on the balance sheet in order of the ease and time involved in converting the assets to cash.

Current liabilities are short-term obligations which require payment within one year. The three major categories are: accounts payable, expenses payable, and notes payable.

Defining Cash in Terms of Other Elements: The balance sheet identity can be written as:

Current assets + Fixed assets = Current liabilities + Long-term debt + Equity

Alternatively, by rearranging terms, this identity can be written:

(Cash + Other current assets) – Current liabilities + Fixed assets = Long-term debt + Equity

Solving this equation for cash:

Cash = Long-term debt + Equity + Current liabilities – Current assets (excluding cash) – Fixed assets

This equation clearly indicates those actions which increase cash and those which decrease cash:

Activities which increase cash:

Increase long-term debt (borrowing long-term);
Increase equity (sell common stock);
Increase current liabilities (borrow short-term);
Decrease current assets other than cash (sell inventory for cash);
Decrease fixed assets (sell fixed assets).

Activities which decrease cash:

Decrease long-term debt (repay long-term debt);
Decrease equity (repurchase common stock);
Decrease current liabilities (repay short-term debt);
Increase current assets other than cash (buy inventory for cash);
Increase fixed assets (buy fixed assets).

Activities that increase cash are called sources of cash; those that decrease cash are called uses of cash. Sources of cash always involve increasing a liability or equity account and/or decreasing an asset account. Uses of cash involve increasing an asset account or decreasing a liability (equity) account.

18.2 THE OPERATING CYCLE AND THE CASH CYCLE

A typical manufacturing firm's short-run operating and financing activities might consist of the following events and decisions:

Events	Decisions
1. Buying raw materials	1. How much inventory to order?
2. Paying cash for purchases	2. To borrow, or draw down cash balance?
3. Manufacturing the product	3. What choice of production technology?
4. Selling the product	4. To offer cash terms or credit terms to customers?
5. Collecting cash	5. How to collect cash?

These activities create cash inflows and outflows that are both unsynchronized and uncertain. Cash flows are unsynchronized because inflows from the sale of a product do not occur at the same time as outflows to acquire raw materials. The uncertainty of cash flows arises from the fact that future sales and costs cannot be predicted with certainty.

Defining the Operating and Cash Cycles: Short-term operating activities and cash flows can be represented by a *cash-flow time line* (see the example in your text). This time line consists of an operating cycle and a cash cycle. The length of the *operating cycle* is equal to the sum of the inventory period and the accounts receivable period. The *inventory period* is the time required from receipt of inventory to sale of the finished goods. The *accounts receivable period* is the time required to collect cash from a credit sale. The *accounts payable period* is the length of time the firm can delay payment on its purchases.

The *cash cycle* is the difference between the operating cycle and the accounts payable period. A cash cycle of 30 days means that inflows occur 30 days after outflows. This mismatch suggests the need for short-term financing, which can be provided either by borrowing or by maintaining a liquid reserve of marketable securities. Alternatively, the cash cycle can be shortened by changing the inventory, accounts receivable or accounts payable periods.

Calculating the Operating and Cash Cycles: The operating and cash cycles can be calculated from balance sheet and income statement information.

An Example: The following information for D. Drysdale & Co., Inc., represents balance sheet data for the beginning and end of 2000, and income statement data for the year 2000:

Balance sheet item	Beginning	Ending	Average
Inventory	$4,500	$5,000	$4,750
Accounts receivable	3,500	4,500	4,000
Accounts payable	2,250	2,500	2,375

Income statement item	Annual
Net sales (all credit)	$18,000
Cost of goods sold	13,300

Calculate the operating cycle and the cash cycle for Drysdale & Co.

The operating cycle is equal to the inventory period plus the accounts receivable period. We compute these from the inventory turnover ratio and the receivables turnover ratio, respectively.

$$\text{Inventory turnover} = \frac{\text{Cost of goods sold}}{\text{Average inventory}} = \frac{\$13,300}{\$4,750} = 2.80 \text{ times}$$

Inventory is 'turned over' 2.80 times per year. Therefore, the inventory period is determined as follows:

$$\text{Inventory period} = \frac{365}{\text{Inventory turnover}} = \frac{365}{2.8} = 130.36 \text{ days}$$

Assuming that all sales are credit sales, then:

$$\text{Receivables turnover} = \frac{\text{Credit sales}}{\text{Average receivables}} = \frac{\$18,000}{\$4,000} = 4.50 \text{ times}$$

$$\text{Receivables period} = \frac{365}{\text{Receivables turnover}} = \frac{365}{4.50} = 81.11 \text{ days}$$

The operating cycle is:

$$\text{Operating cycle} = \text{Inventory period} + \text{Accounts receivable period}$$
$$= 130.36 \text{ days} + 81.11 \text{ days} = 211.47 \text{ days} = 211 \text{ days}$$

In order to determine the cash cycle, we first compute the accounts payable turnover and then the accounts payable period:

$$\text{Payables turnover} = \frac{\text{Cost of goods sold}}{\text{Average payables}} = \frac{\$13,300}{\$2,375} = 5.60 \text{ times}$$

$$\text{Payables period} = \frac{365}{\text{Payables turnover}} = \frac{365}{5.60} = 65.18 \text{ days}$$

Therefore, the cash cycle is:

$$\text{Cash cycle} = \text{Operating cycle} - \text{Accounts payable period}$$
$$= 211.47 \text{ days} - 65.18 \text{ days} = 146.29 \text{ days} = 146 \text{ days}$$

These calculations indicate that, on average, the time between Drysdale's acquisition of inventory and collection of payment on sales is approximately 211 days, and the time between Drysdale's payment for acquisitions and collection of payment on sales is approximately 146 days.

18.3 SOME ASPECTS OF SHORT-TERM FINANCIAL POLICY

A firm's short-term financial policy has two dimensions: the size of the investment in current assets, and the financing of current assets. A *flexible* current-asset policy requires maintaining a relatively high ratio of current assets to sales, while a *restrictive* policy implies a relatively low ratio. A flexible financing policy employs relatively less short-term debt and more long-term debt; a restrictive financing policy requires that current assets are financed primarily by short-term debt.

The Size of the Firm's Investment in Current Assets: A flexible current asset policy implies that the firm maintains relatively high levels of cash, marketable securities and inventories, and grants liberal credit terms resulting in relatively high levels of accounts receivable. Firms with restrictive policies maintain relatively low levels of current assets. In order to determine the optimal levels of current assets, the costs and benefits associated with each policy must be identified.

A flexible policy requires greater initial cash outflows in order to purchase inventory, finance credit sales, and maintain high levels of cash and marketable securities. Future cash inflows, however, should be higher for a flexible policy. Similarly, liberal credit policies also stimulate sales. In addition, the larger cash balances associated with a flexible policy ensure that bills can be paid promptly, thereby increasing discounts taken on accounts payable and reducing borrowing costs required in order to meet expenditures.

The costs associated with managing current assets can be classified as: *carrying costs*, which increase with increases in current assets; and, *shortage costs* which decrease with increases in current assets. Carrying costs are the opportunity costs of investment in current assets because, if the firm holds idle cash, it forgoes the opportunity to earn interest on the investment of that cash. Similarly, investment in inventory also implies an opportunity cost. The two kinds of shortage costs are *trading costs (order costs),* and costs related to safety reserves. Trading (order) costs arise when the firm runs out of cash or inventory and must consequently incur the cost of restocking. Costs related to safety reserves include loss of sales, customer goodwill, or production time when a *stock out (cash out)* occurs.

The figure below illustrates the firm's carrying and shortage costs associated with the investment in current assets. The optimal investment in current assets (CA*) is the level that minimizes *total costs* (that is, the sum of carrying and shortage costs).

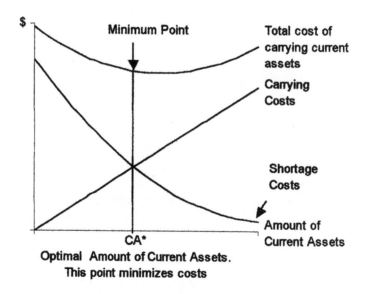

A flexible policy is most appropriate when carrying costs are low relative to shortage costs. This results in a higher optimal level of current assets. This is shown in the graph below.

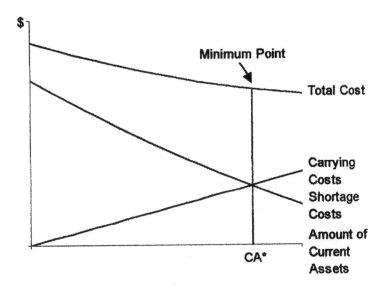

Alternatively, a restrictive policy is most appropriate when carrying costs are high relative to shortage costs. This results in a lower optimal level of current assets as shown in the following graph.

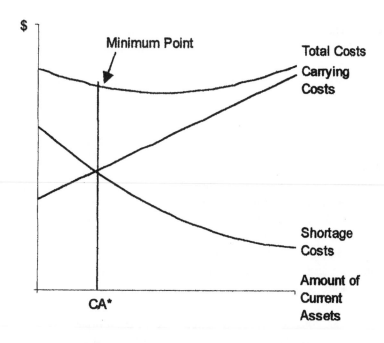

Alternative Financing Policies for Current Assets: For a given level of current assets, different financing policies are feasible. Under ideal circumstances, short-term assets are financed by short-term debts with maturity equal to the life of the assets; net working capital would always be zero.

In the real world, firms almost always require a *permanent investment* in current assets because current assets never decline to zero. This permanent investment is generally a result of growth in sales, seasonal variation, and unpredictable fluctuations. To finance the permanent component of working capital, a firm could use long-term debt. Then the firm will have excess cash available for investment in marketable securities. The alternative to this flexible strategy is a restrictive strategy which involves the use of permanent short-term borrowing to finance any deficit between long-term financing and total assets.

Which Financing Policy is Best?   There is no definitive answer to the question: "How much short-term borrowing is optimal?" Several factors must be considered. First, firms with flexible policies and *cash reserves* are generally less likely to experience financial distress since this policy implies less difficulty in meeting short-term obligations. Second, most firms hedge interest-rate risk by matching debt maturities with asset maturities known as *maturity hedging*. A policy of financing long-term assets with short-term debt is inherently risky since frequent refinancing is needed, and short-term interest rates are more volatile than long-term rates. Finally, short-term interest rates tend to be lower than long-term rates. This implies that, on average, borrowing long-term is costlier.

Flexible policies (F) and *restrictive policies* (R) are extreme cases, since, with F, the firm never does any short-term borrowing, and, with R, the firm never has a cash reserve (an investment in marketable securities). Figure 18.6 on page 615 of your text illustrates these two policies along with a compromise, Policy C.

With a compromise policy, the firm borrows short-term to cover peak financing needs, but maintains a cash reserve in the form of marketable securities during slow periods. As current assets build up, the firm draws down this reserve before engaging in any short-term borrowing.

18.4 THE CASH BUDGET

The *cash budget* is a forecast of estimated cash inflows and outflows over a period of time. It is the primary tool of short-run financial planning. The following example illustrates the preparation of a cash budget.

An Example: C. Erskine & Company has estimated sales for the next four quarters as follows:

	Qtr 1	Qtr 2	Qtr 3	Qtr 4
Sales	$150	$200	$300	$250

Accounts receivable at the beginning of the year are $100. Erskine has a 54-day collection period. Cash outflows consist of: (1) payments to suppliers; (2) wages, taxes, and other expenses; (3) capital expenditures; and, (4) long-term financing payments. Purchases from suppliers during a quarter are equal to 50% of next quarter's forecast sales. Payments to suppliers are equal to the previous period's purchases. In the most recent quarter, Erskine's purchases are (.50 × $150) = $75, which will be paid during the first quarter. Wages, taxes, and other expenses are 30% of sales. Interest and dividends are $20 per quarter. A capital expenditure of $100 is planned in the second quarter. Erskine maintains a $10 minimum cash balance to guard against unforseen contingencies and forecasting errors. Prepare a cash budget for C. Erskine & Co.

Sales and Cash Collections: First, compute the cash collections for each quarter. The 54-day collection period implies that [(90 − 54)/90)] = 40% of the sales in a given quarter will be collected during the current quarter and (54/90) = 60% during the following quarter. That is, sales made during the first (90 − 54) = 36 days of the quarter will be collected before the end of the quarter, while sales during the remaining 54 days will be collected during the following quarter. Therefore, ending receivables for a given quarter are 60% of sales during that quarter. In the first quarter, cash collections are the beginning receivables of $100 plus 40% of sales, or:

Cash collections = Beginning accounts receivable + (40% × Sales)

$$= \ \$100 + (.40 \times \$150) \ = \ \$100 + \$60 \ = \ \$160$$

Cash collections for each quarter are:

	Qtr 1	Qtr 2	Qtr 3	Qtr 4
Beginning Receivables	$100	$ 90	$120	$180
Sales	150	200	300	250
Cash Collections	160	170	240	280
Ending Receivables	90	120	180	150

The cash outflows for Erskine are:

	Qtr 1	Qtr 2	Qtr 3	Qtr 4
Payment of Accounts	$ 75	$100	$150	$125
Wages, taxes, other expenses	45	60	90	75
Capital Expenditures	0	100	0	0
Long-term financing expenses (interest and dividends)	20	20	20	20
Total	$140	$280	$260	$220

Cash Outflows: There are four broad categories of cash outflows. *Payments of accounts payable* are payments for goods and services from suppliers. *Wages, taxes, and other expenses* are the other cash outflows associated with running a business. *Capital expenditures* are cash outflows associated with the acquisition of long-lives assets. Finally, *long-term financing expenses* include dividend and interest payments.

While depreciation may be perceived as a regular cost associated with running a business, there is no actual cash outflow associated with depreciation, hence we do not include depreciation among the categories of cash outflows.

The Cash Balance: The forecasted *net cash inflow* is the difference between cash collections and cash outflows. The net cash inflow is determined as follows:

	Qtr 1	Qtr 2	Qtr 3	Qtr 4
Total cash collections	$160	$170	$240	$280
Total cash disbursements	140	280	260	220
Net cash inflow	$ 20	-$110	-$ 20	$ 60

Erskine maintains a $10 minimum cash balance. Assuming that $10 balance existed at the beginning of the first quarter, we can compute the cumulative surplus, or deficit, at the end of each quarter:

	Qtr 1	Qtr 2	Qtr 3	Qtr 4
Beginning cash balance	$ 10	$ 30	-$ 80	-$100
Net cash inflow	20	- 110	- 20	60
Ending Cash balance	$ 30	-$ 80	-$100	-$ 40
Minimum cash balance	10	10	10	10
Cumulative surplus (deficit)	$ 20	-$ 90	-$110	-$ 50

Beginning in the second quarter, Erskine has a cash shortfall. It occurs because of the seasonal pattern of sales, the delay in collections, and the planned capital expenditure.

18.5 A SHORT-TERM FINANCIAL PLAN

In this section, we use the C. Erskine & Co. example to illustrate a completed short-term financial plan, which includes short-term borrowing of needed funds.

An Example: Erskine will borrow needed funds at a rate of 12 % APR, or (.12/4) = .03 = 3% per quarter. Assume that they begin the year with no short-term debt, and repay short-term debt as soon as possible. Ignore taxes, and assume that the cash surplus during the first quarter does not earn interest. Prepare a complete short-term financial plan for the year.

The complete short-term financial plan is below. With no borrowing, the cumulative deficit at the end of quarter 2 is $90. Consequently, short-term borrowing of $90 is required in quarter 2. Interest of (.03 × $90) = $2.70 must be paid during quarter 3, which increases the cumulative deficit for the quarter from $90 to $92.70. Therefore, additional short-term borrowing of $22.70 is required during the quarter. Ending short-term debt is ($90 + $22.70) = $112.70, which covers the cumulative deficit of $112.70. Interest paid during quarter 4 is (.03 × $112.70) = $3.38, so that ($60 – $3.38) = $56.62 of the $60 cash inflow is available to repay short-term debt.

	Qtr 1	Qtr 2	Qtr 3	Qtr 4
Beginning cash balance	$10	$ 30	$ 10.00	$ 10.00
+ Net cash inflow	20	- 110	- 20.00	60.00
+ New short-term borrowing	90	22.70		
- Interest on short-term borrowing		2.70	3.38	
- Short-term borrowing repaid				56.62
Ending cash balance	$30	$ 10	$ 10.00	$ 10.00
- Minimum cash balance	10	10	10.00	10.00
Cumulative surplus (deficit)	$20	$ 0	$ 0.00	$ 0.00
Beginning short-term borrowing	0	0	90.00	112.70
+ Change in short-term debt	0	90	22.70	- 56.62
Ending short-term debt	$ 0	$ 90	$112.70	$ 56.08

18.6 SHORT-TERM BORROWING

Erskine must finance the cash shortfall beginning in the second quarter. Two options are unsecured and secured short-term financing.

Operating Loans: An *operating loan* is a form of short-term financing which allows the firm to borrow up to a given amount over a specified time period (usually one year). These loans may be either secured or unsecured. These short-term lines of credit are referred to as either *committed* or *noncommitted.* Committed line of credit agreements are more formal than uncommitted agreements. Under a committed agreement, the bank guarantees that funds will be available when needed. For this guarantee, the firm pays a fee, which is usually a percentage of the total committed funds.

Compensating the Bank: The interest rate on an operating loan is usually stated as a specified number of percentage points above the prime rate. In addition, banks often require that a firm maintain a *compensating balance* on deposit in either a low- or zero-interest account. This compensating balance serves to increase the effective rate on the loan because interest on the loan is paid on the full amount borrowed, even though some portion of the loan is not available to the borrower.

An Example: A bank offers a line of credit with a 15% annual interest rate and a 5% compensating balance. How much interest is paid on a $20,000, one-year loan? What is the compensating balance requirement? What is the effective interest rate?

Assuming a single payment at the end of the year, with no compounding of interest, we have the following calculations:

$$\text{Interest paid} \;=\; .15 \times \$20,000 \;=\; \$3,000$$
$$\text{Compensating balance} \;=\; .05 \times \$20,000 \;=\; \$1,000$$

$$\text{Effective interest rate} \;=\; \frac{\text{Interest paid}}{\text{Amount available}} \;=\; \frac{\$3,000}{\$19,000} \;=\; .15789 \;=\; 15.789\%$$

The last calculation indicates that the borrower has only ($20,000 – $1,000) = $19,000 available because $1,000 must be left on deposit at the bank earning no interest. The effective rate is therefore 15.789%, rather than the stated 15%, because the interest paid is computed on the basis of a $20,000 loan, whereas the actual proceeds of the loan to the borrower are only $19,000.

An Example: For the loan terms described above, what size loan is necessary if the borrower requires net proceeds of $25,000? What is the compensating balance requirement? How much interest is paid on the loan for one year? What is the effective interest rate?

The borrower must apply for a loan which is large enough so that 95% of the proceeds of the loan will provide the required $25,000. The size of the loan is the solution to the following equation:

$$(1 - .05) \;\times\; \text{Loan size} \;=\; \$25,000$$
$$\text{Loan size} \;=\; \$25,000\,/\,.95 \;=\; \$26,315.79$$

Therefore, the size of the loan is $26,315.79 and the compensating balance requirement is ($26,315.79 – $25,000) = (.05 × $26,315.79) = $1,315.79.

$$\text{Interest paid} \;=\; .15 \times \$26,315.79 \;=\; \$3,947.37$$

$$\text{Effective interest rate} \;=\; \frac{\$3,947.37}{\$25,000} \;=\; .15789 \;=\; 15.789\%$$

The effective interest rate is 15.789%, as in the previous example, because the interest rate and the compensating balance percentage are constant regardless of the size of the loan. The borrower pays $.15 interest for each $.95 borrowed, or an effective rate of ($.15/$.95) = 15.789%.

Letters of Credit: A letter of credit (LC) is a common arrangement in international finance, where the bank issuing the letter promises to make a loan if certain conditions are met, including that the goods arrive as promised. An LC can be revocable (subject to cancellation) or irrevocable.

Secured Loans: Secured short-term loans usually require either accounts receivable or inventories as security for the loan. In addition, banks routinely limit risk through *covenants* which impose constraints that protect the interest of the debt holder. With accounts receivable financing, accounts are either *assigned* or *factored*.

Under assignment, the lender has a lien on receivables, and the borrower is responsible for bad accounts. The lending agreement establishes a margin (usually 75 %) of current (under 90 days) receivables. As the firm makes sales, it submits its invoices to the bank and can borrow up to 75 % of their value.

Factoring: A factor is an independent company that acts as an 'outside credit department' for the client. In *maturity factoring*, as the accounts are collected, the factor pays the client the face amount of the invoice less a discount (usually below 2 %). If any accounts are late, the factor still pays the firm on an average maturity date determined in advance. Legally, the factor purchases the accounts receivable from the firm, thus providing insurance against bad debts because default or bad debts are the factor's problem. It may also reduce costs associated with granting credit since factors do business with many firms, achieving scale economies and risk reduction through diversification.

Firms which finance their receivables through a chartered bank may also use the services of a factor to improve the receivables' collateral value. Here the factor buys the receivables and assigns them to the bank. This is called maturity factoring with assignment of equity. In the case of *advance factoring*, the factor will provide an advance on the receivables and charge interest at prime plus 2-3 %.

An Example: Pat's Pet Products, Inc. factors receivables by selling them for 98 cents on the dollar; it can also be said that Pat's sells receivables at a 2 % discount. Pat's average collection period is 30 days. What is the effective annual interest rate?

Pat receives $.98 for each dollar of receivables, but does not have to wait thirty days to collect payment. At the end of thirty days, Pat's customers pay the full amount of the receivables to the factor. This is equivalent to paying $.02 to obtain financing of $.98 for 30 days, which is an interest rate of ($.02/$.98) = .020408 = 2.0408% for thirty days. Assuming, for simplicity, twelve thirty-day periods in a year, the effective annual rate is:

$$\text{EAR} \quad = \quad (1.020408)^{12} - 1 \quad = \quad 27.43\%$$

Securitized Receivables - A Financial Innovation: A new approach to receivables financing is *securitized receivables*. Under this arrangement, large corporations may sell securitized receivables to a wholly-owned financial subsidiary. The subsidiary issues debentures and commercial paper backed by a diversified portfolio of receivables. Since receivables are liquid, the subsidiary debt is less risky than lending to the parent company which can benefit from the interest savings.

Inventory loans involve either a *blanket inventory lien* (a lien on all of the borrower's inventory), a *trust receipt* (the borrower holds specific items of inventory 'in trust' for the lender), or *warehouse financing* (a public warehouse company controls the inventory for the lender). The legal form of the security arrangement can be tailored to the type of inventory.

Trade Credit: Another alternative source of financing is trade credit, which is equivalent to borrowing from suppliers.

Suppose a supplier offers terms of 2/10 net 30. If your firm makes a $10,000 purchase, you can pay on the tenth day taking a cash discount or pay the full $10,000 on the thirtieth day. Or, you may be able to 'stretch' your payables by paying the $10,000 after 60 days. The longer you wait, the longer the supplier is providing you with trade credit financing.

An Example: For the $10,000 purchase mentioned above, what should your company do?

The buyer is effectively borrowing $9,800 for 20 days, so that the buyer pays $200 in interest on the 'loan' from the supplier. The interest rate for the 20-day period (net 30 less the discount period of 10 days) is 2.0408% = ($200/$9,800). Since there are 18.25 such periods in a year (365/20), the buyer is paying an effective annual rate (EAR) of:

$$\text{EAR} = (1.020408)^{18.25} - 1 = 44.6\%.$$

If the buyer can stretch and pay in 60 days, the EAR is based on 6.0833 periods a year (365/60):

$$\text{EAR} = (1.020408)^{6.0833} - 1 = 13.08\%.$$

This is a significant improvement for the buyer. However, companies that continually pay their suppliers late risk supplier illwill and possibly a loss in their reputation and credit rating.

Money Market Financing: There are two important money market instruments for firms with excellent credit ratings. *Commercial paper* is offered in denominations of $100,000 and up with maturities ranging from 30 to 90 days (with some up to 365 days). These short-term notes are issued directly by the corporation and backed by a special line of credit. So, the interest rate the firm obtains is below the rate a bank would charge for a direct loan. Also, commercial paper offers the issuer flexibility in tailoring the maturity and size of borrowing.

Bankers acceptances (BAs) are notes backed by the bank which guarantee the paper's principal and interest. When the bank "accepts" paper, it charges a stamping fee ranging from 0.20 % to 0.75 %. The most common buyers of BAs are mutual funds, insurance companies, and banks.

CONCEPT TEST

1. Current assets are defined as cash and other assets expected to be converted to _____ within _____ .

2. The four major categories of current assets are: _____ , _____ , _____ , and _____ . Current assets appear on the balance sheet in order of _____ , which is the ease and time involved in converting the assets to _____ .

3. Short-term obligations which require payment within one year are called _____ . Three major categories are: _____ , _____ , and _____ .

4. The balance sheet identity can be written as: Current assets + Fixed assets = _____ + _____ + _____ . Rearranging terms and solving for cash, cash = _____ + _____ + _____ - _____ - _____ .

5. The equation in (4) indicates those actions which increase cash and those which decrease cash. Activities which increase cash are: (increase/decrease) long-term debt; (increase/decrease) equity; (increase/decrease) current liabilities; (increase/decrease) current assets other than cash; and (increase/decrease) fixed assets. Activities which decrease cash are: (increase/decrease) long-term debt; (increase/decrease) equity; (increase/decrease) current liabilities; (increase/decrease) current assets other than cash; and (increase/decrease) fixed assets.

6.   The length of the operating cycle is equal to the sum of the _____ period and the _____ period.

7.   The cash cycle is the difference between the _____ and the _____ period. A cash cycle of 30 days means that _____ occur 30 days after _____ .

8.   A firm's short-term financial policy has two dimensions: the size of the investment in current assets, and the financing of current assets. A flexible current asset policy implies that the firm maintains relatively (high/low) levels of cash, marketable securities and inventories, and grants (liberal/restrictive) credit terms which result in relatively (high/low) levels of accounts receivable. Restrictive policies mean that the firm maintains relatively (high/low) levels of current assets.

9.   A flexible policy requires (larger/ smaller) initial cash outflows, and future cash inflows should be (larger/smaller) . The (higher/lower) level of inventory associated with a flexible policy (reduces/increases) the likelihood of inventory stockouts, so that sales are (increased/decreased) . Similarly, the (liberal/restrictive) credit policies associated with a flexible policy result in (increased/decreased) sales. Also, the (larger/smaller) cash balances associated with a flexible policy result in (increased/decreased) discounts taken on accounts payable and (reduced/increased) borrowing costs.

10.   A flexible financing policy employs relatively (less/more) short-term debt and (less/more) long-term debt. A restrictive financing policy employs relatively (less/more) short-term debt and (less/more) long-term debt.

11.   The costs associated with managing current assets can be classified as follows: carrying costs, which are costs that (increase/decrease) with increases in the level of investment in current assets; and, shortage costs, which are those that (increase/decrease) with increases in the level of investment in current assets.

12.   Carrying costs are the _____ costs of investment in current assets. The two kinds of shortage costs are: (1) _____ or _____ costs; and, (2) costs related to _____ . The optimal investment in current assets is the level that _____ the sum of the carrying costs and the shortage costs.

13.   Firms almost always require a permanent investment in current assets because _____ . To finance the permanent component of working capital, a firm could use a (flexible/restrictive) strategy for which the amount of long-term debt always exceeds the firm's total asset requirement. The alternative to this strategy is a (flexible/restrictive) strategy which involves the use of permanent short-term borrowing to finance any deficit between long-term financing and total assets. Firms with (flexible/ restrictive) policies are generally less likely to experience financial distress.

14.   Most firms hedge interest-rate risk by matching _____ with _____ .

15.   A policy of financing long-term assets with short-term debt is inherently risky since frequent refinancing is needed, and short-term interest rates are (more/less) volatile than long-term rates. Short-term interest rates tend to be (higher/lower) than long-term rates so that, on average, borrowing long-term is (more/less) costly.

16.   A common arrangement in international finance is known as a _____ where the bank issuing the letter promises to make a loan under certain conditions. This LC can be _____ or _____ .

17.   The _____ is a forecasted estimate of cash inflows and outflows over a period of time. The forecasted net cash inflow is the difference between cash _____ and cash _____ .

18. Short-term borrowing used to cover a temporary cash deficit most often takes the form of _____ loan. A _____ is an informal agreement allowing the firm to borrow without submitting the usual paperwork. A _____ is a formal legal agreement specifying that the bank will lend up to a specified amount to the firm. The interest rate is usually stated as a specified number of percentage points above the _____ .

19. A line of credit arrangement often requires that the firm keep some amount of money on deposit in a low-interest (or zero-interest) account; this arrangement is called a _____ and serves to (increase/decrease) the effective rate on the loan because interest on the loan is paid on the full amount borrowed, even though some portion of the loan is not available to the borrower.

20. Loans which usually require either accounts receivable or inventories as security for the loan are _____ loans. When accounts receivable are sold to the lender, they are said to be _____ . In this case, the (lender/borrower) assumes the risk of default on the part of the borrower's customer. Under the arrangement referred to as _____ of accounts receivable, the lender has a lien on receivables, and the (lender/borrower) assumes the risk of default on the part of the borrower's customer.

21. If the factoring company pays the client the face amount of the invoice less a fee as the accounts are collected, this is referred to as _____ . In the case of _____ , the factor will provide an advance on the receivables and charge interest at _____ plus 2-3 %. If the factor buys the receivables and assigns them to the bank, this is called maturity factoring with _____ .

22. Large corporations may sell _____ to a wholly-owned financial subsidiary. The subsidiary issues debentures and commercial paper which are backed by a diversified portfolio of _____ .

23. When an inventory loan involves a lien on all of the borrower's inventory, the arrangement is referred to as _____ . Inventory loans for which the borrower holds specific items of inventory 'in trust' for the lender involve the use of a _____ . When a public warehouse company controls the inventory for the lender, this arrangement is referred to as _____ .

24. It is (cheaper/more expensive) to purchase supplies from a source with credit terms of 2/15 net 45, whose annual percentage cost is _____ as opposed to another source with credit terms of 2/10 net 30. But you can 'stretch' by paying on the sixtieth day, reducing the annual cost to _____ .

25. _____ are short-term notes issued in denominations of _____ and up, issued by large corporations, with yields that are approximately one percentage (higher/lower) than the bank prime rate.

26. By '_____' the paper, which means the bank guarantees the paper's principal and interest, a _____ is charged which ranges from 0.20 % to 0.75 %.

27. Categories of cash outflows include payments of _____ ; wages, _____ , and other expenses; _____ expenditures; and long-term _____ expenses.

PROBLEMS

Problem 1

The following data for the Bleys Company applies to the year just ended:

1. Accounts payable increased by $20
2. A $10 dividend was paid
3. Inventories were increased by $120
4. Short-term bank borrowing increased by $80
5. Accounts receivable increased by $30

Identify each of the above as either a source or a use of cash.

Some selected items from Oberon Corporation's balance sheets for the beginning and ending of 2000, respectively, and income statement for 2000 are shown below. Use this information to solve Problems 2 - 6:

Balance sheet item	Beginning	Ending	Average
Inventory	$1,000	$1,400	$1,200
Accounts receivable	1,800	2,100	1,950
Accounts payable	900	1,100	1,000

Income statement item	Annual
Net sales (all credit)	$30,000
Cost of goods sold	16,000

Problem 2

Calculate the inventory period.

Problem 3

Calculate the accounts receivable period.

Problem 4

Calculate the accounts payable period.

Problem 5

Calculate the operating cycle.

Problem 6

Calculate the cash cycle.

Problem 7

The balance sheet and income statement date for the Martin Corporation (year 2000) are below.

Balance sheet item	Beginning	Ending	Average
Inventory	$10,500	$8,000	$9,250
Accounts receivable	5,000	6,500	5,750
Accounts payable	2,500	3,250	2,875
Income statement item			
Net sales (all credit)	$17,000		
Cost of goods sold	12,250		

Calculate the inventory period, the accounts receivable period, and the accounts payable period.

Problem 8

What are the operating and cash cycles for Martin Corporation?

Problem 9

The balance sheet and income statement for Iago Corporation for the year 2000 are presented below. Calculate the inventory period, the accounts receivable period, and the accounts payable period.

Balance Sheet Item	Beginning	Ending	Average
Inventory	$27,400	$24,600	$26,000
Accounts Receivable	7,800	8,400	8,100
Accounts Payable	3,200	4,150	3,675
Income State Item			
Net Sales (all credit)	$42,300		
Cost of Goods Sold	$28,000		

Problem 10

What are the operating and cash cycles for Iago Corporation?

Use the following information on Osiris Company to solve Problems 11 - 18:

Osiris has estimated sales for the next four quarters as:

	Qtr 1	Qtr 2	Qtr 3	Qtr 4
Sales	$510	$870	$450	$600

Accounts receivable at the beginning of the year were $210. Osiris has a 60-day accounts receivable collection period. Osiris' purchases from suppliers during a quarter are equal to 50% of the next quarter's forecast sales. Projected sales for each quarter of the year following the current one are uniformly 10% higher than the corresponding quarter's forecast sales during the current year. The accounts payable period is 45 days. Wages, taxes, and other expenses are one-third of sales, and interest and dividends are $10 per quarter. No capital expenditures are planned. Osiris is required to maintain a $10 minimum compensating balance, but currently has a cash balance of $0.

Problem 11

Calculate Osiris's projected cash collections.

Problem 12

Calculate Osiris's projected cash outflows.

Problem 13

Calculate the net cash inflow and cumulative financing surplus (or deficit) for Osiris. What do you observe?

Problem 14

Osiris will borrow needed funds at an interest rate of 16 % APR, or (.16/4) = .04 = 4% per quarter. Assume that Osiris begins the year with no short-term debt, and repays short-term debt as soon as possible. Ignore taxes, and assume that any cash surplus does not earn interest. Prepare a short-term financial plan for Osiris for the year.

Problem 15

Suppose that the following changes occur: the accounts receivable collection period decreases from 60 days to 30 days, and the accounts payable period increases from 45 days to 72 days. Calculate Osiris's projected cash collections.

Problem 16

Calculate Osiris's projected cash outflows, based on the changes described in Problem 15.

Problem 17

Calculate the net cash inflow and cumulative financing surplus (or deficit) for Osiris.

Problem 18

Prepare a complete short-term financial plan for Osiris for the year.

Some selected items from Isis Company's balance sheets for the beginning and ending of 2000, respectively, and income statement for 2000 are shown below. Use this information to solve Problems 19-24.

	Beginning	Ending	Average
Inventory	$600	$ 700	$650
Accounts receivable	800	900	850
Accounts payable	200	250	225

Income statement item	Annual
Net sales (all credit)	$10,000
Cost of goods sold	6,000

Problem 19

Calculate the inventory turnover period, the accounts receivable turnover period and the operating cycle.

Problem 20

Calculate the accounts payable period and the cash cycle for Isis.

Problem 21

Suppose that Isis is able to reduce its inventory period from 39.54 days to 30 days. How will this affect the firm's short-term financing requirements?

Problem 22

Suppose that Isis is able to reduce its accounts receivable turnover period from 31.04 days to 25 days. How will this affect its short-term financing requirements?

Problem 23

Suppose that Isis is able to extend its accounts payable period to 18 days, from the current 13.69 days. How will this affect the firm's short-term financing requirements?

Problem 24

Given the changes presented in Problem 21-23, what is the new operating cycle? What is the new cash cycle?

Problem 25

A bank offers a line of credit with a 13% annual interest rate and a 6% compensating balance. How much interest is paid on a $400,000, one-year loan? What is the compensating balance requirement? What is the effective interest rate?

Problem 26

Refer to the loan terms described in Problem 25. What size loan is necessary if the borrower requires net proceeds of $500,000? What is the compensating balance requirement? How much interest is paid on the loan for one year? What is the effective interest rate?

Problem 27

Kristy Konstruction Supplies, Inc. factors its receivables at a 2.5 % discount. The firm's average collection period is 40 days. What is the effective annual interest rate? Assume 360 days in a year.

ANSWERS TO CONCEPT TEST

1. cash; one year

2. cash; marketable securities; accounts receivable; inventory; accounting liquidity; cash

3. current liabilities; accounts payable; expenses payable; notes payable

4. current liabilities; long-term debt; equity; long-term debt; equity; current liabilities; current assets (excluding cash); fixed assets

5. increase; increase; increase; decrease; decrease; decrease; decrease; decrease; increase; increase

6. inventory; accounts receivable

7. operating cycle; accounts payable; inflows; outflows

8. high; liberal; high; low

9. larger; larger; higher; reduces; increased; liberal; increased; larger; increased; reduced

10. less; more; more; less

11. increase; decrease

12. opportunity; trading; order; safety reserves; minimizes

13. current assets never decline to zero; flexible; restrictive; flexible

14. debt maturities; asset maturities

15. more; lower; more

16. letter of credit; revocable; irrevocable

17. cash budget; collections; outflows

18. an unsecured short-term bank; noncommitted line of credit; committed line of credit; prime rate

19. compensating balance; increase

20. secured short-term; factored; lender; assignment; borrower

21. maturity factoring; advance factoring; prime; assignment of equity

22. securitized receivables; receivables

23. a blanket inventory lien; trust receipt; warehouse financing

24.   more expensive; 17.81%; 13.08%

25.   commercial paper; $100,000; lower

26.   accepting; stamping fee

27.   accounts payable, taxes, capital, financing

PROBLEM SOLUTIONS

Problem 1:   1.   source of cash.
                 2.   use of cash.
                 3.   use of cash.
                 4.   source of cash.
                 5.   use of cash.

Problem 2: First compute the inventory turnover ratio:

$$\text{Inventory turnover} = \frac{\text{Costs of goods sold}}{\text{Average inventory}} = \frac{\$16,000}{\$1,200} = 13.33 \text{ times}$$

$$\text{Inventory period} = \frac{365}{\text{Inventory turnover}} = \frac{365}{13.33} = 27.38 \text{ days}$$

The inventory turnover period is the average length of time required to order, produce and sell a product. Inventory turned over every 27.38 days, on average.

Problem 3: First, compute the accounts receivable turnover ratio:

$$\text{Receivables turnover} = \frac{\text{Credit sales}}{\text{Average receivables}} = \frac{\$30,000}{\$1,950} = 15.38 \text{ times}$$

$$\text{Receivables period} = \frac{365}{\text{Receivables turnover}} = \frac{365}{15.38} = 23.73 \text{ days}$$

Receivables turned over 15.38 times during the year, or every 23.73 days, on average.

Problem 4: First, compute the accounts payable turnover ratio:

$$\text{Payables turnover} = \frac{\text{Cost of goods sold}}{\text{Average payables}} = \frac{\$16,000}{\$1,000} = 16.0 \text{ times}$$

$$\text{Payables period} = \frac{365}{\text{Payables turnover}} = \frac{365}{16.0} = 22.81 \text{ days}$$

Payables turned over 16 times during the year, or every 22.81 days, on average.

Problem 5: Using the results from Problems 2 and 3, the operating cycle is:

$$\text{Operating cycle} = \text{Inventory period} + \text{Accounts Receivable period}$$
$$= 27.38 \text{ days} + 23.73 \text{ days} = 51.11 \text{ days} = 51 \text{ days}$$

Problem 6: Using the results from Problems 4 and 5, the cash cycle is:

$$\text{Cash cycle} = \text{Operating cycle} - \text{Accounts payable period}$$
$$= 51.11 \text{ days} - 22.81 \text{ days} = 28.30 \text{ days} = 28 \text{ days}$$

Problem 7:

$$\text{Inventory Turnover} = \$12,250 / \$9,250 = 1.32 \text{ times}$$
$$\text{Inventory period} = 365 / 1.32 = 275.52 \text{ days}$$

$$\text{Receivables Turnover} = \$17,000 / \$5,750 = 2.96 \text{ times}$$
$$\text{Accounts receivable period} = 365 / 2.96 = 123.31 \text{ days}$$

$$\text{Payables Turnover} = \$12,250 / \$2,875 = 4.26 \text{ times}$$
$$\text{Accounts payable period} = 365 / 4.26 = 85.68 \text{ days}$$

Problem 8:

$$\text{Operating cycle} = \text{Inventory period} + \text{Accounts receivable period} = 276.52 + 123.31 = 399.83 \text{ days}$$
$$\text{Cash cycle} = \text{Operating cycle} - \text{Accounts payable period} = 399.83 - 85.68 = 314.15 \text{ days}$$

Problem 9:

$$\text{Inventory Turnover} = \$28,000 / \$26,000 = 1.08 \text{ times}$$
$$\text{Inventory period} = 365 / 1.08 = 337.96 \text{ days}$$

$$\text{Receivables Turnover} = \$42,300 / \$8,100 = 5.22 \text{ times}$$
$$\text{Accounts receivable period} = 365 / 5.22 = 69.92 \text{ days}$$

$$\text{Payables Turnover} = \$28,000 / \$3,675 = 7.62 \text{ times}$$
$$\text{Accounts payable period} = 365 / 7.62 = 47.90 \text{ days}$$

Problem 10:

$$\text{Operating cycle} = 337.96 + 69.92 = 407.88 \text{ days}$$
$$\text{Cash cycle} = 407.88 - 47.90 = 359.98 \text{ days}$$

Problem 11: With a 60-day collection period, Osiris collects $(30/90) = 1/3$ of sales in the quarter in which they occur; 2/3 of sales are collected the following quarter. Cash collections for the first quarter are:

$$\text{Cash collections} = \text{Beginning accounts receivable} + (1/3 \times \text{Sales})$$
$$= \$210 + (1/3 \times \$510) = \$210 + \$170 = \$380$$

Cash collections for each quarter are indicated in the following table:

	Qtr 1	Qtr 2	Qtr 3	Qtr 4
Beginning Receivables	$210	$340	$580	$300
Sales	510	870	450	600
Cash Collections	380	630	730	500
Ending Receivables	340	580	300	400

Problem 12: With a 45-day accounts payable period, half of purchases from suppliers are paid in the quarter in which they are ordered and half are deferred one quarter. Projected sales in the first quarter of the next year are ($510 × 1.10) = $561. The projected cash outflows are:

	Qtr 1	Qtr 2	Qtr 3	Qtr 4
Payment of Accounts	$345	$330	$263	$290
Wages, taxes, other expenses	170	290	150	200
Long-term financing expenses (interest and dividends)	10	10	10	10
Total	$525	$630	$423	$500

Problem 13:

	Qtr 1	Qtr 2	Qtr 3	Qtr 4
Total cash collections	$380	$630	$730	$500
- Total cash disbursements	525	630	423	500
Net cash inflow	-$145	$ 0	$307	$ 0

The cumulative surplus (or deficit) is computed as follows:

	Qtr 1	Qtr 2	Qtr 3	Qtr 4
Beginning cash balance	$ 0	-$145	-$145	$162
+ Net cash inflow	- 145	0	307	0
Ending cash balance	- 145	- 145	162	162
Minimum cash balance	10	10	10	10
Cumulative surplus (deficit)	-$155	-$155	$152	$152

Osiris has a highly seasonal sales pattern. Because purchases are made in advance and collections are deferred, Osiris will have an ongoing pattern of short-term deficits followed by surpluses.

Problem 14: The complete short-term financial plan is presented in the following table:

	Qtr 1	Qtr 2	Qtr 3	Qtr 4
Beginning cash balance	$ 0	$ 10.00	$ 10.00	$149.35
+ Net cash inflow	– 145	0.00	307.00	00.00
+ New short-term borrowing	155	6.20		
– Interest on short-term borrowing		6.20	6.45	
–Short-term borrowing repaid			161.20	
+Ending cash balance	$ 10	$ 10.00	$149.35	$149.35
–Minimum cash balance	10	10.00	10.00	10.00
Cumulative surplus (deficit)	$ 0	$ 0.00	$139.35	$139.35
Beginning short-term borrowing	$ 0	$155.00	$161.20	$ 0.00
+Change in short-term debt	155	6.20	- 161.20	0.00
Ending short-term debt	$ 155	$161.20	$ 0.00	$ 0.00

With no borrowing, the cumulative deficit at the end of quarter 1 is $155. Consequently, short-term borrowing of $155 is required in quarter 1. Interest of $(.04 \times \$155) = \$6.20$ must be paid during quarter 2, and additional short-term borrowing of $6.20 is required during the quarter because the net cash inflow is zero. Ending short-term debt is $(\$155 + \$6.20) = \$161.20$. Interest paid during quarter 3 is $(.04 \times \$161.20) = \$6.45$, and the net cash inflow of $307 is more than sufficient to pay the total short-term debt of $161.20.

Problem 15: With a 30-day collection period, Osiris collects $(60/90) = 2/3$ of sales in the quarter in which they occur; 1/3 of sales are collected the following quarter. Cash collections for the first quarter are:

$$\text{Cash collections} = \text{Beginning accounts receivable} + (2/3 \times \text{Sales})$$
$$= \$210 + (2/3 \times \$510) = \$210 + \$340 = \$550$$

Cash collections for each quarter are indicated in the following table:

	Qtr 1	Qtr 2	Qtr 3	Qtr 4
Beginning Receivables	$210	$170	$290	$150
Sales	510	870	450	600
Cash Collections	550	750	590	550
Ending Receivables	170	290	150	200

Problem 16: With a 72-day accounts payable period, 20% of purchases from suppliers are paid in the quarter in which they are ordered and 80% are deferred one quarter. Only payment of accounts, and, consequently, total cash outflows are affected by the change in the accounts payable period. The projected cash outflows are:

	Qtr 1	Qtr 2	Qtr 3	Qtr 4
Payment of accounts	$291	$393	$240	$296
Wages, taxes, other expenses	170	290	150	200
Long-term financing expenses (interest and dividends)	10	10	10	10
Total	$471	$693	$400	$506

Problem 17: The net cash inflows are:

	Qtr 1	Qtr 2	Qtr 3	Qtr 4
Total cash collections	$550	$750	$590	$550
- Total cash disbursements	471	693	400	506
Net cash inflow	$ 79	$ 57	$190	$ 44

The cumulative surplus (or deficit) is computed as follows:

	Qtr 1	Qtr 2	Qtr 3	Qtr 4
Beginning cash balance	$ 0	$ 79	$136	$326
+ Net cash inflow	79	57	190	44
Ending cash balance	79	136	326	370
Minimum cash balance	10	10	10	10
Cumulative surplus (deficit)	$ 69	$126	$316	$360

In comparing the results of this problem with those of Problem 13, we note that Osiris now expects a positive cash inflow for all four quarters, and that the firm has a cumulative surplus throughout the year. In the earlier problem, a deficit occurs during the first two quarters due to delays in collections. The differences in this problem result primarily from the earlier collections, although the delayed payments also contribute. It is important to note that total collections and outflows for the year do not change substantially. Rather, it is the timing of cash flows which produce the results observed here.

Problem 18: The complete short-term financial plan is presented in the following table:

	Qtr 1	Qtr 2	Qtr 3	Qtr 4
Beginning cash balance	$ 0	$ 79	$ 136	$ 326
+ Net cash inflow	79	57	190	44
+ New short-term borrowing				
– Interest on short-term borrowing				
–Short-term borrowing repaid				
+Ending cash balance	$ 79	$ 136	$ 326	$ 370
–Minimum cash balance	10	10	10	10
Cumulative surplus (deficit)	$ 69	$ 126	$ 316	$ 360
–Beginning short-term borrowing	$ 0	$ 0	$ 0	$ 0
+Change in short-term debt	0	0	0	0
Ending short-term debt	$ 0	$ 0	$ 0	$ 0

There are no deficits, and we have assumed that a surplus does not earn interest. The complete financial plan does not add any information not already apparent from the solution to Problem 17.

Problem 19: The inventory period is 39.54 days, the accounts receivable period is 31.04 days, and the operating cycle is 70.58 days.

Problem 20: The accounts payable period is 13.69 days, and the cash cycle is 56.89 days.

Problem 21: An inventory period of 30 days is equivalent to inventory turnover of $(365/30) = 12.17$ times per year. With cost of goods sold equal to $6,000 per year, the average inventory level which would be required is: $6,000 / Average inventory $=$ 12.17

The solution to the above equation is $493.02, which is a reduction of $($650 – 493.02) = $156.98 in the level of inventory. Consequently, the firm will require, on average, $156.98 less short-term financing with this reduction in the inventory turnover period.

Problem 22: An accounts receivable turnover period of 25 days is equivalent to accounts receivable turnover of 14.60 times per year. The average level of accounts receivable is determined by : $10,000 / average receivables $=$ 14.60

Therefore, the new level of accounts receivable is $684.93, which represents a reduction of $($850 – 684.93) = $165.07 in the average level of accounts receivable and, consequently, in the average amount of short-term financing required by the firm.

Problem 23: An accounts payable period of 18 days is equivalent to accounts payable turnover of $(365/18) = 20.28$ times per year. The average level of accounts payable which results from this increase is indicated by: $6,000 / Average payables $=$ 20.28

The new level of accounts payable increases to $295.86, which is an increase of ($295.86 – $225) = $70.86 in the level of accounts payable and consequently a decrease in the amount of short-term financing required from other sources.

Problem 24: The operating cycle is 55 days and the cash cycle is 37 days. We have indicated a reduction in the cash cycle here and a resulting reduction in short-term financing requirements as calculated in Problem 17-19. However, it is important to realize that changes such as those suggested above cannot be achieved without incurring related costs. Therefore, the benefit associated with reductions in financing requirements must be weighed against costs such as potential loss of sales due to reduction in credit period.

Problem 25: Assuming a single payment at the end of the year, with no compounding of interest, we have the following calculations:

$$\text{Interest paid} = .13 \times \$400,000 = \$52,000$$
$$\text{Compensating balance} = .06 \times \$400,000 = \$24,000$$

$$\text{Effective interest rate} = \frac{\text{Interest paid}}{\text{Amount available}} = \frac{\$52,000}{\$376,000} = .13830$$

The effective rate is 13.830%, rather than the stated 13%, because the interest paid is computed on the basis of a $400,000 loan, whereas the actual proceeds of the loan to the borrower are only $376,000. The effective interest rate can also be computed on a per dollar basis. The interest paid per dollar borrowed is $0.13, and the actual amount available per dollar borrowed is $0.94, so that the effective interest rate is ($0.13/$0.94) = 13.830%.

Problem 26: The size of the loan is the solution for the following equation:

$$(1 - .06) \times \text{loan size} = \$500,000$$
$$\text{loan size} = \$500,000 / .94 = \$531,914.89$$

The size of the loan is $531,914.89 and the compensating balance requirement is ($531,914.89 – $500,000) = (.06 × $531,914.89) = $31,914.89

$$\text{Interest paid} = .13 \times \$531,914.89 = \$69,148.94$$

$$\text{Effective interest rate} = \frac{\$69,148.94}{\$500,000} = .13830$$

The effective interest rate is 13.830%, as computed in Problem 25.

Problem 27: Kristy receives 97.5 cents for each dollar of receivables, but does not have to wait forty days to collect payment. At the end of forty days, Kristy's customers pay the full amount of the receivables to the factor. This is equivalent to paying 2.5 cents to obtain financing of 97.5 cents for 40 days, which is an interest rate of ($.025 / $.975) = .025641 = 2.5641% for forty days. Assuming 360 days in a year, and therefore nine forty-day periods in a year, the effective annual rate is:

$$\text{EAR} = (1.025641)^9 - 1 = 25.59\%$$

19 Cash and Liquidity Management

CHAPTER HIGHLIGHTS

Corporations hold cash to provide the liquidity necessary for efficient operations. Holding cash, however, means foregoing the return that could be earned by investing in marketable securities. Cash management involves evaluating the tradeoff between the benefits of liquidity and the opportunity cost of foregone interest. Effective cash management requires that financial managers address three basic concerns. First, how much cash should the firm keep on hand? Second, how should the firm manage cash collection and disbursement? Third, how should 'excess' cash be invested?

19.1 REASONS FOR HOLDING CASH

There are three reasons for holding cash: the precautionary motive, the speculative motive, and the transaction motive.

Speculative and Precautionary Motives: The speculative motive is the need for cash to take advantage of investment opportunities which might arise in the future. The precautionary motive is the need to hold cash as a financial reserve in the event of unanticipated decreases in cash inflows. Both of these motives can be satisfied by access to reserve borrowing ability and holding of marketable securities, rather than holding cash. Consequently, it would be more appropriate to refer to these as motives for liquidity, rather than motives for holding cash.

The Transaction Motive: Firms require cash to meet their regular disbursements. This reason for holding cash is referred to as the transaction motive. The need arises because the timing of cash inflows and outflows do not exactly match.

Compensating Balances: Additionally, firms may hold cash in the form of compensating balances. A compensating balance is a minimum deposit required by a commercial bank as compensation for bank services. Compensating balance requirements together with the minimum necessary transactions balance establish the minimum total cash requirement.

Costs of Holding Cash: Firms with cash balances in excess of the minimum total cash requirement incur opportunity costs. The opportunity cost is the interest income foregone by holding cash rather than investing in marketable securities, for example. However, firms with low cash balances run the risk of not meeting required disbursements.

19.2 DETERMINING THE TARGET CASH BALANCE

The opportunity costs of holding cash are carrying costs, which are costs which increase with an increase in the cash balance. The costs of holding too little cash are shortage costs, or adjustment costs. The target cash balance is the firm's desired level of cash, which is the cash balance that minimizes the sum of carrying costs and shortage costs.

Firms with a flexible working capital policy hold marketable securities to satisfy the transaction and precautionary motives. The adjustment costs incurred are the trading costs associated with buying and selling marketable securities. Firms with restrictive policies face adjustment costs in the form of interest expense and other expenses associated with short-term debt.

A firm which holds an extremely low cash balance incurs high trading costs, but little or no opportunity costs. These firms sell marketable securities to meet a cash shortage, and then buy marketable securities with excess cash balances. As the cash balance increases, the firm's opportunity costs increase, while trading costs decrease; sales and purchases of marketable securities are less frequent because cash shortages occur less frequently. With extremely high cash balances, opportunity costs are very high, but trading costs are very low, cash shortages are infrequent, so that sales and purchases of securities are infrequent. The optimal cash balance, or target cash balance, is the cash balance which minimizes the sum of the opportunity costs and the trading costs.

Other Factors Influencing the Target Cash Balance: Firms can raise cash by borrowing, rather than by selling securities. However, the interest rate on short-term debt is usually higher than the rate the firm would have earned on marketable securities. And, firms with greater cash flow variability and low investment in marketable securities typically have to borrow more; thus, interest costs are higher.

For large firms, the transaction cost of buying and selling Treasury bills is almost certainly less than the interest that can be earned on T-bills, even for an overnight investment. As a result, the primary reasons for such firms to hold cash relate to compensating balance requirements. A large firm may have thousands of accounts so that it may not be worthwhile to manage them all on a daily basis.

19.3 UNDERSTANDING FLOAT

The amount of cash on a firm's financial statements (the 'book' or 'ledger' balance) is not the same as the firm's bank balance (the firm's 'available' or 'collected' balance). The difference between the firm's available balance and its book balance is called float.

Disbursement Float: Cheques written by the firm reduce the book balance immediately, but do not affect the available balance until the cheque is actually presented to the firm's bank for payment. The difference in the balances is called *disbursement float*. For example, suppose you have $100 on deposit in a checking account, and you write a cheque for $100 to pay for supplies. Once you write the cheque, you show a balance of zero on your books (i.e., in your cheque book), but the bank shows an available balance of $100 during the time that the cheque is clearing. You have a positive disbursement float of $100 during that time. The firm can obtain the benefits of this cash while the cheque is clearing by temporarily investing the balance in marketable securities.

Prior to writing the cheque, you have zero disbursement float:

$$\text{Float} = \text{Available balance} - \text{Book balance} = \$100 - \$100 = \$0$$

Once you write the cheque, but before the cheque is presented to your bank:

$$\text{Float} = \text{Available balance} - \text{Book balance} = \$100 - \$0 = \$100$$

When the cheque is presented to your bank:

$$\text{Float} = \text{Available balance} - \text{Book balance} = \$0 - \$0 = \$0$$

Collection Float and Net Float: Cheques received increase your book balance but not your available balance until payment is actually received by the bank. The difference is called *collection float*. If you deposit a $200 pay cheque, then you show an increase in your book balance of $200, but your bank balance does not increase by $200 until the cheque clears. This difference is a negative collection float equal to –$200. That is, when the cheque is deposited:

$$\text{Float} \quad = \quad \text{Available balance} - \text{Book balance} \quad = \quad \$0 - \$200 \quad = \quad -\$200$$

When the cheque has cleared, so that the $200 is available to you:

$$\text{Float} \quad = \quad \text{Available balance} - \text{Book balance} \quad = \quad \$200 - \$200 \quad = \quad \$0$$

Net float is the sum of collection and disbursement floats. Suppose you deposit the $200 pay cheque at the same time that you write the $100 cheque to pay for supplies. At that time, the book balance is $200 (i.e., the $200 pay cheque which has been deposited), but the available balance is $100 (i.e., the original $100 balance in the account). Therefore the net discrepancy, or the net float is negative.

$$\text{Float} \quad = \quad \text{Available balance} - \text{Book balance} \quad = \quad \$100 - \$200 \quad = \quad -\$100$$

This negative net float is a disadvantage since, if you were to write another cheque for $150, the bank balance would not be sufficient to cover the cheque even though your book balance is sufficient. Financial managers are more concerned with the available balance than with the book balance.

Float Management: Float management involves speeding up collections and delaying disbursements. Float can be broken down into three parts: *mail float* (the time the cheque is in the mail), *processing float* (the time between the receipt and deposit of a cheque), and *availability float* (the time required to clear the cheque through the banking system). Study Figure 19.2 on page 635 of your text to see the relationship between the three different types of float.

Measuring Float: The size of the float depends on both the dollar amount and the time delay involved. Suppose a customer places an order through a mail-order catalogue; the customer mails a $300 cheque to the firm from another province. It takes four days for the cheque to reach the firm, and one day for the firm to deposit the cheque in the bank. The bank holds out-of-province cheques for two days before crediting the firm's account. The total float is $[\$300 \times (4 + 1 + 2)] = \$2,100$. Assume, for simplicity, that this is the only cheque received by the firm during the month. The average daily float is computed as follows:

$$\text{Average daily float} \quad = \quad \frac{\text{Total float}}{\text{Total days}} \quad = \quad \frac{\$2,100}{30} \quad = \quad \$70$$

During the month, the firm's book balance is, on average, $70 greater than the available balance.

An Example: Suppose that the firm receives two cheques every month: one cheque is for $2,000 and is delayed a total of 15 days; the other is for $3,000 and is delayed 5 days. Compute the total float and the average daily float.

The total float is: $(\$2,000 \times 15) + (\$3,000 \times 5) \quad = \quad \$45,000$

The average daily float, assuming a 30-day month, is: Average daily float $= \quad \$45,000 / 30 \quad = \quad \$1,500$

Alternatively, the average daily float can be computed by first calculating the weighted average delay. For the above example, total receipts for the month are $(\$2,000 + \$3,000) = \$5,000$. The weighted average delay is:

$$[(\$2,000/\$5,000) \times 15] \quad + \quad [(\$3,000/\$5,000) \times 5] \quad = \quad 9 \text{ days}$$

The calculation indicates that $(\$2,000/\$5,000) = 40\%$ of the firm's receipts are delayed 15 days, and $(\$3,000/\$5,000) = 60\%$ of the receipts are delayed 5 days, so that the weighted average delay is 9 days. Average daily receipts are $(\$5,000/30) = \$166.67$. Since this amount is delayed 9 days, on average, then the average daily float is:

Average daily float = Average daily receipts × Weighted average delay = $166.67 × 9 = $1,500

Cost of the Float: The cost of float is the opportunity cost resulting from not being able to use the money. The calculation of this cost is based on the average daily float. Suppose a firm received a $100 payment each day from its customers, and the cheques require three days to clear through the banking system. Therefore, a cheque received Day 1 is available to the firm on Day 4, and float, as of Day 4, is $300. Float remains constant at $300, and the firm receives payment of $100 each day while a cheque deposited three days earlier becomes available each day. Now, suppose that, as of Day t, the three-day delay could be completely eliminated, so that all payments were available immediately; what would such a change be worth to the firm? The answer is $300. On day 5, $400 would become available, representing the $100 payment received from customers on Day t plus payments received from customers on each of the three preceding days. This results in an incremental cash inflow of $300, and float would be reduced from $300 to $0 on Day t. On Day (t + 1), and on every subsequent day, the firm would continue to receive $100 per day. Therefore, the only change in cash flows is the additional $300 received on Day t.

Suppose that, instead of a reduction from a three-day delay to no delay, the reduction is from a three-day delay to a one-day delay. What is the value of this reduction to the firm? Float will decrease from $300 to $100, a $200 decrease, and the incremental cash flow will be $200, the same as the reduction in float. That is, on Day t, $300 becomes available, rather than $100, because cheques which were deposited on Days (t–3), (t–2) and (t–1) all become available on Day t. With the previous arrangement, only the cheque deposited on Day (t–3) would become available on Day t.

A reduction in float has value to the firm, but there is generally a cost associated with accomplishing such a reduction. Some procedures for reducing float are described in the remainder of this section. Adopting these techniques is appropriate only if they have positive net present value; that is, the benefit derived from the reduction in float must exceed the cost of implementing a change.

Accelerating Collections: Techniques to accelerate collections include systems to expedite mail and cheque processing, lockboxes, concentration banking, and wire transfers.

The key tasks of the firm's cash flow information system are tracking payments through the system and providing up-to-date cash balances and investment rates. Linking the manager's terminal with the bank's on-line, real time system, gives the financial manager access to account balances and transactions and information on money market rates. Electronic banking systems also allow the manager to transfer funds and make money market investments. Today *smart cards* are much like an Automated Teller Machine Card and are used within corporations to control access to information by its employees.

Over-the-Counter Collections: Most large retailers and other firms receive collections over the counter at field offices or at stores. Firms also may instruct customers to mail cheques to a given collection point address. By distributing these collection points locally, the firm can reduce mail float (instead of collecting at head office).

Lockboxes: A *lockbox* is the most common approach used to accelerate collections. A firm arranges for customers to mail payments to a post office box maintained by a local bank. The bank collects the cheques from the post office box several times a day, and deposits them in the firm's account. Lockboxes reduce mailing time, because customers mail payment to a local post office rather than to company headquarters. Use of lockboxes also eliminates the time the corporation would spend processing cheques prior to making the deposit.

Electronic Collection Systems: Many firms today use some type of electronic funds transfer system. Examples in Canada include *pre-authorized payments,* which are paperless transfers of installment payments from the customer's account directly to the firm's (mortgage payments, rent, insurance, cable TV etc.); *point-of-sales transfers* which use *debit cards* to transfer funds directly from a customer's bank account to a retailer's, and *electronic trade payables* (discussed later under disbursements).

Cash Concentration: With a *concentration banking system*, a firm's sales offices are used to receive and process cheques. Since customer payments are then deposited in local banks, this process speeds up cheque-clearing because customer's cheques also tend to be drawn on local banks. In addition, mailing time is reduced because cheques are mailed to local sales offices. Surplus funds are subsequently transferred to the firm's main bank (or to a small number of banks), called the concentration bank (or concentration banks). Concentration banking is often combined with lockboxes.

Controlling Disbursements: There are three common approaches to controlling delaying disbursements by delaying receipt of payment. The first is to make payments from as far away as possible. For example, pay Vancouver suppliers with cheques drawn on a Montreal bank, thus increasing the disbursement float by increasing the time required for the cheque to clear. The second is to postmark a payment, but delay mailing it. The third is to mail cheques from remote post offices.

A cheque is drawn on a bank while a draft is drawn on the issuer (the firm) and cannot be paid until it is presented to, and accepted by, the issuer. The issuer then deposits the required amount in order to cover payment of the draft. The use of drafts slows up payments and allows the firm to keep a lower cash balance than would otherwise be required.

Electronic payments made from disbursement accounts (for example, payroll, vendor disbursements, customer refunds etc.) are kept separate from the concentration account to ease accounting and control. Firms use *zero balance accounts* to avoid carrying extra balances in each disbursement account. A zero balance is maintained by transfers of funds from a master account in an amount only large enough to cover cheques presented.

It is often possible for firms to draw on and invest uncollected funds. A systematic policy of exploiting the float is potentially quite profitable, though it presents ethical and legal questions.

19.4 INVESTING IDLE CASH

Canadian chartered banks offer arrangements in which the bank takes all excess available funds at the close of each business day and invests them for the firm.

Idle cash can be invested in short-term securities. The market for these securities is called the money market. Most large firms do their own investing in money-market securities. Smaller firms often rely on money-market mutual funds, some of which specialize in corporate cash management. These funds buy money market instruments and manage them for a fee.

Temporary Cash Surpluses: Temporary cash surpluses help finance seasonal or cyclical activities, as well as planned or possible expenditures. Some firms, such as retailers, have a predictable seasonal cash flow pattern. These firms regularly invest in marketable securities during periods of surplus cash flows and sell securities, or obtain bank loans, during deficit periods. Firms frequently accumulate cash in anticipation of a large expenditure on a new plant, for example. Stocks and bonds might be sold to finance the expenditure; the proceeds are then temporarily invested and drawn down as construction progresses.

Characteristics of Short-term Securities: The most important characteristics of short-term marketable securities are the maturity, default risk, marketability, and tax status of the securities.

Most firms limit their investments in money-market securities to those with maturity of 90 days or less. This strategy virtually eliminates interest-rate risk, which is the change in the value of an asset resulting from changes in interest rates. Firms also restrict their short-term investments to highly-rated securities with little or no default risk. Firms usually prefer to invest in securities which are highly marketable, or liquid, meaning that they can be quickly sold without loss of value. Finally, interest earned on money market securities is subject to federal and provincial tax.

Some Different Types of Money-Market Securities: *Treasury bills* are direct obligations of the federal government. At weekly auctions, they are issued with maturities of 90 and 180 days. At monthly auctions, the maturities are 270 and 360 days. These securities are actively traded by banks and investment dealers over the counter.

Commercial paper is short-term, unsecured debt, issued by businesses with maturities ranging from a few weeks to 270 days. Since there is no active secondary market for commercial paper, marketability is low. DBRS and CBRS publish quality ratings and default risk varies with the issuer's strength.

Repurchase agreements are transactions involving the purchase of an instrument (usually Treasury securities) and a simultaneous agreement to sell it back at a higher price in the future. *Dollar Swaps* are foreign currency deposits that will be converted or swapped back into Canadian dollars at a predetermined rate. They allow the manager to place funds in major money markets outside Canada without measuring foreign exchange risk.

CASH MANAGEMENT MODELS (APPENDIX 19A)

The BAT Model: The Baumol-Allais-Tobin (BAT) model is the simplest formal approach to establishing a target cash balance. Consider the following example:

T = \$240 = the total cash needed for transactions over a period (e.g., a year);
F = \$1 = the fixed cost of making a securities trade to replenish cash balances;
R = 10% = the interest rate on marketable securities (i.e., the opportunity cost);
C = \$10 = the beginning cash balance.

We assume the cash balance is initially at C and declines to zero. When the balance reaches zero, it is replenished to the level C by the sale of marketable securities. Therefore, the average cash balance over the period is $[(C + 0)/2]$ = (\$10/2) = \$5. The total opportunity cost is the average cash balance times the interest rate on marketable securities:

Opportunity costs = $(C/2) \times R$ = \$5 × .10 = \$.50.

The number of times that the cash balance is replenished during the year is: (T/C) = (\$240/\$10) = 24 times.

The total trading cost for the year is:

Trading costs = $(T/C) \times F$ = 24 × \$1 = \$24

The following figure illustrates the characteristic 'sawtooth' pattern of the BAT model.

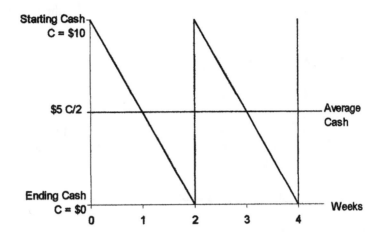

The BAT model identifies the cash balance (C*) which minimizes the sum of the two costs. The total cost is:

Total cost = Opportunity costs + Trading costs

$$= [(C/2) \times R] + [(T/C) \times F]$$

It can be shown that C* is the value of C for which opportunity costs and trading costs are equal:

$$(C^*/2) \times R = (T/C^*) \times F$$

Solving this equation for C*:

$$C^* = [(2T \times F) / R]^{1/2}$$

For our example, the target cash balance is:

$$C^* = [(2 \times \$240 \times \$1) / .10]^{1/2} = (4,800)^{1/2} = \$69.28$$

The BAT model is simple to apply, but it has several deficiencies. The model is based on the assumption that cash disbursements are the same every day, and cash disbursements are known with certainty. To the extent that these assumptions are inconsistent with reality, the model may not be applicable for a particular firm.

The Miller-Orr Model: A More General Approach: The BAT model assumes certainty in the firm's cash flows; the Miller-Orr model allows for cash-flow variability. The essence of the Miller-Orr model is that the firm sets a lower limit (L) on cash holdings, based on the likelihood of a cash shortfall and the firm's willingness to tolerate the risk of a shortfall; then an upper limit (U*) and a target cash balance (C*) are determined by applying the model. When the cash balance reaches U*, the firm returns to its target balance C* by investing (U* – C*) dollars in marketable securities. When the balance declines to L, the firm sells (C* – L) dollars of marketable securities in order to increase the cash balance to C*. As long as the firm's cash balance is between L and U*, no transactions are made.

Given L, the values of C* and U* which minimize expected total cost are determined as follows:

$$C^* = L + [(3/4 \times F \times \sigma^2)/R]^{1/3}$$

$$U^* = (3 \times C^*) - (2 \times L)$$

where F is the cost per transaction of buying and selling marketable securities, σ^2 is the variance of the firm's net cash flows per period, and R is the interest rate, per period, on marketable securities.

The average cash balance is determined as follows:

$$\text{Average cash balance} \quad = \quad [(4 \times C^*) - L]/3$$

Suppose that the daily variance of cash flows is $4, the daily interest rate is .02% (.0002), and that management has determined that a lower limit of $10 is desirable. Using the other data from the BAT model example in the previous section, we calculate C*, U*, and the average cash balance:

$$C^* \quad = \quad \$10 + [(3/4 \times \$1 \times \$4)/.0002]^{1/3} \quad = \quad \$34.66$$

$$U^* \quad = \quad (3 \times \$34.66) - (2 \times \$10) \quad = \quad \$83.98$$

$$\text{Average cash balance} \quad = \quad [(4 \times \$34.66) - \$10]/3 \quad = \quad \$42.88$$

CONCEPT TEST

1.   The desire to take advantage of investment opportunities which might arise in the future is the _____ motive for holding cash. The need to hold cash as a financial reserve in the event of unanticipated increases in cash outflows or unanticipated decreases in cash inflows is the _____ motive. Both of these motives can be satisfied by access to _____ and holding of _____ . Therefore, these might be referred to as motives for _____ .

2.   The need to hold cash for regular disbursements and collections is the _____ motive. An additional need to hold cash arises from the need to keep a _____ , which is a minimum deposit required by a commercial bank as compensation for bank services.

3.   A firm which holds a cash balance in excess of the minimum balance required for transactions and compensating balances incurs a(n) _____ cost. This cost is the interest income which the firm foregoes by holding cash rather than investing the cash. This cost is a carrying cost, which (increases/decreases) with an increase in the cash balance.

4.   A firm whose cash balance is too low is subjected to the risk of being unable to meet required disbursements, which then requires the firm to either _____ or _____ . The costs of holding too little cash are called _____ costs, or _____ costs.

5.   A firm with a (restrictive/flexible) working capital policy holds marketable securities to satisfy the transaction motive and the precautionary motive, while a firm with a (restrictive/flexible) policy relies on short-term borrowing to meet unanticipated cash requirements. In the former case, the shortage costs are _____ costs, and in the latter case, the shortage costs are _____ expenses.

6.   A firm that holds a low cash balance incurs (high/low) shortage costs and (high/low) opportunity costs. As the cash balance increases, opportunity costs (increase/decrease) while shortage costs (increase/decrease). With high cash balances, opportunity costs are (high/low) and shortage costs are (high/low).

7. The optimal cash balance, or target cash balance, is the cash balance which minimizes the sum of _____ and _____ costs.

8. The amount of cash on a firm's financial statement is called the _____ balance or the _____ balance. The firm's bank balance is called the _____ balance or the _____ balance. The difference between the firm's available balance and its book balance is called _____.

9. Cheques written by the firm reduce the _____ balance immediately, but do not affect the _____ balance until the cheque is actually presented to the firm's bank for payment. The difference in the balances is called _____ float.

10. Cheques received increase the _____ balance but do not increase the _____ balance until payment is actually received by the bank. The difference is called _____ float.

11. Net float is the sum of _____ float and _____ float. Float management involves speeding up _____ and delaying _____.

12. Float can be broken down into three parts: _____ float is the time during which a cheque is in the mail; _____ float is the time between the receipt and deposit of a cheque; and, _____ float is the time required to clear the cheque through the banking system.

13. The size of the float depends on both the dollar amount and the time delay involved. The total float is equal to _____ times _____. The average daily float is equal to _____ divided by _____. The average daily float can also be computed as _____ times _____.

14. The cost of float is the _____ cost resulting from not being able to use the money.

15. The most common approach used to accelerate collections is the _____. This approach reduces _____ float, because customers mail payment to a local post office, and eliminates _____ float.

16. A second approach to accelerating collections is a _____ system, in which a firm's sales offices are used to receive and process cheques. Since customer payments are then deposited in local banks, this process reduces _____ float. Also, _____ float is reduced because cheques are mailed to local sales offices. Surplus funds are subsequently transferred to the firm's main bank, called the _____ bank. The fastest way to transfer funds to the firm's concentration bank is _____.

17. Idle cash can be invested in _____, or _____, securities, which are securities with maturity of less than one year. The market for these securities is called the _____ market.

18. Most firms limit their investments in money-market securities to those with maturity of _____. This strategy virtually eliminates _____ risk, which is the change in the value of an asset resulting from changes in interest rates. Firms also restrict their short-term investments to highly-rated securities with little or no _____ risk. That is, these securities have a very low probability that interest and principal will not be paid when due. Firms also prefer to invest in securities which are highly _____, or _____, meaning that they can be quickly sold without loss of value.

19. _____ is short-term, unsecured debt, issued by businesses, with maturities ranging from a few weeks to 270 days.

20.   _____ are time deposits in banks. _____ are transactions involving the purchase of an instrument and a simultaneous agreement to sell it back at a higher price in the future.

21.   In the BAT model, we assume that the cash balance is initially at C and declines to _____, at which time it is replenished to the level _____ by the sale of marketable securities. The average cash balance over the period is _____. The total opportunity cost is the _____ times the _____, or expressed algebraically, _____. The number of times that the cash balance is replenished during the year is equal to _____. The total trading cost for the year is equal to _____.

22.   The BAT model identifies the cash balance (C*) which minimizes the total cost, which is the sum of the _____ cost and the _____ cost. Expressed algebraically: Total cost = _____. C* is the value of C for which _____ costs and _____ costs are equal, and is computed as follows: C* = _____.

23.   In applying the Miller-Orr model, the firm sets a _____ limit (L) on cash holdings, and then an upper limit (U*) and a target cash balance (C*), which minimizes _____, and are determined as follows: C* _____, U* _____. The average cash balance is determined as follows: Average cash balance = _____.

24.   When the cash balance reaches U*, the firm returns to its target balance C* by investing _____ dollars in _____. When the balance declines to L, the firm sells _____ dollars of _____ in order to increase the cash balance to C*.

PROBLEMS

Problem 1

On a typical business day, a firm writes cheques for a total of $5,000. On average, these cheques clear in 8 days. Simultaneously, the firm receives cheques whose total is $7,000. On average, the cash is available in 4 days. Calculate the disbursement float, the collection float, and the net float. Interpret your answer.

Problem 2

A real estate firm receives 100 rental cheques a month. Of these, 70 are for $300 and 30 are for $200. The $300 cheques are delayed 4 days on average; the $200 cheques are delayed 5 days on average. Calculate the average daily collection float, and interpret your answer.

Problem 3

Using the data from Problem 2, calculate the weighted average delay. Use the weighted average delay to calculate the average daily float.

Problem 4

A mail order company typically receives three cheques every month: one is for $1,500 and is delayed for 10 days; one is for $2,000 and is delayed for 17 days, and the last is for $1,200 and is delayed for 12 days. What is the total float and average daily float?

Problem 5

Gill Corporation is a fish tank manufacturer and writes $4,300 worth of cheques each day. These cheques clear in 6 days. Gill also receives cheques worth $5,900 each, although these cheques take 5 days to clear. What is Gill's disbursement float, collection float, and net float?

Problem 6

Suppose that, for the data of Problem 2, a bank has offered to operate a lockbox system which will reduce float by two days. The bank's fee is $200 per year, payable at the end of the year, and the annual interest rate is 9%. Calculate the net present value of this system.

Problem 7

Consider the data from Problems 2-3 and 6. What is the maximum amount the firm would pay to reduce the float by two days?

Problem 8

Your firm has an average receipt size of $100. A bank has approached you concerning a lockbox system that will decrease your collection float by three days. Your firm typically receives 10,000 cheques per day. The daily interest rate is .02%. The bank's fee for the lockbox service is $.05 for each cheque processed. Should the lockbox service be adopted?

Problem 9

Suppose that the bank described in Problem 8 charges an annual fee of $5,000, payable at the end of the year, in addition to the variable fee; is the lockbox service still acceptable?

Problem 10

Suppose that, in addition to the fixed annual fee and the variable fee described in Problems 8 and 9, the bank requires that the firm maintain a compensating balance of $500,000. Should the lockbox service be adopted?

Problem 11

Given the bank fees identified in Problems 8 and 9, what compensating balance would leave the firm indifferent as to whether it adopts the lockbox service?

Problem 12

A company has all of its collections handled by a bank located in the same city as its home office. The bank requires a compensating balance of $100,000 and handles collections of $750,000 per day. The firm is considering a concentration banking system which would require total compensating balances of $450,000, but would accelerate collections by two days. The Treasury-bill rate is 6%. Should the company implement the new system?

Problem 13

Healy's Music Store requires a total of $1,000,000 cash for transactions during a year. Healy's fixed order cost is $25, and its annual interest rate is 20%. Using the BAT Model, determine the target cash balance for Healy's Music Store.

Problem 14

Calculate Healy's opportunity cost, trading cost, and total cost for the cash balance determined in Problem 13.

Problem 15

Try this one on your own. Your firm mails out 15,000 cheques, with a total value of $500,000, during a typical day. You have determined that if the cheques were mailed from Outer Mongolia, mail time would be increased by three days, on average. However, it would cost an extra $.10 per cheque in postage and handling. The daily interest rate is .00015. Should you adopt this method of delaying disbursements?

Problem 16

Given the following information, use the BAT model to calculate the target cash balance:

Annual interest rate	10%
Fixed order cost	$50
Total cash needed	$ 2,500,000

Problem 17

Calculate the opportunity cost, the trading costs, and the total cost for holding the target cash balance determined in Problem 16.

Problem 18

Using the data given in Problem 16, calculate the opportunity cost, the trading costs and the total cost assuming that a $25,000 cash balance is held. Calculate the costs assuming that a $100,000 cash balance is held.

Problem 19

Suppose that, for the data in Problem 16, the fixed order cost increased from $50 to $200. How does this affect the target cash balance, and the costs computed in the solution to Problem 2?

Problem 20

Suppose that, for the data in Problem 16, the interest rate decreased from 10% to 5%. How does this affect the target cash balance?

Problem 21

Suppose that the fixed cost, per transaction, to buy and sell marketable securities is $100, the daily interest rate is .03%, and the standard deviation of daily net cash flows is $50. Management has set a lower limit of $200 on cash holdings. Calculate the target cash balance, upper limit and average cash balance, using the Miller-Orr model.

ANSWERS TO CONCEPT TEST

1. speculative; precautionary; reserve borrowing ability; marketable securities; liquidity

2. transaction; compensating balance

3. opportunity; increases

4. sell marketable securities; borrow; shortage; adjustment

5. flexible; restrictive; trading; interest

6. high; low; increase; decrease; high; low

7. opportunity; shortage

8. book; ledger; available; collected; float

9. book; available; disbursement

10. book; available; collection

11. disbursement; collection; collections; disbursements

12. mail; processing; availability

13. number of days delay; dollar amount of cheque; total float; total days; average daily receipts; weighted average delay

14. opportunity

15. lockbox; mail; processing

16. concentration banking; availability; mail; concentration; wire transfer

17. short-term; marketable; money

18. 90 days or less; interest-rate; default; marketable; liquid

19. commercial paper

20.   certificates of deposit; repurchase agreements

21.   zero; C; [(C + 0)/2]; average cash balance; interest rate on marketable securities; [(C/2) × R]; (T/C); [(T/C) × F]

22.   opportunity; trading; {[(C/2) × R] + [(T/C × F]}; opportunity; trading; [(2T x F)/R]$^{1/2}$

23.   lower; expected total cost; {L + [(3/4 × F × σ^2)/R]$^{1/3}$}; [(3 × C*) – (2 × L)]; {[(4 × C*) – L]/3}

24.   (U* – C*); marketable securities; (C* – L); marketable securities

PROBLEM SOLUTIONS

Problem 1: The disbursement float is (8 × $5,000) = $40,000. The collection float is   [4 × (–$7,000)] = – $28,000. The net float is the sum of the disbursement float and the collection float: [$40,000 + (–$28,000)] = $12,000.

At any given time, the firm typically has disbursed cheques, which have not yet cleared, with a total value of $40,000. That is, $40,000 is the available balance and the book balance is zero. In addition, the firm has received cheques with a total value of $28,000, which are not yet available. Therefore, the available balance is zero and the book balance is $28,000. The firm's book balance is typically $12,000 less than its bank cash.

Problem 2: The total float during the month is: (70 × $300 × 4) + (30 × $200 × 5) = $114,000. Assuming a 30-day month, the average daily float is: $114,000 / 30 = $3,800. On an average day, the firm has $3,800 in the mail or otherwise uncollected.

Problem 3: Total monthly collections are: (70 × $300) + (30 × $200) = $27,000. The weighted average delay is: [($21,000/$27,000) × 4] + [($6,000/$27,000) × 5] = 4.2222 days. Average daily receipts are ($27,000/30) = $900. The average daily float is: Average daily receipts × Weighted average delay = $900 × 4.2222 = $3,800

This is the same as the result computed in Problem 2.

Problem 4:

Total float = ($1,500 x 10) + ($2,000 x 17) + ($1,200 x 12) = $63,400

Assuming a 30-day month,

Average daily float = $63,400 / 30 = $2,113.33

Problem 5: The disbursement float is (6 x $4,300) = $25,800. The collection float is (5 x $5,900) = $29,500. Net float is $25,800 - $29,500 = - $3,700.

Note: Collection means that the firm is *not* collecting funds. So, when you calculate net float as the sum of disbursement and collection floats, you must reverse the sign for collection float.

Problem 6: If the weighted average delay is reduced from 4.2222 days to 2.2222 days, then:

$$\text{Average daily float} = \text{Average daily receipts} \times \text{Weighted average delay} = \$900 \times 2.2222 = \$2,000$$

Therefore float is reduced by: $(\$3,800 - \$2,000) = (2 \times \$900) = \$1,800$

Since this $1,800 becomes available to the firm at the time that the lockbox system is instituted, the present value of the change is $1,800. This $1,800 is available to the firm as long as the lockbox system is in effect. The cost of maintaining the lockbox is $200 per year. The present value of the perpetuity is $(\$200/.09) = \$2,222.22$. Therefore, the net present value of the lockbox system is $(\$1,800 - \$2,222.22) = -\$422.22$, so that the system is unacceptable.

Problem 7: The maximum fee the firm would pay is the amount such that the net present value of the lockbox system is zero. This is the amount such that the present value of the fee is equal to the present value of the system. To determine the maximum fee, solve the following equation:

$$\text{Lockbox fee} / .09 = \$1,800$$
$$\text{Lockbox fee} = \$1,800 \times .09 = \$162$$

If the firm pays $162 per year, the present value of the fee is $(\$162/09) = \$1,800$, and the net present value is zero.

Problem 8: Average daily collections are $(\$100 \times 10,000) = \$1$ million. Speeding collections by 3 days will increase the firm's collected bank balance by $(3 \times \$1 \text{ million}) = \$3$ million, so the present value of the lockbox is $3 million. The daily cost of the variable fee is $(\$.05 \times 10,000) = \$500$. Since this is a perpetuity, the present value is $(\$500/.0002) = \$2,500,000$. The net present value of the service is $(\$3,000,000 - \$2,500,000) = \$500,000$, so that the service should be adopted.

An alternative approach to computing the net present value is to first assume that the firm invests the $3 million collected balance at the daily rate of .02%. The daily interest earned is then $(.0002 \times \$3,000,000) = \$600$. Since the cost of the system is $500 per day, the daily net benefit is $100. The present value of this perpetuity is $(\$100/.0002) = \$500,000$.

Problem 9: In order to compute the present value of the annual $5,000 fee, we first compute the annual interest rate as follows: $(1.0002)^{365} - 1 = .07572 = 7.572\%$

In order to maintain the benefit of the lockbox system, the $5,000 fee must be paid every year. Therefore, the present value of this perpetuity is $(\$5,000/.07572) = \$66,033$. The total present value of the costs is $(\$2,500,000 + \$66,033) = \$2,566,033$. The net present value is $(\$3,000,000 - \$2,566,033) = \$433,967$. The lockbox service is still acceptable.

Problem 10: The $500,000 can be viewed as a reduction in the $3 million available cash calculated in Problem 8, so that the present value of the lockbox system is $2,500,000. Since the present value of the costs, as computed in the solution to Problem 9, is $2,566,033, the net present value of the service is $-\$66,033$. The service should not be adopted.

Problem 11: The firm will be indifferent if the present value of the cost of the lockbox service is exactly equal to the $3,000,000 present value computed in the solution to Problem 8. Since the present value of the costs, without the compensating balance, is $2,566,033, then the compensating balance which leaves the firm indifferent is $(\$3,000,000 - \$2,566,033) = \$433,967$. Given this figure, the bank might then negotiate the size of the compensating balance.

The firm would adopt the lockbox service only if the bank agreed to accept a compensating balance significantly below this figure. Otherwise, the lockbox service has little or no value to the firm.

Problem 12: The concentration banking system would increase the firm's collected bank balance by ($750,000 × 2) = $1,500,000, but an additional $350,000 would be required for compensating balances. The net result would be that ($1,500,000 – $350,000) = $1,150,000 can be invested at a 6% annual rate, providing net savings of ($1,150,000 × .06) = $69,000. Therefore, the concentration banking system should be implemented.

Problem 13:

> T = Cash needed = $1,000,000
> F = Fixed order cost = $25
> R = annual interest rate = 20%

Using the BAT Model, the target cash balance is:

$$C^* = [(2 \times \$1,000,000 \times \$25) / .20]^{\frac{1}{2}}$$

$$= \$250,000,000^{1/2} = \$15,811.39$$

According to the BAT Model, Healy's Music Store should maintain a cash balance of $15,811.39 because this is the balance which equalizes the opportunity and trading costs.

Problem 14:

Average cash balance	=	$15,811 / 2 = $7,905.50
Annual opportunity cost	=	$7,905.50 x 0.2 = $1,581.10
Orders per year	=	$1,000,000 / $15,811 = 63.25 = 64
Annual trading cost	=	64 x $25 = $1,600
Total holding cost	=	$1,581.10 + $1,600 = $3,181.10

Problem 15: The firm could increase its disbursement float by $1.5 million. Investing this amount generates $225 per day. The extra cost would be $1,500 per day. The firm should not adopt the plan.

Problem 16: The target cash balance is:

$$C^* = [(2T \times F)/R]^{1/2} = [(2 \times \$2,500,000 \times \$50) / .10]^{1/2} = [\$2,500,000,000]^{1/2} = \$50,000$$

Problem 17: The average cash balance is: $(C + 0)/2 = \$50,000/2 = \$25,000$.
The annual opportunity cost is: $(C/2) \times R = \$25,000 \times .10 = \$2,500$
The number of orders during the year is: $T/C = \$2,500,000/\$50,000 = 50$
The annual trading cost is: $(T/C) \times F = 50 \times \$50 = \$2,500$
Total cost is the sum of the opportunity cost and the trading cost: $(\$2,500 + \$2,500) = \$5,000$.

The fact that the opportunity cost and the trading cost are equal is not coincidental. The fact that this must always be true for the target cash balance identified by the BAT model can be demonstrated from the mathematical derivation of the model.

Problem 18: If a $25,000 balance is held, the opportunity, trading, and total costs are $1,250, $5,000, and $6,250, respectively. For a $100,000 balance, the costs are $5,000, $1,250, and $6,250 respectively. Note that the total costs for both the $25,000 and $100,000 balances are higher than the total costs for the $50,000 balance as calculated in the previous problem. This result is, of course, to be expected because the BAT model identifies the cash balance which minimizes the sum of these costs.

Problem 19: There are two approaches to computing the new target cash balance for this problem. First, we can compute the solution directly by substituting the appropriate values in the equation for C*. The alternative approach is to note that the value of F in this problem is four times the value in Problem 16. Since F is in the numerator of the fraction, the value of the figure inside the square root sign is now four times its value in Problem 16. Since we take the square root of this figure, the value of C* is twice the value in Problem 16, because the square root of four is two. Consequently, the target cash balance here is (2 × $50,000) = $100,000.

Since the target cash balance is double that of Problem 16, the opportunity cost is also double: (C/2) × R = ($100,000/2) × .10 = $5,000.

It is not necessary to compute the trading costs, because the opportunity costs and the trading costs are equal when the firm holds a cash balance equal to C*. Therefore, the trading costs are $5,000 and the total costs are $10,000.

This problem demonstrates the fact that there is a direct relationship between the fixed transaction cost of selling marketable securities and the target cash balance. This is an intuitively reasonable result, because the increased cost of selling securities makes it more economical to hold larger cash balances.

Problem 20: As in the solution to Problem 19, the result here can be computed directly. Alternatively, we can take note of the fact that, since r is now half of its previous value, the fraction doubles in value. Consequently, the target cash balance here is equal to the solution in Problem 16 times the square root of 2: $50,000 x $2^{1/2}$ = $70,710.68.

This solution demonstrates the inverse relationship between the interest rate and the target cash balance. As the interest rate decreases, the target cash balance increases because the opportunity cost of holding additional cash decreases. Similarly, as the interest rate increases, the target cash balance decreases because it becomes more expensive to hold larger balances.

Problem 21: The variance of the daily cash flows is $\sigma^2 = (50)^2 = 2,500$. The target cash balance is:

$$C* = L + [(3/4 \times F \times \sigma^2)/R]^{1/3} = \$200 + [(3/4 \times \$100 \times \$2,500)/.0003]^{1/3} = \$200 + \$855 = \$1,055$$

The upper limit is: $U* = (3 \times C*) - (2 \times L) = (3 \times \$1,055) - (2 \times \$200) = \$2,765$

The average cash balance is: $[(4 \times C*) - L]/3 = [(4 \times \$1,055) - \$200]/3 = \$1,340$

When the cash balance reaches U* = $2,765, the firm returns to its target balance C* = 1,055 by investing (U* − C*) = $1,710 in marketable securities. When the balance declines to L = $200, the firm sells (C* − L) = $855 of marketable securities in order to increase the cash balance to C* = $1,055.

20   Credit and Inventory Management

CHAPTER HIGHLIGHTS

A firm may require cash on or before delivery in payment for its products, or it may decide to extend credit to its customers. If credit is extended, then the firm must establish a credit policy involving three distinct components: the terms of sale, credit analysis, and collection policy.

20.1 CREDIT AND RECEIVABLES

Granting credit to a customer results in the creation of an account receivable. This process is referred to as either trade credit or consumer credit, depending on whether the customer is another business firm or an individual consumer. Since approximately 15 % of all of the assets of Canadian industrial firms are in the form of accounts receivable, credit management (or receivables management) is an important aspect of a firm's short-term financial policy.

Components of Credit Policy: In managing its credit policy, a firm must establish its terms of sale, procedures for credit analysis, and its collection policy. The firm's terms of sale consist of the following aspects of a credit sale: the credit period, the cash discount and discount period, and the type of credit instrument. Credit analysis is the process of attempting to distinguish between customers who are likely and not likely to make payment on an account. A firm's collection policy is the set of procedures the firm uses to collect payment on accounts.

The Cash Flows from Granting Credit: A firm's accounts receivable period is the time period required for the firm to collect payment on a credit sale. The sequence of events during the accounts receivable period is: (1) the credit sale is made; (2) the customer sends a cheque to the firm; (3) the firm deposits the cheque; and, (4) the firm's account is credited for the amount of the cheque. In this chapter, we discuss the impact of the firm's credit policy on the accounts receivable period.

The Investment in Receivables: Consider a firm with credit sales of approximately $5,000 per day, and an average collection period (ACP) of 40 days. At any given time, the firm has not collected payment on the preceding forty days' sales. Consequently, at any given time, the firm's accounts receivable are equal to ($5,000 × 40) = $200,000. In general:

$$\text{Accounts receivable} \ = \ \text{Average daily sales} \times \text{ACP}$$

A firm's credit policy has an impact on both average daily sales and the average collection period. This means credit policy is a determinant of the level of the firm's investment in accounts receivable.

20.2 TERMS OF THE SALE

The terms of sale involve: the credit period, the cash discount and discount period, and the type of credit instrument.

Why Trade Credit Exists: In practice, trade credit helps overcome certain market imperfections. If buyers and sellers have imperfect information, the buyer may prefer credit terms which give time to return defective products while the seller offering credit 'signals' potential customers that the product is high-quality. Also, any firm which grants credit lacks perfect information on the credit worthiness of the borrower, but a seller which has been granting trade credit to a purchaser likely has it already. Information advantages may allow the seller to offer more attractive and flexible credit terms. Finally, it may be cheaper to initialize credit from the seller than to set up a borrowing facility or to borrow in money markets.

The Basic Form: Credit terms might be quoted, for example, as *5/20, net 60*. This means a customer can take a 5% discount from the stated price if payment is made within 20 days of the invoice date (usually the shipping date or date of sale). Otherwise, the full amount of the sale is due within 60 days. A customer who makes a $2,000 purchase under these terms has the following alternatives: (1) pay [$2,000 × (1 − .05)] = $1,900 within 20 days; or, (2) pay $2,000 within 60 days.

Credit Period: The credit period is the length of the time before the customer is obligated to make payment. When a discount is offered, the credit period has two components. The first is the net credit period, which is the total amount of time the customer has to make payment. The second is the cash discount period, which is the time period during which the discount is available to the customer.

The invoice is the written statement of merchandise delivered to the buyer. The invoice date is the beginning of the credit period.

The firm must consider many factors when setting the *length of the credit period*. Since the seller's credit terms become the buyer's payable period, the buyer's inventory period and operating cycle are important considerations in setting the length of the credit period. Suppose Firm A's inventory period and accounts receivable period are 40 days and 30 days, respectively, so the operating cycle is 70 days. Firm B, however, provides a credit period of 70 days. Firm A could purchase inventory from Firm B on credit, sell the product to its customers, and collect payment in 70 days. Firm A can then use the proceeds from the sale of the product to pay the accounts payable to Firm B. In this scenario, Firm B has financed Firm A's entire operating cycle. Firm A would find a 70-day credit period desirable, and Firm B might attract additional business as a result. On the other hand, Firm B incurs an opportunity cost during the credit period. These considerations must be weighed by Firm B in determining its credit period.

Other factors which influence the length of a firm's credit period are:

1. *Perishability and collateral value.* Credit periods are shorter for perishable goods because they have rapid turnover and low collateral value.
2. *Consumer demand.* Successful products have more rapid turnover and shorter credit periods.
3. *Cost, profitability and standardization.* Relatively inexpensive products, as well as standardized goods and raw materials, tend to have high turnover and short credit periods.
4. *Credit risk.* The greater the credit risk of the buyer, the shorter the credit period.
5. *The size of the account.* The credit period is shorter for small accounts, which are expensive to manage and less important to the seller.
6. *Competition.* Longer credit periods are sometimes offered to attract customers from competitors.
7. *Customer type.* A seller might have different credit periods for wholesale and retail customers.

A longer credit period is, in effect, a reduction in the price paid by the purchaser. Consequently, a longer credit period generally results in an increase in sales.

Cash Discounts: Cash discounts speed up collections of receivables because they provide an incentive to pay earlier. Discounts also provide firms with a way to effectively charge higher prices to credit customers, thus avoiding regulations prohibiting charging different prices for the same products.

Suppose we have a customer who routinely places a $100 order every month and pays the entire amount 60 days later. This customer is offered the alternative of paying within 10 days of the invoice date in exchange for a 3% discount. The alternative payment schedules are: (1) pay $97 in 10 days, or; (2) pay $100 in 60 days. Given these alternatives, the customer is actually obtaining $97 of financing for fifty days, from day 10 to day 60. The cost of the financing is the additional $3 which must be paid if payment is on day 60. The interest rate for this fifty-day period is ($3/$97) = .030928 = 3.0928%. Since there are (365/50) = 7.3 fifty-day periods in a year, the effective annual rate is: EAR = $(1.030928)^{7.3} - 1$ = 0.24901 = 24.901%

A customer who doesn't take the discount is paying an effective annual rate of 24.901% to finance the $97 payment.

If the cash discount encourages customers to pay early, it will shorten the receivables period and generally reduce the firm's investment in receivables.

An Example: A firm offers terms of net 30 and has an average collection period (ACP) of 30 days. If it offers terms of 2/15, net 30, then 40 % of the customers will pay in 10 days, and the remainder will pay on average in one month. If annual sales are $10 million before discounts, what will happen to the ACP and to the investment in receivables?

The new ACP will be: ACP = .40 (10 days) + .60 (30 days) = 22 days. Average daily sales are $10 million/365 = $27,397.26 per day. Receivables will thus fall by $27,397.26 × 10 = $273,972.60.

Credit Instruments: A credit instrument is an evidence of indebtedness. Most trade credit is offered on *open account*, which means the credit instrument is the invoice. The customer signs the invoice when the goods are received. Alternatively, the selling firm may require a *promissory note,* which is basically an IOU. This is not common, except when the order is large, there is no cash discount, and the credit risk is poor.

A *commercial draft* is a demand for payment sent to a customer's bank, along with shipping invoices. The buyer signs the draft before goods are shipped to the buyer. If the draft requires immediate payment, it is called a *sight draft*. If the bank 'accepts' the draft for future payment, it is called a *banker's acceptance* because the bank accepts responsibility for making payment. The banker's acceptance is then sent back to the seller of the goods, who can then sell this acceptance (at a discount) or keep it until payment is made.

A firm can also use a conditional sales contract as a credit instrument. In this case, the firm retains title to the goods until payment is completed, and payment is often made in installments.

20.3 ANALYZING CREDIT POLICY

Credit Policy Effects: The decision regarding whether to grant credit depends on the following:

1.   *Revenue effects.* Granting credit results in both a delay in revenue collections and an increase in total revenue.
2.   *Cost effects.* Granting credit results in increased costs directly associated with the credit process and, if sales increase, increased variable costs.
3.   *The cost of debt.* The cost of financing receivables must be considered.
4.   *The probability of nonpayment.* Some buyers will default.
5.   *The cash discount.* Some customers pay during the discount period.

Evaluating a Proposed Credit Policy: The relevant variables in analysing credit policy are:

P = Price per unit
v = Variable cost per unit
Q = Current quantity sold per month
Q' = Quantity sold under new policy
R = Monthly required return

An Example: Suppose that a firm is considering granting credit terms of net 30 days. Consider the following information regarding this decision:

P = $11
v = $ 5
Q = 100
Q' = 120
R = 1%

Should the firm grant credit terms of net 30 days to its customers?

If the firm does not extend credit:

Monthly sales are: $P \times Q$ = (11×100) = $1,100

Monthly variable costs are: $v \times Q$ = (5×100) = $500

The cash flow is: Cash flow (old policy) = $(P - v) \times Q$ = ($11 - $5) \times 100$ = $600

If credit is granted, then:

Cash flow (new policy) = $(P - v) \times Q'$ = ($11 - $5) \times 120$ = $720

The incremental cash flow is defined as:

Incremental cash flow = Cash flow (new policy) – Cash flow (old policy)

= $(P - v) \times (Q' - Q)$ = ($11 - $5) \times (120 - 100)$ = $120

This incremental cash flow is in the form of a monthly annuity so that the present value of the annuity is:

$$PV = \frac{(P - v) \times (Q' - Q)}{R} = \frac{\$120}{.01} = \$12,000$$

The cost of the change in credit policy is the sum of two components. First, the variable cost of producing the additional units:

$v(Q' - Q)$ = $5 \times (120 - 100)$ = $100

Second, the first month's sales which would be collected under the old policy are not collected until thirty days later under the new policy. Since collections are permanently delayed by thirty days, this cost is:

$$PQ = \$11 \times 100 = \$1,100$$

The sum of these costs is:

$$PQ + v(Q' - Q) = \$1,100 + \$100 = \$1,200$$

The net present value of the change in credit policy is:

$$NPV = -[PQ + v(Q' - Q)] + \frac{(P - v) \times (Q' - Q)}{R} = -\$1,200 + \$12,000 = \$10,800$$

Therefore, the change in credit policy to terms of net 30 days is beneficial in this example.

20.4 OPTIMAL CREDIT POLICY

Firms must also consider the optimal amount of credit to be granted. In performing this analysis, the firm must consider two categories of costs: the carrying costs associated with granting credit and investing in accounts receivables, and the opportunity costs which result from a refusal to grant credit. The carrying costs include the required return on the investment in receivables, losses from bad debts, and the costs of managing credit and credit collections. The opportunity costs are the foregone profits from the lost sales if the firm denies credit. The optimal amount of credit minimizes the sum of the carrying costs plus the opportunity costs which is the total *credit cost curve*. This is depicted in the figure below.

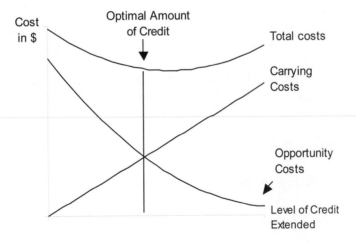

Carrying costs are the cash flows that must be incurred when credit is granted. They are positively related to the amount of credit extended. *Opportunity costs* are the lost sales from refusing credit. These costs go down when credit is granted.

In general, all other things being equal, it is likely that firms with (1) excess capacity, (2) low variable operating costs, and (3) repeat customers will extend credit more liberally than otherwise.

Organizing the Credit Function: Firms that grant credit may contract out all or part of the credit function to a factor, an insurance company or a capture finance subsidiary. Some firms buy credit insurance through an insurance company that covers up to a pre-set dollar limit for accounts. For example, exporters may qualify for credit insurance through the Export Development Corporation owned by the federal government. Setting up the credit function as a legal entity may allow more debt and save on borrowing costs.

20.5 CREDIT ANALYSIS

Credit analysis is the process of estimating the probability that a customer will not pay, and then deciding whether to extend credit to that customer. The firm must first gather relevant information, and then determine the creditworthiness of the customer.

When Should Credit be Granted?: Consider a customer who purchases one unit on credit at a price of $P' = \$100$ per unit. The variable cost is \$70 per unit and the monthly required return is $r = 1\%$. Assume that this is a one-time sale and the customer pays in two months. The probability of default is $\pi = 25\%$. Should the firm grant credit to the new customer?

The net present value is the cost minus the present value of the cash inflow:

$$NPV = -v + \frac{(1 - \pi) \times P'}{(1 + R)^2} = -\$70 + \frac{\$75}{(1.01)^2} = \$3.52$$

Since the net present value is positive, the firm should extend credit to the new customer.

Repeat Business: In the preceding example, we assumed that the firm has no repeat business. In the next example, we analyze the credit decision under the following assumption about repeat business: A new customer who does not default on his first purchase will remain a customer indefinitely and will never default.

An Example: Assume the following data from the previous example: $P' = \$100$, $v = \$70$, and $\pi = 25\%$. Also, the firm's required return for a two-month period is 2%. Assuming that a customer who does not default will purchase one unit every other month forever, should the firm extend credit to a new customer?

The cost to the firm is the variable costs $v = \$70$. In two months, the customer will either default, or he will pay $P' = \$100$ and purchase another unit. The probability that he will not default is $(1 - .25) = 75\%$ and the expected net cash inflow in two months is:

$$(1 - \pi) \times (P' - v) = .75 \times \$30 = \$22.50$$

The net present value of the decision to grant credit is:

$$NPV = -v + \frac{(1 - \pi) \times (P' - v)}{R} = -\$70 + \frac{\$22.50}{.02} = \$1,055$$

Since the net present value is positive, it is beneficial for the firm to extend credit to the new customer.

Credit Information: Useful information commonly used to assess creditworthiness can be obtained from financial statements, credit reports on the customer's payment history with other firms, banks, and the customer's payment history with the firm. Credit reports can be purchased from several sources in North America.

Credit Evaluation and Scoring: The traditional guidelines for assessing the probability of default are the five Cs of credit: *character* (willingness to pay), *capacity* (ability to pay), *capital* (financial reserves), *collateral*, and *conditions* (general business conditions). These criteria are applied in a subjective manner in determining creditworthiness.

Credit scoring is the process of computing a numerical rating as a guideline for assessing creditworthiness. Statistical procedures, called credit-scoring models, are used by some firms to forecast the probability that a customer will default. In general, credit is extended if the score is sufficiently high to indicate that the customer is likely to pay. Government regulations prohibit the denial of credit based on ethnic background, age, or gender.

Computerized scoring models employ a statistical technique called *multiple discriminant analysis* (MDA) to predict which customers will be good or bad accounts. MDA chooses a set of variables which best differentiate between good and bad credits with hindsight. For example, certain ratios like total asset turnover, gross profit margin, etc., may be the relevant variables for certain business customers used in the MDA. Statistic scoring models are more useful in consumer credit and not as popular with business customers because of the relatively smaller sample size in Canada than in the U.S.

20.6 COLLECTION POLICY

Collection policy is the process of monitoring receivables and obtaining payment of overdue accounts.

Monitoring Receivables: Two of the tools which firms use to monitor outstanding accounts are the average collection period (ACP) and the aging schedule. The relationship between the ACP and the firm's credit terms indicate whether customers are generally paying accounts when due.

An aging schedule for a firm with credit terms of 2/10, net 30, might appear as follows:

Age of account	Amount	Percent of total value of accounts receivable
0 – 10 days	$400,000	40%
11 – 30 days	$400,000	40%
31 – 50 days	$100,000	10%
Over 50 days	$100,000	10%

Since the terms require payment within 30 days, 80% of receivables are currently on time, but 20% of receivables are late. If this pattern is not typical or appropriate for the firm, then it is a signal that collection efforts should be intensified. Firms with seasonal sales find that the ACP changes during the year, and different aging schedules are typical at different times of the year.

Collection Effort: Collection effort generally involves a series of steps such as: (1) sending a delinquency letter, (2) calling the customer, (3) hiring a collection agency, and (4) initiating legal action.

20.7 INVENTORY MANAGEMENT

For most Canadian manufacturing operations, inventory often exceeds 15 % of assets and for retailers, inventory could represent more than 25 % of assets. Since a firm's operating cycle consists of its inventory period and its receivables period, we discuss these two topics together.

The Financial Manager and Inventory Policy: Typically, other functional areas in addition to finance, such as purchasing, production, and marketing will normally share decision making authority.

Inventory Types: For a manufacturer, inventory can be classified as *raw material* (whatever the firm uses as a starting point in its production process), *work-in-progress* (unfinished product), and *finished goods* (products ready to ship and sell). Keep in mind that one company's raw materials could be another's finished goods. Furthermore, different types of inventory can be different in terms of their liquidity with work-in-progress being the most illiquid. Finally, demand for an inventory item that becomes part of another is referred to as derived or *dependent* demand whereas demand for finished goods is said to be *independent.*

Inventory Costs: *Carrying costs* represent all of the direct and opportunity costs of keeping inventory on hand such as *storage and tracking costs; insurance and taxes;* losses due to *obsolescence, deterioration or theft* and the *opportunity cost of capital* on the invested amount. The sum of these costs can range from 20 to 40 % of inventory value per year. *Shortage costs* are associated with having inadequate inventory on hand and include *restocking costs* (costs of placing an order) and costs related to *safety reserves* (lost sales and loss of customer good will). The goal of inventory management is to minimize the sum of these carrying and shortage costs.

20.8 INVENTORY MANAGEMENT TECHNIQUES

Cost minimization techniques include the simplistic to the very complex which are described below.

The ABC Approach: The idea is to divide inventory into groups which present portions of inventory value. For example, group A may constitute only 10 % of inventory by count, but represent 50 % of the value of inventory. Group A items are therefore monitored closely and inventory levels kept relatively low. At the other end, basic items such as nuts and bolts are grouped separately, and because these are crucial and inexpensive, large quantities are handled.

The Economic Order Quantity (EOQ): As illustrated in your text, inventory carrying costs rise as inventory levels increase, while, at the same time, restocking costs decrease. Restocking costs are increased when the firm holds a small quantity of inventory. Carry costs are increased when there is a large quantity of inventory on hand. Total costs are the sum of the carrying and restocking costs.

With the EOQ model we attempt to specify the minimum total cost point Q*. This is not the actual cost of the inventory since the *total* amount of inventory a firm needs in a given year depends on sales. What we are determining is how much the firm should have on hand at any particular time or the order size it should place when it restocks its inventory.

Total Costs and the EOQ: For now we will assume that the firm's inventory is sold off at a steady rate until it hits zero and the firm replenishes its inventory back to some optimal level instantaneously. Suppose Q is the quantity of inventory ordered each time, then Q/2 would represent the average level of inventory. This is illustrated in Figure 20.6 on page 694 of your text.

Recall that carrying costs such as storage, insurance, obsolescence, etc., are normally directly proportional to inventory levels. If CC is the carrying costs per unit per year, the total carrying costs will be:

$$\text{Total carrying costs} = \text{average inventory} \times \text{carrying costs per unit}$$

$$= (Q/2) \times CC$$

For now, let us also assume that, if we ignore safety reserves, the only shortage cost consists of restocking costs. These restocking costs (of placing an order) are normally fixed, so that if the firm orders Q units each time, then it will need to place T/Q orders, where T represents the firm's total unit sales per year. So, total restocking costs are:

Total restocking costs   =   fixed cost per order × number of orders   = $F \times (T/Q)$

Since the total costs with holding inventory are the sum of carrying and restocking costs, we have:

Total costs   =   carrying costs + restocking costs

   = $(Q/2) \times CC$ + $F \times (T/Q)$

To find the precise cost-minimizing quality we can equate carrying costs with restocking costs and solve for Q*. The value of Q* is:

Q*   = $[(2T \times F)/CC]^{1/2}$

Where Q* is the economic order quantity (EOQ) which minimizes the total inventory cost.

An Example: Suppose Fullfill Corporation starts out with 7,200 units of inventory. If weekly sales are 1,800 units (annual sales are 93,600 units) then after 4 weeks, all the inventory of 7,200 will be sold and another order of 7,200 will instantly replenish the company's inventory level. Carrying costs are $1.50 per unit per year while ordering costs are $100 per order. What are Fullfill's average level of inventory, total carrying and restocking costs, and the EOQ?

Since Q is 7,200 units, the average level of inventory is 7,200/2 = 3,600 units. The carrying costs are average inventory × carrying cost per unit, or, 3,600 × $1.50 = $5,400. The restocking costs are fixed costs per order × number of orders, or, $100 × (93,600/7,200) = $1,300 per year. Total costs are the sum of carrying and shortage costs, or, $5,400 + $1,300 = $6,700. The EOQ is:
$[(2T \times F)/CC]^{1/2}$ = $[2(93,600)(\$100)/\$1.50]^{1/2}$ =   3,532.7 or 3,533 units

An Example: Given the EOQ for Fullfill Corporation, what are the carrying and restocking costs at Q*?

Carrying costs   =   (3,532.7/2)($1.5)   = $2,649.53

Restocking costs   = $100 × (93,600/3,532.7)   = $2,649.53

Notice, we derived Q* by equating carrying and restocking costs.

Safety Stocks: In reality, a firm reorders before its inventory goes to zero because it wants to minimize the risk of a stockout and when a firm does reorder, there will be some time lag before the order is replenished. Since a *safety stock* is the minimum level of inventory that a firm keeps on hand, inventories are reordered whenever the quantity falls to the safety stock level. Figure 20.7 on page 685 of your text illustrates how a safety stock is incorporated into the EOQ model.

Reorder points: *Reorder points* are the inventory levels at which the firm will actually place its inventory orders. The result is a generalized EOQ in which the firm orders in advance of anticipated needs and also keeps a safety stock to guard against unforeseen fluctuations in demand and delivery times.

An Example: Suppose Fullfill Corporation which was discussed earlier, wishes to hold a safety stock equal to seven days of sales. What is the safety stock and reorder point if the lead time required for the order to arrive is 4 days?

The safety stock is $7/365 \times 93,600 = 1,795$.

The reorder point is the lead time required $\times$ the daily usage plus the safety stock $= 4$ days $\times (93,600/365) + 1,795$
$= 1,025.75$ or $1,026$ units $+ 1,795 = 2,821$ units.

The figure below depicts the results for Fullfill Corporation when both the safety stock and reorder point are incorporated with the EOQ.

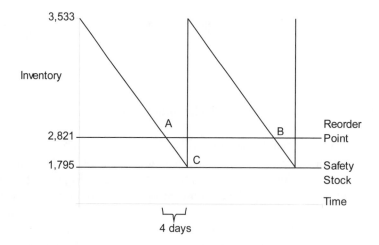

Fullfill will reorder at point A when the inventory level is 2,821 units. The order arrives 4 days later at point C when the minimum safety stock level is reached and the cycle continues thereafter.

Materials Requirements Planning (MRP): Computer-based systems for ordering and/or scheduling production of demand-dependent inventories allows a firm to schedule backward from finished goods inventories to the dependent nature of work-in-progress and raw materials inventories. It is particularly important for firms that use a variety of components are needed to create the finished product.

Just-In-Time Inventory: With JIT, the idea is that raw materials, parts, and other work-in-process should be delivered at the exact time they are needed on the factory floor so that the levels of inventory are minimized. Making JIT work requires extensive materials requirements planning so that all stages of production can be 'recoupled' and coordinated. There are no inventory buffers to fall back on to cover planning errors or equipment downtime.

MORE ON CREDIT POLICY ANALYSIS (APPENDIX 20A)

We will evaluate two alternative approaches to the credit policy analysis described in the chapter. Then we will consider the impact of cash discounts and defaults on credit policy decisions.

The One-Shot Approach: This approach is based on computing the net present value of a change in credit policy under the assumption that the change is in effect for only one time period . Since the change is actually permanent, the NPV of the change is then computed by treating the one-period NPV as a perpetuity. For the example in the chapter, the firm invests $(v \times Q') = (\$5 \times 120) = \$600$ in production costs today. In addition, they forgo a net cash inflow of $[(P - v) \times Q] = [(\$11 - \$5) \times 100] = \$600$ which would be received this month under the existing credit policy. Under the new credit policy, the firm then receives $(P \times Q') = (\$11 \times 120) = \$1,320$ cash inflow from payments thirty days later. The present value of this inflow is $(\$1,320/1.01) = \$1306.9307$. The net present value of this transaction, if we regard this as a one-month change in policy, is:

$$NPV = \$1306.9307 - (\$600 + \$600) = \$106.9307$$

Since we can regard this NPV as repeating itself each month, the NPV of the change in credit policy is:

$$NPV = \$106.9307 + (\$106.9307/.01) = \$10,800$$

The Accounts Receivable Approach: The second approach is based on viewing the change in credit policy as an investment in accounts receivable. The monthly carrying cost, or opportunity cost, of the investment in receivables is compared to the monthly net benefit resulting from the change in policy. The firm's investment in accounts receivable is comprised of two parts. The first part is the amount the firm would have received during the current month if the existing credit policy remained unchanged, which is $(PQ) = (\$11 \times 100) = \$1,100$. The second part of the investment in receivables is the increase in the investment in receivables which results from the increase in sales. The firm must invest $[v(Q' - Q)] = [\$5 \times (120 - 100)] = \$100$ in producing the additional quantity to be sold after the change in credit policy. The total incremental investment in receivables is:

$$(PQ) + [v(Q' - Q)] = \$1,100 + \$100 = \$1,200$$

The required return on this investment for one month is:

$$\text{Carrying cost} = [(PQ) + v(Q' - Q)] \times R = \$1,200 \times .01 = \$12$$

The monthly benefit derived from the investment in receivables is:

$$(P - v) \times (Q' - Q) = (\$11 - \$5) \times (120 - 100) = \$120$$

The monthly net benefit is $(\$120 - \$12) = \$108$ and the net present value of the change in credit policy is $(\$108/.01) = \$10,800$, as computed previously.

Discounts and Default Risk: In this section, we consider the impact of discounts and default risk on the credit decision. The additional variables considered in this section are:

π = Percentage of credit sales that go uncollected
d = Percentage discount allowed for cash customers
P' = Credit price

To clarify the analysis, we make two assumptions. First, we assume a change in credit policy does not affect the firm's sales quantity, Q. Second, we assume all customers buy on credit.

An Example: A company currently sells $Q = 50$ units of a product at a price $P = \$97$. The firm is considering a credit policy which allows customers sixty days to pay. The price for credit customers will be $P' = \$100$, while the cash price will remain \$97. The firm expects that the percentage of credit sales which will go uncollected is $\pi = 1\%$. Variable cost per unit is $v = \$70$ and the firm's required return for a two-month period is 2%. Should the firm adopt the new credit terms?

First, we compute the NPV of the change in credit terms. The cost of the change is the firm's investment in production costs plus the firm's foregone net cash inflow. However, since we have assumed here that Q and Q′ are equal, we can simplify the calculation of this cost as follows:

$$(v \times Q) + [(P - v) \times Q] \ = \ P \times Q \ = \ \$97 \times 50 \ = \ \$4,850$$

To determine the net cash inflow from the change in credit policy, we first compute the monthly cash inflow for the current policy:

$$(P - v) \times Q \ = \ (\$97 - \$70) \times 50 \ = \ \$1,350$$

Next, compute the monthly cash inflow for the proposed policy. If all sales were collected, cash inflow would be $[(P' - v) \times Q]$. However, since π is the percent of sales which are uncollected, then the percent of sales which are collected is $(1 - \pi)$, and the monthly cash inflow is:

$$[(1 - \pi)P' - v] \times Q \ = \ [(.99 \times \$100) - \$70] \times 50 \ = \ \$1,450$$

The net incremental cash flow is therefore ($1,450 – $1,350) = $100. This can also be computed as follows:

$$\text{Net incremental cash flow} \ = \ P' \times Q \times (d - \pi)$$
$$= \ \$100 \times 50 \times (.03 - .01) \ = \ \$100$$

The net present value of the change in credit policy is:

$$\text{NPV} \ = \ -(P \times Q) + \frac{P' \times Q \times (d - \pi)}{R} \ = \ -\$4,850 + \frac{\$100}{.02} \ = \ -\$4,850 + \$5,000 \ = \ \$150$$

Since the net present value of the change in credit policy is positive, the firm should make the change.

CONCEPT TEST

1.   Granting credit to a customer results in the creation of a(n) _____ for the seller, and a(n) _____ for the buyer. This process is referred to as _____ credit if the customer is another business firm, or _____ credit if the customer is an individual consumer.

2.   Collectively, the credit period, the cash discount and discount period, and the type of credit instrument are the _____ .

3.   The process of attempting to distinguish between customers who are likely to make payment on an account and those who are not likely to make payment is referred to as _____ . The set of procedures the firm uses to collect payment on accounts is called the firm's _____ .

4.   The time period required for the firm to collect payment on a credit sale is the firm's _____ or _____ . The firm's level of accounts receivable is equal to the product of the firm's _____ and the _____ . That is: Accounts receivable = _____ × _____

5. The length of the time period during which the customer is obligated to make payment is called the _____ period. When a discount is offered, this period has two components. The first is the _____ period, which is the total amount of time the customer has to make his payment. The second is the _____ period, which is the time period during which the discount is available to the customer.

6. The written statement of merchandise delivered to the buyer is the _____ . The beginning of the credit period is the _____ date.

7. Most trade credit is offered on open account, which means that the credit instrument is the _____ . Alternatively, the selling firm may require a(n) _____ , which is a basic IOU.

8. A(n) _____ draft is a demand for payment sent to a customer's bank. If the draft requires immediate payment, it is called a(n) _____ draft. Otherwise, if the bank 'accepts' the draft for future payment, it is called a(n) _____ .

9. A firm can also use a(n) _____ contract as a credit instrument. The firm retains title to the goods until payment is completed, and payment is often made in installments.

10. When deciding whether to extend credit, the financial manager must compute the _____ of the change in credit terms. Assuming no discount period and a thirty-day credit period, the incremental cash flow for a change in credit terms is : Incremental cash flow is _____ . Since this incremental cash flow is in the form of an annuity, the present value of the annuity is: PV = _____

11. The cost of the change in credit policy is the sum of two components. First, the variable cost of producing the additional units which will be sold with the new credit policy is equal to _____ . Second, the first month's sales which would be collected under the old policy are not collected until thirty days later under the new policy. Since collections are permanently delayed by thirty days, this cost is _____ . The sum of these costs is _____ .

12. The net present value of the change in credit policy is: NPV = _____

13. An additional issue which must be considered is the determination of the optimal amount of credit to be granted. In performing this analysis, the firm must consider two categories of costs: the _____ costs associated with granting credit and making the corresponding investment in accounts receivable, and the _____ costs which result from a refusal to grant credit. The optimal amount of credit minimizes the _____ of the _____ costs plus the _____ costs.

14. The traditional guidelines for assessing the probability that a customer will not pay are the 'five C's' of credit: (1) willingness to pay (i.e., _____); (2) ability to pay (i.e., _____); (3) financial reserves (i.e., _____); (4) general business conditions (i.e., _____); and (5) _____ .

15. The process of computing a numerical rating as a guideline for assessing creditworthiness is called _____ . Statistical procedures, called _____ , are used by some firms to forecast the probability that a customer will default.

16. The process of monitoring receivables and obtaining payment of overdue accounts is referred to as _____ . Two of the tools which firms use to monitor outstanding accounts are the _____ period and the _____ schedule.

17.   _____ inventory is what the firm uses as a starting point in its production process; _____ represents products that are ready to sell, while _____ is classified as unfinished products.

18.   Storage and tracking costs are examples of _____ , while the costs of placing an order and costs related to safety reserves are called _____ .

19.   The basic idea behind the _____ is to divide inventory into groups which represent portions of inventory value.

20.   As inventory levels increase, carrying costs _____ while, at the same time, restocking costs _____ .

21.   Total inventory costs can be calculated by specifying total carrying costs, which are equal to _____ plus total restocking costs, which are equal to _____ .

22.   To find the precise _____ quantity we specify Q*, which represents the _____ . This can be computed using the following formula: _____ .

23.   The minimum level of inventory a firm keeps on hand is referred to as the _____ which minimizes the risk of a _____ and allows for the time lag before the inventory is _____ .

24.   The _____ can be calculated by multiplying the _____ which is the time it takes for the order to arrive, by the _____ and to this we add the _____ .

25.   Managing the Japanese based _____ method of minimizing inventory requires extensive _____ so that all stages can be '_____' and coordinated.

PROBLEMS

Problem 1

Icarus Company (a well-known 'high flyer') manufactures suntan lotion. Its credit terms are 2/20, net 40. Suppose that a retailer purchases 10 cases of suntan lotion for $200 per case. If the retailer takes the full credit period to pay, how much should the retailer remit to Icarus? When should payment be made?

Problem 2

For the data of Problem 1, when must the retailer pay in order to receive the discount offered by Icarus? If the retailer takes the discount, how much should be remitted to Icarus? If the retailer does not take advantage of the discount, how many days' credit do they receive?

Problem 3

If the retailer in Problem 1 does not take the discount, what is the effective interest rate paid for trade credit?

Problem 4

Suppose that the Icarus Company described in Problem 1 finds that, historically, 80% of its customers take the discount. What is the firm's average collection period?

Problem 5

Suppose that the Icarus Company described in Problem 1 sells 600 cases of suntan lotion each month, at a price of $200 per case. What is its average balance sheet amount in accounts receivable?

Problem 6

Suppose that the Icarus Company described in Problem 1 has production costs equal to 80% of selling price. What is the firm's average investment (i.e., its actual cost, as opposed to the balance sheet amount) in receivables?

Problem 7

Daedulus Company has an average collection period of 30 days and an average level of accounts receivable of $600,000. What are the firm's annual credit sales? What is the receivables turnover ratio?

Problem 8

A firm offers credit terms of 3/15, net 60. What effective annual interest rate does the firm earn when a customer does not take the discount?

Problem 9

For each of the following credit terms, compute the effective annual rate: 1.5/20, net 45; 1/10, net 40

Problem 10

For each of the credit terms identified in Problems 8 and 9, determine whether a firm should take the discount or pay the net amount of the invoice. Assume that the firm would have to borrow from a bank at a 15% annual interest rate in order to take advantage of the discount.

Problem 11

Krishna, Inc., is considering a new credit policy. The current policy requires cash payment, while the new policy would extend credit for one month. The following information has been collected:

	Current policy	New policy
Price per unit	$50	$50
Cost per unit	$40	$40
Sales per period, in units	300	345

Also, the required return is 1.5% per month, and there will be no defaults. Should Krishna make the change in credit policy?

Problem 12

Rita's Bakery is considering changing its credit policy by offering credit terms of net 30 days. Given the information below, should they grant credit terms to their customers?

$$P = \$8$$
$$v = \$3$$
$$Q = 500$$
$$Q' = 575$$
$$R = 5\%$$

Problem 13

Verify the calculation for Problem 11 by computing the net present value of the change in credit policy using the following alternative approach. First compute the NPV of the change under the assumption that the change is in effect for one time period only, and then treat the one-period NPV as a perpetuity.

Problem 14

Verify the calculation for Problem 11 by computing the net present value of the change in credit policy using the following accounts receivable approach. Compare the opportunity cost of the investment in accounts receivable to the monthly net benefit resulting from the change in credit policy.

Problem 15

Brahma Company is considering a change in its credit policy. The current policy requires cash payment, while the new policy would extend credit for one month. The following information has been collected:

	Current policy	New policy
Price per unit	$195	$200
Cost per unit	$150	$150
Sales per period, in units	1,000	1,000

Also, the required return is 1% per month, and all customers will buy on credit. Brahma expects that 2% of its customers will default. Should Brahma make the change in credit policy?

Problem 16

Mary Kavanaugh is a manager at Witty Corporation and must decide whether to implement a new credit policy which would extend credit for one month. The current policy allows for cash sales only. If the required return is 2% per month, should Kavanaugh implement the change? Assume there are no defaults. The following information has been collected.

	Current Policy	New Policy
Price per unit	$30	$35
Cost per unit	25	25
Sales per period, in units	450	525

Problem 17

A new customer, Mr. Hernandez, intends to purchase 200 units of a product from the Gooden-Carter Company, Inc. The price of the product is $500 per unit and the variable cost of producing the product is $350. Mr. Gooden must decide whether to extend credit to Mr. Hernandez for a one-month time period. Mr. Gooden has concluded that the probability of default is 30%, and the required return is 1% per month. Should Gooden-Carter extend credit to Mr. Hernandez? (Assume that this is a one-time sale and that Mr. Hernandez will not buy from Gooden-Carter if credit is not extended.)

Problem 18

Muir Inc. sells Bunsen burners to high school chemistry labs. If the company sells 125,000 burners annually and the carrying costs per unit and shortage costs are $0.95 and $55, respectively, what is the EOQ? What is the total cost if Muir uses the EOQ?

Problem 19

Consider the following additional information for Problem 17: If Mr. Hernandez does not default, then he will continue to purchase 200 units each month for the foreseeable future. Should Gooden-Carter extend credit to Mr. Hernandez?

Problem 20

Anna operates a bookstore where managing inventory is an important activity. It costs here $50 to place an order, and her carrying costs are $1.50 per unit per year. Anna's total sales per year are 400,000. What is Anna's EOQ and the total cost of ordering the EOQ?

Problem 21

Bajaba Inc., sells high quality hockey pucks and has an annual demand of 90,000 units. The carrying costs are $0.60 per unit and the shortage costs are $30. What is the EOQ?

Problem 22

What is the total cost if Bajaba orders the EOQ?

Problem 23

Suppose Bajaba meets a supplier who is willing to give a 1 % discount on materials it normally sells for $1.00 per unit if orders were made in lot sizes of 6,000 units. Should Bajaba purchase from this supplier?

Problem 24

Considering the original information for Bajaba in Problem 21, assume the lead-time of placing an order is 6 days. Assume Bajaba is in business 360 days a year, and a 7 day safety stock is kept on hand. On average, how many units are sold per day? How much safety stock does Bajaba have on hand?

Problem 25

What is Bajaba's reorder point?

Problem 26

Suppose the EOQ of a firm is 1,000 units, the sales are 5,000 units per year and the shortage costs are $500 per order. What are the carrying costs in dollars per unit of inventory?

Problem 27

Cameron Ltd. needs 250,000 units per year. The carrying costs per unit are $100, shortage costs are $200 per order and the safety stock is 8,000 units. What is the EOQ?

Problem 28

What is the optimal number of orders Cameron should place each year?

Problem 29

Assuming a 360 business day year and that the expected delivery time for Cameron is 8 days, at what inventory level should the firm reorder?

Problem 30

Fill out the following table for Cameron Ltd.

Order Size	Q/2	Q/2 x CC	T/Q	F x T/Q	Total Cost
800					
1,000					
1,200					

ANSWERS TO CONCEPT TEST

1.   account receivable; account payable; trade; consumer

2.   terms of sale

3.   credit analysis; collection policy

4.   accounts receivable period; average collection period (ACP); average daily sales; average collection period; average daily sales; ACP

5.   credit; net credit; cash discount

6.   invoice; invoice

7.   invoice; promissory note

8.   commercial; sight; banker's acceptance

9.   conditional sales

10.   net present value; $[(P - v) \times (Q' - Q)]$; $[(P - v) \times (Q' - Q)]/R$

11. $v(Q' - Q)$; $P \times Q$; $PQ + v(Q' - Q)$

12. $-[PQ + v(Q' - Q)] + [(P - v) \times (Q' - Q)]/R$

13.   carrying; opportunity; sum; carrying; opportunity

14.   character; capacity; capital; conditions; collateral

15.   credit scoring; credit-scoring models

16.   collection; average collection; aging

17.   raw materials; finished goods; work-in-progress

18.   carrying costs; shortage costs

19.   ABC approach

20.   increase; decrease

21. $(Q/2) \times CC$; $F \times (T/Q)$

22.   cost-minimizing; economic ordering quantity (EOQ); $[(2T \times F) / CC]^{1/2}$

23.   safety stock; stockout; replenished

24.   reorder point; lead time; daily usage; safety stock

25.   just-in-time; materials requirements planning; recoupled

PROBLEM SOLUTIONS

Problem 1: If the retailer does not take the discount, then they must pay the net amount: ($200 × 10) = $2,000. Payment must be made within forty days after the invoice date. For a seasonal product such as this, the invoice date might be May 1, for example, regardless of whether the shipment is made prior to that date. In this case, the $2,000 payment would be due within forty days of the May 1 invoice date.

Problem 2: The retailer must pay within 20 days of the invoice date. If, for example, the invoice is dated May 1, then the retailer must pay by May 21. The discount is 2% in this example, so that the retailer must remit:

$$(1 - .02) \times \$200 \times 10 = \$1,960$$

If the retailer does not take advantage of the discount, they can pay the net amount within 40 days, rather than 20 days, thus receiving 20 days credit.

Problem 3: By not taking the discount, the customer is actually obtaining $1,960 of financing for twenty days, from day 20 to day 40. The cost of financing is the additional $40 which must be paid if payment is on day 40. The interest rate for this twenty-day period is ($40/$1,960) = .020408 = 2.0408%. There are (365/20) = 18.25 twenty-day periods in a year. The effective annual rate is: EAR = $(1.020408)^{18.25} - 1 = 1.44585 = 44.585\%$

A customer who does not take the discount is paying an effective annual rate of 44.585% for the financing of the $1,960 payment.

Problem 4: If we assume that all customers who take the discount pay on the twentieth day, while all customers who do not take the discount pay on the fortieth day, then the average collection period (ACP) is: $(.80 \times 20 \text{ days}) + (.20 \times 40 \text{ days}) = 24$ days.

Problem 5: Icarus has average daily sales of [($200 × 600)/30] = $4,000. The average collection period, as computed in the solution to Problem 4, is 24 days. Therefore, the average level of accounts receivable is: Average daily sales × ACP = $4,000 × 24 = $96,000.

Problem 6: The solution to Problem 5 indicates that average daily sales are $4,000. Therefore, the daily investment in accounts receivable is (.80 × $4,000) = $3,200. The average collection period is 24 days, as computed in Problem 4. Therefore, the average investment in receivables is ($3,200 × 24) = $76,800.

Problem 7: To solve this problem, we first note the following relationship:

Accounts receivable = Average daily credit sales × ACP

Solving for average daily credit sales, we have:

$600,000 = Average daily credit sales × 30 days
Average daily credit sales = $600,000/30 = $20,000

Therefore, annual credit sales equal ($20,000 × 365) = $7,300,000.

The receivables turnover is: $7,300,000 / $600,000 = 12.17 days

Problem 8: Suppose the product costs $100. The firm receives $97 if the discount is taken. If the discount is not taken, then the firm receives $3, or ($3/$97) = 3.0928%, more. This 3.0928% is earned by extending (60 – 15) = 45 additional days credit. There are approximately (365/45) = 8 such periods per year. The effective annual rate is therefore: EAR = $(1.030928)^8 - 1 = .27593 = 27.593\%$

The EAR does not depend on the cost of the product since the 3.0928% would apply regardless of purchase price.

Note that the interest rate the firm earns is the same as the interest rate the customer pays by not taking the discount. Consequently, from the customer's point of view it is generally not reasonable to pay an interest rate in excess of that which would be paid by financing the purchase through an alternative source.

Problem 9: For a 365-day year and terms of 1.5/20, net 45,   EAR $=$ $(1.015228)^{14.6} - 1$ $=$ .24689 $=$ 24.689%
For terms of 1/10, net 40, EAR $=$ $(1.010101)^{12.17} - 1$ $=$ .1301 $=$ 13.01%

Problem 10: For terms of 3/15, net 60, the firm would have to borrow 97% of the invoice amount in order to take advantage of the discount. Interest on the loan would then accumulate at the rate of 1.5% per month, or approximately 2.25% for 45 days, at which time we assume that the firm would repay the bank loan. Let x represent the net amount, so that the bank loan is .97x and interest plus principal of (.97x × 1.0225) = .9918x is repaid to the bank after 45 days. Since this is less than the net amount of the invoice, the firm is better off borrowing from the bank than paying the net amount.

In general, if the annualized effective rate is greater than the rate at which the firm borrows, the firm is better off borrowing from the bank in order to take advantage of the discount. Therefore, for terms of 1.5/20, net 45, the firm should borrow in order to take the discount, but for terms of 1/10, net 40, the firm should pay the net amount.

Problem 11: The relevant data for Krishna is: P = $50;   v = $40; Q = 300;   Q′ = 345; R = 1.5%

For the current policy:

Monthly sales are: P × Q $=$ ($50 × 300) $=$ $15,000
Monthly variable costs are: v × Q $=$ ($40 × 300) = $12,000
The cash flow is: Cash flow (old policy) $=$ (P – v) × Q $=$ ($50 – $40) × 300 $=$ $3,000

If credit is granted: Cash flow (new policy) $=$ (P – v) × Q′ $=$ ($50 – $40) × 345 $=$ $3,450

The incremental cash flow is: Cash flow (new policy) – Cash flow (old policy) = (P – v) × (Q′ – Q) = ($50 – $40) × (345 – 300) = $450

Since the incremental cash flow is in the form of a monthly annuity, the present value is:

$$PV = \frac{(P - v) \times (Q' - Q)}{R} = \frac{\$450}{.015} = \$30,000$$

The cost of the change in credit policy is the sum of two components. First, the variable cost of producing the additional units: v(Q′ – Q) = $40 × (345 – 300) = $1,800

Second, since collections are permanently delayed by thirty days, the following cost is also incurred: PQ = $50 × 300 = $15,000

The sum of these costs is: PQ + v(Q′ – Q) $=$ $15,000 + $1,800 $=$ $16,800

The net present value of the change in credit policy is:

$$NPV = -[PQ + v(Q' - Q)] + \frac{(P - v)(Q' - Q)}{R} = -\$16,800 + \$30,000 = \$13,200$$

Therefore, the change in credit policy to terms of net 30 days is beneficial.

Problem 12:

If Rita does not extend credit:

>   Monthly sales   = $8 x 500   = $4,000
>   Monthly variable costs   = $3 x 500   = $1,500
>   Cash flow   = $4,000 - $1,500   = $2,500   or   ($8 - $3) x 500   = $2,500

If credit is granted, the new cash flow is:

>   ($8 - $3) x 575   = $2,875

Incremental cash flow   = $2,875 - $2,500   = $375

The present value of the incremental flow, treated as a monthly annuity is:

>   PV   = $375 / .05   = $7,500

The cost of the change in credit policy is the sum of the increase in variable costs plus the costs of delaying the collection period by 30 days.

>   VC   = $3 (575 - 500)   = $225

>   Cost of delayed collections   = $8 x 500   = $4,000

>   Total cost   = $225 + $4,000   = $4,225

For Rita's Bakery, the NPV of changing its credit policy is:

>   NPV   =   -$4,225 + $7,500   = $3,275

The NPV is positive, so Rita's Bakery should change its credit policy to terms of net 30 days.

Problem 13: The firm invests the following amount in production costs today: $(v \times Q') = (\$40 \times 345) = \$13,800$

Also, the firm foregoes the following net cash inflow, which would be received this month under the existing credit policy: $(P - v) \times Q = (\$50 - \$40) \times 300 = \$3,000$

Under the new credit policy, the firm then receives the following cash inflow from payments thirty days later: $(P \times Q') = (\$50 \times 345) = \$17,250$

The present value of this inflow is $(\$17,250/1.015) = \$16,995.0739$. The net present value of this transaction, if we regard this as a one-month change in policy, is: $\$16,995.0739 - (\$13,800 + \$3,000) = \$195.0739$

Since this NPV actually repeats itself each month, the NPV of the change in credit policy is: $\$195.0739 + (\$195.0739/.015) = \$13,200$

This is the same as the NPV computed in the solution to Problem 11.

Problem 14: The firm's investment in accounts receivable is comprised of two parts. The first part is the amount the firm would have received during the current month if the existing credit policy remained unchanged: $P \times Q = \$50 \times 300 = \$15,000$

The second part of the investment in receivables is the increase in the investment in receivables which results from the increase in sales: $v + (Q' - Q) = \$40 \times (345 - 300) = \$1,800$

The total incremental investment in receivables is: $(PQ) + [v(Q' - Q)] = \$15,000 + \$1,800 = \$16,800$

The required return on this investment for one month is: Carrying costs $= [(PQ) + v(Q' - Q)] \times R = \$16,800 \times .015 = \$252$

The monthly benefit derived from the investment in receivables is: $(P - v) \times (Q' - Q) = (\$50 - \$40) \times (345 - 300) = \$450$

The monthly net benefit is $(\$450 - \$252) = \$198$. The NPV of the change in credit policy is $(\$198/.015) = \$13,200$.

Problem 15: The relevant data for Brahma can be represented as follows: $P = \$195$; $P' = \$200$; $v = \$150$; $Q = 1,000$; $R = 1.0\%$; $\pi = 2.0\%$; $d = 2.5\%$

The cost of the change is the firm's investment in production costs plus the firm's foregone net cash inflow. Since the change in credit policy does not affect Q, this cost can be computed as follows: $(v \times Q) + [(P - v) \times Q] = P \times Q = \$195 \times 1,000 = \$195,000$.

The monthly cash inflow for the current policy: $(P - v) \times Q = (\$195 - \$150) \times 1,000 = \$45,000$
The monthly cash inflow for the proposed policy is: $[(1 - \pi)P' - v] \times Q = [(.98 \times \$200) - \$150] \times 1,000 = \$46,000$

The net incremental cash flow is therefore $(\$46,000 - \$45,000) = \$1,000$. The net incremental cash flow can also be computed as follows: $P' \times Q \times (d - \pi) = \$200 \times 1,000 \times (.025 - .020) = \$1,000$

The net present value of the change in credit policy is:

$$\text{NPV} = -(P \times Q) + [P' \times Q \times (d - \pi)] / R = -\$195,000 + \$1,000 - .10 = -\$95,000$$

Since the net present value of the change in credit policy is negative, the firm should not make the change.

Problem 16: For the current policy:

    Monthly sales   = $30 x 450 = $13,500
    Monthly variable costs = $25 x 450 = $11,250
    Cash flow (old policy) = ($30 - $25) x 450 = $2,250

If credit is granted: Cash flow (new policy) = ($35 - $25) x 525 = $5,250

The incremental cash flow is $5,250 - $2,250 = $3,000. The present value is $3,000 / 0.02 = $150,000.

The cost of the change in policy is the increased variable cost plus the cost of the delayed payment. The increased variable cost is $25 x (525 - 450) = $1,875. The cost of the delayed payment is $30 x 450 = $13,500. The total cost of the change is $1,875 + $13,500 = $15,375.

The NPV of the change in credit policy is $150,000 - $15,375 = $134,625. The firm should change its policy.

Problem 17: The relevant data for this problem can be represented as follows: $P' = \$500$; $Q = 200$; $v = \$350$; $R = 1.0\%$; $\pi = 30.0\%$

The cost of granting credit to Mr. Hernandez is the variable cost of the product, which must be expended this month: $v \times Q = \$350 \times 200 = \$70,000$

The cash inflow to Gooden-Carter in one month is: $(1 - \pi) \times P' \times Q = .70 \times \$500 \times 200 = \$70,000$

The net present value is:

$$\text{NPV} = -(v \times Q) + \frac{(1 - \pi) \times P' \times Q}{R} = -\$70,000 + \frac{\$70,000}{1.01} = -\$693.07$$

Since the net present value is negative, Gooden-Carter should not extend credit to the new customer.

Problem 18:

$$\text{EOQ} = [(2 \times 125,000 \times \$55) / \$0.95]^{\frac{1}{2}} = 3,804.43 = 3,804$$

$$\text{Total cost} = (3,804 / 2) \times \$0.95 + (125,000 / 3,804) \times \$55 = \$3,614.21$$

Problem 19: The cost to Gooden-Carter of extending credit is still $70,000, as in the solution to Problem 17. In one month, Mr. Hernandez will either default, or he will pay $(P' \times Q) = \$10,000$ and purchase an additional 200 units. The probability that he will not default is $(1 - \pi) = 70\%$ and the expected net cash inflow in one month is: $(1 - \pi) \times (P' - v) \times Q = .70 \times (\$500 - \$350) \times 200 = \$21,000$

The net present value of the decision to grant credit is: NPV = -$70,000 + $21,000 / .01 = $2,030,000. Since the net present value is positive, it is beneficial for the firm to extend credit to the new customer.

Problem 20:

$$\text{EOQ} = [(2 \times 400,000 \times \$50) / \$1.50]^{\frac{1}{2}} = 5,163.98 = 5,164 \text{ units}$$

The cost of ordering the EOQ is:

$$\text{Total cost} = (5,164 / 2) \times \$1.50 + (400,000 / 5,164) \times \$50 = \$3,873 + \$3,873 = \$7,746$$

Problem 21: EOQ $= [(2 \times 90,000 \times \$30) / \$0.60]^{1/2} = 3,000 \text{ units}$

Problem 22: Total Cost $= (Q/2) \times CC + F \times (T/Q) = (3,000/2) \times \$0.60 + \$30 \times (90,000/3,000) = \$900 + \$900 = \$1,800$

Problem 23: Total Cost $= (6,000/2) \times \$0.60 + \$30 \times (90,000/6,000) - 90,000 \times \$1.00 \times .01 = \$1,800 + \$450 - \$900 = \$1,350$

Notice the total cost is reduced by the savings of the purchase price (the discount) so that Bajaha is better-off ordering in lots of 6,000.

Problem 24: On average, Bajaba sells $90,000/360 = 250$ units per day, so the safety stock is $250 \times 7 = 1,750$ units.

Problem 25: The reorder point is equal to the lead time × the daily usage + the safety stock = $(6 \times 250) + 1,750 = 3,250$ units.

Problem 26: Solve the EOQ equation for the value of carrying costs (CC):

$$1,000 = [(2 \times 1,000 \times \$500) / CC]^{1/2}$$

$$1,000,000 = \$1,000,000 \ CC$$

$$CC = \$1.00$$

Problem 27: EOQ $= [(2 \times 250,000 \times \$200) / \$100]^{1/2} = 1,000$ units

Problem 28: Number of orders $= 250,000/1,000 = 250$ orders

Problem 29: Reorder point $= 8 \times (250,000/360) + 8,000 = 13,556$ units

Problem 30:

Order Size	Q/2	Q/2 x CC	T/Q	F x T/Q	Total Cost
800	400	$40,000	312.5 = 313	$62,600	$102,600
1,000	500	50,000	250	50,000	100,000
1,200	600	60,000	208.3 = 209	41,800	101,800

21   International Corporate Finance

CHAPTER HIGHLIGHTS

The basic principles of corporate finance apply to international corporations just as they do to domestic corporations. That is, international corporations seek to invest in positive NPV projects and to arrange financing that creates value for shareholders. However, application of these principles in international finance is complicated by differences in foreign exchange, interest rates, accounting methods, tax rates, and government intervention.

21.1 TERMINOLOGY

As in all specialized subject areas, international finance has a unique vocabulary. Some of the most important terms are defined in this section.

1. **Belgian Dentist:** a stereotype of an investor who purchases Eurobonds because the income derived from these anonymous-bearer bonds is untraceable.
2. **Cross rate:** the exchange rate between two currencies when both are quoted in a third currency.
3. **Eurobond:** a bond issue denominated in a particular currency, sold simultaneously in several European countries, issued in bearer form.
4. **Eurocurrency:** money deposited in financial institutions outside the country whose currency is involved. Eurodollars, the most important Eurocurrency, are American dollars deposited in banks outside the U.S. EuroCanadians are Canadian dollar bank deposits outside Canada.
5. **Foreign bonds:** bonds issued by foreign borrowers in another country and denominated in the currency of the country where issued.
6. **Gilts:** British and Irish government securities.
7. **London Interbank Offered Rate (LIBOR):** the rate on overnight Eurodollar loans between major international banks. Interest rates on short-term debt of corporate and government borrowers are frequently based on this rate.
8. **Swaps:** a currency swap is an agreement to exchange currencies; an interest rate swap is an exchange of a debt with a floating-rate payment for a debt with a fixed-rate payment (or vice versa).
9. **Export Development Corporation (EDC):** a federal crown corporation which promotes Canadian exports by making loans to foreign purchasers.

21.2 FOREIGN EXCHANGE MARKETS AND EXCHANGE RATES

The foreign exchange market is the world's largest financial market. It is strictly an over-the-counter market, consisting of a worldwide telecommunications network among traders in major commercial and investment banks around the world. Most of the trading takes place in a small number of major currencies, including the U.S. dollar, German Deutsche mark (DM), British pound sterling (£), Japanese yen (¥), Swiss franc (SF), and French franc (FF). Participants in the foreign exchange market include importers and exporters, portfolio managers, foreign exchange brokers, traders and speculators.

Exchange Rates: An *exchange rate* is the price of one country's currency expressed in terms of the currency of another country. Thus the French franc (FF) might be quoted at FF 10/$1, indicating that it takes ten francs to buy one dollar. A quote of units of foreign currency per dollar is called an *indirect quote* or *European quote*. A rate can also be quoted in terms of the number of American dollars required to buy one unit of foreign currency: for example, $.10/FF 1. This is a *direct quote* or *American quote*. The direct quote and the indirect quote are reciprocals of each other. In practice, almost all exchange rates are quoted in terms of U.S. dollars.

Cross-Rates and Triangle Arbitrage: Suppose the following exchange rates exist:

> French francs / German D-marks: 5
> French francs / U.S. dollars: 10
> German D-marks / U.S. dollars: 3

You could convert $1 into 3 marks. Next, convert 3 marks to 15 francs and then convert the francs to dollars. At the exchange rate of 10 francs to the dollar, you will have $1.50, or a 50% risk-free return! This outcome is, of course, impossible in an efficient market. This activity is referred to as *triangle arbitrage*. The data of this example are equivalent to two different prices for the dollar at the same point in time. The exchange rate for French francs is quoted here as FF 10/$1. The other two exchange rates are equivalent to an exchange rate of FF 15/$1. In other words, exchanging $1 for DM 3, and then exchanging DM 3 for [DM 3 × (FF 5/DM 1)] = FF 15 is equivalent to exchanging $1 for FF 15. The above triangle arbitrage is equivalent to selling $1 for FF 15, and then buying $1 for FF 10.

Since arbitrage opportunities do not exist in an efficient market, the above exchange rates cannot exist simultaneously. If $1 buys DM 3, and $1 buys FF 10, then the cross rate must be:

> (DM 3/$1) / (FF 10/$1) = DM 3 / FF 10 = DM .3 / FF 1

Types of Transactions: Two basic kinds of transactions exist in the foreign exchange market. Spot trades involve agreement on the exchange rate today, called the *spot exchange rate*, for settlement in two business days. *Forward trades* involve agreement today on an exchange rate for settlement in the more distant future. The exchange rate in this case is the *forward exchange rate*, and settlement is typically one to fifty-two weeks in the future.

When a foreign currency is more expensive in the forward market than in the spot market, it is said to be selling at a *premium* relative to the dollar. For example, if the Japanese yen costs $.0075 in the spot market and $.0080 in the forward market, the Japanese yen is selling at a *premium* relative to the dollar. Equivalently, it is said that the dollar is selling at a *discount* relative to the Japanese yen.

As noted earlier, exchange rates are typically quoted in terms of U.S. dollars. That is, exchange rates are generally stated in terms of indirect quotes, which indicate the amount of the foreign currency per U.S. dollar. Throughout this chapter, we use indirect exchange rates in our discussion.

21.3 PURCHASING POWER PARITY

In this section, we address the following two questions: (1) What are the factors which determine the level of the spot exchange rate? (2) What are the determinants of the rate of change in exchange rates? The concepts of *absolute purchasing power parity* and *relative purchasing power parity* provide part of the answer to these questions.

Absolute Purchasing Power Parity

Absolute purchasing power parity is based on the concept that a particular commodity must have the same price regardless of the currency used to purchase the commodity or the country in which it is purchased. For example, suppose that a litre of gasoline sells for $2 in Canada and for 30 French francs (FF 30) in France. If the exchange rate is FF 10/$1, then you could purchase a gallon of gasoline in Canada for $2, sell the gasoline in France for FF 30, and then exchange the 30 francs for $3. The profit for the transaction is $1. This transaction is analogous to the triangle arbitrage described in the previous section. The transaction is equivalent to buying and selling an asset (i.e., a gallon of gasoline) at two different prices (i.e., $2 in Canada, and FF 30, or $3, in France) at the same time.

As is true in the case of triangle arbitrage, the above scenario could not continue to exist; the stated prices and/or exchange rate would adjust in such a way as to eliminate the arbitrage profit for this transaction. This profit is eliminated if:

$$P_{FF} = S_0 \times P_{CDN}$$

where P_{FF} is the current price of a commodity in France, P_{CDN} is the current price in Canada, and S_0 is the spot exchange rate (i.e., the number of francs required to purchase one Canadian dollar). If, for example, the prices remain the same, then, in order for absolute purchasing power parity to prevail, S_0 must equal:

$$S_0 = P_{FF} / P_{CDN} = FF\ 30 / \$2 = FF15 / \$1$$

In the preceding example, we assumed that prices remained constant. In general, however, absolute purchasing power parity implies that both prices and exchange rates adjust. For instance, the profit opportunity indicated in the example would result in both increased demand for gasoline in Canada and increased supply in France, so that price would increase in Canada and decrease in France. In addition, the demand for francs would decrease and the demand for dollars would increase, thereby increasing the exchange rate.

The above argument is strictly accurate only if there are no shipping or other transactions costs, no barriers to trade, and commodities are identical in both countries. Clearly, these conditions are rarely met, so that, in general, we do not expect absolute purchasing power parity to apply precisely.

Relative Purchasing Power Parity: The concept of *relative purchasing power parity* provides the answer to the second question posed at the beginning of this section. That is, the rate of change in an exchange rate over time is determined by relative inflation rates in the two countries.

Suppose that the French franc / Canadian dollar exchange rate is FF 10 / $1. Further, assume that the expected inflation rates in France and Canada during the coming year are 9% and 0%, respectively. What is the expected exchange rate one year from now? Recall that the exchange rate is the number of francs required to purchase one dollar. Since prices in France are expected to increase by 9% during the coming year, while prices in Canada are expected to remain constant, then, by the end of the year, 9% more francs will be required to purchase one dollar. In other words, the exchange rate at the end of the year is expected to be (FF 10 × 1.09) = FF 10.9/ $1. It now takes more francs to buy one dollar because the higher inflation rate in France makes the franc worth relatively less.

If the expected inflation rate in Canada is 5%, rather than 0%, then, relative to prices in Canada, prices in France are expected to increase by (9% – 5%) = 4%. Therefore, the exchange rate at the end of the year is expected to be (FF 10 × 1.04) = FF 10.4 / $1.

To summarize this concept, we will use the following notation:

S_0	=	Current spot exchange rate
$E[S_t]$	=	Expected exchange rate in t periods

h_{CDN} =   Inflation rate in Canada
h_{FC} =   Inflation rate in foreign country

The expected percentage change in the exchange rate during the next year is represented as: $(E[S_1] - S_0)/S_0$. Relative purchasing power parity states that the expected change in the exchange rate is equal to the difference in the inflation rates:

$$\frac{E[S_1] - S_0}{S_0} = h_{FC} - h_{CDN}$$

This statement of relative purchasing power parity can be algebraically rearranged, as follows:

$$E[S_1] = S_0 \times [1 + (h_{FC} - h_{CDN})]$$

If the inflation rates remain constant for the next two years, then the above relationship could be applied to the second year, as follows:

$$E[S_2] = E[S_1] \times [1 + (h_{FC} - h_{CDN})]$$

Now, using the above, $E[S_2]$ can then be computed as follows:

$$E[S_2] = S_0 \times [1 + (h_{FC} - h_{CDN})^2]$$

Alternatively, $E[S_2]$ can be computed as follows:

$$E[S_2] = S_0 \times [1 + (h_{FC} - h_{CDN})]^2$$

$$= (FF\ 10/\$1) \times (1.04)^2 = FF\ 10.816/\$1$$

In general, for any time period t, relative purchasing power parity is stated as follows:

$$E[S_t] = S_0 \times [1 + (h_{FC} - h_{CDN})]^t$$

21.4 INTEREST RATE PARITY, UNBIASED FORWARD RATES, AND THE INTERNATIONAL FISHER EFFECT

In this section, we investigate the relationship between spot exchange rates, forward exchange rates, and interest rates. The additional notation required in this section is:

F_t =   Forward exchange rate for settlement at time t
R_{CDN} =   Nominal risk-free interest rate in Canada
R_{FC} =   Nominal risk-free interest rate in foreign country

Covered Interest Arbitrage: An investor who makes an investment in a risk-free asset (i.e., Treasury bills) in Canada receives a return equal to R_{CDN}. On the other hand, an investor who makes an investment at the risk-free rate in a foreign country must first convert dollars to that foreign currency, invest in the risk-free asset, and then convert the foreign currency to dollars. Therefore, the return on this latter investment depends on not only the nominal risk-free interest rate in the foreign country, RFC, but also the spot exchange rate (S_0) and the forward exchange rate (F_t). Note that, if the exchange rate in effect in the future could not be established today, then the investment in the foreign country would not be risk-free; the actual return would depend on the spot exchange rate in effect at time t. Since the forward rate can be established today, the investment is risk-free, but the return is not the same as R_{FC}. If the actual rate on this investment differs from R_{CDN}, then an arbitrage opportunity exists.

We will use the following data to demonstrate these points:

$$
\begin{aligned}
S_0 &= \text{FF } 10.0 \,/\, \$1 \\
F_1 &= \text{FF } 9.6 \,/\, \$1 \\
R_{CDN} &= 9\% \\
R_{FF} &= 6\%
\end{aligned}
$$

An investor who invests $1 in T-bills for one year will have, at the end of one year, ($1 × 1.09) = $1.09. An investor who invests at the risk-free rate available in France proceeds as follows:

1. Convert $1 to ($1 × S_0) = [$1 × (FF 10/$1)] = FF 10.

2. Simultaneously, the investor enters into a forward agreement to convert dollars to francs at the forward rate F_1 = FF 9.6/$1.

3. Invest FF 10 at the rate R_{FF} = 6%, so that, at the end of one year, the investor has [(FF 10) × 1.06] = FF 10.6.

4. Convert FF 10.6 to dollars at the rate established in (2) above, so that the investor has [(FF 10.6/$1) / (FF 9.6/$1)] = $1.10417.

Clearly, the investor prefers the latter investment; the actual rate of return is 10.417%, compared to R_{CDN} = 9%.

The existence of the discrepancy in rates of return on risk-free investments gives rise to an arbitrage opportunity, referred to as *covered interest arbitrage*. Suppose a Canadian investor can borrow $100,000 at R_{CDN} = 9%, and invest the $100,000 at the French risk-free rate, as described above. At the end of the year, the investor would repay ($100,000 × 1.09) = $109,000 on the loan. On the other hand, the investor would have ($100,000 × 1.10417) = $110,417 from the investment at the French risk-free rate. The arbitrage profit is ($110,417 − $109,000) = $1,417.

Interest Rate Parity (IRP): In an efficient market, arbitrage opportunities, such as the covered interest arbitrage of the preceding example, do not exist. Therefore, the return for each of the risk-free investments must be the same. The return per dollar for the investment at the risk-free rate R_{CDN} is [$1 × (1 + R_{CDN})]. The return per dollar for the investment in the foreign risk-free investment is:

$$[\, \$1 \times S_0 \times (1 + R_{FC}) \,] \,/\, F_1$$

The interest rate parity condition states that these two returns must be equal:

$$(1 + R_{CDN}) = S_0 \times (1 + R_{FC}) \,/\, F_1$$

Alternatively, this can be rearranged algebraically, as follows:

$$F_1 / S_0 \;\; = \;\; (1 + R_{FC}) / (1 + R_{CDN})$$

Interest rate parity indicates that the relationship between the forward and spot exchange rates is a function of the relationship between foreign and domestic interest rates. An approximation to this statement of IRP can further clarify the relationship. This approximation states that the percentage forward premium or discount is equal to the difference between the foreign and domestic interest rates:

$$(F_1 \; - \; S_0) / S_0 \;\; = \;\; R_{FC} \; - \; R_{CDN}$$

This approximation is often algebraically rearranged as follows:

$$F_1 \;\; = \;\; S_0 \times [1 + (R_{FC} - R_{CDN})]$$

This statement can be extended to any number of time periods, t, as follows:

$$F_t \;\; = \;\; S_0 \times [1 + (R_{FC} - R_{CDN})]^t$$

Forward Rates and Future Spot Rates: The *unbiased forward rates* (UFR) condition is the statement that the forward rate (F_1) is equal to the expected future spot rate ($E[S_1]$):

$$F_1 \;\; = \;\; E[S_1]$$

UFR can also be stated for any number of time periods:

$$F_t \;\; = \;\; E[S_t]$$

Essentially, these statements indicate that the forward rate must be equal to the market consensus expectation regarding the future spot rate. UFR can also be thought of as a long-run average; that is, on average, the one-period forward rate for a particular currency is equal to the spot rate one period from now. Equivalent statements apply to the forward rate for any time period t.

"Putting It All Together"   To this point, we have developed three basic relationships of international finance: absolute purchasing power parity (PPP), interest rate parity (IRP), and unbiased forward rates (UFR). These concepts can be stated as:

$$\text{PPP:} \quad E[S_1] = S_0 \times [1 + (h_{FC} - h_{CDN})]$$

$$\text{IRP:} \quad F_1 \quad = S_0 \times [1 + (R_{FC} - R_{CDN})]$$

$$\text{UFR:} \quad F_1 \quad = E[S_1]$$

F_1 is on the left side of both IRP and UFR. Therefore, the right-hand sides of these equations must be equal:

$$E[S_1] \;\; = \;\; S_0 \times [1 + (R_{FC} - R_{CDN})]$$

This statement is referred to as *uncovered interest parity* (UIP), which can be stated for t time periods as follows:

$$E[S_t] \quad = \quad S_0 \times [1 + (R_{FC} - R_{CDN})]^t$$

The right-hand sides of PPP and UIP must also be equal:

$$S_0 \times [1 + (h_{FC} - h_{CDN}) \quad = \quad S_0 \times [1 + (R_{FC} - R_{CDN})$$

This statement can be simplified as:

$$h_{FC} - h_{CDN} \quad = \quad R_{FC} - R_{CDN}$$

That is, the difference in foreign and domestic inflation rates is equal to the difference in foreign and domestic interest rates. This equation can be rearranged:

$$R_{CDN} - h_{CDN} \quad = \quad R_{FC} - h_{FC}$$

This statement is referred to as the *international Fisher effect* (IFE). It indicates that *real* interest rates in different countries are equal. In the absence of differences in attitudes toward risk from one country to another and barriers to the movement of money, the international Fisher effect is simply another implication of efficient markets. If the IFE did not apply to two countries, money would flow to the country with the higher real rate. This would increase values and lower returns in that country, while having the opposite effect in the country with the lower real rate.

21.5 INTERNATIONAL CAPITAL BUDGETING

International capital budgeting decisions are made using the same net present value criterion used for domestic capital budgeting. The difference is that, for international capital budgeting decisions, we must compute the net present value in dollars even though cash flows are in another currency. Two equivalent approaches to accomplishing this objective are considered in this section: the *home currency approach* and the *foreign currency approach*. We will illustrate the two alternatives with the following example.

A firm is considering building a factory in Slobovia. The factory is a 3-year project, which will cost 100 slobs (SL 100) to build and will produce after-tax cash inflows of SL 40 per year. The current spot exchange rate is SL 2 = \$1. The one-year risk-free rates for Canada and Slobovia are quoted at 5% and 3%, respectively, and the appropriate cost of capital for *dollar* cash flows is 10%.

Method 1 - The Home Currency Approach: To calculate the net present value using the home currency approach, first convert the SL cash flows to dollar flows, and then discount the dollar cash flows at the 10% cost of capital. In order to convert the foreign currency cash flows to dollar cash flows, we compute the expected future exchange rates, using the uncovered interest parity (UIP) relationship:

$$E[S_t] \quad = \quad S_0 \times [1 + (R_{FC} - R_{CDN})]^t$$

$$= \quad (SL\ 2) \times [1 + (.03 - .05)]^t$$

$$= \quad (SL\ 2) \times [1 + (-.02)]^t \quad = \quad (SL\ 2) \times (.98)^t$$

The expected spot exchange rates for years 1, 2 and 3 are presented in the following table:

Year	Expected exchange rate
1	$(SL\ 2) \times (.98)^1 = SL\ 1.9600$
2	$(SL\ 2) \times (.98)^2 = SL\ 1.9208$
3	$(SL\ 2) \times (.98)^3 = SL\ 1.8824$

These exchange rates are then used to convert cash flows to dollars:

Year	Cash flow (in SL)	Expected exchange rate	Cash flow (in CDN $)
0	-SL 100	SL 2.0000	-$50.0000
1	SL 40	SL 1.9600	$20.4082
2	SL 40	SL 1.9208	$20.8247
3	SL 40	SL 1.8824	$21.2495

Using the 10% opportunity cost, the net present value of the investment in the new factory is +$1.7285.

Method 2 - The Foreign Currency Approach: The foreign currency approach requires that we discount the cash flows, measured in the foreign currency. The resulting net present value, measured in the foreign currency, is then converted to a dollar NPV. The foreign currency cash flows are not discounted at the firm's cost of capital. However, the cost of capital is converted to an appropriate rate for the foreign currency, using the international Fisher effect, before computing the net present value of the foreign currency cash flows.

The international Fisher effect indicates the difference in the nominal rates:

$$h_{FC} = h_{CDN} = R_{FC} - R_{CDN} = .03 - .05 = -.02$$

Therefore, the firm's 10% cost of capital is reduced by 2%, to 8%. The net present value of the cash flows for the project, measured in the foreign currency, and discounted at 8%, is SL 3.0839. Using the spot exchange rate, this net present value is converted to dollars:

$$(SL\ 3.0839) / (SL\ 2/\$1) = \$1.5420$$

(Note that this net present value differs somewhat from the NPV obtained using the home currency approach. The reason for the difference is the approximation used in the previous section in deriving the international Fisher effect.)

Unremitted Cash Flows: A foreign subsidiary can remit funds to a parent via dividends, management fees for central services and royalties on the use of trade names and patents.

The example above assumes that the cash flows from the project are remitted to Canada as they are earned. However, in reality, this assumption is frequently not appropriate. First, foreign countries often place limitations on the ability of international firms to remit cash flows. Second, the issue of remittance is affected by foreign taxes. For example, tax incentives may make it advantageous for an international firm to reinvest foreign cash flows in the foreign country. Total taxes paid by a multinational firm may be affected by the timing of remittances. Therefore, the timing of remittances may alter the net present value of a foreign investment.

21.6 FINANCING INTERNATIONAL PROJECTS

The Cost of Capital for International Firms: The required return for international projects could be different from that of similar domestic projects if international financial markets were *segmented* (barriers preventing shareholders in Canada from holding foreign securities) and / or foreign political risk of expropriation, foreign exchange, and taxes existed. Empirical evidence suggests that internationally diversified portfolios have a lower variance than purely domestic stock portfolios. And, because investors are not fully diversified internationally, firms can benefit from a lower cost of capital for international projects which provide diversification services for the firm's shareholders.

International Diversification and Investors: Financial engineering is aiding investors to overcome barriers and information costs. As investors diversify globally, the cost of capital advantage to firms will likely decline. For example, an *Index Participation* (IP) on the Standard & Poor's 500 Index is a vehicle for international diversification which gives the investor both liquidity and reduced trading costs. Furthermore, recently, the maximum allowable foreign holding for Canadian pension funds was recently increased to 30 %.

Sources of Short and Intermediate Term Financing: For short and medium-term cash, Canadian multinationals can borrow from a charted bank at the Canadian rate or borrow EuroCanadian or Eurocurrency from a bank outside Canada. These *Eurobanks* make loans and accept deposits in foreign currencies. Loans are usually made on a floating rate basis, set at a fixed margin above LIBOR.

Under a *Note Issuance Facility* (NIF), a large borrower issues short-term notes with maturities ranging from three months to one year underwritten by a bank(s). When banks sell NIFs to investors, the Euronotes issued are called *Euro-Commercial paper* (ECP), and unlike domestic commercial paper, the ECP issued in the unregulated Eurocredit market offers greater flexibility and possibly lower cost.

21.7 EXCHANGE RATE RISK

Exchange rate risk is the risk of loss in value resulting from fluctuations in exchange rates over time. The three categories of exchange rate risk, or exposure are: short-run exposure, long-run exposure, and translation exposure.

Short-Run Exposure: Firms dealing in international trade are subject to exchange rate risk because they both make payments in foreign currencies and receive foreign currencies in payments. Suppose the spot exchange rate for the Japanese yen is ¥ 125 / $1 and that a company has receivables of ¥ 1,500,000 to be collected in 90 days. At the current exchange rate, the firm will be able to exchange ¥ 1,500,000 for [(¥ 1,500,000)/(¥ 125/$1)] = $12,000. But, if the exchange rate in 90 days is ¥ 150 / $1, the firm will receive only [(¥ 1,500,000) / (¥ 150/$1)] = $10,000. Of course, it is also possible that the exchange rate will decrease during the next 90 days; this would result in an increase in the dollar value of the future payment. The firm's exchange rate risk is the uncertainty associated with the dollar value of the future payment in the foreign currency.

Corresponding exchange rate risk is associated with an obligation to make a payment in a foreign currency at a future date. In the example above, if the firm has payables of ¥ 1,500,000 due in 90 days, the increase in the exchange rate from ¥ 125 to ¥150 decreases the cost to the firm, measured in dollars. Similarly, a decrease in the exchange rate increases the cost to the firm.

The forward market provides a means for hedging exchange rate risk. Suppose that, in the receivables example above, the 90-day forward rate is ¥ 140. The firm can eliminate exchange rate risk by purchasing a forward contract and promising to deliver yens for dollars. At the ¥ 140 forward exchange rate, the firm is certain to receive [(¥ 1,500,000)/(¥ 140/$1)] = $10,714.29 ninety days from now. That is, hedging in the forward contract means that, when the firm receives the payment of ¥ 1,500,000 90 days from now, it will be able to exchange this sum for $10,714.29. This eliminates the risk associated with fluctuations in the exchange rate over the next ninety days.

Hedging is generally considered advantageous because, in an efficient market, exchange rate speculation is a zero NPV activity. That is, the UFR condition indicates that the forward rate is equal to the expected future spot rate so that, on average, there is no gain from speculating on the direction of the exchange rate. In addition, the costs of hedging are generally quite low.

Long-Run Exposure: Long-run exposure to exchange rate risk arises from, for example, a long-term commitment to purchase resources, such as labour or materials, in a foreign country. Since such commitments are denominated in the foreign currency, the dollar value of future payments is subject to exchange rate risk. In general, such long-run exposure to exchange rate risk can be hedged in the forward markets only to a limited extent, because forward contracts generally have maturities of one year or less. Protection against long-run exposure is generally accomplished by matching inflows and outflows in the foreign currency. Then, when changes in the exchange rate result in a decrease in the dollar value of the firm's inflows, these changes are offset by a decrease in the dollar value of the outflows. Exchange rate risk can also be hedged by obtaining financing in the country where the investment is to be made. The risk reduction occurs because changes in the value of the investment will be partially offset by changes in the value of the liabilities.

Translation Exposure: When a Canadian firm prepares its financial statements, the data for foreign operations must be translated into dollars. The major issues which arise from this process are: first, the determination of the appropriate exchange rate; and second, accounting for gains and losses from foreign currency translation. In the U.S., Financial Accounting Standards Board Statement Number 52 requires that all assets and liabilities be translated at current, rather than historical, exchange rates. Gains and losses from exchange rate fluctuations are carried as a separate item in the shareholder's equity portion of the balance sheet, but are not recognized on the income statement. In Canada, firms typically use the rules provided by the Canadian Institute of Chartered Accountants (CICA) rule 1650. This rule sets the guidelines for calculating the firm's translation exposure.

21.8 POLITICAL RISK

Political risk is the risk of loss of values due to political actions. Political actions can range from actions such as changes in regulation or tax laws to outright business interruption or confiscation, though these latter actions are typically associated with relatively unstable political environments.

Political risk can affect both domestic and international firms. One example of domestic firms facing political risk is the risk faced by Quebec based firms, given the possibility that Quebec may choose to separate from Canada. Indeed, one Canadian study finds that the stock market typically reacts positively to announcements of relocation to Toronto, Ontario.

The greater the exposure to political risk that a firm faces when investing in a country, the greater the compensation the firm will demand in terms of higher returns. The degree of exposure to political risk is also a function of the nature of the business. For example, even in an unstable political environment, it is unlikely that a government would confiscate a manufacturing plant that produces parts that are only valuable to the parent company located overseas. Conversely, businesses focused on natural resource development are particularly tempting targets for confiscation, given the value of the natural resource.

Firms facing political risk can hedge these risks in a number of ways. For example, the Export Development Corporation can provide insurance. Further, a firm can seek to finance the overseas operation locally, as the fear that the firm would refuse to satisfy its interest obligations should confiscation occur can act as a disincentive against confiscation.

CONCEPT TEST

1. When the exchange rates for two currencies are quoted in a third currency, the exchange rate between the two currencies is a(n) _____ .

2. A bond issue denominated in a particular currency, sold simultaneously in several European countries, issued in bearer form, is a(n) _____ .

3. American money deposited in banks outside the U.S. is referred to as _____ .

4. Bonds issued by foreign borrowers in another country and denominated in the currency of the country where issued are called _____ .

5. The rate on overnight Eurodollar loans between major international banks is the _____ .

6. An agreement to exchange currencies is a(n) _____ .

7. An exchange of floating-rate debt for fixed-rate debt is a(n) _____ .

8. The price of one country's currency expressed in terms of the currency of another country is a(n) _____ . A quote of units of foreign currency per dollar is called a(n) _____ quote or _____ quote. A rate can also be quoted in terms of the number of dollars required to buy one unit of foreign currency; this is a(n) _____ quote, or _____ quote.

9. The simultaneous purchase and sale of the same asset (or similar assets) at different prices at the same time is called _____ . Conversions among three currencies, in order to profit from discrepancies in spot exchange rates, is called _____ . Such opportunities do not exist in a(n) _____ market.

10. Spot trades involve agreement on the exchange rate today, called the _____ exchange rate, for settlement in _____ business days. Forward trades involve agreement today on an exchange rate for settlement in the more distant future. The exchange rate in this case is the _____ exchange rate. When a foreign currency is more expensive in the forward market than in the spot market, it is selling at a _____ relative to the dollar; equivalently, it is said that the dollar is selling at a _____ relative to the foreign currency.

11. If a commodity has different prices when purchased with different currencies, this is a violation of the concept of _____ . This scenario creates opportunities for _____ profits if the following three conditions are also met: (1) there are no _____ costs; (2) there are no barriers to _____ ; and (3) the commodities are _____ in both countries.

12. In efficient markets, the opportunity for profits such as those just described cannot exist, so that the following condition applies: $P_{FC} =$ _____ × _____ . In an efficient market, any deviation from this condition results in adjustments in both _____ and _____ .

13.   The concept of relative purchasing power parity indicates that the rate of change in an exchange rate over time is determined by _____ in the two countries. Relative purchasing power parity states that the expected change in the exchange rate is equal to the _____ , as indicated in the following equation: _____ = _____ . This statement of relative purchasing power parity can be algebraically rearranged, as follows: $E[S_1] =$ _____ .

14.   In general, for any time period t, relative purchasing power parity is stated as follows: $E[S_t] =$ _____ .

15.   The rate of return on an investment in a risk-free asset in a foreign country depends not only on the minimal risk-free interest rate in the foreign country, but also on the _____ exchange rate and the _____ exchange rate. If the actual rate on this investment differs from the risk-free rate in Canada, then an opportunity exists for a(n) _____ profit; the process of taking advantage of this opportunity is referred to as _____ .

16.   In an efficient market, such opportunities do not exist. The statement that these two returns must be equal is called the _____ condition, which is stated mathematically as follows:_____ = _____ . This statement can be rearranged algebraically as follows: $F_1/S_0 =$ _____ .

17.   An approximation of the above equation states that the percentage forward premium or discount is equal to the difference between the foreign and domestic interest rates: _____ = _____ . This approximation is often algebraically rearranged as follows: $F_1 =$ _____ . This statement an be extended to any number of time periods, t, as follows: $F_t =$ _____ .

18.   The statement that the forward rate is equal to the expected future spot rate is referred to as the _____ condition, which is stated mathematically as follows: _____ = _____ . Essentially, this statement indicates that the forward rate must be equal to the _____ expectation regarding the _____ rate.

19.   The condition referred to as uncovered interest parity is stated as follows: $E[S_1] =$ _____ . This condition can also be stated for t time periods as follows: $E[S_t] =$ _____ .

20.   The international Fisher effect is derived by equating the right-hand sides of the PPP and UIP relationships, as follows: _____ = _____ . This statement can be simplified as: $h_{FC} - h_{CDN} =$ _____ . That is, the difference in foreign and domestic inflation rates is equal to the difference in foreign and domestic _____ . This equation can be algebraically rearranged: $R_{CDN} - h_{CDN} =$ _____ .

21.   The international Fisher effect indicates that _____ in different countries are equal. In the absence of differences in attitudes toward risk from one country to another, and barriers to the movement of money, the international Fisher effect is an implication of _____ markets.

22.   International capital budgeting decisions are made using the _____ criterion. The _____ approach requires that foreign currency cash flows are converted to dollar cash flows. This conversion requires the calculation of _____ exchange rates, using the _____ relationship, as follows: $E[S_t] =$ _____ . The dollar cash flows are then discounted using the required rate of return for dollar cash flows.

23. The _____ approach to international capital budgeting requires that we discount the cash flows, measured in terms of the _____ . The resulting net present value is then converted to a net present value measured in _____ . The foreign currency cash flows are not discounted at the firm's cost of capital. However, the cost of capital is converted to an appropriate rate for the foreign currency, using the _____ relationship. This net present value is converted to dollars, using the _____ exchange rate.

24. The risk of loss of value resulting from fluctuations in exchange rates over time is referred to as _____ risk. Firms dealing in international trade are subject to exchange rate risk because they both make payments in foreign currencies and receive foreign currencies in payments. Consequently, changes in exchange rates can result in losses; this is considered _____ exposure. For example, a firm which has receivables denominated in a foreign currency, experiences a(n) (increase/decrease) in the dollar value of the receivables when the exchange rate increases; the firm experiences a(n) (increase/decrease) in the dollar value of the receivables when the exchange rate decreases. Similarly, a firm which has payables denominated in a foreign currency, experiences a(n) (increase/decrease) in the dollar value of the payables when the exchange rate increases.

25. The _____ risk is the uncertainty associated with the dollar value of the future payment in the foreign currency. A means of hedging exchange rate risk is provided by the _____ market. The firm can eliminate exchange rate risk by _____ a forward contract and promising to deliver the foreign currency in exchange for dollars.

26. A long-term commitment to purchase resources, such as labour or materials, in a foreign country results in a _____ exposure to exchange rate risk. Protection against such exposures is generally accomplished by _____ in the foreign currency. When a Canadian firm prepares its financial statements, the information on foreign operations must be translated into dollars; this process results in _____ exposure. The American Financial Accounting Standards Board Statement Number 52 requires that all assets and liabilities be translated at _____ exchange rates. Gains and losses from exchange rate fluctuations are carried as a separate item in the _____ portion of the balance sheet, but are not recognized on the income statement.

PROBLEMS

Problem 1

The direct exchange rate for German Deutsche marks is $.50/DM 1. The direct exchange rate for British pounds is $1.50/£ 1. If you have 1 Deutsche mark, how many pounds can you buy? (That is, what is the cross rate?)

Problem 2

Suppose that, for the data in Problem 1, the cross rate is DM 3.3/£ 1, rather than the calculated result of DM 3/£ 1. Describe the triangle arbitrage opportunity which would exist under these circumstances.

Problem 3

Suppose that, for the data in Problem 1, the cross rate is DM 2.7/£ 1. Describe the triangle arbitrage opportunity which would exist under these circumstances.

Use the following data to solve Problems 4 through 7:

The spot exchange rate for the British pound is $1.80/£ 1, and the ninety-day forward rate is $1.75/£ 1. The spot rate and ninety-day forward rate for the Swiss franc are $.80/SF 1, and $.75/SF 1, respectively. The spot rate and ninety-day forward rate for the German Deutsche mark are $.65/DM 1, and $.70/DM 1, respectively.

Problem 4

Compute the indirect exchange rate for each of the exchange rates quoted above. Which of these currencies are selling at a premium relative to the dollar? For which currencies is the dollar selling at a premium relative to the foreign currency?

Problem 5

What is the cross-rate, in the spot market, for pounds in terms of Deutsche marks? What is the cross-rate, in the spot market, for Deutsche marks in terms of pounds?

Problem 6

Suppose that the cross-rate for pounds in terms of Deutsche marks is actually £ .35/DM 1, rather than the result computed in the solution to Problem 5. Describe the triangle arbitrage opportunity which would exist under these circumstances.

Problem 7

Suppose that the cross-rate for pounds in terms of Deutsche marks is actually £ .37/DM 1, rather than the result computed in the solution to Problem 5. Describe the triangle arbitrage opportunity which would exist under these circumstances.

Problem 8

An ounce of silver costs $5 in Canada The exchange rate with Japan is ¥ 150 = $1. Is this an equilibrium situation: Suppose that a trader has $500 available; can the trader earn an arbitrage profit?

Problem 9

Suppose that, for the data of Problem 8, the price of silver in Canada and Japan does not change. What is the equilibrium exchange rate which is consistent with absolute purchasing power parity?

Problem 10

Suppose that, for the data in Problem 8, the price of silver in Japan is ¥ 700 per ounce. Describe the arbitrage profit opportunity for a trader with $500 available.

Problem 11

The direct spot exchange rate for marks is $.50/DM 1 and the 90-day forward rate is $.51/DM 1. Is the mark selling at a premium or discount? Compute the indirect spot and forward rates.

Problem 12

Suppose that, in Problem 11, the Canadian 90-day risk-free rate is $R_{CDN} = 3\%$. What is the German risk-free rate, R_G?

Problem 13

In three years, the inflation rate in Canada is expected to be 4%, while in France it is expected to be 10%. The current exchange rate is $\$1 = FF\ 2.50$. What is the expected spot exchange rate three years from now?

Problem 14

Using the above spot rate and forward exchange rate, assume that a risk-free asset in Canada earns a 14% return, while in France the risk-free interest rate is 12%. Is there a covered interest arbitrage opportunity?

Problem 15

The exchange rate for the French franc is \$0.25 / 1FF and the rate for the British pound is \$1.50 / £ 1. What is the cross rate for the French franc and the British pound?

Problem 16

If the actual cross rate were £1 / 5FF, how could an investor take advantage of an arbitrage opportunity?

Problem 17

Suppose the Swiss inflation rate is forecasted to be 2% during the coming year and the United States rate over the same period will be 5%. The current exchange rate is \$1.50 = SF 1. What is the expected spot exchange rate in one year?

Problem 18

The current yen/dollar exchange rate is ¥ 150/\$1. The risk-free interest rate in Japan is 6% and in Canada is 8%. What is the expected spot exchange rate in one year?

Problem 19

Suppose that, for the data Problem 18, the Canadian inflation rate is expected to be 4%. What is the expected spot exchange rate in five years?

Use the following information to solve Problems 20 and 21.

You have been asked to evaluate a proposed investment in the country of Westfield. Westfield's home currency is the Sar, abbreviated SA. The current exchange rate is SA 2/\$1. The inflation rate in Westfield is expected to be 10% higher than in Canada. The project will cost SA 1,000 and is expected to generate SA 300 per year for three years. The project will then be sold for an estimated SA 400. The appropriate discount rate for dollar flows of this risk level is 12%.

Problem 20

What is the expected spot exchange rate at the end of the project's life?

Problem 21

Use the home currency approach to compute the net present value of the proposed investment in dollars.

ANSWERS TO CONCEPT TEST

1.   cross rate

2.   Eurobond

3.   Eurodollars

4.   foreign bonds

5.   London Interbank Offered Rate

6.   currency swap

7.   interest rate swap

8.   exchange rate; indirect; European; direct; American

9.   arbitrage; triangle arbitrage; efficient

10.   spot; two; forward; premium; discount

11.   absolute purchasing power parity; arbitrage; transactions; trade; identical

12. S_0; P_{CDN}; prices; exchange rates

13.   inflation rates; difference in the inflation rates; $[E(S1) - S_0] / S_0$; $(h_{FC} - h_{CDN})$; $S_0 \times [1 + (h_{FC} - h_{CDN})]$

14. $S_0 \times [1 + (h_{FC} - h_{CDN})]^t$

15.   spot; forward; arbitrage; covered interest arbitrage

16.   interest rate parity; $\$1 \times (1 + R_{CDN})$; $S_0 \times (1 + R_{FC}) / F_1$; $(1 + R_{FC}) / (1 + R_{CDN})$

17. $(F_1 - S_0) / S_0$; $(R_{FC} - R_{CDN})$; $S_0 \times [1 + (R_{FC} - R_{CDN})]$; $S_0 \times [1 + (R_{FC} - R_{CDN})]^t$

18.   unbiased forward rates; F_t; $E[S_t]$; market consensus; future spot

19. $S_0 \times [1 + (R_{FC} - R_{CDN})]$; $S_0 \times [1 + (R_{FC} - R_{CDN})]^t$

20. $S_0 \times [1 + (h_{FC} - h_{CDN})]$; $S_0 \times [1 + (R_{FC} - R_{CDN})]$; $(R_{FC} - R_{CDN})$; interest rates; $(R_{FC} - h_{FC})$

21.   real interest rates; efficient

22.   net present value; home currency; expected future; uncovered interest parity; $S_0 \times [1 + (R_{FC} - R_{CDN})]^t$

23.   foreign currency; foreign currency; dollars; international Fisher effect; spot

24.   exchange rate; short-run; decrease; increase; decrease

25.   exchange rate; forward; purchasing

26.   long-run; matching inflows and outflows; translation; current; shareholders' equity

PROBLEM SOLUTIONS

Problem 1: One Deutsche mark will buy $.50. With $.50, you can buy 1/3 of a pound. The cross rate is M 3/£ 1.

Problem 2: Use the one Deutsche mark to purchase $.50, and then exchange the $.50 for £ (1/3). At the cross rate of DM 3.3/£ 1, 1/3 pound can be exchanged for DM 1.1. This results in an arbitrage profit of 10%.

Problem 3: Exchange DM 1 for £ (1/2.7) = £ .37037, and then purchase £ .37037 × ($1.50/£ 1) = $.55556. At the exchange rate of DM 2/$1, $.55556 can be exchanged for [$.55556 × (DM 2/$1)] = 1.1111 marks. This result represents an arbitrage profit of 11.11%.

Problem 4: The direct (or American) exchange rate is the number of dollars per unit of foreign currency; the exchange rates given above are quoted as direct exchange rates. The indirect exchange rate is the number of units of the foreign currency per dollar. To convert the direct spot exchange rate for the British pound to the indirect exchange rate, divide both sides of the direct exchange rate quote by 1.80: $1.80 / 1.80 = £ 1/1.80. So, $1.00 = £ .5556

Therefore, the indirect exchange rate is £ 0.5556. In general, the indirect exchange rate is the reciprocal of the direct exchange rate. For the British pound, the ninety-day direct exchange rate is (£ 1/1.75) = £ 0.5714. For the Swiss franc, the spot and ninety-day forward rates are SF 1.2500 and SF 1.3333, respectively. For the Deutsche mark, the respective rates are DM 1.5385 and 1.4286.

The German Deutsche mark is more expensive in the future than it is today (i.e., $.70/DM 1 and $.65/DM 1, respectively), so the Deutsche mark is selling at a premium relative to the dollar. Equivalently, the dollar is selling at a discount relative to the Deutsche mark. On the other hand, the British pound is less expensive in the future than it is today (i.e., $1.75/£ 1 and $1.80/£ 1, respectively), so the pound is selling at a discount relative to the dollar. And, the dollar is selling at a premium relative to the pound. These latter conclusions also apply to the Swiss franc.

Problem 5: The spot rate for British pounds is £ 0.5556/$1; the spot rate for the Deutsche mark is DM 1.5385/$1. Therefore, £ 0.5556 and DM 1.5385 are equivalent, so that the cross-rate for pounds in terms of Deutsche marks is: £ 0.5556 / DM 1.5385 = £ .3611 / DM 1.

The cross rate for pounds in terms of Deutsche marks is: DM 1.5385 / £ 0.5556 = DM 2.7691 / £ 1

Note that the cross-rate for pounds in terms of Deutsche marks is simply the reciprocal of the cross-rate for Deutsche marks in terms of pounds.

Problem 6: Given the circumstances of this problem, the Deutsche mark is less expensive in terms of pounds than it is in terms of dollars. Therefore, the triangle arbitrage opportunity requires purchasing Deutsche marks using pounds, and then selling Deutsche marks for dollars. That is, buy Deutsche marks at the lower price and then sell Deutsche marks at the higher price. Specifically, first convert $1 to £ 0.5556. Next, convert pounds to Deutsche marks: £ .35 = DM 1. So, (£ 0.5556) / .35 = DM 1.5874.
Then convert DM 1.5874 to dollars: DM 1.5385 = $1, and (DM 1.5874) / 1.5385 = $1.0318.

Thus, $1 has been converted to $1.0318, using triangle arbitrage.

Problem 7: Now, the Deutsche mark is less expensive in terms of dollars than it is in terms of pounds. Therefore, the triangle arbitrage opportunity requires purchasing Deutsche marks using dollars, and then selling Deutsche marks for pounds. That is, buy Deutsche marks at the lower price and then sell Deutsche marks at the higher price.

Convert $1 to DM 1.5385. Next, convert DM 1.5385 to pounds. The cross-rate for Deutsche marks in terms of pounds is the reciprocal of the rate for pounds in terms of Deutsche marks: DM (1/.37) / £ 1 = DM 2.7027 / £ 1.

Therefore, DM 1.5385 are converted to [£ (1.5385/2.7027)] = £ 0.5692. Pounds are now converted to dollars: £ 0.5692 = [$(.5692/.5556)] = $1.0245.

Problem 8: The trader can purchase ($500/$5) = 100 ounces of silver in Canada. This can then be sold for (100 × ¥ 800) = ¥ 80,000 in Japan. At an exchange rate of ¥150/$1, the trader can exchange ¥80,000 for (¥ 80,000 / (¥ 150/$1)] = 533.33; the arbitrage profit is ($533.33 – $500) = $33.33. This is not an equilibrium situation; it is a violation of the concept of absolute purchasing power parity. The demand for silver in Canada will cause the dollar price of silver to increase and the supply of silver will cause the yen price to decrease in Japan. Also, the exchange rate will increase due to the increased demand for dollars and the decreased demand for yen.

Problem 9: The condition for absolute purchasing power parity is: $P_{FC} = S_0 \times P_{CDN}$. Therefore, in order for absolute purchasing power parity to prevail, S_0 must equal: $S_0 = P_{FC} / P_{CDN} = $ ¥ 800 / $5 = ¥ 160 / $1

Problem 10: In this situation, the trader can exchange $500 for [$500 × (¥ 150/$1)] = ¥ 75,000. With ¥ 75,000, the trader can then purchase (75,000/700) = 107.1429 ounces of silver in Japan. He can sell the silver for ($5 × 107.1429) = $535.71, for an arbitrage profit of $35.71.

Problem 11: The indirect rates are the reciprocal of the direct rates; therefore, the spot rate is DM (1/.50) = DM 2.0000 and the forward rate is DM 1.9608.

Problem 12: From the interest rate parity condition:

$$F_1 / S_0 = (1 + R_G) / (1 + R_{CDN})$$

Substituting the known values and solving for R_G, we have:

$$1.9608 / 2.000 = (1 + R_G) / 1.03$$
$$2 \times (1 + R_G) = 1.9608 \times 1.03$$
$$1 + R_G = 1.009812$$
$$R_G = .009812$$

Therefore, the German risk-free rate is .9812%, or approximately 1%.

Problem 13: This can be calculated using relative purchasing power parity:

$$E[S_t] = S_0 \times [h_{FF} - h_{CDN}]^t = (FF\ 2.50\ /\ \$1) \times [1 + (.10 - .04)]^3$$

$$= (FF\ 2.50\ /\$1) \times (1.06)^3 = FF\ 2.978\ /\ \$1$$

Problem 14: By investing \$1 in a risk-free Canadian asset for three years, an investor will earn $\$1 \times (1.14)^3 = \$1.4815$. By investing the same amount in a risk-free asset in France, the investor receives:

Convert \$1: $\$1 \times (FF\ 2.50 \times \$1) = FF\ 2.50$
The investor may enter a forward agreement at a rate of $F_3 = FF\ 2.978\ /\ \$1$
Investing the FF 2.50, the investor will have $[FF\ 2.50 \times (1.12)^3] = FF\ 3.5123$ at the end of three years
Converting the FF 3.5123 to dollars at the rate established above, the investor has $[(FF\ 3.5123\ /\ \$1)\ /\ (FF\ 2.978\ /\ \$1)]$ = \$1.1794

There is a covered interest arbitrage opportunity, because the investor will prefer to earn 17.94% rather than the Canadian rate of 14%.

Problem 15: With 1£, you can buy \$1.50. With this you can then buy 6 FF. The cross rate is therefore £1 / 6FF.

Problem 16: Using £1, you could purchase \$1.50 which could then be exchanged for 6 FF. This represents an arbitrage profit of 20%.

Problem 17: From relative purchasing power parity: $(E[S_1] - S_0)\ /\ S_0 = h_{FC} - h_{CDN}$

Since the exchange rates here are in terms of units of foreign currency per dollar, the relevant spot rate here is $S_0 = SF\ (1/1.50) = SF\ 2/3 = SF\ 0.66667$. Therefore, substituting into the relative purchasing power parity relationship: $(E[S_1] - 2/3)\ /\ 0.6667 = .02 - .05$, and $E[S_1] = .64667$.

Solution note: You must be careful here to use the exchange rate expressed as units of foreign currency per dollar. The difference between the Swiss and the Canadian inflation rates is (-3%), so the price of a dollar, measured in terms of Swiss francs will decrease by approximately 3%: $[(SF\ .66667) \times .97] = SF\ .64667$.

Problem 18: From the interest rate parity condition: $F_1\ /\ S_0 = (1 + R_J)\ /\ (1 + R_{CDN})$

Substituting the known values and solving for F_1, we have: $F_1\ /\ 150 = 1.06\ /\ 1.08$.
Therefore, the forward rate is ¥ 147.22/\$1.

Problem 19: Using the international Fisher effect, the Japanese inflation rate (h_J) can be determined as follows:

$$R_{CDN} - h_{CDN} = R_J - h_J$$
$$.08 - .04 = .06 - h_J$$
$$h_J = .02 = 2\%$$

The expected spot exchange rate five years from now is determined using the relative purchasing power parity relationship:

$$E[S_t] = S_0 \times [1 + (h_{FC} - h_{CDN})]^t$$

$$E[S_5] = S_0 \times [1 + (h_j - h_{CDN})]^5$$

$$= (¥\,147.22) \times [1 + (.02 - .04)]^5 = ¥\,133.08$$

Problem 20: The expected spot exchange rate is determined using the relative purchasing power parity relationship:

$$E[S_t] = S_0 \times [1 + (h_{FC} - h_{CDN})]^t$$
$$E[S_3] = S_0 \times [1 + (h_{FC} - h_{CDN})]^3$$

$$= (SA\,2) \times [1.10]^3 = SA\,2.662$$

Problem 21: The expected spot exchange rates for years 1, 2 and 3 are presented in the following table:

Year	Expected exchange rate
1	$(SA\,2) \times (1.10) = SA\,2.200$
2	$(SA\,2) \times (1.10)^2 = SA\,2.420$
3	$(SA\,2) \times (1.10)^3 = SA\,2.662$

These exchange rates are then used to convert cash flows to dollars:

Year	Cash flow (in SA)	Expected exchange rate	Cash flow (in $)
0	-SA 1,000	SA 2.000	-$500.0000
1	SA 300	SA 2.200	$136.3636
2	SA 300	SA 2.420	$123.9669
3	SA 700	SA 2.662	$262.9602

At a 12% discount rate, the NPV in dollars is –$92.25.

22 Leasing

CHAPTER HIGHLIGHTS

Leasing is a form of financing for businesses to use plant, property, equipment and other assets. Our focus will be on long-term leases that are typically more than five years, which we will compare with the alternative of buying an asset financed by long-term debt.

22.1 LEASES AND LEASE TYPES

A lease is a contracted agreement between the *lessee*, the user of the equipment, and the *lessor,* who is the owner. The lease agreement establishes the right of the lessee to use the asset by making periodic payments to the lessor.

Leasing Versus Buying: The decision to lease or to borrow and buy requires a comparison of alternative *financing* arrangements for the use of an asset. This implies that the capital budgeting decision has already been made.

When the leasing company purchases the asset from the manufacturer, the arrangement is called a *direct lease.* Here the leasing company arranges the financing, purchases the asset, and holds title to it. If a company leases its own assets from wholly-owned subsidiaries, the latter are referred to as *captive finance companies.*

Operating Leases: An operating or *service lease* is usually a short-term lease, meaning the life of the lease is less than the economic life of the asset. The lessor is responsible for insurance, taxes and upkeep. Operating leases are often cancellable on short notice, and the value of a cancellation clause depends on whether technological and/or economic conditions are likely to make the value of the asset to the lessee less than the value of the future lease payments under the lease.

Financial Leases: Payments made under a *financial lease* are usually sufficient to cover fully the lessor's cost of purchasing the asset and pay the lessor a return on the investment. Therefore, financial leases are typically a longer-term, fully amortized lease under which the lessee is responsible for the upkeep. These leases are usually noncancellable, at least not without a significant penalty. Two special types of financial leases include a *sale and lease back* arrangement and a *leveraged lease.*

Sale and Lease Back Arrangements: A *sale and lease back* arrangement occurs when a company sells an asset to another firm and simultaneously leases it back. In other words, the lessee receives cash from the sale of the asset and continues to use the asset. A sale and lease back is typically motivated by the realization of tax benefits.

Leveraged Leases: A *leveraged lease* is a tax-oriented lease involving three or more parties which at least include a lessee, a lessor, and a lender. The lessor usually puts up no more than 40 to 50 % of the financing, is entitled to the lease payments but must pay interest to the lenders. The lenders supply the remaining financing but cannot turn to the lessor in case of a default. However, the lenders have a first lien on the asset and may actually receive the lease payments by deducting the principal and interest portion and then forwarding the remainder to the lessor.

Leveraged leases make sense when the lessee cannot fully use CCA and/or tax credits that come with owning the asset so that these benefits are passed on to the lessor. Of course, the lessor may return a portion of these tax benefits to the lessee in the form of lower lease costs.

22.2 ACCOUNTING AND LEASES

Before 1979, lessees only had to report information on leasing activity in footnotes accompanying their financial statements. Thus, leasing was frequently called *off balance sheet financing*. This meant that firms could acquire a substantial number of assets with significant financial commitment via financial leases, yet not disclose the impact of this debt in their financial statements. To discourage companies from understating their financial leverage, the Canadian Institute of Chartered Accountants (CICA) implemented new rules for lease disclosure which meant that the present value of lease payments must be calculated and reported along with other liabilities of the lessee's balance sheet.

In order to determine whether a lease must be *capitalized* and appear in the balance sheet and declared as a financial lease, *one* of the following criteria must apply to the lease transaction:

1.   The lease transfers ownership of the property to the lessee by the end of the term of the lease.

2.   The lessee has an option to purchase the asset at a price below fair market value when the lease expires, commonly referred to as a bargain purchase option.

3.   The lease term is 75 % or more of the estimated economic life of the asset.

4.   The present value of lease payments is at least 90 % of the fair market value of the asset at the start of the lease.

22.3 TAXES, CCRA, AND LEASES

Basically, Canada Customs and Revenue Agency (CCRA) requires that a lease be primarily for business purposes and not merely for tax avoidance. Normally, the lessee gets a tax deduction for the full lease payment. In a *Conditional Sales Agreement*, only the interest position of the payment is deductible. If CCRA detects one or more of the following, including sale and lease backs, the lease will be disallowed:

1.   The lessee automatically acquires title after payment of a specified amount in the form of rentals,

2.   The lessee is required to buy the property from the lessor during or at the termination of the lease,

3.   The lessee has the right during (or at the expiration of) the lease to acquire the property at a price less than fair market value.

Current regulations allow lessors to deduct CCA from leasing income only and unused CCA tax shields cannot be passed along to other companies owned by the same parent holding campany.

22.4 THE CASH FLOWS FROM LEASING

The Incremental Cash Flows: The following example illustrates the incremental after-tax cash flows from leasing instead of borrowing.

An Example: Your firm needs one hundred new machines to support a tremendous growth in sales. Each machine can be purchased for $20,000 which will reduce operating costs on the existing equipment by $12,000 per machine per year, for the next five years. The machines can be depreciated for tax purposes at CCA rate of 30 % and are expected to have $1,000 residual value after 5 years. Your firm has also contacted Welease Inc., which requires beginning of year lease payments of $5,000 per year for each machine over the five year period. With the lease, your firm is responsible for maintenance, insurance and operating expenses. Your firm's tax rate is 40 %. What are the cash flow consequences of leasing instead of buying? First compute the tax shield on CCA and the tax shield on the terminal loss that will occur in year 5.

The schedule below shows the CCA and UCC schedule for one machine. The half year rule has been incorporated.

Year	UCC	CCA	Tax Shield
1	$10,000	$3,000	$1,200
2	17,000	5,100	2,040
3	11,900	3,570	1,428
4	8,330	2,499	999.6
5	5,831	1,749.3	699.72
6	4,081.7		1,232.68

In Year 5, the UCC balance after the sale is positive ($4,081.7 − $1,000) but there are no assets left in the pool because each of the machines are scrapped for $1,000 salvage. This results in a terminal loss tax shield of $3,081.7 (.40) = $1,232.68.

To calculate the relevant cash flow for each of the next 5 years, a few points should be noted. First, the $12,000 reductions of operating costs on the existing equipment will be realized whether the machines are leased or purchased and therefore, because these are not incremental, they must be ignored in the analysis. Second, if the machine is leased there is a tax shield of $5,000 (.40) = $2,000 each year so that the after-tax cost is $3,000. However, because payments are made at the beginning of each period the tax shield will lag by one period. In other words, the $2,000 tax shield will be realized at the end of each year. Third, if the machines are leased, your firm cannot claim CCA for tax purposes. This foregone tax shield represents an outflow for your firm. Note: Unlike the payment shield the CCA tax shield has not been lagged for one period. Finally, the initial investment of $20,000 per machine represents an inflow for your firm since by leasing them, this money does not have to be spent. However, the salvage of $1,000 represents an outflow since this amount is forgone if the firm leases the machine. These points are summarized below.

	Year					
	0	1	2	3	4	5
Investment	$20,000					
Salvage					(1,000)	
Lease Payment	(5,000)	(5,000)	(5,000)	(5,000)	(5,000)	
Payment Shield		2,000	2,000	2,000	2,000	2,000
Forgone CCA Tax Shield	(1,200)	(2,040)	(1,428)	(999.6)	(699.72)	(1,232.68)
Total Cash Flow	$13,800	(5,040)	(4,428)	(3,999.6)	(3,699.72)	(232.68)

22.5 LEASE OR BUY?

A Preliminary Analysis: Suppose your firm were to borrow $20,000 today and make after-tax payments equal to the cash flows shown above. What is the interest rate your firm is paying on this 'loan?' To find the unknown rate we solve the following equation:

$$0 = \$13,800 - \frac{\$5,040}{(1+i)} - \frac{\$4,428}{(1+i)^2} - \frac{\$3,999.6}{(1+i)^3} - \frac{\$3,699.72}{(1+i)^4} - \frac{\$232.68}{(1+i)^5}$$

The discount rate works out to 10.41 %. In other words, your firm has arranged financing from Welease Inc., at an after-tax rate of 10.41 %. This rate should be compared to the after-tax cost of the term loan that your firm could obtain from a financial institution.

An Example: Your firm has secured a 5 year term loan from the Loyal bank at 14 % interest rate. Should your firm lease or go with the bank?

Your firm should go with the bank because the after-tax interest rate would be .14 (1 − .4) = 8.4 % which is less than the 10.41 % implicit after-tax rate on the lease.

Three Potential Pitfalls: First, as we saw earlier, leasing would have been preferred to borrowing if the implicit rate on leasing was *lower* than the after-tax rate of borrowing. Normally, the higher the IRR, the better, but with this cash flow pattern, the IRR represents the rate we pay, so the *lower* the IRR the better. Second, a related pitfall is that we were calculating the advantage of leasing instead of borrowing, which is why a lower IRR from the cash flows of leasing is preferred over the after-tax borrowing rate. Third, some analysts mistakenly calculate the IRR of leasing by totally excluding the borrow-to-buy decision. This is incorrect because the incremental cash flows are misspecified because the CAA tax shields and salvage value are ignored.

NPV Analysis: Since we know that the relevant rate for evaluating a lease versus buy decision is the firm's after-tax borrowing cost, the NPV is simply discounting the cash flows in the above table   .14 (1 − .4) = 8.4 percent:

$$NPV = \$13,800 - \frac{\$5,040}{(1.084)} - \frac{\$4,428}{(1.084)^2} - \frac{\$3,999.6}{(1.084)^3} - \frac{\$3,699.72}{(1.084)^4} - \frac{\$232.68}{(1.084)^5}$$

The NPV of −$592.71 reinforces our decision earlier to buy and is often called the *net advantage to leasing* (NAL).

A Misconception: Some argue that the $20,000 your firm would borrow is not equivalent to the present value of after-tax interest plus principal repayments that are paid over 5 years. In fact, it can be shown that for any loan amortized over any given period, the present value of the after-tax interest plus principal repayments is always equal to the amount of the loan as long as the discount rate used is the loan rate after-tax. This is demonstrated in Problem 10 at the end of the chapter.

An Example: Suppose your firm was able to negotiate a lease payment of $4,000 per year. What is the IRR and NPV of the lease?

The table below shows the new calculations.

	0	1	2	3	4	5
			Year			
Investment	$ 20,000					
Salvage						(1,000)
Lease Payment	(4,000)	(4,000)	(4,000)	(4,000)	(4,000)	
Payment Shield		1,600	1,600	1,600	1,600	1,600
Forgone CCA Tax Shield	(1,200)	(2,040)	(1,428)	(999.6)	(699.72)	(1,232.68)
Total Cash Flow	$14,800	(4,440)	(3,828)	(3,399.6)	(3,099.72)	(632.68)

The IRR for leasing is 1.64 % and the NPV using the after-tax loan rate of 8.4 % is $2,109.75. Since the IRR is less than the after-tax cost of borrowing and the NPV is positive, your firm should now favour leasing over buying.

In the original example for your firm, since all of the machines were sold, the asset pool was closed with a resulting terminal loss. Suppose that your firm has other assets in the same class so that the unused UCC is depreciated from zero to infinity. In this case, we use the CCA tax shield formula developed in earlier.

$$NAL = I - \left[L \sum_{t-1}^{n-1} \frac{L(1-T)}{(1+i)^t} - \frac{L(T)}{(1+i)^n} \right] - \left[\frac{TdI}{(1+d)} \times \frac{1+i/2}{(1+i)} \right] + \left[\frac{SdT}{(i+d)} \times \frac{1}{(1+i)^n} \right] - \frac{S}{(1+i)^n}$$

While the formula looks formidable, the application is pretty straightforward. Notice the terms within the first set of brackets. These represent the present value of lease payment after-tax, taking into account the lag in the tax shields from the lease payments. The second set of brackets contains the familiar formula to compute the present value of infinite CCA tax savings, except that the sign preceding the formula is negative. This is because, by leasing, the tax savings are foregone. The third set of brackets contains the reduction in tax savings due to salvage for which, again, we reverse signs. The final term is the present value of salvage preceded by a negative sign, since it represents a forgone opportunity for leasing.

An Example: Referring the original information provided for your firm, but assuming that there will be other machines in the assets class, what is your firm's NAL?

$$NAL = \$20,000 - \$5,000 + \$5,000(1.-.4)(PVIFA8.4\%,4) - \frac{\$5,000(.4)}{(1.084)^5}$$

$$- \frac{(.4)(.3)(\$20,000)}{.084+.3} \times \frac{1+.084/2}{1.084} + \frac{\$1,000(.3)(.4)}{.084+.3} \times \frac{1}{(1.084)^5} - \frac{\$1,000}{(1.084)^5}$$

$$= \$20,000 - \$13,512.31 - \$6,007.84 + \$208.79 - \$668.12 = \$20.52$$

With the full tax shield on CCA available instead of just the write-off in year 5, the NAL increases from the original value of −$592.72 to +$20.52. Of course, if your firm acquires 100 machines, the NAL could be $2,052.

22.6 A LEASING PARADOX:

The cash flows from the lessor's perspective for WeLease are presented below.

	Year					
	0	1	2	3	4	5
Investment	$(20,000)					
Salvage						1,000
Lease Payment	5,000	5,000	5,000	5,000	5,000	
Payment Shield		(2,000)	(2,000)	(2,000)	(2,000)	(2,000)
CCA Tax Shield	1,200	2,040	1,428	999.6	699.72	1,232.68
Total Cash Flow	$(13,800)	5,040	4,428	3,999.6	3,699.72	232.68

NAL = $592.71

The cash flows to Welease Inc. are exactly the opposite of the cash flows to your firm. The investment is an outflow today, the lease payments after taxes are reflected, and the benefit from the CCA tax shield is shown. This implies a zero-sum game where the positive NPV of one party (Welease, in our example) is the negative NPV of the other (your firm). In this case, Welease hopes that your firm will do the deal.

Resolving the Paradox: A lease contract is not a zero sum game, if the effective tax rates between the lessee and lessor differ. In this case, both sides may benefit. For example, the tax benefits of leasing and CCA tax shields can be shared between the two firms by setting the lease payments at the appropriate level and shareholders of both firms will benefit (CCRA will lose). The firm in the higher tax bracket should be the lessor in order to take advantage of CCA (especially in the early years) and debt financing, some of which are passed on to the lessee through lower lease payments.

22.7 REASONS FOR LEASING

Good Reasons: First, *taxes* may be reduced by leasing because a potential tax shield that cannot be used by one firm can be transferred to another by leasing. Second, certain types of *uncertainty* may be reduced that may otherwise decrease the value of the firm. Transferring the uncertainty about the residual value insures the lessee and is especially valued in industries facing changes in technology and rapid obsolescence. Third, *transactions costs* such as those associated with changes in ownership can be lower for a lease contract than for buying an asset.

Bad Reasons: As mentioned earlier, *classification* of a lease as operating or financial (or capital) in nature may affect debt and profitability ratios, but this impact is not likely to fool anyone. The NPV gained or lost is far more important than the effect of the lease on a firm's financial statements. It is claimed that leasing provides *100 % financing* whereas secured equipment loans require a down payment. However, lease payments are often made in advance, and implicitly secured by assets of the firm.

Other reasons specific to a firm may motivate it to engage in leasing. For example, circumventing capital expenditure control systems, a liquidity crisis, application of unused capital losses, and so on, may be factors for companies to find leasing advantageous.

CONCEPT TEST

1. Leases are _____ agreements between the user of the asset, the _____ and the _____, the _____ of the asset.

2. If the leasing company purchases the asset directly from the manufacturer, this is called a _____. However, a firm may lease its own assets from a wholly-owned subsidiary, sometimes also known as a _____.

3. _____ are often cancellable on short notice and are short-term whereas _____ are fully amortized where the lessee is responsible for upkeep.

4. Tax benefits and the need for liquidity may result in a _____ transaction where a company _____ an asset and _____ it back.

5. Three parties or more are included in a _____ transaction where _____ benefits are shared between the lessee, lessor and _____.

6. The four criteria that determine whether a lease should be _____ include: the lease transfers ownership to the _____ by the end of the term; there is an _____ at a price below fair market value; the term of the lease is _____ or more than the estimated economic life of the assets; and that the present value of the _____ is at least 90 % of the _____ of the asset.

7. For tax purposes, normally the lease payment is fully _____ . However, in a _____ only the _____ portion of the payment is deductible.

8. Lessors cannot use CCA deductions to increase _____ .

9. For the company leasing the asset, the incremental cash flows include the initial investment, an _ (inflow/outflow) ; the salvage value, an (inflow/outflow); the lease payments, an (inflow/outflow) ; the payment shield, an (inflow/outflow) ; and the foregone _____ , which is an (inflow/outflow) .

10. The discount rate which makes the net advantage to leasing (NAL) equal to zero should be (higher/lower) than the after-tax rate on the loan for the NPV to be positive. In other words, a _____ IRR from the cash flows of leasing is preferred over the after-tax borrowing rate.

11. The appropriate discount rate for leasing is the _____ after tax.

12. The present value of a loan adjusted for tax savings on interest is equal to the _____ if the discount rate is the loan rate _____ .

13. If no other assets remain in the asset class when the pool is terminated, then the salvage value can result in taxes saved on a _____ or taxes paid on _____ income.

14. A _____ refers to the notion that the positive NPV of the lessee is exactly equal to the _____ NPV of the lessor. However, if the effective _____ of the lessee and lessor differ, then the lease contract need not be a _____ .

15. Reduction in _____ , _____ and _____ are cited as good reasons for leasing, whereas accounting classification and 100 % financing are considered to be bad reasons.

PROBLEMS

The following information pertains to Problems 1 through 12

A & Sons Inc., is considering buying $80,000 worth of equipment, at a 20 % discount from a wholesaler, financed by a 15 %, 5-year term loan from the Bank of Notreal. On the other hand, the equipment may be leased from Rigget Leasers Co., requiring beginning-of-year lease payments of $20,000 per year over the five-year period. The equipment can be depreciated at a CCA rate of 30 % worth $5,000 residual value at the end of the fifth year.

Problem 1

If A & Sons are responsible for the upkeep of the equipment, what is the CCA tax shield on the equipment, assuming a tax rate of 40 %?

Problem 2

If there are no assets left in the equipment, pool calculate the tax shield on the terminal loss in year 5.

Problem 3

Calculate the incremental cash flows for A & Sons.

Problem 4

Calculate the implicit IRR for leasing from the incremental cash flow in Problem 3.

Problem 5

If the Bank of Notreal is charging 15 % interest, should A & Sons lease or buy?

Problem 6

What is the NPV of leasing?

Problem 7

Suppose there is other equipment in the asset pool. What is the NAL?

Problem 8

Why, and by how much, did the NAL change from negative in Problem 6 to a positive amount in Problem 7?

Problem 9

At what level of lease payments will A & Sons be indifferent towards leasing or buying? Assume that other equipment is in the pool so that the tax write-off in year 5 is ignored.

Problem 10

Demonstrate that, if we use the after-tax loan rate as the appropriate discount rate, the present value after-tax cost of the loan is equal to the loan. Set up a loan amortization table to arrive at your conclusion.

Problem 11

What are the cash flows from the lessor's perspective?

Problem 12

What is the implicit rate of return for the lease company if you consider the lease payments and the investment in equipment, ignoring taxes?

Problem 13

Digital Manufacturing wishes to lease a microcomputer that costs $800,000 for lease payments of $210,000 per year, made in advance, for each of the next five years. The equipment has a 5 year useful life with no expected salvage value and a CCA rate of 30 %. The firm's marginal tax rate is 40 %. The after-tax cost of borrowing is 9 %. What is the present value of the foregone CCA tax shield if Digital decides to lease?

Problem 14

What is the present value of after-tax lease payments for Digital, if the tax shield on the payments lagged by one period?

Problem 15

What is the net advantage of leasing for Digital?

ANSWERS TO CONCEPT TEST

1.   contracted; lessee; lessor; owner

2.   direct lease; captive finance company

3.   operating leases; financial leases

4.   sale and leaseback; sells; leases

5.   leveraged lease; tax; lender

6.   capitalized; lessee; option to purchase; 75 %; lease payments; market value

7.   deductible; conditional sales agreement; interest

8.   operating losses

9.   inflow; outflow; outflow; inflow; CCA tax shield; outflow

10.   lower; lower

11.   loan rate

12.   loan; after-tax

13.   terminal loss; recaptured

14.   leasing paradox; negative; tax rates; zero-sum game

15.   taxes; uncertainty; transactions costs

PROBLEM SOLUTIONS

Problem 1:

Year	UCC	CCA	Tax Shield
1	$40,000	$12,000	$4,800
2	68,000	20,400	8,160
3	47,600	14,280	5,712
4	33,320	9,996	3,998.4
5	23,324	6,997.2	2,798.88
6	16,326.8		4,530.72 (See Solution 2)

Problem 2: The UCC balance in year 5, prior to the sale is $16,326.8 and is reduced by the residual value of $5,000 to give a terminal loss of $11,326.8. The tax shield is $11,326.8 x .4 = $4,530.72

Problem 3:

	Year					
	0	1	2	3	4	5
Investment	$ 80,000					
Salvage						(5,000)
Lease Payment	(20,000)	(20,000)	(20,000)	(20,000)	(20,000)	
Payment Shield		8,000	8,000	8,000	8,000	8,000
Forgone CCA						
Tax Shield	(4,800)	(8,160)	(5,712)	(3,998.4)	(2,798.88)	(4,530.72)
Total Cash Flow	$55,200	(20,160)	(17,712)	(15,998.4)	(14,798.88)	(1,530.72)

Problem 4: The implicit IRR is the unknown discount rate for the net advantage of leasing when the NPV is equal to zero:

$$NPV = \$55,200 - \frac{\$20,160}{(1+i)} - \frac{\$17,712}{(1+i)^2} - \frac{\$15,998.4}{(1+i)^3} - \frac{\$14,798.88}{(1+i)^4} - \frac{\$1,530.72}{(1+i)^5}$$

The IRR for leasing is 10.73 %.

Problem 5: The after-tax interest rate will be .15(1 - .4) = 9 % if the loan is taken. This is cheaper than the implicit IRR for leasing (10.73 %). So, A & Sons should buy.

Problem 6: Discounting the cash flows at 9% gives us the NPV:

$$NPV = \$55,200 - \frac{\$20,160}{(1.09)} - \frac{\$17,712}{(1.09)^2} - \frac{\$15,998.4}{(1.09)^3} - \frac{\$14,798.88}{(1.09)^4} - \frac{\$1,530.72}{(1.09)^5}$$
$$= -\$2,035.71$$

Problem 7:

$NAL = \$80,000 - [\$20,000 + \$20,000 (.60) (3.239720) - (\$20,000) (.6)/(1.09)^5] -$

$[(.4)(.3)(\$80,000) / (.09 + .3) \times (1.045/1.09)] + [\$5,000(.3) (.4) / (.09 + .3)$
$\times 1 / (1.09)^5] - \$5,000 / (1.09)^5 = \$3,073.62$

Problem 8: The NAL favoured leasing when A & Sons had other equipment in the asset pool which allowed for the full tax shield on CCA instead of the write-off in year 5. The NAL changed by $5,109.33 (-$2,035.71 to $3,073.62).

Problem 9: In the NAL equation used in solution 7, we equate NAL to zero and solve for the unknown lease payments which equal $21,203.51 or approximately $21,204. At this level of payment, A & Sons will be indifferent between leasing and buying.

Problem 10:

Period	Loan Payments (a)	Balance (b)	Interest (c)	Tax Shield (d)	After-Tax Payment (e)	Present value Equivalent (f)
1	23,865	80,000	12,000	4,800	19,065	17,491
2	23,865	68,135	10,220	4,088	19,777	16,646
3	23,865	54,490	8,174	3,270	20,595	15,903
4	23,865	38,799	5,820	2,328	21,537	15,257
5	23,865	20,752	3,113	1,245	22,620	14,701

a) $80,000 / PVIFA (15%,5) = $80,000 / 3.352155 = $23,865.24
b) Outstanding loan less amortized portion of the payment. For example, amortized portion of year 1 payment is $23,865 - $12,000 = $11,865. Similarly, year 2 portion of payment is $23,865 - $10,220 = $13,645.
c) Loan balance times the interest rate of 15%.
d) Interest times the tax rate of 40%.
e) Payments less tax shield
f) Discounted at the after-tax loan rate of 9%

The sum of all present value equivalents in the last column are equal to $79,998, which is equal to the loan of $80,000 (The $2 difference is due to rounding).

Problem 11:

	Year					
	0	1	2	3	4	5
Investment	$(80,000)					
Salvage						5,000
Lease Payment	20,000	20,000	20,000	20,000	20,000	
Payment Shield		(8,000)	(8,000)	(8,000)	(8,000)	(8,000)
CCA Tax Shield	4,800	8,160	5,712	3,998.4	2,798.88	4,530.7
Total Cash Flow	$(55,200)	20,160	7,712	15,998.4	14,798.88	1,530.7

NAL = $2,035.71

Problem 12: The implicit return earned by Rigget Lease Co., can be found by solving for the interest rate in the following equation: $80,000 = $20,000 + $20,000 x (PVIFA i%,4). The solution is i = 12.59%.

Problem 13: The foregone CCA tax shield is:

$$\frac{(\$800,000)\,(.4)\,(.3)}{.09 + .3} \times \frac{1.045}{1.09} = \$235,992$$

Problem 14: The present value of the first payment is $210,000 plus the present value of the next 4 after-tax payments is $210,000 (.60) (PVIFA 9%,4) = $408,205 minus the present value of the lagged tax shield is $210,000 (.4) (PVIFA 9%,5) = $326,731. This adds up to $210,000 + $408,205 - $326,731 = $291,474..

Problem 15: The NAL is $800,000 - $291,474 - $235,992 = $272,534. Digital should prefer leasing.

23 Mergers and Acquisitions

CHAPTER HIGHLIGHTS

In principle, the decision to acquire another firm is a capital budgeting decision. However, since the net present value of such an acquisition is difficult to measure, the subject of mergers and acquisitions warrants specific attention.

Mergers differ from ordinary investment decisions in at least four ways. First, the value of a merger may depend on benefits, referred to as strategic fits and synergies. Second, the accounting, tax, and legal aspects of a merger are complex. Third, mergers often involve issues of corporate control (related to the conflict between managers and shareholders). Finally, mergers are often 'unfriendly' transactions because management and/or shareholders of the sought-after firm do not want the firm to be acquired and may resort to defensive tactics.

23.1 THE LEGAL FORMS OF ACQUISITIONS

The legal mechanism used by one firm to acquire another takes one of the following forms: (1) merger or consolidation, (2) stock acquisition, or (3) asset acquisition. In discussing acquisitions, the acquiring firm is referred to as the *bidder*; the firm that is being bought is the *target firm;* and the cash or securities offered to the target firm is the *consideration*.

Merger or Consolidation: A merger is the absorption of one firm by another; the acquiring firm retains its identity while the acquired firm ceases to exist. In a consolidation, an entirely new firm is created. The shareholders of each firm exchange their shares for shares of the new firm. Both the Canadian and Ontario Business Corporation Acts refer to combinations of firms as amalgamations. We will use the general term merger to refer to any type of reorganization.

The primary advantage of a merger is its legal simplicity. A disadvantage of a merger is the fact that the shareholders of each firm must vote to approve a merger; usually, a two-thirds majority is required for approval.

Acquisition of Stock: Another way to acquire a firm is to buy the target firm's voting stock directly from shareholders. This is most often accomplished through a tender offer. This means the acquiring firm makes an offer directly to the shareholders of a firm to buy the firm's common stock.

A tender offer does not require a shareholder vote for approval; those wishing to keep their stock simply do not 'tender' their shares to the acquiring firm, and they thereby retain their ownership interest in the target firm. A tender offer bypasses both the board of directors and the management of the target firm. This is important because the management of the target firm may be opposed to the acquisition. However, management's resistance can make this form of acquisition quite expensive. Often, a minority of shareholders choose not to sell their shares, so that the firm is not completely absorbed; complete absorption requires a merger. Many stock acquisitions are subsequently completed as a formal merger.

Acquisition of Assets: A firm can acquire another firm by purchasing the assets of the target firm. This procedure involves a costly legal transfer of title to the assets and must be approved by the shareholders of the selling firm.

Acquisition Classifications: Acquisitions can be classified as *horizontal, vertical*, or *conglomerate*. A horizontal acquisition involves two firms which compete in the same product market. A vertical acquisition involves firms in different stages of the production process. Conglomerate acquisitions involve firms in unrelated lines of business.

A Note on Takeovers: A *takeover* is the transfer of control of a firm from one group to another. The acquiring firm, or bidder, makes an offer to pay cash or securities in order to acquire the target firm. A takeover can occur by acquisition (as described above), a *proxy contest*, or a *going-private transaction.*

A proxy authorizes another party to cast a shareholder's votes. In a proxy contest, a group of dissident shareholders seeks to obtain enough proxies from the firm's existing shareholders to gain control of the board of directors. In a going-private transaction, a small group of investors buys all of the firm's common stock. The stock is then delisted, so that it no longer trades on a stock exchange. Since a substantial portion of the financing for these transactions is generally obtained by borrowing, going-private transactions are often referred to as *leveraged buyouts* (LBOs). The term *management buyout* is used when the bidding group includes existing management.

23.2 TAXES AND ACQUISITIONS

The acquisition of one firm by another may or may not be a taxable transaction.

Determinants of Tax Status: The primary issue in determining the tax status of an acquisition is whether the shareholders of the acquired firm have sold their shares, resulting in a realized, taxable capital gain, or exchanged their shares for new shares of equal value. The former is a *taxable acquisition,* while the latter is a *tax-free acquisition.* The general requirements for tax-free status are that the acquisition involves two Canadian corporations subject to corporate income tax and that there be continuity of equity interest.

For a taxable acquisition, the shareholders of the acquired firm have a realized, taxable capital gain equal to the difference between the price they receive for their shares and the initial purchase price of their stock. In addition, the acquiring firm may elect to 'write-up' the value of the assets acquired, based on the cost of the acquisition. This has the advantage of increasing the firm's subsequent depreciation expenses. However, such a write-up also requires that the firm treat the acquisition price of the asset as currently taxable income.

23.3 ACCOUNTING FOR ACQUISITIONS

For accounting purposes, an acquisition is treated as either a purchase or a pooling of interests.

The Purchase Method: The *purchase accounting method* for an acquisition requires that the assets of the acquired firm be reported at fair market value on the financial statements of the acquiring firm. The difference between the purchase price and the fair market value of the acquired assets is identified as 'goodwill' on the balance sheet of the acquiring firm. The goodwill is amortized over a period of years, but this amortization is not a tax-deductible expense. This means that the purchase method accounting results in lower reported net income than the pooling accounting method. This, in turn has a negative effect on traditional accounting measures of performance, such as ROA and ROE.

Pooling of Interests: With a *pooling of interests,* the balance sheets of the two firms are simply combined. Asset values are not adjusted to market value and, therefore, no goodwill is created.

Which is Better: Purchase or Pooling of Interests? Income reported to shareholders after an acquisition is lower for the purchase method because the amortization of goodwill and the write-up of asset values result in higher depreciation expenses. Neither of these considerations has any effect on the firm's taxable income. Therefore, these alternative accounting treatments do not have any consequences for cash flow or net present value determinations.

23.4 GAINS FROM ACQUISITION

In this section, we analyze the source of value derived from an acquisition.

Synergy: If Firm A (with value V_A) is acquiring Firm B (with value V_B), then the acquisition is beneficial to the shareholders of Firm A if:

$$V_{AB} > V_A + V_B$$

where V_{AB} is the value of the combined firm.

The incremental net gain derived from the acquisition (ΔV) is:

$$\Delta V = V_{AB} - (V_A + V_B)$$

If ΔV is positive, the acquisition is said to generate synergy. In this case, the value of the whole (V_{AB}) is greater than the value of the sum of its parts ($V_A + V_B$). Another way of looking at this relationship is to define the value of Firm B to Firm A as the sum of ΔV and V_B:

$$V^*_B = \Delta V + V_B$$

where V^*_B is defined as the value of Firm B to Firm A. If A and B are public companies, their values as separate companies can be observed in the marketplace. Synergy exists when the cash flow for the combined firm is greater than the sum of the cash flows for the two firms as separate entities. The gain from the merger is the present value of this difference in cash flows.

The incremental cash flow (ΔCF) can be represented in terms of four components:

$$\Delta CF = \Delta EBIT + \Delta Depreciation - \Delta Tax - \Delta Capital\ Requirements$$

$$= \Delta Revenue - \Delta Cost - \Delta Tax - \Delta Capital\ Requirements$$

where the four components are the difference in revenues, costs, taxes and capital requirements, respectively. Therefore, the synergy from an acquisition results from one or more of the following: (1) revenue enhancement, (2) cost reduction, (3) lower taxes, or (4) lower capital requirements.

Revenue Enhancement: Increased revenues may result from marketing gains, strategic benefits, and increases in market power. Marketing gains are produced by more effective advertising, an improved distribution network, and a more balanced product mix. Strategic benefits are the opportunities presented by options to enter and exploit new lines of business. Finally, a merger may reduce competition, and thereby increase market power, allowing the company to increase prices and obtain monopoly profits. Such mergers, of course, may run afoul of laws designed to limit takeovers that may limit market competition. In general, there is little evidence that market power has been a major motivation for acquisitions.

Cost Reductions: Under some circumstances, larger firms operate more efficiently than two smaller firms. Horizontal mergers sometimes generate 'economies of scale'. This means that the average production cost decreases following the merger. A vertical merger may allow a firm to save by more closely coordinating production and distribution; vertical mergers often allow for transfer of technology among different products. Economies may also be achieved when firms have complementary resources (e.g. one firm has excess production capacity and another has insufficient capacity). Some acquisitions also serve to remove inefficient management.

Tax Gains: Tax gains resulting from a merger may arise because of unused tax losses, unused debt capacity, surplus funds, or the ability to write-up the value of depreciable assets. A profitable firm may find it advantageous to acquire a firm that has *net operating losses* (NOL). The profitable firm can then use these losses to reduce taxes on current income. A firm with NOL can 'carry back' losses for three years and 'carry forward' losses for up to seven years. However, the benefit of an acquisition must be greater than the tax benefit the acquired firm could derive from its own losses. In addition, the tax credit may not be allowed if the primary purpose of the acquisition is to avoid taxes.

Unused Debt Capacity: Debt financing provides tax benefits because interest payments are tax deductible. Acquisition of a firm with a relatively low level of debt can be beneficial to the acquiring firm since the combined firm can then obtain additional debt financing. That is, the merged firm may be able to increase its debt capacity, thereby producing significant tax savings.

Surplus Funds: A firm with surplus funds may have motivation for acquiring another firm. The alternatives for a firm with surplus funds are the distribution of surplus funds as a dividend or the repurchase of some of the firm's outstanding shares. However, the former alternative increases shareholders' income taxes, while the latter may be illegal if the sole purpose is to avoid taxes. With an acquisition, no income taxes are paid by the shareholders of the acquiring firm.

Changing Capital Requirements: Reduced capital requirements might result from an acquisition if one of the merged firms has excess capacity while the other requires additional capacity in order to expand.

Avoiding Mistakes: In evaluating the profitability of an acquisition, an analyst must be aware of sources of potential errors. First, market values should be used to establish the value of an opportunity. Second, only cash flows that are incremental to the acquisition are relevant; the value of a target firm as a separate entity already reflects the value of its existing cash flows. Third, the discount rate used should reflect the risk associated with the incremental cash flows. The acquiring firm, for example, should not use its own cost of capital to value the cash flows of a firm to be acquired. Finally, acquisition generally involves significant fees and costs which are incremental expenses and therefore must not be ignored.

A Note of Inefficient Management: For some firms, a change in management can lead to increased value. One method of replacing weak management is through a merger. Note that the expression "weak management" should not be construed to refer to management that is dishonest, incompetent or negligent. Instead, management skills may vary across different managers, with some managers endowed with superior skills than others. Alternatively, some managers may be particularly proficient in a specific area of management from which the firm can benefit, such as technology management. Finally, some managers may receive excessive compensation or may overexploit their access to corporate perks such as private jets and country club memberships.

The Negative Side of Takeovers: Critics of takeovers, and particularly leveraged buyouts, argue that the costs associated with takeovers are high. They argue that the pursuit of efficiency following takeovers can lead to actions that are costly to society, such as layoffs and plant closures. These actions are costly due to the cost that society must incur to place unemployed workers in new jobs, and to adapt the closed plants for other purposes. Critics also argue that takeovers weaken the relation between management and the labour force, which reduces efficiency. Critics argue that outside directors should be placed on the board to increase efficiency.

23.5 SOME FINANCIAL SIDE EFFECTS OF ACQUISITIONS

Two important financial side effects associated with an acquisition are EPS growth and diversification. As we demonstrate in this section, neither of these effects has any impact on the value of the combined firm.

EPS Growth: Firm A has decided to acquire Firm B through an exchange of stock. Both firms are 100% equity. The following is some pre-merger information:

	Firm A	Firm B
Total earnings	$100	$200
Shares outstanding	200	500
Price per share	$ 10	$ 2

Firm B has a market value of ($2 × 500) = $1,000. To acquire Firm B, Firm A will have to give ($1,000/$10) = 100 shares to the shareholders of Firm B. The combined firm will have 300 shares outstanding.

Before the merger, earnings per share (EPS) for Firm A are ($100/200) = $ .50. After the merger, the combined firm will have $300 in earnings and 300 shares, so EPS will be $1 per share, a 100% growth! Of course, no real change has occurred. Firm A has a higher value per share than does Firm B, so B's 500 shares are replaced with 100 shares of A. Naturally, EPS rises, but this increase has no cash flow consequences, and, as a result, no impact on value.

Diversification: Diversification is often cited as a benefit in mergers. However, diversification by itself does not create value because the shareholders of the acquiring firm can accomplish the same thing by purchasing stock in the target firm.

To understand that a merger does not provide a diversification benefit to the shareholders of the acquiring firm, recall that variability of returns consists of unsystematic and systematic components. Systematic variability cannot be eliminated by any form of diversification, including merger. Unsystematic variability can be reduced by diversification. However, an individual investor can achieve this diversification very inexpensively by purchasing shares of stock in different companies.

23.6 THE COST OF AN ACQUISITION

The incremental net gain derived from a merger is:

$$\Delta V = V_{AB} - (V_A + V_B)$$

We define the value of Firm B to Firm A as:

$$V^*_B = \Delta V + V_B$$

The net present value of a merger is:

$$NPV = V^*_B - \text{Cost to Firm A of the acquisition}$$

The NPV of the merger can be calculated from the following information for Firm A and Firm B:

	Firm A	Firm B
Price per share	$ 10	$ 5
Number of shares	20	20
Total market value	$ 200	$ 100

Both firms are all-equity firms. The incremental net gain (ΔV) is $80 and Firm B will agree to the acquisition at a price of $150. The difference between the acquisition price and V_B is referred to as the *merger premium*. In this example, the merger premium is ($150 – $100) = $50.

To compute the net present value of the acquisition, we first compute the value of Firm B to Firm A.

$$V^*_B = \Delta V + V_B = \$80 + \$100 = \$180$$

Next, we determine the cost to Firm A of the acquisition. Even though Firm B agrees to be acquired for $150, the cost of the acquisition to Firm A varies with the means of payment from Firm A to Firm B. The two methods of payment are a cash acquisition and a stock acquisition.

Case I - Cash Acquisition: If the cost of the acquisition is paid in cash, then the net present value is:

$$NPV = V^*_B - Cost = \$180 - \$150 = \$30$$

Since the net present value of the acquisition is positive, the acquisition is beneficial to the shareholders of Firm A. The value of the merged firm after the acquisition is equal to the value of the combined firm less the cash paid for Firm B:

$$V_{AB} = V_A + V^*_B - Cost = \$200 + \$180 - \$150 = \$230$$

After the merger, the value of the merged firm's stock will increase to [($380 – $150)/20] = $11.50 per share. The increase of $1.50 per share above the price of Firm A stock is the net present value of $30 on a per share basis, or ($30/20) = $1.50 per share gain.

Case II - Stock Acquisition: Suppose Firm A pays the $150 acquisition cost by giving 15 shares of stock to the shareholders of Firm B. The cost appears to be $150. However, this is an underestimate of the actual cost. After the merger, the value of the firm is:

$$V_{AB} = V_A + V_B + \Delta V = \$200 + \$100 + \$80 = \$380$$

The merged firm has (20 + 15) = 35 shares outstanding, the price per share is ($380/35) = $10.857. Therefore, the actual cost of the acquisition is (15 × $10.857) = $162.86, and the net present value of the merger is:

$$NPV = V^*_B - Cost = \$180 - \$162.86 = \$17.14$$

Note that the $10.857 per share value in this case is less than the $11.50 value indicated above for a cash acquisition. The difference arises from the fact that a portion of the $30 net present value for the cash acquisition now goes to the new shareholders. The 15 new shares of stock are each worth ($10.857 – $10) = $.857 more than the pre-merger value of Firm A stock, for a total of (15 × $.857) = $12.86 to the former shareholders of Firm B. That is, as indicated above, the shareholders of Firm B actually receive $162.86 in this merger.

In a cash merger, the potential gains of the merger go entirely to the shareholders of the acquiring firm. When a merger is financed by an exchange of stock, the benefits are shared by the stockholders of both firms.

Cash versus Common Stock: The decision as to whether an acquisition should be financed with cash or stock depends on three factors. First, the use of stock means that the shareholders of the acquired firm will share in any gains from the merger; on the other hand, if the merger is unsuccessful, then the acquired firm's shareholders will share in the loss. Second, a cash acquisition is usually a taxable transaction; this consideration may result in a higher price for the target firm. Third, a cash acquisition does not affect control of the acquiring firm.

23.7 DEFENSIVE TACTICS

Management of a target firm frequently resists takeover attempts. This resistance may enable shareholders to subsequently receive a higher price for their shares. On the other hand, management resistance to a takeover may be based largely, if not exclusively, on management's desire to protect its own interests. The defensive tactics commonly used by the management of a target firm in order to resist takeovers are described below.

The Control Block and the Corporate Charter: The *corporate charter* consists of the firm's articles of incorporation and the corporate bylaws. These documents specify the firm's governance rules. The charter can be amended to make acquisition difficult for the acquiring firm. For example, the charter can be amended to require that an 80% majority of shareholders must vote to approve a merger. Such a 'super majority' provision is in contrast to the usual two-thirds majority required for approval of a merger. Another strategy is the 'staggering' of the election of board members so that only a few board members are elected at any one time. This makes it more difficult to change the membership of the board quickly.

Repurchase/Standstill Agreements: A *standstill agreement* specifies that the bidding firm will limit its holdings in the target firm. Such agreements often precede a *targeted repurchase;* under this arrangement, the target firm buys back its own stock from the bidder. Since this repurchase is usually at a premium above market price, the premium is viewed by critics as a bribe, and is frequently termed *greenmail.*

Exclusionary Offers: In an *exclusionary self-tender*, the target firm offers to buy back its own stock, at a premium, from all shareholders except the bidder. By excluding the bidder, the firm effectively transfers wealth to other shareholders by reducing the value of the bidder's stock.

Poison Pills and Share Rights Plans: A *poison pill* is a procedure designed to force a bidder to negotiate with the management of a target firm, rather than acquire the firm by means of a tender offer. Such procedures are sometimes called *share rights plans* (SRPs). The potential target firm's shareholders receive share rights which entitle them to purchase shares of stock at a specified price. This exercise price is substantially below the current market price of the firm's stock. Normally, the rights cannot be exercised or sold. However, the rights are 'triggered' when a tender offer is announced, or when an investor acquires 20 % of the target firm's stock. At that point, the rights can be exercised. This essentially allows shareholders of the target firm to purchase shares in the merged firm at 'bargain' prices. This makes the takeover less attractive to potential buyers.

Going Private and Leveraged Buyouts: A privately-owned firm is not subject to unfriendly takeovers. A publicly-traded firm 'goes private' when a group, which usually includes the existing management, buys all of the firm's publicly held stock and takes it off the market. Although such a buyout might be regarded as a takeover defence by the target firm's management, the target firm's shareholders view the buyout as a takeover itself.

23.8 SOME EVIDENCE ON ACQUISITIONS

The impact of acquisitions on shareholder wealth has been extensively studied. Some empirical evidence regarding this issue is considered here.

There is little doubt that the shareholders of the acquired firm benefit substantially from an acquisition. Excess returns for these shareholders are approximately 20% for mergers and 30% for tender offers. Tender offers are typically made when a proposed friendly merger is rejected by the management of the target firm. Subsequent tender offers must generally be at a higher price, resulting in the larger abnormal returns.

The gains to the shareholders of acquiring firms are difficult to measure. The best evidence suggests that these shareholders gain little, if anything, from an acquisition, and in fact, losses in value subsequent to merger announcements are not unusual. Some studies indicate that excess returns to shareholders of the acquiring firm average approximately 4% for tender offers and zero for mergers, while other studies indicate significant losses. These results seem to suggest that overvaluation of the target firm by the bidding firm is common. An alternative explanation of the evidence is that management is simply not pursuing the best interests of the shareholders in such cases.

CONCEPT TEST

1.   The following terminology is often used when discussing acquisitions: the acquiring firm is referred to as the _____ ; the firm that is being sought is the _____ ; and, the cash or securities offered to the target firm is the _____ .

2.   Several different legal mechanisms are used by firms seeking to acquire other firms. The absorption of one firm by another, so that the acquiring firm retains its identity while the acquired firm ceases to exist, is called a(n) _____ . In a(n) _____ , an entirely new firm is created; the shareholders of each of the two firms involved exchange their shares for shares of the new firm. Another way to acquire a firm is to buy the target firm's voting stock directly from shareholders; this is generally accomplished through a process called a(n) _____ . A firm can also buy another firm by purchasing the _____ of the target firm.

3.   If the two firms compete in the same product market, the acquisition is called a(n) _____ acquisition. A reorganization of firms at different stages of the production process is a(n) _____ acquisition. Acquisitions involving firms in unrelated lines of business are called _____ acquisitions.

4.   The transfer of control of a firm from one group to another is called a(n) _____ ; the acquiring firm makes an offer to pay cash or securities in order to acquire the target firm. A takeover can occur by acquisition or in two other alternative ways. A proxy authorizes another party to _____ . In a(n) _____ contest, a group of dissident shareholders seeks to obtain enough proxies from the firm's existing shareholders in order to gain control of the board of directors. In a(n) _____ transaction, a small group of investors buys all of the firm's common stock; since a substantial portion of the financing for these transactions is generally obtained by borrowing, these transactions are often referred to as _____ . When the bidding group includes existing management, the term _____ is used.

5. The acquisition of one firm by another may or may not be a taxable transaction. The primary issue in determining the tax status is whether the shareholders of the acquired firm have sold their shares, resulting in a realized _____ , or exchanged their shares for new shares of equal value. The former (is/is not) a taxable acquisition, while the latter (is/is not) a taxable acquisition.

6. For accounting purposes, an acquisition is treated in one of two alternative ways. The _____ method requires that the assets of the acquired firm be reported at fair market value on the financial statements of the acquiring firm; the difference between the purchase price and the fair market value of the acquired assets is identified as _____ on the balance sheet of the acquiring firm. The second alternative treatment is a(n) _____ ; in this case, the balance sheets of the two firms are simply combined and asset values are not adjusted to market value.

7. If Firm A (with value V_A) is acquiring Firm B (with value V_B), then the acquisition is beneficial to the stockholders of Firm A if: $V_{AB} >$ _____ ,where V_{AB} is the value of the combined firm. The incremental net gain derived from the acquisition (ΔV) is: $\Delta V =$ _____ . If ΔV is positive, the acquisition is said to generate _____ . Another way of looking at this relationship is to define the value of Firm B to Firm A as the sum of ΔV and V_B. That is: $V^*_B =$ _____ , where V^*_B is defined as the value of Firm B to Firm A.

8. When the cash flow for the combined firm is greater than the sum of the cash flows for the two firms as separate entities, the acquisition is said to generate _____ . The gain from the merger is the present value of this difference in cash flows. The incremental cash flow (ΔCF) can be represented in terms of four components: $\Delta CF = \Delta$ _____ $- \Delta$ _____ $- \Delta$ _____ $- \Delta$ _____ . Therefore, the synergy from an acquisition results from one or more of the following: (1) increase in _____ , (2) decrease in _____ , (3) decrease in _____ , or (4) decrease in _____ .

9. The NPV of a merger is: _____ $-$ _____ . The difference between the acquisition price and V_A is the _____ . The cost of the acquisition varies with the means of payment from Firm A to Firm B. The two methods of payment are a(n) _____ acquisition and a(n) _____ acquisition.

10. If the cost of the acquisition is paid in cash, then the net present value is: $NPV =$ _____ $-$ _____ . The value of the merged firm after the acquisition is equal to the value of the combined firm less the cash paid for Firm B: $V_{AB} =$ _____ $+$ _____ $-$ _____

11. In a cash merger, the benefits of the merger go entirely to _____ . For a stock acquisition, a portion of the net present value for the cash acquisition goes to _____ . When a merger is financed by an exchange of stock, the benefits are shared by _____ .

12. Several different defensive tactics are commonly used by the management of a target firm in order to resist takeovers. The firm's articles of incorporation and the corporate bylaws constitute the _____ ; these documents can be amended to make acquisition difficult for the acquiring firm by requiring that an 80% majority of shareholders must vote to approve a merger. An agreement which specifies that the bidding firm will limit its holdings in the target firm is called a(n) _____ agreement. Such agreements often precede a _____ ; under this arrangement, the target firm buys back its own stock from the bidder. The premium paid in such arrangements is viewed by critics as a bribe, and is frequently termed _____ . In a(n) _____ , the target firm offers to buy back its own stock, at a premium, from all shareholders except the bidder. A(n) _____ is a procedure designed to force a bidder to negotiate with the management of a target firm, rather than acquire the firm by means of a tender offer; such procedures are sometimes called _____ .

PROBLEMS

Problem 1

PMG Corporation wants to acquire JPH Corporation through a cash acquisition. The incremental gain is $400, and JPH Corp. will agree to the acquisition at the price of $1,000. Given the information below, what is the NPV of the acquisition? What is the value of the merged firm after the acquisition?

	PMG	JPH
Price per share	$15	$ 8
Number of shares	120	100
Total market value	$1,800	$800

Problem 2

Suppose PMG Corporation decides to acquire JPH Corporation through an exchange of shares. How much will this cost? What is the NPV of the acquisition? Which type of acquisition would the shareholders of PMG Corporation prefer? Why?

Use the following information to solve Problems 3 through 10. Firms A and B have no debt outstanding.

	Firm A	Firm B
Total earnings	$3,500	$1,400
Shares outstanding	700	350
Price per share	$ 50	$ 20

Problem 3

Firm A is considering the acquisition of Firm B. Firm A has estimated that the value of the combined firm will be $43,000. Firm B has indicated that it would accept a cash purchase offer of $22 per share. Should Firm A proceed with the acquisition?

Problem 4

For the data of Problem 3, what is the synergy from the merger? What is the merger premium paid for the acquisition? Use the synergy and the premium to determine the net present value of the acquisition.

Problem 5

For the data of Problem 3, what is the price of Firm A's stock after the merger?

Problem 6

For the data of Problem 3, what is the net present value of the merger if Firm A pays for the acquisition with common stock, based on the current market prices? What is the post-merger price of the stock?

Problem 7

For the data of Problem 6, what is the synergy from the merger? What is the merger premium paid for the acquisition? Use the synergy and the premium to determine the net present value of the acquisition. Why is the net present value lower for the acquisition through exchange of stock in Problem 4 compared to the acquisition for cash in Problem 3?

Problem 8

Problem 3 indicates that the shareholders of Firm B are willing to accept $7,700 for the acquisition. How many shares of Firm A stock should Firm B shareholders receive so that they actually receive the $7,700 price?

Problem 9

Suppose that, for the data in Problem 3, Firm A acquires Firm B in exchange for stock valued at $21 per share. How will this affect earnings per share for Firm A?

Problem 10

For the data of Problem 9, what is the price per share of the new firm if the market is 'fooled' by this earnings growth (i.e., if the P/E ratio does not change)? What will the P/E ratio be if the market is not 'fooled?'

Problem 11

The following information is available for SMJH Corporation and BDA Corporation.

	SMJH	BDA
Shares outstanding	750	1,000
Price per share	$12	$10

BDA would like to acquire SMJH. The value of the combined firm will have an estimated value of $22,000. BDA will accept a cash offer of $14 per share. Should BDA acquire SMJH?

Problem 12

What is the value of BDA's stock after the merger?

Problem 13

Blizzard Manufacturing, a producer of snow-removal equipment, is analyzing the possible acquisition of Max Motors, a manufacturer of engine components. Blizzard forecasts that the purchase would result in incremental after-tax cash flows of $10,000 per year for the foreseeable future. Current market values of Blizzard and Max are $500,000 and $200,000, respectively. The opportunity cost of capital for the incremental cash flows is 20 %. What is the synergy from the merger?

Problem 14

Suppose that, for the data of Problem 13, Blizzard is considering an offer of $220,000 cash for the acquisition of Max Motors. What is the merger premium for this acquisition? What is the net present value of the merger?

Problem 15

As an alternative to the $220,000 offer described in Problem 14, Blizzard is considering offering 25 % of its stock to the shareholders of Max Motors. What is the net present value of this offer?

Use the following information to solve Problems 16 and 17:

M. Wilson Company, Inc. ($ in thousands)			
Current assets	$ 2,000	Current liabilities	$ 600
Fixed assets	8,000	Long-term debt	3,400
		Equity	6,000
Total	$10,000	Total	$10,000

B. Buckner Company, Inc. ($ in thousands)			
Current assets	$ 1,500	Current liabilities	$ 750
Fixed assets	3,500	Long-term debt	1,000
		Equity	3,250
Total	$ 5,000	Total	$ 5,000

Problem 16

Assume that the balance sheets above are in terms of book values. Construct the balance sheet for M. Wilson Company, assuming that M. Wilson purchases B. Buckner, and the pooling of interests method of accounting is used.

Problem 17

Suppose that the fair market value of Buckner's fixed assets is $5,000, in contrast to the $3,500 book value shown. Wilson pays $7,500 for Buckner and raises the needed funds through an issue of long-term debt. Construct the balance sheet for M. Wilson Company, assuming that the purchase method of accounting is used.

ANSWERS TO CONCEPT TEST

1.   bidder; target firm; consideration

2.   merger; consolidation; tender offer; assets

3.   horizontal; vertical; conglomerate

4.   takeover; cast a shareholder's votes; proxy; going-private; leveraged buyouts; management buyout

5.   capital gain; is; is not

6.   purchase accounting; goodwill; pooling of interests

7. $(V_A + V_B)$; $[V_{AB} - (V_A + V_B)]$; synergy; $(\Delta V + V_B)$

8.   synergy; revenues; cost; taxes; capital requirements; revenues; costs; taxes; capital requirements

9. V^*_B; Cost to Firm A of the acquisition; merger premium; cash; stock

10. V^*_B; Cost; V_A; V^*_B; Cost

11.   the shareholders of the acquiring firm; the new shareholders; the shareholders of both the acquiring and the acquired firm

12.   corporate charter; standstill; targeted repurchase; greenmail; exclusionary self-tender; poison pill; share rights plans

PROBLEM SOLUTIONS

Problem 1: First, compute the net present value of the acquisition of JPH to MG:

$$V^*_{JPH} = \Delta V + V_{JPH} = \$400 + \$800 = \$1,200$$

With a cash acquisition, the cost to PMG Corp. is $1,000 , making the NPV

$$NPV = V^*_{JPH} - Cost = \$1,200 - \$1,000 = \$200$$

The NPV of the acquisition is positive, making it beneficial to PMG corp. The value of the merged firm is:

$$V_{PMG,JPH} = V_{PMG} + V^*_{JPH} - cost = \$1,800 + \$1,200 - \$1,000 = \$2,000$$

Problem 2: To acquire JPH Corp., PMG Corp. will have to pay ($1,000 / $15) = 66 2/3 shares to the shareholders of JPH Corporation. After the merger, the value of the firm will be:

$$V_{PMG,JPH} = V_{PMG} + V_{JPH} + \Delta V = \$1,800 + \$800 + \$400 = \$3,000$$

The merged firm has $(120 + 66\ 2/3) = 186\ 2/3$ shares outstanding. Therefore, the price per share is $3,000 / 186 2/3 = $16.07, making the actual price of the acquisition (66 2/3 x $16.07) = $1,071.33. The NPV of the acquisition is

$$NPV = V^*_{JPH} - Cost = \$1,200 - \$1,071.33 = \$128.67$$

In the cash acquisition, the value of PMG's stock increases to ($3,000 - $1,000) / 120 = $16.67 per share, a gain of 41.67 per share (which is the same as the NPV divided by the number of shares). With a stock acquisition, the new share price is $16.07, a gain of $1.07 per share, because some of the NPV of the merger goes to the shareholders of JPH. So, shareholders of PMG will prefer a cash acquisition because the merger gains go entirely to them.

Problem 3: At $22 per share, Firm A is paying ($22 × 350) = $7,700 to acquire Firm B. The value of Firm A is: $V_A = \$50 \times 700 = \$35,000$. The value of Firm B is: $V_B = \$20 \times 350 = \$7,000$. The incremental net gain derived from the merger is: $\Delta V = V_{AB} - (V_A + V_B) = \$43,000 - (\$35,000 + \$7,000) = \$1,000$. The value of Firm B to Firm A is: $V^*_B = \Delta V + V_B = \$1,000 + \$7,000 = \$8,000$ .The net present value of the merger is: $NPV = V^*_B - Cost$ to Firm A of the acquisition $= \$8,000 - \$7,700 = \$300$. Since the net present value is positive, the acquisition is beneficial to the shareholders of Firm A. Firm A should proceed with the acquisition.

Problem 4: The synergy is equal to the value of the combined firm less the total value of the two separate firms: $\Delta V = V_{AB} - (V_A + V_B) = \$1,000$ as computed in the solution to Problem 3.

The merger premium is the difference between the acquisition price and V_B, the market value of the acquired firm: $(\$22 \times 350) - (\$20 \times 350) = \$700$. The net premium value can be computed as the synergy minus the merger premium, or $(\$1,000 - \$700) = \$300$, as indicated in Problem 3.

Problem 5: The net present value of the merger is $300, so the stock will increase in value by $(\$300/700) = \$.43$ per share. The stock price will be $50.43. Note that, in the case of a cash acquisition, the net present value accrues to the shareholders of the acquiring firm.

This result can be computed in an alternative manner. The value of Firm A (V_A) is $35,000 prior to the merger. The value of the merged firm after the acquisition is: $V_{AB} = V_A + V^*_B - Cost = \$35,000 + (\$8,000 - \$7,700) = \$35,300$. The per share value is thus $(\$35,300/700) = \$50.43$, as previously calculated.

Problem 6: Firm A will have to give $(\$22/\$50) = .44$ shares of its stock for every share of B, or $(.44 \times 350) = 154$ shares. This result is also equal to the cash price of the acquisition divided by the current market value of a share of Firm A stock: $(\$7,700/\$50) = 154$. The new firm will have a total of 854 shares outstanding. After the merger, the value of the firm is: $V_{AB} = V_A + V_B + \Delta V = \$35,000 + \$7,000 + \$1,000 = \$43,000$.

Consequently, the per share value is $(\$43,000/854) = \$50.3513$, and the actual cost of the acquisition is $(154 \times \$50.3513) = \$7,754.10$. the net present value of the merger is: $NPV = V^*_B - Cost = \$8,000 - \$7,754.10 = \$245.90$.

Problem 7: The synergy is $1,000, as indicated in Problem 4. The merger premium is the difference between the acquisition price and the market value of the acquired firm: $\$7,754.10 - (\$20 \times 350) = \$754.10$

The net present value is the synergy minus the merger premium, or $(\$1,000 - \$754.10) = \$245.90$. This NPV is $54.10 less than the $300 NPV of the acquisition for cash. When the acquisition is paid for with an exchange of stock, the shareholders of Firm B receive a proportionate part of the net present value of the acquisition: $(154/854) \times \$300 = \$54.10$.

This difference can also be viewed as the increment in the value of the shares of Firm A which is given to the shareholders of Firm B: $(\$50.3513 - \$50) \times 154 = \$54.10$

Problem 8: In order for the Firm B shareholders to receive $7,700, they must receive stock which has a total value equal to $(\$7,700 / \$43,000) = .17907 = 17.907\%$ of the merged firm. Therefore, the new shares issued must represent 17.907% of the outstanding shares of the merged firm. This value is determined by solving for x in the following equation:

$$[x / (700 + x)] = .17907$$

The number of new shares which should be issued to the shareholders of Firm B is 152.691, so that the total number of shares outstanding will then be $(700 + 152.691) = 852.691$. The price per share will be $(\$43,000/852.691) = \$50.4386$. The shareholders of Firm B receive 152.691 shares worth $50.4286, for a total value of $(152.69 \times \$50.4286) = \$7,700$.

Problem 9: The new firm will have total earnings of $4,900. At $21 per share, Firm A will have to give $[(\$21/\$50) \times 350] = 147$ shares to the shareholders of Firm B, so that the new firm will have 847 shares outstanding. EPS will be $(\$4,900/847) = \$5.785$ per share; this is an increase of $.785 from the pre-merger level of $5 per share.

Problem 10: Before the merger, Firm A had a P/E ratio of ($50/$5) = 10. If the market is fooled, in the sense that this P/E ratio is unchanged after the merger, the stock will rise in value to $(10 \times \$5.785) = \$57.85$.

If the market is not fooled, then the P/E ratio will fall to ($43,000/$4,900) = 8.776, and the price per share will be $(8.776 \times \$5.785) = \$50.77$. This result is also equal to the value of the firm divided by the number of shares: ($43,000/847) = $50.77.

Problem 11: BDA is paying 750 x $14 = $10,500 to acquire SMJH. The value of BDA is 1,000 x $10 = $10,000, and the value of SMJH is $12 x 750 = $9,000. The net gain derived from the merger is $\Delta V = V_{AB} - (V_A - V_B)$ = $22,000 - ($10,000 + $9,000) = $3,000. The value of SMJH to BDA is $V^*_B = \Delta V + V_B = \$3,000 + \$9,000 = \$12,000$. The NPV of the acquisition is $12,000 - $10,500 = $1,500. BDA should acquire SMJH.

Problem 12: The NPV of the merger is $1,500, so the share price will increase by $1,500 / 1,000 = $1.50. The new share price will be $11.50.

Problem 13: The synergy is the present value of the perpetual annuity of $10,000 per year: $\Delta V = V_{AB} - (V_A + V_B)$ = ($10,000/.20) = $50,000. Therefore, Max's value to Blizzard is: $V^*_B = \Delta V + V_B = \$50,000 + \$200,000 = \$250,000$.

Problem 14: The merger premium is ($220,000 – $200,000) = $20,000. The net present value is the synergy minus the merger premium, or ($50,000 – $20,000) = $30,000. The net present value can also be determined as the difference between the value of the acquisition and the cost: $NPV = V^*_B - Cost = \$250,000 - \$220,000 = \$30,000$.

Problem 15: The value of the combined company is: $V_{AB} = V_A + V_B + \Delta V = \$500,000 + \$200,000 + \$50,000 = \$750,000$. Twenty-five percent of the combined company is worth: $.25 \times \$750,000 = \$187,500$

The net present value of this acquisition would be: $NPV = V^*_B - Cost = \$250,000 - \$187,500 = \$62,500$

Blizzard would prefer to acquire Max Motors for 25 % of the firm's stock rather than the $220,000 cash offer described in Problem 14.

Problem 16:

With a pooling of interests, the balance sheets are added together, so the new balance sheet appears as follows:

M. Wilson Company, Inc. ($ in thousands)			
Current assets	$ 3,500	Current liabilities	$ 1,350
Fixed assets	11,500	Long-term debt	4,400
		Equity	9,250
Total	$15,000	Total	$15,000

Problem 17: Buckner's fair market value is $5,000 plus $1,500 in current assets, or $6,500 total. The ($7,500 – $6,500) = $1,000 premium paid is goodwill. Wilson's fixed assets would be $8,000 (the book value of Wilson's premerger fixed assets) plus $5,000 (the market value of Buckner's assets), or $13,000 total. The balance sheet appears as follows:

M. Wilson Company, Inc. ($ in thousands)			
Current assets	$ 3,500	Current liabilities	$ 1,350
Fixed assets	13,000	Long-term debt	10,150
Goodwill	1,000	Equity	6,000
Total	$17,500	Total	$ 17,500

Solution note: Buckner's assets are ($5,000 + $1,500) = $6,500. Assuming that the current liabilities and long-term debt are shown at market value, the equity in Buckner is worth ($6,500 − $750 − $1,000) = $4,750. Wilson pays a $1,000 premium, so the total amount of debt that Wilson must raise is ($4,750 + $1,000) = $5,750. The total long-term debt after the merger is ($5,750 + $3,400 + $1,000) = $10,150, as shown.

24 Risk Management: An Introduction to Financial Engineering

CHAPTER HIGHLIGHTS

Risk management is one of the most important aspects of modern financial management. In this chapter, we introduce you to some of the basic concepts associated with the field of risk management.

24.1 HEDGING AND PRICE VOLATILITY

The term *hedging* refers to the reduction of a firm's exposure to either price or interest rate fluctuations. Alternatively, this process is also referred to as *immunization*. One aspect of the financial manager's job is to use existing financial instruments to create new ones that allow firms to hedge against specific risks. This process is called *financial engineering*. Corporate risk management frequently involves the use of *derivative securities* - securities that represent a claim to another financial asset. The process of financial engineering often involves creating new derivative securities or combining existing derivatives to accomplish the firm's hedging goals.

Price Volatility - A Historical Perspective: Although price changes have slowed down recently, volatility has greatly increased in three areas: interest rates, exchange rates, and commodity prices. Because of increased uncertainty about future interest rates, today's firms are less able to plan and predict future borrowing costs. Also, because global operations have become increasingly more important, exchange rates (and their volatility) play an increasingly important role in corporate finance. In addition, prices of various commodities have become more uncertain (for example, oil), increasing the need for risk management.

24.2 MANAGING FINANCIAL RISK

Whether increased volatility in interest rates, exchange rates, and commodity prices affects a given firm depends on both the nature of the firm's operations and its financing. We discuss some of the relevant issues below.

The Risk Profile: A firm's *risk profile* shows the relationship between changes in the price of a particular good, service, or rate and changes in the firm's value. The concept is quite similar to the concept of a sensitivity analysis developed in Chapter 11.

Reducing Risk Exposure: Depending on the nature of the firm, fluctuations in the price of any good or service may have different effects on firm value. For example, an increase in the price of a raw material might mean an increase in cash flows for one firm but a decrease in cash flows for another firm. Both firms are subject to risk if prices change. Negotiations for an arrangement between the firms, however, can eliminate much of the risk.

For example, consider a firm that uses rice to make a popular brand of cereal. If the price of rice increases, the firm that raises and processes the rice will benefit; the firm that uses the rice in its cereal will lose. By signing a contract specifying that the rice producer will deliver a certain quantity of rice at a certain price, the cereal manufacturer has reduced (or eliminated) the uncertainty about the cost of rice. At the same time, the rice producer has eliminated uncertainty about the price they will receive for the processed rice.

Hedging Short-Run Exposure: Short-term price fluctuations due to unexpected events or shocks are referred to as *transitory* changes. Even though a business may be financially sound in the long run, these price fluctuations may force the firm into financial distress. Short-run financial risk is called *transactions exposure*. Various alternatives for managing this risk are discussed later in this chapter.

Hedging Long-Term Exposure: Some price fluctuations may reflect permanent changes due to a fundamental shift in the underlying economics of a business. Exposure to this type of risk is referred to as *economic exposure*. This type of risk is much more difficult to hedge than short-term exposure.

24.3 HEDGING WITH FORWARD CONTRACTS

Forward contracts are among the oldest tools for risk management. In this section, we discuss how they can be used to hedge financial risk.

Forward Contracts - The Basics: A *forward contract* is a legal agreement between two parties in which they agree today on the price of an asset or product to be delivered at a future date. The delivery date of the goods is called the *settlement date*, and the agreed-upon price is the *forward price*. The *buyer* of the contract must take delivery and pay for the goods; the *seller* must make the delivery and accept payment for the goods. If prices increase before the delivery date, the buyer benefits. If prices decrease, the seller benefits.

The Payoff Profile: A *payoff profile* is a plot that depicts the gains and losses on a futures that result from unexpected price changes.

Hedging with Forwards: The basic idea is to use a risk profile to identify the firm's exposure to a given type of financial risk. Then, financial managers try to find a financial arrangement (for example, a forward contract) that has an offsetting payoff profile. Because the two payoff profiles exactly offset each other, the firm's cash flow will not be affected by changes in the underlying variable (interest rates, etc). This eliminates financial risk.

It is important to remember that, while hedging with forward contracts eliminates the risk associated with unfavourable price adjustments, it also eliminates any potential gain from favourable price adjustments. In a later section, we will discuss ways that a firm can hedge against only unfavourable price changes.

Credit Risk: Because no money changes hands until a forward contract is actually completed, there is a credit risk involved. The party on the losing end of the deal has an incentive to default on the agreement. Variations in forward contracts can reduce the risk of default by either party to the agreement.

24.4 HEDGING WITH FUTURES CONTRACTS

Futures contracts are identical to forward contracts with one exception. With a forward contract, gains and losses are recognized only on the settlement date. With futures contracts, gains and losses to the buyer or seller are recognized on a daily basis. This daily settlement feature is referred to as *marking-to-market*. This daily settlement greatly reduces the default risk associated with forward contracts. Because of this, organized trading in futures contracts is much more common than in forward contracts.

Trading in Futures: Futures contracts for many items are routinely bought and sold around the world. There are two main types of futures contracts: commodity futures, and financial futures. The underlying asset in a commodity future is essentially anything except a financial asset. The underlying asset in a financial future is any type of financial asset (stock, bond, etc.).

Futures Exchanges: Probably the largest futures exchange is the Chicago Board of Trade (CBOT). Other major exchanges include the Chicago Mercantile Exchange (COMEX), the London International Financial Futures Exchange (LIFFE), the New York Futures Exchange (NYFE), and the Winnipeg Commodity Exchange (WPG).

Hedging With Futures: Essentially, a hedge created with futures contracts is conceptually the same as a hedge created with forward contracts. The payoff profiles are drawn in the same way. The only difference is that a firm hedging with futures must maintain an account with an investment dealer. That account will be debited or credited each day as the contract is market to market.

Although there is a large variety of futures contracts available, many firms will not be able to find the precise hedging instrument they need. So, firms typically use *cross-hedging*. They buy contracts on a related, but not identical asset, to establish their hedge.

It should be noted that, in practice, futures contracts are very rarely held to maturity. Firms usually sell and buy contracts, reversing their financial position before the contract matures. In addition, firms wishing to hedge long-term contracts may need to roll over a series of short-term contracts. This increases the risk to the firm.

24.5 HEDGING WITH SWAP CONTRACTS

A *swap contract* is an agreement between two parties to exchange specified cash flows at specified intervals. In essence, a swap contract is a series of forward contracts. The major difference is that there are multiple exchanges, whereas forward contracts involve only one exchange. The three major categories of swaps are: currency swaps, interest rate swaps, and commodity swaps.

Currency Swaps: In a *currency swap*, the two parties agree to exchange a specific amount of one currency for a specific amount of another currency at a specified future date. For example, a Canadian firm doing business in France may want to use debt financing. Because the cash flows related to the project in France are mostly in French francs, the firm may want to make its debt payments in French francs as well. If the firm doesn't have good access to French capital markets, it may enter into a currency swap with a French firm that needs financing denominated in Canadian dollars. The firms agree to exchange Canadian dollars for French francs at a fixed rate on a future date (or dates). This eliminates the exposure to exchange rate changes for both firms.

Interest Rate Swaps: In an *interest rate swap,* firms typically exchange fixed-rate loans for floating-rate loans (and vice versa). Frequently, interest rate swaps are combined with currency swaps. Here, one firm will obtain fixed-rate financing in one currency and then swap it for floating-rate financing in another currency. The floating rate loan is always based on some index, such as the one-year Treasury bill rate.

Commodity Swaps: A *commodity swap* is an agreement to exchange a specified quantity of some commodity at a specified future date. This is the newest type of swap and, to date, the market for commodity swaps is relatively small compared to the other swap markets.

The Swap Dealer: Swap contracts are not traded on organized exchanges because, to date, the contracts are not sufficiently standardized. So, the *swap dealer* plays a major role in these transactions. When a firm enters into a swap contract, the dealer takes the opposite side of the agreement. Then, the dealer tries to find another party to establish an offsetting transaction. If this is not possible, dealers hedge their positions with futures contracts.

A dealer's contracts are detailed in a *swap book*. In general, dealers try to keep a balanced book (called a *matched book*) to limit their net exposure.

24.6 HEDGING WITH OPTION CONTRACTS

An *option contract* differs from forward, futures and swap contracts in that the owner of the contract has the *right*, but *not* the *obligation*, to buy or sell an asset for a specified price at a specified date.

Option Terminology: The two types of options are puts and calls. The owner of a *call option* has the right to *buy* the underlying asset; the owner of a *put option* has the right to *sell* the asset. The fixed price at which the asset may be bought or sold is the *strike price* or *exercise price*. To actually buy or sell the underlying asset is referred to as *exercising* the option. The *expiration date* is the last date at which an option may be exercised.

Options Versus Forwards: There are two main differences between option contracts and forward contracts. First, as discussed above, the transaction associated with an option contract is only completed if the owner of the option chooses to exercise it. Second, when the buyer of an option obtains the right to purchase the underlying asset, that right is valuable. Consequently, the buyer of an option must pay for that right. The price paid is called the *option premium*. In a forward contract, on the other hand, no money changes hands until the transaction is completed.

Option Payoff Profiles: Study the option payoff profiles in your text. For a call option, the owner begins to make a profit when the price of the underlying asset rises above the strike price. From the seller's viewpoint, any gain to the owner of the option is a loss to the seller of the option. For a put option, the owner begins to make a profit when the price of the underlying falls below the strike price. Again, a gain to the buyer of a put option is a loss to the seller of the option.

Option Hedging: This works in essentially the same way as hedging with a forward or futures contract. The basic idea is to use options to create a payoff profile exactly the opposite of the cash flows expected. Because of the nature of options, firms can use option contracts to hedge against the downside risk caused by adverse price movements. At the same time, however, they can retain the potential for upside benefits if prices move in the desired direction.

Hedging Commodity Price Risk with Options: In addition to futures contracts for commodities, there are now options available on the same commodities. Usually, the options traded on commodities are really options on futures contracts; they are referred to as *futures options*. The owner of a futures call option receives a futures contract on the underlying commodity; in addition the owner receives the difference between the strike price on the option and the current futures price. This difference is paid in cash.

Hedging Exchange Risk with Options: Futures options are also available on foreign currencies. These allow firms to create additional hedges against exchange rate risk. Typically, firms wishing to hedge against adverse changes in the exchange rate do so by purchasing put options.

Hedging Interest Rate Risk with Options: There are a number of ways to use options to hedge against interest rate risk. One possibility is to buy a put option on a bond. This protects the firm in case interest rates increase. Firms can also buy call options on interest rates from a bank. These are called *interest rate caps*. If interest rates rise above an agreed-upon ceiling, the bank pays the cash difference between the actual payment and the interest rate ceiling. In contrast, a *floor* is a put option on an interest rate. Firms can buy a cap and sell a floor, creating a *collar*. If rates increase, the firm never pays above the ceiling price. If rates drop, though, the firm's rate will never be below the floor price. The result is that the firm knows its interest rate will always be between the floor and ceiling rates.

Other Interest Rate Options: There are two relatively new types of interest rate options. The *swaption* allows a firm to buy an option on an interest rate swap. This gives the firm the possibility to convert a floating-rate loan to a fixed-rate loan (or vice versa) at a future date. A *compound option* is an option on an option. The popularity of these financial instruments is growing.

CONCEPT TEST

1.   The term hedging refers to the reduction of a firm's exposure to _interest rate_ or _price_ fluctuation. This process is also referred to as _immunization_ .

2.   The process of using existing financial instruments to create new ones that allow firms to hedge against specific risk is called _fin engineer._ .

3.   Price changes have slowed down recently, but volatility has increased in the areas of _interest rates_, _exch. rate_ , and _commi. prices_ .

4.   A firm's _risk profile_ shows the relationship between changes in the price of a particular good, service, or rate and changes in the firms value.

5.   Short-term price fluctuations due to unexpected events or shocks are called _transitory_ changes. Short-run financial risk due to these changes is called _transactions exp._ .

6.   Exposure to price changes due to permanent changes in the underlying economics of a business are referred to as _econ. exp._ . It is typically (more/less) difficult to hedge against this type of risk than against short-term exposure.

7.   A _forward agreement_ is a legal agreement between two parties in which they agree today on the price of an asset or product to be delivered in the future. The date of delivery is the _settlement date_ and the agreed upon price is the _forward price_. If prices increase before the delivery date, the (buyer/seller) benefits. If prices decrease, the (buyer/seller) benefits.

8.   Firms can use a _payoff profile_ to identify their exposure to a given type of financial risk. Then, financial managers try to find a financial arrangement that has an _offsett. p.p._ . The result is that the firm's cash flow (will/will not) be affected by changes in the underlying variable.

9.   Futures contracts are identical to forward contracts except that, with a forward contract, gains and losses are recognized on the _____ . With a futures contract, gains and losses are recognized on a ____ _____ basis. This is known as _____ . This feature (increases/decreases) the default risk associated with the contracts.

10.   When firms cannot find the precise instrument they need to hedge against a particular type of risk, they buy contracts on a related asset. This is known as _____ .

11.   A _____ is an agreement between two parties to exchange specified cash flows at specified intervals. Essentially, this is a series of _____ . The main difference is that there are_____ exchanges, whereas _____ involve only one exchange.

12.   In a _____ , the parties exchange specified amounts of one currency for specified amounts of another. In an _____ , firms typically exchange fixed-rate loans for floating-rate loans (or vice versa.) In a _____ , firms agree to exchange specified quantities of a commodity at a future date.

13.   Since swap contracts aren't traded on organized exchanges, the _____ plays a major role in the transaction. The swap dealer takes the _____ side of the transaction and tries to find another party to take an _____ position. If this is not possible, the dealers hedge their position with _____ .

14.   A dealer's contracts are listed in a _____ . A balanced book is referred to as a _____ .

15.   An option gives the owner the _right_ but not the _obligation_ to buy or sell an asset for a specified _price_ at a specified _date_ .

16.   The two types of options are a _call_ option, giving the owner the right to buy an asset, and a _put_ option, giving the owner the right to sell an asset.

17.   The main difference between an option contract and a forward contract is that an option contract is only _executed_ if the owner of the option chooses to _exercise_ the option. This choice has value to the owner. The price paid for the right to make this choice is called the _option premium_

18.   Options can be used to hedge against changes in interest rates. The two main ways to do this are with _____ and _____ . If a firm buys a _____ and sells a _____ , then the interest rate paid will always be between the _____ and the _____ rates.

ANSWERS TO CONCEPT TEST

1.   price; interest rate; immunization

2.   financial engineering

3.   interest rates; exchange rates; commodity prices

4.   risk profile

5.   transitory; transactions exposure

6.   economic exposure; more

7.   forward contract; settlement date; forward price; buyer; seller

8.   payoff profile; offsetting payoff profile; will not

9.   settlement date; daily; marking-to-market; decreases

10.   cross-hedging

11.   swap contract; forward contracts; multiple; forward contracts

12.   currency swap; interest rate swap; commodity swap

13.   swap dealer; opposite; offsetting; futures contracts

14.   swap book; matched book

15.   right; obligation; price; date

16.   call; put

17.   completed; exercise; option premium

18.   interest rate caps; floors; cap; floor; ceiling; floor

25 Options and Corporate Securities

CHAPTER HIGHLIGHTS

Options such as the call provision on corporate debt have been described in previous chapters. This chapter concerns the valuation of options in general. In addition, we discuss the fact that corporate securities such as common stock and bonds can be thought of as options. Consequently, we can gain additional insight into many financial problems and decisions by viewing them as options. Warrants and convertible securities, which involve options issued by corporations to investors, are also discussed in this chapter.

25.1 OPTIONS: THE BASICS

An option gives the owner of the option the right, but not the obligation, to buy or sell a certain asset at a fixed price (called the strike price or exercise price) during a specified period of time. Options on stock and other assets are examples of *derivative securities*. The value of an option is derived from the price and other features of the underlying assets. The act of purchasing or selling the underlying asset, as specified in the option contract, is referred to as *exercising* the option. The maturity date of the option is called the *expiration date*; the owner of the option cannot exercise the option after the expiration date. An *American option* can be exercised anytime up to the expiration date. A *European option* can be exercised only on the expiration date. Options on stocks and bonds are traded on several exchanges, the largest of which is the Chicago Board Options Exchange (CBOE). Option trading in Canada began in 1975 on the Montreal Exchange. All options traded in Canada are cleared through Trans-Canada Options Inc.

Puts and Calls: A *call option* gives the owner of the option the right to *buy* a specified asset. The most common call options are options on stocks. For example, a call option to buy 100 shares of The Bank of Montreal (BOM) common stock for $30 per share can be purchased on the Montreal Exchange. A *put option* gives the owner of the option the right to *sell* the underlying asset. You might purchase a put option if you expect the value of the underlying stock to decline.

Suppose that, on October 1, an investor purchases a call option to buy 100 shares of BOM common stock: the expiration date is the third Friday in December; the exercise price is $30; the price of the option is quoted as $1½; the current market price of BOM stock is $27½. How much does the investor pay for the option? What is the investor's gain (or loss) if the price of BOM stock declines between October 1 and the third Friday in December? What is the investor's gain (or loss) if the price of BOM stock increases?

The price of the option is $1½ per share, or a total cost of $150. Trading takes place in *round lots* (multiples of 100 shares), so one option *contract* costs $1½ × 100 = $150. If the price of BOM stock declines to $25, the investor would not exercise the option. That is, he would not choose to purchase 100 shares of stock for $30 per share at a time when the market price of the stock is less than $30 per share. When the market price of the stock is less than the exercise price of the call option, the option is said to be 'out of the money.' If, on the expiration date, the market price of the stock is less than the exercise price of the option, then the option is worthless; the investor has lost $150 on the transaction, the purchase price of the option, because the option expired out of the money.

If the price of the stock exceeds the exercise price, then the option is 'in the money.' For example, suppose that the price of the stock is $32¾ on the expiration date; the owner of the option could exercise the option for a profit. The investor can exercise the option and purchase 100 shares of stock for ($30 × 100) = $3,000, and then immediately sell the shares for ($32.75 × 100) = $3,275. The investor's profit is ($3,275 – $3,000) = $275, less the $150 purchase price of the option, for a net profit of ($275 – $150) = $125.

These transactions can also be viewed from the seller's perspective. The seller, or writer, of the call option must sell the stock at the exercise price if the buyer exercises the option. If the option expires out of the money, the writer keeps the purchase price of the option. In the example above, the seller (writer) would have a profit of $150. That is, the buyer's $150 loss is the seller's gain.

Now assume the price of the stock is $32¾ on the expiration date. The writer of the option must sell 100 shares of BOM stock for ($30 × 100) = $3,000. If the writer does not own the stock, he must buy it in the market for ($32¾ × 100) = $3,275. His loss will be ($3,000 – $3,275) = $275. This is partially offset by the $150 received for selling the option, so the actual loss is ($275 – $150) = $125. Again the seller's loss is the same as the buyer's profit.

The size of the option writer's loss does not depend on whether he owns the stock. Assuming the writer above owned the stock, he would be selling at $30 per share stock actually worth $32¾ per share. In other words, the loss is still $275 (less the $150 received for selling the option).

An Example: On October 1, an investor purchases a Times Mirror December 30 put, currently quoted at $3. The market price of Times Mirror stock is $27½. What is the investor's gain (or loss) if the price of Times Mirror stock declines between October 1 and the third Friday in December? What is the investor's gain (or loss) if the price of Times Mirror stock increases?

A put is in the money if the market price is less than exercise price and is out of the money if market price exceeds the exercise price. If the market price of Times Mirror stock is $25 on the expiration date, the investor will exercise the option. That is, she will buy 100 shares in the market for ($25 × 100) = $2,500, and then sell the 100 shares to the writer of the call option for ($30 × 100) = $3,000. The profit from this transaction is ($3,000 – $2,500) = $500. Since the purchase price of the option is ($3 × 100) = $300, the investor's net profit is ($500 – $300) = $200. The writer of the option incurs a loss of $500 when the put is exercised; he is obligated to purchase, for $3,000, stock with a market value of only $2,500. This loss is partially offset by the $300 he received when he sold the option, so that his net profit is ($300 – $500) = –$200, or a $200 loss.

If the market price exceeds the exercise price, the put owner will not exercise the option. If, for example, the market price is $32 on the expiration date, the owner of the option would not choose to exercise an option to sell, at $30 per share, stock which can be sold in the market for $32 per share. Consequently, the option expires out of the money; the buyer of the option loses the $300 she paid to acquire the option, while the option writer has a net profit of $300.

25.2 FUNDAMENTALS OF OPTION VALUATION

In this section, we introduce the basic factors that determine the value of an option. Although the discussion focuses on call options, the basic principles discussed here also apply to put options.

Value of a Call Option at Expiration: The following notation is used in the discussion of option valuation:

S_1	=	Stock price at expiration (in one period)
S_0	=	Stock price today
C_1	=	Value of the call option on the expiration date (in one period)
C_0	=	Value of the call option today
E	=	Exercise price on the option

The value of a call option on the expiration date (C_1) is zero if the stock price (S_1) is less than the exercise price (E). This statement can be written:

$$C_1 = 0 \text{ if } S_1 \leq E$$

This relationship can also be stated as follows:

$$C_1 = 0 \text{ if } (S_1 - E) \leq 0$$

A call option is in the money if $S_1 > E$. The value of a call option that is in the money at expiration is $(S_1 - E)$. This relationship can be stated in either of the following ways:

$$C_1 = (S_1 - E) \text{ if } S_1 > E$$
$$C_1 = (S_1 - E) \text{ if } (S_1 - E) > 0$$

An Example: Suppose that the exercise price is \$100. On the expiration date, the option is in the money if $S_1 > \$100$, and the value of the option is $(S_1 - \$100)$. For example, if S_1 is \$120, then the owner of the option can exercise it to buy the stock for \$100, and then immediately sell the stock for \$120, for a \$20 gain. If $S_1 < \$100$ on the expiration date, the option is out of the money and has no value. The call cannot have a negative value because the owner of the call is not obligated to exercise the option.

The Upper and Lower Bounds on a Call Option's Value: Since a call option is simply the right to buy the stock, the option cannot be worth more than the stock. Therefore, the upper bound on the value of a call option can be expressed as follows:

$$C_0 \leq S_0$$

The lower bound on the value of a call option depends on whether the option is in or out of the money. We established that the value of a call option at expiration is zero if the option is out of the money. However, prior to expiration, an out of the money option has a value greater than zero if the investor believes that the price of the stock might increase enough so that, at some time prior to expiration, the option is in the money. Therefore, the lower bound for the value of an out of the money call option, prior to the expiration date, can be written as:

$$C_0 \geq 0 \text{ if } (S_0 - E) < 0$$

A call that is in the money prior to expiration is worth at least the difference between the value of the stock and the exercise price of the call. Suppose the stock is selling for \$80 and the option to buy the stock at \$60 is selling for \$15. You could buy the option for \$15, exercise it by purchasing the stock for another \$60, and then sell the stock for a guaranteed profit of \$5. Consequently, the price of the call must be at least \$20; at a lower price, the existence of arbitrage opportunities would immediately drive the price of the option higher. The price of the option generally exceeds the difference between the stock price and the exercise price due to the opportunity for additional profit if the price of the stock increases further prior to the expiration date. This relationship can be summarized as follows:

$$C_0 \geq (S_0 - E) \text{ if } (S_0 - E) \geq 0$$

The lower bound on the value of a call option is referred to as the *intrinsic value* of the option.

The upper bound on a call's value is given by the value of the stock ($C_0 \leq S_0$). The lower bound is either $S_0 - E$ or 0, whichever is larger.

A Simple Model: To establish a precise value for a call option, we will initially assume that future stock prices can have only two possible values.

An Example: Suppose a share of stock is currently selling for $100, and the risk-free rate (R_f) is 10%. Also assume that, one year from now, the stock price will be either $105 or $120. A call option with expiration in one year has an exercise price of $100. How much is the call worth today?

One year from now, the stock will be worth either $105 or $120. If you buy the option today, you will have either ($105 – $100) = $5 or ($120 – $100) = $20 one year from now. Suppose that, in addition to buying the option today, you also lend an amount equal to the present value of the exercise price: ($100/1.10) = $90.91. At the end of the year, you have $100 from the repayment of the loan and either $5 or $20 from the exercise of the option; the total return is either ($100 + $5) = $105 or ($100 + $20) = $120. Notice that the strategy of buying the option and lending $90.91 has the same possible future returns as does the strategy of simply buying the stock. Since the two strategies have the same future returns, they must have the same value today. Therefore, the value of the call option plus the present value of the exercise price must be the same as the price of the stock:

$$C_0 + \$90.91 \ = \ \$100$$

The value of the call option is $9.09. In general, this result can be written as:

$$C_0 \ + \ \frac{E}{(1 + R_F)} \ = \ S_0$$

$$C_0 \ = \ S_0 \ - \ \frac{E}{(1 + R_F)}$$

Although this result is based on the unrealistic assumption that the stock price will be one of only two possible values at the expiration date, it can be generalized to the case where the stock price at the expiration date will be any value greater than or equal to the exercise price of the option.

If the option expires in t time periods, then the value of the call option is:

$$C_0 \ = \ S_0 \ - \ \frac{E}{(1 + R_F)^t}$$

Four Factors Determining Option Values: If we assume that a call option is certain to expire in the money, then the result of the previous section indicates that four factors determine the option's value. (If the option can expire out of the money, then a fifth factor influences the option's price; this fifth factor is discussed in the next section.) The four factors are:

1.   *The stock price.* As the price of the stock (S_0) increases, the value of the option increases.

2.   *The exercise price.* A higher exercise price (E) makes the option less valuable.

3.   *The time to expiration.* The value of the option decreases as the time to expiration (t) decreases. The longer the term to expiration, the greater the value of the option, because it provides the holder of the option a longer period of time during which to exercise.

4.   *The risk-free rate.* The value of the call increases as the risk-free rate (R_f) increases. The purchaser of a call option will pay the exercise price at some future date. The higher the interest rate, the lower the present value of this future amount. Thus, the higher the interest rate, the more the call option is worth.

25.3 VALUING A CALL OPTION

In this section, we discuss the valuation of a call option under the more realistic assumption that the option might expire out of the money. As in the previous section, we initially assume that only two future stock prices are possible.

A Simple Model - Part II: In order to identify the factors which determine the value of an option which might expire out of the money, we first consider a modification of the example of the previous section.

An Example: Assume again that the current price of the stock is $100, that the possible stock prices at the expiration of the option are $105 and $120, and that the risk-free rate is 10%. A call option with an exercise price of $115 expires out of the money if the stock price is $105, and is in the money if the stock price is $120. What is the value of the call option with an exercise price of $115?

To establish the value of this option, we develop a strategy of investing in the risk-free asset and purchasing call options which duplicate the possible returns resulting from owning the stock.

The strategy which duplicates the payoff on the stock is: invest ($105/1.10) = $95.45 in the risk-free asset, and buy three call options. One year from now, the value of the investment in the risk-free asset is $105, which is the lower of the two possible stock prices. If, one year from now, the stock price is $105, then the three call options are out of the money, and the total value of the investor's position is [$105 + (3 × $0)] = $105. On the other hand, if the stock price is $120, then the call options are in the money, and the value of each call option is ($120 – $115) = $5. The total value of the investor's position is then [$105 + (3 × $5)] = $120. Therefore, the strategy of investing $95.45 in the risk-free asset and buying three call options has the same possible future returns as does the stock. Consequently, the current value of the two strategies must be the same:

$$(3 \times C_0) + \frac{\$105}{(1 + R_F)} = S_0$$

$$(3 \times C_0) + \frac{\$105}{(1.10)} = \$100$$

Solving for C_0, we find that the value of a call option is $1.52.

Option valuation is based on the fact that it is always possible to duplicate a stock's possible future returns with a combination of options and either lending or borrowing. The required number of calls is equal to ($\Delta S/\Delta C$), where ΔS is the difference in possible future stock prices and ΔC is the difference in possible future option values. In the above example, this fraction is equal to [($120 – $105)/($5 – $0)] = 3, indicating the purchase of three call options. The logic of this result is straightforward. When the option is in the money, the options purchased must provide a return equal to the difference in possible stock prices; since one in-the-money option provides a return of ΔC, the number of options required to provide a return of ΔS is ($\Delta S/\Delta C$).

The Fifth Factor: For an option which might expire out of the money, the fifth factor influencing the value of the option is the variability in the price of the underlying asset. The more variable the price of the underlying asset, the greater the value of the option. Imagine that you own a call on a riskless asset which is currently selling for $100 and will yield a 10% return for the year. What is the value of a call option to buy this asset for $120? Obviously, the value is zero because this asset can never be worth more than $110 during the year. If this asset's value were variable, however, then there would be a possibility that it would sell for more than $120, and the call would have value. The greater the variability, the greater the chance for profit, and consequently, the greater the value of the option.

An Example: Suppose the possible stock prices are $100 and $125, the risk-free rate is 10%, and the current price of the stock is $100. What is the value of a call option with an exercise price of $115?

The possible values of the option at the expiration date are: $0 and ($125 – $115) = $10. The investment strategy which duplicates the returns from an investment in the stock is as follows: invest ($100/1.10) = $90.91 in the risk-free asset, and purchase $(\Delta S/\Delta C)$ = [($125 – $100)/($10 – $0)] = 2.5 call options. The value of a call option is the solution for C_0 in the following equation:

$$(2.5 \times C_0) \; + \; \frac{\$100}{(1 + R_F)} \; = \; S_0$$

$$(2.5 \times C_0) \; + \; \frac{\$100}{(1.10)} \; = \; \$100$$

The value of the call option is $3.64. In the example of the preceding section, the value of the option is $1.52. The value of an option which might expire out of the money increases when the possible stock prices are more variable.

25.4 EMPLOYEE STOCK OPTIONS

An Employee Stock Option (ESO) gives an employee the right to purchase shares of a stock at a fixed price for a fixed period. ESO are quite common; one study found that at the end of 1994, 90% of firms listed on the Toronto Stock Exchange used stock options.

ESO Features: ESOs are call options, but include several unique features. ESOs tend to have longer lives than regular options, typically 10 years, and cannot be sold. For a period of time known as the "vesting" period the ESO cannot be exercised. Holders of ESOs may be forced to exercise following resignation from the company.

Firms grant ESOs to align shareholder and management interests and to motivate employees. Executives granted many ESOs can become very wealthy if the firm does well. Firms also grant ESOs when they do not have enough cash to pay ordinary wages. Because ESOs do not require any cash outlay upfront, they provide a tempting alternative form of compensation.

ESO Repricing: When issued, the strike price associated with the ESO is equal to the stock price. While the ESO is "at the money," the intrinsic value is zero. The term "underwater" is used to describe situations where the stock price falls significantly. ESO repricing may occur in such situations, through designating a new strike price. Repricing occurs to maintain the incentive associated with ESOs. But some critics argue that repricing represents and award for failing, effectively undercutting the motivational benefits associated with ESOs.

25.5 EQUITY AS A CALL OPTION ON THE FIRM'S ASSETS

The financial decision-making process can often be reformulated in terms of options. In this section, we view corporate securities as options on the value of the firm.

Suppose a firm has a single debt issue coming due in one year. At that time, the shareholders will have a choice. If the value of the firm (V_1) exceeds the face value of the debt (B_1), then the shareholders will pay off the debt and the stock will be worth $S_1 = (V_1 - B_1)$. By paying off the debt, the shareholders own the assets of the firm. However, if V_1 is less than B_1, then the shareholders will not exercise their option to acquire the firm's assets, and the bondholders will own the firm. The stock is worth zero in this case. Consequently, the equity in a firm with debt can be viewed as a call option on the assets of the firm. The bondholders' position can be described as follows: the bondholders own the firm and they have written a call option against the value of the firm, with an exercise price equal to the value of the debt. The value of the bonds is then equal to the value of the firm's assets less the value of the call option held by the shareholders.

An Example: A firm has a pure-discount $500 debt issue due in one year. The risk-free rate is 10%, and the current market value of the firm's assets is $475. One year from now, the value of the firm's assets will be either $525 or $550. What is the value today of the equity in the firm?

The firm's shareholders own a call option on the firm's assets. The exercise price of the option is $500. The value of their option is the current value of the underlying asset minus the present value of the exercise price:

$$C_0 = S_0 - \frac{E}{(1 + R_F)^t} = \$475 - \frac{\$500}{(1.10)} = \$20.45$$

Therefore, the firm's equity is worth $20.45.

The conclusion in this example can be verified by noting that the firm's debt is risk-free; therefore, the current value of the debt is ($500/1.10) = $454.55. Since the current value of the firm is $475, the value of the firm's equity is ($475 − $454.55) = $20.45.

25.6 WARRANTS

A warrant gives the holder the right to buy common stock directly from the company at a fixed price during a specified time period. To the holder, a warrant is essentially a call option, although warrants usually have longer maturities. Typically, warrants are attached to the bond with which they are issued; however, some warrants are detachable, which means the warrants can be sold separately from the bond.

The Difference Between Warrants and Call Options: To the firm, a warrant is substantially different from a call option. A call option sold on the firm's stock is a private transaction between investors, in which the firm is not directly involved. In contrast, a warrant is a security issued by the firm. When a call option is exercised, existing stock merely changes hands, but when a warrant is exercised, the firm must issue new stock.

Warrants and the Value of the Firm: An example best illustrates the difference between warrants and calls; the following example also demonstrates the manner in which the exercise of a warrant affects the value of the issuing firm.

An Example: The Vinson Company is financed entirely with equity. The firm has assets valued at $9,000 and has 900 shares outstanding. Elizabeth and Steve Vinson each own 450 shares. Each has decided to sell a call option on 150 shares to Claire Vinson. The call option has an exercise price of $12. Now, suppose the company's assets increase in value to $13,500. Each share is now worth ($13,500/900) = $15. Claire will exercise her options by paying a total of ($12 × 300) = $3,600 to Steve and Elizabeth, and she will acquire a total of 300 shares. At this point, 900 shares are still outstanding and each share is still worth $15. Claire has made a profit of [300 × ($15 − $12)] =

$900, but, from the corporation's point of view, no change has taken place. That is, the number of shares outstanding remains the same and no new financing becomes available to the firm.

Alternatively, suppose that Steve and Elizabeth have sold warrants entitling Claire to buy 300 shares at $12 per share. Assume again that the assets increase in value to $13,500 and the warrants are about to expire. The value of the firm can be thought of as either the value of its assets or the value of its equity, because the firm is financed entirely through equity. Since both the existing common stock and the warrants represent a claim on the firm's assets, prior to the expiration of the warrants, the total value is equal to the value of the common stock plus the value of the warrants.

If Claire exercises her warrants, the firm issues 300 new shares and receives ($12 × 300) = $3,600. The firm is now worth ($13,500 + $3,600) = $17,100 and 1,200 shares are outstanding. Each share is worth ($17,100/1,200) = $14.25. Claire's profit is [300 × ($14.25 − $12)] = $675, because she owns shares worth $14.25 for which she paid only $12. Immediately prior to the expiration of the warrants, the common stock is worth ($14.25 × 900) = $12,825 and the warrants are worth $675, for a total of $13,500. The reason the shares are worth $14.25, instead of $15, is that the warrants, which represent a direct claim on the firm's assets and cash flow, have value.

Even though the terms of the call and the warrant appear comparable, the consequences of the exercise of these options differ. In the case of the call option, the value of the firm and the value of a share are unaffected by the exercise of the option. Both before and after exercise, the firm has 900 shares outstanding, each share is worth $15 and the total value of the firm is $13,500. Claire's profit is $900 since she exercises an option on each of 300 shares, and earns a $3 profit on each share. On the other hand, when Claire exercises the warrant, 300 new shares are issued and the value of the firm increases by the $3,600 payment. The exercise of the warrant changes the total number of shares from 900 to 1,200; the value of each share is $14.25, rather than $15; the value of the firm is $17,100 rather than $13,500. Since each share is worth $14.25, Claire's profit on the exercise of the warrant is $675, compared to her $900 profit when she exercises the call.

The exercise of the warrants results in an increase in the number of shares, so that earnings per share will be diluted. Firms with a significant number of warrants outstanding report EPS in two ways: 'primary' (earnings divided by outstanding shares) and 'fully-diluted' (earnings divided by the number of shares that would be outstanding if all warrants were converted to stock).

25.7 CONVERTIBLE BONDS

A convertible bond is a corporate bond that can be exchanged for a fixed number of shares of the firm's common stock, at the holder's option, at any time prior to the maturity of the bond. A convertible preferred stock is similar to a convertible bond except that it has no maturity date.

Features of a Convertible Bond: Consider a convertible subordinated debenture with a face value of $1,000 and a $50 *conversion price*. The bondholder can exchange this bond for ($1,000/$50) = 20 shares of stock; that is, the *conversion ratio* is 20. When a convertible bond is issued, the conversion price typically exceeds the stock price. The difference between the conversion price and the market value of the stock is called the *conversion premium*. If the market value of the firm's stock is $40, then the conversion premium is ($50 − $40) = $10. The conversion premium is often expressed as a percent of the market value of the stock. In this example, the conversion premium is ($10/$40) = .25 = 25% of the market value of the stock.

Value of a Convertible Bond: The value of a convertible bond can be thought of in terms of its value as a bond and the value of the conversion feature.

The *straight bond value* is the price at which the bond would sell if it were not convertible. A convertible sells at a price only slightly above its straight bond value when the conversion price greatly exceeds the stock price. The straight bond value is the present value of the coupon payments and the maturity value, and is therefore dependent on the appropriate discount rate for bonds with a given risk level.

The *conversion value* is the value of the bond if it were immediately converted into common stock. That is, conversion value equals the conversion ratio times the current stock price. The conversion value is another minimum value for a convertible bond since the bond cannot sell for less than its conversion value. If the stock price exceeds conversion value, the value of the convertible bond depends primarily on the conversion value, because the conversion value is significantly greater than the straight bond value. The minimum or 'floor' value of a convertible bond is either its straight bond value or its conversion value, whichever is higher.

The value of a convertible bond exceeds both the straight bond value and the conversion value because the holder has the right, but not the obligation, to convert. Essentially, the bondholder has a call option that increases the value of the bond. The option to wait has value, and it raises the value of the convertible bond over its floor value. The total value of the convertible is equal to the sum of the floor value and the option value.

25.8 REASONS FOR ISSUING WARRANTS AND CONVERTIBLES

A bond that is convertible or has warrants attached pays a lower coupon rate than does an identical straight bond. This interest saving is an apparent advantage to the issuing firm. Warrants and convertibles may also provide the firm with the opportunity to issue stock at a premium over current prices. This argument is based on the fact that the warrant or convertible is usually 'out of the money' initially, so that exercise will take place only if the stock price increases. These arguments seem to indicate that warrants and convertibles are 'no lose' propositions for the issuer. As explained below, this conclusion is incorrect.

The 'Free Lunch' Story: Suppose that a firm can issue either straight subordinated debentures with a 13% coupon rate or convertible subordinated debentures, with a conversion price of $50, and a 10% coupon rate. The firm's common stock currently sells for $40 per share. If the stock declines in value, then the bonds will not be converted, and the firm will have succeeded in issuing debt at 10%, rather than 13%.

If the stock price increases, then conversion will occur, but the company will effectively be selling stock for $50 per share, or $10 more than the stock was worth at the time the convertible was issued. It *appears* that the convertible bond is preferable to either new common stock or straight debt as a source of long-term financing. However, the flaw in the above argument lies in the fact that we are comparing convertible-debt financing with each of the two alternatives only under the circumstances which make convertibles appear more attractive. That is, convertibles are preferable to straight-debt financing when the price of the stock declines, but not when the price increases; convertibles are preferable to common stock financing when the price of the stock increases, but not when the price decreases.

The 'Expensive Lunch' Story: An argument can be constructed which *appears* to indicate that convertible securities are never the preferable alternative. For example, one could argue that, if the stock price declines subsequent to the issuing of the convertibles, then the firm would have been better off issuing common stock when its value was high. In comparison with common stock financing, a valuable opportunity is lost by issuing convertibles if the stock price subsequently declines.

Similarly, if the stock price subsequently rises, then the bondholders convert and reap some of the benefits of the company's success. The firm's existing shareholders would have been better off if the firm had issued straight debt, so that the gains to shareholders would not be diluted. In comparison with straight-debt financing, the existing shareholders are at a relative disadvantage when the firm issues convertibles and the stock price subsequently increases.

A Reconciliation: Neither of the above analyses is correct. In an efficient market, issuing convertibles (or any other financial instrument) is a zero NPV transaction. From the perspective of the firm's existing shareholders, issuing convertibles is generally less desirable than issuing straight-debt and preferable to issuing stock if the company subsequently prospers. If the company does not fare as well, then the reverse is true. Of course, there is no way of knowing in advance whether stock price will increase or decrease, so it is not possible to determine which financing alternative is preferable.

25.9 OTHER OPTIONS

Besides the options discussed above, many other options exist in business as well. This section reviews several examples of such options.

The Call Provision on a Bond: A call provision gives a bond issuer the right to purchase outstanding bonds for a fixed price during a fixed period of time. Effectively, this right represents a call option, and the cost of the option is incurred by the bond issuer. Convertible bonds are an example of bonds that are typically callable. Therefore, convertible bonds can be perceived as a package of three financial securities: The call option held by the bondholders; the call option held by the bond issuer; and the bond itself.

Put Bonds: A bondholder holding a put bond can force the bond issuer to repurchase outstanding bonds for a fixed price during a fixed period of time. Effectively, this right represents a put option, and the cost of the option is incurred by the bondholder.

The Overallotment Option: The overallotment option is the option that an underwriter may be granted to purchase additional shares following an initial pubic offering (IPO) it has underwritten. This right represents a valuable warrant, and therefore represents a portion of the underwriters compensation.

Insurance and Loan Guarantees: Insurance and loan guarantees can be perceived as a put option, as the holder of the insurance or loan guarantee can force the insurance or guarantee provider to "purchase" the insured entity or loan when the value of the entity or loan has drastically decreased.

For example, if you insure your house for $1,000,000 and it burns down in a fire, then the insurance company must "purchase" the house from you for $1,000,000. As another example, consider an individual that chooses to deposit cash at a financial institution. Effectively, the deposit is a loan between the individual and the financial institution. If the financial institution is a member of the Canada Deposit Insurance Corporation (CDIC) then the loan is insured up to $60,000. Should the financial institution fail, the CDIC agrees to "purchase" the loan.

Loan guarantees are costly, as demonstrated by bank failures in Canada and the savings and loan collapse in the U.S. To ensure that these costs are recognized in financial statements, the Canadian auditor general has urged accountants to force government agencies to report guarantees.

Managerial Options: managerial options are options that managers can exploit if certain events occur in the future. These options are designated *real options*, as the option payoffs are in terms of real goods and not asset prices. For example, a manager may have to choose between two production facilities: one is cheaper to build, but can only produce one type of product. The other is more expensive to build, but can produce multiple products. The greater range of product types associated with the second potential production facility is valuable, due to the flexibility it provides the firm when reacting to changes in product demand.

CONCEPT TEST

1. An option gives the owner of the option the right, but not the obligation, to buy or sell a certain asset at a fixed price during a specified period of time. The asset specified in the option contract is referred to as the _____ asset. The price specified in the option contract is the _____ price or the _____ price. The act of purchasing or selling the underlying asset is referred to as _____ the option. The maturity date of the option is called the _____ date.

2. A call option gives the owner of the option the right to (buy/sell) a specified asset. A put option gives the owner of the option the right to (buy/sell) a specified asset. The writer of an option is the individual who (buys/sells) the option. The writer of a call is obligated to (buy/sell) the stock if the buyer of the option chooses to exercise. The writer of a put is obligated to (buy/sell) the stock should the buyer of the put elect to exercise the option.

3. A call is out of the money when the market price of the stock is (less/greater) than the exercise price of the call. On the expiration date, a call is worthless if the market price of the stock is (less/greater) than the exercise price of the option. A call is in the money when the market price of the stock is (less/greater) than the exercise price of the call.

4. A put is out of the money when the market price is (less/greater) than the exercise price and is in the money when the market price is (less/greater) than the exercise price. The owner of the put option will not exercise the option if the market price is (less/greater) than the exercise price.

5. Because the profit earned by one party to an options contract is a loss to the other party, it is said that options represent a _____.

6. If, on the expiration date, the stock price (S_1) is less than the exercise price (E) of a call option, then the value of the call (C_1) is _____. That is: $C_1 =$ _____ if _____. The value of a call option that is in the money at expiration is _____. That is: $C_1 =$ _____ if _____

7. The upper bound on the value of a call option prior to expiration (C_0) is _____. Prior to expiration, an out of the money call option has a value (less/greater) than _____ if the investor believes that the price of the stock might increase sufficiently so that, at some time prior to expiration, the option is in the money. The lower bound for the value of an out of the money call option, prior to the expiration date, can be written as follows: C_0 _____ if _____ ≥ 0. A call that is in the money prior to expiration is worth at least the difference between the _____ and the _____. That is: $C_0 \geq$ _____ if _____ ≥ 0

8. Option valuation is based on the fact that it is always possible to duplicate a stock's possible future returns with a combination of options and either lending or borrowing. When valuing call options, the required number of calls is equal to _____, where ΔS is the difference in _____ and ΔC is the difference in _____. For a call option which is certain to expire in the money, the value of the option prior to expiration (C_0) is equal to the _____ minus the present value of the _____. That is: $C_0 =$ _____

9. For a call option which is certain to expire in the money, the following four factors determine the option's value: (1) _____; (2) _____; (3) _____; (4) _____.

10. In order to establish the value of a call option which might expire out of the money, a strategy is developed which duplicates the possible _____ which result from owning _____. This strategy consists of investing in _____ and purchasing _____. The value of the call option prior to expiration (C_0) is then determined by equating the _____ of the two strategies; that is, the total value of the _____ plus the present value of the _____ is equal to the _____.

11. For an option which might expire out of the money, the fifth factor influencing the value of the option is the _____ in the price of the _____. The greater the _____, the greater the value of the option.

12. The financial decision-making process can often be reformulated in terms of _____. The equity in a firm with debt can be viewed as a _____ option on _____. The bondholders own the firm and they have written a _____ option against the _____, with an exercise price equal to _____. The value of the bonds is then equal to the value of _____ less the value of _____ held by the shareholders.

13. A warrant gives the holder the right to buy _____ from the issuing company at a fixed price during a specified time period. To the holder, a warrant is essentially a _____ option. Warrants are generally issued in combination with _____. To the firm, a warrant is substantially different from a call option. A _____ sold on the firm's stock is a private transaction between investors, while a _____ is a security issued by the firm. Existing stock merely changes hands when a _____ is exercised, but the firm must issue new stock when a _____ is exercised.

14. In the case of the _____, the value of the firm and the value of a share are unaffected by the exercise of the option. Both the value of the firm and the value of a share are affected by the exercise of a _____; the value of the firm (increases/decreases) and the value of a share generally (increases/decreases).

15. A convertible bond is a corporate bond that can be exchanged for a fixed number of _____ at any time prior to _____. The conversion ratio specifies the _____ into which the bond can be converted. The face value of the convertible bond divided by the conversion ratio is equal to the _____. When a convertible bond is issued, the conversion price is typically (less/greater) than the price of the firm's common stock. The difference between the conversion price and the market value of the stock is called the _____, which is often expressed as a percent of the _____.

16. The value of a convertible bond can be thought of in terms of its value as a _____ and the value of the _____ feature. The straight bond value is the price at which the bond would sell if it were _____. The straight bond value is the _____ of the coupon payments and the maturity value, and is dependent on the appropriate _____ for bonds with a given risk level. The conversion value is the value of the bond if it were _____. The conversion value equals the _____ multiplied by the _____. The value of a convertible bond exceeds both the _____ and the _____.

17. In an efficient market, issuing convertibles is a _____ transaction. From the perspective of the firm's existing shareholders, issuing convertibles is generally (more/less) desirable than issuing straight-debt and (more/less) desirable than issuing stock if the company subsequently prospers. If the company does not fare as well, then issuing convertibles is generally (more/less) desirable than issuing straight-debt and (more/less) desirable than issuing stock.

PROBLEMS

Problem 1

Common shares in Stone Company are currently trading at $25, and the risk-free rate is 12%. There is a call option that expires in one year with an exercise price of $30. How much should an investor pay for 100 calls today?

Use the following information to solve Problems 2 through 6:

The price of Walden Corporation common stock will be either $60 or $80 at the end of the year. A call option contract for the purchase of 100 shares of Walden stock has an expiration date in one year. The risk-free rate is 8%.

Problem 2

Suppose the current price of Walden stock is $65 and the exercise price of the call is $70. What are the possible values of the call contract on the expiration date?

Problem 3

For the data in Problem 2, what is the current value of the call contract?

Problem 4

Suppose the option described in Problem 2 has an exercise price of $50. What is the value of the call contract?

Problem 5

Suppose a call contract for 100 shares of Walden common stock, with an exercise price of $65, sells for $1,000. What is the current value of the stock?

Problem 6

Calculate the value of the call if the current stock price is $50 and the exercise price is $70.

Problem 7

The common stock of Hanna Corporation is currently selling at $50 per share. Assume that the continuously compounded interest rate is 10% and that the price of the Hanna stock is certain to increase at that rate. What is the value of a call option to buy one share of Hanna stock for $40, if the expiration date is one year from today?

Problem 8

Calls on Barbera Corporation common stock are currently selling for $10; puts are selling for $8. The exercise price is $80 and the expiration date of both options is in one year. Barbera common stock is currently selling for $73 2/8 per share. Suppose that an investor buys a put and holds it until the expiration date. What is the profit (or loss) if the price of the stock, on the expiration date, is $65? $75? $80? $85? $95? What is the maximum return possible?

Problem 9

For the data in Problem 8, compute the gain (or loss) to the writer of the put if the price of the stock on the expiration date is $65? $75? $80? $85? $95? What is the maximum return the writer of the put can earn? What is the maximum possible loss for the writer of the put option?

Problem 10

At the end of the year, a share of Dobrowolski Corporation, currently trading at $93, will be worth either $95 or $110. If a call expires at the end of the year and has an exercise price price of $90, what is the value of the call contract? The risk-free rate is 9.5%.

Problem 11

For the Barbera Corporation common stock described in Problem 8, assume that an investor buys a call and holds the call until the expiration date. What is the investor's profit (or loss) if the price of the stock, on the expiration date, is $65? $75? $80? $85? $95? What is the maximum return the investor can earn?

Problem 12

For the data in Problems 8 and 10, compute the gain (or loss) to the writer of the call if the price of the stock, on the expiration date, is $65? $75? $80? $85? $95? What is the maximum return the writer of the call can earn? What is the maximum possible loss for the writer of the call option?

Problem 13

A firm has a pure-discount debt issue due in one year with a maturity value of $5,000. The risk-free rate is 11%, and the current market value of the firm's assets is $4,600. One year from now, the value of the firm's assets will be either $5,100 or $5,500. What is the value today of the equity in the firm? What is the value of the firm's debt?

Problem 14

From the data in Problem 13, suppose that the possible values of the firm's assets one year from now are $4,500 or $5,500. What is the value today of the equity in the firm? What is the value of the firm's debt? What is the interest rate on the firm's debt?

Problem 15

A convertible bond issued by Erving Manufacturing, Inc., a manufacturer of medical supplies, has a face value of $1,000, a coupon interest rate of 12%, and matures in 18 years. Interest is paid annually. The Erving bond is rated BB; non-convertible, BB-rated corporate bonds currently yield 13%. At the holder's option, the bond can be exchanged for 16 shares of Erving common stock, which currently sells for $45 per share. What is the conversion ratio for the Erving Bond? What is the conversion price? What is the conversion premium?

Problem 16

Compute the straight bond value for the bond described in Problem 15.

Problem 17

Compute the conversion value for the Erving bond described in Problem 15. What is the floor value of the bond?

Problem 18

A bond with ten detachable warrants has been offered for sale at a price of $1,000. The bond matures in 30 years and has an annual coupon payment of $100. Each warrant gives the owner the right to purchase five shares of stock at $15 per share. Ordinary bonds (i.e., bonds without warrants) of similar quality are priced to yield 14%. What is the value of a warrant?

Problem 19

Using the data from Problem 18, determine the maximum current price of the firm's stock.

Problem 20

Tasha holds a convertible debenture in a firm with a $1,000 face value and a conversion price of $25. How many shares of stock can Tasha exchange the bond for? What is the conversion ratio? If the market value of the firm's stock is $18, what is the conversion premium?

Problem 21

Billy Shakespeare holds a convertible debenture of the Globe Theatre, Inc. which has a face value of $1,000 and a conversion price of $20. Globe shares currently trade at $16.16. As a percentage, the How many shares can Shakespeare trade his bond for? What is the conversion premium?

Problem 22

BabyFoot, Inc. (BFI) sells animal-themed footwear suitable for very young children, BFI has decided to open a new production facility, and must choose between a flexible facility that would allow it to switch between two different footwear designs, zebra or giraffe, or a facility that is limited to the zebra footwear design. The flexible facility requires a larger investment than the inflexible facility. The following chart details the expected present value of the cash flows in the future:

Future market demand	Flexible Facility	Inflexible Facility
Zebra-themed footwear remains popular	$75,000,000	$95,000,000
Giraffe-themed footwear becomes popular	$125,000,000	$45,000,000

There is a 50% chance of each future market demand scenario occurring. What is the additional present value associated with the flexible facility?

ANSWERS TO CONCEPT TEST

1. underlying; strike; exercise; exercising; expiration

2. buy; sell; sells; sell; buy

3.   less; less; greater

4.   greater; less; less

5.   zero-sum game

6.   zero; zero; $S_1 \leq E$ or $(S_1-E) \leq 0$; (S_1-E); (S_1-E); $S_1 > E$ or $(S_1-E) > 0$

7.   the price of the stock; greater; zero; ≥ 0; (S_0-E); value of the stock; exercise price; (S_0-E); (S_0-E)

8. $\Delta S / \Delta C$; possible future stock prices; possible future option values; stock price; exercise price; $S_0 - [E/(1+R_F)^t]$

9.   the stock price; the exercise price; the time to expiration; the risk-free rate

10.   future returns; the stock; risk-free assets; call options; current value; call options; exercise price; price of the stock

11.   variability; stock; variability

12.   options; call; the assets of the firm; call; value of the firm; the value of the firm's debt; the firm's assets; the call option

13.   common stock; call; privately placed debt; call option; warrant; call option; warrant

14.   call option; warrant; increases; decreases

15.   shares of the firm's common stock; maturity; number of shares; conversion price; greater; conversion premium; market value of the stock

16.   bond; convertibility; not convertible; present value; discount rate; converted into common stock; conversion ratio; current stock price; straight bond; conversion value

17.   zero–NPV; less; more; more; less

PROBLEM SOLUTIONS

Problem 1: C_0 = $30 - \$25 / 1.12$ = $7.68

The cost of the call option for 100 shares is $7.68 x 100 = $768.

Problem 2: On the expiration date, Walden stock will be worth either $60 per share or $80 per share. That is, S_1 = $60 or S_1 = $80. If the stock is worth $60 per share, the option to buy at $70 is worthless; that is $C_1 = 0$ if $S_1 \leq E$. If the stock is worth $80 per share on the expiration date (i.e., $S_1 > E$), then the value of call option for one share of Walden stock is: C_1 = $S_1 - E$ = $80 - \$70$ = $10

Consequently, the value of a call option contract for 100 shares is (10×100) = $1,000.

Problem 3: If you buy the call, then, at the end of the year, you will have either $0 or $1,000. The number of options per share that must be purchased is equal to:

$$\frac{\Delta S}{\Delta C} \ = \ \frac{\$80 \ - \$60}{\$10 \ - \$0} \ = \ 2$$

A total of $(2 \times 100) = 200$ call options must be purchased.

The strategy which duplicates the returns from one share of stock is: invest $[\$60/(1 + R_f)] = (\$60/1.08) = \$55.56$ in the risk-free asset, and buy two call options. The current value of these two strategies must be the same:

$$(2 \times C_0) \ + \ \frac{\$60}{(1 + R_F)} \ = \ S_0$$

$$(2 \times C_0) \ + \ \frac{\$60}{(1.08)} \ = \ \$65$$

Solving this equation for C_0, the value of a call option for one share is $4.72; the value of the call option contract for 100 shares is $(\$4.72 \times 100) = \$472$.

Problem 4: If the exercise price is $50, then the option is certain to expire in the money. If you buy a call option for one share of stock, then the return at the end of the year will be either $(\$60 – \$50) = \$10$ or $(\$80 – \$50) = \$30$. For an option which is certain to expire in the money, the number of options required for the strategy to replicate the returns for the stock is:

$$\frac{\Delta S}{\Delta C} \ = \ \frac{\$80 \ - \$60}{\$30 \ - \$10} \ = \ 1$$

In addition to buying the option today, you also lend an amount equal to the present value of the exercise price: $(\$50/1.08) = \$46.30$. The strategy of buying the option and lending $46.30 has the same possible future returns as does the strategy of simply buying the stock. Since the two strategies have the same future returns, they must have the same value today, as indicated in the following equation:

$$C_0 \ = \ S_0 \ - \ \frac{E}{(1 + R_F)} \ = \ \$65 \ - \ \$46.30 \ = \ \$18.70$$

The cost of the call option contract for 100 shares of Walden common stock is $(\$18.70 \times 100) = \$1,870$.

Problem 5: The possible returns for a share of Walden stock are $80 and $60. The possible returns for a call option for one share of Walden stock are $(\$80 – \$65) = \$15$ and $0. The number of options required for the strategy to replicate the returns for the stock is:

$$\frac{\Delta S}{\Delta C} \ = \ \frac{\$80 \ - \$60}{\$15 \ - \$0} \ = \ 1 \ 1/3$$

To duplicate the returns for a call option for one share, invest the following amount in the risk-free asset:

$$\frac{\$60}{(1 + R_F)} \ = \ \frac{\$60}{1.08} \ = \ \$55.56$$

The strategy of buying the call options and investing at the risk-free rate has the same returns as does the strategy of buying the common stock. Therefore, the current value of these two strategies must be the same:

$$(1\ 1/3 \times C_0)\ +\ \frac{\$60}{(1 + R_F)}\ =\ S_0$$

$$(1\ 1/3 \times \$10)\ +\ \frac{\$60}{(1.08)}\ =\ S_0$$

Solving this equation for S_0, the current value of the stock is $68.89 per share.

Problem 6: The possible returns for a share of Walden stock are $80 and $60. The possible returns for a call option for one share of Walden stock are ($80 – $70) = $10 and $0. The number of options required for the strategy to replicate the returns for the stock is:

$$\frac{\Delta S}{\Delta C}\ =\ \frac{\$80 - \$60}{\$10 - \$0}\ =\ 2$$

To duplicate the returns for a call option for one share, invest the following amount in the risk-free asset:

$$\frac{\$60}{(1 + R_F)}\ =\ \frac{\$60}{1.08}\ =\ \$55.56$$

The current value of the two strategies must be the same:

$$(2 \times C_0)\ +\ \frac{\$60}{(1 + R_F)}\ =\ S_0$$

$$(2 \times C_0)\ +\ \frac{\$60}{(1.08)}\ =\ \$50$$

Solving this equation for C_0, the current value of the call option is (–$2.78) per share, or $[(-\$2.78 \times 100] = (-\$278)$. Since an option cannot have a negative value, the call is worthless.

How can the option to buy a share of stock, that may be worth $80, for only $70 be worth nothing?   The inconsistency here arises from the fact that the current stock price cannot be $50. You can borrow $50 at an 8% interest rate, and buy one share of stock. Under the worst case scenario, the share will be worth $60, but you will have to repay only ($50 × 1.08) = $54 on the loan. As a result, you would earn, at a minimum, a costless, riskless $6. There is an arbitrage opportunity here because the return on the stock is always greater than the riskless 8% interest rate. Therefore, the stock must sell for more than $50 per share.

Problem 7: If there is no uncertainty, then the value of Hanna stock one year from now will be: $\$50e^{.10} = \$55.26$. The payoff on the option at that time is thus ($55.26 – $40) = $15.26. The value of the call is the present value of the future payoff: $\$15.26e^{-.10} = \$13.81$

Problem 8: If the price of the stock on the expiration date is $65, the investor will exercise the put, thereby selling the stock for $80. The gain on the exercise of the put is $(E - S_1) = (\$80 - \$65) = \$15$ since the investor can purchase a share in the market for $65 and sell the share for $80. Since the investor paid $8 to purchase the put, the net gain is $(\$15 - \$8) = \$7$.

If the price of the stock is $75 on the expiration date, the investor will exercise the put for a gain of $(E - S_1) = (\$80 - \$75) = \$5$. The net gain to the investor is $(\$5 - \$8) = -\$3$, or a net loss of $3. If the price of the stock is the same as the exercise price of the option, the investor will not exercise the option. If the investor did exercise the option, there would be no gain or loss on the transaction, which is the same result as if the option were discarded. The net loss would be the $8 purchase price of the option.

At a price of $85 or $95 (or at any stock price such that $E < S_1$), the investor will not exercise the option, so that the net loss is the $8 purchase price of the option. The maximum return the investor can earn is $80 per share, less the $8 price of the option. That is, if the market value of the stock declines to zero on the expiration date, the investor can sell, for $80, stock which has a value of $0.

Problem 9: If the price of the stock on the expiration date is $65, the buyer of the put will exercise the option, thereby selling the stock for $80. The writer of the put must therefore purchase, for $80, a share of stock with a market value of only $65; the gain on this transaction is $(\$65 - \$80) = -\$15$, or a loss of $15. The loss to the writer of the put is equal to the gain to the buyer of the put, as indicated by the solution to Problem 7. Since the writer of the put receives the $8 purchase price of the option, the net loss to writer $(-\$15 + \$8) = -\$7$. Again, since options are a 'zero-sum game,' the net loss to the writer is the same as the net gain to the buyer of the option.

If the price of the stock on the expiration date is $75, then the gain to the writer is $(\$75 - \$80) = -\$5$, or a loss of $5; the net gain is $(-\$5 + \$8) = \$3$.

Since the option will not be exercised if the price of the stock is $80 or more on the expiration date, the gain to the writer of the put is the $8 purchase price of the option.

The maximum return to the writer of the put is the $8 purchase price of the put. If the price of the stock falls to zero on the expiration date, the loss to the writer of the put is $(-\$80 + \$8) = \$72$.

Problem 10: For one share, the return at year end will be either $5 or $20. The number of options required for the strategy to replicate the returns for the stock is:

$$\Delta S / \Delta C = (\$110 - \$95) / (\$20 - \$5) = 1$$

In addition to buying the option today, you could also lend the present value of the exercise price: $90 / 1.095 = $82.19. The two strategies have the same future returns, so the value of the call is

$$C_0 = S_0 - E / (1 + R_F)^t \quad \$93 - \$82.19 = \$10.81$$

The cost of the contract for 100 shares of Dobrowolski Corporation is $1,081.

Problem 11: The value of the call option (C_1) is zero if the value of the stock is less than the exercise price of the option (i.e., if $S_1 \leq E$). Therefore, the investor's net loss is the $10 purchase price of the call for S_1 equal to $65, $75 or $80. If S_1 is $85 on the expiration date, the investor will exercise the option for a gain of $(S_1 - E) = (\$85 - \$80) = \$5$. The net gain is $(\$5 - \$10) = -\$5$, or a net loss of $5. If S_1 is $95, the gain on the exercise of the option is

$(S_1 - E) = (\$95 - \$80) = \$15$, and the net gain is $(\$15 - \$10) = \$5$. In principle, there is no upper limit to the return on the call; the higher the price of the stock on the expiration date, the greater the net gain to the investor.

Problem 12: If the price of the stock on the expiration date is less than or equal to the exercise price (i.e., if $S_1 \leq E$), then the buyer of the call option will not exercise the option and the net gain to the writer of the option is the $10 purchase price. Note that this is the same as the loss to the buyer of the option, as indicated in Problem 9, because the writing of a call option is a zero-sum game.

The buyer of the call will exercise the option if the price of the stock is $85 on the expiration date, forcing the writer of the call to sell, for $80, a share of stock whose market value is $85. Therefore, the exercise of the option results in a $5 loss to the writer of the option; the net gain to the writer of the option is $(\$10 - \$5) = \$5$. If the price of the stock is $95, the exercise of the option results in a $15 loss to the writer of the option, and a net gain of $(-\$15 + \$10) = -\$5$, or a loss of $5.

The maximum return to the writer of the call is the $10 purchase price of the call. The writer earns this amount if $S_1 \leq E$, so that the call is not exercised. The maximum loss to the writer of the call is, theoretically, unlimited; as the price of the stock increases, the loss to the writer of the option increases.

Problem 13: The firm's shareholders own a call option on the firm's assets, with an exercise price of $5,000. The option is certain to expire in the money, since the value of the firm's assets will exceed the exercise price on the expiration date of the option. Consequently, the value of the option is equal to the current value of the underlying asset (i.e., the firm's total assets) minus the present value of the exercise price of the call option:

$$C_0 \;=\; S_0 \,-\, \frac{E}{(1 + R_t)} \;=\; \$4,600 \,-\, \frac{\$5,000}{(1.11)} \;=\; \$95.50$$

Therefore, the firm's equity is worth $95.50. The current value of the debt is $(\$5,000/1.11) = \$4,504.50$.

Problem 14: If, one year from now, the value of the firm's assets is $4,500, then the shareholders will elect to default on the firm's debt. That is, since the option is out of the money, the call option is worthless. On the other hand, if the value of the firm's assets is $5,500, then the value of the call option is $(S_1 - E) = (\$5,500 - \$5,000) = \$500$. The strategy which replicates the possible values of the underlying asset is an investment of $(\$4,500/1.11) = \$4,054.05$ in the risk-free asset and the purchase of an appropriate number of call options, computed as follows:

$$\frac{\Delta S}{\Delta C} \;=\; \frac{\$5,500 \,-\, \$4,500}{\$500 \,-\, \$0} \;=\; 2$$

The current value of the firm must be equal to the value of the two call options plus the present value of the investment in the risk-free asset: $\$4,600 \;=\; (2 \times C_0) + \$4,054.05$.

Solving for C_0, we find that the value of the firm's equity is $272.97. The value of the firm's debt is the total value of firm less the value of the equity: $\$4,600 - \$272.97 \;=\; \$4,327.03$

The firm's debt has a maturity value of $5,000, so that the interest rate on the firm's debt is: $(\$5,000/\$4,327.03) - 1 \;=\; .15553 \;=\; 15.553\%$

Problem 15: The bond can be converted into 16 shares of common stock, so that the conversion ratio is 16. The conversion price is the face value of the bond divided by the conversion ratio: $1,000 / 16 = $62.5. The conversion premium is the difference between the conversion price and the market price of the common stock: ($62.50 – $45) = $17.50. The conversion premium as a percent of the market price is: ($17.50/$62.50) = .28 = 28%.

Problem 16: The straight bond value of a convertible bond is the price at which the bond would sell if it were not convertible. As discussed earlier, the value of a bond is the present value of the future coupon interest payments plus the present value of the maturity value, which is computed as follows: $PV = [\$120 \times PVIFA(13\%,8)] + \$1,000 / (1.13)^{18} = (\$120 \times 6.839905) + (\$1,000 \times .1108123) = \$931.60$.

Problem 17: The conversion value is equal to the conversion ratio multiplied by the current price of the stock: $16 \times \$45 = \$720$. The floor value of a convertible bond is the greater of the straight bond value and the conversion value; for the Erving bond, the floor value is $931.60.

Problem 18: If there were no warrants, the value of the bond would be the present value of the future coupon interest payments plus the present value of the $1,000 maturity value. Using the procedure described earlier, the value of the bond is $719.89. The total value of the warrants is ($1,000 – $719.89) = $280.11. Since there are ten warrants, each is worth $28.01.

Problem 19: The straight bond value is $719.89. Each bond enables the owner to buy a total of 50 shares of stock for $15 per share. The minimum value of the warrants is [50 × (S – $15)]; the solution to Problem 18 indicates that the total value of the warrants is $280.11. Therefore, the current stock price is at most the value of S in the equation: 50 × (S – $15) = $280.11.

Solving for S, we find that the current stock price is at most: S = $15 + ($280.11/50) = $20.60.

Problem 20: Tasha can exchange the bonds for ($1,000/$25) = 40 shares. The conversion ratio is 40. With a market value of $18 per share, the conversion premium is ($25-$18) = $7; expressed as a percent of the market value of the stock, the conversion premium is ($7 / $18) = 38.89% of the market value of the stock.

Problem 21: Shakespeare can trade his bond for $1,000 / $20 = 50 shares of the Globe Theatre, Inc. The conversion ratio is 50 and the conversion premium is $20 - $16.16 = $3.84. As a percentage, the premium is $3.84 / $16.16 = 0.2376 = 23.76%

Problem 22: The additional present value is equal to the expected present value of the flexible facility minus the expected present value of the inflexible facility. The present values of the two facilities are as follows:

Expected PV (Flexible Facility) = 0.5 x $75,000,000 + 0.5 x $125,000,000 = $100,000,000

Expected PV (Inflexible Facility) = 0.5 x $95,000,000 + 0.5 x $45,000,000 = $70,000,000

It follows that the additional present value = $100,000,000 - $70,000,000 = $30,000,000.